The Nurturing Home

The Nurturing Home

Living with Kotoisa, the Finnish Way to Happiness

Susanna Laiho Hawkins

Photography by Simon Bevan

Mitchell Beazley

Contents

What Kotoisa Means to Me

One of my earliest childhood memories is of my grandparents' island cabin. My grandma is cooking in the kitchen, standing next to the wood-burning stove wearing a floral dress, with a linen apron tied around her waist. She is looking focused while stirring a pot of something on the stove, most likely fish soup. The kitchen is small but has high ceilings; there's probably too much pine on show for this room ever to be featured in a design magazine, and the light-blue kitchen cabinets have seen better days. I'm standing by the door watching her quietly.

That image has stayed with me for over 40 years. When I think about what kotoisa means to me, I think about that moment. It is that feeling of belonging to a place, like the way you feel when you come home – relaxed and at ease.

Origins and meaning

At its heart, kotoisa is a Finnish concept that translates loosely to 'cosy' or 'homely', but its essence runs far deeper than mere aesthetics. It's about creating a home that feels aligned with your personality, memories and daily life – a place where comfort, connection and calm intertwine. A kotoisa home is one where you can exhale deeply, where details reflect care and intention, and where the warmth isn't just physical, but emotional.

Growing up, I didn't have a word for kotoisa, but I felt it – at home, and every time I visited my grandparents' little island cottage. Neither of them were perfect, but both felt like home: safe, cosy and relaxing. The scent of freshly brewed coffee seemed to greet us before the door even opened. This wasn't about style or perfection. It was about the way the spaces invited you in, made you linger and left you feeling nurtured long after you'd left.

Kotoisa is about the relationship between home and well-being. Finns have long understood that the spaces we inhabit shape how we feel. A home can be a haven or a source of stress, depending on how it is designed. The beauty of kotoisa is its balance of functionality and comfort. It prioritizes simplicity and practicality while infusing spaces with warmth and personality.

My happy place

The terrace at my family's island cottage, where the air smells like sun-warmed pine and time seems to slow. This is my blueprint for kotoisa: calm, simple and close to nature.

Kotoisa is deeply rooted in Finnish cultural values, particularly an appreciation for simplicity, imperfection and authenticity. One of the most poignant expressions of this is the word *kotikutoisuus*, which loosely translates to 'homespun quality'. This refers to the charm of something homemade and crafted with care rather than precision. In a kotoisa home, you might find hand-knitted blankets, ceramic bowls with uneven edges, or a faded quilt that has been passed down through generations. These things aren't perfect, but they carry a kind of soul – a story that makes them irreplaceable.

I remember once, as a child, trying to 'fix' the frayed edges of a blanket my father had when he was young. I thought it looked worn and shabby. My mum stopped me gently, saying, 'It's not broken, it's loved.' That idea stayed with me: things don't have to be flawless to be valuable. In fact, their imperfections are often what make them feel most alive, most kotoisa.

Simplicity is another cornerstone of Finnish life and, by extension, kotoisa. It's not about minimalism for the sake of aesthetics, but about clearing away what doesn't matter to make room for what does. It's the joy of a few well-loved books on a shelf rather than rows of untouched ones; neatly stacked firewood in a woven basket or a small gathering of family around a single candle instead of a lavish, showy display.

Unlike trends that prize perfection or stark minimalism, kotoisa celebrates the lived-in and the real: the muddy boots by the door after a long walk, the mismatched coffee mugs that tell their own stories, and the aroma of wood smoke lingering in the air after a cosy winter evening. These things make a house feel alive – not perfectly curated, but deeply cared for.

When I think of kotoisa, I think of all those little moments that breathe life into a home: a child's drawing taped crookedly to the fridge, a woollen throw draped over a sofa, or the scent of cardamom in the kitchen. These are the things that ground us, making a house a sanctuary rather than just a structure.

Kotoisa is more than a design philosophy. It is a way of living. It's about embracing imperfection, infusing your space with personality and prioritizing what makes you feel happy, calm and connected. In a world that often prizes glossy perfection, kotoisa reminds us that home is where life happens – messy, beautiful and utterly real.

An instant welcome
This is my favourite kind of hosting: nothing fancy, just coffee, cake, a few candles and my best cups on an otherwise ordinary day.

About me

I grew up in rural south-west Finland, surrounded by forests, lakes and the long, golden summers of the north. With not much in the way of entertainment, books became my world. My mother was an avid reader, too, and every week we made the trip to our local library, returning home with stacks of books.

Stories were everywhere: told around the kitchen table, passed down through generations, and found in the pages of those well-loved books. I loved words and the way they could build entire worlds, but I took a more scientific path at first, earning a master's degree in neurobiology. My plan was to start a PhD.

I felt the pull of something different, however, so I swapped my PhD plans for an adventure and moved to New York City to take a job as a research assistant. During this period, on a spontaneous trip to the Caribbean, I met my future husband. Two years later, I found myself in London, working in pharmaceutical research, before eventually stepping away from the corporate world to pursue a more creative life.

For the past decade, I've worked as a stylist, writer and content creator, weaving stories through images more than using words. Writing has always been there in the background, but it took me a long time to feel confident writing in my second language. Now, I'd love for my next chapter to be all about storytelling, because, in the end, it brings me back to where it all began: to the magic of the written word and the power of a well-told tale.

I live in the Cotswolds with my husband, our two children, an energetic cocker spaniel named Laila, and Ebba, our beautiful but permanently grumpy cat.

My beginning
I come from rural Finland, with summers spent in a family island cabin and winters fuelled by library books. I started out working in science, then took the scenic route into a creative life.

CHAPTER 1

What is Kotoisa?

If you ask a Finn what kotoisa means, you'll likely get a small smile and a gentle shrug. It's one of those words that is felt more than defined – trying to define it is like trying to describe the scent of morning coffee, or the way your favourite jumper feels after a long day. You know it when you experience it.

Technically speaking, it translates to something like 'cosy' or 'homely', but as anyone who's lived it knows, that barely scratches the surface. Kotoisa isn't about plush throws and designer lights (although it can include those). It's about emotional warmth – the kind that seeps in quietly, unnoticed at first, but brings with it deep comfort. It's the soft landing at the end of a hard day – the quiet exhale of breath you didn't know you were holding.

At its core, kotoisa is the opposite of pretence. It's not about having the latest sofa or nailing the paint colour of the moment. It's about making space for life to happen. The concept is deeply personal, which is why no two kotoisa homes ever look the same. One might be a light-filled modern flat with big houseplants and curated stacks of books. Another might be a creaky old cottage with lumpy cushions and a kitchen that smells perpetually of cinnamon. The magic is in the feeling it gives you: ease, comfort, belonging.

Kotoisa is also a quiet rebellion against the constant pursuit of newness and perfection. In a world that tells us to upgrade and reinvent, kotoisa reminds us to notice what is already here, and to work with what we have – to find joy in the old wooden spoon, the blanket with the worn edges, the chair that squeaks a little when you lean back but is just the perfect shape.

All this is not to say that aesthetics don't matter – they do. But in a kotoisa home, beauty is often subtle, layered and slow to show itself. It might be revealed in the way afternoon light hits the floorboards, or how a table setting, however mismatched, feels just right, or how a single shelf can tell an entire life story, through objects gathered over time.

There's also a rhythm to kotoisa, a sense of seasonality and ritual. You are invited to live in sync with the world outside your windows: to bring in branches in spring, berries in summer, candles in winter; to let your home change with you, gently, like an old friend who knows how to keep you grounded.

In Finland, we don't often talk about these things in grand terms. We let the silence speak for us. But this, in many ways, is our secret superpower. We know how much our environment matters – how a soft light or a quiet corner can shape an entire day. Kotoisa is this wisdom, passed down quietly. Not a set of rules, but a way of seeing.

Once you start seeing your home through that lens – not as a project to finish, but a story to live in – it changes everything. You stop chasing perfection and start building something deeper. Something that welcomes you home.

The four pillars of kotoisa

If you've ever walked into a house and immediately felt yourself breathe easier – not because it was grand or stylish, but because it felt lived in, welcoming, real – then you've felt what I'd call kotoisa. This is an atmosphere, a softness, a kind of quiet confidence, in a home that doesn't try too hard.

When I started thinking more deeply about how to define what makes a home kotoisa, I realized it came down to a few core ideas. Not rules – I'm not big on those – but guiding principles. These are the ideas I return to when I'm stuck with a room, or trying to understand why a space feels just right, or not quite right.

I've come to think of these as the four pillars of kotoisa. They aren't fancy or complicated, and they definitely aren't about achieving perfection. They are about creating a home that supports you, reflects you and grows with you – a home that works for your real life, not just the version you post on Instagram. Most importantly, these pillars are about how your home feels, not how it looks.

Let's start with the first one: comfort.

Room to breathe
Two homes can look nothing alike and still share the same feeling: calm, lived-in, welcoming – inviting you to stop striving and just be.

Comfort

When we first moved into our house, it didn't feel like home. It was cold and echoey – things hadn't found their right place. New spaces make me instinctively lower my voice in response to this feeling. I remember making coffee that first afternoon and realizing that I had no idea where to sit – not because there wasn't furniture (there was), but because none of it felt like mine.

When most people think of comfort, they picture something soft: a plump sofa, fluffy slippers, a thick blanket draped over the end of the bed. And yes, those things are lovely. But in a kotoisa home, comfort runs deeper than that – beyond physical softness and to a place of psychological ease. This is the sense of being able to fully exhale and let your guard down. Comfort means not having to apologize for the mess, or feel like you should be tidying up before someone comes over. It means living in your space the way you actually live, not the way you think you're supposed to be living.

In a way, a comfortable home invites you to be comfortable in your self, too. It allows you to dress how you want: to potter about in your favourite old jumper or those old knitted socks. You can make a cup of tea and sit for a moment just because you feel like it, and not just because you've finally ticked off everything on your to-do list.

Kotoisa comfort extends to how you nourish yourself. It's not about Instagram-worthy meals or restrictive food rules, but about cooking something simple and satisfying – a bowl of soup with a slice of homemade bread, however wonky. This is the kind of food that feels good in your body, not just on the plate.

The feeling of being at home – truly at home – is the same as the feeling of being comfortable in your own skin. There's a quiet joy in that. Comfort, I've learned, arrives slowly.

Permission to relax
Comfort, to me, is psychological as much as physical. Flowers cut from the garden, loosely arranged, a sofa you can sink into and the permission to live here without apologizing.

THE PIG
KINFOLK

Comfort doesn't come from buying the right sofa or following some strict formula. It comes from using a space and from inhabiting it in your own, slightly wonky way. In kotoisa, comfort is the way a home lets you drop your shoulders. It's the feeling of slipping into something familiar – not just your favourite jumper, but your favourite version of yourself.

And that comfort extends to how we live within these walls, so that you're able to move through your day without feeling like you're failing some invisible test: food that soothes rather than impresses, clothes you actually want to wear, routines that work for your family (even if they'd never pass as 'aspirational' on social media). There's something so grounding about living in a space that truly works in this way – where everything has a place and you don't have to overthink daily life.

Comfort is personal. What feels cosy and safe to me might feel cluttered or chaotic to someone else. That's why kotoisa isn't about copying a look or following a formula. It's about paying attention to how your home makes you feel, and making adjustments based on that. If you feel calm in a room – if your body softens a little just by being there – that's a good sign. And if you don't? Well, it probably doesn't mean you need to buy something new. Maybe the sofa's in the wrong place. Maybe there's too much going on, visually. Maybe the lighting's a bit harsh or there's nowhere to set down a cup of tea. These are all easy things to fix.

And yes, there's a physical element too. A room with the right textures – the softness of worn linen, the warmth of wood, the gentle glow of a lamp – invites you in. But those same things mean very little if the room also makes you feel like you can't breathe.

When we were renovating, I remember obsessing over finishes. I wanted everything to be 'just so'. But the spaces to which we now gravitate most, like the sofa next to the window, the chair in the kitchen corner, are the ones that came together a bit haphazardly. These are the places where function quietly won out over form.

Really, comfort is the one thing that doesn't age. It holds steady even as trends shift. You won't fall out of love with it in a season. It's the feeling that welcomes you in from the rain, the one that lets you cry quietly on the sofa, laugh until your stomach aches or eat toast at midnight.

A comfortable home, a truly kotoisa one, isn't there to impress. It's there to hold you, gently, in all your everyday mess and beauty.

Moments of calm

This is what I mean by 'inhabiting' a space: not styling it into submission, but letting it work with and for your real life. Here, everything has a place, and you can stop overthinking.

Functionality

One of the most liberating things I've learned over the years is that practicality isn't the enemy of beauty – it's often the foundation of it. A functional home isn't boring or utilitarian. It just means you're not hunting for light switches or tripping over baskets, or muttering about why the cupboard opens the wrong way.

When we first moved in, our house didn't function well at all. It had long, narrow corridors that seemed designed purely to house all the doors leading to small, boxy rooms. The windows were so high you could see nothing but a sliver of sky. It was always a house with a lot of potential, but the layout didn't support our family life. It felt more like a collection of rooms we happened to pass through.

More on our renovation later (see chapter 3), but I can say this: living in the house – previously dark, awkward and non-functioning – felt entirely different afterwards. That, at its heart, is the kotoisa approach to functionality: intuitive and rooted in your real life. It's not about designing your life around your home, it's about shaping your home around your life.

Practical functionality starts with asking questions:

- Where do you spend the most time? Is it easy to move around in that space?
- What annoys you daily? That cupboard you always bang your hip on? The lamp that gives off harsh light, or the plug that's always in the wrong place?
- What do you need close at hand, and what could be put away?
- How do you want this room to feel, and is that feeling currently being supported or hindered?

Sometimes, functionality means a full renovation: rethinking a layout, adjusting doorways, swapping rooms around. Often, though, little shifts can yield results: adding a narrow console table in the hallway to catch keys and post, installing shelves where clutter gathers, or just moving the kettle to a more sensible spot.

Foundations of beauty
Kotoisa functionality means your home supports your life: a kitchen island that earns its keep, light where you need it, and the everyday bits left out on purpose.

I keep a basket near our back door for gardening gloves, torches and dog leads. It's not especially stylish, but it's saved me from countless moments of panicked rummaging.

Kotoisa isn't about rigid organization or clever storage systems (though both can help). It's about creating spaces that ease your day rather than add to its weight. A functional home allows your attention to rest where it matters – on the people you live with, the dinner you're making, the book you've been meaning to finish – and not on all the little things that aren't working. This form of emotional functionality is sometimes easy to overlook, but centres on how moving through the space supports your state of mind. Can you make a cup of coffee without feeling hemmed in? Is there a seat where the light falls in the afternoon? Are there corners that invite rest?

I've always loved beautiful things. I'm an aesthete at heart, and I believe that our surroundings deeply affect how we feel. I care about colour, about texture, about light falling just right on a wooden surface. But as much as I love a beautifully styled room, if a space doesn't function well, it never truly feels good.

So I try to design for real life, not a magazine spread. I've learned that function is often about small, almost invisible decisions: making sure the things we use every day are within reach, choosing layouts that support how we move through a space and defining areas for the different aspects of life. A reading chair by the window, a table that doubles as a workspace, a hallway that doesn't feel like an obstacle course – these aren't grand gestures, but they make life smoother.

Lighting plays a big role. A single harsh overhead light can flatten even the most beautiful room. I rely on layers instead – all kinds of lamps. Each kind of light has its place, supporting different moods and times of day. And when form and function come together – when a space is both beautiful and supportive of the way we live – that, to me, is the heart of kotoisa.

It doesn't matter if you have a huge house or a tiny flat. Functionality is about paying attention – it means being honest about what's working and what isn't, and having the courage to change it. Because when your home functions well, you feel better in it. You're not constantly compensating. You're not quietly irritated. You're free to relax, to notice the good stuff, to let go.

Everyday display
Plates you love, wood ready for the fire, baskets by the door – when what you use is also what you see, life feels easier and more enjoyable.

Authenticity

If comfort is how a space makes you feel and functionality is how it works, then authenticity is what anchors it all to you. It's the soul of kotoisa – the part that makes your home unmistakably yours.

I've always been drawn to homes that feel lived in – not in a cluttered or chaotic way, but with that quiet, reassuring sense that someone really lives there. You can sense it in the artwork that isn't quite straight, the forgotten mug on the coffee table, slippers by the front door and the books that linger around the house. There's a kind of softness in those imperfections that makes a space feel more welcoming and more human.

Authenticity doesn't mean a fixed style or aesthetic. It means reflecting your own story, your history and your values. For some, that might mean a perfectly pared-back space with only a handful of meaningful pieces. For others, it's layered and full: a mix of inherited furniture, found objects, handmade pieces and things picked up on travels or in charity shops. For me, it's often a bit of both. I have a weakness for old ceramics – vases with texture, and anything that shows the hand of the maker.

I'm not interested in trends for the sake of trends. I'd rather live with things that carry a memory or a mood. There's something very freeing about letting go of the idea that your home needs to impress anyone. When you stop trying to keep up with what's 'in' and start noticing what feels good to you, your home naturally starts to take shape. A worn chair that reminds you of your grandfather, a mismatched table setting that somehow always sparks conversation: these are the kinds of things that create emotional warmth – and that's what authenticity is really all about.

It's also worth saying that a truly authentic home doesn't need to look the same every year. It shifts with your life. New objects come in, old ones are passed along. Rooms get rearranged, painted, stripped back. I find this comforting – the idea that our homes grow with us. Authenticity isn't something you achieve and then tick off a list. It's something you live, day by day.

Character, not clutter
The little clues that say 'someone lives here': a favourite object left out, books that never quite make it back to the shelf, a mug on the table.

å

Imperfection

There's a Finnish word I come back to often: *kotikutoisuus*. It means something like homemade, but not in the prim, perfect bake-off kind of way. It's the cardigan your grandma knitted slightly too big, or the curtain hem that isn't quite square. It's charm, warmth and story stitched into everyday things.

I used to apologize when the house wasn't tidy, but I don't anymore, because I've realized that people don't come to see your perfectly styled mantel. They come to feel welcome. A little chaos, a little texture, a little evidence of life – that's what makes a home feel lived in, not just looked at. Accepting, or even celebrating, imperfection, I've come to believe, is less about showing off and more about showing up – letting stories breathe life into rooms. It's not something you jump into one day, it's the home you build softly, step by step.

This doesn't mean letting everything go. I still love beauty – I'll happily faff with cushions or rearrange furniture until the balance and rhythm feels right. But I've learned to stop when it feels good, not when it looks perfect, and that's a big difference. You can spend years chasing perfection and still feel like your home isn't 'done'. Or you can decide 'this is enough'. This clean but permanently stained tea towel, this rug that never quite lies flat – it's enough. It's beautiful in its own way. Just like us.

The magic of imperfection is that it frees you. You can experiment more. Take risks. Be bolder. You can let your house evolve over time instead of trying to get it 'finished' all at once. That slow layering of objects, colours, memories and little flaws is how the most beautiful homes are built.

Over the last 18 years, I've lived in five different homes. Each one came with its quirks and flaws; each one became a backdrop to some part of our life. And when I think back to them now, I don't remember the carefully chosen colour palettes or how I arranged the cushions on the sofa. I couldn't even tell you what my bedside lamps looked like. What I do remember are the things that made each place a home.

Lovely imperfection
This wall, with its layers of paint, faded pattern and traces of time, is a reminder that a home can be beautiful without being flawless.

1984
AE
LISA

When we moved into our first flat together, it was also the first time my husband and I had lived in the same country. The flat was petite and the hallway often smelled faintly of someone else's cooking. That's where I found out I was pregnant for the first time. I remember standing in the hallway, gripping the test with both hands, heart racing. When my husband came through the front door after work, I didn't even wait for him to take off his coat. I just blurted out, 'I'm pregnant'. That moment is fixed in my memory: the hallway lino bubbling at the edges, the bright red door, the halogen lighting – and the excited nervousness that filled the space.

Not long after that, we moved into a 1960s semi-detached house in a village outside London. A boxy, practical house that didn't look like much, this was nevertheless a good setting for the most intense and chaotic years of our life. It's where we brought our son home from hospital; where we padded across cold floors in the middle of the night, trying to settle him – bleary-eyed and whispering so we didn't wake the neighbours. The night before our daughter was born, we had friends over for dinner. I remember feeling odd all evening: distracted, a bit foggy, putting things in the wrong cupboards, leaving the fridge open more than once. The next morning, she arrived in a rush. I came home the same evening holding this tiny bundle of a person, and our son peered at her with a mix of suspicion and curiosity from the side of her basket bed.

I don't remember what throw cushions we had on the sofa at that point. I couldn't tell you what was hanging on the walls. But I do remember how I slept on the sofa with our little girl when she had terrible chicken pox, and how I sometimes went to hide in the loft with a cup of coffee, ignoring the washing up, because I finally had five quiet minutes to myself.

These homes were not perfect. Most of the time they weren't even close. But they held us through new babies, career changes, illness, birthdays, sleepless nights, long-awaited news and ordinary Tuesday dinners that turned out to be the best part of the week.

Kotoisa is about recognizing that a home's worth isn't in its finishes or styling, but in how it makes you feel. It's in the rituals that shape your days and the stories you collect along the way – stories you'll never find in a floor plan or a paint chart.

Looking back, I wouldn't change a thing. Because in each of those homes, life happened. Messy, joyful, ordinary life. And honestly, that's all I ever wanted. A home that felt like ours: not perfect, but perfectly us. That's what makes a house kotoisa.

Collected, layered, personal
Vintage pieces bring instant soul, without trying too hard. The patina, the quirks, the little imperfections – all add up to a kotoisa home.

How kotoisa differs from *hygge* and *lagom*

Kotoisa often gets grouped together with its better-known Nordic cousins *hygge* and *lagom*, and while they share some values – simplicity, warmth, a sense of balance – the terms come from different roots and lead to slightly different places.

Hygge, the Danish concept that has swept through Pinterest boards and bookstore shelves, is all about creating moments of cosiness. Think sheepskin throws, candlelight, warm drinks and being tucked up indoors while the rain patters on the windows. It's about atmosphere, and the fleeting beauty of comfort in a particular moment. *Lagom*, the Swedish philosophy, is more about moderation – the 'just enough' approach to living. Not too much, not too little; a kind of minimalist mindfulness.

Kotoisa, though, feels less curated and more personal – less about creating a moment, and more about building a feeling that lasts. Where *hygge* might light the candle and *lagom* would make sure you only had one, kotoisa asks whether the candle has a memory attached to it – was it picked up on holiday or given by someone you love? Does it sit somewhere meaningful? It's less about aesthetics or even balance, and more about the emotional connection you have with your space.

It's a feeling that is built slowly, layer by layer. Not because a stylist has chosen the right neutral palette or the proportions are perfect, but because the room knows you, and you know it. It remembers the stories. A kotoisa home isn't trying to impress. It's trying to hold you. It is comforting and calm, but also practical, working quietly in the background to support your daily rhythms.

Kotoisa is not a lifestyle you adopt, but a way of being at home – one that embraces imperfection, celebrates the homespun and makes space for both the joyful rituals and the messy, mundane moments of real life. Kotoisa is emotional. It's instinctive. It's the feeling of being grounded, and of moving through your space with ease and comfort. It's a lived-in, fully functional life, filled with personal touches and moments of care.

Rather than stripping back or staging, kotoisa celebrates the space in-between. It holds space for mess and meaning, for rituals and routines, and for the quiet, everyday moments that make life feel full. And while *hygge* and *lagom* might have become familiar, kotoisa is an idea that feels ready for right now – a reminder that home isn't a performance, but a place to belong.

A place to belong
Kotoisa asks 'does it feel like you?' It creates an easeful home, built layer by layer and full of memories.

CHAPTER 2

The Lived-In Home

RICE

There's a certain kind of silence in a house that hasn't been lived in: not the peaceful, contented quiet of a slow Sunday afternoon, but a sort of hollowness, a sense that the rooms are waiting for something to happen, for someone to arrive and bring them to life.

When we first moved back into our house after renovating it over nine months, it felt exactly like that. The house wasn't quite finished either, so we shared our space with the builders for a few weeks while the last jobs were done. The walls were bare. Even once we were able to start unpacking our things, it didn't feel like *home*. Not yet.

It took time, much more than I expected. Time to learn how the light moved across the floor during the day, and how the smallest changes – a rug here, a hook there – began to soften the space. Slowly, quietly, it started to feel like ours. This chapter is about *that* feeling.

What turns a house into a home isn't just what you put in it. It's how it makes you feel. In Finland, we aren't known for talking too much about emotions, but our homes say so much. They reflect who we are, how we live, what we value. A kotoisa home is layered with the rituals and stories of daily life – imperfect, beautiful, evolving. It's the candleholder that's seen better days but always finds its place on the table, and the lopsided picture you never get around to straightening; it's the softness of a throw at the end of the bed, the smell of toast on a rainy morning, a lamp clicked on at dusk. It's a feeling more than a look, and something you sense the moment you step through the door.

In the pages that follow, I want to take you through what it really means to live kotoisa. We'll talk about how our surroundings shape us, the role of light and layout, the comfort of imperfection and the quiet rituals that bring joy to ordinary days. I'll also share the story of how we transformed our own house from a dark shell into a warm, lived-in space that finally felt like home.

So much of this is about noticing the little things and trusting that they matter. Because they do.

Home is a feeling
Your surroundings shape your moods more than you might realize. Here we're talking about why some spaces calm us instantly, and how to build that sense of ease in real life.

The emotional power of home

We often underestimate just how much our environment can influence our inner state. Sometimes it's obvious, like when you walk into a room filled with harsh lighting, clashing colours and nowhere comfortable to sit. Other times, it's subtler: a hallway that's always cluttered, a kitchen that never quite works, or a bathroom where towels never dry. Over time, those little friction points chip away at our sense of ease.

I have lived in various homes over the years, and while most were small and full of compromises, I enjoyed living in all of them. When I was living in New York I rented a room that was just about big enough to contain a double bed and a narrow hanging storage unit. I shared a kitchen and bathroom with two other girls, and we had a living room, too, so there was ample communal space. There was not much space for decorating as such, but I had a big window and a fire-escape staircase, where I used to sit and listen to the city noises. I was young and fun and, in those days, always out, so the room worked fine.

I remember the feeling of coming back after a long day, cracking the window open and watching the neighbouring buildings flicker to life one by one. There was a corner deli on the next block where I used to order coffee and perfect bagels. That tiny room felt like an adventure. Looking back now, I realize it wasn't the space itself that mattered so much, but what the space *held*. That's the emotional power of home. It doesn't have to be big or beautifully styled – it just has to feel like it's *yours*.

There's science behind this. Studies show that our physical surroundings impact our stress levels, sleep patterns and even our relationships. Homes with natural light, thoughtful layout and soothing textures are linked to better well-being. But you don't need data to know this – you feel it: when you walk into a sunlit room, or your eyes come to rest on a tidy surface, or when you settle down in a well-worn corner that's entirely yours.

So when we talk about creating a kotoisa home, it starts with awareness. Not of trends or what everyone else is doing, but of how your home makes you feel. Which are the spaces you gravitate towards? What drains you? What delights you in ways you can't always explain? Once you notice that – once you start tuning in – you'll begin to understand how your home can be your ally in creating a life that feels grounded and joyful.

Light

There's a reason we're all drawn to well-lit homes. Light changes not only how a room looks but also how it feels. Making the most of daylight is important, but so is artificial lighting, as it creates homes that are warm and inviting. No amount of styling or beautiful furniture can save a space if the lighting is wrong – too cold, too harsh, too bright or dim in the wrong places. Something will always feel 'off'. Paying attention to the *quality* of light is also important.

A simple, layered lighting plan will help you create effective lighting for each space. Most rooms will benefit from at least three of these layers, and often four if the space allows. You don't need to install everything at once, but knowing what's missing can help you understand why a room doesn't feel quite right.

When it comes to lighting, the details matter. I always recommend using dimmers wherever possible. They're one of those small changes that can make a huge difference. Being able to soften the lighting in the evening or brighten things up on a grey afternoon gives you control over the mood, without having to rely on multiple switches. Another simple but effective idea is to group lighting sources at different heights. Light at floor level, eye level and overhead adds a sense of depth to a room that a single ceiling pendant simply can't achieve. Think about how a floor lamp in one corner, a low table lamp by the sofa and a soft ceiling glow can work together to create a space that feels cocooning and calm.

And while we're on the subject of glow – pay attention to the temperature of your bulbs. This sounds technical but it's honestly not. A 'warm white' bulb, somewhere around 2700K, will almost always be your friend. It mimics the light at dusk, or candlelight – the kind of light to which we're drawn. Anything cooler than that and you start to move into blue-toned territory, which might be fine for a dentist's office but is not going to do your kitchen or bedroom any favours.

You can absolutely mix lamp styles – in fact, I'd encourage it. A mix of shapes, finishes and shades can add visual interest. But what you *don't* want is a mismatch of light tones. One bright-white LED next to a soft amber glow is jarring to the eye, even if you can't put your finger on why. Try to keep bulbs consistent in warmth, even if the lamps themselves don't match.

Lastly, don't forget that lighting is part of your decor. A beautiful lamp, even when it's switched off, adds character to a space. Lighting doesn't have to be purely functional.

Instant glow

If a room feels 'off', check the light before you change the furniture. The best lighting is functional, but it should make you feel something, too. Try warm bulbs, a dimmer and light sources at different heights.

I like to think of lighting like layering an outfit. One layer alone rarely does the job. You need a combination:

- ***Ambient lighting*** is your general, overall light, the kind that fills the room softly and evenly, giving you a base level of illumination. Often a combination of a pendant light and wall lights and table or floor lamps works well – a gentle wash of light that comes from multiple sources working together.
- ***Task lighting*** is focused light for doing things. Think of reading lamps by the sofa, under-cabinet lighting in the kitchen, or a desk lamp in your workspace. This is where form meets function.
- ***Mood or accent lighting*** creates small pools of light that soften a space and draw your eye to certain corners. Wall lights, picture lights, fairy lights, a lamp on a shelf or candlelight by the bath – these are the soul of the room.
- ***Statement lighting*** (optional but lovely) is not just practical but beautiful, too: a pendant over the dining table, a sculptural floor lamp or a chandelier in an unexpected room. These all help to give a room personality.

Layered lighting
Aim for a mix of soft ambient light, practical task lighting, a little mood in the corners, and one statement piece for personality.

vesper

Layout and flow

I've always cared about how a home feels, but it wasn't until our first renovation that I really noticed how much layout impacts that feeling.

It's not just about open-plan versus separate rooms or where the plug sockets are (though both are important). It's about whether your space works with the way you actually live. Can you walk from one room to the next without awkward detours? Do you end up piling bags in the hallway because there's nowhere else for them to go? Are the spots in which you naturally linger – by a window, near the kettle – easy to use and lovely to be in?

When we moved into our old house, the whole place felt chopped up and disconnected. The windows were small and so high that you could barely see out. It didn't feel welcoming, even though the bones of the house were beautiful. One of the biggest changes we made was rethinking how we wanted to live in the house and how the light travelled throughout the day. We moved the kitchen to the sunnier west side of the house and made the north-facing kitchen into our living room. We opened out the boxy rooms and narrow corridors, and added bigger windows. The house felt bigger without increasing the footprint: lighter and so much more inviting.

- ***Walk through your home as if you were a guest.*** Notice where you pause, where you get stuck. What's in your way? Is there a cabinet door that always bangs into something? A narrow passage between the dining chairs and the wall?
- ***Observe your daily routes.*** Where do you put your bag down? What do you reach for every day? Is the bin easy to access? Little irritations add up, and fixing them often doesn't require anything fancy. Sometimes you just need to move a piece of furniture or rethink a shelf height.
- ***Think about transitions between spaces.*** Do they feel natural? Or do you find yourself looping around the long way just to get from one room to another? Visual connection helps, too – even a glimpse of a favourite corner as you pass by can make a space feel more coherent.
- ***Allow space to breathe.*** Not every surface needs styling. Not every wall needs art. Sometimes what a room needs most is a bit of empty space – somewhere for your eye to rest and your shoulders to drop.

One of the best bits of advice I've ever heard about layout is this: don't decorate around problems. Fix the flow first, then add the beauty. It's tempting to rush into the fun part – paint colours, textiles, lighting – but no cushion can fix a tight hallway that you have to shimmy through, or a dining room where no one can fit round the table.

When your layout works, your home does the hard parts for you, and that, to me, is deeply kotoisa.

A warm welcome
Our hallway, post-renovation. We added big windows on both external walls, so the space stopped feeling like a corridor and started feeling like a welcome.

Layers and textures

Soft edges, gentle warmth, somewhere to rest your hand or your eyes – these elements are the heartbeat of a home, and what makes a space feel alive. No matter how minimalist or maximalist your style is, a room without texture usually feels flat. It's like dressing head-to-toe in sackcloth: technically fine, but something's missing.

Natural materials like linen, wool and cotton always feel more inviting, and they age beautifully, too. They've got a softness that's hard to fake. I love the look of slightly crumpled linen bedding, or a faded wool rug that's been walked over a thousand times. Nothing too precious, just pieces that are made to be lived with.

On the sofa, I tend to rotate throws with the seasons: heavier knits and richer tones in winter, something lighter and softer in spring. Cushions, too, change the mood of a space without much effort. I rarely go in for perfectly matching sets. A mix of sizes, patterns and materials feels more relaxed, like the room evolved over time rather than being styled all at once.

But texture isn't just about fabric. Think about woodgrain, ceramic glaze, the softness of a sheepskin; a smooth wall next to a rough brick one, or a sleek surface with a chunky handmade bowl on top. You want some contrast – a bit of tension between smooth and rough, cool and warm. One of the simplest ways to bring more texture into a space is using everyday items that you already have in circulation.

I often find myself instinctively running my hands along surfaces when I'm in a new space. A smooth marble worktop, a linen tablecloth, a battered old wooden dining table that's been sanded back so many times that it feels like silk – these are the details that make a space feel welcoming, inviting you to touch, pause, feel grounded in the moment. And of course, light plays a part, too. The way it hits different textures adds yet another layer of depth.

If you're not sure where to start with layering, try this: pick one area of your home, like a reading nook or your bedroom. Add three textures to the space – maybe a knitted blanket, a smooth ceramic and a soft lamp light. Live with it for a while. Notice how it changes the mood.

A home that's rich in texture feels generous. It doesn't ask for perfection. It just offers softness, warmth and welcome.

Beautiful details

I'm always drawn to materials that age beautifully: linen that gets softer, wood that shows its grain. A few tactile pieces can change the whole mood of a room.

Embracing imperfection and *kotikutoisuus*

I've always believed that homes are at their most beautiful when they're not trying too hard. Real life is rarely tidy, and the kind of home I love the most is one that makes space for the frayed edges – neither too perfect, too polished nor too posed.

In Finland, we have a word that captures this beautifully: *kotikutoisuus*. It's the feeling of something being created with care, not expertise: the lopsided cake your child ices with fierce concentration, a knitted jumper with a crooked sleeve, wool socks pieced together from leftover yarn. These things transmit warmth because they carry the marks of the maker's hand.

At our small red cottage in Finland, we've been renovating slowly. And I do mean *slowly*. The place smells faintly of woodsmoke. The kitchen came with a single free-standing unit: low, battered, almost unusable, and too full of history to throw away. By luck, my parents had an almost identical unit stored in a barn, from a previous renovation, and we're restoring both to use together. There's quiet comfort in knowing I'll chop vegetables where my grandma once did, decades ago.

In a world that constantly shouts for our attention and promotes gleaming newness, there's power in choosing the gently worn – objects with history. A chipped tile that's been there longer than you have, a table with water rings and stories in the grain: these pieces don't audition for approval, they tell your story. They are specific and personal – already part of a house's memory.

Of course, not every old thing is worth keeping. Kotoisa doesn't mean cluttered or chaotic. It's about balance: letting in what adds warmth and letting go of what gets in the way. A good rule of thumb: if it makes you smile every time you pass it, it has earned its place. If you're forever stepping around it, it hasn't.

Embracing imperfection is more than a design choice; it's a gentler way to live. If we can be at ease with the wobbly coffee table or the paint that never quite dried right in the corner, perhaps we can be at ease with the day that runs off course, the plan that changes, the version of life that looks different to the one in our heads. Perfection is brittle; lived-in is generous.

Homes, like people, get better with time – not because they stay flawless, but because they gather meaning. That's the beauty of a kotoisa home: it only asks you to be yourself. And it will meet you there, scuffs and all.

The simple life
Our red cottage in south-west Finland – no running water, patina aplenty – is rough around the edges, and that's exactly the point.

The power of nostalgic, meaningful objects

If you've ever caught yourself smiling at an old teacup or hanging onto a threadbare teddy bear long past its prime, you already understand the quiet power of meaningful objects. These things don't have to be valuable or even particularly beautiful, they just have to mean something to you.

I have a wooden butter knife that my dad made from a juniper bush that used to grow behind my parents house. It gets used almost daily. It's not fancy, and probably a bit too big to be especially practical, but every time I reach for it, there's a small flicker of comfort. It reminds me of childhood summers on the island, rye bread breakfasts and my dad's hands – always warm, always busy. Objects like these don't just fill a space, they anchor us. They carry memories; they have a lineage.

That said, there's a fine line between surrounding yourself with meaningful things and keeping everything just because it has a story. Not every sentimental object needs to be on display. Some treasures are best kept tucked away, and pulled out every now and then like old letters, their magic intact precisely because they aren't part of the daily visual noise.

One of the simplest ways to create a home that feels kotoisa is to give space to the things that mean something to you. Not as clutter, not as decoration for decoration's sake, but as reminders of where you've come from and what you love.

If you're not sure where to begin, try this: walk through your home and notice what makes you pause, what makes you smile or remember. Maybe it's a lamp inherited from a parent, or a small chipped bowl from your first flat. These objects are the threads that tie your present life to all the others you've lived before.

Pieces with a story
A familiar picture on the wall, a well-used chest, something inherited or found; this is how kotoisa builds itself, one meaningful object at a time.

Daily rituals and small joys

I think most of us underestimate just how much our days are made up of tiny moments. Not the big milestones or once-a-year events, but the little, familiar rituals that string the hours together like beads on a thread. I like drinking coffee from my favourite mug every morning, and the smell of freshly washed sheets as I crawl into bed; I like lighting a candle for the dinner table, even if we're just having leftovers on an average Thursday night. These are the things that make a house feel lived-in and, more importantly, loved.

I look forwards to these little rituals when I come home. They help me appreciate the ordinary day. Some of mine are tiny and entirely unspectacular, like rearranging the cushions the way I like them on the sofa every night before I sit down with a cup of tea. I'm not sure why, but this feels like a small act of intention. Loading up the coffee machine in the evening, ready for the next morning, is not about perfection or productivity. It's just ... gentle. Familiar. A way to say 'I'm here. This is my home. This is my life.'

Wiping down the kitchen counters after dinner, not in a rush to finish, but as a way to signal that the day is slowing down. Tucking a wool throw over the end of the bed just because it looks comforting. Keeping a big stack of books on the nightstand, even if I never quite finish any of them. There's something deeply kotoisa in these acts – a sense that your home is holding you in return.

The beauty of these small joys is that they're completely individual. Your rituals won't look like mine. Maybe you always light incense before work, or you put fresh herbs in a glass on the windowsill, or you change the hand towel in the bathroom every Friday afternoon. These things don't have to be impressive. They just have to be yours.

So often we chase big lifestyle changes hoping that they'll transform our daily experience. But more often than not, it's the reverse – these small, consistent, tender gestures truly change how we feel.

Tiny moments of joy

Most of life is made up of tiny moments – the familiar routines that say 'I'm here'. A cup of tea in the same spot, or a lamp switched on at dusk.

Morning rituals

Small beginnings make the whole day softer, setting a calm mood that inflects your daytime routine from wake-up to dusk. You can play soft music while you get ready to focus the mind, or draft a short to-do list every morning. Here are a few ideas to inspire your morning ritual. These are not rules, just options. Borrow what fits, leave the rest.

- Open a window for a breath of fresh air and morning sounds.
- Make coffee or tea and enjoy the process as much as the drink.
- Sit in a favourite spot for five quiet minutes before the day begins.
- Light a candle or incense while you get ready.
- Stretch gently – no yoga mat needed.
- Read a few pages of a book, a poem or a quote that inspires you.
- Open the curtains and let natural light flood in.
- Tidy one surface – a calm visual cue for the day ahead.
- Make the bed, smoothing sheets and fluffing pillows.
- Take a short walk outside, even if it's just to the garden or postbox.
- Choose your clothes based on how you want to feel, not how you think you should look.
- Pause to notice something beautiful or seasonal outside.
- Have a slow breakfast – mindfully. Sit at the table to eat, even if just for five minutes.
- Use the 'good' mug or plate – every day is worthy.
- Set out one small thing that will bring you joy (a book, candle, blanket).
- Put on cosy socks or a soft jumper as a small comfort cue.
- Roll your shoulders and stretch your neck while the kettle boils.
- Swap out the tea towel to start fresh.
- Do a 60-second tidy of the living room or hallway.
- Add lemon or herbs to your water for a sensory lift.
- Place fresh fruit in a bowl where it's easy to reach.
- Step outside with bare feet on grass or stone (weather permitting!).
- Keep your phone in airplane mode for the first hour.

Kotoisa mood reset
A hot drink in a favourite spot, a few minutes enjoying the view through the window, a simple flower arrangement – all ways to start the day with calm and intention.

Evening rituals

Evenings are an invitation to soften the edges of the day. The pace slows, the light shifts and you can settle back into yourself. I'm a homebody and love staying in – evenings at home are my favourite. I wear something comfortable, dim the lights and cosy up on the sofa for a moment, even if the day has been long and bedtime is looming. Even if things have been chaotic, a few small rituals can gently mark the shift into rest. They don't need to be elaborate or time-consuming – just simple signals to your body and mind that it's time to exhale.

- Switch off the main lights and turn on a table lamp or two.
- Light candles, even just one at the dinner table or on the windowsill.
- Prepare a warm drink of choice – for me it's always mint tea.
- Tidy one surface, so you wake up to a calmer space.
- Close the curtains and fluff the sofa cushions.
- Fold a blanket over the arm of a chair or bed.
- Brush hair slowly or apply hand cream as a moment of self-care.
- Water any thirsty plants before bed.
- Write a few lines in a journal or jot down a highlight of the day.
- Lay out clothes or prep lunches for the next day if that feels helpful.
- Put away your phone or switch to airplane mode for the night.
- Burn incense or use a pillow spray to cue rest.
- Read a chapter or a few pages of a favourite book.
- Stretch gently or take a few deep breaths to release tension.
- Have a warm bath or shower.
- Diffuse essential oils or place lavender sachets near the bed.
- Change into cosy house clothes.
- Take a moment outside – just a few deep breaths.

Gentle shift into rest
My favourite kind of evening ritual is simple: candlelight, a soft pool of lamp light, curtains closed, cushions fluffed. Nothing dramatic, just a soothing transition into night-time.

JO MALONE

Simple pleasures

Afternoon *kahvit* – coffee time, in Finland – was always part of the day when I was growing up: expected in the way that routines often are. Someone would suggest 'isn't this now a perfect time for coffee?' (I don't remember anyone ever disagreeing), and soon the familiar smell would drift from the faithful coffee machine and through the house. We'd gather in the kitchen – sometimes all together, sometimes just whoever happened to be around. There'd usually be something my mum had baked: cinnamon buns, *tiikerikakku* or a tray of *mustikkapiirakka* if it was blueberry season.

It wasn't a big occasion, but it mattered. It was a small pause, a reset – a chance to sit down, catch up, maybe have a quiet moment with a newspaper or just your thoughts. It never felt rushed. There was no performance to it. Just a warm cup, something sweet and the sense that everything else could wait.

There's joy in these small acts: putting on music while you cook, slicing strawberries for a weekend pancake breakfast, the good wine opened for no reason, a candle lit on the kitchen table even just for you. I like to set the table nicely even when we're having leftover pasta from the fridge, just because it makes me pause and appreciate the moment.

You don't need to do anything big or elaborate to feel joy at home. Often, the simplest pleasures are the ones that stay with you longest.

Everyday ceremony
You don't need a special occasion to set the table: a striped cloth, a few pretty plates, a candle and whatever you've got on hand, creating a little corner of light.

Simple pleasures to savour at home

- Bake a small batch of oat biscuits or a banana cake, just because.
- Flip through an old cookbook and pick a recipe that you haven't made in years.
- Eat lunch in the garden or outdoors, even if it's just a sandwich.
- Roast apples or pears with a pinch of cinnamon for a warming afternoon treat.
- Cook your favourite Saturday-night dinner, even if it's just for you.
- Use linen napkins on a Wednesday – no guests needed.
- Set the table with candles.
- Sit at the table long after the meal is done.
- Bake something nostalgic from your childhood and eat it warm.
- Plate your food like it matters, even leftovers.
- Bring out your favourite wine glasses for fizzy water.
- Eat from your prettiest plate.
- Have a meal-prep day.
- Eat outside whenever the weather allows.
- Rearrange a corner of a room for the joy of seeing it with fresh eyes.
- Change your pillowcases to freshly washed linen midweek.
- Warm a jumper on the radiator before you put it on.
- Sit by the window to watch the weather shift.
- Take ten minutes to have a stretch.
- Fold clean laundry into neat stacks.
- Light a candle for no reason at all.
- Hang a new postcard or photo on the fridge or noticeboard.
- Tidy a single drawer or shelf.
- Brush a wool throw to keep it looking soft and loved.
- Write a list of things you're looking forwards to.
- Swap out cushion covers or throws for the season ahead.
- Sit on the floor with a book or a blanket.
- Dust a bookshelf and get lost in a title you forgot you had.

Function and form
I like homes where useful things are also the pretty things: glass jars out on the shelf, cups on hooks and wooden boards ready to grab.

Kotoisa across life stages

How our homes evolve – and how to keep them feeling kotoisa through it all

One of the most comforting things about kotoisa is that it doesn't require any one particular style, size of home or stage of life. It's not something you achieve once and for all, it's something that flexes and softens and rearranges itself alongside you.

The home that suited you at 25 won't be the one you need at 45; seasons shift, people come and go, routines alter. The work is to notice those changes and adjust in small, practical ways so that ease returns. The layout, the way you use each space – all of it shifts. Sometimes it happens gradually, almost without you noticing. Other times, life throws you into a new season and suddenly nothing about your home feels quite right anymore.

This chapter is about recognizing those changes and responding to them in small, thoughtful ways. How do you stay connected to a sense of ease and belonging, even as everything around you – and inside you – evolves and shifts?

A feeling you build over time
Your first home is a practice run in listening to yourself. What helps you settle? What makes you exhale? Start there: soft light, one comfortable spot, a few easy rituals.

Your first home (or just your first time living alone)

There's a particular kind of joy in your very first home. Maybe it's a rented studio with noisy neighbours, or a house-share, where your bedroom is the only space that's fully yours. It might not be your dream place, and that's part of the charm. What matters is the feeling of ownership. You get to choose what goes where, what to keep, what to get rid of.

You're learning how to live with yourself: what time you like to eat, how tidy you are, what your routines look like without anyone else shaping them. That's no small thing.

Make it work now

- Pick one corner to get just right – it's easier to feel settled when at least one space feels good.
- Don't fill it too fast. Let your space evolve with you.
- Spend where it counts: a decent pillow, a supportive chair, warm lamp light (2700K).
- Add light layers rather than overhead glare: a bedside lamp with plug-in dimmer and a paper shade.
- Use removable solutions: command hooks, free-standing shelves, rugs to zone space.
- Start two rituals: a five-minute reset before bed and a ten-minute tidy on Sunday.

Living with flatmates or a partner

Sharing a home is a negotiation of space, sound and tempo. Aim for 'mine, yours, ours' zones and agree the baseline: tidy enough to be kind, flexible enough to be lived in.

It's a dance, really. In these years, home is a negotiation. You might be blending tastes, or figuring out how to carve out quiet in a house that's always buzzing with someone else's energy.

This is where kotoisa can offer a bit of ease, by creating small rituals, softening shared spaces and making room for everyone's way of being.

Make it work now

- Map traffic and friction points (hallway, fridge, laundry). Put the best storage where the pressure is highest.
- Create personal pockets in shared rooms: a chair that's 'yours', a small tray for your bits, a shelf each.
- Establish quick resets for each room: kitchen counters clear, surfaces dusted, bathroom towels hung and floor dry.
- Write a simple chores cadence that suits your schedule (15 minutes, three times a week). Put it on the fridge and keep it light.

Space for everyone
When you live with other people, home becomes a series of small compromises. Little choices can make space for everyone to exist together peaceably.

Family life (with small children)

This is the chapter where your home fills up fast, and not just with stuff – though there's plenty of that – but with noise and joy and chaos and the kind of mess that signals life is happening. It's easy to feel like you're drowning in plastic toys and laundry piles, but it can also be the most alive your home has ever felt.

Kotoisa doesn't mean tidy or quiet. It means welcoming, forgiving, warm. A family home that works is one where there's flow, softness, storage that makes sense and spaces for everyone.

Design for flow

- Push storage to the edges and keep floors clear: low baskets for toys, closed cupboards for visual calm.
- Choose materials that age well: scrubbed timber, washable slip-covers, rugs with patterns that hide a little life.
- Put kid-height hooks, a shoe tray and a basket for hats and gloves by the door. (If it's easy, it happens.)
- Aim for multi-use: a bench with storage, a coffee table that can be lifted out of the way, a play mat that becomes a reading rug.
- Keep everyday rituals simple and consistent: breakfast at the table, music during bath time.
- Let your children's presence be visible – art on the wall, a few toys in shared spaces – but not overwhelming.
- Let go of the pressure to 'finish' the home. You're living in a work in progress.

The teen years (and transitional phases)

The teenage years and other big shifts – a divorce, a move, a job change – bring a different energy to the home. Sometimes it's unsettled. Sometimes it's stretched thin. And that's OK. A kotoisa home doesn't fix the chaos, but it can offer pockets of calm within it.

These phases ask us to be flexible. What used to work might not anymore. Rooms might need to change purpose. And sometimes, simply acknowledging that can be a relief.

Build buffers

- Revisit your layout. Could a rarely used dining room become a study space?
- Create 'catch points': a basket on the stairs, a tray in the hall, a hook for headphones, a hamper where laundry actually lands.
- Lean on sensory rituals: soft lighting, familiar meals, warm blankets on the sofa.
- Let teens personalize their space, even if it's not your taste – it helps them feel at home.
- Keep some things constant – Friday film, Sunday pancakes – routines are soothing.

Empty nest (or living alone again)

When the house suddenly gets quiet, it can feel both spacious and strangely sad. You might find yourself moving through rooms differently, not quite sure what to do with all that space or silence. But this season is also a beautiful opportunity to reclaim your home as your own.

You get to decide what stays and what goes, what brings comfort and what feels heavy. This is a time for renewal – gentle, slow, but powerful.

Ideas for kotoisa living

- Refresh a room or two, just for you: a reading nook, a painting space, a sewing table.
- Keep the good dishes out – every day is worth a little beauty.
- Keep objects that bring joy, not guilt. Let go of things you've outgrown.
- Make space for guests, even if they're rare.
- Add small pleasures to your everyday: fresh flowers, new linen, an afternoon ritual.

Ageing in place

This stage is about simplicity and ease – less about 'making over' and more about making things work – softly, safely, beautifully.

Design with grace

- Prioritize good lighting, especially in darker corners and hallways.
- Add handrails or seating where needed, but choose ones that blend into your style.
- Keep favourite items within easy reach – books, blankets, your favourite cup.
- Put everyday things between knee and shoulder height, heavy items at waist height.
- Let your home reflect your life, and not just your age.

Yours in every season

Home changes because life changes. Teen years, big transitions, the house going quiet again, ageing in place – it's all about making your space flex to suit you.

CHAPTER 3

Our Home Story

We weren't looking to buy a house in Bath. The search had been focused in an entirely different part of the country, where we'd already fallen for and lost a few houses. It was the usual story: long drives, dashed hopes, a growing sense that maybe we were being too picky, or just weren't lucky enough.

Bath wasn't even on the list. We had no ties to the city, no practical reason to consider it (other than the fact we had honeymooned there many years ago). But then this house popped up for sale. I can't remember what I was supposed to be doing that day – something productive, probably – but instead I was scrolling through listings and saw it. A very interesting looking modern house on a beautiful plot, close to the city centre but backing onto a field; trees everywhere, space to breathe. We booked a viewing on our way to visit friends, thinking it would just be a detour.

And then we pulled up outside.

It wasn't love at first sight. A 1960s bungalow that had clearly had a 1990s renovation, the house was practical, well-looked-after and, well, a bit odd. Lots of cherry-coloured wood; a lot of questionable layout choices; narrow, windowless corridors that led into an array of boxy rooms with high windows. The bathrooms were comically large, the bedrooms poky. But we both felt something shift as we walked around. We could see it – not as it was, but as it *could* be. More than that, we liked the way it felt: quiet, calm and settled.

There were already three offers on the table. We put ours in, held our breath, and – surprisingly – had it accepted. For 12 hours, it was ours.

And then it wasn't. Gazumped. Just like that.

It was disappointing, of course, but we had to move in time for the new school year, so had to move on. We found a charming farmhouse in Oxfordshire, made an offer and imagined ourselves there. I even allowed myself to start planning what colours I'd paint the walls. And then the survey came back – the kind of report that makes you take a deep breath and sit down for a moment. I read it while sitting on a granite rock on a small island in the Finnish archipelago, and all I could think was: *this is not our house*. I didn't even need to finish the report.

A few days later, the Bath agent called. The other buyer had pulled out. Were we still interested? We were.

It still wasn't the house I thought I wanted – I had visions of something Georgian and grand, not a boxy, brown bungalow – but it felt good, and the potential made up for the lack of period features, at least for the moment. The process of unlocking that potential would take time (and dust, and mess and more than a few layout debates).

This house gave us a new chapter, and this book is the story of what we've done with it. It's about creating a home that feels lived-in and loved, even if it didn't start out as the obvious choice. Sometimes, the house *isn't* the dream, but the home you build there is.

Where it all began
Before: not exactly love at first sight. During: the messy middle (plans, rubble, and a thousand small decisions to make).

The house as it was

The setting was beautiful: a generous plot, surrounded by mature trees, with glimpses of open countryside and views over the city of Bath.

Inside, things were less charming. A 1990s extension had left the layout disjointed and boxy – a maze of corridors and awkward walk-through rooms. The windows were oddly high, so you couldn't see the views unless you were standing. Most of the bedrooms were small, but the bathrooms were huge, and not in a luxurious spa-like way, just in a slightly baffling one.

At the back of the house stood a plastic-framed sun lounge. It was far too hot in the summer, freezing in the winter, and not particularly pleasant at any time in-between; it also blocked all the natural light that would otherwise fall into the adjacent living room.

Still, it had good bones. It was solid and well cared for and full of potential, and we were excited to get started.

Dreaming what it could be

Even when the house still felt awkward and dark, we could see what it might become. We realized straight away that we could add a new floor at the bedroom end, opening up the volume of the house and making the most of the incredible views. That one decision unlocked everything else, bringing more light, more flow and a chance to reconfigure the layout completely.

I wanted rid of the sun lounge without hesitation. It sat awkwardly off the living room, blocking the light and interrupting the view. In its place, we imagined a seamless extension that would look like it had been part of the house since the start: vaulted ceilings, exposed timber, soft white walls, and the sort of nook where you'd actually want to sit with a cup of tea and watch the trees move in the wind.

We sketched out a new kitchen that connected to the dining area, with room for a long table, tall shelves and a big, glass-fronted cabinet for our everyday dishes. A proper utility room was non-negotiable. Building a bedroom storey above the old bedrooms created a triple-height hallway, and we wanted both of the external walls glazed.

The original layout felt disjointed. Our dream was to create a layout that was calm and coherent and made the house feel generous. At the heart of it all was light: how to let more in, how to stretch the ceilings, how to make each room feel taller, brighter, softer. We didn't extend the footprint of the house, just worked with what was there already. It was about creating a home that felt right for the way we lived as a family.

From house to home

When you take on a house that's full of potential but also full of problems, it can be hard to know where to begin. Ours had a beautiful plot, a baffling layout and plenty of potential to keep us hooked. But buying the house was the easy part. The real work began once the paperwork was signed and we started figuring out how to turn a tired, awkward space into somewhere that felt like home. What needed to change? What could be kept? And how could we shape it all into something that worked for our family, now and in the future?

Start with a wishlist

Before we thought about finishes or tiles or paint colours, we made a wishlist – not a Pinterest board, but an actual written list of the things we hoped to include in the renovation. Some ideas were practical, like creating better flow between the kitchen and garden. Others were a bit more out-there, like creating a mezzanine library over the living space or views from the bed in the new loft.

Having this list meant we had a starting point when we began working with our architect. It was a way to communicate how we wanted to live in the house. It helped focus the design and streamline decisions, and it reminded us what really mattered when things got complicated.

Work with professionals early

We brought an architect on board early, before we made any big structural decisions. We walked them through the house, talking about what worked and what didn't, and what we were hoping to change. They helped us figure out what was possible, what wasn't and what might be more expensive than it was worth. That early collaboration shaped the entire project and meant we didn't waste time or budget chasing impossible ideas.

Think about how you actually live

It's easy to get caught up in what looks good, but the best renovations come from thinking about how you use a space. For us, that meant more storage in the hallway, a separate grown-up living room and places for the kids to hang out without taking over the kitchen. We planned for mess, for everyday life and for our family.

Plan the space before you plan the details

In our case, getting the layout right meant removing awkward corridors, knocking rooms together and reworking the entire floorplan to make the most of the space available. The result? Higher ceilings, more light, improved views and a home that actually worked for how we live.

Only once that structure was in place did we start thinking about materials, finishes and details. By then, the house had already begun to take shape in our heads.

Welcome home
The view from our front door towards the living space: an open-plan kitchen-diner and living room.

Planning and layout: rethinking the bones

We focused on reworking the interior layout of our home – improving the flow and finding ways to bring in light where it was lacking. Enlarging windows was key to making the most of the views. Removing internal walls opened up the long, windowless corridors. We worked closely with our architect to design a home that would fit our life, without falling foul of planning restrictions.

The budget shaped every decision. We began with a very long wishlist and then sat down to sort it into 'essentials' and 'nice-to-haves'. This was a useful way to prioritize and stretch the budget without losing sight of what mattered most. One of the biggest decisions was adding another floor. There were low lofts above all the rooms originally, and we wanted to build upwards to make the most of the views and bring height into the living spaces. This gave us a new main bedroom and studio above, and allowed us to move rooms around downstairs to create a better layout.

Once our planning permission came through, we commissioned detailed technical drawings. These not only helped us visualize the final layout, but also gave us the level of detail needed to get accurate quotes from builders. Unsurprisingly, the quotes varied wildly, and were all nearly double our original budget. So if your architect tells you that you can achieve X, Y and Z for a certain amount, brace yourself. You might be lucky to get just the X.

We wanted to plan for the future as well as the present. We imagined teenagers needing more space, guests staying for longer visits, parents spending more time with us. So we carved out a second living room, which could one day become a den or snug, we gave the kids built-in storage and en-suites, and we added a flexible guest room that doubles as a home office. One of the best decisions we made was adding a utility and boot room just off the back entrance to the house. It became one of the hardest working rooms.

Wishlist items
The pantry/display cabinet was on my wishlist before we even started renovating. It's hard to believe that this used to be a low-ceilinged, windowless room.

Tips for budgeting: renovating without compromise

Tweak to save money

For our windows, we chose a slightly thicker frame profile, which gave us the same look but at a much lower cost – it ended up saving us nearly 30 per cent. Ask suppliers what similar alternatives they offer.

Plan early

The earlier you start sourcing finishes (tiles, taps, flooring), the more opportunities you'll have to find better prices and avoid rushed, expensive, last-minute decisions.

Reuse where you can

Internal doors, bathroom units, flooring – is there something worth saving from the old layout?

Focus your budget where it matters

We invested in better flooring and cabinetry because they're used daily, but spent less on things like lighting fixtures and furnishings.

Challenge the architect if needed

Our architect was keen on giving the children small bedrooms and a big playroom with a climbing wall. Lovely in theory, but expensive, and likely to be ignored once the novelty wore off. Instead, we made the bedrooms bigger, downsized the playroom to a cosy snug and skipped the climbing wall altogether. More practical, and a much better solution for us.

Choose off-the-shelf with a twist

Flat-pack or standard units with custom handles, a bespoke worktop or creative layout can look high-end but with a smaller price tag.

Ask trades for their advice

Builders often know clever ways to save time or materials that designers don't suggest. Don't be afraid to ask 'Is there a cheaper way to do this?'

Buy ahead, store later

If you spot something you love in a sale (like radiators or lighting), snap it up. As long as you've got somewhere to keep it, it can save hundreds down the line.

Know when to wait

Not everything has to be done in phase one. Some of our best decisions came out of living in the house for a while (and it spread the spending).

Planning your layout: a few things we learned

- Keep a measuring tape in your bag. We were measuring everywhere we went: kitchens, bathrooms, shower enclosures, corridor widths, the space needed between the fridge and a kitchen island.
- Prioritize light, views and flow over square footage.
- Be ruthless about what you don't need.
- Think about your daily life: where bags and shoes go, where you fold laundry, where you store muddy wellies or wash your dog's feet.
- Get as many builder quotes as you can, based on detailed drawings.
- Keep your budget realistic, and leave breathing room for extra costs.

Subtle savings
One of our best money-savers: we had our handyman build this media unit for us. Custom look for far less than bespoke joinery.

Moving the kitchen

In the original layout, the kitchen sat in the north-east corner of the house. It got the least light during the day, felt tucked away from everything else (you had to walk through a dark corridor to reach it) and was the one room I actively disliked. The colours were unflattering and the layout was so terribly non-functioning that I tried to spend as little time there as possible.

So we moved it. The new location made no obvious sense on paper, but had potential. This room – tucked in the corner of the house, facing one side of the plastic sun lounge – had no windows and a ceiling so low I could nearly touch it with my fingers. But once the sun lounge came down, the ceiling was stripped out and two huge window openings were created in the back corner, the whole thing started to make sense.

The kitchen wraps around three walls, anchored by a generous island at its centre. We kept the layout simple but hardworking: no upper cabinetry, just open shelving for everyday things and tall units to house the fridge-freezer and ovens. One corner of the room had an odd kink in the outer wall, which we worked into the design by building a full-height cabinet: one side stores our crockery, the other hides a small-but-mighty walk-in pantry for dry goods.

The tall corner windows opened up beautiful long views over the city of Bath and brought in so much light the room felt twice the size. About ten months after finishing the renovation, we commissioned tall, steel-framed glass doors to complete the space. As functional as it is pretty, this kitchen is now where we spend most of our time.

Our dining and seating area (pages 80–83) are adjacent to the kitchen in the new open-plan layout, in what was originally the living room. This was quite a nice space, with a high ceiling, even if the green carpet and yellow walls weren't my personal favourite. The shape of the room made it feel a little like a corridor, though, and the sloping ceiling was stained a peculiar dusty mauve. The sliding doors at the far end looked out not onto a garden, but onto the back of that draughty plastic conservatory. Despite facing south, it was always a dim room that felt like a bit of a lost opportunity.

Post-renovation, with the new kitchen positioned at the far end, the whole room finally came into its own. Three rooflights bring in natural light from above, while wide openings into the kitchen create a much better sense of flow. The dining table now sits in the centre of the room, which has become one of the most used spaces in the house.

At the end of this space, where that sun lounge was, we created a smaller seating area. Just a rug, a sofa and an armchair, and a low coffee table. It's where weekend coffee is drunk, evening drinks are sipped and guests settle when they arrive early for dinner. It softens the open-plan layout, making the space feel lived-in rather than just large.

Heart of the home

I love this view from our dining space towards the kitchen. Light pouring in, and the island right at the centre of everyday life.

Zoning the living room

The space that's now our living room used to be the kitchen, although you'd barely recognize it. Low ceilings, a cluttered layout and barely any natural light – there was a single, small window over the sink – made this one of the least inspiring parts of the house. It felt boxed in, though the ceiling was high above a low false one and the space backed onto the garden.

We opened it all up. The empty loft space above was removed to reclaim the full height, and we made a new, tall window opening to bring in more daylight and draw the eye upwards. We also knocked through the wall between this room and the old dining area to create a much larger footprint. The result is a generous living space that's both cosy and open.

At one end, we created a TV nook with a built-in media unit and bookshelves that span the full wall. This is where we all pile in to watch films, the dog curled up under someone's feet. It's snug and simple, painted in the same soft neutral as the rest of the open-plan space, but it feels like a hideaway.

Next to it, we added a second seating area, arranged for conversation rather than watching screens. It's where guests settle with a glass of wine or where we find ourselves reading on Sunday afternoons. Together, these two zones help the open-plan layout feel more human-scaled; they flow naturally into one another but are broken up just enough to give each space a clear purpose.

Flowing open plan
The sightlines between TV room, living and dining spaces create those calm, in-between views that make an open-plan home feel cosy and connected.

å

Open-plan zoning: tips to make it work

Start with purpose

Think about how you want to use each area. Will one end be for TV watching? Is there a place you naturally gather for coffee, or where you settle to read? Once the purpose is clear, layout choices follow naturally.

Use soft barriers

Rugs, lighting, curtains and ceiling treatments can all help zone a space without blocking light or flow. Pendant lights over a dining table or a different paint colour in a reading nook go a long way to define an area.

Let furniture do the dividing

Use the backs of sofas, open shelving or even a change in flooring direction to subtly signal where one zone ends and another begins. It keeps things open but purposeful.

Mind the movement

Leave natural walkways between zones. If people have to zigzag awkwardly around sofas or chairs, rethink the flow. Think of paths like water – they want to find the easiest route.

Vary the lighting

Use a mix of task lighting, low-level lamps and ceiling fixtures to match the mood of each zone. You want the kitchen to be bright and functional, the seating area warm and dimmable.

Avoid the furniture showroom look

Too many matching pieces can make an open-plan room feel flat and uninspired. Let each zone have its own character – even a different coffee table style or rug texture can help.

Don't forget acoustic zones

Open spaces can echo. Textiles like curtains, rugs and upholstery help dampen sound, but you can also consider acoustic panels or cleverly placed bookshelves to keep things comfortable.

Open plan, with clear zones
Dining in the centre, kitchen behind and living area tucked beyond the table – everything has a purpose and it flows.

Creating the perfect bedroom

The main bedroom

The bedroom sits up on the new first floor that we added to the house, and as soon as the space began to take shape, it felt like we were making a treehouse bedroom, thanks to the centuries-old beech growing nearby. We created generous ceiling height here and views over the fields behind the house as well as out towards Bath. There was even enough room for a skinny 'Juliet' balcony – a total indulgence, yes, but one I've never regretted for a second. It became a perfect little hideaway.

Before the build, this floor didn't exist. The old main bedroom was a floor below – a low-ceilinged box with a scant window, tired carpet and walls painted in patchy magnolia. Upstairs, the new bedroom gave us the freedom to start fresh. We kept the layout simple and the palette soft and muted. A calm, restful space emerged, with more breathing room than any bedroom I've ever had. It wasn't filled with furniture or decoration, just the essentials: a lovely big bed, bedside tables, brass wall lights and a small sofa at the foot of the bed.

The back wall felt bare and boring, though, so we added a full-height panelled wall in a clean square pattern. This brought some texture to the space without overpowering the room. We painted it in a soft and muted warm beige.

There's a dressing room tucked away off to one side, and a pocket door that leads through to the en suite. I wanted the bedroom to feel like a proper retreat: quiet, airy and just a little bit indulgent. That little balcony might not make it onto anyone's list of 'essential bedroom features', but on summer mornings, with the doors flung open and the trees brushing against the sky, it felt like one of the best decisions we had made.

The en-suite bathroom

The en suite sits just off the bedroom, tucked behind a pocket door that disappears into the wall. It's not an enormous room, but it feels generous. More sanctuary than squeeze. Because we added it as part of the new first floor, we had a completely blank canvas to work on here. No awkward pipework or outdated tiles to wrestle with, just the opportunity to create something calm and considered.

At first, I worked with a bathroom designer, but we weren't aligned. He kept dismissing my ideas, especially about where the toilet should go, and eventually I took over the design myself. Thanks to the posi-joists in the floor construction, we could run the waste pipe exactly where we wanted, which meant the toilet could be neatly tucked away, rather than front and centre, as it was in the bathroom designer's plan.

Instead, the focal point is the free-standing bath, positioned just in front of the window. Being able to soak while looking out at Bath was high on my wishlist, and it felt like such a treat. Opposite is a walk-in shower with a stone-effect tray and a bronze-framed screen that adds a bit of quiet contrast. The palette, again, is soft and muted: mint-green tiles line the walls, and white hexagonal tiles add texture to the floor.

It is the finishes that make this room. I chose brushed-gold fittings for their quality and simplicity. I loved the concrete double sinks – the softness of their shape and the classic concrete-grey colour, and how they sit against the light oak vanity unit. That unit was a lucky find after a long search. Most options were too shiny or modern for my taste, but this one struck the right balance.

There is a rattan pendant with simple wall lights placed either side of the mirrors. We added a small bamboo shelf for everyday bits and pieces, and I brought in some colour with a bright bath mat, and added a couple of candles and a stool for coffee and books.

A simple sanctuary
Our bedroom and en suite were a completely new addition, so we could design them from scratch. We kept everything simple, soft and airy.

Lessons learned: what I would do again

Every renovation comes with a learning curve, but some choices consistently prove their worth. There are a few decisions I'd make all over again without a second thought.

Prioritize natural light over obvious layout

Sometimes the room that makes the most sense on paper isn't the one that feels best in reality. Repositioning key spaces, like a kitchen or seating area, to make the most of sunlight and views can completely transform how a home feels and functions.

Invest in what gets used daily

Finishes like switches, handles, flooring and taps are touched and used constantly. These small details shape the everyday experience of living in a home. Good-quality, well-designed pieces last longer and feel better, too.

Make room for soft, social spaces

In open-plan layouts, carving out smaller corners for sitting, reading or quiet moments can stop a large space from feeling cold or echoey. A rug, a couple of chairs and a low table might be all it takes to turn a thoroughfare into a lived-in, well-loved spot.

Build storage into structure

Designing storage into walls, alcoves and unused corners makes it easier to keep a home feeling calm and collected. Think walk-in pantries, utility cupboards or a place near the back door for bags and boots, not as afterthoughts, but as essential parts of the layout.

Let in light
Adding this kitchen window was one of our best decisions. More light and views over the city. I'd do it again in a heartbeat.

KINFOLK

Design with the future in mind

A well-planned layout should adapt to changing needs, growing children, unexpected guests, and changes to work-life balance. Consider flexible spaces, rooms that can serve more than one purpose and a layout that allows for life's inevitable changes.

Create a second living space if possible

A smaller seating nook off the main kitchen or dining area can become one of the most used parts of a home. It gives guests a place to perch, creates a morning suntrap for coffee breaks, and brings softness to open-plan layouts. Even a compact space can feel inviting when treated with intention.

Live in the space before decorating it fully

It's tempting to furnish everything straight away, but holding off allows time for you to understand how the light moves, where people tend to gather, and what's actually needed. Rooms that remain unfinished for a while often evolve into the most intentional.

Phase the project where needed

Not everything has to be done at once. Some of the most satisfying features can come later, once the space has settled and needs become clearer. Giving a home time to breathe between phases allows for smarter decisions and results in fewer regrets.

Pay attention to instinct

There's no shortage of advice during a renovation, but not all of it fits every house or every family. When a choice feels right – even if it goes against convention – it's usually worth trusting. Intuition often picks up on things logic overlooks.

Trust yourself
Your instincts matter. If something feels right, it usually is. These small choices ended up shaping the whole feel of the house.

CHAPTER 4

The Well-Lived Home

The seven-step process of creating a kotoisa home

If you feel like your home isn't as cosy, inviting and kotoisa as you'd like, here are seven gentle steps to help you change it. This chapter is a practical route map. It won't ask you to buy a trolley full of new things or to force your home to conform to someone else's style. It will help you block out the noise, notice what you already have and make a series of small, confident decisions that add up to a kinder, easier place to live.

Think of the seven steps as a loop rather than a ladder. You'll circle them more than once as your life shifts: first home to shared home, babies to teens, busy seasons to quieter ones. Start where you are. If the clutter is shouting, begin there. If your vision is foggy, build the vision board. If a room is nearly there but not quite, style, snap and adjust. Each step is designed to lower your shoulders, sharpen your eye, and bring your home closer to the way you actually live.

How to use this chapter:

- Move at your pace – five minutes a day is still progress.
- Do the steps in order the first time, then dip back in as needed.
- Spend money last; spend attention first.
- Choose 'good enough for Tuesday' over 'perfect someday'.
- Write small notes as you go – what works, what doesn't, what to try next.

By the end, you'll have a clearer sense of what you want your home to do for you, and a framework you can return to whenever life changes shape. Not a makeover, but a method. Not perfection, but ease.

Now, let's begin at the simplest, most transformative place: letting go of what you don't need.

Fresh perspective
Morning light, the doors wide open and the table clear and ready for whatever the day brings.

Step 1: Declutter first

Yes, really. Unless you're already living in a strictly spartan space (and if you are, feel free to skip this and move to the next step), this is hands-down the most powerful thing you can do to shift the energy of your home. It doesn't matter how many lovely throws you buy or how perfectly you style your shelves – if the room is full of clutter, it's just not possible to create a beautiful space that soothes your soul and calms your senses.

We're not aiming for minimalist perfection here – unless, of course, that's your happy place. What we're really after is breathing space. The point of decluttering is to keep only what serves a purpose or brings you joy. Think of it as editing your space to make room for the things that truly matter.

When I recently tackled the clutter in our home, I realized I'd been holding onto items I didn't even like. There was a vase from a distant relative that I felt I 'should' keep but didn't love, and stacks of magazines I was convinced I needed to re-read someday. Letting go of those things made space – physically and mentally – for pieces that made me happy.

Quick tips for decluttering

- Start small: one drawer, one shelf, one basket. Trying to declutter the entire house in one go is the fast track to burnout.
- Make categories: keep, donate, recycle and 'I'm not sure yet'. Sometimes we need a little time to let go.
- Ask questions as you go: do I use this? Does it make my life better in some way? Would I buy this again today?
- Don't get stuck organizing clutter. It's tempting to rearrange it instead of actually removing it, but the magic happens when it actually leaves the house.

Decluttering doesn't have to be a grand event either. I often do it while I'm waiting for the kettle to boil or as part of my evening wind-down – one drawer here, a shelf there. It all adds up.

This isn't about living in a showroom. It's about clearing the decks so you can see and enjoy what's already good. Your home will feel more peaceful, more intentional and you'll wonder why you left it so long.

Delightful chaos

I'm a big fan of organized, pretty clutter. This step is about editing, not stripping the personality out of your home.

Step 2: Vision board

How to make one, how to use it

If there's one step in the design process that feels the most fun, it's this one: sitting down with a cup of coffee, surrounded by magazines, Pinterest boards and swatches, and letting yourself dream. But vision boarding isn't just about the dreaming, it's one of the most useful tools at your disposal. Not only does it help clarify your ideas, it's also one of the best ways to understand your personal style and stay focused throughout the design process.

Finding your style can sometimes feel overwhelming. With so many trends and beautiful homes out there, it's easy to get distracted. A vision board cuts through the noise. It brings your preferences into sharper focus and helps you spot patterns – tones, shapes, materials that you're naturally drawn to. Limiting your options is the best way to eliminate 'analysis paralysis'. Understanding your interior style means making more confident decisions, avoiding expensive mistakes, and creating a home that truly reflects you.

What to include in your vision board?

Start with the big picture. What's the atmosphere you want to create? Cosy and layered? Calm and minimal? Lived-in and full of patina? Think about how you want to *feel* in the space – relaxed, energized, nostalgic or maybe playful? Then move to the specifics. Collect images of:

- Rooms you love
- Materials that speak to you (wood, linen, terracotta, marble, etc.)
- Colours that you find calming or uplifting
- Furniture or layout ideas that inspire you or could work in your space
- Lighting styles you gravitate towards
- Architectural details that catch your eye

You don't need to limit yourself to interiors either. Nature, fashion, travel, books, packaging — all can spark something meaningful. What matters is that each image makes you feel something, even if you're not quite sure why.

Digital or physical?

There's no right answer. Some people prefer creating digital boards using tools like Pinterest, Canva or Milanote. These are quick, easy to organize and you can share them with your designer or architect if you're working with one.

Others love a physical version – cutting up magazines, printing images, pinning fabric swatches. The tactile element can be inspiring in itself. Pin it to your wall or keep it in a folder so you can refer back as your ideas evolve.

Visualizing ideas
Colours, textures, materials and combinations – a vision board is a great way to test and clarify your ideas before committig to the real thing.

How to analyze your board

Once you've pulled together 20–30 images, take a step back. Look for common themes.

- Do you lean towards warm or cool colours?
- Is there a certain material that appears again and again?
- Are your spaces more traditional, rustic or minimal?
- Do you gravitate towards open, airy rooms or snug and layered ones?

Circle, tag or note down the elements you love most. It might be the way a certain light falls on a textured wall, or a specific colour combination. The goal here isn't to replicate someone else's home but to understand what resonates with *you*, so you can recreate that feeling in a way that works for your own space.

How to use your vision board

Once your board is ready, treat it like your compass. You can refer back to it every time you're about to make a decision, from choosing tiles to buying a sofa. If something doesn't sit comfortably with the vision you've created, it's probably not the right fit.

A vision board also keeps you grounded when you're overwhelmed with options or tempted by trends that don't actually suit your space or lifestyle. That rustic black kitchen might look dreamy online, but if all your favourite inspiration images show pale timber and white walls, it's probably time to follow your gut instinct.

Tips to get the most out of your vision board

- Don't overthink. Save anything that gives you a *feeling* of 'yes'.
- Don't aim for perfection. This isn't a moodboard for a magazine shoot, it's for *you*.
- Include words or phrases that help define your vision: welcoming, quiet, tactile, joyful.
- Revisit and edit. As your ideas sharpen, refine your board to reflect the strongest direction.
- Use it to communicate with anyone involved in the process: builders, designers, even your partner.

Creating a vision board is about uncovering the threads that connect you to a space. It's one of the simplest but most powerful ways to start building a home that feels unmistakably yours.

Your style compass

Your vision board is something that you can add to, refer back to and refine as you go. When you're feeling overwhelmed, it will help guide you back to your intentions.

Step 3: Take stock

What you have, what you need, and what might just need a fresh perspective

Before you dive headfirst into choosing paint colours or pinning layout ideas, it helps to pause and take a proper look at what you already have. This step is easy to skip, but it's often the one that saves the most time, money and stress later.

Start by walking through your home with fresh eyes. What is working well? What has always annoyed you? Are there pieces you love but don't know how to use? Are you short on storage, or do you have more than you need? Which spaces and places do you gravitate towards? Which rooms feel 'dead'? Is your hall always cluttered with coats and bags? Do you have too many chairs, but nowhere comfy to curl up? This kind of everyday noticing is what leads to smart, responsive design.

This is also the moment to get practical. Measure up your rooms, note window heights, the placement of sockets and heating pipes and the spots where light falls in the afternoon. This information will be invaluable when you start planning layouts or buying furniture.

In one of my previous renovations, I drew out the floorplans by hand, then made tiny paper cut-outs of all the key pieces of furniture, to scale. It might sound tedious, but it was incredibly helpful, both in visualizing the space and also understanding the proportion and flow. When a sofa felt too big, or a bed left no room to open the wardrobe, I could see it instantly, long before buying a single thing.

The first and best upgrade
Sometimes the biggest upgrade is simply putting things where you use them. What's working? What's always in the way? What needs a better spot?

Take stock: your measurement checklist

Use this list to gather the essential details that will help you design with confidence:

- Room dimensions (length, width and height)
- Ceiling heights (especially if they vary)
- Window sizes and sill heights
- Radiator and vent locations
- Socket and light switch placements
- Door swings and clearance space
- Direction of natural light
- Fixed features (like alcoves, beams, or fireplace recesses)
- Existing storage (built-ins, wardrobes, awkward corners)
- Circulation space (how you move through the room)
- Sightlines (what you see when you walk in)

Once you've got these details noted down, they'll become your reference point for every design decision that follows. At this point, you're not committing to anything. You're just getting a clearer view of what you're working with, and that clarity is a brilliant place to begin.

Taking stock starts here
Measure the room, then notice the light. In a room like this, where the most beautiful tall windows set the mood, the decor can be kept simple.

ATWOOD
Girl, Woman, Other
HARPER LEE
GO SET A WATCHMAN

Step 4: Work with what you have

One of the things I love most about kotoisa is that it's not about throwing everything out and starting from scratch. A kotoisa home grows slowly, layer by layer, shaped by what you already own and love. The most soulful spaces are rarely filled with brand-new purchases. They are made up of pieces that each have a story – things that have been moved, reinvented or made to work in quietly clever new ways.

Most homes already have a lot of potential – we just forget to look at them with fresh eyes. That side table you're bored of in the bedroom? It might be exactly what your living room needs. A forgotten ceramic bowl from the back of a kitchen cupboard could become the perfect place for keys in the hallway. There's something so satisfying about discovering new uses for what you already have. It makes your home feel alive and evolving – not static or overly 'done'.

I've done this more times than I can count. A bench that lived unloved in our spare room now sits happily under a window with a few folded blankets and a book or two. A mirror from the hallway ended up over the mantelpiece, where it suddenly made the whole room feel bigger and brighter. Sometimes just switching two rugs between rooms can bring new energy to both spaces.

This is a mindset shift rather than a design rule. Instead of thinking 'what do I need to buy?', ask 'what do I already have that could work here?' It's more sustainable, more creative, and almost always more personal. You don't have to be wildly inventive, just a little bit curious.

Ideas to help you start shopping your own home:

- *Rearrange furniture to suit how you live.* If your armchair is never used in the corner where it is, try moving it near a window and add a floor lamp to make a reading nook.
- *Repurpose with purpose.* A vintage trunk can double as a coffee table. An old ladder can become a towel rail.
- *Rotate your decor.* That art print you've stopped noticing in the hallway might feel fresh above the bed. A stack of books from the living room might work better on your bedroom shelf.
- *Move soft furnishings.* Cushions, throws and rugs are wonderfully flexible. A throw from the sofa might cosy up your hallway bench or an old cushion might be just the thing your workspace needs.
- *Combine forgotten things.* Grouping smaller items on a tray or shelf – a candle, a small vase – can make them feel more considered.
- *Elevate the everyday.* A worn wooden chopping board leaning against the backsplash or a cluster of attractive mugs on an open shelf can be both practical and beautiful.

Cosy corners with familiar pieces
A bookshelf, a well-loved chair, mirrors and artworks, lamps and throws – these can be made 'new' again by moving them around.

Step 5: Add personality

How to make a house feel like it's yours

There's a moment in every decorating journey when everything is *technically* done – the paint's dry, the sofa's in, the shelves are up – but the room still feels a bit flat, like it's waiting for something. This is where you get to have a little fun. This is the part that doesn't follow rules or moodboards or paint charts.

This step is all about adding the details that make your home feel personal, and not just like a space copied from a magazine. It's what gives a room warmth, character and that hard-to-define *feeling* that makes people want to sit down and stay a while.

I once heard someone call this 'working in the weird', though I prefer to think of it as adding in the personality. These are the moments that tell a story, sometimes just to you, but often to the people who visit, too. These weird and wonderful touches are real conversation starters.

You don't need to go out and buy anything new. In fact, most of these touches probably already live in your cupboards or storage boxes: a stack of dog-eared books you've read more than once; a framed photo that makes you laugh; a faded print you've had since university, or a throw blanket from a holiday long ago. These are the things that carry memory, and memory is what gives a space soul.

Think about the things you're drawn to again and again. Maybe you love vintage market finds or mid-century shapes; maybe it's textiles with history, or earthy ceramics, or black-and-white photography. Those small leanings are worth paying attention to – they're breadcrumbs leading you back to your own style.

Don't be afraid of mixing things up. A contemporary kitchen can still have a battered wooden stool in the corner. A calm, minimalist living room might look better with a bright painting that doesn't 'match'. These juxtapositions are what make a room feel lived in, layered and real. If it means something to you, it belongs. That's really the only rule.

If your home still feels like it hasn't quite found its voice, don't rush to fill it. Sit with it. Let it breathe. Add slowly, with intention and trusting that the most beautiful spaces are made up of not grand gestures, but the quiet, imperfect details that belong to you.

Tell your story
Layer in personal items that carry stories, like a favourite print, a little stack of pictures, a quirky lamp and plants that will soften the corners. These don't have to match perfectly.

Step 6: Style, snap, adjust

Now that the big pieces are in place and your home is slowly coming together, it's time to add the layers that give it life – all the styling details. A kotoisa home feels welcoming, lived-in and a bit undone. Not every cushion needs plumping, and not every shelf need hold a perfectly curated vignette.

Start with just one corner. A coffee table, a shelf, a windowsill – something small enough that you can play around without getting overwhelmed. It helps to put on some music and treat this like a creative session. Try things out, move pieces around. Add, subtract, shift. Don't aim for finished, aim for feeling.

There's no rulebook, but there *are* a few tricks that can help. Varied heights and mixed textures work well. Soften harder edges with something round or organic. Layer books, bowls, candles, ceramics and textiles. Leave some breathing space, as clutter can quickly take the magic out of even the loveliest objects.

This is also the moment to ask: what's this corner for? Does it invite you in? Does it feel calm or considered? If not, strip it back. Keep the pieces that feel meaningful and work with the space. It's better to have fewer things that matter than too many that don't.

Once you're happy with a corner, take a photo. This might sound unnecessary, but somehow the camera spots the things our own eyes skim past: an awkward gap, an object that's slightly off-centre, a combination that doesn't quite work. It's much easier to tweak once you've got a picture in front of you. A camera (even just your phone) helps you see if something is off-balance, too crowded, or just not quite working. Snap your styled corner from a few angles: straight-on, at an angle and with a close-up or two. If the photo feels flat, tweak the arrangement. Maybe the lamp needs turning, or the books need angling slightly. Maybe it's just the wrong vase altogether. Try again.

Natural light is your friend. Turn off the overheads and take your photos in daylight. It makes everything feel more natural and soft. You don't need filters or editing tricks – just a bit of patience.

Let it be a little undone. That cushion that isn't quite straight? Leave it. The throw that's loosely draped rather than perfectly folded? Even better. The goal isn't perfection, it's ease. You want it to look like someone might walk in, sink into the sofa and feel instantly at home.

Take a break if you need to. Come back later with fresh eyes. Often, that one little vase or lamp you couldn't make work will suddenly find its place. And don't forget to trust your gut. If it makes you smile, if it feels like home, it's working.

Move one thing, then live with it
Step 6 is the gentle tweaking stage.

Tips for styling photos

- ***Shoot in natural light.*** Turn off overhead lights and wait for good daylight. Direct sun is often too harsh, whereas morning or late afternoon usually give the softest light.
- ***Turn off the flash.*** Flash can flatten everything and distort colours. If you're struggling with blur, prop your phone on a shelf or tripod.
- ***Capture a few angles.*** Take one shot straight-on, one from a three-quarter angle and one close-up. Imagine you're flipping through a magazine: variety helps you see what's working.
- ***Style it as you'd actually live.*** Loosen throws, let a cushion slump a little. Real homes aren't stiff and styled, they have warmth and ease.
- ***Step back and look again.*** A photo will show you things you won't spot in real life: an awkward gap, a missing texture, a too-perfect arrangement. Trust the camera.
- ***Don't rely on filters.*** Natural is best. If you must tweak, adjust warmth or brightness slightly. Avoid overly filtered looks that age quickly.
- ***Compare and adjust.*** Try two versions of a vignette side by side. Which feels calmer? Which looks more lived-in? Style isn't about being 'right', it's about what feels good.
- ***Ask this one question.*** If you saw this in a magazine, would you pause and look closer? If not, change something.

Compare and adjust
Styling photos is really just training your eye. Try a few angles, chase soft natural light and keep the scene simple. Take the shot, then tweak one thing and shoot again.

Step 7: Refresh

You did it! Maybe your space even looks exactly how you hoped it would and you love it ... for a while. Chances are you will want to spruce things up after a while. Homes are forever evolving; they're not museums or film sets. They shift, soften and change with the people who live in them.

That's why refreshing your home regularly is such a lovely habit to get into. We're not talking frantic, rip-it-all-out-and-start-again change, but small, seasonal, satisfying tweaks: a different vase on the shelf, a new arrangement of books, swapping cushions from one room to another. These small, almost imperceptible changes can make a space feel alive again.

When things start to feel a little stale or uninspired, a quiet afternoon of pottering and adjusting can do more than a trip to the shops. Think of your home as something you're in a gentle conversation with, not a project to be 'completed'. The objects you live with might stay the same, but the way you see them doesn't have to. The light changes, the seasons shift and the way your home is styled can shift, too.

If you're someone who tends to overthink or strive for perfection, remember: none of this is permanent. It's all movable – swappable. Try something new, live with it for a while and change it again if it doesn't quite feel right.

Refreshing your space is a way of caring for it and for yourself. It's a way to mark the small chapters of daily life, to notice what you need right now and to make sure your home continues to feel like your own – a little lighter, a little lovelier, and still full of life.

Permission to make changes
Small shifts can make a room feel new again. Swap in fresh linen, move a chair, pull out a different rug or bring in a few stems from the garden.

Seasonal refresh ideas

Here are some simple ways to keep your home feeling fresh throughout the year.

Spring

- Change your curtains to lighter and brighter ones.
- Bring in branches of blossom or greenery from the garden.
- Swap heavy throws and pillowcases for linen blankets or cotton quilts in softer, pastel colours.
- Add a bowl of lemons or pots of herbs on the kitchen counter.
- Rotate artwork or prints to include lighter tones and florals.

Summer

- Display fresh flowers in simple glass vases.
- Move a favourite chair near the garden doors or next to a window that opens wide and claim this as your summer reading spot.
- Style the kitchen simply: a bowl of tomatoes, a jug of herbs, linen napkins folded in a drawer.
- Switch to a sheer curtain or pull back fabric entirely to let in light on the long evenings.
- Keep a small, pretty tray ready with your warm-weather ritual: two glasses, your favourite cordial or aperitif, a sprig of mint.

Autumn

- Switch to warmer colours in cushions or bedding. Rust browns, olives and ochres work well.
- Bring in texture with knits, velvets or sheepskins.
- Layer in quiet textures: velvet cushions, wool throws, a runner over the dining table.
- Bring in branches with berries or coppery leaves and let them dry in place.
- Change lampshades for added texture: raffia, pleated linen or fabric gathered on a wire frame.
- Scent the house subtly, with dried orange peel on the woodburner or clove-studded apples in a bowl.

Winter

- Embrace ambient light: table lamps in every room, warm bulbs, a candle in the bathroom.
- Add weight and warmth: flannel sheets, velvet curtains, an old quilt folded at the end of the bed.
- Bring in a few evergreen sprigs in ceramic jugs, or a basket of kindling by the fire.
- Switch artworks to wintery scenes: landscapes and charcoal sketches, with darker frames.
- Create rituals: lighting a candle with breakfast, a blanket over the kitchen chair, mulled wine simmering by late afternoon.

Closing thoughts

By now, you've hopefully started to see your home a little differently: not as a blank canvas waiting to be made perfect, but as a living space that can hold more of your life, your ideas, your quirks – a place that reflects how you want to live, not just how you want things to look.

This chapter has walked you through a simple but powerful process. You have taken time to think about how you want your home to feel. You've made a vision board to capture your style and shape your direction. You've looked at what you already have and taken stock of your space. You've explored ways to build a layout that works and learned how to bring in personality, not by copying trends but by letting your own story shine through.

You've styled, stepped back, tweaked and taken photos to help you see with fresh eyes. And, most importantly, you've given yourself permission to keep changing things. Because a home is never really finished; it grows and shifts as you do.

At the heart of all this is the idea of home as something deeply personal. That's what makes a space kotoisa. It's about noticing what makes you feel grounded, relaxed and happy. It's about choosing details that make daily life smoother or more beautiful, as well as leaving space for the unexpected.

The good news is, there are no rules you need to follow. If something feels too precious or too perfect, loosen it. If a corner feels flat, bring in something that tells a story. If you fall out of love with a piece of furniture or a colour, change it. These small choices are where your home really begins to take shape.

So trust yourself. Your eye is sharper than you think. Your gut is wiser than you realize. You don't need a fancy budget or a decorator's degree. You just need a little time, a bit of curiosity, and a willingness to experiment. You've got this. And your home is already better for it.

Grounded and calm
Trust your eye and keep it flexible. A home isn't finished, it's lived in.

CHAPTER 5

The Rooms

69

Living room

The living room in our house growing up was the heart of the home. I remember my brother and I lounging side by side on the sofa in our matching pyjamas, glued to *Knight Rider* or *MacGyver*, burying our faces in the cushions when things got too scary. It's where we played endless rounds of Monopoly with our own set of rules, built Lego towns across the rug and made elaborate dens out of blankets and chairs when friends came over.

Every Christmas eve morning, a wonky Christmas tree would appear in the corner – always a bit too sparse and often leaning in one direction. My dad would cut it in from the spruce woods near our house, and while I envied the perfect, thick trees I saw in American Christmas films, ours had its own charm. The 'good' trees were always left to grow tall, so we usually got the crooked one left behind. We never seemed to mind too much, though.

That room felt alive. It was the space we all ended up in, where you could fall asleep under a blanket on a Sunday afternoon or curl up with a book on a rainy day. It wasn't trying too hard – it just *was*.

When I think about the kind of living room I want to create now, it's about capturing that same sense of ease I remember from childhood. I want a space that's considered, yes, and full of beautiful things, but never too precious to enjoy – somewhere that invites you in to relax or gather with friends for a lazy Sunday afternoon.

The cushions might not stay perfectly in place, the coffee table may carry the remains of snacks and last night's candle, but that's the point. A kotoisa living room is as stylish as it is soft around the edges. It's a room that looks good and feels even better: inviting, warm and lived-in in the best possible way.

That, to me, is the essence of a kotoisa space: beautiful and personal, intentional and easy. It is a room that reflects who you are and makes everyone who walks in feel instantly at home.

Heart-of-the-home feeling
A soft sofa, a floral footstool, books within reach and living greenery. The kind of room you can actually relax in, nothing too precious to enjoy.

Layout and seating

When I'm thinking about how to arrange a living room, I don't start with measurements or moodboards. I start by imagining how I want the room to feel. Is it a place to gather with friends? Or a spot where the kids can sprawl across the floor with Lego? Function comes first. Kotoisa design always circles back to how a room supports your life – not some version of it you aspire to, but the real, daily life you live.

Think about your room as a conversation, not a display. Sofas and chairs should face each other, not just the TV. A side table close enough for a cup of tea matters more than a perfectly styled shelf seen across the room. And always, always test how your space flows. Can you walk through it comfortably without squeezing past furniture? Does it invite you in or ask you to perch politely and not touch anything?

We had a sofa in our last house that looked great in photos but was awkward in real life: too far from the other seats, facing away from the light. No one ever chose to sit there. As soon as we moved it a few feet closer to the armchair and added a rug to anchor the space, it started working *with* us, not against us.

A few things to consider:

- Make sure there's enough seating for your household, plus extra. Floor cushions, ottomans or a bench tucked nearby can all be pressed into service.
- Group furniture in a way that encourages connection. A small L-shaped sofa or two chairs angled together make conversation feel natural.
- Leave space around furniture so you can move, but don't let everything float aimlessly. A rug can help pull a seating area together.

Textures and soft furnishings

Texture is what makes a room feel welcoming before you've even properly taken it in. It's what you actually feel when you sit down, curl up or brush past something on your way to get another cup of tea. Softness is the slouch of a linen cushion, the way a sheepskin flops over the arm of a chair, the flicker of candlelight against a velvet curtain. And it doesn't have to be fancy. Some of the most comforting rooms I've been in had that well-worn and much-loved look but they invited you to sit, to relax and to stay a while.

I always like to build a room around layers of textures: a linen-covered sofa with wool throws; cushions in a mix of fabrics and textures (maybe something a bit unexpected, like a nubby, oversized knit); a rug underfoot to soften the room and add a bit of hush. None of it is precious; all of it gets moved about regularly. Soft furnishings are allowed to shift and change, they're supposed to.

We have a wool blanket in our house that has been around for years. It isn't especially beautiful, and definitely not what you'd call pristine. But it's soft and *familiar* and it always ends up on someone's lap by the end of the evening. That's the thing with sentimental pieces. They don't have to be perfect to earn their place. What matters is how they make you feel.

But don't hold onto everything just because it has a story. A few well-chosen pieces can add soul to a room, but too many and the space starts to feel crowded. Rooms need breathing space. Your eyes need quiet places to land. Sometimes the best thing you can give a space is a bit of emptiness.

A few things to consider:

- Use a mix of textures to add depth, especially if you're keeping your colour palette calm.
- Throws aren't just decorative. I have a few on every sofa and chair and people use them, especially in winter.
- Rugs do more than warm your toes – they anchor the space, define zones and help a room feel finished.
- Don't be afraid of imperfection. A faded cushion cover or unravelled fringe often adds character.

Practical and comfortable
With white sofas and a cocker spaniel puppy, the big blanket wasn't a styling choice so much as a survival plan. Soft layers make the space feel welcoming; they're moved about and really used.

MAISON D'ART

CHANEL
lord Boontje

Colour and lighting

Lighting is one of the most overlooked parts of home design, but it has the power to completely change the mood of a space. In the living room, where we read, nap, chat, scroll and snack, the right lighting should be adaptable. One central ceiling light might technically illuminate the space, but it will never make it feel cosy – you need layers.

Here's a simple way to think about it:

- ***Ambient lighting*** is your base layer. It gives the room an overall glow and helps you move through the space safely. This could be a ceiling pendant, a row of wall sconces or even a few larger lamps placed at opposite corners of the room. Soft, warm bulbs are key here – look for anything around 2700K and, if at all possible, add a dimmer switch. It's the easiest way to change the feel of a room from 'daily chores' to 'evening unwind'.
- ***Task lighting*** is what you add for specific activities. Your reading nook will need a lamp close by – preferably one with a shade that casts light downwards. It's all about function, but that doesn't mean it has to look functional. Vintage desk lamps, clipped-on wall lights or tall floor lamps tucked behind the sofa can all do the job beautifully.
- ***Accent lighting***, or decorative lighting, is what gives the room that soft twinkle and makes the space feel alive. It's the glow of a candle on the mantle, a fairy-light strand inside a vintage glass jar or a small ceramic table lamp with a fabric shade tucked into a corner. None of these are technically necessary but they make a big difference to the atmosphere. These are the details that turn a space from ordinary to kotoisa.

When you're layering lighting, mix the heights too. A ceiling light, mid-level table lamps and low floor lighting will create a sense of depth and softness that flat, overhead-only lighting can't. Lampshades matter, too; fabric diffuses light more gently than plastic or glass, and a warm-toned shade will give you a softer glow than something pure white or cool-toned. Your light sources are part of your decor. A well-chosen lamp can be just as impactful as a piece of art. If you're investing in something, make it something you'll enjoy looking at, on or off.

Colour is emotional. It can calm us down, lift us up or quietly act in the background to energize us. So the colour choices you make here need to work hard without shouting for attention.

Personally, I love a soft, layered palette – a combination that doesn't immediately declare itself, but gently unfolds the longer you spend time in the room. I've tried the deep, dramatic tones and I've done the bright-white-everything look (I liked it at the time but it feels a bit stark these days). What I've found works best is something in-between: colours that are soft, natural and muted, with just enough depth to feel cosy without closing in the room.

Bold choices, warm mood
Warm light softens strong contrasts like dark paint and bold pattern, making the space feel calmer and more inviting.

A few things to consider:

- ***Start with how you want the room to feel.*** Do you want it to be calm and restful? Lean into soft blues, warm greys, oatmeal tones or muted greens. Want it to feel fresh and bright? Try warm whites, pale putty or stony pinks but with a hint of warmth. If you want something bolder or more characterful, go for earthy ochres, moss greens or chalky navy – colours that feel grounded, not glossy.
- ***Look at how the light behaves in your space.*** North-facing rooms often need warmer tones to stop them feeling flat or cold. South-facing rooms can handle cooler hues. Try large samples on multiple walls and live with them for a few days. Paint has a funny way of changing depending on the time of day, the weather and even what colour your floor or sofa is.
- ***Colour doesn't just live on the walls.*** If you're not ready to commit to painting a whole room, start small. A deep-green velvet cushion or a faded rust-coloured throw can completely shift the tone of a space. Don't underestimate the power of soft furnishings to carry colour in a way that feels changeable and relaxed.
- ***Mix, but don't clash.*** You don't need everything to match, but it should all feel like it belongs to the same conversation. If your walls are pale sage and your sofa is beige, maybe add cushions in soft plum or dusty rose. Think of the room like an outfit: a few layered neutrals, a pop of personality, and something grounding to tie it all together.
- ***Test in daylight and lamplight.*** A colour that looks beautifully warm in the morning may turn murky in the evening under your overhead bulb. I always test with my actual lighting on, especially if it's a room we use after dark (which, let's be honest, is most of them).
- ***And lastly – you are allowed to change your mind.*** Colours evolve as the spaces do, as the seasons change and as our lives shift. That's part of the joy of a kotoisa home. It's always adjusting, settling in, softening around the edges.

Colour, unleashed
A reminder that colour doesn't have to live on the walls. This gorgeous baby-blue sofa does a lot of heavy lifting, setting the mood even in neutral surrounds.

Slow evenings

I've always loved the idea of adding small pauses into the day, and the living room is the perfect place for that. But evenings weren't always something I gave much thought to. For years, I'd just collapse into bed at the end of a long day. I thought winding down simply meant 'stopping' – closing the laptop, brushing teeth, lights out. Done.

I've always been a talented sleeper, so it felt like I didn't need to change anything. But once I started adding a few gentle wind-down rituals to my evenings, something shifted. My mornings got better, too. A simple and repeatable evening routine (it needs to be easy for me to stick to it) has profound effects on the quality of the next day.

For me, winding down starts with the room, not a to-do list. When the living room is still in 'day mode', my brain stays there too. So the goal is to help the space shift gears, from practical and bright to softer and slower. I lower the light levels and switch on a few lamps so everything feels gentler. I clear one surface, not as a deep clean, but to remove the visual noise that keeps you mentally switched on. Then I add one small cue that tells my body it's evening. For me, that's peppermint or liquorice tea. We're also lucky to have a separate TV room, which in winter is used for nothing else. It becomes the place where we properly end the day. In summer, it changes completely because the doors open onto the patio, so it becomes part inside, part outside. Same room, different season, and it still does the same job: it makes slowing down feel natural rather than forced.

A simple day-to-evening reset:

- ***Lower the light levels.*** Switch on a few lamps and turn the room down a notch. Softer light changes the whole mood, especially in the evening.
- ***Add a sensory cue.*** A familiar tea or scent helps signal 'day is done'. For me, it's peppermint or liquorice tea, plus a candle to soften the mood.
- ***Edit one surface.*** Clear the coffee table or one shelf so your eye has somewhere to rest. Not a full tidy is needed, just one calm patch.
- ***Contain the day.*** Have one basket/tray where chargers, post, and loose bits can disappear quickly. The room instantly feels less busy.

A slow-evening corner
A few candles, a warm fire and comfortable seating. The point isn't to do more, it's to wind down.

Hosting

There's something quietly magical about a living room that makes people want to linger. You know the kind, where the light is soft, the cushions are slightly rumpled and there's always somewhere to perch with a glass in hand – a room that doesn't try too hard, but still manages to feel just right. That's the kind of living room I try to create: one that draws people in and makes them want to stay a little longer than they had planned.

Part of the effect is down to how the room is laid out. I've found that arranging furniture in a way that encourages conversation, so that people face one another and can talk without shouting across the room, makes all the difference. Just think about where people naturally sit, how the space flows when there are more than a couple of you in it and where someone might feel comfortable sitting down. Sofas are great, but I love adding a few extra options, too: an armchair pulled close, a stool that can double as a side table or even a pouffe tucked by the fire. These little additions mean people can shift and settle without needing to ask, and smaller groupings often lead to the best chats.

If I've learned anything from watching people gather, it's that most of us love to have something to hold – a cup of tea, a glass of wine, a bowl full of crisps we pretend to share. That means side tables are essential. They are a small gesture, but one that makes guests feel considered and makes it feel easier to relax.

For casual gatherings, a drinks station is a great addition. It does not need to be a fancy set-up – just a surface for a few glasses, a bottle, mixers, a few garnishes and perhaps a jug of water with lemon. When friends are over, it gives them somewhere to help themselves. I'm not a formal host, so I like set-ups that invite people to get stuck in. If you've got space, a moveable trolley is fun, too, and makes it look like you've planned the whole thing, even when you haven't.

What makes a room feel warm and full of personality is the presence of personal items. You don't have to display your entire life history on every surface, but one or two meaningful pieces can be great sparks for conversation.

None of this requires perfection or big budgets. It's more about intent. A kotoisa living room holds space for conversation, quiet moments and shared laughter. It makes room for connection. And once you've felt that in someone else's home, you'll know exactly what I mean.

Something sweet
The easiest way to make people feel welcome is to give them something to reach for. A pot of tea, a treat and a tray that can sit happily on the coffee table or the arm of the sofa.

Kitchen and dining room

In every house I've ever lived in, the kitchen has been the unofficial gathering place, even when it wasn't particularly nice. Everyone ended up leaning on the counters, chatting next to the hob or perching awkwardly on a stool that was never meant for sitting.

I've always loved creating beautiful kitchens. In every home we've had, the kitchen has been a showpiece in some way – often the first space we renovated and where most of the budget has been spent, and always the room that sets the tone of the house. This is the space where we spend most of our waking hours, so it has often been the most important room to get 'right'. Of course, it was not all about good looks. Function is equally important – it's a hard-working room after all. There's a rhythm to how things are laid out – not necessarily according to any grand design theory, but because it suits the way you cook, live and gather. There's thought behind the flow, so that you don't have to even think about it day-to-day – it just works.

This is where dinner gets pulled together at speed while someone helps with homework at the island. It's where music plays while you chop vegetables or make coffee, where platters come out for friends who have just popped in. It might be styled to perfection on the surface – and there's nothing wrong with that – but the real beauty is in how easily it folds into everyday life.

Dining spaces work in the same way. I love a long table, soft lighting and the ritual of setting out cloth napkins and candles, but the best meals are never the most complicated ones. A leftover curry eaten on mismatched plates, a slow Sunday breakfast with toast crumbs and endless coffee refills, a last-minute gathering that turns into something far lovelier; that's what I want from a dining area. It should be a space that adapts to real life, and that holds everything from solo lunches to birthday dinners without needing to reinvent itself every time.

Natural gathering place
Kitchens are where people hover, chat, help, and somehow end up staying. A good one earns its keep by working hard and flowing well.

Joy in everyday function

- ***Design for the way you live.*** Group things by how you actually use them. Coffee and tea bits go together; everything for school lunches in one cupboard. If you always make toast and smoothies in the morning, those appliances should live side by side. Let function dictate form.
- ***Keep the dishwasher near the sink.*** This one's worth repeating. It keeps mess in one zone and loading becomes less of a juggling act. Same goes for bins: keep them where scraps naturally end up. Minimize back and forth.
- ***Watch your walkways.*** Make sure there's enough space for people to pass behind chairs or island stools without having to do that awkward sideways shuffle. Around 90cm (approx. 35 inches) is ideal.
- ***Add moments of contrast.*** A mostly pale or neutral space benefits from a little punctuation – a dark wood chair at the dining table, a colourful bowl on the island or textured linen napkins to break up the 'smooth'.
- ***Don't overdo wall units.*** Too many high cupboards can make a kitchen feel top-heavy. Mix in open shelves or keep walls clear for a lighter, more open feel.
- ***Use the full height.*** If you have tall ceilings, don't leave all the visual interest at waist level. Hang a big pendant over the table, or stack ceramics on high open shelves. A little something to draw the eye up makes the room feel taller and more intentional.
- ***Let the dining table breathe.*** If all the chairs are tucked in too neatly, pulling one out just a little adds a sense of life.
- ***Create a corner of calm.*** Whether it's a small armchair near a window or a bench tucked beside the table, these soft spots make the room more inviting and give you somewhere to sit with a cup while the pasta boils.
- ***Style for ease.*** Think about what you reach for daily – olive oil, salt, serving spoons – and make them beautiful enough to leave out. The right tray, pot or chopping board can bridge form and function effortlessly.

Function and form
Group the things you use together, keep the dishwasher near the sink and leave proper walkways so no one has to do an awkward side-shuffle.

Table settings

I'm a happy collector of pretty things: bowls that wink at me from village fêtes, saucer-less teacups with hairline cracks that only make the gold rim sweeter. Setting the table is my favourite part of any gathering: a chance to let all these characters take a bow. It's not about perfection so much as intention.

When we have friends over, I keep it simple. I'd rather chat than hover at the stove, so I cook things that can be prepped beforehand and then mostly mind themselves. I only throw casual dinners and invite people I feel relaxed around. The aim is always the same: spend time together, keep the glasses topped up and serve plenty of good food.

A quick table setting that always looks considered

- Start with texture: a runner or plain linen cloth.
- Mix plates, but keep one thread consistent (colour, rim or material).
- Place short flowers or herbs in jam jars – thyme, mint, a bay sprig.
- Candles at two heights: low tea lights and one taller pair.
- A 'useful pretty' at every place: a bowl for salt, a slice of lemon.

Five tiny upgrades

- Cloth napkins in a basket by the table
- Water jug on the table, not the counter
- A little dish for olive stones or butter
- A pinch pot and pepper mill within reach
- A tray for bread and a serrated knife

The kotoisa place setting (loose rules, high reward)

- Dinner plate with bowl on top (handles soup, salad or pudding)
- Spoon next to the fork (left side, outermost)
- Glass for water, tumbler for wine or juice
- Name card, only if you're more than six

Ready to celebrate
Lay the table before you start cooking. It buys calm, turns a Tuesday into a celebration, and lets those pretty pieces earn their keep.

Meals together

In our house, I do most of the cooking; my husband is a steadfast sous-chef and world-class washer-upper. The children mostly join in later in the process and lay the table for family dinners; the children's friends often stay for a plate, too. My cooking is not fancy, and I still often cook foods my mum made for us growing up: a lot of stews, soups and oven bakes. What matters isn't a clever menu so much as the rituals around dining: soft light, water and glasses within reach and everyone helping themselves.

We keep a few house rules. Dinner-time attendance is non-negotiable, and we always eat at the table. Candles are lit by whoever reaches the matches first and phones are tucked out of reach, on silent. We do a quick day check-in – how is everyone, how was school, what was for lunch, the day's highlight – while we eat. Dinners together should feel like a soft landing to the end of the day.

Our family's top ten dinners (no particular order)

- ***Fish soup.*** Creamy and soothing. Lots of dill, chunks of potato, carrot and fish. Served with Finnish rye bread and butter.
- ***Lasagne.*** Slow-cooked ragu, plenty of bechamel and a cheeky extra layer of pasta, baked until the top is crisp. Green salad on the side.
- ***Fajitas.*** We keep flatbread dough in the freezer and fry these up just before eating. So good with a red pepper-heavy filling. Add yoghurt, avocado, grated cheese and coriander.
- ***Spicy lentil soup and bread.*** Red lentils, all the leftover veggies from the fridge and a spoon of yellow curry paste. Ready in under 30 minutes.
- ***Spaghetti bolognese.*** Comfort in a bowl. Rich sauce, al dente spaghetti, a snowfall of parmesan. Peas on the table for good measure.
- ***Chilli con carne.*** Deep, smoky and forgiving. Cook ahead if you can. Serve with rice, yoghurt, grated cheddar and lime.
- ***Homemade sushi.*** Rolls and bowls. Short-grain rice, salmon or veg, cucumber, avocado and soy, pickled ginger and wasabi.
- ***Gyros with feta salad.*** Warm homemade pittas or flatbread, garlicky chicken, lamb or halloumi, and heaps of feta salad.
- ***Chickpea halloumi curry.*** Halloumi cubes in a spiced tomato-coconut sauce with chickpeas and cauliflower. Rice or naan alongside.
- ***Spinach pancakes.*** Crepes with blitzed spinach in the batter. Eat with lingonberry jam and grated cheese. Crisp edges are the goal!

Dining etiquette
Small rules can keep you at the table a little longer: phones away, candles lit and everyone carrying something to the dishwasher at the end.

Dining area design

A good dining area earns its keep every day. Design for what really happens at your table: quick breakfasts, homework and snacks, week-day suppers, Sunday lunches, the odd birthday tea. Beauty helps, but function is what makes the room inviting on a wet Tuesday and generous on a Saturday night.

Start with circulation. Give chairs honest room to move so people can sit, stand and pass behind without feeling cramped. If the space is narrow, slide the table off-centre to create one clear lane. Keep door swings and radiators in mind when you place the ends of the table. If there's a view or fireplace, align the table so it can be enjoyed.

Light does the heavy lifting. Aim for a pendant that spreads light evenly across the table, hung low enough to feel intimate but high enough for flowers and conversation. Add a couple of lamps to warm the corners and soften the room after dark. Light candles for meals and switch the overheads off unless you are clearing up.

Choose forgiving materials: a table that can be scrubbed; chairs with a little flex and a seat you can linger on. If you use a rug, pick one that hides crumbs and extends well past the chair legs so they never catch. Keep storage close by: a dresser or sideboard for plates, napkins, candles and serving spoons, with one shallow drawer for matches, a corkscrew and the bits that vanish when you need them. A bench to one side is brilliantly useful for extra guests and school bags.

Make space for a small, everyday centrepiece that never needs clearing: a tray with salt, pepper, a bud vase and a box of matches. Everything else arrives and departs with the meal so the surface can be reset quickly.

Keep it simple, comfortable and ready. If the room helps you sit, talk and pass a bowl without fuss, you have designed it well.

Different flavours of design
Keep it comfortable, keep it practical and keep it flowing. Everything else is just decoration.

YIYUN LI

Bedroom

A restful bedroom is a simple machine: it manages light, sound, temperature and touch, while keeping decisions and visual noise to a minimum. Design it first for sleep and second for waking. Beauty follows naturally when comfort leads.

Start with the bed. Choose the best mattress you can sensibly afford and set the bed at roughly knee height so that getting in and out is effortless. Use breathable natural fibres for bedding: cotton percale for crisp coolness, linen for relaxed texture. I like to keep patterns quiet so that the room reads as calm, but go with bold patterns if they are your love language.

Lighting should be helpful for both sleeping and waking up. Aim for layers you can control: blackout blinds for proper darkness and curtains to soften and dress the window, with sheers for daytime privacy. Bedside lamps with warm bulbs (around 2700K) and fabric shades create a soft pool of light at reading height; overheads are worthwhile when they are on a dimmer and used sparingly. If dawn light wakes you too early, add a liner to curtains or a secondary roller blind. For gentle mornings, sheers diffuse brightness without gloom.

Rugs, curtains, upholstered headboards and small seating can hush echoes and soften hard corners. Keep the bedroom cooler than the rest of the home and rely on layers rather than heat. I love sleeping in fresh air, so we always have a window open, even during the winter.

Good storage is essential for calm spaces. Keep what you reach for daily at hand and rotate the rest out of sight. Closed wardrobes and drawers create visual quiet, and a single landing zone – a tray or shallow bowl – keeps glasses, jewellery and hair ties from roaming. Bedside tables need only night-time essentials: books, water, lip cream. Hide chargers, tidy cables and resist turning the surface into a second desk.

Colour works best as a whisper. Misty greens, mineral blues, oatmeal neutrals and gentle clays will shift beautifully with the light. If you crave depth, keep the walls soft and bring richer tones to a headboard, throw or cushions; this way the overall mood stays restful. Choose matt, tactile finishes that absorb light rather than bouncing it around.

The layout should feel unhurried. Place the bed on the calmest wall and keep walking lines clear at the sides and foot. In narrow rooms, slide the bed slightly off-centre to create one generous circulation lane rather than two tight ones. Wall lights can free up small bedside spaces; a slim console or floating shelf will suit these rooms. A large rug under the bed will make the room feel larger and kinder underfoot.

If the bedroom must work harder – hosting a desk or dressing area – mark zones clearly so the bed can remain the star. A screen, a curtain across open shelves and a lidded basket for your laptop allow work to disappear after-hours. Keep mirrors where natural light is kind, and add a small lamp at the dressing table for flattering evening light. Hooks behind the door are for tomorrow's outfit, not a textile mountain; if a chair collects laundry, remove the chair.

A soft landing

Minimize visual noise, and use gentle light and textures that make you exhale the second you walk in.

Small rooms need softness, not shyness. Hang curtains high and wide to enlarge the window, choose a shallow headboard and slim bed frame to gain floor area, and consider mirrored wardrobes to bounce light around the room. Two runners beside the bed can stand in for one large rug. Store spare linen in under-bed drawers or lidded boxes, but leave breathing space so the room does not feel packed. Keep surfaces mostly empty and let texture do the work.

Seven peaceful evening rituals for better sleep

- *Dim the lights after dinner*. Let your home wind down with you. Switch off anything too bright and turn on a couple of lamps or a soft overhead light. It doesn't have to be perfect, just enough to gently signal the end of the day.
- *Change into something soft*. Old pyjamas, a worn-in jumper, thick socks – the kind of clothes that feel like an exhale. This is a quiet cue to your body that it can start letting go of daily stresses.
- *Write one sentence*. Something you're grateful for; something that annoyed you; something you're glad is over – a few words in a notebook to get things out of your head and onto paper.
- *Step outside and stare at the stars (or night sky)*. I love doing this, often just before going upstairs to bed. It also acts as the final outing for our dog. There is something deeply meditative about it – I often think of all the people who have done the same thing, perhaps standing in the very same spot.
- *Put your phone away*. You knew this one was coming, didn't you? Screens before bedtime are a bad idea and not an easy habit to break, so start small. Even ten phone-free minutes before bed can make a difference.
- *Read a few pages*. It does not need to be something Nobel prize-winning or groundbreaking – just a book you enjoy or a poem that helps you slow your thoughts. It doesn't matter if you don't finish the chapter either. There is always tomorrow.
- *Make time for your skincare routine*. It's hard to enjoy a moment of self-care when you're half-asleep and counting the seconds until you can lie down. Lately, I've started doing my evening skincare routine earlier – usually after dinner – when I still have the energy to enjoy it. This feels less like a chore and more like a small act of kindness, done calmly and without the rush.

Evening rituals for calm
Candle lit, phone away and the day can be left behind. You can finally unwind.

ENID BLYTON
CORALIE BICKFORD-SMITH

Bathroom

A good bathroom is equal parts sanctuary and workhorse. It wakes you up kindly, scrubs small knees and muddy paws, stores your cosmetics and still holds enough calm to host a quiet bath at the end of the day. Design should follow those realities. Start with the feeling you want to achieve – clean, warm, unhurried – and let every choice support that.

Think about the route you take through the room. Where do towels live so that you can grab one without dripping across the floor? Can two people move about without the toothbrush tango? A layout that works on an ordinary Tuesday is the one that will feel lovely on Sunday night.

Surfaces and materials

Bathrooms have short tempers with the wrong finishes, so choose forgiving ones. Porcelain or ceramic tiles on the floor are hearty, easy to clean and kinder to budgets than stone. If you dream of timber, go for a water-resistant, engineered option and treat it properly, then add a deep bathmat. On the walls, tiling where water splashes and paint everywhere else keeps the room from feeling clinical. A satin or eggshell paint resists steam and wipes down without protest. Natural stone is glorious, but needs sealing and the odd gentle pat rather than bleach – commit only if you love a little maintenance.

Light, always in layers

Overhead light makes cleaning straightforward; wall lights at face level flatter and ease the morning mirror moment. A dimmer allows the room to shift from practical to peaceful. Pick warm bulbs for rooms without windows, and add candles to brighten gloomy shelves and corners. Daylight is precious – keep windows as clear as privacy allows and hang curtains high and wide, or use frosted film rather than heavy blinds.

Ventilation

Steam is inevitable; mould is optional. An efficient extractor fan that runs on after you leave is one of the most worthwhile upgrades you can make. If you can open a window for ten minutes after a bath or shower, even better. Warm towels help rooms dry faster, so a heated rail earns its place even in a tiny cloakroom.

Room with a view
I had one non-negotiable for this bathroom: the bath had to go in front of the window. I love watching the trees, sky and the view over the city of Bath.

Storage saves mornings

Keep what you use every day within arm's reach and hide the rest. A mirrored cabinet swallows toothbrushes, face cloths and other boring but essential things. Drawers beat cupboards because nothing vanishes at the back. Decant only what helps – handwash into a nice pump, bath salts into a jar – and label anything that could cause a frantic 7am mix-up. Hooks are more forgiving than towel bars for children; baskets under a vanity catch spare loo rolls and hand towels. If space is tight, add a narrow shelf above the door for both back-stock and bandages.

Water and warmth

If you can put both a shower and a bath in, wonderful; if not, choose the one you will use the most and make it excellent. Walk-in showers feel generous in small rooms because sightlines stay open; a single fixed pane is easier to keep clean than a folding door. Invest in a proper thermostatic valve so temperature is reliable and your hands are free. Underfloor heating is a quiet luxury, but a good rug and a warm towel can do similar work.

Mirrors and medicine

A large mirror doubles the light and makes even a narrow room feel more open. If shaving or meticulous skincare is part of your life, add a small magnifying mirror that can tuck away. Keep medicine safely out of reach and out of the sun, and separate first-aid from beauty so that plasters appear when they're actually needed.

Colour and mood

Bathrooms take colour beautifully. Crisp white with warm brass is classic, but soft greens, plaster pinks and smoky blues are wonderfully soothing. If you prefer neutrals, bring interest through texture: zellige-style tiles, linen blinds, a timber stool or woven baskets. Plants – ferns or pothos – thrive here if you have natural light available.

Easy cleaning

Choose grout that hides a little life and squeegee glass after showers to keep the limescale from winning. Store cleaning spray and a cloth in the room to turn 'I'll do it later' into a 30-second habit. If you live in a hard-water area, keep vinegar on hand for taps and a gentle cream cleaner for basins.

Quiet functionality
A bathroom that works well is one that's easy to use on a busy morning. Keep the everyday essentials within reach, add warmth where you can and choose finishes that age kindly.

APOLLO

Rituals and self-care

In Finland, sauna is not a luxury or a spa day; it is part of the culture. Heat, rest, rinse, repeat – a simple cycle that relaxes the mind as much as muscles. The word to know is *löyly*: the living steam created when water hits hot stones – a soft cloud that first prickles your skin and then feels like a hug. Contrast is part of the magic: warmth followed by cool air, a cold shower, a plunge in a lake or a roll in the snow. You emerge pink-cheeked and clear-headed having shed all your worries.

Most families have a set day for sauna. In my childhood it was Saturday. Ours was heated with birch logs, and sometimes my brother and I were given a bottle of sparkling green lemonade to share as a sauna-break treat. Afterwards we ate my mum's homemade pizza and watched TV. In summer we moved to my family's island cabin, where sauna was part of our evening routine every day. We would jump squealing into the chilly Baltic Sea, run back into the sauna to warm up, then head out again for more jumping and swimming. It was a very important part of our daily ritual, and it stitched the days together.

Kotoisa without sauna

You may not have a built-in sauna at home, but the principles travel beautifully to an ordinary bathroom. Start with warmth. Run a hot bath or a steamy shower and let the room heat gently while you gather what you need: a warm towel, a glass of water, a clean robe close by. Add calm light – wall lights or candles rather than bright overheads. Keep scent simple and recognizable: birch, eucalyptus and pine echo the forested feel of a Finnish sauna; lavender lowers the shoulders before bed.

Then invite contrast. Finish a bath with a cool rinse of legs and arms, or step into cooler air for a minute before wrapping up. In summer, open the window and breathe in evening air; in winter, rest by the window for a few breaths before returning to warmth. Contrast sharpens the senses and makes the heat feel more generous (without the need for any properly cold plunges).

Ritual is really about attention. Move slowly. Use a wooden brush or a soft cloth to wake the skin and encourage circulation. Sip water or a mint tea. Put your phone out of reach. Give your products time to work – hair mask, face oil, body balm – and read a few pages while they do. The goal is not 'treatment' so much as punctuation – a clear comma between the day and whatever comes next.

If you are designing from scratch, a compact barrel sauna outside or a small infra-red cabin indoors can be transformative, but you can also nod to sauna life with simpler choices: timber stools, a bucket and ladle for bath time, hooks for linen wraps, a cool jug in the fridge. Keep towels in generous sizes, and have one set that feels special for slow evenings. And remember common sense: avoid extreme heat if you are unwell or pregnant, keep water nearby and always listen to your body.

Whether a weekly sauna session, a slow Sunday bath or three calm minutes with warm water and a clean towel, the effect is the same: you leave the room feeling more yourself than when you entered.

Heat, rest, rinse, repeat
You don't need a sauna to borrow the feeling, just a warm shower, a towel within reach and one small 'I'm looking after myself' detail.

Home offices and workspaces

Work at home is not one thing. It is a laptop at the kitchen table before school runs, a quiet desk for deep focus, a craft bench for making and a corner where bills are paid and life admin gets tamed. The aim is not to build a miniature corporate office, but to create spaces that help you think clearly, do your best work, then switch off.

A kotoisa workspace is calm, practical and ready for work. It helps you to start without faff, keeps you comfortable while you focus, and lets you put the day away quickly. When work is contained and has a set space, the rest of the house has room to feel like home again.

Start by deciding what the space needs to do on an ordinary day. Do you write, code, sketch, sew, take calls? All of the above? List the top three tasks and design for those first. If you can dedicate a room, brilliant; if not, a well-planned corner can do more than you think. The rules are the same either way: clear surfaces, good light, a supportive chair and storage that stops small things from breeding.

After sleep, light is the biggest performance enhancer. Place the desk where you can borrow daylight without fighting glare; side light is kinder than a window directly in front or behind you. Sheer fabrics can soften a bright window, and a simple blind will help you manage the late-afternoon sun. Add a warm task lamp with a directional shade at eye level to prevent screen reflections. Overheads are best for cleaning and finding paperclips, not for working under all afternoon. If you take video calls, face the window or a lamp rather than having it behind you.

Ergonomic design pays you back daily. Aim for the top of your screen to sit around eye height and about an arm's length away. Keep shoulders relaxed, with elbows at roughly 90 degrees and wrists neutral, not perched on a sharp edge. A footrest can work wonders if your chair is a touch high, and a folded blanket can rescue an unforgiving seat. If you swap between laptop and paper, give each a defined spot so that you are not juggling piles. Movement matters, so consider a sit-stand set-up if you will actually use it, or build simple movement into the day with a timer and a short stretch between tasks.

Sound can be attention's friend or enemy. Rugs, curtains and bookshelves absorb echo in hard rooms. A door that shuts is gold; if you cannot have that, noise-cancelling headphones are the next best thing. On calls, use a soft-furnished backdrop if you can, and park the microphone away from keyboard clatter. If home is lively, agree on some signals: headphones on means 'please don't interrupt', a small lit lamp means you are on a call.

Inspiring, creative spaces
I love this little studio space: coffee within reach, a moodboard in progress, and enough room to make, edit, think and start again.

Be brutally honest about storage. Keep what you use weekly at arm's reach. Monthly items can live one step away. Anything used more rarely goes high, low or out of the room. Drawers beat open shelves for small things. Label liberally and use shallow trays inside drawers so your work surface does not become a jumble. A rolling cart is ideal if your work needs to appear and disappear daily. For craft spaces, clear jars and lidded boxes keep colour visible but dust at bay. Keep a shredder or recycling bag close so that paper leaves as quickly as it arrives.

If your workspace has another function, a folding screen, curtain on a ceiling track or even a change of rug can mark zones and help your brain switch modes. On the dining table, work from a tray or shallow crate so that everything can lift away in one go. Keep chargers and cables in a single pouch for easy access. A wall shelf holds files without eating up floor space, and a pinboard or rail keeps important bits in sight.

Colour and texture set the tempo. Softer, lower-saturation colours help concentration for most people: olive, clay, mineral blue, warm neutrals. If you thrive on energy, reserve bolder tones for a chair, a lamp or a single wall rather than the whole envelope. Matt finishes read calmer on camera and in real life. Natural textures help rooms feel less tech-heavy: timber, linen pinboards, wool rugs, a ceramic mug that lives on a coaster. Add one living plant if you can keep it alive; your eyes will thank you for a patch of green.

Personalize lightly and usefully: one or two photos, a small object with meaning, a calendar you will actually consult. Clutter gets tired quickly. Art at seated eye height beats a gallery wall that scrambles behind your head on calls. If you need whiteboard space, paint a panel with magnetic whiteboard paint and frame it with timber so it feels intentional.

Spaces that work

- ***The closed-door study.*** A classic desk facing the door or window, a task lamp, a supportive chair, books and a small armchair for reading; add a dimmer so the room can shift from focus to free thinking. Use a rug to soak up sound and as a finishing touch.
- ***The quiet corner.*** A 120cm (approx. 47-inch) desk tucked against a wall with a pinboard above, slim drawers and a floor lamp that throws light across the work surface. A curtain or screen can separate work from life in the evening.
- ***The table worker.*** A large tray holds a laptop, charger, notebook, pen pot and mouse. A folding laptop stand and compact keyboard live inside. Everything lifts away when dinner is ready. Keep a shallow basket nearby for papers that need revisiting.
- ***The maker's bench.*** Sturdy table, task light on an arm, pegboard or rail for tools and a rolling cart for materials. Stand on a cushioned mat if you are cutting or assembling for hours. Add a shelf for in-progress pieces so the surface can be reset.

Give work a home
A separate desk, a quiet corner with a pinboard, even the kitchen table – the trick is giving work a 'home', however portable, so that it doesn't take over the whole house.

Tech without the tangle

Route cables behind the desk with adhesive clips and a simple cable tray. Label chargers and keep duplicates where you use them. A small Uninterruptible Power Supply (UPS) can save your desktop during brief power cuts. If fans whirr loudly, lift the laptop on a stand for airflow. For calls, a simple external microphone and headphones beats the laptop mic in a lively room. Place the camera slightly above eye level and look towards light, not away from it.

Well-being while you work

Breaks make work better. Use a 50–10 or 45–15 rhythm and actually stand up when you stop. Look at something far away for 20 seconds every 20 minutes to rest your eyes. Stretch your chest and hips after long periods of sitting. Keep a short walk on your calendar after lunch. If you can, change posture through the day: sit, stand, perch on a stool, then back to the chair. End the day with a small closing ritual.

Sharing the space

Agree on quiet hours and call windows. Keep a shared calendar visible. Use baskets or labelled trays for each person's in-progress piles so they do not sprawl. Headphones are essential, not rude. A second lamp and set of chargers prevents silent wars. If children do homework nearby, give them a dedicated box of supplies and a defined finish time.

Useful measurements

- ***Desk height.*** Around 73–75cm (approx. 30 inches) for most, paired with a chair that lets your feet rest flat and elbows sit near 90 degrees.
- ***Screen.*** Top at or just below eye height, about an arm's length away from your face.
- ***Task lamp.*** Bottom of shade roughly at seated eye level to reduce glare.
- ***Chair seat height.*** 44–50cm (approx. 17–20 inches), with lumbar support or a small cushion at the curve of your back.
- ***Clearance.*** 90cm (approx. 35 inches) behind your chair.
- ***Pinboard height.*** Centre around 120–30cm (approx. 47–51 inches) from the floor when seated is your reference.

Conducive to creativity
Not everything needs to be perfectly set up to be useful. Sometimes the best workspaces are the ones that feel light, lived-in and quietly inspiring.

Kotoisa outdoors

Start where you are

A kotoisa garden can come in different sizes and shapes. A balcony not much more than the size of a tea towel can feel generous if it holds a chair and a pot of herbs. A long, narrow garden can become a string of small rooms. A windswept roof terrace can be tamed with planters and a windbreak so that it finally invites you out with your morning mug.

Begin by watching. Where does the sun land at breakfast, lunch and late evening? Where does the wind swirl? Which corner stays soggy, and which one bakes? Look out from the windows you use the most often – what do you want to see in February when everything is grey? Maybe a little table and a chair, or a pot with an evergreen plant in it, or a small tree with pale bark. Note the views you love and the ones you would rather hide. Screens, climbers and a single well-placed shrub can tidy sightlines more kindly than a fence.

Set the brief the way you would indoors. What must this space do in a normal week? Coffee outside before work; supper with friends during the warmer months; a place for the dog to run and the children to kick a ball; a spot for herbs; a composting corner; and a washing line that does not photobomb every picture.

Scale is your friend. Big pots look calmer than lots of small ones. Fewer, larger perennials are easier to manage than dozens of tiny 'bits'. Keep surfaces simple and safe: stable paths, non-slip decking, steps with a handrail if you need one. If you can, put a light outside on a timer and a socket for a string of lamps or to power the hedge trimmer. This small-scale infrastructure makes daily life smoother.

Quick wins to make any space kinder

- One seat with a backrest where the nicest light falls
- A pot you see from indoors, planted for winter interest
- Hooks for tools and a lidded box for cushions
- A watering can that lives outside and a hose on a reel

Waiting for dusk to fall
One table, a few chairs and a lantern lit for evening is sometimes all a garden needs to feel inviting. All the better if you can see it from indoors.

Garden types (and how to make the most of them)

Balcony or tiny patio

Think vertical and multi-use. A slim bench against the wall provides seating and storage underneath. Rail planters free the floor and offer herbs at nose level. Use one large pot as a focal point rather than a clutter of small ones: a dwarf fruit tree, an olive or a cloud-pruned evergreen. Choose light-coloured outdoor rugs to reflect light and soften concrete. Add a collapsible bistro set that you can fold away when you need the space.

Planting should work hard: rosemary, thyme, mint (in a pot), chives, strawberries, trailing cherry tomatoes, hardy geraniums, heucheras, grasses like carex. One scented plant close to the seat makes evenings feel like a holiday: jasmine, *trachelospermum* or a rose in a big pot.

Long, narrow garden

Break it into short chapters, so that the eye and the feet have reasons to travel: a small terrace near the house for weekday meals, a 'green room' in the middle for lawn or play and a tucked-away seat at the far end for a private cup of tea. Keep a single repeated line to tie it together, like the same edging on each bed or the same timber for seats and planters. Use tall, see-through plants to zone the space without blocking light or flow.

Courtyard or town garden

Think of it as an outdoor room. Hard surfaces can be softened with planters the size of barrels and climbers on wires or a grid. Water is transformative here; even a small wall spout running into a trough adds movement and calming sound. Lanterns on ledges, a fireplace or a chiminea for colder seasons, and an overhead sail for summer shade, make the space usable for more months of the year.

Opt for plants that thrive in shelter: ferns, hostas, hydrangeas, camellias for acid soil, scented daphnes near the door, evergreen jasmine on a trellis. In full sun, try salvias, nepeta, rosemary, bay in a pot and a small multi-stem tree for shade and sculptural winter branches.

No two gardens alike
However much space you have, think about what you most want to use it for – relaxing or entertaining, growing plants for food, scent or colour. Make it work for you.

Family lawn with play

Keep the centre clear and push planting to the edges. Choose a surface you can repair easily. Put the sandpit in partial shade and use a lidded box for toys and tools at night. Add a simple outdoor tap children can reach, a hook for skipping ropes and a chalkboard on a fence panel. Plant tough perennials that forgive stray balls: hardy geraniums, lavender, ornamental grasses, catmint and small shrubby herbs.

Kitchen garden

You do not need a field. Two sleepers stacked to form a 1.2 x 2.4m (4 x 8ft) raised bed will feed a household with heroic amounts of salad and herbs. Add a second bed if you are keen and a slim bed along a fence for beans and peas. Keep paths wide enough for a wheel barrow, use woodchip to keep mud down and store tools neatly. Plant what you actually eat weekly: cut-and-come-again lettuces, rocket, parsley, strawberries, chives, courgettes, tomatoes, a steady rotation of radishes and spring onions. Blueberries in pots reward anyone with patience.

Wildlife-friendly gardens

Aim for layers: canopy, shrubs, perennials, groundcover. Leave some seedheads for winter food and structure. Areas of water, however small, are great for attracting wildlife – try a shallow dish with stones for birds, or a buried trug as a tiny pond, with a beachy edge so that hedgehogs can get out. Avoid pesticides. Plant native plants and flowers loved by pollinators. A log pile in a quiet corner is a whole neighbourhood.

A garden that works for you
Make the garden easy to live with, not another job. Grow what you love to look at (or eat), add inviting seating and lighting, and leave a little space for nature.

Make it liveable

By the time friends arrive, the garden has done that lovely dusk thing where edges soften and the night animals are getting ready for their day. The lamps click on by themselves – a timer is the quiet hero here – and path lights hover at ankle height so that no one trips over the lavender. A single uplight grazes the small tree and suddenly the whole space feels taller, like the garden put on a formal jacket.

The calm you feel in this garden is mostly storage doing its job. Cushions vanish into the storage box with the lift-up lid, tools hang on hooks instead of sulking in corners and bird seed lives in a lidded box that the fox can't open. Even the bins look respectable behind a simple timber screen with a climber working its way up. By the back door there's a weatherproof pot with secateurs and gloves so the five-minute jobs actually happen when you think of them.

People drift naturally to the seats because there are two obvious places to be: a small table near the house for first glasses and easy breakfasts, and a deeper perch that catches the last of the sun. A basket by the door holds cushions that don't mind a bit of drizzle, and the table is the right size for the number we often are, rather than the once-a-year crowd. When more bodies appear, a folding trestle table comes out or we throw blankets on the grass and call it charming.

It's a garden arranged to be kind after 6pm: light where you need it, water features without faff, places to sit that invite you to stay, and the mess hidden so that the evening can be about the people, not the stuff.

Shared and borrowed spaces

If you have access to a communal courtyard or a shared green, treat it like an extension of home. Bring a blanket, a thermos, a frisbee. Know the polite rules and add to the space: a bird bath everyone can enjoy, a stack of spare chairs, a small pot of herbs with a 'please pick' sign. If all you have is a window, make the sill a tiny stage: pots of basil and thyme, a jar of branches that change with the season, a candle for evenings. The goal is the same: nature within reach, a seat in the light and a reason to step outside for five minutes every day.

The happiest people in the world

Start with the ordinary and you'll discover the Finnish approach to happiness. It's a stack of practical, ordinary things done well: trust that things work, spend time outside in all weather, repeat small rituals and find that calm sense of 'enough'. The World Happiness Report puts Finland at the top again and again largely because daily life runs smoothly and the majority of people feel looked after.

Kotoisa – Finnish for homelike, cosy and at ease – belongs at the centre. A kotoisa home or life isn't polished to impress; it's made for you. It helps you to do the ordinary things that make you feel well, and to feel satisfied with *enough* instead of restless for more.

That, more or less, is the Finnish happiness thesis in miniature.

Happiness research keeps circling back to trust. In Finland, people tend to trust one another and the systems around them: schools, healthcare, public services. The welfare net is strong enough that a setback doesn't become a spiral – fewer people fall through the cracks – and corruption is low enough that paying your taxes feels like a collective project rather than a personal loss. That kind of social contract gives everyday life a reliable baseline. It doesn't manufacture joy but it reduces preventable misery, which in the long run matters more. Think of it like insulation in a house: invisible when it's working, costly when it's not.

The best kind of self-care
A quick walk under trees steadies the mind and resets breathing. Make it easy: boots and waterproof coat by the door, and go.

Nature within arm's reach

In Finland, nature is everywhere and easily accessed, even in the cities. 'Every person's right' (*jokamiehenoikeus*) lets anyone roam forests and lake shores, forage berries and mushrooms, and camp for a night – regardless of who owns the land – as long as you do it respectfully. Access is the point. Nature isn't a destination you book, it's a neighbour you visit. The result is a society where fresh air and trees are part of ordinary, daily life.

Nature is a shortcut to feeling human again. Ten minutes under trees reduces mental noise; a horizon line steadies your breathing. It isn't mystical, it's mechanical: light helps set your body clock, fresh air nudges you to breathe deeper, greens and blues give your brain something gentle on which to rest. After time outside, you come back softer at the edges and a bit more yourself.

In Finland this is baked into daily life: you step out into the woods because they're there, not because you've blocked out time for it. Ease is the point. When nature is close and uncomplicated, it becomes a habit rather than an event, and habits are what shape well-being.

At home, you can make nature ordinary, too. Open the window first thing in the morning and last thing at night. Keep shoes and a basket by the door so a quick walk is frictionless. Bring in branches, herbs or a pot of something living; they do more for the mood than a bunch of flowers wrapped in cellophane. Let daylight into your life. Use materials that feel honest under your hand: timber, wool, linen, clay. They age well, they're quiet to look at and they anchor you when the day is busy.

Catch small doses of that air. Stand outside with your mug for two minutes. Eat lunch on the step. Walk the long way to the bin. In rain, a good coat, waterproof trousers and boots change everything – there is no such thing as bad weather, only the wrong kit. In winter, chase sky where you can; in summer, shade is as nourishing as sun.

If you need a nudge, create practical prompts: a peg for your raincoat, a torch by the back door, a basket for hats and gloves, a spot to dry wet boots. Reduce the faff and you'll go out more. And when you come back in, let the house meet you halfway: somewhere to hang damp things, a mat that actually catches grit. Bit by bit, the boundary softens: outside comes in, inside steps out, and your days get that little bit kinder.

Enough over excess

A thread in Finnish thinking is the idea of 'enough'. Happiness doesn't seem to grow with more stuff or more noise. Research by Finnish scholars echoes this: life satisfaction improves when society minimizes extreme unhappiness and supports autonomy, rather than when people are chasing constant highs. What you get is a calmer, more workable everyday life. Kotoisa is the interior version of enoughness.

How to build kotoisa happiness at home (wherever you live)

- ***Design for everyday, not someday.*** If weekday mornings are the pinch point, solve those first: pegs at child height, breakfast bowls in a low drawer, a lamp on a timer to nudge you awake.
- ***Layer your light.*** Have bright light for cleaning and finding splinters, soft light for evenings. Warm bulbs and dimmers change the room from 'chore mode' to 'kind mode' in a second and your nervous system notices.
- ***Keep nature close.*** A bench by the door, boots ready and a small basket make 'ten minutes outside' a habit, not a chore. Inside the house, add sheer curtains to soften daylight and open the window for five minutes morning and night. The Finnish right-to-roam may not exist where you are, but the impulse to go outside often, for no reason, is portable.
- ***Make one weekly ritual untouchable.*** A longer bath on Sundays with a cool rinse at the end, or a family walk that ends with tea – put it in the diary. Treat it like a train you mean to catch.
- ***Design for trust.*** Put essentials where your future self will actually look for them: towels in reach of the shower, chargers by the desk, the good mugs at the front. Reduce daily frictions and you raise a room's kindness levels.

Less is more
Choose fewer and better things, keep surfaces clear and let colour and detail do the heavy lifting. Put essentials where you actually use them and daily life feels calmer.

Acknowledgements

Writing a book about the art of making a home feel truly kotoisa, warm, safe, deeply yours, has been one of the great joys of my life. But no home, and no book, comes together alone.

To my brilliant literary agent Oscar Janson-Smith – thank you for believing in this book from day one, for seeing what it could be before I could quite see it myself, and for championing it with such conviction and care. None of this would exist without you.

To my fantastic publisher Alison Starling – thank you for taking a chance on *The Nurturing Home*, for your wisdom, your warmth and for guiding me through this process with such grace. You made a first-time author feel entirely held. Huge thank you also to editor Rachel Silverlight, art director Juliette Norsworthy and the whole team at Octopus.

To Simon Bevan, whose photography brings every page of this book to life – you have the most extraordinary eye. The way you found the light, the stillness, the soul in each home is something I will never stop being grateful for.

To all the wonderful homeowners who opened their doors to us, shared their stories, and trusted us to do justice to the spaces they have so lovingly created – thank you from the bottom of my heart. Your generosity is woven into every chapter.

To my family – my greatest constants – thank you for your support, your encouragement and your unwavering belief that dreams are worth chasing.

To my friends, who listened, encouraged, distracted me when I needed it and rallied when I didn't. You know who you are, and you are everything.

To my wonderful children – never stop dreaming. Watch what happens when you don't.

And to Paul. You kept me going on the hard days, celebrated the good ones and never once doubted me, even when I doubted myself. This book is for you too.

Resources

A YEAR IN THE COTSWOLDS
shnordic.substack.com
I share many of my own finds and the stories behind them on my Substack. It's worth browsing if you're curious about how I put rooms together.

AARIKKA
aarikka.com
A Finnish lifestyle design brand founded in 1954, beloved for its crisp Scandinavian lines, round wooden forms and use of natural materials. Known for jewellery, home decoration and seasonal pieces.

ANTHROPOLOGIE
anthropologie.com
Bohemian-inspired furniture, textiles, homewares and accessories.

BLOOMINGVILLE
bloomingville.com
A Danish homewares brand. Lots of lovely furniture, ceramics, tableware, textiles, lighting and decorative accessories – all at accessible prices.

BUNGALOW DK
bungalow.dk
A Danish brand rooted in the ancient craft of block printing. The resulting range – tablecloths, tea towels, cushions, napkins, ceramics and glassware – is vibrant and joyful, handmade by artisans using techniques thousands of years old.

CASTLERY
castlery.com
A global furniture design brand born in Singapore in 2013, offering timeless sofas, beds, dining tables, storage and accessories. Pieces are crafted with a focus on quality materials, designed to live with you and improve with time.

EBAY
ebay.com
An online marketplace for new, used and vintage items. An endlessly rewarding hunting ground for one-off home finds, secondhand furniture and collectables at every price point.

ETSY
etsy.com
A global marketplace connecting buyers with independent makers, vintage sellers and small creative businesses. Perfect for finding handmade ceramics, prints, textiles and unique decorative pieces that bring genuine character to a home.

FACEBOOK MARKETPLACE
facebook.com/marketplace
A local buying and selling platform where preloved furniture, homewares and curiosities change hands every day. One of the best places to find affordable secondhand pieces and give them a new life.

H&M HOME
hm.com
The home arm of H&M brings affordable, well-designed textiles, ceramics, candles and accessories to the high street. A reliable port of call for seasonal updates, everyday basics and the kind of simple, considered pieces that layer well with older finds.

IITTALA
iittala.com
A Finnish design brand founded as a glassworks in 1881, now producing some of my favourite tableware and glassware.

LA REDOUTE
laredoute.com
A French lifestyle brand with a long history of bringing relaxed, continental style to the home. Strong on furniture, bed linen, rugs and accessories, and consistently good value- particularly when you catch one of their sales.

MADAM STOLTZ
madamstoltz.dk
Brand that beautifully blends Scandinavian simplicity with Indian and global artisan traditions, producing handwoven textiles, bamboo furniture, stoneware ceramics, brass pieces and rattan homewares – all with an earthy, bohemian warmth that feels lived-in.

NEPTUNE
neptune.com
Makers of kitchens, furniture, lighting and home accessories. Rooted in British heritage and traditional cabinet-making, every piece is designed to age beautifully and last a lifetime. Their stores – over 30 across the UK and Europe – feel like real homes rather than showrooms.

OLIVER BONAS
oliverbonas.com
A British lifestyle brand offering clothing, jewellery, gifts and an ever-changing collection of distinctive homewares.

PIGLET IN BED
pigletinbed.com
Best known for its linen and linen-blend sheets in a range of timeless colours and classic patterns- gingham, stripe, chambray – all of which soften and improve with every wash.

RUGGABLE
ruggable.com
Washable rugs and home textiles in a wide range of designs and sizes. A practical, design-conscious solution for real homes- the two-piece system means covers can be removed and machine-washed, making them as hardworking as they are good-looking.

THE SOHO LIGHTING COMPANY
soholighting.com
A family-owned British lighting brand founded in 2017. Pendants, wall lights, switches and sockets are designed in London and hand-finished by artisans in Cornwall.

SUNBURY ANTIQUES MARKET AT KEMPTON PARK
sunburyantiques.com
A large antiques fair selling everything from furniture and ceramics to silverware, vintage fashion, paintings and garden pieces. An unmissable day out for anyone who loves the thrill of the find. Beyond Kempton, some of my favourite things have come from local charity shops, car boot sales and regional antique fairs.

TAT LONDON
tat-london.co.uk
A wonderful and endlessly browsable vintage and antique shop, great for unusual decorative pieces.

TOAST
toa.st
A British lifestyle brand best known for its clothing, Toast also offers a considered range of homewares, including linen bedding, ceramics, glassware, throws and decorative pieces.

VINTERIOR
vinterior.co
Vinterior is a marketplace for pre-owned, vintage and antique furniture and homewares with a strong sustainability ethos. A well-curated alternative to the endless scroll of eBay – easier to search by style, decade or piece type.

ZARA HOME
zarahome.com
A high street favourite for affordable, beautiful homewares, textiles and accessories. Reliably good for updated seasonal pieces, bedding, glassware and those finishing touches that pull a room together.

Index

G

H

I

J

K

L

Index

First published in Great Britain in 2026 by
Mitchell Beazley, an imprint of Octopus Publishing
Group Ltd, Carmelite House, 50 Victoria
Embankment, London EC4Y 0DZ
www.octopusbooks.co.uk

An Hachette UK Company
www.hachette.co.uk

The authorized representative in the EEA is Hachette
Ireland, 8 Castlecourt Centre, Dublin 15, D15 XTP3,
Ireland (email: info@hbgi.ie)

Distributed in the US by Hachette Book Group
1290 Avenue of the Americas, 4th and 5th Floors
New York, NY 10104

Distributed in Canada by Canadian Manda Group
664 Annette St., Toronto, Ontario, Canada M6S 2C8

ISBN: 978-1-84601-621-9
eISBN: 978-1-84601-622-6

A CIP catalogue record for this book is available
from the British Library.

Printed and bound in China.

10 9 8 7 6 5 4 3 2 1

MIX
Paper | Supporting responsible forestry
FSC www.fsc.org FSC® C008047

Publishing Director: Alison Starling
Art Director: Juliette Norsworthy
Senior Developmental Editor: Rachel Silverlight
Copy Editor: Faye Robson
Design: Studio Brannan
Photography: Simon Bevan
Assistant Production Manager: Allison Gonsalves

ANALYSIS OF
THIN CONCRETE
SHELLS

A circular ground level reservoir of 6.75 million litres capacity having a central dome and fan shaped shell for the roof (Clients: Bangalore Water Supply and Sewerage Board, Courtesy: H.K. Nanjundaswamy, Consulting and Construction Engineer, Bangalore).

A ground level reservoir having a trough type folded plate wall and funicular shells for roof with a capacity of 22.5 million litres (Clients: Bangalore Water Supply and Sewerage Board, Courtesy: H.K. Nanjundaswamy, Consulting and Construction Engineer, Bangalore).

ANALYSIS OF THIN CONCRETE SHELLS

(SECOND REVISED EDITION)

K CHANDRASHEKHARA

BE, ME, PhD, DSc.

Emeritus Fellow

Department of Civil Engineering

Indian Institute of Science

Bangalore, Karnataka

NEW AGE REFERENCE

An Imprint of

NEW AGE INTERNATIONAL (P) LIMITED, PUBLISHERS

LONDON • NEW DELHI • NAIROBI

Bangalore • Chennai • Cochin • Guwahati • Hyderabad • Kolkata • Lucknow • Mumbai

Visit us at **www.newagepublishers.com**

Published by New Age International (P) Ltd., Publishers
First Edition: 1995
Reprint: 2017

GLOBAL OFFICES

- **New Delhi** **NEW AGE INTERNATIONAL (P) LIMITED, PUBLISHERS**
7/30 A, Daryaganj, New Delhi-110002, (INDIA)
Tel.: (011) 23253771, 23253472, **Telefax:** 23267437, 43551305
E-mail: contactus@newagepublishers.com • Visit us at www.newagepublishers.com
- **London** **NEW AGE INTERNATIONAL (UK) LTD.**
27 Old Gloucester Street, London, WC1N 3AX, UK
E-mail: info@newacademicscience.co.uk • Visit us at www.newacademicscience.co.uk
- **Nairobi** **NEW AGE GOLDEN (EAST AFRICA) LTD.**
Ground Floor, Westlands Arcade, Chiromo Road (Next to Naivas Supermarket)
Westlands, Nairobi, KENYA, **Tel.:** 00-254-713848772, 00-254-725700286
E-mail: kenya@newagepublishers.com

BRANCHES

- **Bangalore** 37/10, 8th Cross (Near Hanuman Temple), Azad Nagar, Chamarajpet, Bangalore- 560 018
Tel.: (080) 26756823, **Telefax:** 26756820, **E-mail: bangalore@newagepublishers.com**
- **Chennai** 26, Damodaran Street, T. Nagar, Chennai-600 017, **Tel.:** (044) 24353401
Telefax: 24351463, **E-mail: chennai@newagepublishers.com**
- **Cochin** CC-39/1016, Carrier Station Road, Ernakulam South, Cochin-682 016
Tel.: (0484) 2377303, **Telefax:** 4051304, **E-mail: cochin@newagepublishers.com**
- **Guwahati** Hemsen Complex, Mohd. Shah Road, Paltan Bazar, Near Starline Hotel
Guwahati-781 008, **Tel.:** (0361) 2513881, **Telefax:** 2543669
E-mail: guwahati@newagepublishers.com
- **Hyderabad** 105, 1st Floor, Madhiray Kaveri Tower, 3-2-19, Azam Jahi Road, Near Kumar Theater
Nimboliadda Kachiguda, Hyderabad-500 027, **Tel.:** (040) 24652456, **Telefax:** 24652457
E-mail: hyderabad@newagepublishers.com
- **Kolkata** RDB Chambers (Formerly Lotus Cinema) 106A, 1st Floor, S N Banerjee Road
Kolkata-700 014, **Tel.:** (033) 22273773, **Telefax:** 22275247
E-mail: kolkata@newagepublishers.com
- **Lucknow** 16-A, Jopling Road, Lucknow-226 001, **Tel.:** (0522) 2209578, 4045297, **Telefax:** 2204098
E-mail: lucknow@newagepublishers.com
- **Mumbai** 142C, Victor House, Ground Floor, N.M. Joshi Marg, Lower Parel, Mumbai-400 013
Tel.: (022) 24927869, **Telefax:** 24915415, **E-mail: mumbai@newagepublishers.com**
- **New Delhi** 22, Golden House, Daryaganj, New Delhi-110 002, **Tel.:** (011) 23262368, 23262370
Telefax: 43551305, **E-mail: sales@newagepublishers.com**

ISBN: 978-81-224-0797-6
C-16-11-9780

Printed in India at Glorious Printers, Delhi.
Typeset at Jayanti Graphics, Delhi.

NEW AGE INTERNATIONAL (P) LIMITED, PUBLISHERS
7/30 A, Daryaganj, New Delhi-110002
Visit us at **www.newagepublishers.com**
(CIN: U74899DL1966PTC004618)

Preface to the Second Edition

In this second edition, all the matter of the first edition has been retained. However, at number of places explanations have been enlarged to provide a better understanding to the reader. Further, a chapter on bending analysis of shells of revolution subjected to asymmetric load and some additional numerical examples have been added. Typographical errors found in first edition have been corrected. I am thankful to my students Dr. B.S. Kumar, Sri K.S. Nanjunda Rao and Sri D.V.T.G. Pavan Kumar for carefully checking most of the mathematical equations and numerical examples as well as for helping me in correcting proofs of this edition. I would also like to thank Sri R. Narayanaswamy for his neat typing of some parts of this edition and Sri V.B. Prasad for producing neat additional figures. The financial support for preparing the manuscript for this edition was provided by the Curriculum Development Cell. I gratefully acknowledge the financial assistance provided by the Curriculum Development Cell established at the Indian Institute of Science, Bangalore by Ministry of Human Resources Development, Govt. of India

MAY, 1995 **K. CHANDRASHEKHARA**

Preface to the Second Edition

Preface

Preface

Shell structures are being increasingly used nowadays to roof large spans and to provide column-free space in industrial buildings, auditoriums, etc,. Although application of shells in civil engineering has been largely limited to roofs, there have been many examples where the entire structural system of a building combining the roof and enclosing walls consisted of one structurally continuous shell. Apart from this, water tanks, silos, cooling towers are essentially shell structures. Recently, shells are also finding application as foundation structures. It has been found that shell foundations result in considerable economy of materials compared to traditional foundation structures. With the rapid utilization of shell structures, the conventional method of design based on empirical or approximate solutions is giving way to more realistic and sound mathematical analysis. Several books have been written recently on shell structures which either overemphasize the mathematical analysis or the design aspect. In this book I have tried to keep some sort of a balance between these two approaches.

The main objective of this book is to help the reader understand the mechanics of shells through the development of basic equations, methods of analysis and discussion of results of the analysis. The methods of analysis presented make use of the well-known methods of solving ordinary and partial differential equations. No attempt has been made to present computer-based numerical methods like finite element method for the analysis of shell structures. The methods of analysis presented here can be used not only for the analysis and design of concrete shells but also for the design of shells made of other linearly elastic materials. However, the application and examples considered in the text are from concrete shell structures and hence I preferred to give the present title, *Analysis of Thin Concrete Shells*.

The book is essentially based on the lecture notes of a course offered by me on shell structures, for over a decade, to graduate students as well as lectures delivered at refresher courses for engineering college teachers and design engineers. The subject-matter covered in this book can form a four-credit course (four hours per week) for one-semester for postgraduate students. Of late, some

Universities in India have also introduced an introductory course on shell structures in their undergraduate curriculum and for them some parts of the book can also be effectively used. I make no claim to have treated the subject-matter comprehensively in this book by providing all the available knowledge. However, I have attempted to provide a systematic development of analysis of shell structures by restricting to only certain types of shell structures and these have been presented in six chapters (Chapters 2 to 7).

In the first chapter some results of differential geometry are given which are essential in the analysis of thin shells. The basic assumptions made in the theory of thin shells and its implications have also been discussed in this chapter. In the second chapter, first the basic equations for the membrane analysis of an arbitrary doubly curved shell are given and later these have been applied to shells of revolution subjected to asymmetric as well as axisymmetric load. In Chapter 3, the membrane theory is developed for shells of translation. Though it is shown in these two chapters that neglecting the bending resistance of shells simplifies the analysis considerably, there are some serious shortcomings of the membrane theory which have been highlighted with examples at appropriate places in these chapters. However, it is desirable to select such a shape and provide such a support condition to a shell structure that the load is carried by the shell predominantly by developing membrane stresses. From the designer's point of view a near membrane state of stress in a shell is a most satisfactory and desirable solution.

In Chapter 4, bending analysis of a circular cylindrical shell has been discussed in detail. Solutions for boundary conditions normally met with in cylindrical shell roofs have been presented. A number of examples are given to highlight several points of interest in the analysis of concrete cylindrical shell roofs. In Chapter 5, bending analysis of shells of revolution subjected to axisymmetric edge loads has been discussed. Solutions for cylindrical, conical and spherical shells subjected to edge forces are presented. It is shown through examples that by combining the membrane and bending analysis, problems of practical interest could be easily solved. In Chapter 6, bending analysis of doubly curved shell is presented based on the shallow shell theory. Solutions for certain typical type of support conditions have been developed and their applications have been illustrated through examples. In Chapter 7, analysis of folded plate structure is developed. Solutions applicable for short and long folded plate structures have been developed. Analysis of long folded plate structures have been illustrated through examples. In Chapter 8, a brief description of how an experimental analysis would provide a designer not only a better idea about the actual boundary condition but also would provide the necessary physical insight into the problem for sound engineering judgement and design. I have not made any attempt to provide a bibliography on the subject at the end as the publications on the analysis and design of shell structures in the last three decades are so many that the list would run to several hundreds. Hence, I have taken recourse to providing only some references at appropriate places which the reader could consult for more details.

I wish to thank all those who made many suggestions and helped me directly or indirectly in writing this book. The financial support for preparing this manuscript was provided by the curriculum development cell. I gratefully acknowledge the financial assistance provided for the preparation of the manuscript by the curriculum development cell established at the Indian Institute of Science by the Ministry of Education and Culture, Government of India. I am grateful to the publishers McGraw-Hill, E. and F. N. Spon Ltd and VEB Verlag für Bauwesen for permitting to quote from their publications. I am also grateful to Sri H.K. Nanjundaswamy for providing the photographs of shell structures included in this book. I wish to thank Mr. R. Narayanaswamy for excellent typing of the manuscript and Mr. V.B. Prasad for preparing neat diagrams.

K. CHANDRASHEKHARA

Contents

Definitions of Some Commonly Used Terminologies

THIN SHELL	Curved structure in space in which the thickness is small compared to the radius and other dimensions.
GENERATRIX, DIRECTRIX	A curve which moves parallel to itself over another stationary curve to generate a surface is called the generatrix and the stationary curve the directrix.
GAUSS CURVATURE	Product of two prinicipal radii of curvature at any point on the surface of the shell.
SYNCLASTIC SURFACE	A surface for which Gauss curvature is positive.
DEVELOPABLE SURFACE	A surface for which Gauss curvature is zero.
ANTICLASTIC SURFACE	A surface for which Gauss curvature is negative.
SHELLS OF REVOLUTION	Shells that are obtained when a plane curve is rotated about an axis of symmetry.
SHELL OF TRANSLATION	Shells that are generated when one curve moves parallel to itself along another curve, the plane of the two curves being at right angles to each other.
RULED SURFACES	Surfaces that can be obtained entirely by straight lines. The surface is said to be 'singly ruled' if at every point on the surface a single straight line can be ruled and 'doubly ruled' when at every point on the surface two straight lines can be ruled.

CYLINDRICAL SHELLS	Singly curved shells in which the generatrix (or directrix) is a straight line. The surface is generated by moving the straight line against a plane curve.
CIRCULAR CYLINDRICAL SHELLS	Singly curved shells in which the plane curve is an arc of a circle.
NON-CIRCULAR CYLINDRICAL SHEELS	Singly curved shells in which the plane curve is other than an arc of a circle like catenary, cycloid, parabola, etc.
MULTIPLE CYLINDRICAL SHELLS	A series of parallel cylindrical shells that are transversely continuous.
CONTINUOUS CYLINDRICAL SHELLS	Cylindrical shells which are longitudinally continuous over the supports.
BARREL SHELLS	Cylindrical shells which are symmetrical about the crown.
TRAVERSES (or DIAPHRAGMS)	Traverses or end frames are structures provided to support the shell and preserve the geometry of the surface.
PRISMATIC FOLDED PLATE	Folded plate structure made up of a number of rectangular slabs of constant width and thickness inclined to one another and joined monolithically along their common edges.

Chapter One

General Introduction to Shell Theory

1.1 INTRODUCTION

In recent years, thin shell structures are finding wide applications in many branches of technology such as space vehicles, nuclear reactors, pressure vessels, roofs of industrial buildings and auditoriums. From the point of view of architecture, the development of shell structures offered unexpected possibilities and opportunities for the combined realisation of functional, economic and aesthetic aspects. Further, shell structures have become common particularly for industrial buildings and auditoriums where large column-free space is required. Hence the practical utility of shell structure has helped in developing a wide variety of solutions for some important and basic shell problems. This has also led to a thorough study of the foundation of the theories of thin shell on which these solutions are based.

A thin shell can be defined as a curved slab whose thickness is very small compared to the other dimensions of the shell. Alternatively, a shell can also be defined as a body that is bounded by two closely spaced curved surfaces. The middle or reference surface, which is the locus of points that are equidistant from the two bounding surfaces, defines the shape of the shell. The thickness of the shell at a given point is the distance between the two bounding surfaces measured along the normal to the middle surface passing through a point. The thickness of a shell need not be constant throughout and a shell having a linearly varying thickness is very common in practice. A shell which does not have edges or boundaries other than inner and outer curved surface is referred as complete or closed shell, while a shell having edges or boundaries is referred as an incomplete or open shell.

Generally, any shell surface can be classified as a thin shell or a thick shell. According to Novozhilov[1.1], a shell can be called thin if the maximum value of the ratio of thickness of the shell to the radius of curvature of its middle surface is very small compared to unity. Shells which do not satisfy this requirement can be classified as thick shells. This division of shells into two categories, however, is not fully defined as long as a definite statement regarding the absolute value of this ratio is made. For most of the practical problems, this ratio for thin shells can be taken less than 0.05. This classification has an important bearing in the theory of shells, as in thin shells, certain stress and strain components can be safely neglected, thus making the analysis somewhat simpler. On the other hand, thick shell problems have to be solved using three-dimensional theory of elasticity and hence, their analysis are much more involved compared to the analysis based on thin shell theory.

The behaviour of a shell made of a given material, entirely depends on the geometry of the middle or reference surface. Hence, it becomes necessary to first study the fundamental properties of the surfaces. A study of the properties of the curves and surfaces is included in the subject of differential geometry[1,2]. In what follows, we will discuss only certain specific results of differential geometry which are essential for the classification of shell surfaces as well as in the derivation of certain basic equations in the theory of thin shells.

1.2 THEORY OF SURFACE

A surface can be defined as the locus of all points such that the position vector **r** from a fixed point O can be written as (Fig. 1.1).

$$\mathbf{r} = ix + jy + kz \tag{1.1}$$

where, i, j and k are the unit vectors directed along x, y and z directions. The surface can also be defined in parametric form as

$$\mathbf{r} = \mathbf{r}\ (\alpha, \beta) \tag{1.2}$$

or by the three parametric equations.

$$x = f_1(\alpha, \beta),\ y = f_2(\alpha, \beta),\ z = f_3(\alpha, \beta) \tag{1.3}$$

where f_1, f_2 and f_3 are single valued and continuous functions of the parameters α and β.

If we now assume that β = constant, then we obtain the vector **r** as a function of the single independent variable α and hence Eq. (1.2) will be the equation of a curve on the surface. Hence by taking β constant we can get a family of curves which may be called α-curves and similarly we can get a second family of curves called β-curves by taking α as constant. Here (α, β) are called as the curvilinear coordinates and α-and β-curves as coordinate or parametric curves. Hence a surface is completely defined by two families of coordinate lines.

By eliminating α and β from the three parametric equations (Eq. 1.3), we can obtain the equation of a surface in the form

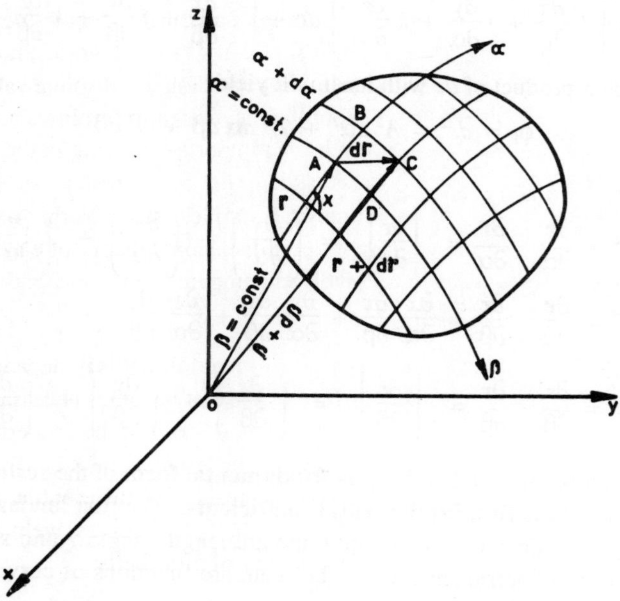

Fig. 1.1 Surface with the coordinate system

$$\mathbf{F}(x, y, z) = 0 \tag{1.4a}$$

and if z is expressed as a function of the other variables, then we can define the surface in explicit form as

$$z = f(x, y) \tag{1.4b}$$

1.2.1 First Fundamental Form

Let us consider two points A and C on the surface specified by the position vector $\mathbf{r}$ and $\mathbf{r} + d\mathbf{r}$ (Fig. 1.1). The corresponding curvilinear coordinates of points A and C will be (α, β) and $(\alpha + d\alpha, \beta + d\beta)$ respectively. The length of the elementary arc ds, connecting the points A and C, will be equal to the absolute value of the vector $d\mathbf{r}$. Hence,

$$ds = |d\mathbf{r}| = \left| \frac{\partial \mathbf{r}}{\partial \alpha} d\alpha + \frac{\partial \mathbf{r}}{\partial \beta} d\beta \right| \tag{1.5}$$

The square of the elementary arc length ds will be equal to the scalar product of $d\mathbf{r}$ with itself. Thus,

$$ds^2 = d\mathbf{r} \cdot d\mathbf{r} = |d\mathbf{r}|^2 \tag{1.6}$$

Using Eq. (1.1), $d\mathbf{r}$ can be written as

$$d\mathbf{r} = \left(i\frac{\partial x}{\partial \alpha} + j\frac{\partial y}{\partial \alpha} + k\frac{\partial z}{\partial \alpha} \right) d\alpha + \left(i\frac{\partial x}{\partial \beta} + j\frac{\partial y}{\partial \beta} + k\frac{\partial z}{\partial \beta} \right) d\beta \quad (1.7)$$

Now the scalar product of $d\mathbf{r}$ with itself will yield

$$\phi_1 = ds^2 = A^2\, d\alpha^2 + 2F\, d\alpha\, d\beta + B^2\, d\beta^2 \quad (1.8)$$

where

$$A^2 = \frac{\partial \mathbf{r}}{\partial \alpha} \cdot \frac{\partial \mathbf{r}}{\partial \alpha} = \left| \frac{\partial \mathbf{r}}{\partial \alpha} \right|^2 = \left(\frac{\partial x}{\partial \alpha} \right)^2 + \left(\frac{\partial y}{\partial \alpha} \right)^2 + \left(\frac{\partial z}{\partial \alpha} \right)^2$$

$$F = \frac{\partial \mathbf{r}}{\partial \alpha} \cdot \frac{\partial \mathbf{r}}{\partial \beta} = \frac{\partial x}{\partial \alpha}\frac{\partial x}{\partial \beta} + \frac{\partial y}{\partial \alpha}\frac{\partial y}{\partial \beta} + \frac{\partial z}{\partial \alpha}\frac{\partial z}{\partial \beta}$$

$$B^2 = \frac{\partial \mathbf{r}}{\partial \beta} \cdot \frac{\partial \mathbf{r}}{\partial \beta} = \left| \frac{\partial r}{\partial \beta} \right|^2 = \left(\frac{\partial x}{\partial \beta} \right)^2 + \left(\frac{\partial y}{\partial \beta} \right)^2 + \left(\frac{\partial z}{\partial \beta} \right)^2$$

The function ϕ_1 is called the **first fundamental form** of the surface and A, F and B are called the **first fundamental coefficients**. The first fundamental coefficients play a basic role in computing the arc length, angle χ and surface area. The fundamental coefficients, as can be seen, are functions of curvilinear coordinates and can be determined from

$$A = \left| \frac{\partial \mathbf{r}}{\partial \alpha} \right|, \quad B = \left| \frac{\partial \mathbf{r}}{\partial \beta} \right|, \quad F = \left| \frac{\partial \mathbf{r}}{\partial \alpha} \right| \left| \frac{\partial \mathbf{r}}{\partial \beta} \right| \cos \chi \quad (1.9)$$

where χ is the angle between the vector $\partial \mathbf{r}/\partial \alpha$ and $\partial \mathbf{r}/\partial \beta$.

According to Eq. (1.8), the element length AB (which is along the coordinate line β = constant) will be

$$ds_1 = A\, d\alpha \quad (1.10a)$$

and similarly, the elemental length AD will be

$$ds_2 = B\, d\beta \quad (1.10b)$$

If the coordinate lines α and β are orthogonal, then $F = 0$, and the arc length ds will be given by

$$ds = \sqrt{ds_1^2 + ds_2^2} = \sqrt{A^2\, d\alpha^2 + B^2\, d\beta^2} \quad (1.11)$$

The area of the element $ABCD$ can be obtained by taking the cross product of the two vectors $\partial \mathbf{r}/\partial \alpha$ and $\partial \mathbf{r}/\partial \beta$ as

$$dA = \frac{\partial \mathbf{r}}{\partial \alpha}\, d\alpha \times \frac{\partial \mathbf{r}}{\partial \beta}\, d\beta = \left| \frac{\partial r}{\partial \alpha} \right| \left| \frac{\partial r}{\partial \beta} \right| \sin \chi\, d\alpha\, d\beta$$
$$= \sqrt{A^2 B^2 - F^2}\, d\alpha\, d\beta \quad (1.12)$$

If the surface is defined by an equation of the form

$$z = f(x, y)$$

then the three parametric equations (Eq. 1.3) will be

$$x = x, y = y, z = f(x, y) \tag{1.13}$$

For such a case, the first fundamental form can be written as

$$ds^2 = A^2 \, dx^2 + 2F \, dx \, dy + B^2 \, dy^2 \tag{1.14}$$

where

$$A^2 = (1 + p^2), \quad B^2 = (1 + q^2), F = pq$$

and

$$p = \frac{\partial z}{\partial x}, \quad q = \frac{\partial z}{\partial y}$$

The expression for the area of the element *ABCD* will now be

$$dA = \sqrt{1 + p^2 + q^2} \, dx \, dy \tag{1.15}$$

1.2.2 Second Fundamental Form

At a point *P* (Fig. 1.2) on the surface defined by **r** (α, β), one can draw a series of different curves passing through it. The tangents drawn to these curves at point *P* will all lie in a plane tangent to the surface at *P* (Fig. 1.2). This plane is called the tangent plane and a normal to the tangent plane is called the principal normal **N** to the surface at the point *P*. A normal section of a surface at point *P* is a section made by a plane that contains the normal to surface at that point. This section is a plane curve, whose principal normal has the same direction as the normal to the surface at the point *P*. The tangent plane contains the two vectors, namely (∂**r**/∂α) and (∂**r**/∂β) which are tangents to the curves α and β at *P*. If we denote the unit tangent vector to a curve, say *s* on the surface by (∂**r**/∂*s*), then

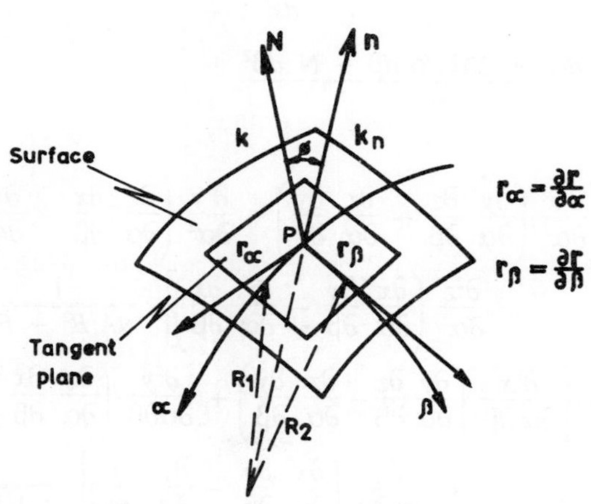

Fig. 1.2 Surface with the tangent plane and normal

$$\frac{\partial \mathbf{r}}{\partial s} = \frac{\partial \mathbf{r}}{\partial \alpha}\frac{d\alpha}{ds} + \frac{\partial \mathbf{r}}{\partial \beta}\frac{d\beta}{ds} \tag{1.16}$$

According to Serret-Frenet formula[1.2] for a space curve

$$\frac{d^2\mathbf{r}}{ds^2} = \frac{1}{R}\cdot\mathbf{n} = k\cdot\mathbf{n} \tag{1.17}$$

where R is the radius of curvature
k is the curvature (= 1/R)
$\mathbf{n}$ is unit (normal) vector along the principal normal

The unit normal vector $\mathbf{n}$ can be determined as

$$\mathbf{n} = \frac{\dfrac{\partial \mathbf{r}}{\partial \alpha}\times\dfrac{\partial \mathbf{r}}{\partial \beta}}{\left|\dfrac{\partial \mathbf{r}}{\partial \alpha}\times\dfrac{\partial \mathbf{r}}{\partial \beta}\right|} \tag{1.18}$$

Differentiating Eq. (1.16) with respect to s gives

$$\frac{d^2\mathbf{r}}{ds^2} = k\cdot\mathbf{n} = \frac{\partial^2\mathbf{r}}{\partial\alpha^2}\left(\frac{d\alpha}{ds}\right)^2 + 2\frac{\partial^2\mathbf{r}}{\partial\alpha\,\partial\beta}\left(\frac{d\alpha}{ds}\right) \times\left(\frac{d\beta}{ds}\right) + \frac{d^2\mathbf{r}}{\partial\beta^2}\left(\frac{d\beta}{ds}\right)^2 + \frac{\partial\mathbf{r}}{\partial\alpha}\left(\frac{d^2\alpha}{ds^2}\right) + \frac{\partial\mathbf{r}}{\partial\beta}\left(\frac{d^2\beta}{ds^2}\right) \tag{1.19}$$

To determine k, we can take the scalar product of the two vectors $d^2\mathbf{r}/ds^2$ and $\mathbf{n}$ to obtain

$$k = \frac{\mathbf{n}\cdot\dfrac{\partial^2\mathbf{r}}{\partial\alpha^2}\,d\alpha^2 + 2\dfrac{\partial^2\mathbf{r}}{\partial\alpha\,\partial\beta}\cdot\mathbf{n}\,d\alpha\,d\beta + \mathbf{n}\cdot\dfrac{\partial^2\mathbf{r}}{\partial\beta^2}\,d\beta^2}{ds^2}$$

$$= \frac{L\,d\alpha^2 + 2\mathbf{M}\,d\alpha\,d\beta + \mathbf{N}\,d\beta^2}{ds^2} \tag{1.20}$$

where

$$L = \mathbf{n}\cdot\frac{\partial^2\mathbf{r}}{\partial\alpha^2} = \left[\frac{\partial^2 x}{\partial\alpha^2}\left(\frac{\partial y}{\partial\alpha}\frac{\partial z}{\partial\beta} - \frac{\partial z}{\partial\alpha}\frac{\partial y}{\partial\beta}\right) + \frac{\partial^2 y}{\partial\alpha^2}\left(\frac{\partial z}{\partial\alpha}\frac{\partial x}{\partial\beta} - \frac{\partial x}{\partial\alpha}\frac{\partial z}{\partial\beta}\right) + \frac{\partial^2 z}{\partial\alpha^2}\left(\frac{\partial x}{\partial\alpha}\frac{\partial y}{\partial\beta} - \frac{\partial y}{\partial\alpha}\frac{\partial x}{\partial\beta}\right)\right]\frac{1}{\sqrt{A^2B^2 - F^2}}$$

$$M = \mathbf{n}\cdot\frac{\partial^2\mathbf{r}}{\partial\alpha\,\partial\beta} = \left[\frac{\partial^2 x}{\partial\alpha\,\partial\beta}\left(\frac{\partial y}{\partial\alpha}\frac{\partial z}{\partial\beta} - \frac{\partial z}{\partial\alpha}\frac{\partial y}{\partial\beta}\right) + \frac{\partial^2 y}{\partial\alpha\partial\beta}\left(\frac{\partial z}{\partial\alpha}\frac{\partial x}{\partial\beta} - \frac{\partial x}{\partial\alpha}\frac{\partial z}{\partial\beta}\right) + \frac{\partial^2 z}{\partial\alpha\,\partial\beta}\left(\frac{\partial x}{\partial\alpha}\frac{\partial y}{\partial\beta} - \frac{\partial y}{\partial\alpha}\frac{\partial x}{\partial\beta}\right)\right]\frac{1}{\sqrt{A^2B^2 - F^2}}$$

$$N = \mathbf{n} \cdot \frac{\partial^2 \mathbf{r}}{\partial \beta^2} = \left[\frac{\partial^2 x}{\partial \beta^2} \left(\frac{\partial y}{\partial \alpha} \frac{\partial z}{\partial \beta} - \frac{\partial z}{\partial \alpha} \frac{\partial y}{\partial \beta} \right) + \frac{\partial^2 y}{\partial \beta^2} \left(\frac{\partial z}{\partial \alpha} \cdot \frac{\partial x}{\partial \beta} - \frac{\partial x}{\partial \alpha} \frac{\partial z}{\partial \beta} \right) \right.$$
$$\left. + \frac{\partial^2 z}{\partial \beta^2} \left(\frac{\partial x}{\partial \alpha} \frac{\partial y}{\partial \beta} - \frac{\partial y}{\partial \alpha} \frac{\partial x}{\partial \beta} \right) \right] \frac{1}{\sqrt{A^2 B^2 - F^2}}$$

and $\mathbf{n}$ is determined from Eq. (1.18).

In the above equation, the numerator

$$\phi_2 = L\, d\alpha^2 + 2M\, d\alpha\, d\beta + N\, d\beta^2$$

is called the **second fundamental form** of the surface, which characterises the external geometry of the surface, radius of curvature and coordinates of its points. It should be noted that A, B, F, L, M and N are all functions of (α, β) and are constant at a given point. Further, it may be observed from Eq. (1.20) that the normal curvature depends only on the direction $(\partial\alpha/\partial\beta)$. Hence, it can be said that all the curves passing through a point on a surface which are tangent to the same direction have the same normal curvature.

If the surface is defined by the equation

$$z = f(x, y),$$

then it can be shown that

$$L = \frac{r}{\sqrt{1 + p^2 + q^2}}, \quad M = \frac{s}{\sqrt{1 + p^2 + q^2}}, \quad N = \frac{t}{\sqrt{1 + p^2 + q^2}} \tag{1.21}$$

where $r = \dfrac{\partial^2 z}{\partial x^2}, \quad s = \dfrac{\partial^2 z}{\partial x\, \partial y}, \quad t = \dfrac{\partial^2 z}{\partial y^2}$

1.2.3 Principal Curvature

We will now find those directions $(d\beta/d\alpha)$ for which the normal curvature k has a maximum or minimum. By setting $(d\beta/d\alpha) = \lambda$, Eq. (1.20) can be written as

$$k = \frac{L + 2M\lambda + N\lambda^2}{A^2 + 2F\lambda + B^2\lambda^2} \tag{1.22}$$

The extremum values of k are determined by making $(dk/d\lambda) = 0$. Differentiating Eq. (1.22), we get

$$(A^2 + 2F\lambda + B^2\lambda^2)(M + N\lambda) - (L + 2M\lambda + N\lambda^2)(F + B^2\lambda) = 0 \tag{1.23}$$

or
$$[A^2 + F\lambda + \lambda(F + B^2\lambda)]\,(M + N\lambda) - [L + M\lambda + \lambda(M + \lambda N)]\,(F + B^2\lambda) = 0$$

or
$$(A^2 + F\lambda)(M + N\lambda) = (L + M\lambda)(F + B^2\lambda). \tag{1.24}$$

An equation for determining the direction λ corresponding to the extremum curvatures can be found by expanding Eq. (1.24) as

$$(B^2M - NF)\lambda^2 + (LB^2 - NA^2)\lambda + (FL - A^2M) = 0. \tag{1.25}$$

The above quadratic equation yields two roots, λ_1 and λ_2, (provided $B^2M - NF \neq 0$), corresponding to two directions of extremum curvature. These two directions are called as the principal directions and curves on the surface that everywhere have the principal directions (λ_1, λ_2) are called as the lines of principal curvature. It can be shown that the principal directions are always orthogonal.

From Eq. (1.24), we have

$$(M + N\lambda) = \frac{(L + M\lambda)(F + B^2\lambda)}{(A^2 + F\lambda)} \tag{1.26}$$

Substituting Eq. (1.26) in Eq. (1.22), we obtain

$$k = \frac{L + M\lambda}{A^2 + F\lambda} = \frac{M + N\lambda}{F + B^2\lambda} \tag{1.27}$$

It is often convenient to select the coordinate lines such that they coincide with the lines of principal curvature. Hence, if the lines of principal curvature are coordinate lines, then $M = F = 0$. In such a case, Eq. (1.22) yields

$$k = \frac{L + N\lambda^2}{A^2 + B^2\lambda^2} \tag{1.28}$$

The extreme values of k, as determined from the above equation, are obtained for $\lambda = 0$ and $\lambda = \infty$, then the principal curvatures are

$$k_1 = \frac{L}{A^2},\ k_2 = \frac{N}{B^2} \tag{1.29}$$

If the lines of curvature do not coincide with the coordinate lines, then we have to determine the principal curvatures k_1 and k_2 from Eq. (1.27). Equation (1.27) yields

$$(A^2k - L) + \lambda(Fk - M) = 0$$

and

$$(Fk - M) + \lambda(B^2k - N) = 0 \tag{1.30}$$

where k is the principal normal curvature. The above equation can provide a value of λ if, and only if

$$\begin{vmatrix} (A^2k - L), & (Fk - M) \\ (Fk - M), & (B^2k - N) \end{vmatrix} = 0 \tag{1.31}$$

or $$(A^2B^2 - F^2)k^2 - (LB^2 + A^2N - 2MF)k + (LN - M^2) = 0 \tag{1.32}$$

The roots (k_1, k_2) of the above equation satisfy the relation

$$M = (k_1 + k_2) = \frac{LB^2 + A^2N - 2MF}{A^2B^2 - F^2} \tag{1.33}$$

$$K = k_1k_2 = \left(\frac{LN - M^2}{A^2B^2 - F^2}\right) \tag{1.34}$$

In the above, the variable M is called the mean curvature and K is called the Gaussian or total curvature. If M and K are determined, then we can easily determine k_1 and k_2..

It is clear from Eq. (1.34) that the Gauss curvature will be positive, zero or negative according as

$$LN - M^2 \gtreqless 0$$

or

$$rt - s^2 \gtreqless 0$$

A surface is called synclastic, developable or anticlastic at a point according as the Gauss curvature is positive, zero or negative at that point. It is to be emphasized that k_1 and k_2 are not necessarily the curvatures of the lines of principal curvature; they are the curvatures of the normal sections in the direction of the lines of principal curvature. For example, any curve on a sphere may be regarded as a line of principal curvature, yet the curvature of any normal section of the sphere is $1/R$, where R is the radius of the sphere.

For a surface of negative curvature, the tangent plane cuts the surface into two curves that intersect at the point where the plane is tangent to the surface. The directions of these curves are called the asymptotic directions on the surface. The direction of principal curvature bisects the angle between the asymptotic directions. For a normal section in asymptotic direction, the curvature is zero. Curves on the surface that have, everywhere, the asymptotic direction, are called as asymptotic lines. Hence, for a surface for which Gaussian curvature is negative, we have real asymptotic lines. For a point for which Gaussian curvature is zero, the two asymptotic directions coincide, while for a point of positive Gaussian curvature, the asymptotic lines are imaginary.

If the four parameters A, B, L and N, which are functions of (α, β), are arbitrarily chosen, then, in general, they will not define a surface. These parameters may be considered as Lame parameters and principal radii of curvature of the surface, only when they satisfy the conditions of Gauss and Codazzi. It may be shown[1.1, 1.4] that the Lame parameters are connected to the principal curvature through Codazzi equations as

$$\frac{\partial}{\partial \alpha}(k_2 B) = k_1 \frac{\partial B}{\partial \alpha} \tag{1.35}$$

and
$$\frac{\partial}{\partial \beta}(k_1 A) = k_2 \frac{\partial A}{\partial \beta}$$

and through the equations of Gauss as

$$\frac{\partial}{\partial \alpha}\left(\frac{1}{A}\frac{\partial B}{\partial \alpha}\right) + \frac{\partial}{\partial \beta}\left(\frac{1}{B}\frac{\partial A}{\partial \beta}\right) = -k_1 k_2 AB \tag{1.36}$$

The above Gauss–Codazzi conditions are the necessary and sufficient conditions to be satisfied by parameters of first and second fundamental form for a definite surface. Often the Gauss–Codazzi conditions are referred as compatability conditions in the theory of surfaces.

1.3 CLASSIFICATION OF SHELL SURFACES[1.3]

Before classifying the shell surface, it is appropriate to define some of the terminologies used in the classification.

A ruled surface is defined as a surface formed by the motion of a straight line which is known as the generator or ruling. A surface is said to be singly ruled if, at every point on the surface, a single straight line can be ruled and doubly ruled if, at every point, two straight lines can be ruled. Ruled surfaces have a practical advantage in that they may be cast on straight forms. Examples of single ruled surfaces are conical shells, conoids and cylinders, and doubly ruled surfaces are hyperbolic paraboloid, and hyperbolic paraboloid of revolution.

A surface of translation is generated by the motion of a plane curve parallel to itself over another curve, the planes containing the two curves being at right angles to each other. Examples are elliptic paraboloid and hyperbolic paraboloid.

A surface of revolution is obtained by rotating a plane curve called the meridian about an axis, lying in the plane of the curve. This plane is known as the meridian plane. Examples are circular domes, paraboloid of revolution, and hyperboloid of revolution.

Shell surfaces may be broadly classified as singly curved and doubly curved. Singly curved surfaces are developable and the Gauss curvature is zero for such shell surfaces. This type of shell structure tend to flatten out under load and structurally are not so efficient, compared to doubly curved shells, which are nondevelopable. The doubly curved shells may have either positive or negative Gaussian curvature. Shells with positive Gaussian curvatures are called as synclastic shells, while those with negative curvatures are called as anticlastic shells. A developable surface can be both a translational and ruled surface, like for example, a cylindrical shell.

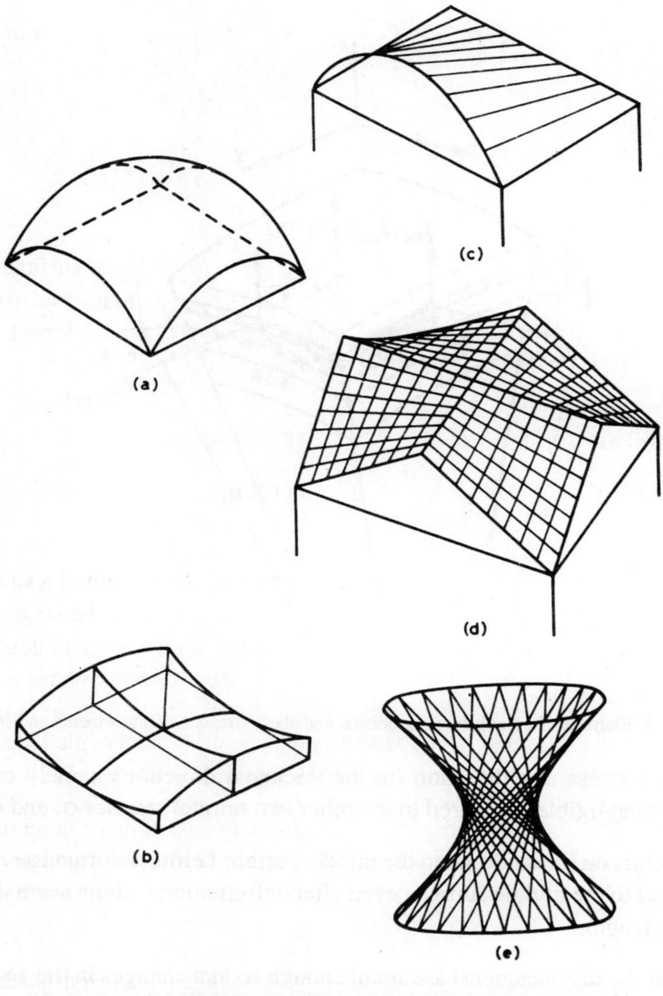

Fig. 1.3 (a) Elliptic paraboloid, (b) Hyperbolic paraboloid, (c) Conoid, (d) Hyperbolic paraboloid (doubly ruled), (e) Hyperboloid of revolution

Similarly, an anticlastic shell can be a shell of revolution and ruled surface, as in the case of hyperbolic paraboloid of one sheet. There are shell surfaces like corrugated shells, funicular shells, which cannot be classified under any one single category. They are normally partly synclastic and partly anticlastic. Some of the common types of shell surfaces, that are used in practice, are shown in Fig. 1.3a to 1.3e.

1.4 ASSUMPTIONS

The following general assumptions are made while deriving the basic equations in the theory of thin elastic shells (Fig. 1.4).

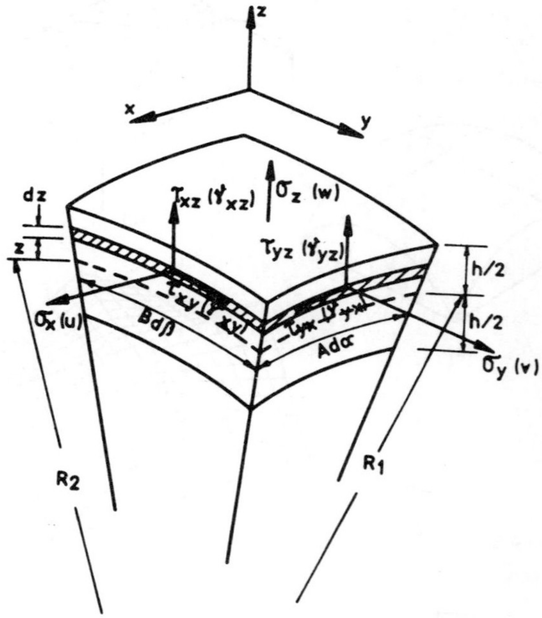

Fig. 1.4 Element of a shell showing normal and shear stresses, displacements and strains

(a) The stress in z-direction (in the thickness direction) namely σ_z may be considered negligible compared to the other two normal stresses σ_x and σ_y.

(b) Points on lines normal to the middle surface before deformation remain on line, normal to the middle surface, even after deformation and the normal does not change its length.

(c) All the displacements are small enough so that changes in the geometry of the shell will not alter the static equilibrium of the shell.

(d) The material is homogeneous, isotropic and exhibits linear elastic behaviour (follows Hooke's law).

The above assumptions reduce the three-dimensional problem to two-dimensional one, describing reasonably the behaviour of thin elastic shells and was first proposed by Love. The first assumption implies that, as the shell is assumed thin, whatever happens in the thickness direction (z-direction) is without significance. The second assumption is equivalent to Bernoulli's hypothesis of plane sections for straight beams. It implies that the shear strains γ_{xz} and γ_{yz} are zero. It also means that the displacement of any point, normal to the middle surface is constant and is equal to the displacement w of the corresponding point on the middle surface. The third assumption results in linear differential equations, which are not very difficult to solve. The fourth assumption is made use of in the linear elastic theory of thin isotropic shells. A reinforced concrete shell should, in order to be called homogeneous and isotropic, be reinforced in the same way all over the shell area, which is not usually done. However, for all practical purposes, a reinforced concrete shell can be considered as homogeneous and isotropic. If a shell is provided with closely spaced stiffening ribs, then such a shell can be generally considered as anisotropic shell.

1.5 STRUCTURAL ACTION OF A SHELL

A shell resists the external load by developing direct stresses (normal and shear stresses), lying in the plane of the shell, accompanied by bending stresses. Hence, a shell structure makes use of both extensional and flexural rigidities in carrying the external load unlike flat slab structure, which carries the load purely by flexure. The direct stresses are caused by inplane forces which are normally referred as membrane forces. Figure 1.5a shows an element of a shell being acted upon by membrane forces only. Sometimes, the bending forces in a shell, are so small that these forces can be safely neglected. In such a case, the shell is said to have been analysed according to the membrane theory. If the shell is purely under a membrane state of stress, then the unknown internal forces in the shell will be N_x, N_y, $N_{xy} = N_{yx}$ and these internal forces can be completely determined from the three static equilibrium equations, provided the supporting system is statically determinate. Thus the membrane analysis of a shell can be done without considering the deformation of the shell. But often, the membrane analysis yields displacements and reactions along the boundaries of the shell, which do not normally comply with the actual boundary conditions. Hence, in such shells, it is not possible to have a pure membrane state of stress. However, the membrane theory can be used with reasonable approximation in certain types of shells far away from the edges. The bending forces are considered only in the edge zones in such shells and these forces are often referred as perturbational forces or edge disturbances. The bending analysis is not only required along the edges, because of the support conditions, but also in the vicinity of concentrated load, near the openings, near the stiffening ribs, and at sections where there is a sudden change in curvature or thickness. The bending analysis includes the consideration of internal bending and twisting moments, radial shear forces as well as membrane forces. Figure 1.5b shows the bending and twisting moments, radial shear forces and load acting on an element of a shell.

1.6 STRESS RESULTANTS

In general, a shell carries the external load by developing direct and bending stresses. The stresses in a shell can be defined with respect to a chosen coordinate system. A thin shell being a two-dimensional structure, we need two coordinates to define the position of a point on it. Let us, for convenience, assume an x, y

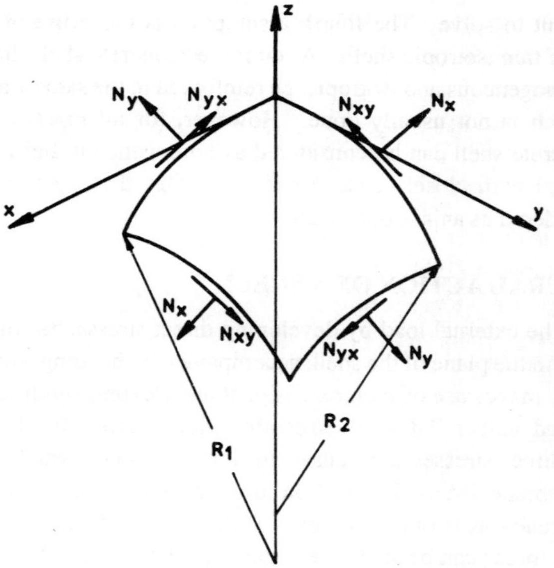

Fig. 1.5a Membrane forces on a shell element

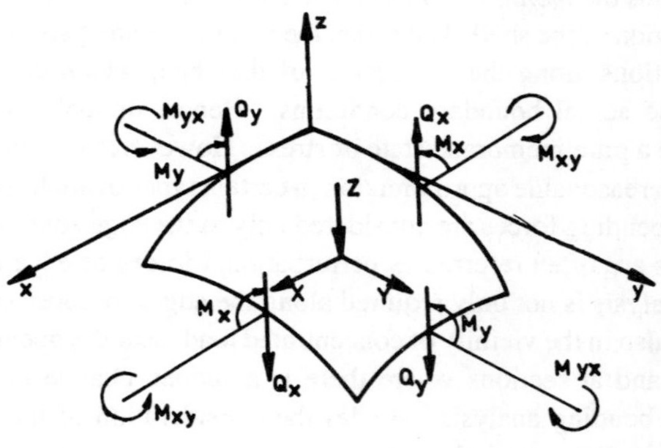

Fig. 1.5b Bending and twisting moments, shear force and load acting on a shell element

coordinate system, such that lines x = constant, and y = constant, are orthogonal (that is the coordinate lines are along the principal curvature directions). Figure 1.6 shows an element of shell cut along the two pairs of adjacent coordinate lines. Let the length of the element be $A\, d\alpha$ and $B\, d\beta$ and it is possible that the element length of opposite sides will be slightly different in length. However, we will not consider this difference here.

If we consider the side of the element x = constant, the area of this side will be $B\,d\beta \cdot h$. The stresses acting on this area will have certain resultant which depends on the length $B\,d\beta$. If $B\,d\beta$ is made to approach zero, the resultant decreases proportionately and the force divided by the length $B\,d\beta$ will have a finite limit. This is referred as the stress resultant and will be a force per unit length.

It is possible to express the stress resultants as integrals of stresses acting on a section. For example, on the section x = constant, the total force normal to the section is $N_x\,B\,d\beta$. This force is the resultant of the stress σ_x which acts on this area. Now consider a small shaded area (Fig. 1.4) at a distance z from the middle surface. Its length is $Bd\beta\,(1 + z/R_2)$ and the force on this element area is $\sigma_x\,Bd\beta\,(1 + z/R_2)\,dz$. The total normal force is determined by integrating this quantity over the thickness. Hence,

$$N_x\,Bd\beta = \int_{-h/2}^{+h/2} \sigma_x Bd\beta\,(1 + z/R_2)\,dz$$

or

$$N_x = \int_{-h/2}^{+h/2} \sigma_x\,(1 + z/R_2)\,dz \tag{1.37a}$$

In the same way, the shear stresses τ_{xy} and τ_{xz} are to be integrated to determine the forces N_{xy} and Q_x. Hence,

$$N_{xy} = \int_{-h/2}^{+h/2} \tau_{xy}\,(1 + z/R_2)\,dz \tag{1.37b}$$

$$Q_x = -\int_{-h/2}^{+h/2} \tau_{xz}\,(1 + z/R_2)\,dz \tag{1.37c}$$

The minus sign for Q_x indicates that the shear stress τ_{xz} is acting in the opposite direction with respect to the positive direction of the shear force Q_x.

In a similar way, by considering a section y = constant, we can write three more equations for the other three stress resultants. These are

$$N_y = \int_{-h/2}^{+h/2} \sigma_y\,(1 + z/R_1)\,dz \tag{1.37d}$$

$$N_{yx} = \int_{-h/2}^{+h/2} \tau_{yx}\,(1 + z/R_1)\,dz \tag{1.37e}$$

$$Q_y = -\int_{-h/2}^{+h/2} \tau_{yz}\,(1 + z/R_1)\,dz \tag{1.37f}$$

It is interesting to note from Eqs. (1.37b) and (1.37e) that even if the shear stresses τ_{xy} and τ_{yx} are equal, in general, the shear force N_{xy} will not be equal to N_{yx}. However, the two shear forces N_{xy} and N_{yx} will be equal if $R_1 = R_2$ or when τ_{xy} is independent of z.

The normal stresses σ_x, σ_y and shear stress τ_{xy} will not only result in the normal forces N_x, N_y and shear force N_{xy}, but also will result in bending moments M_x, M_y and twisting moments M_{xy}, M_{yx}. Following the same procedure described above, we can obtain the following relations between bending and twisting moments with normal and shear stresses.

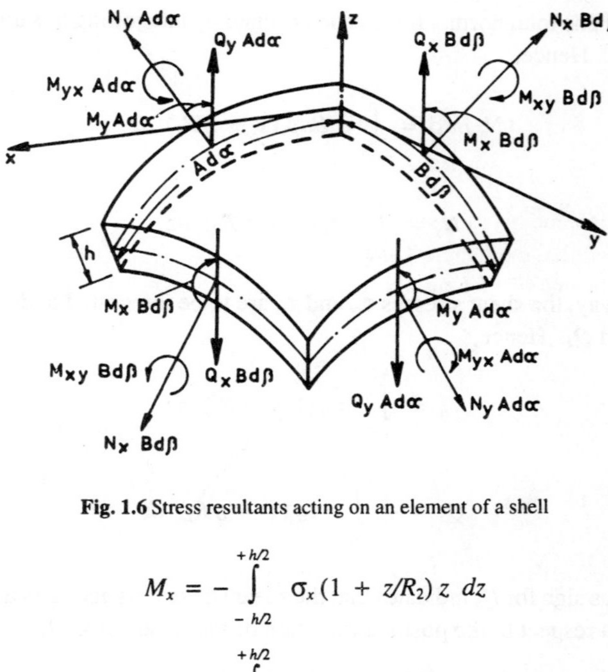

Fig. 1.6 Stress resultants acting on an element of a shell

$$M_x = - \int_{-h/2}^{+h/2} \sigma_x (1 + z/R_2)\, z\, dz \tag{1.37g}$$

$$M_y = - \int_{-h/2}^{+h/2} \sigma_y (1 + z/R_1)\, z\, dz \tag{1.37h}$$

$$M_{xy} = - \int_{-h/2}^{+h/2} \tau_{xy} (1 + z/R_2)\, z\, dz \tag{1.37i}$$

$$M_{yx} = - \int_{-h/2}^{+h/2} \tau_{yx} (1 + z/R_1)\, z\, dz \tag{1.37j}$$

It may be again observed from Eqs. (1.37i) and (1.37j) that the twisting moments M_{xy} and M_{yx}, in general, will not be equal even if the shear stresses τ_{xy} and

τ_{yx} are equal. The ten forces N_x, N_y, N_{xy}, N_{yx}, M_x, M_y, Q_x, Q_y, M_{xy} and M_{yx} are now related to the stresses σ_x, σ_y, τ_{xy}, τ_{xz} and τ_{yz} through the Eqs. (1.35a–j).

Alternatively, if the stress resultants are known, the stresses can be found by elementary methods. In the case of a thin shell, the stress distribution is generally not far from linear and hence the stresses can be obtained by using the following relations:

$$\sigma_x = \frac{N_x}{h} \pm \frac{12M_x z}{h^3} \tag{1.38a}$$

$$\sigma_y = \frac{N_y}{h} \pm \frac{12M_y z}{h^3} \tag{1.38b}$$

$$\tau_{xy} = \frac{N_{xy}}{h} \pm \frac{12M_{xy} z}{h^3} \tag{1.38c}$$

$$\tau_{yx} = \frac{N_{yx}}{h} \pm \frac{12M_{yx} z}{h^3} \tag{1.38d}$$

If the bending and twisting stresses are linearly distributed, then the transverse shear stresses will have parabolic distribution similar to the parabolic shear stress distribution in beams of rectangular cross-section. Hence, the shear stresses τ_{xz} and τ_{yz} can be determined from

$$\tau_{xz} = -\frac{3Q_x}{2\,h}\left(1 - \frac{4z^2}{h^2}\right) \tag{1.39a}$$

$$\tau_{yz} = -\frac{3Q_y}{2\,h}\left(1 - \frac{4z^2}{h^2}\right) \tag{1.39b}$$

1.7 SELECTION OF SHELL TYPE

It is rather difficult to lay down rules for the selection of proper type of shell for any given situation, as the shell shapes are numerous and their possible uses are so varied. However, it is possible to give some general guideline for the selection of shell type. Where the width of the building to be covered over is very large in comparison with its length, multiple cylindrical shell, with edge-beams, could be used. The limiting span of reinforced concrete shell with edge-beams is about 30m. For larger spans, either continuous cylindrical shells or cylindrical shells with prestressed edge-beams may be preferred. Folded plates are generally competitive with cylindrical shells in the span range of 12 to 25 m. If good day-lighting is desired, several alternatives are possible. A northlight cylindrical shell, a northlight folded plate, a conoid and a hyperbolic paraboloid are some of the possible shapes. If the plan of the building is square or nearly square, then an elliptic paraboloid may be a satisfactory shape for the roof.

1.8 SUMMARY

In the preceding sections, we have developed all the necessary concepts and presented results from differential geometry. We will be making use of the first fundamental form and the associated first fundamental quantities later in the analysis of thin shells. Making use of the second fundamental form, the lines of principal curvature, mean and Gauss curvatures have been defined. Based on Gauss curvature index, it is shown that a systematic classification of shell surfaces can be made.

REFERENCES

1.1 Novozhilov, V.V., *Thin shell theory* (translated from Russian by P.G. Lowe), P. Noordhoff, Groningen, Netherlands, 1964.

1.2 Struik, D.J., Lectures on Classical Differential Geometry, Addison-Wesley, Reading, Mass, 1950.

1.3 *Criteria for the design of reinforced shell structures and folded plates, Indian Standard* 2210–1962, Indian Standard Institution, New Delhi, 1963.

1.4 Kraus, H., *Thin elastic shells*, John Wiley and Sons, 1967.

Chapter Two

Membrane Theory for Shells of Revolution

2.1 INTRODUCTION

In the previous chapter, it has been indicated that in general, a thin elastic shell resists the external load by developing direct forces and bending moments. For a given geometry of shell under some appropriate loading and support conditions, it is possible that the bending moments developed in the shell are either zero or too small, so that they can be safely neglected. In such a case, the shell will resist the external forces through direct or membrane forces. The shell is then said to be under a membrane state of stress. Since, in the membrane theory, the bending moments are neglected, sometimes this theory is also referred as momentless theory of shells. The membrane theory is much simpler as compared to the bending theory, since in this theory, the membrane forces can be directly determined from equilibrium equations. Because of its simplicity, the membrane theory is often used as a reasonable basis for design. However, it must be noted that the membrane theory would be reasonably valid if, at least, the following two conditions are satisfied.

(a) The load varies smoothly over the surface of the shell.

(b) The supports provide such forces or displacements as required by the membrane stress resultants.

We will discuss later, in little more detail, the limitation of membrane theory.

In this chapter, we will first develop the membrane equations for a general shell surface and later apply this to shells of revolution. A surface of revolution is generated by rotating a plane curve about an axis in its plane. The generating curve is normally called as a meridian. Thin shell structures of this description are widely used in the construction of water tanks, roofs, silos, pressure vessels, cooling towers, etc.

2.2 EQUILIBRIUM EQUATIONS

Figure 2.1 shows an element ABCD, taken from an arbitrary shell surface at the middle plane. The geometry of the element will be defined using a curvilinear coordinate system which coincides with the lines of principal curvature of the surface. The length of the sides of the element are

$$AD = A\,d\alpha, \qquad AB = B\,d\beta$$

$$BC = \left(A + \frac{\partial A}{\partial \beta}\,d\beta\right)d\alpha, \quad CD = \left(B + \frac{\partial B}{\partial \alpha}\,d\alpha\right)d\beta \tag{2.1}$$

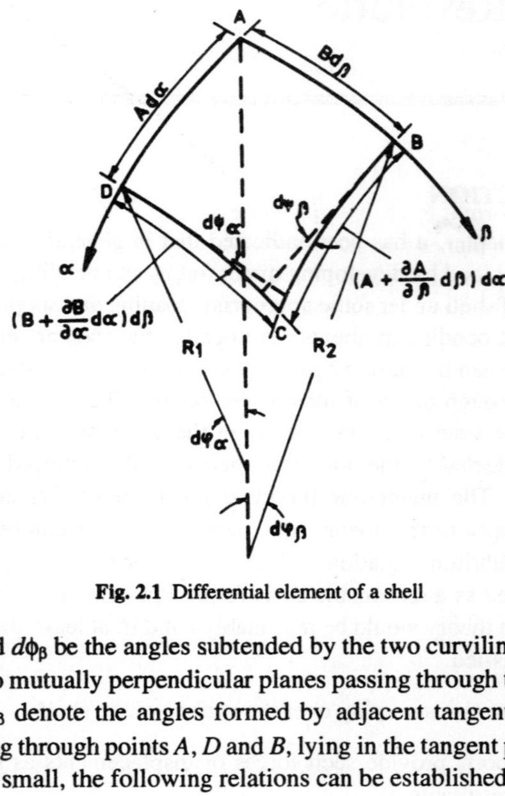

Fig. 2.1 Differential element of a shell

Let $d\phi_\alpha$ and $d\phi_\beta$ be the angles subtended by the two curvilinear sides AD and AB lying in two mutually perpendicular planes passing through the point A. Also let $d\psi_\alpha$ and $d\psi_\beta$ denote the angles formed by adjacent tangents to the lines of curvature passing through points A, D and B, lying in the tangent plane. Assuming these angles are small, the following relations can be established:

$$d\phi_\alpha = \frac{A\,d\alpha}{R_1}, \quad d\phi_\beta = \frac{B\,d\beta}{R_2} \tag{2.2}$$

$$d\psi_\alpha = \frac{1}{B}\frac{\partial A}{\partial \beta}\,d\alpha, \quad d\psi_\beta = \frac{1}{A}\frac{\partial B}{\partial \alpha}\,d\beta$$

Figure 2.2 shows the element of the shell, taken at the middle plane, acted upon by the internal membrane forces and external loading. Let N_α and N_β

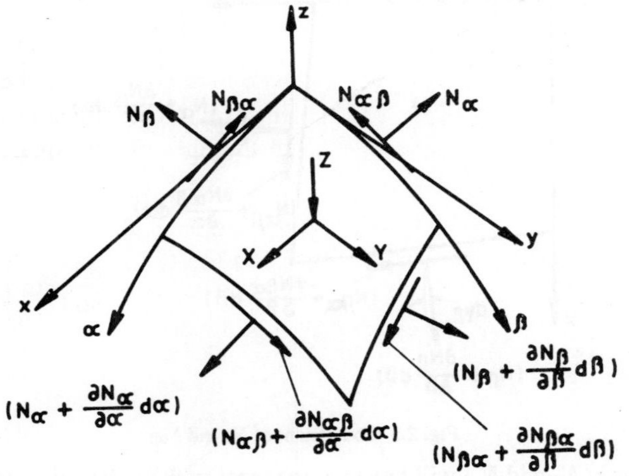

Fig. 2.2 Membrane forces and load on a shell element

represent the normal forces per unit length, $N_{\alpha\beta}$ and $N_{\beta\alpha}$ the shear forces per unit length acting on planes normal to α and β direction, respectively. Let X, Y and Z denote the component of external loading per unit area directed along the tangents to the coordinate lines β-constant and α-constant, as well as a normal to the surface.

First let us use the condition of equilibrium of forces in the three directions, viz. x, y and z and later on, examine the moment equilibrium conditions. To this end, we will now consider the equilibrium of forces in the x-direction. The following will be the components of the forces in the x-direction:

The force N_α will have a resultant component in the x-direction given by

$$- N_\alpha B\, d\beta + \left(N_\alpha + \frac{\partial N_\alpha}{\partial \alpha} d\alpha \right) \left(B + \frac{\partial B}{\partial \alpha} d\alpha \right) d\beta$$

which can be simplified as (neglecting small-order terms)

$$\frac{\partial}{\partial \alpha} (B N_\alpha)\, d\alpha\, d\beta \qquad \text{(a)}$$

Next, the resultant component of force $N_{\beta\alpha}$ in the x-direction will be

$$- N_{\beta\alpha} A\, d\alpha + \left(N_{\beta\alpha} + \frac{\partial N_{\beta\alpha}}{\partial \beta} d\beta \right) \left(A + \frac{\partial A}{\partial \beta} d\beta \right) d\alpha$$

which can be simplified as (neglecting small-order terms)

$$\frac{\partial}{\partial \beta} (A N_{\beta\alpha})\, d\alpha d\beta \qquad \text{(b)}$$

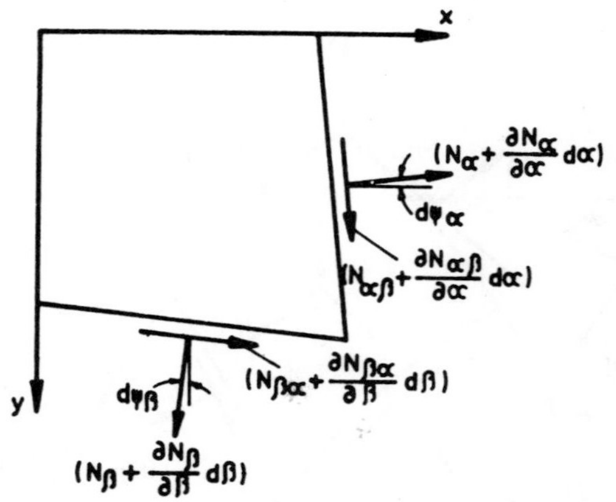

Fig. 2.3 Component of N_β and $N_{\alpha\beta}$

The forces N_β and $N_{\alpha\beta}$ will have components in the x-direction and neglecting small-order terms, these can be determined as

$$-N_\beta A \; d\alpha \; d\psi_\beta \text{ and } N_{\alpha\beta} B \; d\beta \; d\psi_\alpha$$

which, after substituting for $d\psi_\alpha$ and $d\psi_\beta$, from Eq. (2.2), can be written as

$$-N_\beta \left(\frac{\partial B}{\partial \alpha} \right) d\alpha \; d\beta \text{ and } N_{\alpha\beta} \left(\frac{\partial A}{\partial \beta} \right) d\alpha \; d\beta \tag{c}$$

Finally, the component of the external load in the x-direction is:

$$X \; AB \; d\alpha \; d\beta \tag{d}$$

Summing up all the resultant components of the forces in the x-direction and dividing throughout by $d\alpha$ and $d\beta$, we get

$$\frac{\partial}{\partial \alpha} (BN_\alpha) + \frac{\partial}{\partial \beta} (AN_{\beta\alpha}) - N_\beta \frac{\partial B}{\partial \alpha} + N_{\alpha\beta} \frac{\partial A}{\partial \beta} + XAB = 0 \tag{2.3a}$$

Similarly, considering the equilibrium of forces in the y-direction, we get

$$\frac{\partial}{\partial \beta} (AN_\beta) + \frac{\partial}{\partial \alpha} (BN_{\alpha\beta}) - N_\alpha \frac{\partial A}{\partial \beta} + N_{\beta\alpha} \frac{\partial B}{\partial \alpha} + YAB = 0 \tag{2.3b}$$

Lastly, considering the equilibrium of forces in the z-direction, the forces N_α and N_β will have components in the z-direction. These can be determined as (Fig. 2.4)

$$\left(N_\alpha + \frac{\partial N_\alpha}{\partial \alpha} d\alpha \right) \left(B + \frac{\partial B}{\partial \alpha} d\alpha \right) d\beta \sin d\phi_\alpha$$

and

$$\left(N_\beta + \frac{\partial N_\beta}{\partial \beta} d\beta \right) \left(A + \frac{\partial A}{\partial \beta} d\beta \right) d\alpha \sin d\phi_\beta \tag{e}$$

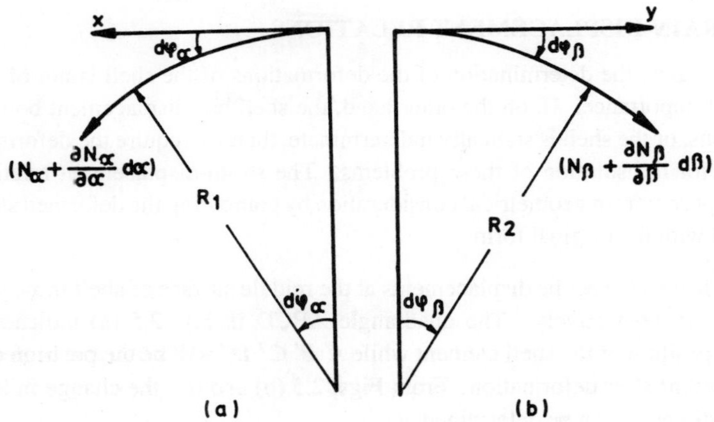

Fig. 2.4 Components of forces N_α and N_β

Substituting for $d\phi_\alpha$ and $d\phi_\beta$ from Eq. (2.2) and after neglecting small-order terms, we get

$$\frac{N_\alpha AB\, d\alpha\, d\beta}{R_1} \text{ and } \frac{N_\beta AB\, d\alpha\, d\beta}{R_2} \tag{f}$$

The component of the external load in the z-direction is

$$ZAB\ d\alpha\ d\beta \tag{g}$$

Summing up all the components of forces in the z-direction and dividing throughout by $AB\ d\alpha\ d\beta$, we get

$$\frac{N_\alpha}{R_1} + \frac{N_\beta}{R_2} + Z = 0 \tag{2.3c}$$

Now let us examine the moment equilibrium equations. Since the membrane forces act on the middle surface of the shell, they cannot produce moments about the x-and y-axis. The equilibrium of moments about the z-axis leads to the condition

$$N_{\alpha\beta} = N_{\beta\alpha} \tag{2.3d}$$

Considering the above identity, we have three equilibrium equations [Eqs. (2.3a – c)] involving three unknown forces, namely, N_α, N_β and $N_{\alpha\beta}$. The three forces can be determined directly by integrating these equations. Hence it may be said that the membrane theory is statically determinate internally. However, the above statement does not take into account the support conditions and it is possible that the shell problem may become complex because of external statical indeterminacy.

2.3 STRAIN-DISPLACEMENT RELATIONS

In many cases, the determination of the deformations of the shell is not of much practical importance. If, on the other hand, the shell has displacement boundary conditions, or the shell is statically indeterminate, then we require the deformation of shell for the solution of these problems. The strain-displacement relation is derived purely from geometrical consideration by comparing the deformed state of the shell with the original form.

Let u, v and w be the displacements at the middle surface of shell in x-, y- and z-directions, respectively. The quadrangle ABCD in Fig. 2.5 (a) indicates the original position of the shell element while $A'\,B'\,C'\,D'$ will be the position of the shell element after deformation. From Figs. 2.5 (b) and (c), the change in length in the x-direction can be determined as:

$$\frac{\partial u}{\partial \alpha}\, d\alpha + v\, d\psi_\alpha + w\, d\phi_\alpha \tag{a}$$

In the above equation, the first term represents the change in length along the x-direction, the second term represents the change in length caused by the lateral movement of the element because of the increase in length in the x-direction and the third term represents the contraction due to decrease in the radius of curvature associated with the radial displacement (Fig. 2.5c). Dividing the above equation by $A\, d\alpha$, we get the strain.

The strain in the x-direction at the middle surface is now given by

$$\varepsilon_{\alpha 0} = \frac{1}{A}\frac{\partial u}{\partial \alpha} + \frac{v}{AB}\frac{\partial A}{\partial \beta} + \frac{w}{R_1} \tag{2.4a}$$

Similarly, the strain in the y-direction at the middle surface can be obtained as

$$\varepsilon_{\beta 0} = \frac{1}{B}\frac{\partial v}{\partial \beta} + \frac{u}{AB}\frac{\partial B}{\partial \alpha} + \frac{w}{R_2} \tag{2.4b}$$

The shear strain at middle surface is determined as the relative change in the angle BAD (Fig. 2.5a) included between the edges AD and AB and depends only on the displacements u and v. The shear strain $\gamma_{\alpha\beta 0}$ can be determined as the sum of the following two quantities:

$$\gamma'_{\alpha\beta} = \frac{1}{B\, d\beta}\left(\frac{\partial u}{\partial \beta}\, d\beta\right) - v\,\frac{d\psi_\beta}{B\, d\beta} \tag{b}$$

$$\gamma''_{\alpha\beta} = \frac{1}{A\, d\alpha}\left(\frac{\partial v}{\partial \alpha}\, d\alpha\right) - u\,\frac{d\psi_\alpha}{A\, d\alpha} \tag{c}$$

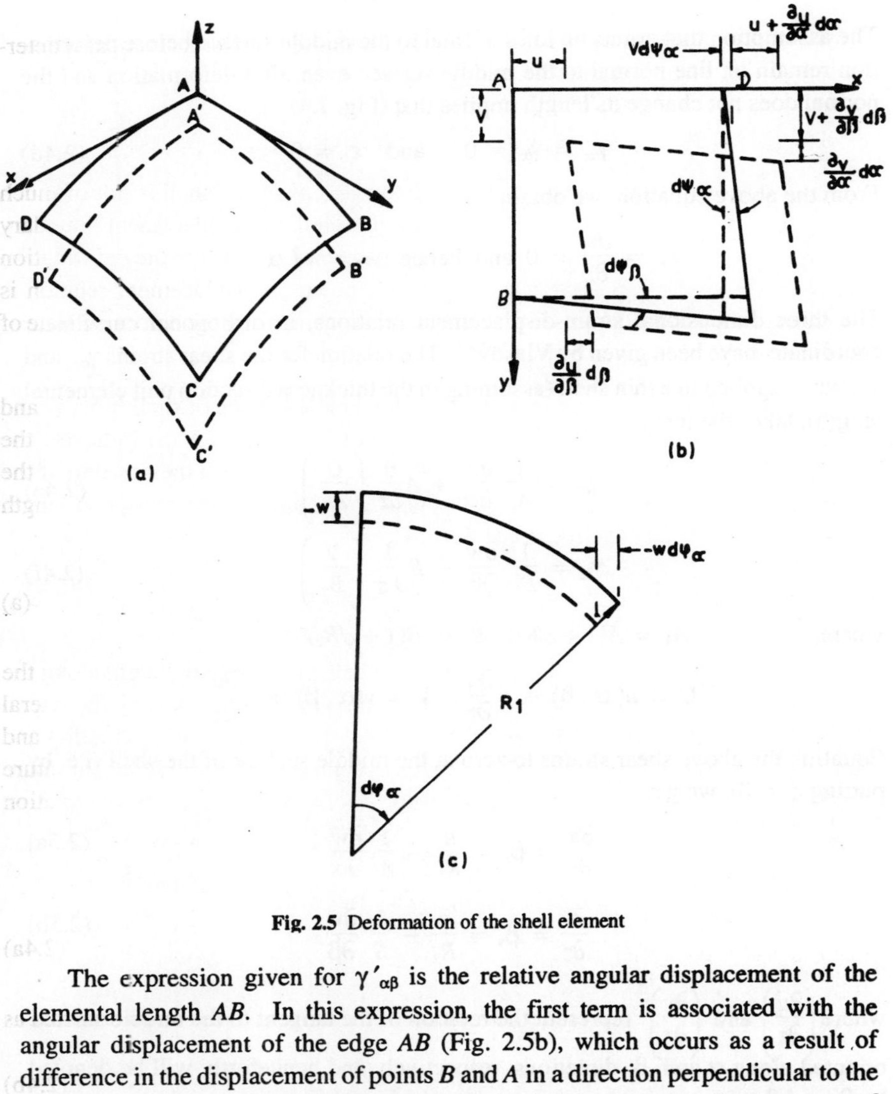

Fig. 2.5 Deformation of the shell element

The expression given for $\gamma'_{\alpha\beta}$ is the relative angular displacement of the elemental length *AB*. In this expression, the first term is associated with the angular displacement of the edge *AB* (Fig. 2.5b), which occurs as a result of difference in the displacement of points *B* and *A* in a direction perpendicular to the edge *AB*. The second term corresponds to the relative angular displacement of edge *AB*, which occurs as a result of the displacement *v* directed along the edge *AB*. The minus sign for this angular displacement is used, as it is in a direction opposite to that of the first term. Similarly, the expression given for $\gamma''_{\alpha\beta}$, which is the angular displacement of edge *AD*, can be obtained. Hence, the shear strain $\gamma_{\alpha\beta o}$ at the middle surface can be obtained as (after making use of the relations given in Eq. (2.2))

$$\gamma_{\alpha\beta o} = \frac{1}{A}\frac{\partial v}{\partial \alpha} + \frac{1}{B}\frac{\partial u}{\partial \beta} - \frac{u}{AB}\frac{\partial A}{\partial \beta} - \frac{v}{AB}\frac{\partial B}{\partial \alpha} \qquad (2.4c)$$

The assumption that points on lines normal to the middle surface before deformation remain on line normal to the middle surface even after deformation and the normal does not change its length implies that (Fig. 1.4)

$$\gamma_{\alpha z} = \gamma_{\beta z} = 0 \quad \text{and} \quad \varepsilon_z = 0 \tag{2.4d}$$

From the above equation, we obtain

$$\varepsilon_z = \frac{\partial w}{\partial z} = 0 \text{ and hence, } w = w(\alpha, \beta)$$

The three dimensional strain-displacement relations, in orthogonal curvilinear coordinate, have been given by Vlasov[2.7]. The relation for the shear strains $\gamma_{\alpha z}$ and $\gamma_{\beta z}$, when applied to a thin shell (assuming in the thickness direction unit elemental length), takes the form

$$\gamma_{\alpha z} = \frac{1}{A_1}\frac{\partial w}{\partial \alpha} + A\frac{\partial}{\partial z}\left(\frac{U}{A_1}\right) \tag{2.4e}$$

$$\gamma_{\beta z} = \frac{1}{B_1}\frac{\partial w}{\partial \beta} + B\frac{\partial}{\partial z}\left(\frac{V}{B_1}\right) \tag{2.4f}$$

where, $A_1 = A(1 + z/R_1),\ B_1 = B(1 + z/R_2)$

$$U = u(\alpha, \beta) + z\frac{\partial u}{\partial z}, \quad V = v(\alpha, \beta) + z\frac{\partial v}{\partial z}$$

Equating the above shear strains to zero at the middle surface of the shell (i.e. by putting $z = 0$), we get

$$\frac{\partial u}{\partial z} = \beta_x = \frac{u}{R_1} - \frac{1}{A}\frac{\partial w}{\partial \alpha} \tag{2.5a}$$

$$\frac{\partial v}{\partial z} = \beta_y = \frac{v}{R_2} - \frac{1}{B}\frac{\partial w}{\partial \beta} \tag{2.5b}$$

where $\left(\frac{\partial u}{\partial z}\right)$ and $\left(\frac{\partial v}{\partial z}\right)$ represent the rotation of the tangent to the middle surface oriented along α and β directions, respectively and henceforth, will be denoted by β_x and β_y.

The rotation is considered positive, if it is clockwise and negative if it is counter-clockwise.

The strain can be related to the stresses through the stress–strain relations and later, to the stress resultants. Assuming that the shell material is isotropic, linearly elastic and follows Hooke's law, the strains can be related to the stress resultants as

$$\varepsilon_{\alpha 0} = \frac{1}{Eh}(N_\alpha - \nu N_\beta) \tag{2.6a}$$

$$\varepsilon_{\beta o} = \frac{1}{Eh} (N_\beta - \nu N_\alpha) \tag{2.6b}$$

$$\gamma_{\alpha\beta o} = \frac{N_{\alpha\beta}}{Gh} \tag{2.6c}$$

where E = modulus of elasticity, ν = Poisson's ratio, G = shear modulus and h = thickness of shell.

If the stress resultants are known, then the displacements in the shell can be determined from Eqs. (2.4a–c) and (2.6a–c).

2.4 BOUNDARY CONDITIONS

The equilibrium Eqs. (2.3a) and (2.3b) are partial differential equations of first order and if necessary, they can be combined together, resulting in a second order differential equation, the solution of which will determine the forces. Alternatively, we can first obtain the force-displacement relations using Eqs. (2.6a–c) together with Eqs. (2.4a–c). Then we can substitute the force-displacement relation in the equilibrium equations and reduce to a single fourth-order differential equation in terms of displacement. However, it is always convenient to solve the equilibrium equations in terms of forces first and then determine displacements later. From this point of view, in membrane theory only two boundary conditions can be specified at each edge of the shell. These could be either in terms of forces or displacements or a combination of force and displacement. Hence, along an edge α, equal to constant N_α and $N_{\alpha\beta}$ may be specified, or u and v may be specified. Solutions to several problems based on membrane theory will now be obtained, using the basic equations given here.

2.5 MEMBRANE ANALYSIS OF SHELLS OF REVOLUTION

As a first application of the general membrane theory developed above, let us consider shells of revolution whose reference surfaces have straight line generators. There are two types of shells in this category, namely cylindrical and conical shells. We will first consider the analysis of cylindrical shells subjected to arbitrary loading and later subjected to axisymmetric load. The latter type of load leads to great simplification in the analysis. Later, we will carry out similar analysis for conical and spherical shells.

2.5.1 Membrane Analysis of Cylindrical Shells

Figure 2.6 shows a cylindrical shell with a chosen (x, θ) coordinate system.

For the chosen coordinate system, the following identity can be written with respect to the curvilinear coordinate system (Fig. 2.7).

$$\alpha = x, \ \beta = \theta, \ A = 1, \ B = R, \ R_1 = \infty, R_2 = R$$

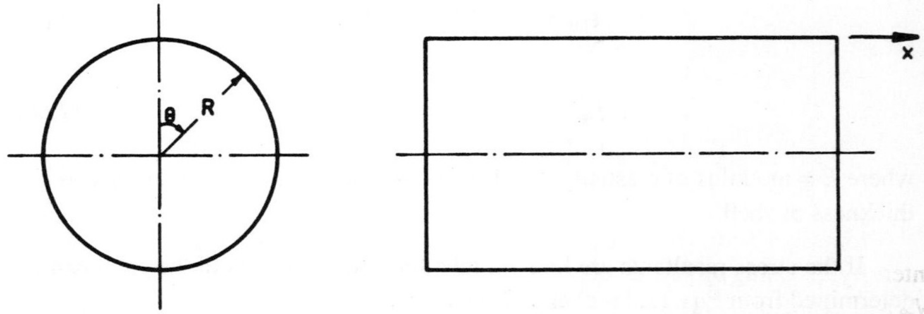

Fig. 2.6 Geometry of a cylindrical shell

and $$N_\alpha = N_x,\ N_\beta = N_\theta,\ N_{\alpha\beta} = N_{x\theta}$$

Using the above identity in Eqs. (2.3a–c), the following equilibrium equations for a cylindrical shell can be obtained

$$\frac{\partial N_x}{\partial x} + \frac{\partial N_{x\theta}}{R\,\partial\theta} + X = 0 \tag{2.7a}$$

$$\frac{\partial N_\theta}{R\,\partial\theta} + \frac{\partial N_{x\theta}}{\partial x} + Y = 0 \tag{2.7b}$$

$$\frac{N_\theta}{R} + Z = 0 \tag{2.7c}$$

The strain-displacement relations can also be obtained, using the above identity in Eqs. (2.4a – c) as

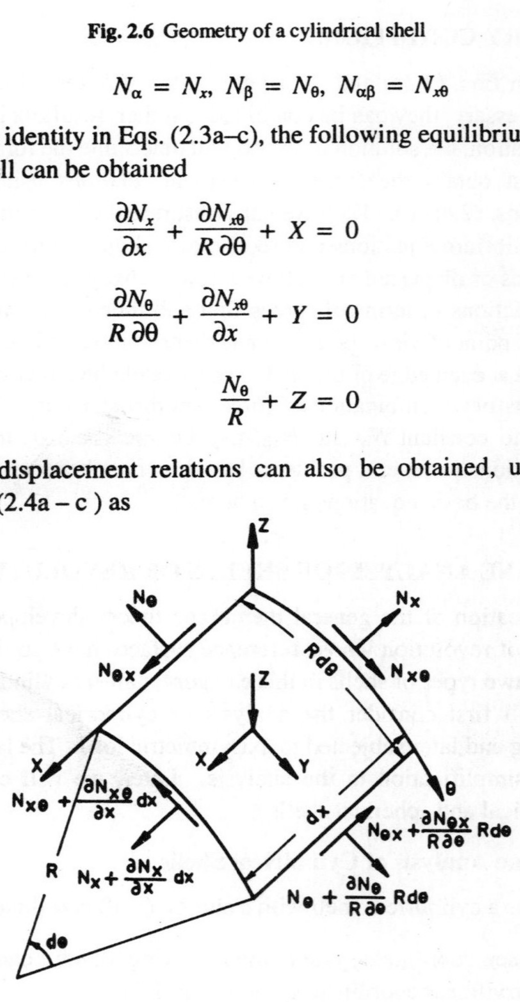

Fig. 2.7 Membrane forces on an element of a cylindrical shell

$$\varepsilon_{x0} = \frac{\partial u}{\partial x} \tag{2.8a}$$

$$\varepsilon_{\theta 0} = \frac{\partial v}{R\,\partial \theta} + \frac{w}{R} \tag{2.8b}$$

$$\gamma_{x\theta 0} = \frac{\partial v}{\partial x} + \frac{1}{R}\frac{\partial u}{\partial \theta} \tag{2.8c}$$

From Eq. (2.7c), we can immediately determine N_θ for a given normal load of intensity Z. Using this value of N_θ, Eq. (2.7b) may be integrated first to determine $N_{x\theta}$ and later Eq. (2.7a) may be integrated to determine N_x. Each of these integrations yields integration constants, which would be functions of θ only and can be determined from the two boundary conditions. The expressions for the membrane forces in a cylindrical shell can now be written in a general form as:

$$N_\theta = -ZR \tag{2.9a}$$

$$N_{x\theta} = -\int \left(Y + \frac{\partial N_\theta}{R\,\partial \theta} \right) dx + f_1(\theta) \tag{2.9b}$$

$$N_x = -\int \left(X + \frac{\partial N_{x\theta}}{R\,\partial \theta} \right) dx + f_2(\theta) \tag{2.9c}$$

where f_1 and f_2 are integration constants.

The general equations for the displacements can now be obtained in terms of the stress resultants. By substituting the strain-displacement relations (Eq. 2.4a – c) in Eq. (2.6a – c), we obtain the following equations:

$$\frac{\partial u}{\partial x} = \frac{1}{Eh}\,(N_x - \nu N_\theta) \tag{a}$$

$$\frac{w}{R} + \frac{\partial v}{R\,\partial \theta} = \frac{1}{Eh}\,(N_\theta - \nu N_x) \tag{b}$$

$$\frac{\partial v}{\partial x} + \frac{\partial u}{R\,\partial \theta} = \frac{N_{x\theta}}{Gh} \tag{c}$$

The equation for displacements can be obtained by simple integration of the above equations as

$$u = \frac{1}{Eh}\int (N_x - \nu N_\theta)\,dx + f_3(\theta) \tag{2.10a}$$

$$v = \frac{1}{Gh}\int N_{x\theta}\,dx - \frac{1}{R}\int \frac{\partial u}{\partial \theta}\,dx + f_4(\theta) \tag{2.10b}$$

$$w = R\left[\frac{1}{Eh}\,(N_\theta - \nu N_x) - \frac{\partial v}{R\,\partial \theta}\right] \tag{2.10c}$$

where f_3 and f_4 are integration constants.

The integration constants in the above equations can easily be determined by making use of the boundary conditions for a given problem.

The use of the above expressions for determining the membrane stress resultants and displacements in cylindrical shells, subjected to different types of loading and support conditions, will now be illustrated through examples.

2.5.1.1 Examples

(a) Circular-cylindrical shell filled with a liquid:

Figure 2.8 shows a circular-cylindrical shell of radius a and length L filled with a liquid of density γ.

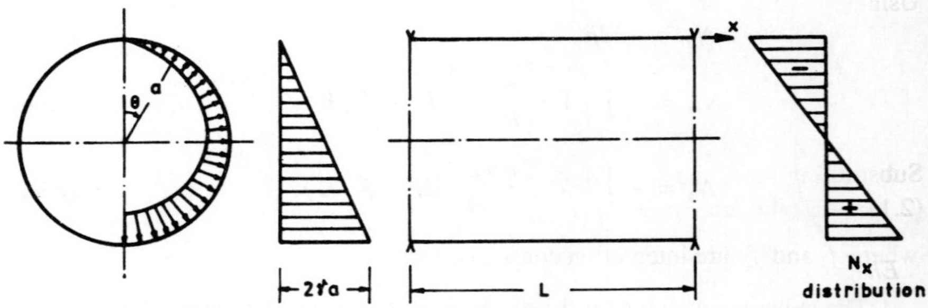

Fig. 2.8 Circular-cylindrical shell filled with a liquid

For this case, the load components can be determined as $X = Y = 0$, $Z = -\gamma a(1 - \cos\theta)$

Substituting this in Eqs. (2.9a – c) and after integration, the membrane forces are determined as

$$N_\theta = \gamma a^2 (1 - \cos\theta) \tag{a}$$

$$N_{x\theta} = -\gamma a x \sin\theta + f_1(\theta) \tag{b}$$

$$N_x = \frac{\gamma x^2}{2}\cos\theta - \frac{x}{a}\frac{\partial f_1}{\partial\theta} + f_2(\theta) \tag{c}$$

The integration constants f_1 and f_2 are determined so as to satisfy the required boundary conditions. In the present problem, we shall assume that the shell is supported at the two ends in such a way that the end supports cannot resist a normal force. This leads to the following boundary conditions:

$$\text{at } x = 0 \quad \text{and} \quad x = L, \quad N_x = 0 \tag{d}$$

Using the above condition, f_1 and f_2 can be determined as

$$f_1 = \frac{\gamma L a}{2}\sin\theta, \; f_2 = 0 \tag{e}$$

Substituting for f_1 and f_2 in Eqs. (a) - (c), we get

$$N_\theta = \gamma a^2 (1 - \cos\theta) \tag{2.11a}$$

$$N_{x\theta} = \gamma a \left(\frac{L}{2} - x\right) \sin\theta \tag{2.11b}$$

$$N_x = -\frac{\gamma x}{2} (L - x) \cos\theta \tag{2.11c}$$

The displacements can be determined using Eqs. (2.10 a–c) and (2.11a–c). The integration constants f_3 and f_4 in Eq. (2.10a, b) have to be determined so as to satisfy the displacement boundary conditions. Since we have assumed that the support is flexible in the x-direction and it is only the $N_{x\theta}$ force that can get transmitted to the support, it will be appropriate to assume $v = 0$ at $x = 0$ and L. Using this condition, the constants f_3 and f_4 can be determined as

$$f_3 = \frac{\gamma L}{2\,Eh} \left[\frac{L^2}{12} \cos\theta + \nu a^2 (1 - \cos\theta)\right] \tag{f}$$

$$f_4 = 0 \tag{g}$$

Substituting for f_3 and f_4 in Eqs. (2.10a, b) and the stress resultants given in Eqs. (2.11a – c) and after simplification, we get the displacements as

$$Ehu = -\frac{\gamma a^2 \nu (2x - L)}{2} + \frac{\gamma \cos\theta\,(2x - L)}{2} \left\{\frac{2x^2 - 2xL - L^2}{12} + \nu a^2\right\} \tag{2.12a}$$

$$Ehv = \frac{\gamma \sin\theta\; x(L - x)}{2} \left\{(2 + \nu)\,a - \frac{x^2 - xL - L^2}{12a}\right\} \tag{2.12b}$$

$$Ehw = \gamma a^3 (1 - \cos\theta) - \frac{\gamma \cos\theta\; x\,(L - x)}{2} \left\{2a + \frac{L^2 - x^2 + xL}{12a}\right\} \tag{2.12c}$$

It may be observed from the above equations, that the radial displacement w would not be zero at the support. If the support is rigid in its own plane, then the displacement must be zero. Hence, to satisfy this condition, additional edge radial load has to be applied to nullify the membrane radial displacement, causing local bending of the shell.

From the above expressions of stress resultants, it may be noted that the weight of the liquid is carried by the pipe between the supports $x = 0$ and L by producing bending of the pipe. Incidentally, the distribution of N_x will be linear, similar to that of bending stress variation in simple beam theory (see N_x diagram in Fig. 2.8). Also the span-wise distribution of N_x and $N_{x\theta}$ will be of the same form as in the case of a beam.

(b) Cylindrical shell subjected to wind loading

Figure 2.9 shows a circular cylindrical shell of radius a and height L subjected to wind load. Wind loads on shell structures depend on the Reynolds' number, surface roughness, shape of structure as well as the aspect ratio (height to diameter ratio). For static analysis of shell structures due to wind load, it becomes necessary to know the wind pressure distribution in the circumferential and longitudinal directions. For an open-end cylinder, Rish[2.1] has suggested the following approximate equation for a strong wind of uniform velocity.

$$p_1 = p_0\,(-\,0.387 + 0.338\,\cos\theta + 0.533\,\cos 2\theta + 0.471\,\cos 3\theta$$
$$+\,0.166\cos 4\theta - 0.066\,\cos 5\theta - 0.055\,\cos 6\theta)$$

which can be written as

$$p_1 = p_0 \sum_{n=0}^{6} A_n \cos n\theta$$

where p_0 = dynamic pressure on the front face = 0.6 × (wind velocity in m/sec²). In this case the dimensions of p_0 will be in Newton's per square metre (SI units). It may be noted that $n = 0$ corresponds to a uniform pressure all round the shell (axisymmetric) and solution for such a case will be discussed later.

The wind pressure in the vertical direction varies from zero at the ground level to maximum value at some height called the gradient height, beyond which it is practically constant. For simplicity, the wind pressure distribution in the vertical direction can be taken as constant. For determining the membrane stress resultant here, we will restrict ourselves to one term in the series ($n = 1$) and hence the wind pressure distribution can be taken as (Fig. 2.9)

$$p_1 = p\cos\theta, \text{ (assuming } A_1 = 1\text{)}$$

For this type of wind load, the load components can be determined as

$$X = Y = 0,\; Z = p\cos\theta \tag{a}$$

Substituting the above load components in Eqs. (2.9a–c), we get, after integration,

$$N_\theta = -\,pa\cos\theta \tag{b}$$

$$N_{x\theta} = -\,px\sin\theta + f_1(\theta) \tag{c}$$

$$N_x = \frac{px^2\cos\theta}{2a} - \frac{x}{a}\frac{\partial f_1}{\partial\theta} + f_2(\theta) \tag{d}$$

Assuming that the top end of the cylindrical shell is free, we can write the following boundary conditions:

$$\text{at } x = L,\; N_x = N_{x\theta} = 0$$

Using these boundary conditions, the integration constants f_1 and f_2 can be determined as

$$f_1 = rL\sin\theta,\; f_2 = \frac{pL^2}{2a}\cos\theta \tag{e}$$

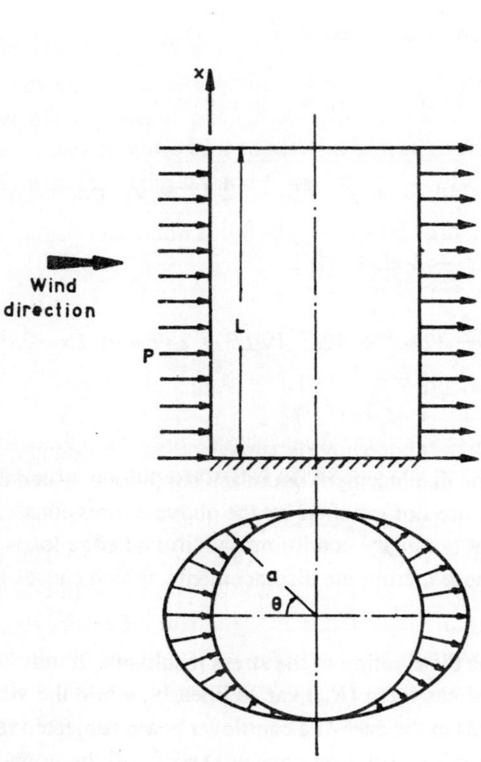

Fig. 2.9 Cylindrical shell subjected to wind load

Substituting the above values for f_1 and f_2 in Eqs. (c) and (d), we get the membrane forces as

$$N_\theta = -\,pa\cos\theta \qquad (2.13a)$$

$$N_{x\theta} = p\,(L - x)\sin\theta \qquad (21.3b)$$

$$N_x = \frac{p}{2a}\,(L - x)^2\cos\theta \qquad (2.13c)$$

The displacements can be determined using Eqs. (2.10a–c) and Eqs. (2.13a–c). Since the shell is fixed at the bottom end, the displacements u, v, w and the slope $\partial w/\partial x$ should be zero. However, we have only two constants namely f_3 and f_4 in Eqs. (2.10a–b) and these constants can be determined by using only two displacement boundary conditions. Taking the boundary conditions along the fixed edge as

$$\text{at} \qquad x = 0,\ u = v = 0 \qquad (f)$$

we find

$$f_3 = f_4 = 0 \qquad (g)$$

The displacements can now be obtained as

$$Ehu = \frac{px\cos\theta}{6a}\left[(3L^2 - 3xL + x^2) + 6\nu a^2\right] \tag{2.14a}$$

$$\begin{aligned} Ehv = \frac{px\sin\theta}{24a^2} & [48\,(1+\nu)\,a^2L - 12\,(2+\nu)\,a^2x \\ & + x\,(6L^2 - 4\,xL + x^2)] \end{aligned} \tag{2.14b}$$

$$\begin{aligned} Ehw = \frac{-p\cos\theta}{24a^2} & [24a^4 + 12a^2\,\{\nu L^2 + 2\,(2+\nu)\,Lx - 2x^2\} \\ & + x^2\,(6L^2 - 4Lx + x^2)] \end{aligned} \tag{2.14c}$$

It may be seen that the displacement boundary conditions, w and $\partial w/\partial x$ to be zero along the fixed end, are not satisfied by the above expressions. In order to satisfy these displacement boundary conditions, additional edge loads have to be applied so as to nullify these membrane displacements, which causes local bending of the shell.

Figure 2.10 shows the distribution of the stress resultants. It may be observed from this figure that the shear force ($N_{x\theta}$) varies linearly, while the vertical force (N_x) varies parabolically, as in the case of a cantilever beam subjected to a uniform load. As mentioned earlier, this solution does not satisfy all the boundary conditions corresponding to the fixed edge at the bottom. Hence, in the rigorous sense, the membrane solution is not valid for this problem. However, it will be shown later (Chapter – 6) that the nonsatisfaction of the boundary conditions at the fixed edge will have a localised effect and for a major portion of the shell (away from the fixed edge), the membrane solution would be acceptable.

(c) Cylindrical tank filled with a liquid

Consider a circular tank of radius a, height L and filled with a liquid of density γ; the load is symmetrical about the axis of revolution (Fig. 2.11).

Hence, the membrane forces will be independent of θ and all the derivatives with respect to θ in Eqs. (2.7a) and (2.7b) will disappear. Further, as the load is symmetrical, the shear force $N_{x\theta}$ will not exist.

The equilibrium Eqs. (2.7a–c) then reduces to

$$\frac{dN_x}{dx} + X = 0 \tag{2.15a}$$

$$\frac{N_\theta}{a} + Z = 0 \tag{2.15b}$$

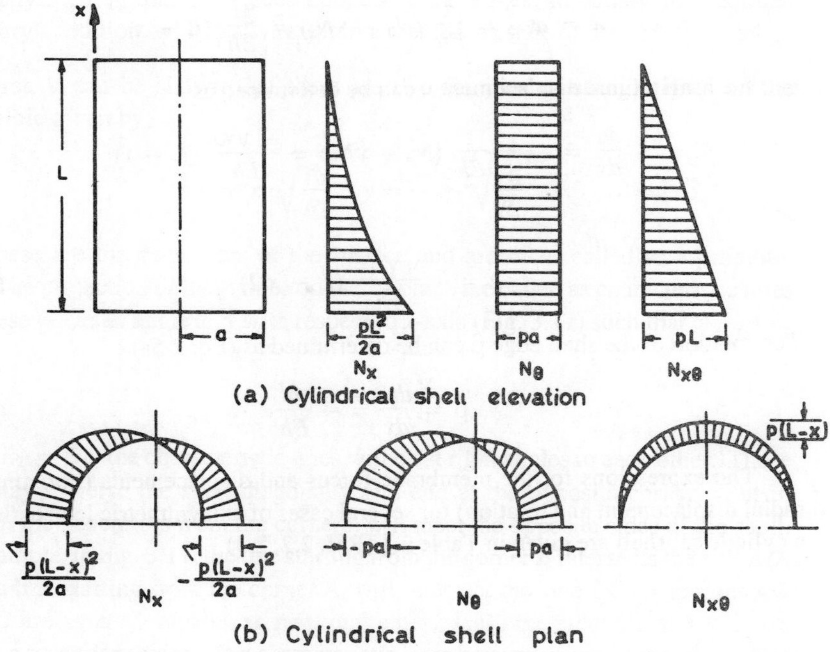

Fig. 2.10 Variation of forces in a cylindrical shell subjected to wind load

Since the load is axisymmetric, the tangential displacement v would be zero. The strain-displacement relation given in Eqs. (2.8a–c) will now reduce to

$$\varepsilon_{x0} = \frac{du}{dx} \tag{2.16a}$$

$$\varepsilon_{\theta 0} = \frac{w}{a} \tag{2.16b}$$

For the liquid pressure considered here, the load components can be determined as

$$X = 0,\; Z = -\,\gamma\,(L - x) \tag{a}$$

Substituting this in Eqs. (2.15a) and (2.15b), we get

$$N_\theta = \gamma a\,(L - x) \tag{2.17a}$$

$$N_x = 0 \tag{2.17b}$$

It may be observed that the hoop force N_θ varies linearly over the height of the tank.

Using Eq. (2.16b), the radial displacement w can be determined as

$$w = a\varepsilon_{\theta 0} = \frac{a}{Eh}(N_\theta - \nu N_x) = \frac{\gamma a^2}{Eh}(L - x) \tag{2.18}$$

and the longitudinal displacement u can be determined as

$$\frac{du}{dx} = \varepsilon_{x0} = \frac{1}{Eh}(N_x - \nu N_\theta) = \frac{-\nu\gamma a}{Eh}(L - x)$$

or

$$u = -\frac{\nu\gamma ax}{Eh}(L - x/2) \tag{2.19}$$

The rotation of the shell edge β can be determined as (Eq. 2.5a)

$$\beta = \frac{dw}{dx} = -\frac{\gamma a^2}{Eh} \tag{2.20}$$

The expressions for the membrane forces and displacements (horizontal or radial displacement and rotation) for several cases of axisymmetric load acting on a cylindrical shell are given in Table 2.1 (Ref. 2.2, 2.3).

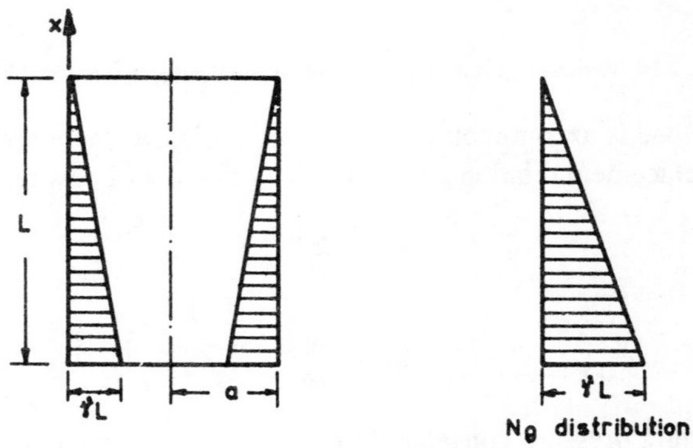

Fig. 2.11 Cylindrical tank filled with a liquid

2.5.2 Membrane Analysis of Conical Shells

The following identity can be written down between the chosen coordinate system (x, θ) for the conical shell here and the general curvilinear coordinate system used earlier (Fig. 2.12)

$$\alpha = x,\ \beta = \theta,\ A = 1,\ B = r,\ R_1 = \infty\ ,\ R_2 = r_2$$

$$N_\alpha = N_x,\ N_\beta = N_\theta,\ N_{\alpha\beta} = N_{x\theta}$$

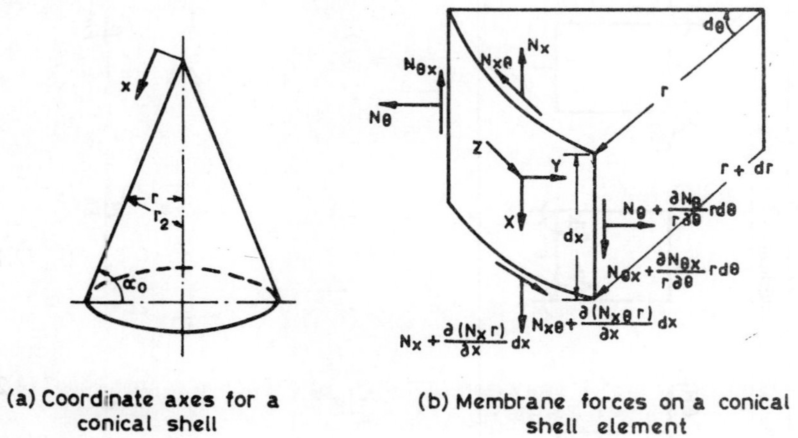

Fig. 2.12 Conical shell

Using the above identity in Eqs. (2.3a–c), the equilibrium equations for a conical shell can now be written as

$$\frac{\partial}{\partial x}(N_x r) + \frac{\partial N_{x\theta}}{\partial \theta} - N_\theta \frac{\partial r}{\partial x} + Xr = 0 \tag{a}$$

$$\frac{\partial N_\theta}{\partial \theta} + \frac{\partial}{\partial x}(N_{x\theta} r) + N_{x\theta} \frac{\partial r}{\partial x} + Yr = 0 \tag{b}$$

$$\frac{N_\theta}{r_2} + Z = 0 \tag{c}$$

It can be shown that (Fig. 2.12a)

$$r = x \cos \alpha_0,\ r_2 = x \cot \alpha_0, \text{ and } \frac{\partial r}{\partial x} = \cos \alpha_0 \tag{d}$$

Substituting the above relations in Eqs. (a)–(d), we get

$$x \frac{\partial N_x}{\partial x} + \frac{1}{\cos \alpha_0} \frac{\partial N_{x\theta}}{\partial \theta} + (N_x - N_\theta) + Xx = 0 \tag{2.21a}$$

$$\frac{1}{\cos \alpha_0} \frac{\partial N_\theta}{\partial \theta} + 2N_{x\theta} + x \frac{\partial N_{x\theta}}{\partial x} + Yx = 0 \tag{2.21b}$$

$$N_\theta + Zx \cot \alpha_0 = 0 \tag{2.21c}$$

Using the above identity, the strain-displacement relations given in Eqs. (2.4a–c) can be transformed as

Table 2.1 Membrane forces and displacements for a cylindrical shell for different types of loading

Shell geometry and loading condition	Membrane forces		Boundary displacements			
	N_x	N_θ	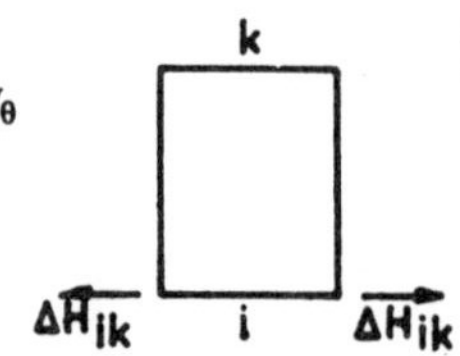	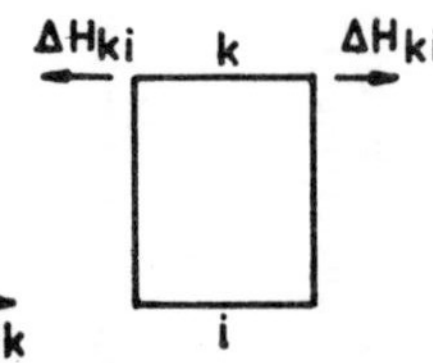	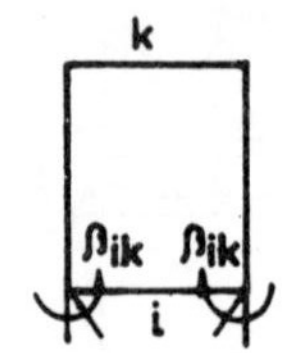	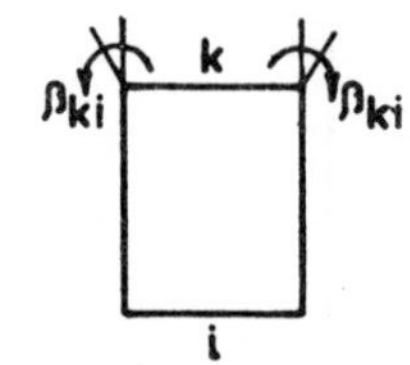
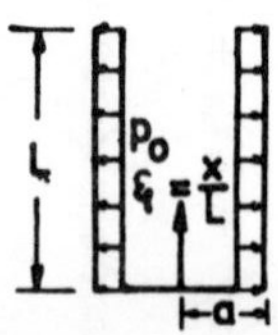	0	$p_0 a$	$\frac{p_0 a^2}{Eh}$	$\frac{p_0 a^2}{Eh}$	0	0
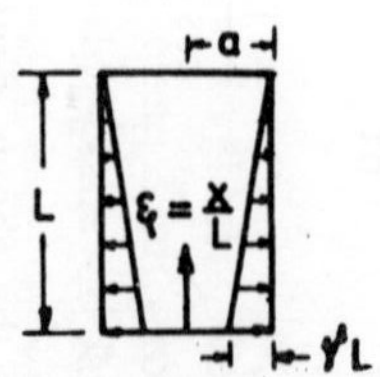	0	$\gamma La(1-\xi)$	$\frac{\gamma La^2}{Eh}$	0	$-\frac{\gamma a^2}{Eh}$	$-\frac{\gamma a^2}{Eh}$

Table 2.1 (*Continued*)

Shell geometry and loading condition	Membrane forces		Boundary displacements			
	N_x	N_θ	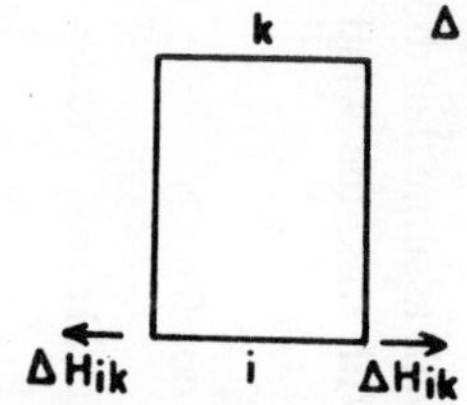	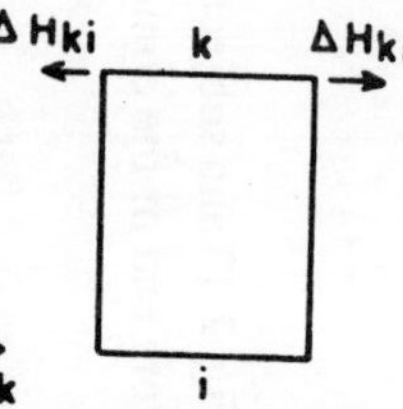		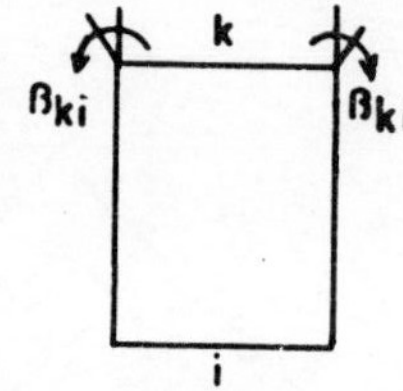
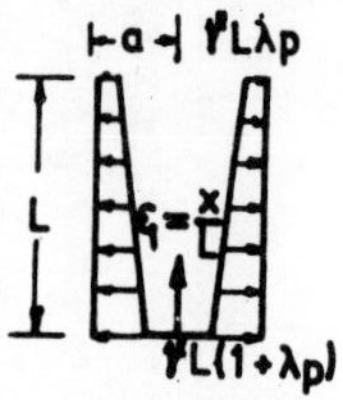	0	$\gamma La(1 + \lambda_p - \xi)$	$\frac{\gamma La^2}{Eh}(1 + \lambda_p)$	$\frac{\gamma La^2}{Eh}\lambda_p$	$-\frac{\gamma a^2}{Eh}$	$-\frac{\gamma a^2}{Eh}$
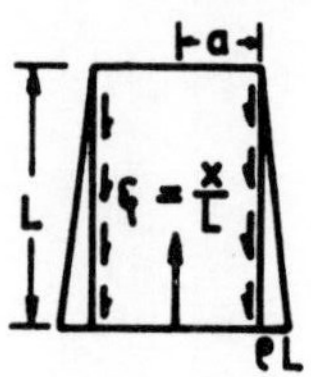	$-\rho L^2\left(\frac{1}{2} - \xi + \frac{\xi^2}{2}\right)$	0	$\frac{\rho L^2 a\nu}{2Eh}$	0	$-\frac{\rho La\nu}{Eh}$	0

$$\varepsilon_{x0} = \frac{\partial u}{\partial x} \tag{2.22a}$$

$$\varepsilon_{\theta 0} = \frac{1}{x \cos \alpha_0} \frac{\partial v}{\partial \theta} + \frac{u}{x} + \frac{w}{x} \tan \alpha_0 \tag{2.22b}$$

$$\gamma_{x\theta 0} = \frac{\partial v}{\partial x} + \frac{1}{x \cos \alpha_0} \frac{\partial u}{\partial \theta} - \frac{v}{x} \tag{2.22c}$$

The use of the above equations to determine the membrane stress resultants, in a conical shell subjected to different types of load, will now be illustrated through some examples.

2.5.2.1 Examples

(a) Conical shell subjected to wind load

A conical shell supported at the centre, as shown in Fig. 2.13 and subjected to wind load, will be considered. It is assumed that the bottom end of the conical shell is free.

As we did in the case of a cylindrical shell, we will assume that the wind load varies as $\cos \theta$ in the circumferential direction. With this, the wind load components can now be determined as

$$X = Y = 0, \quad Z = p \sin \alpha_0 \cos \theta \tag{a}$$

First, N_θ can be straight away determined from Eq. (2.21c) as

$$N_\theta = - px \cos \alpha_0 \cos \theta \tag{2.23a}$$

Equation (2.21b) can be rewritten as

$$\frac{\partial}{\partial x} (N_{x\theta}\, x^2) + \frac{x}{\cos \alpha_0} \frac{\partial N_\theta}{\partial \theta} = 0 \tag{b}$$

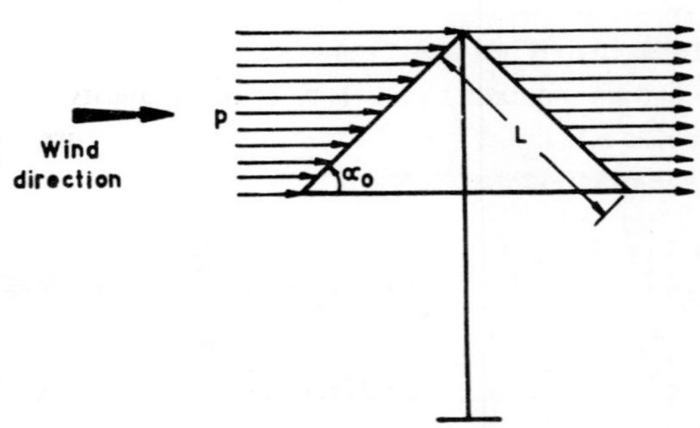

Fig. 2.13 Conical shell under wind load

Substituting for N_θ, the expression given in Eq. (2.23a) and after integration, we get

$$N_{x\theta} = -\frac{px\sin\theta}{3} + \frac{f_1}{x^2} \tag{c}$$

where f_1 is the integration constant.

Using the boundary condition that at $x = L$, $N_{x\theta} = 0$, we can determine f_1 as

$$f_1 = \frac{pL^3\sin\theta}{3} \tag{d}$$

Substituting for f_1 in Eq. (c), the expression for $N_{x\theta}$ can be written as

$$N_{x\theta} = \frac{p\sin\theta}{3}\left(\frac{L^3 - x^3}{x^2}\right) \tag{2.23b}$$

Equation (2.21a) can be re-written as

$$\frac{\partial(N_x x)}{\partial x} + \frac{1}{\cos\alpha_0}\frac{\partial N_{x\theta}}{\partial\theta} - N_\theta = 0 \tag{e}$$

Substituting for $N_{x\theta}$ and N_θ from Eqs. (2.23b) and (2.23a) and after integration, we get

$$N_x = -\frac{p\cos\theta}{x\cos\alpha_0}\left(-\frac{L^3}{3x} - \frac{x^2}{6} + \frac{x^2\cos^2\alpha_0}{2}\right) + \frac{f_2}{x} \tag{f}$$

where f_2 is an integration constant which can be determined using the boundary condition, that at $x = L$, $N_x = 0$. From this, f_2 can be determined as

$$f_2 = \frac{pL^2\cos\theta}{2\cos\alpha_0}[\cos^2\alpha_0 - 1] \tag{g}$$

Substituting for f_2 in Eq. (f) and after simplification, we obtain N_x as

$$N_x = \frac{p\cos\theta}{\cos\alpha_0}\left[\frac{L^3 - x^3}{3x^2} - \frac{L^2 - x^2}{2x}\sin^2\alpha_0\right] \tag{2.23c}$$

It can be seen that both N_x and $N_{x\theta}$ tend to infinity as we approach the apex of the conical shell, thus indicating that there is a singularity. However, these forces will be finite at a small distance from the apex. Figure 2.14 shows the distribution of the membrane forces in the conical shell.

For a truncated conical shell fixed at the bottom and free at top (chimney stack) and subjected to wind load, as shown in Fig. 2.15, the following boundary conditions can be used:

$$x = x_1, \; N_x = N_{x\theta} = 0$$

Using the above boundary conditions, the integration constants in Eqs. (c) and (f) can be determined as

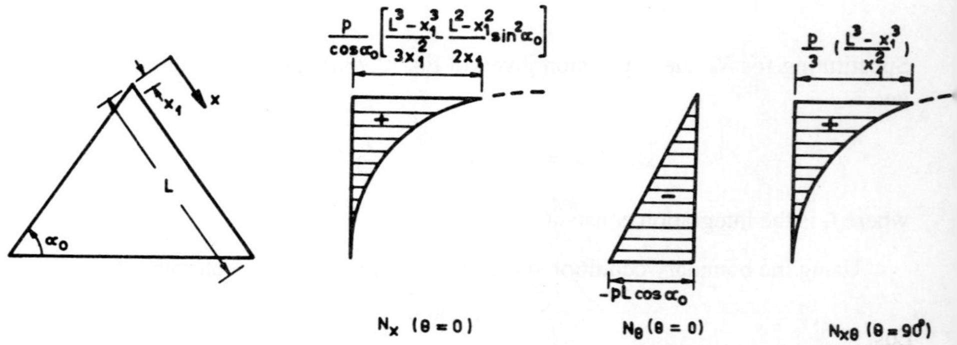

Fig. 2.14 Distribution of membrane forces in a conical shell due to wind load

$$f_1 = \frac{px_1^2 \sin\theta}{3} \tag{h}$$

and

$$f_2 = \frac{px_1^2 \cos\theta}{2\cos\alpha_0}(\cos^2\alpha_0 - 1) \tag{i}$$

Substituting the above constants in Eqs. (c) and (f), the membrane forces can be obtained as

$$N_x = -px\cos\alpha_0\cos\theta \tag{2.24a}$$

$$N_{x\theta} = \frac{px\sin\theta}{3}\left(\frac{x_1^3}{x^3} - 1\right) \tag{2.24b}$$

$$N_\theta = \frac{p\cos\theta}{\cos\alpha_0}\left(\frac{x_1^3 - x^3}{3x^2} - \frac{x_1^2 - x_1^2}{2x}\sin^2\alpha_0\right) \tag{2.24c}$$

Since the bottom end ($x = x_2$) is fixed, the displacements at the bottom end should be zero. The expressions for displacements in terms of the stress resultants can be obtained from Eqs. (2.22a–c) and (2.6a–c) as

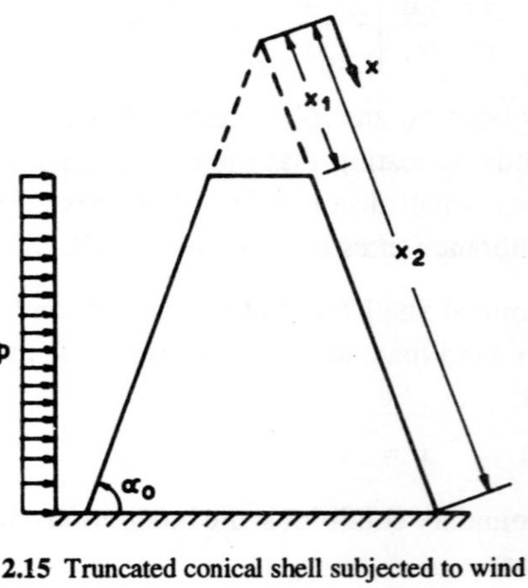

Fig. 2.15 Truncated conical shell subjected to wind load

$$u = \frac{1}{Eh} \int (N_x - \nu N_\theta)\, dx + f_3(\theta) \tag{2.25a}$$

$$v = x\left[\int \left(\frac{N_{x\theta}}{Gxh} - \frac{1}{x^2 \cos\alpha_0} \frac{\partial u}{\partial \theta} \right) dx + f_4(\theta)\right] \tag{2.25b}$$

$$w = \frac{x}{\tan\alpha_0}\left[\frac{1}{Eh}(N_\theta - \nu N_x) - \frac{u}{x} - \frac{1}{x\cos\alpha_0}\frac{\partial v}{\partial \theta}\right] \tag{2.25c}$$

The displacements can now be determined using Eqs. (2.25a–c) together with Eqs. (2.24a–c). Since the shell is fixed at the bottom edge, the displacements u, v, w, as well as slope $\partial w/\partial x$ should be zero. However, we have only two constants viz. f_3 and f_4 in Eqs. (2.25a, b) and hence, we can satisfy only two displacement boundary conditions. Taking the boundary conditions along the fixed edge as

$$x = x_2,\ u = v = 0$$

we can determine the constants f_3 and f_4 as

$$f_3 = -\frac{p\cos\theta}{Eh\cos\alpha_0}\left[-\frac{1}{6x_2}(2x_1^3 + x_2^3) - \frac{x_2^2 \sin^2\alpha_0}{4} \times \left(\frac{2x_1^2}{x_2^2}\log x_2 - 1\right) + \frac{\nu x_2^2 \cos^2\alpha_0}{2}\right] \tag{j}$$

$$f_4 = \frac{p\sin\theta}{Eh}\left[\left\{\frac{2x_2\,(1+\nu)}{3} + \frac{x_2}{3\cos^2\alpha_0}\right\}\left(\frac{x_1^3}{2x_2^3} + 1\right) - \frac{x_2\tan^2\alpha_0}{2}\left(\frac{x_1^2}{x_2^2} + 1\right) - \nu x_2\right] \tag{k}$$

The displacements can now be determined as

$$Ehu = \frac{p\cos\theta}{\cos\alpha_0}\left[\frac{x_1^3}{3x}\left(\frac{x}{x_2} - 1\right) - (x^2 - x_2^2) \times \left(\frac{1}{6} - \frac{\nu\cos^2\alpha_0}{2} - \frac{\sin^2\alpha_0}{4}\right) - \frac{x_1^2}{2}\sin^2\alpha_0 \log(x/x_2)\right] \tag{2.26a}$$

$$\begin{aligned} Ehv = p\sin\theta \Bigg[&\left(\frac{1+\nu}{2}\right)\left\{x_2\left(\frac{x_1^3}{x_2^3} + 2\right) - x\left(\frac{x_1^3}{x^3} + 2\right)\right\} \\ &+ \frac{1}{6x^2\cos\alpha_0}\left(x_1^2 - xx_2^2\right)\left(1 - \frac{x}{x_2}\right)^2 + \frac{x_1^2\tan^2\alpha_0}{2x}\log(x/x_2) \\ &+ \tan^2\alpha_0\left\{\frac{1}{4x}\left(x_2^2 + 2x_1^2 + x^2\right) - \frac{1}{2x_2}\left(x_1^2 + x_2^2\right)\right\} \\ &+ \frac{\nu}{2x}(x - x_2)^2 \Bigg] \end{aligned} \tag{2.26b}$$

$$Ehw = -\frac{px^2\cos\theta}{\sin\alpha_0}\left[\cos^2\alpha_0 + \nu\left\{\frac{x_1^3 - x^3}{3x^2} - \frac{x_1^2 - x^2}{2x^2}\sin^2\alpha_0\right\}\right]$$

$$-\frac{Eh}{\sin\alpha_0}(u\cos\alpha_0 + v\cot\theta) \qquad (2.26c)$$

As pointed out in the case of cantilever cylindrical shell subjected to wind load (Sec. 2.5.1.1 b), in this case also, the displacement boundary conditions $w = \partial w/\partial x = 0$, along the fixed edge, are not satisfied by the membrane solution. To satisfy these displacement boundary conditions, additional edge loads along $x = x_2$, have to be applied which causes local bending of the shell.

(b) Conical shell under dead load

Figure 2.16 shows a complete and a truncated conical shell subjected to dead load. Since the load has rotational symmetry, the shear force $N_{x\theta}$ and all the derivatives with respect to θ in the equilibrium Eqs. (2.21a – c) vanish. Hence, the equilibrium equations now reduce to the following form:

$$\frac{dN_x}{dx} + \frac{(N_x - N_\theta)}{x} + X = 0 \qquad (2.27a)$$

$$N_\theta + Zx\cot\alpha_0 = 0 \qquad (2.27b)$$

For the case of dead load, the load components can be determined as

$$X = -g\sin\alpha_0,\ Z = -g\cos\alpha_0 \qquad (a)$$

where g is the dead load per unit area.

From Eq. (2.27b), N_θ can be determined as

$$N_\theta = \frac{gx\cos^2\alpha_0}{\sin\alpha_0} \qquad (2.28a)$$

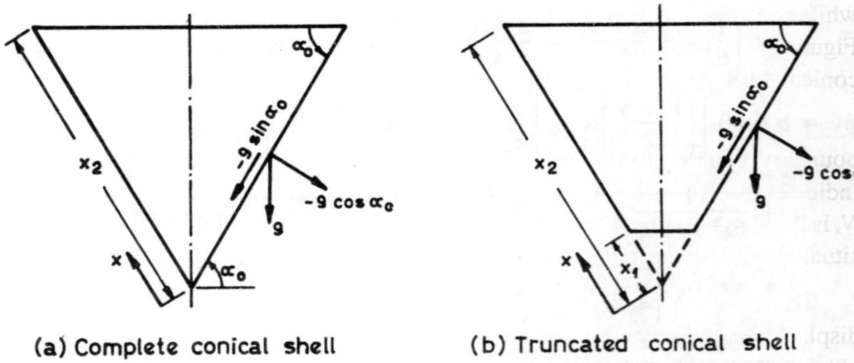

Fig. 2.16 Conical shell subjected to dead load

Equation (2.27a) can be rewritten as

$$\frac{d}{dx}\left(N_x x\right) - N_\theta + Xx = 0 \tag{b}$$

Substituting for N_θ, the expression given in Eq. (2.28a) and for X and integrating, we get

$$N_x = \frac{gx\cos^2\alpha_0}{2\sin\alpha_0} + \frac{gx\sin\alpha_0}{2} + \frac{f_1}{x} \tag{c}$$

where f_1 is an integration constant to be determined from the boundary condition.

For a complete conical shell at $x = 0$, N_x should be finite. To satisfy this condition, the integration constant f_1 must be zero. Hence, the force N_x is given by

$$N_x = \frac{gx}{2\sin\alpha_0} \tag{2.28b}$$

For a truncated conical shell, the following boundary condition may be used (assuming that the top end $x = x_2$ is hinged):

at $$x = x_1\,,\; N_x = 0 \tag{d}$$

Using this condition, the integration constant f_1 may be determined as

$$f_1 = -\frac{gx_1^2}{2\sin\alpha_0} \tag{e}$$

Substituting this in Eq. (c) and after simplification, we get

$$N_x = \frac{gx}{2\sin\alpha_0}\left[1 - \left(\frac{x_1}{x}\right)^2\right] \tag{2.29}$$

It may be noted that for a complete conical shell, both N_x and N_θ vary linearly, while for a truncated conical shell, N_θ varies linearly but N_x variation is nonlinear. Figure 2.17 shows the distribution of N_x and N_θ for a complete and truncated conical shell.

It must be recognized that in the analysis of a complete conical shell, no boundary condition was enforced at the edge $x = x_2$. The membrane theory indicates that N_x force exists at this edge. Hence, unless a support to give this force N_x is provided, a pure membrane state of stress will not exist in the shell. A similar situation also arises in the case of a truncated conical shell at the edge $x = x_2$.

For the above two cases, the displacement can also be determined. The strain displacement relations for a conical shell subjected to axisymmetric load can be obtained from Eqs. (2.22a – b) by omitting the derivatives with respect to θ, as well as the displacement component v.

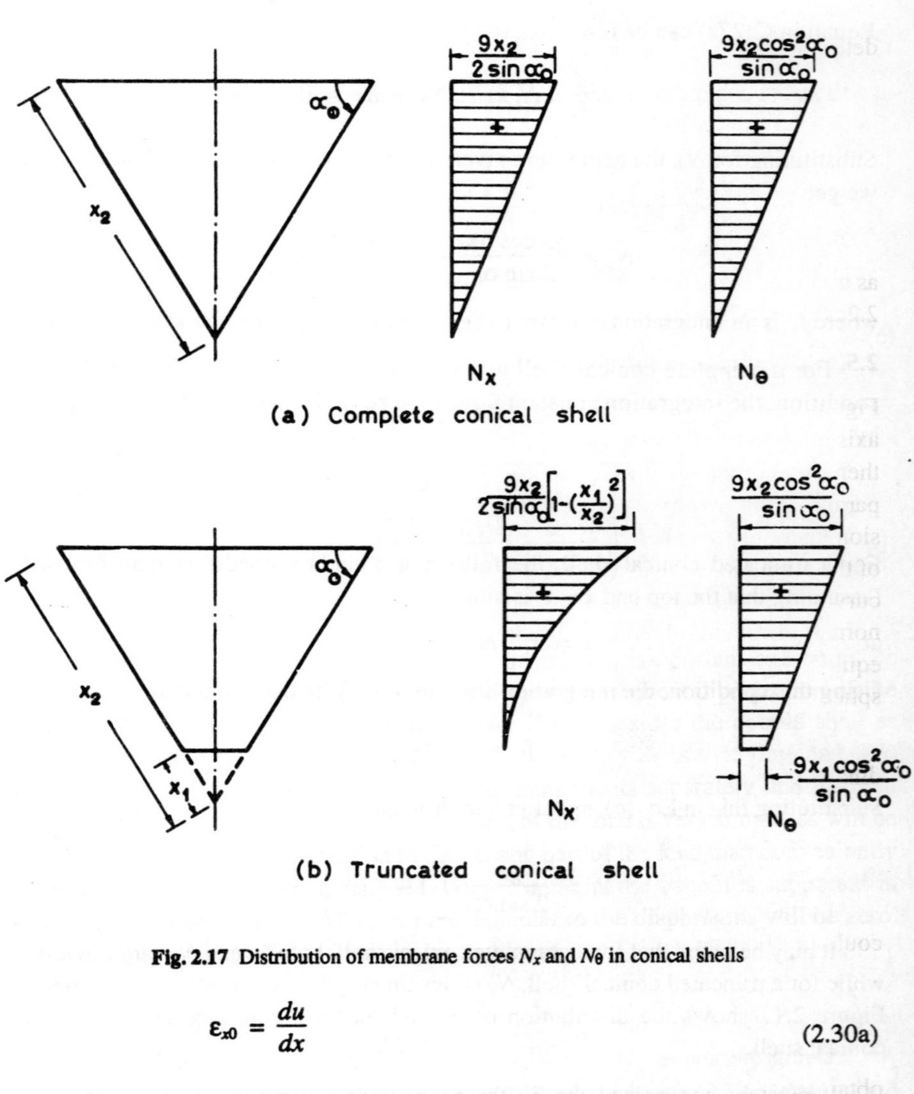

Fig. 2.17 Distribution of membrane forces N_x and N_θ in conical shells

$$\varepsilon_{x0} = \frac{du}{dx} \tag{2.30a}$$

$$\varepsilon_{\theta 0} = \frac{u}{x} + \frac{w}{x} \tan \alpha_0 \tag{2.30b}$$

The horizontal displacement and rotation can be determined from

$$\Delta H = r\varepsilon_{\theta 0} = \frac{r}{Eh} (N_\theta - \nu N_x) \tag{2.31a}$$

$$\beta = \frac{dw}{dx} = \cot \alpha_0 \left(\varepsilon_{\theta 0} + x \frac{d\varepsilon_{\theta 0}}{dx} - \varepsilon_{x0} \right) \tag{2.31b}$$

For a complete conical shell, the horizontal displacement and rotation can be determined as

$$\Delta H = \frac{gx^2}{Eh} \cot \alpha_0 \left(\cos^2 \alpha_0 - \nu / 2 \right) \tag{2.32a}$$

$$\beta = \frac{gx \cos \alpha_0}{Eh \sin^2 \alpha_0} \left[(2+\nu) \cos^2 \alpha_0 - \nu - \frac{1}{2} \right] \tag{2.32b}$$

The expressions for the membrane forces and displacements for complete, as well as truncated conical shells for several cases of axisymmetric load are given in Tables 2.2a, b and 2.3a, b (Ref. 2.2, 2.3).

2.5.3 Membrane Analysis of Spherical Shells

Figure 2.18a shows a shell surface generated by rotating a plane curve about an axis in its plane. If the plane curve is either an arc of a circle, or parabola or ellipse, then the corresponding surface generated would be a spherical surface or a paraboloid of revolution or an ellipsoid of revolution. We will restrict our discussion later only to spherical shells. Referring to Fig. 2.18b, the radius of curvature of the meridian is r_1 and the radius of the parallel circle is r_0. The second radius of curvature of the surface is r_2, which is the length between the intersection of the normal to the meridian surface with the axis of rotation. First, we will give the equilibrium equations valid for a shell of revolution and later on, specialise this for spherical shells.

The following identity can be established between the chosen (θ, ϕ) coordinate system here and the curvilinear coordinate

$$\alpha = \theta, \beta = \phi, A = r_0, B = r_1, R_1 = r_2, R_2 = r_1$$

$$N_\alpha = N_\theta, N_\beta = N_\phi \; N_{\alpha\beta} = N_{\theta\phi}$$

Further, referring to Fig. 2.18b and c, the following geometrical relations could be obtained.

$$r_0 = r_2 \sin \phi, \; \frac{dr_0}{d\phi} = r_1 \cos \phi \tag{a}$$

Using the above identity in Eqs. (2.3a–c) the equilibrium equations can be obtained as

$$\frac{\partial}{\partial \phi} (N_{\theta\phi} r_0) + r_1 \frac{\partial N_\theta}{\partial \theta} + N_{\theta\phi} \frac{\partial r_0}{\partial \phi} + X r_0 r_1 = 0 \tag{2.33a}$$

$$\frac{\partial}{\partial \phi} (N_\phi r_0) + r_1 \frac{\partial N_{\theta\phi}}{\partial \theta} - N_\theta \frac{\partial r_0}{\partial \phi} + Y r_0 r_1 = 0 \tag{2.33b}$$

$$\frac{N_\theta}{r_2} + \frac{N_\phi}{r_1} + Z = 0 \tag{2.33c}$$

Table 2.2a Membrane forces and displacements for a conical shell subjected to different types of load (supported at $x = x_2$)

Membrane force/displacement	Shell geometry and loading	
	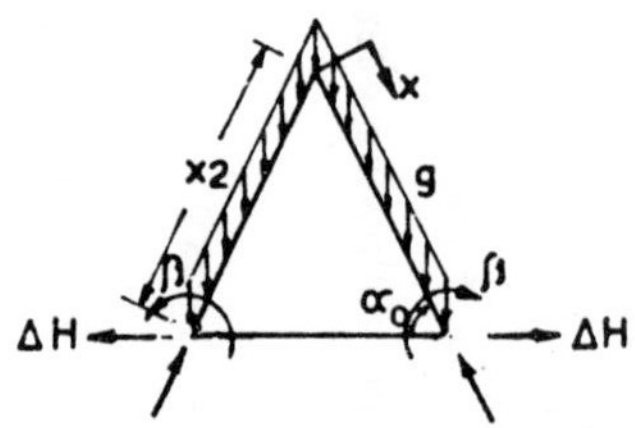 Dead load g (force/unit area)	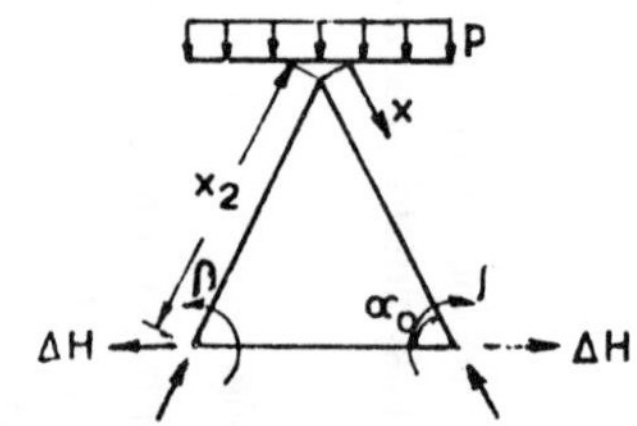 Uniform load p (force/unit area) acting on the horizontal projected area
N_x	$-\dfrac{gx}{2\sin\alpha_0}$	$-\dfrac{px}{2}\cot\alpha_0$
N_θ	$-\dfrac{gx\cos^2\alpha_0}{\sin\alpha_0}$	$-\dfrac{px\cos^3\alpha_0}{\sin\alpha_0}$
ΔH	$-\dfrac{gx_2^2}{Eh}\cot\alpha_0\left(\cos^2\alpha_0-\dfrac{\nu}{2}\right)$	$-\dfrac{px_2^2}{Eh}\cos\alpha_0\cot\alpha_0\left(\cos^2\alpha_0-\dfrac{\nu}{2}\right)$
β	$\dfrac{gx_2}{Eh}\left(\dfrac{\cos\alpha_0}{\sin^2\alpha_0}\right)\left[\cos^2\alpha_0(2+\nu)-\dfrac{1}{2}-\nu\right]$	$\dfrac{px_2}{Eh}\cot^2\alpha_0\left[\cos^2\alpha_0(2+\nu)-\dfrac{1}{2}-\nu\right]$

Table 2.2a (*Continued*)

Membrane force/displacement	Shell geometry and loading	
	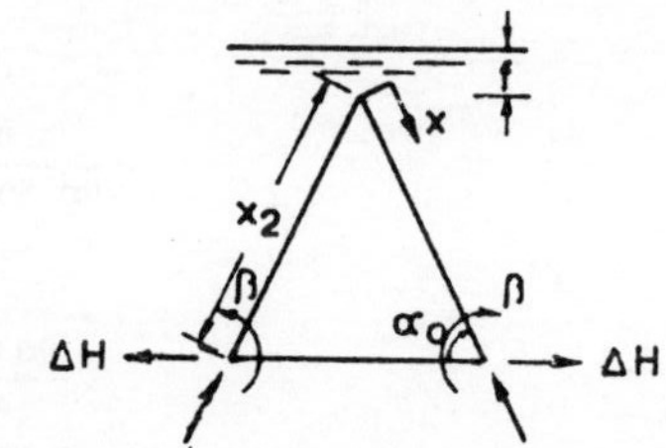 Filled with a liquid of density γ (force/unit volume)	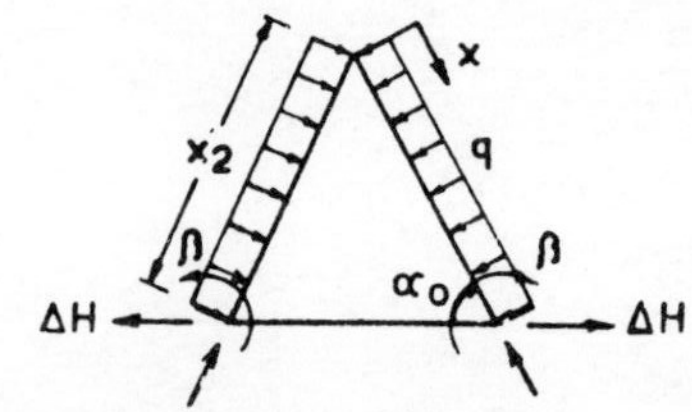 Uniform external pressure q (force/unit area)
N_x	$-\gamma x \cos\alpha_0 \left(\dfrac{f}{2\sin\alpha_0} + \dfrac{x}{3} \right)$	$-\dfrac{qx}{2}\cot\alpha_0$
N_θ	$-\gamma x \cos\alpha_0 \left[\dfrac{f}{\sin\alpha_0} + x \right]$	$-qx\cot\alpha_0$
ΔH	$\dfrac{\gamma x_2^2}{Eh}\cos^2\alpha_0 \left[\dfrac{f}{\sin\alpha_0} \left(\dfrac{\nu}{2} - 1 \right) + x_2 \left(\dfrac{\nu}{3} - 1 \right) \right]$	$-\dfrac{qx_2^2}{Eh}\cos\alpha_0 \cot\alpha_0 \left(1 - \dfrac{\nu}{2} \right)$
β	$\dfrac{\gamma x_2}{Eh}\dfrac{\cos^2\alpha_0}{\sin\alpha_0} \left[\dfrac{3}{2}\dfrac{f}{\sin\alpha_0} + \dfrac{8}{3}x_2 \right]$	$\dfrac{qx_2}{Eh}\left(\dfrac{3}{2} \right)\cot^2\alpha_0$

Table 2.2b Membrane forces and displacements for a conical shell subjected to different types of load (supported at $x = x_2$)

Membrane force/displacement	Shell geometry and loading	
	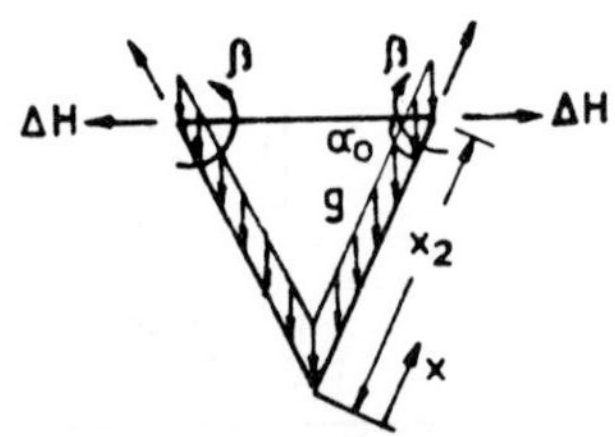 Dead load g (force/unit area)	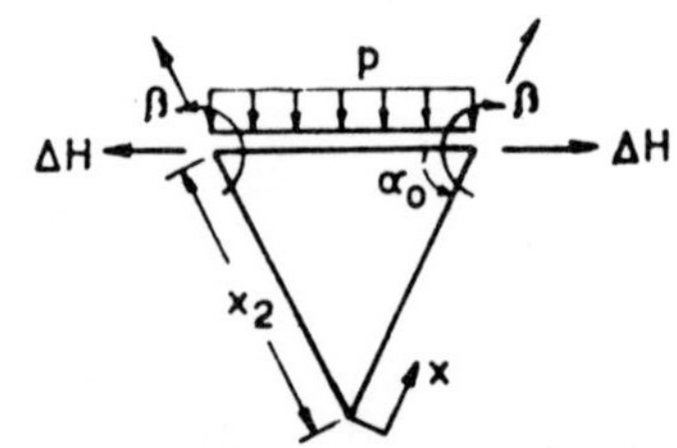 Uniform load p (force/unit area) acting on the horizontal projected area
N_x	$\dfrac{gx}{2\sin\alpha_0}$	$\dfrac{px}{2}\cot\alpha_0$
N_θ	$\dfrac{gx\cos^2\alpha_0}{\sin\alpha_0}$	$\dfrac{px\cos^3\alpha_0}{\sin\alpha_0}$
ΔH	$\dfrac{gx_2^2}{Eh}\cot\alpha_0\left(\cos^2\alpha_0-\dfrac{\nu}{2}\right)$	$\dfrac{px_2^2}{Eh}\cos\alpha_0\ \cot\alpha_0\left(\cos^2\alpha_0-\dfrac{\nu}{2}\right)$
β	$\dfrac{gx_2}{Eh}\dfrac{\cos\alpha_0}{\sin^2\alpha_0}\left[\cos^2\alpha_0(2+\nu)-\dfrac{1}{2}-\nu\right]$	$\dfrac{px_2}{Eh}\cot^2\alpha_0\left[\cos^2\alpha_0(2+\nu)-\dfrac{1}{2}-\nu\right]$

Table 2.2b (*Continued*)

Membrane force/displacement	Shell geometry and loading	
	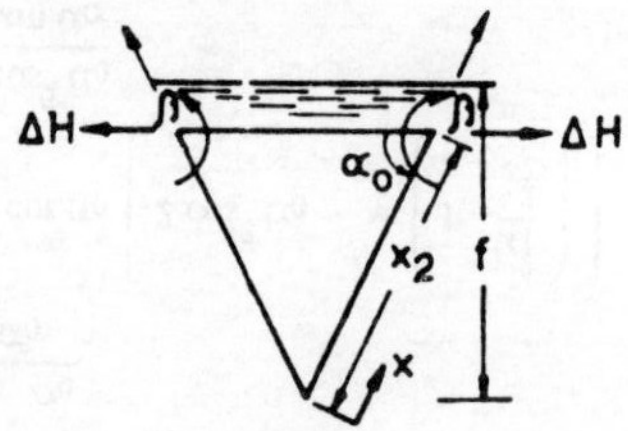 Filled with a liquid of density γ (force/unit area)	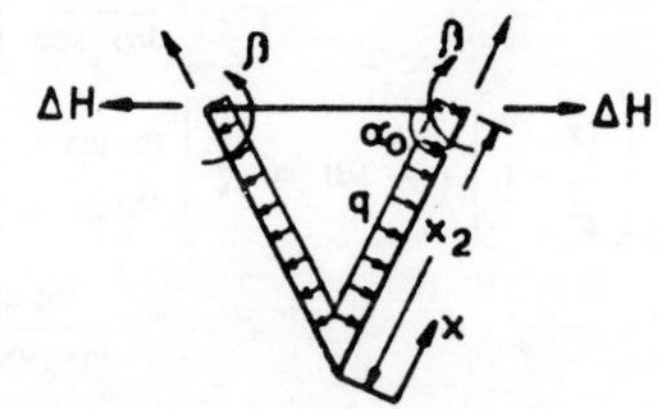 Uniform internal pressure q (force/unit area)
N_x	$-\gamma x \cos\alpha_0 \left(\frac{x}{3} - \frac{f}{2\sin\alpha_0}\right)$	$\frac{qx}{2}\cot\alpha_0$
N_θ	$-\gamma x \cos\alpha_0 \left(x - \frac{f}{\sin\alpha_0}\right)$	$qx\cot\alpha_0$
ΔH	$\frac{\gamma x_2^2}{Eh}\cos^2\alpha_0 \left[x_2\left(\frac{\nu}{3}-1\right) - \frac{f}{\sin\alpha_0}\left(\frac{\nu}{2}-1\right)\right]$	$\frac{qx_2^2}{Eh}\cos\alpha_0\cot\alpha_0\left(1-\frac{\nu}{2}\right)$
β	$\frac{\gamma x_2\cos^2\alpha_0}{Eh\sin\alpha_0}\left(-\frac{8}{3}x_2 + \frac{3}{2}\frac{f}{\sin\alpha_0}\right)$	$\frac{qx_2}{Eh}\left(\frac{3}{2}\right)\cot^2\alpha_0$

Table 2.3a Membrane forces and displacements for a truncated conical shell subjected to different types of load (supported at $x = x_2$)

Membrane force/displacement	Shell geometry and loading		
	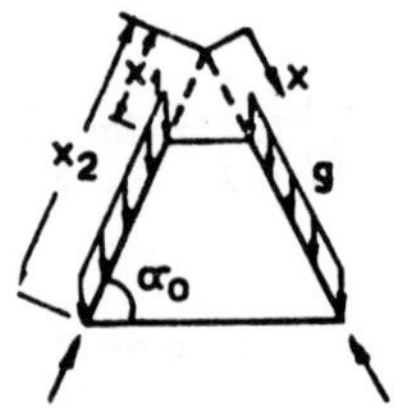 Dead load g (force/unit area)	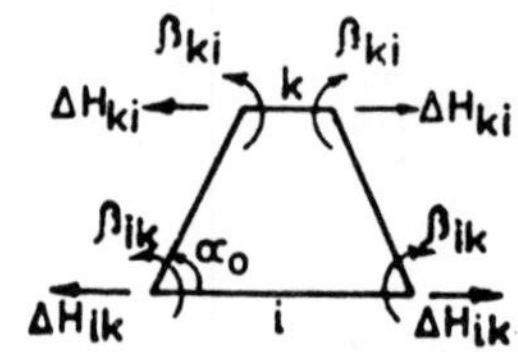 Edge displacements	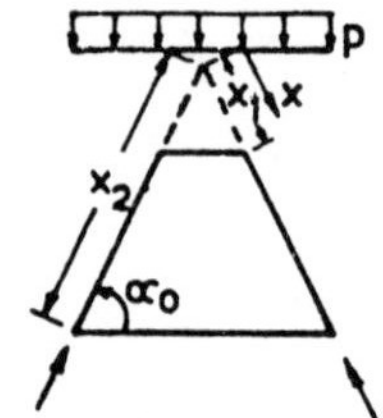 Uniform load p (force/unit area) acting on the horizontal projected area
N_x	$-\frac{gx}{2\sin\alpha_0}\left[1-\left(\frac{x_1}{x}\right)^2\right]$		$-\frac{1}{2}px\left[1-\left(\frac{x_1}{x}\right)^2\right]\cot\alpha_0$
N_θ	$-\frac{gx\cos^2\alpha_0}{\sin\alpha_0}$		$-\frac{px\cos^3\alpha_0}{\sin\alpha_0}$
ΔH_{ik}	$-\frac{gx_2^2}{2\,Eh}\cot\alpha_0\left[2\cos^2\alpha_0-\nu\left(1-\frac{x_1^2}{x_2^2}\right)\right]$		$-\frac{px_2^2}{Eh}\frac{\cos^2\alpha_0}{2\sin\alpha_0}\left[2\cos^2\alpha_0-\nu\left(1-\frac{x_1^2}{x_2^2}\right)\right]$
ΔH_{ki}	$-\frac{gx_1^2}{Eh}\frac{\cos^3\alpha_0}{\sin\alpha_0}$		$-\frac{px_1^2}{Eh}\frac{\cos^4\alpha_0}{\sin\alpha_0}$
β_{ik}	$\frac{gx_2}{Eh}\frac{\cos\alpha_0}{2\sin^2\alpha_0}\left[2\cos^2\alpha_0(2+\nu)-1-2\nu+\left(\frac{x_1}{x_2}\right)^2\right]$		$\frac{gx_2}{Eh}\frac{\cot^2\alpha_0}{2}\left[2\cos^2\alpha_0(2+\nu)-1-2\nu+\left(\frac{x_1}{x_2}\right)^2\right]$
β_{ki}	$\frac{gx_1}{Eh}\frac{\cos\alpha_0}{\sin^2\alpha_0}[\cos^2\alpha_0(2+\nu)-\nu]$		$\frac{px_1}{Eh}\cot^2\alpha_0[\cos^2\alpha_0(2+\nu)-\nu]$

Table 2.3a (Continued)

Membrane force/displacement	Shell geometry and loading		
	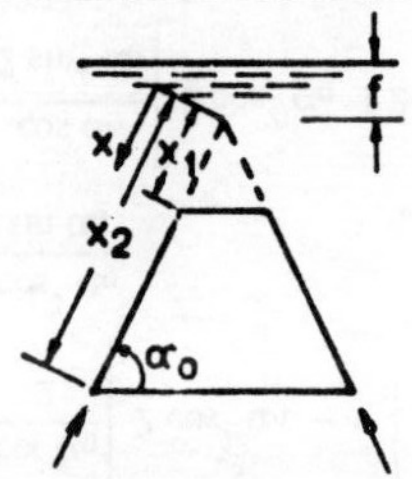 Filled with liquid of density γ (force/unit volume)	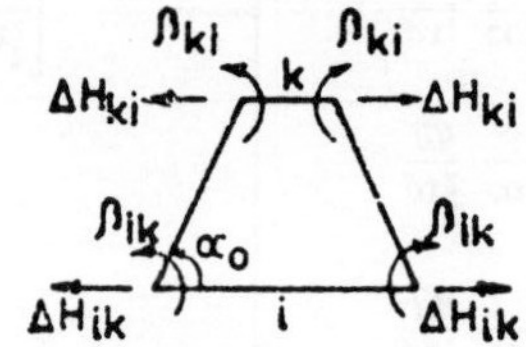 Edge displacements	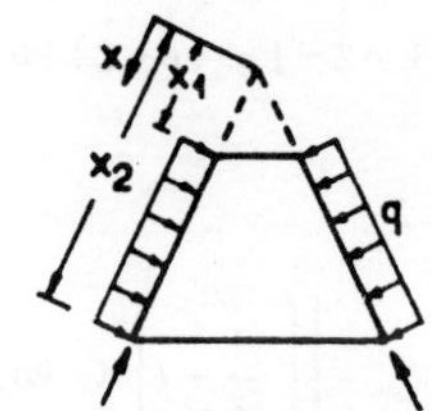 Uniform external pressure q (force/unit area)
N_x	$-\gamma x \cos\alpha_0 \left[\frac{f}{2\sin\alpha_0}\left\{1-\left(\frac{x_1}{x}\right)^2\right\} + \frac{x}{3}\left\{1-\left(\frac{x_1}{x}\right)^3\right\}\right]$		$-\frac{qx}{2}\cot\alpha_0\left[1-\left(\frac{x_1}{x}\right)^2\right]$
N_θ	$-\gamma x\cos\alpha_0\left(\frac{f}{\sin\alpha_0}+x\right)$		$-qx\cot\alpha_0$
ΔH_{ik}	$\frac{\gamma x_2^2}{Eh}\cos^2\alpha_0\left[\nu\left\{\frac{x_2}{3}\left(1-\frac{x_1^3}{x_2^3}\right)+\frac{f}{2\sin\alpha_0}\left(1-\frac{x_1^2}{x_2^2}\right)\right\}-\frac{f}{\sin\alpha_0}-x_2\right]$		$-\frac{qx_2^2}{Eh}\cos\alpha_0\cot\alpha_0\left[1-\frac{\nu}{2}\left(1-\frac{x_1^2}{x_2^2}\right)\right]$
ΔH_{ki}	$\frac{\gamma x_1^2}{Eh}\cos^2\alpha_0\left(-\frac{f}{\sin\alpha_0}-x_1\right)$		$-\frac{q x_1^2}{Eh}\cos\alpha_0\cot\alpha_0$
β_{ik}	$\frac{\gamma x_2}{Eh}\frac{\cos^2\alpha_0}{\sin\alpha_0}\left[\frac{f}{2\sin\alpha_0}\left(3+\frac{x_1^2}{x_2^2}\right)+\frac{x_2}{3}\left(8+\frac{x_1^3}{x_2^3}\right)\right]$		$\frac{q x_2}{Eh}\frac{\cot^2\alpha_0}{2}\left[3+\frac{x_1^2}{x_2^2}\right]$
β_{ki}	$\frac{\gamma x_1}{Eh}\frac{\cos^2\alpha_0}{\sin\alpha_0}\left[\frac{2f}{\sin\alpha_0}+3x_1\right]$		$\frac{2qx_1}{Eh}\cot^2\alpha_0$

Table 2.3b Membrane forces and displacements for a truncated conical shell subjected to different types of load (supported at $x = x_1$)

Membrane force/displacement	Shell geometry and loading	
	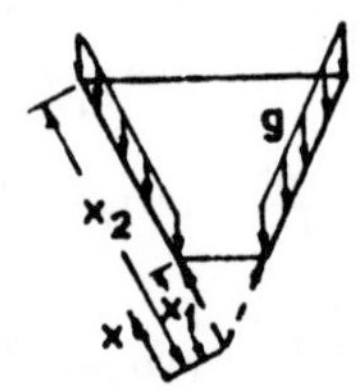 Dead load g (force/unit area) 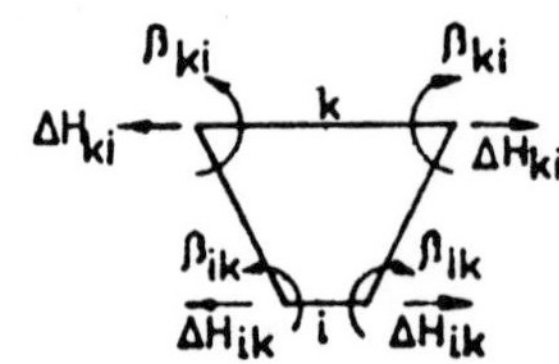 Edge displacements	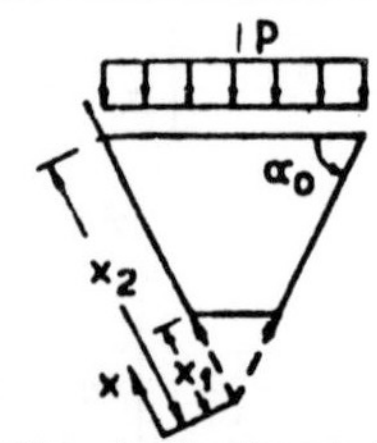 Uniform load p (force/unit area) acting on the horizontal projected area
N_x	$\frac{gx}{2\sin\alpha_0}\left(1-\frac{x_2^2}{x^2}\right)$	$\frac{1}{2}px\left(1-\frac{x_2^2}{x^2}\right)\cot\alpha_0$
N_θ	$gx\,\frac{\cos^2\alpha_0}{\sin\alpha_0}$	$px\,\frac{\cos^3\alpha_0}{\sin\alpha_0}$
ΔH_{ik}	$\frac{gx_1^2}{Eh}\,\frac{\cot\alpha_0}{2}\left[2\cos^2\alpha_0-\nu\left(1-\frac{x_2^2}{x_1^2}\right)\right]$	$\frac{px_1^2}{Eh}\,\frac{\cos^2\alpha_0}{2\sin\alpha_0}\left[2\cos^2\alpha_0-\nu\left(1-\frac{x_2^2}{x_1^2}\right)\right]$
ΔH_{ki}	$\frac{gx_2^2}{Eh}\,\frac{\cos^3\alpha_0}{\sin\alpha_0}$	$\frac{px_2^2}{Eh}\,\frac{\cos^4\alpha_0}{\sin\alpha_0}$
β_{ik}	$\frac{gx_1}{Eh}\,\frac{\cos\alpha_0}{2\sin^2\alpha_0}\left[2\cos^2\alpha_0\,(2+\nu)-1-2\nu+\frac{x_2^2}{x_1^2}\right]$	$\frac{px_1}{Eh}\,\frac{\cot^2\alpha_0}{2}\left[2\cos^2\alpha_0\,(2+\nu)-1-2\nu+\frac{x_2^2}{x_1^2}\right]$
β_{ki}	$\frac{gx_2}{Eh}\,\frac{\cos\alpha_0}{\sin^2\alpha_0}\,[\cos^2\alpha_0\,(2+\nu)-\nu]$	$\frac{px_2}{Eh}\,\cot^2\alpha_0\,[\cos^2\alpha_0\,(2+\nu)-\nu]$

Table 2.3b (*Continued*)

Membrane force/displacement	Shell geometry and loading		
	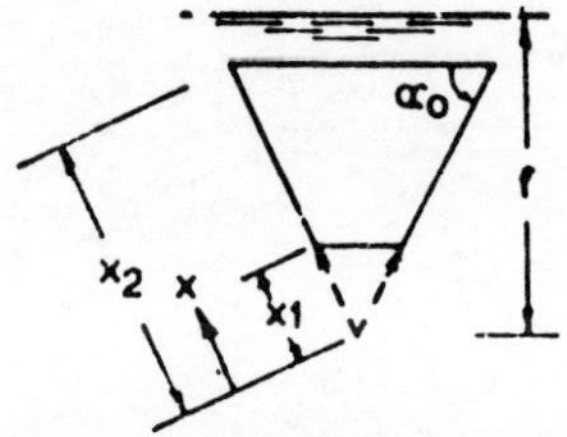 Filled with liquid of density γ (force/unit volume)	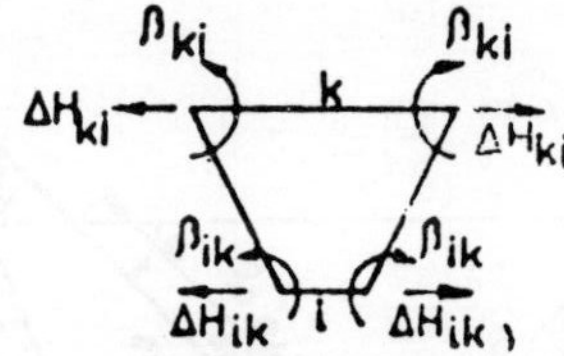 Edge displacements	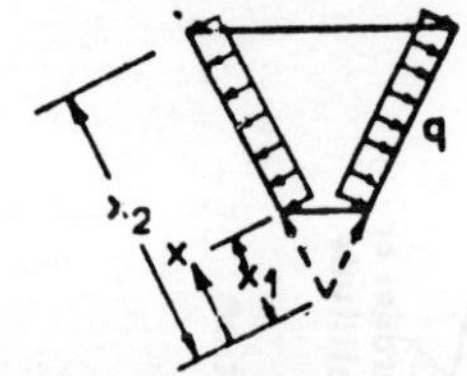 Uniform internal pressure q (force/unit area)
N_x	$-\gamma x \cos\alpha_0 \left\{\frac{x}{3}\left(1-\frac{x_2^3}{x^3}\right)-\frac{f}{2\sin\alpha_0}\left(1-\frac{x_2^2}{x^2}\right)\right\}$		$\frac{qx}{2}\cot\alpha_0\left(1-\frac{x_2^2}{x^2}\right)$
N_θ	$-\gamma x \cos\alpha_0\left(x-\frac{f}{\sin\alpha_0}\right)$		$qx\cot\alpha_o$
ΔH_{ik}	$\frac{\gamma x_1^2}{Eh}\cos^2\alpha_0\left[\nu\left\{\frac{x_1}{3}\left(1-\frac{x_2^3}{x_1^3}\right)-\frac{f}{2\sin\alpha_0}\left(1-\frac{x_2^2}{x_1^2}\right)\right\}+\frac{f}{\sin\alpha_0}-x_1\right]$		$\frac{qx_1^2}{Eh}\cos\alpha_0\cot\alpha_0\left[1-\frac{\nu}{2}\left(1-\frac{x_2^2}{x_1^2}\right)\right]$
ΔH_{ki}	$\frac{\gamma x_2^2}{Eh}\cos^2\alpha_0\left(\frac{f}{\sin\alpha_0}-x_2\right)$		$\frac{qx_2^2}{Eh}\cos\alpha_0\cot\alpha_0$
β_{ik}	$\frac{\gamma x_1}{Eh}\frac{\cos^2\alpha_0}{\sin\alpha_0}\left[\frac{f}{2\sin\alpha_0}\left(3+\frac{x_2^2}{x_1^2}\right)-\frac{x_1}{3}\left(8+\frac{x_2^3}{x_1^3}\right)\right]$		$\frac{qx_1}{Eh}\frac{\cot^2\alpha_0}{2}\left[3+\frac{x_2^2}{x_1^2}\right]$
β_{ki}	$\frac{\gamma x_2}{Eh}\frac{\cos^2\alpha_0}{\sin\alpha_0}\left\{\frac{2f}{\sin\alpha_0}-3x_2\right\}$		$\frac{2qx_2}{Eh}\cot^2\alpha_0$

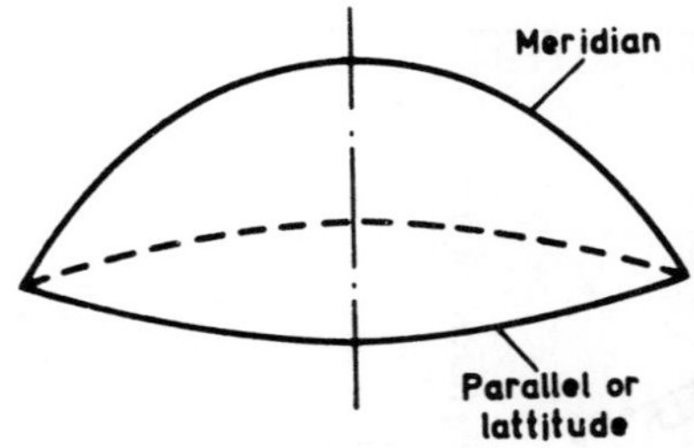

(a) Shell of revolution

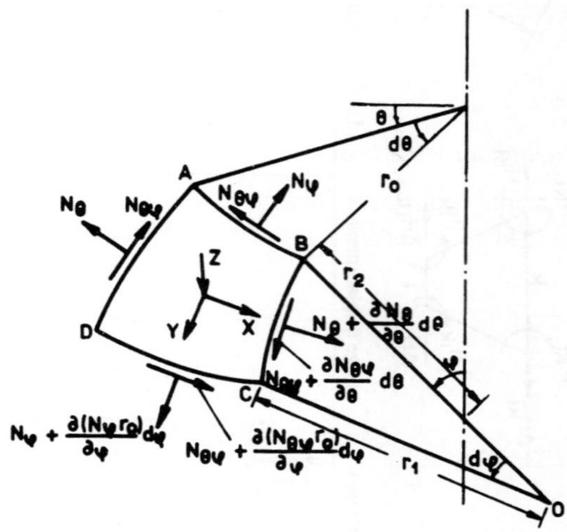

(b) Shell element showing membrane force

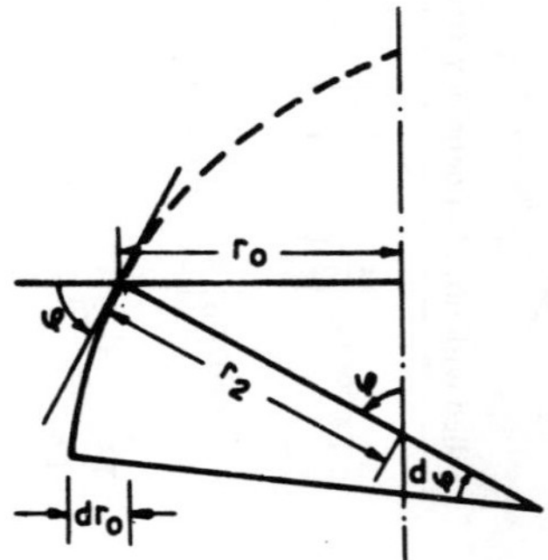

(c) Meridian of a shell of revolution

Fig. 2.18 A general shell of revolution; (a) Shell of revolution; (b) Shell element showing membrane force; (c) Meridian of a shell of revolution

The strain-displacement relation can be obtained, using the above identity in Eqs. (2.4a–c), as

$$\varepsilon_{\theta 0} = \frac{1}{r_0}\frac{\partial u}{\partial \theta} + \frac{v}{r_0\, r_1}\frac{\partial r_0}{\partial \phi} + \frac{w}{r_2} \tag{2.34a}$$

$$\varepsilon_{\phi 0} = \frac{1}{r_1}\frac{\partial u}{\partial \phi} + \frac{w}{r_1} \tag{2.34b}$$

$$\gamma_{\theta\phi 0} = \frac{1}{r_0}\frac{\partial v}{\partial \theta} + \frac{1}{r_1}\frac{\partial u}{\partial \phi} - \frac{u}{r_0\, r_1}\frac{\partial r_0}{\partial \phi} \tag{2.34c}$$

We will consider some examples to illustrate the application of the above equations.

2.5.3.1 Examples

(a) Spherical shell under wind load

Let us consider a spherical dome subjected to windload (Fig. 2.19). As shown earlier, the wind load components are

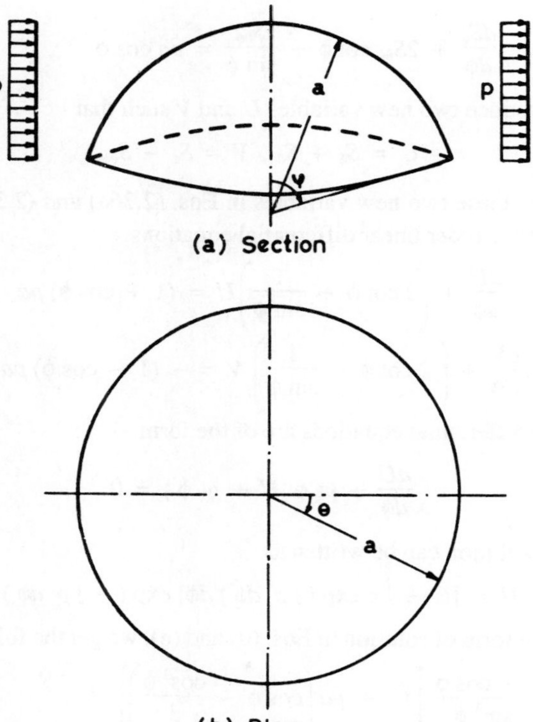

Fig. 2.19 Spherical dome subjected to wind load

$$X = Y = 0, \;\; Z = -\, p \sin\phi \cos\theta \qquad \text{(a)}$$

The three equilibrium Eqs. (2.33a–c) can be reduced to the following two equations by eliminating N_θ from these equations. Further, since we are dealing with a spherical dome, $r_1 = r_2 = a$. Hence, the reduced equations are

$$-\frac{\partial N_\phi}{\partial \theta} + \sin\phi \frac{\partial N_{\theta\phi}}{\partial \phi} + 2N_{\theta\phi}\cos\phi = a\frac{\partial Z}{\partial \theta} \qquad (2.35a)$$

$$\sin\phi \frac{\partial N_\phi}{\partial \phi} + 2N_\phi \cos\phi + \frac{\partial N_{\theta\phi}}{\partial \theta} = -\, Za\cos\phi \qquad (2.35b)$$

The solution can be written in the form

$$N_\phi = S_\phi \cos\theta, \; N_\theta = S_\theta \cos\theta, \; N_{\theta\phi} = S_{\theta\phi}\sin\theta \qquad \text{(b)}$$

where S_ϕ, S_θ and $S_{\theta\phi}$ are functions of ϕ only.

Now introducing Eqs. (a) and (b) into the differential equations (2.35a) and (2.35b), we get the following set of ordinary differential equations:

$$\frac{dS_{\theta\phi}}{d\phi} + 2S_{\theta\phi}\cot\phi + \frac{S_\phi}{\sin\phi} = pa \qquad (2.36a)$$

$$\frac{dS_\phi}{d\phi} + 2S_{\theta\phi}\cot\phi + \frac{S_{\theta\phi}}{\sin\phi} = pa\cos\phi \qquad (2.36b)$$

Let us now introduce two new variables U and V such that

$$U = S_\phi + S_{\theta\phi}, \; V = S_\phi - S_{\theta\phi} \qquad (2.36c)$$

Introducing these two new variables in Eqs. (2.36a) and (2.36b), we get the following two first-order linear differential equations:

$$\frac{dU}{d\phi} + \left(2\cot\phi + \frac{1}{\sin\phi}\right)U = (1 + \cos\phi)\, pa \qquad (2.36d)$$

$$\frac{dV}{d\phi} + \left(2\cot\phi - \frac{1}{\sin\phi}\right)V = -\,(1 - \cos\phi)\, pa \qquad (2.36e)$$

The above two differential equations are of the form

$$\frac{dU}{d\phi} + p(\phi)U + g(\phi) = 0 \qquad (2.36f)$$

whose general solution can be written as

$$U = [C - \textstyle\int g \exp(\int p \; d\phi)\, d\phi] \exp(-\int p \; d\phi) \qquad (2.36g)$$

Using the above form of solution in Eqs. (d) and (e), we get the following solution

$$U = \frac{1+\cos\phi}{\sin^3\phi}\left[C_1 + pa\left(\cos\phi - \frac{\cos^3\phi}{3}\right)\right] \qquad (2.36h)$$

$$V = \frac{1-\cos\phi}{\sin^3\phi}\left[C_2 - pa\left(\cos\phi - \frac{\cos^3\phi}{3}\right)\right] \qquad (2.36i)$$

Using now the following relation, which can be obtained from Eqs. (b) and (c),

$$N_\phi = \left(\frac{U+V}{2}\right)\cos\theta,\ N_{\theta\phi} = \left(\frac{U-V}{2}\right)\sin\theta \tag{2.36j}$$

We can now obtain N_ϕ and $N_{\theta\phi}$ as

$$N_\phi = \frac{\cos\theta}{\sin^3\phi}\left[\frac{C_1+C_2}{2} + \frac{C_1-C_2}{2} \times \cos\phi + pa\left(\cos^2\phi - \frac{1}{3}\cos^4\phi\right)\right] \tag{2.36k}$$

$$N_{\theta\phi} = \frac{\sin\theta}{\sin^3\phi}\left[\frac{C_1-C_2}{2} + \frac{C_1+C_2}{2} \times \cos\phi + pa\left(\cos\phi - \frac{1}{3}\cos^3\phi\right)\right] \tag{2.36l}$$

where C_1 and C_2 are constants. For the spherical shell at $\phi = 0$, the above forces should be finite and this condition gives

$$C_1 = -\frac{2}{3}pa,\ C_2 = \frac{2}{3}pa \tag{2.36m}$$

Substituting for C_1 and C_2 in Eqs. (2.36k) and (2.36l) and after simplification, we get

$$N_\phi = -\frac{pa\cos\theta\cos\phi}{3\sin\phi\ (1+\cos\phi)}\left[(2+\cos\phi)\ (1-\cos\phi)\right] \tag{2.37a}$$

$$N_{\theta\phi} = -\frac{pa\ (2+\cos\phi)\ (1-\cos\phi)}{3\ (1+\cos\phi)\ \sin\phi}\sin\theta \tag{2.37b}$$

Substituting for N_ϕ in Eq. (2.33c), we get N_θ as

$$N_\theta = \frac{pa}{3}\,\frac{(3+4\cos\phi + 2\cos^2\phi)\ (1-\cos\phi)}{(1+\cos\phi)\ \sin\phi}\cos\theta \tag{2.37c}$$

The distribution of these forces for a semicircular dome is shown in Fig. 2.20.

Normally, the membrane force N_ϕ must equilibrate the moment due to wind load, with respect to the diameter $\phi = \pi/2$. As we have considered here a hemispherical shell, all the external forces pass through the centre of the sphere and hence, the moment is zero. It is obvious that for a hemispherical shell, the resultant of wind force is equilibrated by the shear force $N_{\theta\phi}$ at $\phi = \pi/2$. If a support to give this reactive shear force at $\phi = \pi/2$ if provided, then a pure membrane state of stress would exist in the shell.

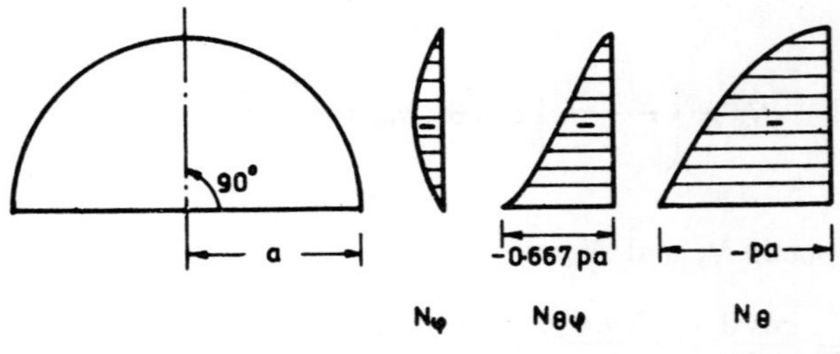

Fig. 2.20 Membrane force distribution in a semicircular dome under wind load

(b) Spherical storage tank

Figure 2.21 shows a complete spherical tank supported on a ring beam and columns at one of its parallel circles *AA*. It is assumed that the tank is completely filled with a liquid of density γ. The analysis is done here considering only the pressure due to the liquid. It is obvious that the load is symmetrical about the axis of revolution. Hence the equilibrium Eqs. (2.33a–c) will now reduce to

$$\frac{d}{d\phi}(N_\phi r_0) - N_\theta \frac{dr_0}{d\phi} + Yr_0 r_1 = 0 \tag{2.38a}$$

$$\frac{N_\theta}{r_2} + \frac{N_\phi}{r_1} + Z = 0 \tag{2.38b}$$

The strain-displacement relation given in Eqs. (2.34a–c) will now reduce to

$$\varepsilon_{\theta 0} = \frac{v}{r_2}\cot\phi + \frac{w}{r_2} \tag{2.39a}$$

$$\varepsilon_{\phi 0} = \frac{dv}{r_1 d\phi} + \frac{w}{r_1} \tag{2.39b}$$

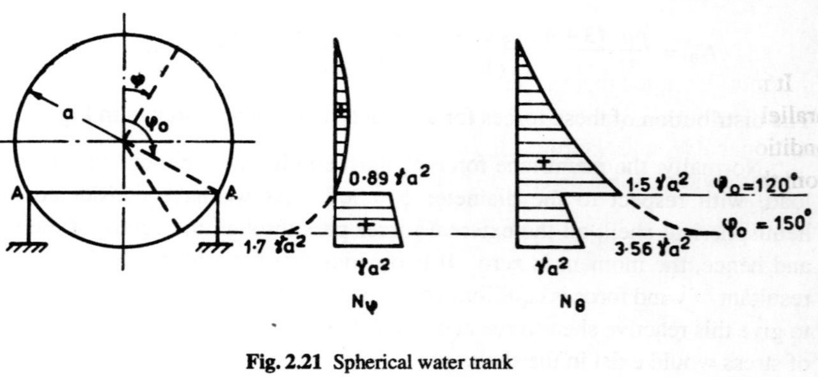

Fig. 2.21 Spherical water trank

Eliminating N_θ from Eq. (2.38a) by using Eq. (2.38b), then using the relation $r_0 = r_2 \sin\phi$, $dr_0/d\phi = r_1 \cos\phi$ and after multiplying throughout by $\sin\phi$, we get

$$\frac{d}{d\phi}\,(N_\phi\, r_2 \sin\phi)\,\sin\phi + r_2\, N_\phi\, \cos\phi \sin\phi = -\,r_1 r_2 \sin\phi\,\,(Z\cos\phi + Y\sin\phi)$$

which can be written as

$$\frac{d}{d\phi}\,(r_2\, N_\phi \sin^2\phi) = -\,r_1 r_2 \sin\phi\,(Z\cos\phi + Y\sin\phi) \qquad \text{(a)}$$

Integrating the above equation, N_ϕ may be determined as

$$N_\phi = -\frac{1}{r_2 \sin^2\phi}\left[\int r_1 r_2 \sin\phi\,\,(Z\cos\phi + Y\sin\phi)\,d\phi + C\right] \qquad (2.40)$$

For the case of a spherical tank completely filled with liquid, we have the load components

$$Y = 0,\;\; Z = -\,\gamma a\,(1 - \cos\phi) \qquad \text{(b)}$$

and $$r_1 = r_2 = a$$

Substituting this in Eq. (2.40), we get

$$N_\phi = \frac{\gamma a^2}{6\sin^2\phi}\,\left[(2\cos\phi - 3)\,\cos^2\phi + 6C\right]$$

To determine the integration constant C, we enforce the condition that N_ϕ must be finite at $\phi = 0$. From this condition, we determine $C = 1/6$. Hence, the expression for N_ϕ can now be written as

$$N_\phi = \frac{\gamma a^2}{6}\left(\frac{1-\cos\phi}{1+\cos\phi}\right)(1 + 2\,\cos\phi) \qquad (2.41a)$$

Using the above expression for N_ϕ in Eq. (2.38b), N_ϕ can be determined as

$$N_\phi = \frac{\gamma a^2}{6}\left(\frac{1-\cos\phi}{1+\cos\phi}\right)(5 + 4\,\cos\phi) \qquad (2.41b)$$

It must be noted that the above expressions for N_ϕ and N_θ are valid above the parallel circle AA, i.e. $\phi \le \phi_0$. For the lower part, i.e. $\phi > \phi_0$, we enforce the condition that N_ϕ must be finite at $\phi = \pi$ for determining the integration constant C. From this condition, we determine $C = 5/6$. Hence, for $\phi > \phi_0$, we have

$$N_\phi = \frac{\gamma a^2}{6}\left(\frac{5 - 5\,\cos\phi + 2\cos^2\phi}{1 - \cos\phi}\right) \qquad (2.42a)$$

$$N_\theta = \frac{\gamma a^2}{6}\left(\frac{1 - 7\,\cos\phi + 4\cos^2\phi}{1 - \cos\phi}\right) \qquad (2.42b)$$

It is interesting to note that the expressions for the forces obtained for $\phi \leq \phi_0$ and $\phi > \phi_0$ are not influenced by the position of the support *AA*. In Fig. 2.21, the distribution of membrane forces, for the case $\phi_0 = 120°$ and $150°$, are presented. The results are presented for these two cases to illustrate the effect of the position of the support on the forces.

If the support is provided at an angle of 120°, Eqs. (2.41a) and (2.41b) indicate that both N_ϕ and N_θ will be tensile in region $0 < \phi < 120°$. At the support, N_ϕ and N_θ can be determined as zero and $1.5\ \gamma a^2$ respectively. If, on the other hand, a support is provided at an angle of 150°, then N_ϕ changes to compression in the region $120° < \phi < 150°$ while N_ϕ continues to be tensile (Fig. 2.21). It may be noted that the magnitudes of N_ϕ and N_θ, at the support, computed from Eqs. (2.40a) and (2.40b) and Eqs. (2.42a) and (2.42b) will not be the same. For example, when the support, is provided at an angle of 120° at the support, N_ϕ and N_θ can be determined from Eqs. (2.42a) and (2.42b), as $0.89\ \gamma a^2$ and $0.61\ \gamma a^2$ as compared to zero and 1.5 γa^2, as given by Eqs. (2.40a) and (2.40b). This indicates that the stress resultants are discontinuous at the support.

The calculation of displacements at this section also indicates a discontinuity which physically cannot happen. The continuity of displacement may be rees-tablished by applying additional forces causing bending in the border zone of the two halves. Hence, the membrane stress resultants obtained here for the two halves will be valid only at sections farther away from the support.

(c) Spherical dome under dead load

From Fig. 2.22, the load components can be determined as

$$Y = g \sin \phi, \quad Z = g \cos \phi \tag{a}$$

Introducing this in Eq. (2.40) with $r_1 = r_2 = a$, we get

$$N_\phi = -\frac{1}{a \sin^2 \phi} \int_0^\phi a^2 g \sin \phi \, d\phi + C$$

$$= -\frac{1}{a \sin^2 \phi} [-a^2 g \cos \phi + C] \tag{b}$$

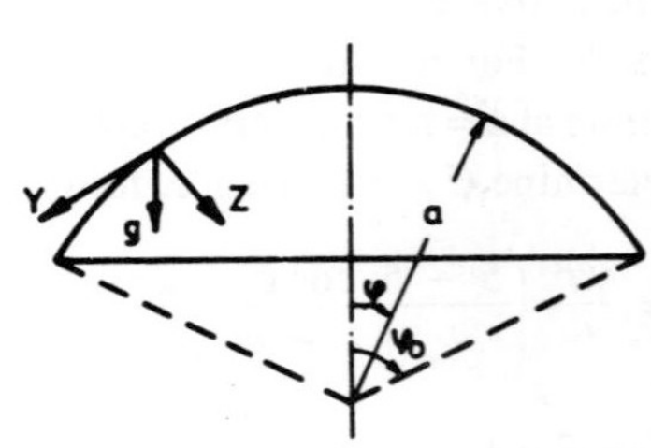

Fig. 2.22 Spherical dome under dead load

The integration constant C is determined by enforcing the condition that at $\phi = 0$, N_ϕ must be finite. This condition results in the following value for C:

$$C = ga^2 \tag{c}$$

Substituting this in Eq. (b) and after simplification, we get

$$N_\phi = -\frac{ga}{1 + \cos\phi} \tag{2.43a}$$

Substituting for N_ϕ from Eq. (2.43a) in Eq. (2.38b), N_θ can be determined as

$$N_\theta = ga\left(\frac{1}{1 + \cos\phi} - \cos\phi\right) \tag{2.43b}$$

It is interesting to note that at $\phi = 0$, both N_ϕ and N_θ are equal and equal to $-ga/2$. With increase in ϕ, N_θ decreases and becomes tensile for $\phi > 51.82°$. Further, at $\phi = \phi_0$ (Fig. 2.22), we find that N_ϕ would not be zero and this force gets transmitted to the supporting member. However, the reaction provided by the supporting member will not be the same and hence the membrane theory breaks down near the edge.

The horizontal displacement, ΔH and rotation β can be determined from

$$\Delta H = r\varepsilon_\theta = \frac{a\sin\phi}{Eh}(N_\theta - \nu N_\phi) \tag{2.44a}$$

$$\beta = \frac{v}{a} - \frac{dw}{a\,d\phi}$$

$$= \frac{\cot\phi}{Eh}(1 + \nu)(N_\phi - N_\theta) - \frac{1}{Eh}\frac{d}{d\phi}(N_\theta - \nu N_\phi) \tag{2.44b}$$

Following the above procedure, spherical domes with different types of load, including lantern load could be solved. The expressions for the membrane forces and displacements for different types of load are given in Tables 2.4a, b and 2.5a, b (Ref. 2.2, 2.3). In all the cases given in these Tables, it is assumed that the edge $\phi = \phi_1$ or ϕ_2 is supported. A spherical dome-shaped water tower is shown in Fig. 2.23.

(d) Ogival shell

In the case of a spherical shell, the meridian meets the axis of revolution at right angles. If, on the other hand, the meridian does not meet the axis of revolution at right angles, then a shell with pointed apex results. We will study now an example of this type of shell. If the meridian of the shell is an arc of a circle whose centre does not lie on the axis of revolution, then we get an Ogival shell (Fig. 2.24). Though one of the radius of curvature r_1 of the meridian is constant (equal to a) in

Table 2.4a Membrane forces and displacements for a spherical shell subjected to different types of load (supported at $\phi = \phi_1$)

Membrane force/displacement	Shell geometry and loading	
	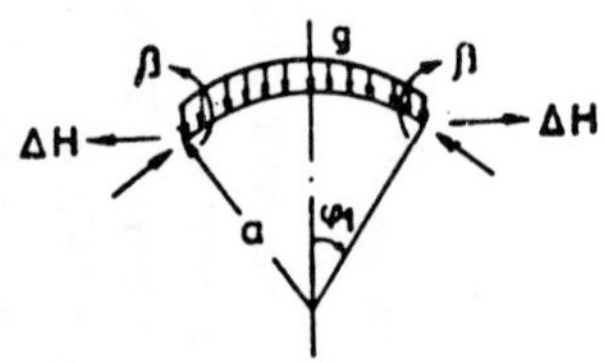 Dead load g (force/unit area)	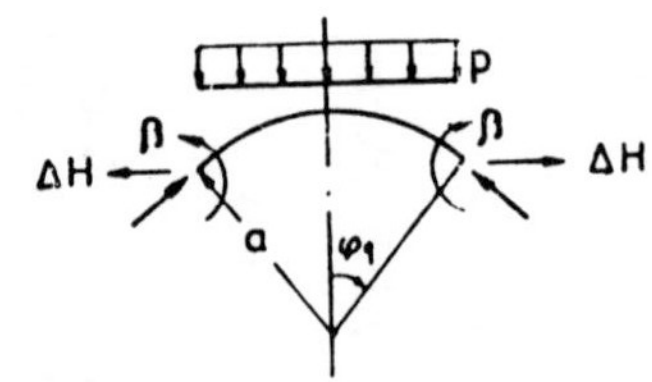 Uniform load p (force/unit area) acting on the horizontal projected area
N_ϕ	$\frac{-g a}{1+\cos\phi}$	$-\frac{pa}{2}$
N_θ	$-ga\left(\cos\phi - \frac{1}{1+\cos\phi}\right)$	$-\frac{pa}{2}\cos 2\phi$
ΔH	$\frac{ga^2}{Eh}\sin\phi_1\left[-\cos\phi_1 + \frac{1+\nu}{\sin^2\phi_1}(1-\cos\phi_1)\right]$	$\frac{pa^2\sin\phi_1}{Eh}\left[-\cos^2\phi_1 + \frac{1+\nu}{2}\right]$
β	$-\frac{ga}{Eh}(2+\nu)\sin\phi_1$	$-\frac{pa}{Eh}(3+\nu)\frac{\sin 2\phi_1}{2}$

Table 2.4a (*Continued*)

Membrane force/displacement	Shell geometry and loading	
	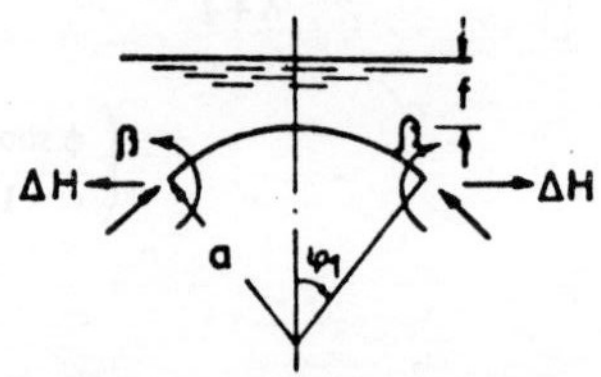 Filled with liquid of density γ (force/unit volume)	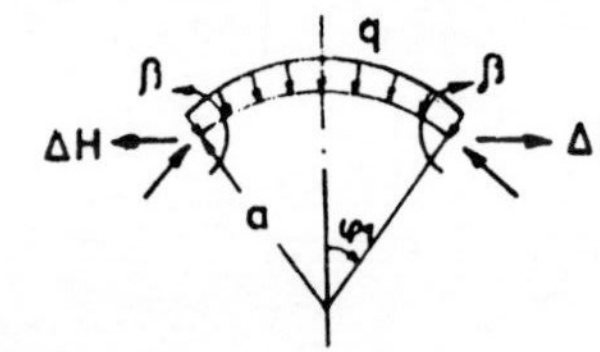 Uniform external pressure q (force/unit area)
N_ϕ	$-\dfrac{\gamma a^2}{6}\left(1+\dfrac{3f}{a}-\dfrac{2\cos^2\phi}{1+\cos\phi}\right)$	$-\dfrac{qa}{2}$
N_θ	$-\dfrac{\gamma a^2}{6}\left(-1+\dfrac{3f}{a}-\dfrac{4\cos^2\phi-6}{1+\cos\phi}\right)$	$-\dfrac{qa}{2}$
ΔH	$-\dfrac{\gamma a^3}{6Eh}\sin\phi_1\left[3\left(1+\dfrac{f}{a}\right)(1-\nu)-6\cos\phi_1-\dfrac{2(1+\nu)}{\sin^2\phi_1}(\cos^3\phi_1-1)\right]$	$-\dfrac{qa^2}{2Eh}(1-\nu)\sin\phi_1$
β	$\dfrac{\gamma a^2}{Eh}\sin\phi_1$	0

Table 2.4b Membrane forces and displacements for a spherical shell subjected to different types of load (supported at $\phi = \phi_1$)

Membrane force/displacement	Shell geometry and loading	
	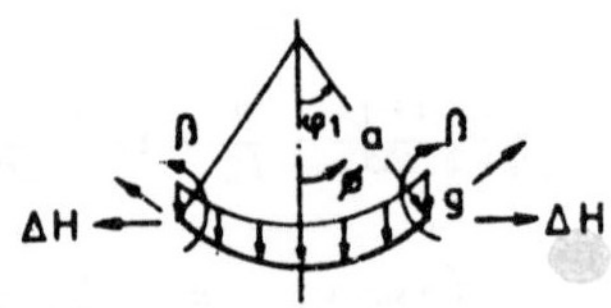 Dead load g (force/unit area)	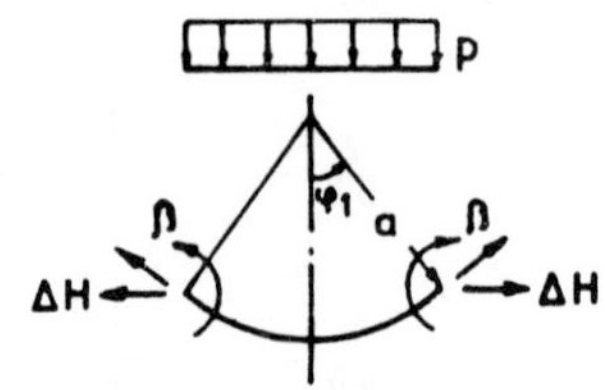 Uniform load p (force/unit area) acting on the horizontal projected area
N_ϕ	$\frac{g\,a}{1+\cos\phi}$	$\frac{pa}{2}$
N_θ	$g\,a\left(\cos\phi - \frac{1}{1+\cos\phi}\right)$	$\frac{pa}{2}\cos 2\phi$
ΔH	$-\frac{g\,a^2}{E\,h}\sin\phi_1\left[-\cos\phi_1 + \frac{1+\nu}{\sin^2\phi_1}(1-\cos\phi_1)\right]$	$-\frac{p\,a^2}{E\,h}\sin\phi_1\left(\frac{1+\nu}{2} - \cos^2\phi_1\right)$
β	$-\frac{ga}{Eh}(2+\nu)\sin\phi_1$	$-\frac{p\,a}{E\,h}(3+\nu)\frac{\sin 2\phi_1}{2}$

Table 2.4b (*Continued*)

Membrane force/displacement	Shell geometry and loading	
	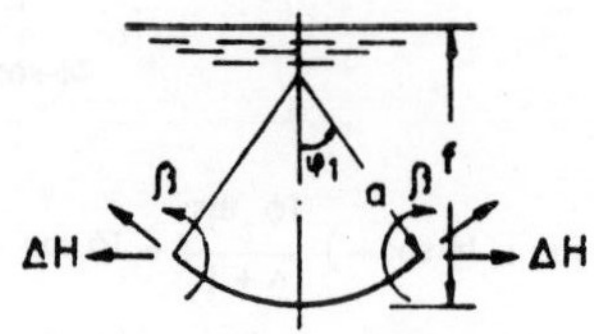 Filled with liquid of density γ (force/unit volume)	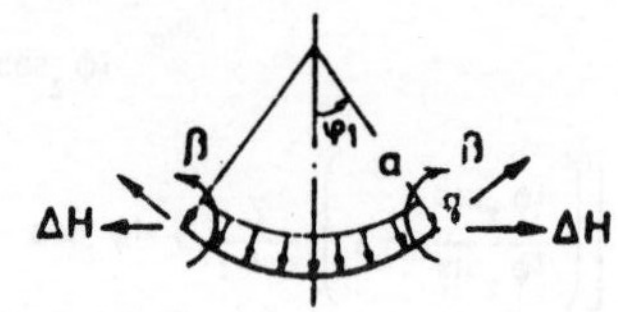 Uniform internal pressure q (force/unit area)
N_ϕ	$\frac{\gamma a^2}{6}\left(-1+\frac{3f}{a}+\frac{2\cos^2\phi}{1+\cos\phi}\right)$	$\frac{qa}{2}$
N_θ	$\frac{\gamma a^2}{6}\left(1+\frac{3f}{a}+\frac{4\cos^2\phi-6}{1+\cos\phi}\right)$	$\frac{qa}{2}$
ΔH	$-\frac{\gamma a^3}{6Eh}\sin\phi_1\left[3\left(1-\frac{f}{a}\right)(1-\nu)\right.$ $\left.-6\cos\varphi_1-\frac{2(1+\nu)}{\sin^2\phi_1}(\cos^3\phi_1-1)\right]$	$\frac{qa^2}{2Eh}(1-\nu)\sin\phi_1$
β	$-\frac{\gamma a^2}{Eh}\sin\phi_1$	0

Table 2.5a Membrane forces and displacements for a segment of a spherical shell subjected to different types of load (supported at $\phi = \phi_1$)

Shell geometry and loading

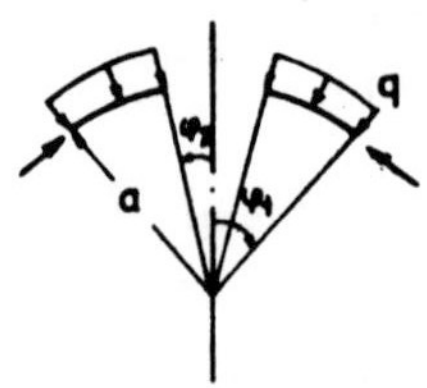

Dead load g (force/unit area)

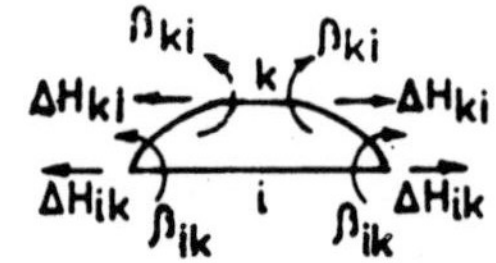

Edge displacements

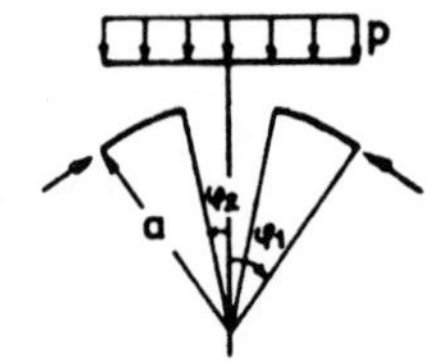

Uniform load p (force/unit area) acting on the horizontal projected area

Membrane force/displacement	Dead load g (force/unit area)	Uniform load p (force/unit area) acting on the horizontal projected area
N_ϕ	$\dfrac{-g\,a}{\sin^2\phi}(\cos\phi_2 - \cos\phi)$	$-\dfrac{pa}{2}\left(1 - \dfrac{\sin^2\phi_2}{\sin\phi}\right)$
N_θ	$-ga\left[\cos\phi - \dfrac{1}{\sin^2\phi}(\cos\phi_2 - \cos\phi)\right]$	$-\dfrac{pa}{2}\left(2\cos^2\phi - 1 + \dfrac{\sin^2\phi_2}{\sin^2\phi}\right)$
ΔH_{ik}	$\dfrac{ga^2}{Eh}\sin\phi_1\left[-\cos\phi_1 + \dfrac{1+\nu}{\sin^2\phi_1}(-\cos\phi_1 + \cos\phi_2)\right]$	$\dfrac{pa^2}{Eh}\sin\phi_1\left[-\cos^2\phi_1 + \dfrac{1+\nu}{2}\left(1 - \dfrac{\sin^2\phi_2}{\sin^2\phi_1}\right)\right]$
ΔH_{ki}	$-\dfrac{ga^2}{Eh}\sin\phi_2\cos\phi_2$	$-\dfrac{pa^2}{Eh}\sin\phi_2\cos^2\phi_2$
β_{ik}	$-\dfrac{ga}{Eh}(2+\nu)\sin\phi_1$	$-\dfrac{pa}{Eh}(3+\nu)\sin\phi_1\cos\phi_1$
β_{ki}	$-\dfrac{ga}{Eh}(2+\nu)\sin\phi_2$	$-\dfrac{pa}{Eh}(3+\nu)\sin\phi_2\cos\phi_2$

Table 2.5a (*Continued*)

Membrane force/displacement	Shell geometry and loading	
	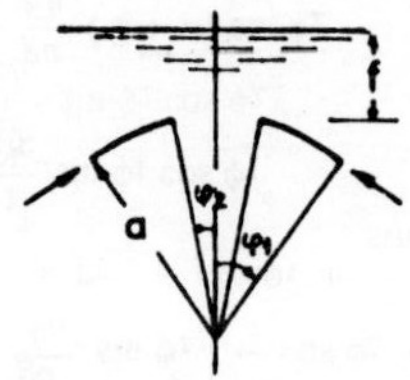 Filled with liquid of density γ (force/unit volume)	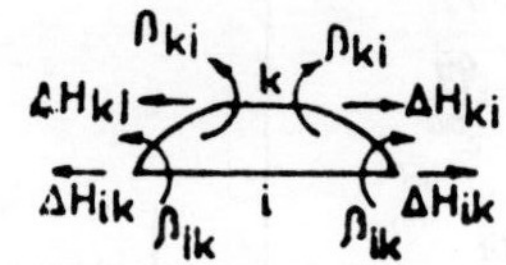 Edge displacement 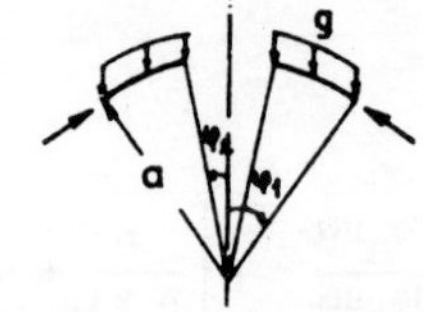 Uniform external pressure q (force/unit area)
N_ϕ	$-\dfrac{\gamma a^2}{6}\left[3\left(1+\dfrac{f}{a}\right)\left(1-\dfrac{\sin^2\phi_2}{\sin^2\phi}\right)-\dfrac{2}{\sin^2\phi}(\cos^3\phi_2-\cos^3\phi)\right]$	$-\dfrac{qa}{2}\left(1-\dfrac{\sin^2\phi_2}{\sin^2\phi}\right)$
N_θ	$-\dfrac{\gamma a^2}{6}\left[3\left(1+\dfrac{f}{a}\right)\left(1+\dfrac{\sin^2\phi_2}{\sin^2\phi}\right)+\dfrac{2(2\cos^3\phi+\cos^3\phi_2)-6\cos\phi}{\sin^2\phi}\right]$	$-\dfrac{qa}{2}\left(1+\dfrac{\sin^2\phi_2}{\sin^2\phi}\right)$
ΔH_{ik}	$-\dfrac{\gamma a^3}{6Eh}\sin\phi_1\left[3\left(1+\dfrac{f}{a}\right)\left\{1-\nu+(1+\nu)\dfrac{\sin^2\phi_2}{\sin^2\phi_1}\right\}-6\cos\phi_1+2(1+\nu)\left\{\dfrac{\cos^3\phi_2-\cos^3\phi_1}{\sin^2\phi_1}\right\}\right]$	$-\dfrac{qa^2}{Eh}\sin\phi_1\left[1-\dfrac{1+\nu}{2}\left(1-\dfrac{\sin^2\phi_2}{\sin^2\phi_1}\right)\right]$
ΔH_{ki}	$-\dfrac{\gamma a^3}{6Eh}\sin\phi_2\left[6\left(1+\dfrac{f}{a}\right)-6\cos\phi_2\right]$	$-\dfrac{qa^2}{Eh}\sin\phi_2$
β_{ik}	$\dfrac{\gamma a^2}{Eh}\sin\phi_1$	0
β_{ki}	$\dfrac{\gamma a^2}{Eh}\sin\phi_2$	0

Table 2.5b Membrane forces and displacements for a spherical segment shell subjected to different types of load (supported at $\phi = \phi_2$)

Membrane force/displacement	Shell geometry and loading		
	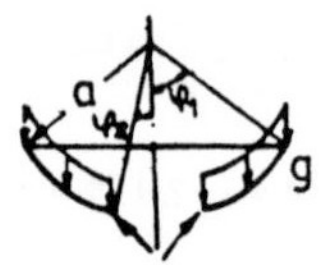 Dead load g (force/unit area)	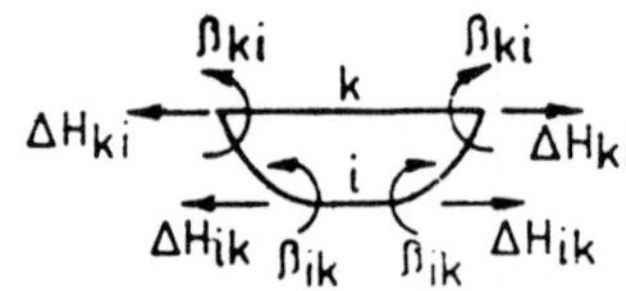 Edge displacements	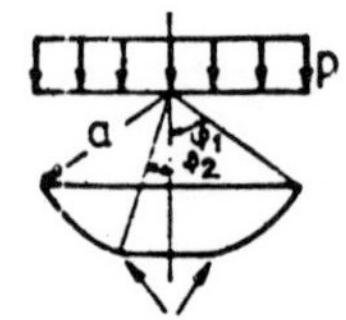 Uniform load p (force/unit area) acting on the horizontal projected area
N_ϕ	$\frac{ga}{\sin^2\phi}(\cos\phi_1 - \cos\phi)$		$\frac{pa}{2}\left(1 - \frac{\sin 2\phi_1}{\sin^2\phi}\right)$
N_θ	$ga\left[\cos\phi - \frac{1}{\sin^2\phi}(\cos\phi_1 - \cos\phi)\right]$		$\frac{pa}{2}\left(2\cos^2\phi - 1 + \frac{\sin^2\phi_1}{\sin^2\phi}\right)$
ΔH_{ik}	$-\frac{ga^2}{Eh}\sin\phi_2\left[-\cos\phi_2 + \frac{1+\nu}{\sin^2\phi_2}(-\cos\phi_2 + \cos\phi_1)\right]$		$-\frac{pa^2}{Eh}\sin\phi_2\left[-\cos^2\phi_2 + \frac{1+\nu}{2}\left(1 - \frac{\sin^2\phi_1}{\sin^2\phi_2}\right)\right]$
ΔH_{ki}	$\frac{ga^2}{Eh}\sin\phi_1\cos\phi_1$		$\frac{pa^2}{Eh}\sin\phi_1\cos^2\phi_1$
β_{ik}	$-\frac{ga}{Eh}(2+\nu)\sin\phi_2$		$-\frac{pa}{Eh}(3+\nu)\frac{\sin 2\phi_2}{2}$
β_{ki}	$-\frac{ga}{Eh}(2+\nu)\sin\phi_1$		$-\frac{pa}{Eh}(3+\nu)\sin\phi_1\cos\phi_1$

Table 2.5b *(Continued)*

Membrane force/displacement	Shell geometry and loading	
	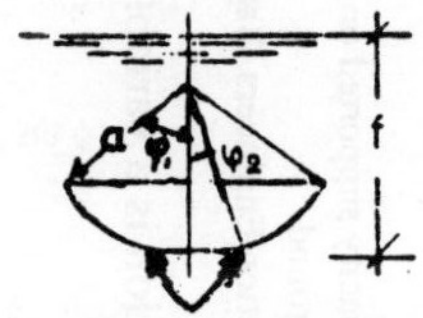 Filled with a liquid of density γ (force/unit volume) 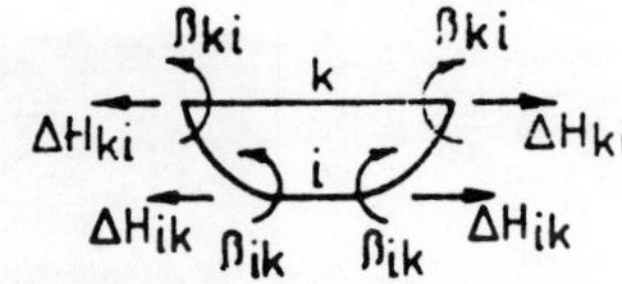 Edge displacements	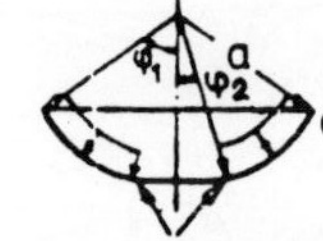 Uniform internal pressure q (force/unit area)
N_ϕ	$-\dfrac{\gamma a^2}{6}\left[3\left(1-\dfrac{f}{a}\right)\left(1-\dfrac{\sin^2\phi_1}{\sin^2\phi}\right)-\dfrac{2(\cos^3\phi_1-\cos^3\phi)}{\sin^2\phi}\right]$	$\dfrac{qa}{2}\left(1-\dfrac{\sin^2\phi_1}{\sin^2\phi}\right)$
N_θ	$-\dfrac{\gamma a^2}{6}\left[3\left(1-\dfrac{f}{a}\right)\left(1+\dfrac{\sin^2\phi_1}{\sin^2\phi}\right)+\dfrac{2(2\cos^3\phi-\cos^3\phi_1)-6\cos\phi}{\sin^2\phi}\right]$	$\dfrac{qa}{2}\left(1+\dfrac{\sin^2\phi_1}{\sin^2\phi}\right)$
ΔH_{ik}	$-\dfrac{\gamma a^3}{6Eh}\sin\phi_2\left[3\left(1-\dfrac{f}{a}\right)\left\{1-\nu+(1+\nu)\dfrac{\sin^2\phi_1}{\sin^2\phi_2}\right\}-6\cos\phi_2+2(1+\nu)\left\{\dfrac{\cos^3\phi_1-\cos^3\phi_2}{\sin^2\phi_2}\right\}\right]$	$\dfrac{qa^2}{Eh}\sin\phi_2\left[1-\left(\dfrac{1+\nu}{2}\right)\left(1-\dfrac{\sin^2\phi_1}{\sin^2\phi_2}\right)\right]$
ΔH_{ki}	$-\dfrac{\gamma a^3}{6Eh}\sin\phi_1\left[6\left(1-\dfrac{f}{a}\right)-6\cos\phi_1\right]$	$\dfrac{qa^2}{Eh}\sin\phi_1$
β_{ik}	$-\dfrac{\gamma a^2}{Eh}\sin\phi_2$	0
β_{ki}	$-\dfrac{\gamma a^2}{Eh}\sin\phi_1$	0

Fig. 2.23 A spherical water tank of 50,000 litres capacity supported on a cylindrical shaft of 20m height from ground.
(Courtesy: H.K. Nanjundaswamy, Consulting and Construction Engineers, Bangalore)

this case, the radius of curvature r_2 in the other direction is a variable and can be shown equal to

$$r_2 = \frac{r_1}{\sin \phi} = a \left(1 - \frac{\sin \phi_0}{\sin \phi}\right) \tag{a}$$

In the limit when ϕ_0 tends to zero, the Ogival shell transforms itself into a spherical shell. If the shell is under dead load only, then the load components can be determined as

$$Y = g \sin \phi, \quad Z = g \cos \phi \tag{b}$$

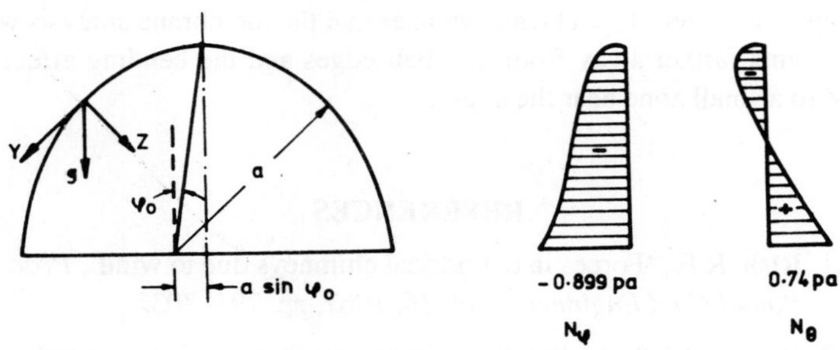

Fig. 2.24 Membrane force distribution in an ogival shell ($\phi_0 = 10°$)

Substituting the above load components in Eq. (2.40), we get

$$N_\phi = \frac{-ga}{\sin\phi\ (\sin\phi - \sin\phi_0)} \int_{\phi_0}^{\phi} (\sin\phi - \sin\phi_0)\, d\phi$$

which after integration results in

$$N_\phi = -ga \left[\frac{(\cos\phi_0 - \cos\phi) - (\phi - \phi_0)\sin\phi_0}{\sin\phi\ (\sin\phi - \sin\phi_0)} \right] \tag{2.45a}$$

The hoop force N_θ may be determined by substituting for N_ϕ the above expression in Eq. (2.38b) as

$$N_\phi = -ga\ [(\phi - \phi_0)\sin\phi_0 - (\cos\phi_0 - \cos\phi) + (\sin\phi - \sin\phi_0)\cos\phi\ \sin\phi] \tag{2.45b}$$

It may be observed that as ϕ_0 tends to zero, the expressions for N_ϕ and N_θ would correspond to the stress resultants of a spherical shell. At the apex ($\phi = \phi_0$) the stress resultant N_θ would be zero and N_ϕ becomes indefinite, but its value can be determined by using L'Hospital rule. It can be shown that N_ϕ also become zero at the apex. In Fig. 2.24, the distributions of N_ϕ and N_θ are shown for $\phi_0 = 10°$.

2.6 SUMMARY

In this chapter, we have developed first, the basic equations for the membrane theory of an arbitrary shell surface defined by curvilinear coordinate system, which coincides with the lines of principal curvature of the surface. We have shown that the equations of equilibrium can be directly integrated to determine the stress resultants. If necessary, the strains can be determined by making use of stress–strain relationship and later on, the displacements can be determined by integrating the strain-displacement equations. We have illustrated the application of membrane theory to shells of revolution like cylindrical, conical and spherical shell subjected to arbitrary and axisymmetric loads. In many examples presented, it is clear that the membrane theory does not provide the complete solution to the problem, since the membrane solution does not satisfy the required boundary conditions. However, it will be shown later that the membrane analysis would be valid at points farther away from the shell edges and the bending effect will be confined to a small zone near the edges.

REFERENCES

2.1 Rish, R.F., 'Forces in cylindrical chimneys due to wind', *Proc. Institution of Civil Engineers,* Vol. 36, 1967, pp. 791–803.

2.2 Hampe, E., *Statik Rotations Symmetrischer Flachentragwerke, Band 2 and 3*, VEB Verlag Fur Bauwesen, Berlin, 1964.

2.3 Baker, E.H., L. Kovalevsky and F.L. Rish, *Structural Analysis of Shells,* McGraw-Hill Book Co., New York, 1972.

2.4 Flugge, W., *Stresses in Shells,* Second edition, Springer-Verlag, Berlin, 1973.

2.5 Kraus, H., *Thin Elastic Shells,* John Wiley and Sons, 1967.

2.6 Fischer, L., *Theory and Practice of Shell Structures*, Wilhelm Ernst and Sohn, Berlin-Munich, 1968.

Chapter Three

Membrane Analysis of Shells of Translation

3.1 INTRODUCTION

In Chapter 2, the membrane theory for shells of revolution has been developed. The simplifications introduced in the general theory of shell of revolution due to rotational symmetry makes it possible to obtain simple solutions to several problems. This point has been sufficiently emphasised in Chapter 2 through examples. In this chapter, we will discuss the membrane analysis of shells of translation. As mentioned earlier, a shell of translation is obtained by moving a plane curve (generatrix) against another plane curve (directrix), the function of the two curves being interchangeable. A shell of translation can fall into the category of developable or synclastic or anticlastic surface. Shells of this type are normally used for roof structure and the common shapes are cylindrical, elliptic or hyperbolic paraboloid, conoid, etc. We will first discuss the membrane analysis of cylindrical shells (open) which can be done using the equilibrium equations already given for a cylindrical shell in Chapter 2. Later, we will develop the membrane theory for shell of arbitrary shape and apply it to synclastic and anticlastic shell surfaces.

3.2 MEMBRANE ANALYSIS OF CYLINDRICAL SHELLS

The middle surface of a cylindrical shell is obtained by moving a plane curve against a straight line or vice versa. The plane curve can be an arc of a circle, a parabola, a catenary, part of an ellipse, etc. Shells for which the plane curve is an arc of a circle are often called as circular-cylindrical shells, while those which have plane curve other than an arc of a circle are called as non-circular-cylindrical shells. A general equation for a family of plane curves can be written in the form (Fig. 3.1).

$$R = R_0 \cos^n \theta \tag{3.1}$$

where R is the radius of curvature at any point

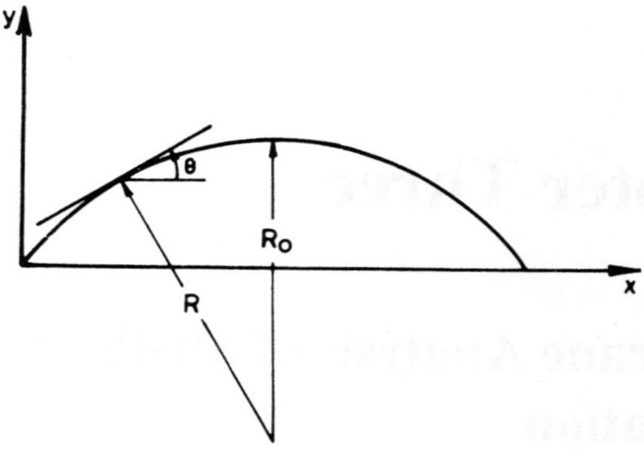

Fig. 3.1 Geometry of a plane curve

R_O is the radius of curvature at the crown

θ is the angle made by the tangent at any point to the horizontal.

It can be shown that if

n = 0, the plane curve will be an arc of a circle,
n = 1, the plane curve will be a cycloid,
n = −2, the plane curve will be a catenary,
n = −3, the plane curve will be a parabola.

Figure 2.7 shows an element of a cylindrical shell with the internal membrane forces and external loading. The membrane equilibrium equations as well as the strain-displacement relations have already been given in Chapter 2 (Eqs. 2.7a–c and 2.8a–c).

The general solution for the membrane-stress resultants in a cylindrical shell can be obtained as follows. First, N_θ can be determined from Eq. (2.7c) as

$$N_\theta = -\ ZR_0 \cos^n \theta \tag{3.2a}$$

Substituting for N_θ in Eq. (2.7b) and integrating, we obtain $N_{x\theta}$ as

$$N_{x\theta} = -\int \frac{1}{R_0 \cos^n \theta} \left(\cdot \frac{\partial N_\theta}{\partial \theta} \right) dx - \int Y\, dx + f_1(\theta) \tag{3.2b}$$

Substituting for $N_{x\theta}$ in Eq. (2.7a) and integrating, we obtain N_x as

$$N_x = -\int \frac{1}{R_0 \cos^n \theta} \left(\frac{\partial N_{x\theta}}{\partial \theta} \right) dx - \int X\, dx + f_2(\theta) \tag{3.2c}$$

where $f_1(\theta)$ and $f_2(\theta)$ are integration constants to be determined from the boundary conditions.

3.2.1 Examples

(a) Simply supported cylindrical shell subjected to dead load

Let g be the weight of shell per unit area of its middle surface. The load components can be determined as (Fig. 3.2)

$$X = 0, \ Y = g \sin \theta, \ Z = g \cos \theta \tag{a}$$

Substituting for the load components in Eqs. (3.2a–c), we get the expressions for the membrane forces as

$$N_\theta = - \ g R_0 \cos^{n+1} \theta \tag{3.3a}$$

$$N_{x\theta} = -(n+2)\, gx \sin \theta + f_1(\theta) \tag{b}$$

$$N_x = \frac{(n+2)\, gx^2}{2 R_0} \cos^{-n+1} \theta + f_2(\theta) \tag{c}$$

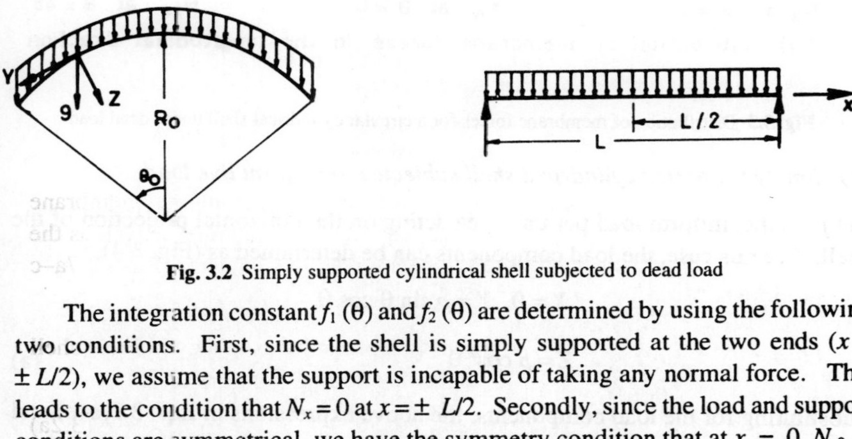

Fig. 3.2 Simply supported cylindrical shell subjected to dead load

The integration constant $f_1(\theta)$ and $f_2(\theta)$ are determined by using the following two conditions. First, since the shell is simply supported at the two ends ($x = \pm L/2$), we assume that the support is incapable of taking any normal force. This leads to the condition that $N_x = 0$ at $x = \pm\ L/2$. Secondly, since the load and support conditions are symmetrical, we have the symmetry condition that at $x = 0$, $N_{x\theta} = 0$. Using these two conditions, the two integration constants $f_1(\theta)$ and $f_2(\theta)$ can be determined as

$$f_1(\theta) = 0 \tag{d}$$

$$f_2(\theta) = \frac{-(n+2)}{2 R_0 \cos^{n-1} \theta} \left(\frac{gL^2}{4} \right) \tag{e}$$

Substituting for $f_1(\theta)$ and $f_2(\theta)$ in Eqs. (b) and (c), the expressions for $N_{x\theta}$ and N_x can be obtained as

$$N_{x\theta} = -(n+2)\, gx \sin \theta \tag{3.3b}$$

$$N_x = -\left(\frac{n+2}{2} \right) \frac{1}{R_0 \cos^{n-1} \theta}\, g \left(\frac{L^2}{4} - x^2 \right) \tag{3.3c}$$

In Eqs. (3.3a–c), if we put $n = 0$, we get the stress resultants for a circular-cylindrical shell and the typical variations of these forces are shown in Fig. 3.3.

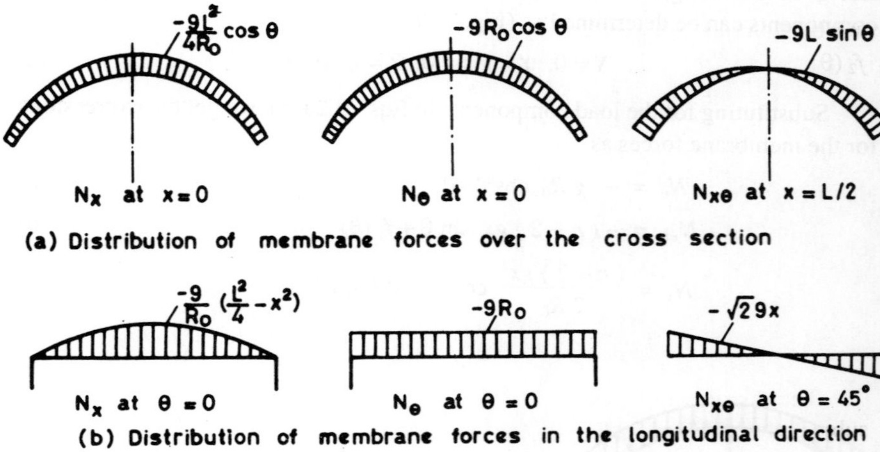

Fig. 3.3 Distribution of membrane forces for a circular cylindrical shell under dead load

(b) Simply supported cylindrical shell subjected to uniform live load

Let p be the uniform load per unit area acting on the horizontal projection of the shell. For this case, the load components can be determined as (Fig. 3.4),

$$X = 0,\; Y = p \sin\theta \cos\theta,$$

$$Z = p \cos^2\theta \tag{a}$$

Substituting for the load components, the above expressions in Eqs. 3.2(a–c) and after integration we obtain

$$N_\theta = -p\, R_0 \cos^{n+2}\theta \tag{3.4a}$$

$$N_{x\theta} = -\,(n+3)\, px \cos\theta \sin\theta + f_1(\theta) \tag{b}$$

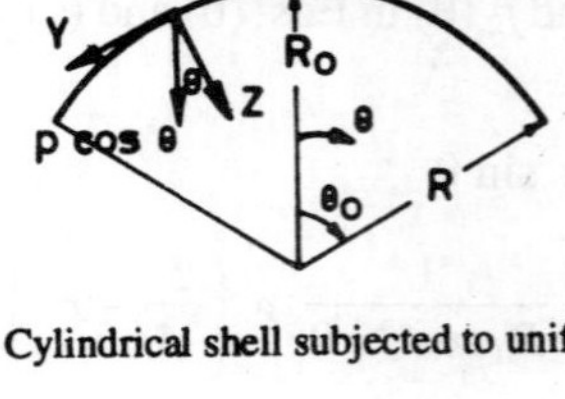

Fig. 3.4 Cylindrical shell subjected to uniform loading

$$N_x = \frac{\cos^2\theta - \sin^2\theta}{2 R_0 \cos^n\theta} (n+3)\, px^2 + f_2(\theta) \tag{c}$$

Using the same conditions as in the previous example, namely, $N_{x\theta} = 0$ at $x = 0$ and $N_x = 0$ at $x = \pm L/2$, we can determine the integration constants $f_1(\theta)$ and $f_2(\theta)$ as

$$f_1(\theta) = 0 \tag{d}$$

$$f_2(\theta) = -(n+3)\frac{pL^2}{4}\frac{\cos^2\theta - \sin^2\theta}{2 R_0 \cos^n\theta} \tag{e}$$

Substituting the above expressions in Eqs. (b) and (c), we get $N_{x\theta}$ and N_x as

$$N_{x\theta} = -(n+3)\, px \cos\theta \sin\theta \tag{3.4b}$$

$$N_x = -\frac{\cos^2\theta - \sin^2\theta}{2 R_0 \cos^n\theta}(n+3)\, p\left(\frac{L^2}{4} - x^2\right) \tag{3.4c}$$

The distribution of membrane forces for a circular-cylindrical shell ($n = 0$) subjected to uniform load is shown in Fig. 3.5.

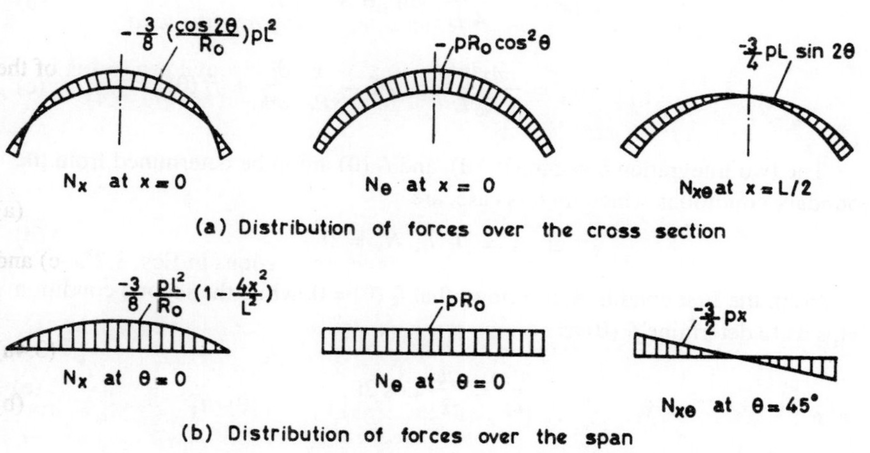

Fig. 3.5 Distribution of membrane forces in a circular-cylindrical shell subjected to uniform load

(c) Simply supported circular-cylindrical shell subjected to triangular loading

Consider a circular-cylindrical shell subjected to a triangular loading in the longitudinal direction and this load is assumed to be acting on the horizontal projection of the shell, as shown in Fig. 3.6.

The load components can be determined as

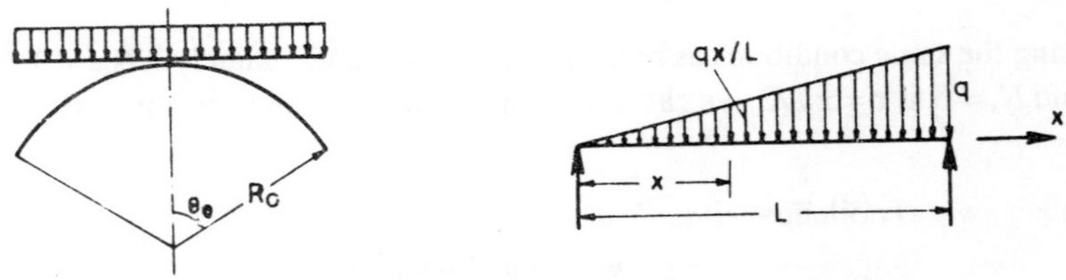

Fig. 3.6 Circular-cylindrical shell subjected to triangular loading

$$X = 0, \; Y = \frac{qx}{L} \sin\theta \cos\theta, \; Z = \frac{qx}{L} \cos^2\theta \tag{a}$$

The following expressions for the membrane stress resultants can be obtained after substituting the above load components in Eqs. (3.2 a-c) and after integration,

$$N_\theta = -\frac{qx}{L} R_0 \cos^2\theta \tag{3.5a}$$

$$N_{x\theta} = -\frac{3\,qx^2}{4\,L} \sin 2\theta + f_1(\theta) \tag{b}$$

$$N_x = \frac{qx^3}{2\,R_0\,L} \cos 2\theta - \frac{x}{R_0} \frac{\partial f_1}{\partial \theta} + f_2(\theta) \tag{c}$$

The two integration constants $f_1(\theta)$ and $f_2(\theta)$ are to be determined from the boundary conditions which, in this case, are

$$\text{at} \quad x = 0, \; L; \; N_x = 0 \tag{d}$$

From the first condition, it follows that $f_2(\theta) = 0$, while the second condition helps us to determine $f_1(\theta)$ as

$$\frac{\partial f_1}{\partial \theta} = \frac{qL}{2} \cos 2\theta \tag{e}$$

which, after integration, gives f_1 as

$$f_1 = \frac{qL}{4} \sin 2\theta + f_3(x) \tag{f}$$

Since the load is symmetrical about x-axis, we have $N_{x\theta} = 0$ for $\theta = 0$. Using this condition in Eqs. (b) and (f), it can be shown that $f_3 = 0$. Hence, the constant f_1 can now be determined as

$$f_1 = \frac{qL}{4} \sin 2\theta \tag{g}$$

Substituting the above expression in Eqs. (b) and (c), $N_{x\theta}$ and N_x can now be determined as

$$N_{x\theta} = -\frac{qL}{4}\sin 2\theta\left(\frac{3x^2}{L^2} - 1\right) \tag{3.5b}$$

$$N_x = \frac{qLx}{2R_0}\cos 2\theta\left(\frac{x^2}{L^2} - 1\right) \tag{3.5c}$$

In Fig. 3.7 the distribution of the membrane stress resultants is shown.

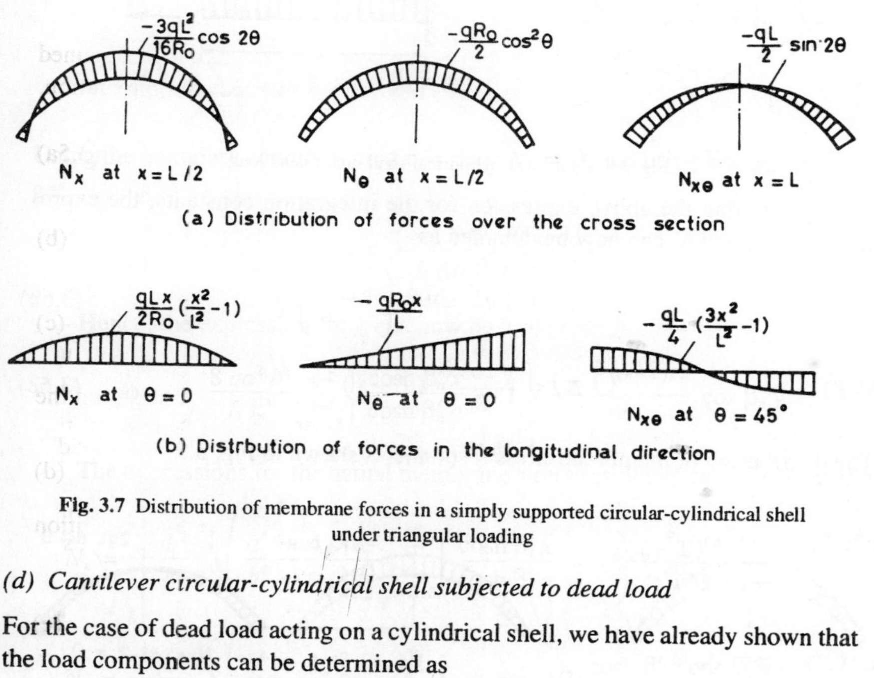

Fig. 3.7 Distribution of membrane forces in a simply supported circular-cylindrical shell under triangular loading

(d) Cantilever circular-cylindrical shell subjected to dead load

For the case of dead load acting on a cylindrical shell, we have already shown that the load components can be determined as

$$X = 0,\ Y = g\sin\theta,\ Z = g\cos\theta \tag{a}$$

and the expressions for the membrane forces can be written down following example (a) as

$$N_\theta = -g R_0 \cos\theta \tag{3.6a}$$

$$N_{x\theta} = -2gx\sin\theta + f_1(\theta) \tag{b}$$

$$N_x = \frac{gx^2}{R_0}\cos\theta - \frac{x\,\partial f_1}{R_0\,\partial\theta} + f_2(\theta) \tag{c}$$

The integration constants $f_1(\theta)$ and $f_2(\theta)$ are determined using the following boundary conditions

$$x = L, N_x = \cdot N_{x\theta} = 0 \tag{d}$$

Using the above conditions, $f_1(\theta)$ and $f_2(\theta)$ can be determined as

$$f_1 = 2\,gL\,\sin\theta \tag{e}$$

$$f_2 = \frac{gL^2}{R_0}\cos\theta \tag{f}$$

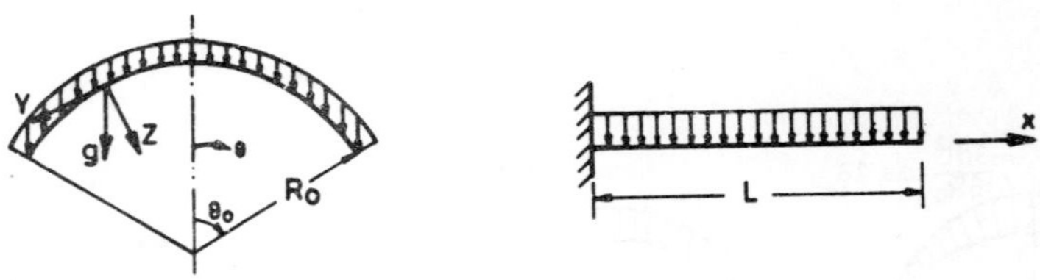

Fig. 3.8 Cantilever cylindrical shell under dead load

Substituting the above expression for the integration constants, the expressions for $N_{x\theta}$ and N_x can now be obtained as

$$N_{x\theta} = 2\,gL\,\sin\theta\left(1 - \frac{x}{L}\right) \tag{3.6b}$$

$$N_x = \frac{g\cos\theta}{R_0}(L - x)^2 \tag{3.6c}$$

The distribution of membrane stress resultants is shown in Fig. 3.9.

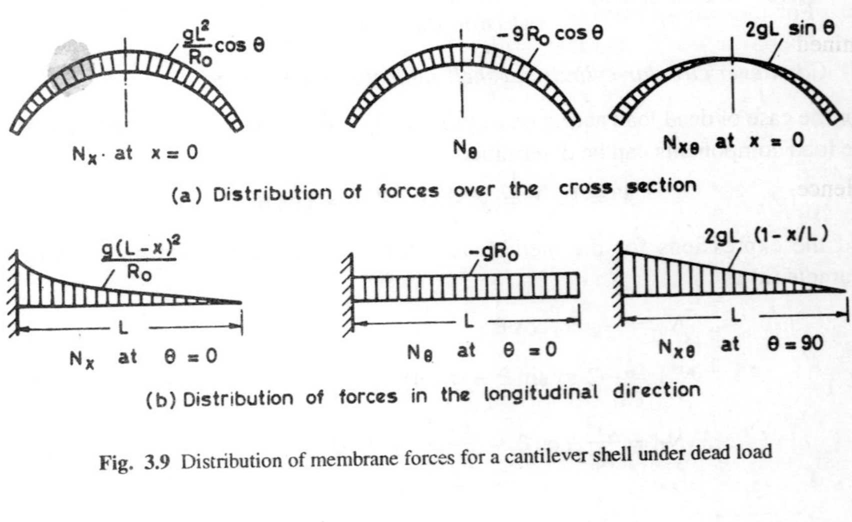

Fig. 3.9 Distribution of membrane forces for a cantilever shell under dead load

3.2.2 Membrane Analysis of Circular-Cylindrical Shell Using Trigonometric Series

The solution given in the previous article is obtained by direct integration of the equilibrium equation, considering that the load is continuous. However, when the loading is discontinuous in the x-direction or when the membrane solution forms the particular integral for the bending theory, then it is desirable to obtain the solution in terms of trigonometric (Fourier) series. The application of trigonometric series for the solution of beam problems is well known. We can extend this to circular-cylindrical shells here. First, we express the load in terms of Fourier series as (Fig. 3.10a)

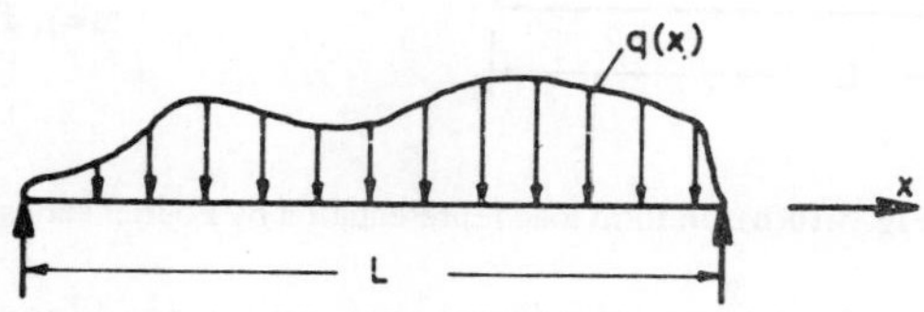

Fig. 3.10(a) Simply supported shell subjected to arbitrary load in the x-direction.

$$q(x) = \sum_{m=1}^{\infty} A_m \sin \frac{m\pi x}{L}, 0 \le x \le L \qquad \text{(a)}$$

The coefficient A_m is determined using the orthogonality condition as

$$A_m = \frac{2}{L} \int_0^L q(x) \sin \frac{m\pi x}{L} dx \qquad \text{(b)}$$

For the case of uniformly distributed load (q = constant), A_m can be determined as

$$A_m = \left(\frac{4q}{m\pi}\right), (m = 1, 3, 5, \cdots) \qquad \text{(c)}$$

Hence, we can now represent the load (q = constant) as follows (Fig. 3.10b)

$$q = \frac{4q}{\pi} \sin \frac{\pi x}{L} + \frac{4q}{3\pi} \sin \frac{3\pi x}{L}$$

$$+ \frac{4q}{5\pi} \sin \frac{5\pi x}{L} + \cdots + \frac{4q}{m\pi} \sin \frac{m\pi x}{L}$$

$$= \frac{4q}{\pi} \sum_{m=1,3}^{\infty} \frac{1}{m} \sin \frac{m\pi x}{L} \qquad \text{(d)}$$

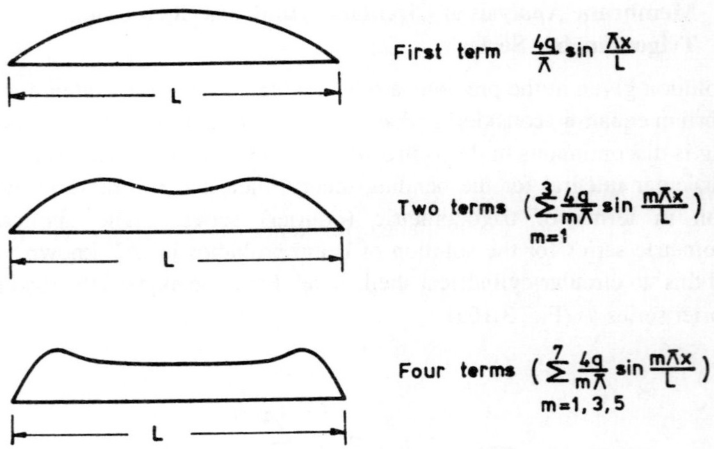

Fig. 3.10(b) Uniform load representation by Fourier series

(a) Simply supported circular-cylindrical shell under dead load

Let g be the dead load per unit area. This load can be expressed in terms of Fourier series as

$$g = \sum_{m=1}^{\infty} C_m \sin\frac{m\pi x}{L} \tag{e}$$

where $C_m = \frac{4g}{m\pi} \cdots (m = 1, 3, 5, \cdots)$

Hence, $$g = \frac{4g}{\pi}\sum_{m=1,3}^{\infty}\frac{1}{m}\sin\frac{m\pi x}{L} \tag{f}$$

As shown earlier, the components of dead load are

$$X = 0,\ Y = g\sin\theta = \frac{4g}{\pi}\sin\theta\sum_{m=1}^{\infty}\frac{1}{m}\sin\frac{m\pi x}{L} \tag{g}$$

$$Z = g\cos\theta = \frac{4g}{\pi}\cos\theta\sum_{m=1}^{\infty}\frac{1}{m}\sin\frac{m\pi x}{L}$$

Substituting the above load components in the equilibrium Eqs. (3.2a–c) with $n = 0$ and after integration, we get

$$N_\theta = -\frac{4gR_0}{\pi}\cos\theta\sum_{m=1,3}^{\infty}\frac{1}{m}\sin\frac{m\pi x}{L} \tag{3.7a}$$

$$N_{x\theta} = \frac{8\,gL}{\pi^2} \sin\theta \sum_{m=1,3}^{\infty} \frac{1}{m^2} \cos\frac{m\pi x}{L} + f_1(\theta) \tag{h}$$

$$N_x = -\frac{8\,gL^2}{R_0\,\pi^3} \cos\theta \sum_{m=1,3}^{\infty} \frac{1}{m^3} \sin\frac{m\pi x}{L} + f_2(\theta) \tag{i}$$

Using the boundary condition that (Fig. 3.10a)

$$\text{at} \quad x = 0,\ L;\ N_x = 0.$$

and symmetry condition

$$N_{x\theta} = 0 \text{ at } x = \frac{L}{2},$$

we determine the integration constants $f_1(\theta) = f_2(\theta) = 0$. Hence, $N_{x\theta}$ and N_x can now be written as

$$N_{x\theta} = \frac{8\,gL}{\pi^2} \sin\theta \sum_{m=1}^{\infty} \frac{1}{m^2} \cos\frac{m\pi x}{L} \tag{3.7b}$$

$$N_x = \frac{-8\,gL^2}{R_0\,\pi^3} \cos\theta \sum_{m=1}^{\infty} \frac{1}{m^3} \sin\frac{m\pi x}{L} \tag{3.7c}$$

In Table 3.1, we compare the values obtained from this solution with the exact solution given in Eqs. (3.3a–c).

Table 3.1 Comparison of series solution result with exact solution

	Series solution		Exact solution
	$m = 1$	$m = 1, 3$	
N_x at midspan	$-0.258\,\frac{gL^2}{R_0}\cos\theta$	$-0.248\,\frac{gL^2}{R_0}\cos\theta$	$-0.25\,\frac{gL^2}{R_0}\cos\theta$
N_θ at midspan	$-1.273\,gR_0\cos\theta$	$-0.849\,gR_0\cos\theta$	$-gR_0\cos\theta$
$N_{x\theta}$ at support	$0.811\,gL\sin\theta$	$0.901\,gL\sin\theta$	$gL\sin\theta$

It may be seen from Table 3.1, that the convergence of series in respect of the force N_x is very good and the first term itself gives result near to the exact solution. However, the convergence of the series, in respect of the forces N_θ and $N_{x\theta}$, is not that good. For the purpose of design, if the forces are computed by limiting to the first term only, then the forces N_x and N_θ would be higher than the exact and would be safe. Hence, the forces are often computed by taking only the first term in the series.

The solution can also be obtained, if the load is symmetric about θ-axis, by taking the origin at the centre. In this case, the load is expressed in terms of Fourier series as

$$g = \sum_{m=1,3}^{\infty} C_m \cos\frac{m\pi x}{L} \tag{j}$$

where

$$C_m = \frac{2}{L} \int_{-L/2}^{+L/2} g \cos \frac{m\pi x}{L} \, dx = \frac{4g}{m\pi} (-1)^{(m-1)/2} \tag{k}$$

Following the same procedure described above, membrane forces can be determined as

$$N_\theta = -\frac{4gR_0}{\pi} \cos\theta \sum_{m=1,3}^{\infty} \frac{(-1)^{(m-1)/2}}{m} \cos \frac{m\pi x}{L} \tag{3.8a}$$

$$N_{x\theta} = -\frac{8gL}{\pi^2} \sin\theta \sum_{m=1,3}^{\infty} \frac{(-1)^{(m-1)/2}}{m^2} \sin \frac{m\pi x}{L} \tag{3.8b}$$

$$N_x = -\frac{8gL^2}{\pi^3 R_0} \cos\theta \sum_{m=1,3}^{\infty} \frac{(-1)^{(m-1)/2}}{m^3} \cos \frac{m\pi x}{L} \tag{3.8c}$$

(b) Simply supported circular-cylindrical shell under uniform load

Let p be the uniform load per unit area on the horizontal projection of the shell. Taking the origin at the centre of the span, the load may be expressed in terms of Fourier series as

$$p = \frac{4p}{\pi} \sum_{m=1,3}^{\infty} \frac{(-1)^{(m-1)/2}}{m} \cos \frac{m\pi x}{L} \tag{a}$$

The components of the load, in terms of Fourier series, can be written as

$$X = 0, \; Y = \frac{2p \sin 2\theta}{\pi} \sum_{m=1,3}^{\infty} \frac{(-1)^{(m-1)/2}}{m} \cos \frac{m\pi x}{L}$$

$$Z = \frac{4p \cos^2\theta}{\pi} \sum_{m=1,3}^{\infty} \frac{(-1)^{(m-1)/2}}{m} \cos \frac{m\pi x}{L} \tag{b}$$

The membrane forces can be determined as (by considering only the first term in the series)

$$N_\theta = -\frac{4pR_0}{\pi} \cos^2\theta \cos \frac{\pi x}{L} \tag{3.9a}$$

$$N_{x\theta} = -\frac{6pL}{\pi^2} \sin 2\theta \sin \frac{\pi x}{L} \tag{3.9b}$$

$$N_x = -\frac{12pL^2}{R_0 \pi^3} \cos 2\theta \cos \frac{\pi x}{L} \tag{3.9c}$$

It must be noted that in the various examples of cylindrical shells considered here, the boundary condition along the longitudinal edges ($\theta = \pm\,\theta_0$) has not been considered. Consequently, the membrane solution does indicate the existence of both N_θ and $N_{x\theta}$ along these edges. Hence a membrane state of stress can exist in the cylindrical shell only when such a support is provided along the longitudinal edges, so as to permit the existence of these forces. Any other type of support will obviously cause the membrane state of stress in the shell to be violated. However, it will be shown later that the membrane solution can be used as an approximate solution for certain dimensions of cylindrical shell (see Sec. 4.4.2).

A parabolic ferrocement shell is shown in Fig. 3.11.

Fig. 3.11 A parabolic ferrocement shell for the entrance of a cathedral - Front: span 9 m, height 6 m; side: span 6 m, height 4.8 m, thickness 4 cm (Courtesy: H.K. Nanjundaswamy, Consulting and Construction Engineer, Bangalore).

3.3 MEMBRANE THEORY OF SHELLS OF DOUBLE CURVATURE

We will develop here a general membrane theory for shells of arbitrary shape and later apply it to some shells of double curvature. The middle surface of the shell is described as

$$z = f(x, y)$$

The basic equations are obtained here by considering an element bounded by sides, tangents to which are not necessarily orthogonal. In other words, the curvilinear coordinates selected do not coincide with the principal curvature of the surface. The equations derived here, when specialised for the case of orthogonal curvilinear coordinate system, reduce to the one given in Chapter 2.

3.3.1 Geometry of Shell

A typical shell element ABCD, taken at the middle surface of a shell of arbitrary shape, is shown in Fig. 3.12. The sides of this element are such that when they are projected onto a horizontal *xy*-plane, results in a rectangle $A'\ B'\ C'\ D'$. The sides of the element in *x*- and *y*-direction are taken as ds_1 and ds_2 while the angle between the sides is taken as θ. The equation defining the surface of such a shell can be written as

$$z = f(x, y) \tag{a}$$

Following the results of differential geometry given in Chapter 1, we have, for the length of sides *AB* and *AD* of the element, the relation

$$ds_1 = \frac{dx}{\cos\phi} = \sqrt{1 + p^2}\ dx \tag{b}$$

$$ds_2 = \frac{dy}{\cos\psi} = \sqrt{1 + q^2}\ dy \tag{c}$$

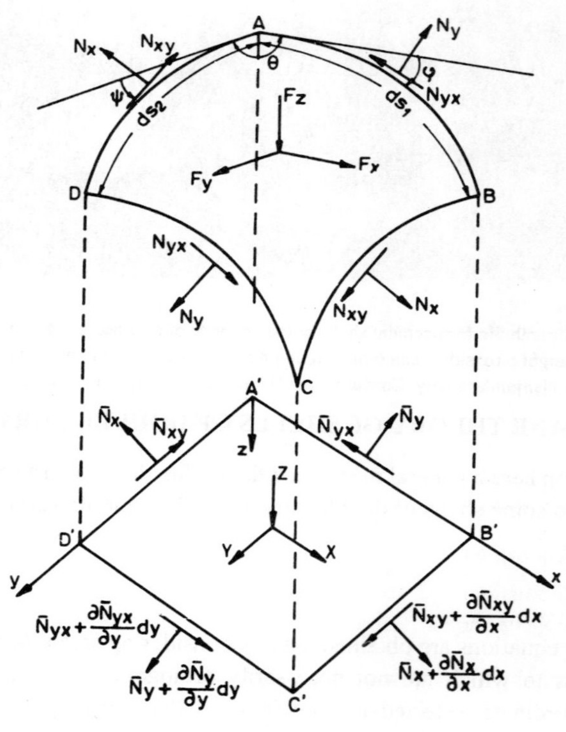

Fig. 3.12 An arbitrary shell element and its projection on *xy*-plane

and the angle between them is determined from

$$\cos\,\theta = \frac{pq}{\sqrt{1+p^2}\,\sqrt{1+q^2}} \tag{d}$$

The area of the element $ABCD$ will be equal to $\sqrt{1+p^2+q^2}\ dx\ dy$. The membrane forces N_x, N_y, N_{xy} and N_{yx} are the actual internal forces acting on the shell element, while $\overline{N}_x$, $\overline{N}_y$, $\overline{N}_{xy}$ and $\overline{N}_{yx}$ are the forces acting on the projected shell element. It must be remembered that the membrane forces N_x, N_y, N_{xy} and N_{yx} are forces per unit length and these are to be multiplied by the length of element on which they are acting, to get the total force. The horizontal component of these forces would be equal to the forces acting on the projected shell element. We can now write the following relations between the actual and the projected stress resultants.

$$\overline{N}_x\ dy = N_x \frac{dy}{\cos\psi}\cos\phi = N_x\sqrt{\frac{1+q^2}{1+p^2}}\ dy \tag{e}$$

$$\overline{N}_{yx}\ dx = N_{yx}\frac{dx}{\cos\phi}\cos\phi = N_{yx}\ dx \tag{f}$$

$$\overline{N}_y\ dy = N_y\frac{dx}{\cos\phi}\cos\psi = N_y\sqrt{\frac{1+p^2}{1+q^2}}\ dx \tag{g}$$

$$\overline{N}_{xy}\ dy = N_{xy}\frac{dy}{\cos\psi}\cos\psi = N_{xy}\ dy \tag{h}$$

Alternatively, we can also write

$$N_x = \overline{N}_x\sqrt{\frac{1+p^2}{1+q^2}}\,,\ N_y = \overline{N}_y\sqrt{\frac{1+q^2}{1+p^2}}\,,$$

$$N_{xy} = \overline{N}_{xy}\,,\qquad N_{yx} = \overline{N}_{yx}$$

Similarly, the actual components of the load, namely F_x, F_y and F_z, acting on the shell element, can be related to the components of load X, Y and Z, acting on the projected shell element through the following relationship.

$$X\ dx\ dy = F_x\ dA = F_x\sqrt{1+p^2+q^2}\ dx\ dy \tag{i}$$

$$Y\ dx\ dy = F_y\ dA = F_y\sqrt{1+p^2+q^2}\ dx\ dy \tag{j}$$

$$Z\ dx\ dy = F_z\ dA = F_z\sqrt{1+p^2+q^2}\ dx\ dy \tag{k}$$

3.3.2 Equilibrium Equations

First, we will consider the stress resultants acting on the projected shell element $A'\,B'\,C'\,D'$ to write the equilibrium equations in x- and y-direction. These are

$$\frac{\partial\overline{N}_x}{\partial x} + \frac{\partial\overline{N}_{yx}}{\partial y} + X = 0 \tag{3.10a}$$

$$\frac{\partial\overline{N}_y}{\partial y} + \frac{\partial\overline{N}_{xy}}{\partial x} + Y = 0 \tag{3.10b}$$

For writing the equilibrium equation in the z-direction, it is necessary to go back to the original shell element *ABCD* and determine the vertical component of all the four stress resultants acting on the sides of the element. It may be seen from Fig. 3.12 that the force N_x will be inclined at an angle ϕ with the tangent plane. Hence the vertical component of force N_x, acting on side *AD*, will be

$$N_x\ ds_2\ \sin\phi = N_x\ \frac{dy}{\cos\psi}\ \sin\phi$$

or, in terms of the stress resultant acting on the projected element, it will be

$$N_x\ \frac{dy}{\cos\psi}\ \sin\phi = \overline{N}_x\ dy \left(\frac{1}{\cos\phi}\right) \sin\phi = \overline{N}_x\ dy\ \tan\phi$$

or

$$N_x \left(\frac{\partial z}{\partial x}\right) dy$$

This force will be acting upwards. Similarly, the vertical component of the force N_x, acting on the side *BC*, will be

$$\overline{N}_x \left(\frac{\partial z}{\partial x}\right) dy + \frac{\partial}{\partial x}\left(\overline{N}_x\ \frac{\partial z}{\partial x}\right) dx\ dy$$

This component will be acting downwards. Hence, the net component of the force will be in the downward direction and is equal to

$$\frac{\partial}{\partial x}\left(\overline{N}_x\ \frac{\partial z}{\partial x}\right) dx\ dy$$

Similar expressions for the vertical component of the forces N_y, N_{xy} and N_{yx} can be obtained. It must be noted that the vertical component of all the resultant forces will be acting in the downward direction. The equilibrium equation in the *z*-direction is obtained by adding the component of the external load, namely $Z\,dx\,dy$, to the resultant component of the forces, as

$$\frac{\partial}{\partial x}\left(\overline{N}_x\ \frac{\partial z}{\partial x}\right) + \frac{\partial}{\partial y}\left(\overline{N}_y\ \frac{\partial z}{\partial y}\right) + \frac{\partial}{\partial x}\left(\overline{N}_{xy}\ \frac{\partial z}{\partial y}\right) + \frac{\partial}{\partial y}\left(\overline{N}_{yx}\ \frac{\partial z}{\partial x}\right) + Z = 0$$

or, in expanded form, taking $\overline{N}_{xy} = \overline{N}_{yx}$ (which can be established from moment equilibrium consideration),

$$\overline{N}_x\ \frac{\partial^2 z}{\partial x^2} + \overline{N}_y\ \frac{\partial^2 z}{\partial y^2} + 2\overline{N}_{xy}\ \frac{\partial^2 z}{\partial x\,\partial y} + \left(\frac{\partial \overline{N}_x}{\partial x} + \frac{\partial \overline{N}_{xy}}{\partial y}\right) p + \left(\frac{\partial \overline{N}_y}{\partial y} + \frac{\partial \overline{N}_{xy}}{\partial x}\right) q + Z = 0$$

By making use of equilibrium Eqs. (3.10a and b), the above equation can be written as

$$\bar{N}_x \frac{\partial^2 z}{\partial x^2} + \bar{N}_y \frac{\partial^2 z}{\partial y^2} + 2\bar{N}_{xy} \frac{\partial^2 z}{\partial x\, \partial y} = Xp + Yq - Z \tag{3.10c}$$

Equations (3.10a–c) are the basic equations governing the membrane theory of a shell of arbitrary shape. As in Chapter 2, we have two first order differential equations (Eqs. (3.10a and b)) and one ordinary linear equation (Eq. 3.10c) with variable coefficients. A direct solution of these equations can be obtained in some cases. However, it is advantageous to reduce this system of equations to a single differential equation of second order. This can be done by recognising the fact that the first two equilibrium equations (Eqs. (3.10a) and (3.10b)) are identical to equilibrium equations of a plane stress system and hence, it is possible to select a variable similar to the stress function. This was first suggested by Pucher[3.1] and here, it will be called as Pucher's stress function. Following the two-dimensional plane stress system, the Pucher stress function ϕ can be defined as

$$\bar{N}_x = \frac{\partial^2 \phi}{\partial y^2} - \int X\, dx \tag{3.11a}$$

$$\bar{N}_y = \frac{\partial^2 \phi}{\partial x^2} - \int Y\, dy \tag{3.11b}$$

$$\bar{N}_{xy} = - \frac{\partial^2 \phi}{\partial x\, \partial y} \tag{3.11c}$$

It may be verified that the above definition of stress resultants in terms of stress function ϕ is such that the first two equilibrium equations, namely Eqs. (3.10a) and (3.10b), are automatically satisfied. Substituting the above relation for the stress resultants in the third equilibrium equation (Eqs. 3.10c), we get the following second order differential equation:

$$r \frac{\partial^2 \phi}{\partial y^2} - 2s \frac{\partial^2 \phi}{\partial x\, \partial y} + t \frac{\partial^2 \phi}{\partial x^2}$$

$$= pX + qY - Z + r \int X\, dx + t \int Y\, dy \tag{3.12}$$

Hence, the membrane analysis of a given doubly curved shell will now reduce itself to obtaining the solution of the differential equation (Eq. 3.12). A partial differential equation of the above form can be called elliptic, if $rt - s^2 > 0$, parabolic, if $rt - s^2 = 0$ and hyperbolic, if $rt - s^2 < 0$. The boundary conditions, which must be prescribed for a unique solution, depends upon the type of equation.

3.4 MEMBRANE THEORY FOR SYNCLASTIC SHELLS

Among synclastic shells, we will consider here, only a shell of translation. The most commonly used shell surfaces under this category are elliptic paraboloid and the rotational paraboloid. These two types of shell surfaces are used to cover large areas, which are either rectangular or square in plan. An elliptic paraboloid is obtained by moving one parabola against another parabola, the planes containing these two parabolas being orthogonal. A section through the elliptic paraboloid with the vertical plane, x = constant or y = constant, leads to a parabola, while a section in the horizontal plane (z = constant) leads to an ellipse. Hence, the surface is called as elliptic paraboloid.

3.4.1 Elliptic Paraboloid

The equation for the surface of a translational shell can be written as

$$z = f(x) + g(y) \tag{a}$$

In the case of an elliptic paraboloid, $f(x)$ and $g(y)$ will be quadratic and hence, the equation to the surface can be written as (Fig. 3.13)

$$z = f_1 \frac{x^2}{a^2} + f_2 \frac{y^2}{b^2} \tag{3.13}$$

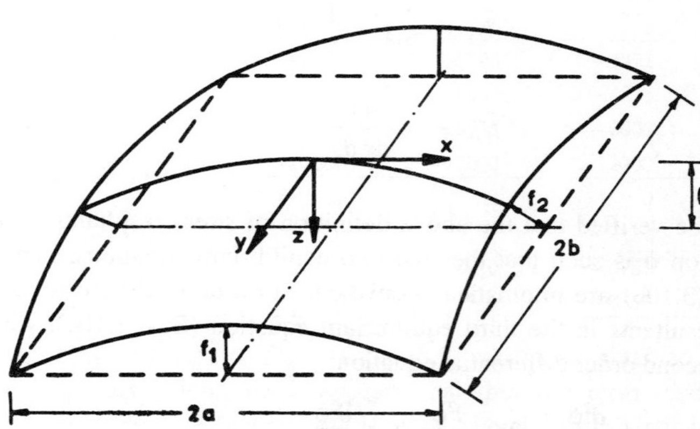

Fig. 3.13 Elliptic paraboloid

If the plan is square (i.e. $a = b$) and the rise of the parabolas are equal, then we obtain a circular paraboloid shell, whose equation may be written as

$$z = \frac{f}{a^2}(x^2 + y^2) \tag{3.14}$$

The rise at the centre of the elliptic paraboloidal shell will be equal to $(f_1 + f_2)$ and if this is less than one-fifth of the diagonal of the rectangle, then we call such a shell as a shallow shell. For a shallow paraboloidal shell, the rise at the centre is selected such that

$$\frac{a+b}{10} \le f_1 + f_2 \le \frac{2}{5}\sqrt{a^2+b^2}$$

which means

$$\min f_1 \ge a/10$$

$$\min f_2 \ge b/10$$

where $2a$ and $2b$ are the plan dimensions (Fig. 3.13).

The slopes and curvatures for an elliptic paraboloid can be determined as

$$p = \frac{2f_1 x}{a^2},\ q = \frac{2f_2 y}{b^2},\ r = \frac{2f_1}{a^2},\ s = 0,\ t = \frac{2f_2}{b^2} \tag{b}$$

If R_1 and R_2 are the two radii of curvature of the generatrix and directrix, then

$$\frac{1}{R_1} = \frac{2f_1}{a^2},\ \frac{1}{R_2} = \frac{2f_2}{b^2} \tag{c}$$

3.4.1.1 Differential equation

Substituting for r, s and t in Eq. (3.12), we get the following differential equation for an elliptic paraboloid

$$\frac{2f_1}{a^2}\frac{\partial^2\phi}{\partial y^2} + \frac{2f_2}{b^2}\frac{\partial^2\phi}{\partial x^2} = pX + qY - Z + r\int X\,dx + t\int Y\,dy \tag{3.15}$$

If we assume that the elliptic paraboloid shell will be subjected to vertical load only, then

$$X = Y = 0$$

and Eq. (3.15) reduces to

$$\frac{2f_1}{a^2}\frac{\partial^2\phi}{\partial y^2} + \frac{2f_2}{b^2}\frac{\partial^2\phi}{\partial x^2} = -Z \tag{3.16}$$

3.4.1.2 Solution

The solution for the differential equation (Eq. 3.16) can be obtained by using different procedures. We will illustrate the several ways by which the solution for the differential equation can be obtained, assuming that the elliptic paraboloid will be supported on shear diaphragms on all the four edges. These shear diaphragms are stiff enough to carry load in their own plane, but cannot resist any load normal to their plane. This type of support condition is often referred as simple support condition in shell analysis. The boundary condition for this type of support condition can be written as (Fig. 3.13),

$$\begin{aligned} x &= \pm a,\ \overline{N}_x = 0 \\ y &= \pm b,\ \overline{N}_y = 0 \end{aligned} \tag{3.17}$$

(a) Solution in terms of double trigonometric series

A solution for ϕ in terms of double trigonometric series, satisfying the boundary conditions given in Eq. (3.17), can be written as

$$\phi = \sum_{m=1\,3}^{\infty} \sum_{n=1,3}^{\infty} A_{mn} \cos \alpha_m x \cos \beta_n y \tag{3.18}$$

where A_{mn} is an undetermined coefficient and

$$\alpha_m = \frac{m\pi}{2a}, \; \beta_n = \frac{n\pi}{2b}$$

The loading can also be expressed in terms of double trigonometric series as

$$Z = \sum_{m=1,3}^{\infty} \sum_{n=1,3}^{\infty} C_{mn} \cos \alpha_m x \cos \beta_n y \tag{3.19}$$

where C_{mn} is determined from

$$C_{mn} = \frac{4}{ab} \int_{-a}^{+a} \int_{-b}^{+b} Z \cos \alpha_m x \cos \beta_n y \, dx\, dy \tag{a}$$

If an uniformly distributed load, including dead load, of intensity q per unit area is acting on the shell then, for such a case, C_{mn} can be determined as

$$C_{mn} = \frac{(-1)^{(m+n-2)/2}\, 16\, q}{mn\pi^2} \tag{b}$$

By substituting for ϕ and Z, the above expressions in Eq. (3.16), A_{mn} can be determined as

$$A_{mn} = \frac{C_{mn}}{\left(\dfrac{2 f_1 \beta_n^2}{a^2} + \dfrac{2 f_2 \cdot \alpha_m^2}{b^2} \right)} \tag{c}$$

Hence, the expression for ϕ can now be written as

$$\phi = \sum_{m=1,3}^{\infty} \sum_{n=1,3}^{\infty} \frac{C_{mn} \cos \alpha_m x \cos \beta_n y}{\left(\dfrac{2 f_1}{a^2}\, \beta_n^2 + \dfrac{2 f_2}{b^2}\, \alpha_m^2 \right)} \tag{3.20}$$

The expressions for projected stress resultants can be obtained as

$$\overline{N}_x = -\sum_{m=1,3}^{\infty}\sum_{n=1,3}^{\infty} \frac{C_{mn}\,\beta_n^2 \cos\alpha_m x \cos\beta_n y}{\left(\dfrac{2f_1}{a^2}\,\beta_n^2 + \dfrac{2f_2}{b^2}\,\alpha_m^2\right)} \tag{d}$$

$$\overline{N}_y = -\sum_{m=1,3}^{\infty}\sum_{n=1,3}^{\infty} \frac{C_{mn}\,\alpha_m^2 \cos\alpha_m x \cos\beta_n y}{\left(\dfrac{2f_1}{a^2}\,\beta_n^2 + \dfrac{2f_2}{b^2}\,\alpha_m^2\right)} \tag{e}$$

$$\overline{N}_{xy} = -\sum_{m=1,3}^{\infty}\sum_{n=1,3}^{\infty} \frac{C_{mn}\,\alpha_m\,\beta_n \sin\alpha_m x \sin\beta_n y}{\left(\dfrac{2f_1}{a^2}\,\beta_n^2 + \dfrac{2f_2}{b^2}\,\alpha_m^2\right)} \tag{f}$$

The actual stress resultants can be determined as

$$N_x = -\frac{b^2}{a^2}\sqrt{\frac{a^4+4f_1^2x^2}{b^4+4f_2^2y^2}}\sum_{m=1,3}^{\infty}\sum_{n=1,3}^{\infty} \frac{C_{mn}\,\beta_n^2 \cos\alpha_m x \cos\beta_n y}{\left(\dfrac{2f_1}{a^2}\,\beta_n^2 + \dfrac{2f_2}{b^2}\,\alpha_m^2\right)} \tag{3.21a}$$

$$N_y = -\frac{a^2}{b^2}\sqrt{\frac{b^4+4f_2^2y^2}{a^4+4f_1^2x^2}}\sum_{m=1,3}^{\infty}\sum_{n=1,3}^{\infty} \frac{C_{mn}\,\alpha_n^2 \cos\alpha_m x \cos\beta_n y}{\left(\dfrac{2f_1}{a^2}\,\beta_n^2 + \dfrac{2f_2}{b^2}\,\alpha_m^2\right)} \tag{3.21b}$$

$$N_{xy} = -\sum_{m=1,3}^{\infty}\sum_{n=1,3}^{\infty} \frac{C_{mn}\,\alpha_m\,\beta_n \sin\alpha_m x \sin\beta_n y}{\left(\dfrac{2f_1}{a^2}\,\beta_n^2 + \dfrac{2f_2}{b^2}\,\alpha_m^2\right)} \tag{3.21c}$$

It may be noted that, the series expressions for the forces converge slowly thus requiring the consideration of large number of terms to get reasonably accurate results.

(b) Solution in terms of single trigonometric series

First, consider the homogeneous differential equation

$$\frac{2f_1}{a^2}\frac{\partial^2\phi}{\partial y^2} + \frac{2f_2}{b^2}\frac{\partial^2\phi}{\partial x^2} = 0 \tag{a}$$

The solution of the above differential equation may be taken as

$$\phi = f(x)\,g(y) \tag{b}$$

where $f(x)$ is a function of x only and $g(y)$ is a function of y only.

The function $g(y)$ can be taken in the form of trigonometric series in such a way that the boundary condition along $y = \pm b$, namely, $\overline{N}_y = 0$ is satisfied. Hence, for the chosen coordinate system (Fig. 3.13), $g(y)$ can be taken as

$$g(y) = \sum_{n=1}^{\infty} g \cos \beta_n y \tag{c}$$

where $$\beta_n = \left(\frac{n\pi}{2b}\right).$$

Substituting Eqs. (b) and (c) in the differential equation (a), we get a second order ordinary differential equation in terms of the variable f as

$$-\left(\frac{2f_1}{a^2}\right)\beta_n^2 f + \frac{2f_2}{b^2}\frac{d^2 f}{dx^2} = 0 \tag{d}$$

or

$$\frac{d^2 f}{dx^2} - \left(\frac{f_1}{f_2}\right)\left(\frac{b^2}{a^2}\right)\beta_n^2 f = 0$$

The solution of the above ordinary differential equation may be obtained as

$$f = A_n \cosh \beta_n' x + B_n \sinh \beta_n' x \tag{e}$$

where $$\beta_n' = \left(\sqrt{\frac{f_1}{f_2}}\right)\beta_n\left(\frac{b}{a}\right)$$

Hence, the solution for the homogeneous part of the differential equation can be written as

$$\phi_0 = \sum_{n=1}^{\infty} (A_n \cosh \beta_n' x + B_n \sinh \beta_n' x) \cos \beta_n y \tag{3.22a}$$

Now the loading also can be expressed in terms of trigonometric series as

$$Z = \sum_{n=1}^{\infty} C_n \cos \beta_n y \tag{f}$$

where $$C_n = \frac{1}{b}\int_{-b}^{+b} Z \cos \beta_n y \, dy$$

For the case of uniform load of intensity q (including dead load) per unit area C_n can be determined as

$$C_n = (-1)^{(n-1)/2}\left(\frac{4q}{n\pi}\right) \cdot\cdot (n = 1, 3, \cdots) \tag{g}$$

The particular integral can now be determined as

$$\phi_p = \frac{a^2}{2f_1}\sum_{n=1,3}^{\infty}\frac{C_n}{\beta_n^2}\cos \beta_n y \tag{3.22b}$$

For the problem considered here, since the loading and boundary condition are symmetrical about y-axis, the constant B_n will be zero. Hence, the complete solution for ϕ can be written as

$$\phi = \phi_0 + \phi_p = \sum_{n=1,3}^{\infty} \left[A_n \cosh \beta_n' x + \frac{a^2}{2 f_1 \beta_n^2} C_n \right] \cos \beta_n y \tag{3.23}$$

The projected membrane forces can be determined as

$$\overline{N}_x = - \sum_{n=1,3}^{\infty} \left(A_n \beta_n^2 \cosh \beta_n' x + \frac{a^2}{2 f_1} C_n \right) \cos \beta_n y \tag{h}$$

$$\overline{N}_y = - \sum_{n=1,3}^{\infty} A_n (\beta_n')^2 \cosh \beta_n' x \cos \beta_n y \tag{i}$$

$$\overline{N}_{xy} = \sum_{n=1,3}^{\infty} A_n \beta_n \beta_n' \sinh \beta_n' x \sin \beta_n y \tag{k}$$

Using the boundary condition, that $x = \pm a$, $\overline{N}_x = 0$, and using Eq. (g) for C_n, we get

$$A_n = - \frac{(-1)^{(n-1)/2} \, 8 \, q a^2 b^2}{f_1 (n\pi)^3 \cosh \beta_n' a} \tag{k}$$

Hence, the expression for ϕ can now be written as

$$\phi = - \frac{8 \, q a^2 b^2}{f_1 \pi^3} \sum_{n=1,3}^{\infty} \left\{ \frac{\cosh \beta_n' x}{\cosh \beta_n' a} - 1 \right\} \frac{(-1)^{(n-1)/2}}{n^3} \cos \beta_n y \tag{3.24}$$

The expressions for the actual membrane stress resultants can be obtained as

$$N_x = \frac{2 \, q b^2}{f_1 \pi} \sqrt{\frac{a^4 + 4 f_1^2 x^2}{b^4 + 4 f_2^2 y^2}} \sum_{n=1,3}^{\infty} \left(\frac{\cosh \beta_n' x}{\cosh \beta_n' a} - 1 \right) \frac{(-1)^{(n-1)/2}}{n \cos \beta_n y} \tag{3.25a}$$

$$N_y = \frac{2 \, q a^2}{f_2 \pi} \sqrt{\frac{b^4 + 4 f_2^2 y^2}{a^4 + 4 f_1^2 x^2}} \sum_{n=1,3}^{\infty} (-1)^{(n-1)/2} \frac{\cosh \beta_n' x \cos \beta_n y}{n \cosh \beta_n' a} \tag{3.25b}$$

$$N_{xy} = - \frac{2 \, q a b}{\sqrt{f_1 f_2} \, \pi} \sum_{n=1,3}^{\infty} (-1)^{(n-1)/2} \frac{\sinh \beta_n' x \sin \beta_n y}{n \cosh \beta_n' a} \tag{3.25c}$$

It must be noted that the above solution has been obtained by taking the particular solution (Eq. (g)) also, in terms of trigonometric series. Hence, while obtaining the membrane forces, it becomes necessary to study the convergence of the particular solution. As indicated earlier, fairly large number of terms are to be considered in the series to represent the uniform load, which means, for the computation of membrane forces, particularly N_x, one has to consider large number of terms in the series. Alternatively, it is possible to express the particular solution in closed form, so that the membrane stress resultants could be computed by considering the first few terms in the series. However, it must be noted that this approach is possible only when the loading is continuous over the shell, so that its variation can be expressed in terms of simple polynomials. This restriction does not apply to the above solution, since the loading and the particular solution have been expressed in terms of trigonometric series and hence, discontinuous loading also can be dealt with. We will now present an alternative solution, in which the particular solution can be written in the closed form as (satisfying the boundary condition)

$$\phi_p = \frac{qa^2}{4f_1}(b^2 - y^2) \tag{l}$$

The solution for ϕ can now be written as

$$\phi = \frac{qa^2}{4f_1}(b^2 - y^2) + \sum_{n=1,3}^{\infty} A_n \cosh \beta'_n x \cos \beta_n y \tag{m}$$

Now, the projected stress resultant $\overline{N}_x$ can be obtained as

$$\overline{N}_x = -\frac{qa^2}{2f_1} - \sum_{n=1,3}^{\infty} A_n \beta_n^2 \cosh \beta'_n x \cos \beta_n y \tag{n}$$

Now, expanding the constant term in the above equation in terms of Fourier series (Eq. (g)) and using the boundary condition that $\overline{N}_x = 0$ at $x = \pm a$, we get

$$A_n = -\frac{(-1)^{(n-1)/2}\, 8\, qa^2 b^2}{f_1 (n\pi)^3 \cosh \beta'_n a} \tag{o}$$

Hence, the complete solution can be written as

$$\phi = \frac{qa^2}{4f_1}\left[(b^2 - y^2) - \frac{32\, b^2}{\pi^3} \sum_{n=1,3}^{\infty} (-1)^{(n-1)/2} \times \frac{1}{n^3} \frac{\cosh \beta'_n x}{\cosh \beta'_n a} \cos \beta_n y\right] \tag{3.26}$$

The expressions for the actual membrane stress resultants can be determined as

$$N_x = \frac{qb^2}{2f_1\pi}\sqrt{\frac{a^4 + 4f_1^2 x^2}{b^4 + 4f_2^2 y^2}}\left(1 - \frac{4}{\pi}\sum_{n=1,3}^{\infty} (-1)^{(n-1)/2} \times \frac{\cosh \beta'_n x}{n \cosh \beta'_n a} \cos \beta_n y\right) \tag{3.27a}$$

$$N_y = \frac{-2qa^2}{f_2\pi}\sqrt{\frac{b^4 + 4f_2^2 y^2}{a^4 + 4f_1^2 x^2}}\sum_{n=1,3}^{\infty} (-1)^{(n-1)/2} \times \frac{\cosh \beta'_n x \cos \beta_n y}{n \cosh \beta'_n a} \tag{3.27b}$$

$$N_{xy} = -\frac{2qab}{\sqrt{f_1 f_2}\,\pi} \sum_{n=1,3}^{\infty} (-1)^{(n-1)/2} \frac{\sinh \beta_n' x \sin \beta_n y}{n \cosh \beta_n' a} \tag{3.27c}$$

It may be noted that the particular solution for N_x in seiies form (Eq. 3.25a) is now replaced by a closed form solution for N_x in Eq. (3.27a). Except for this change, the expressions for N_y and N_{xy} are identical to the ones given in Eqs. (3.25b) and (3.25c). The expressions for N_x and N_y (Eqs. (3.27a) and (3.27b)) indicate that the series converges rapidly, since we have a hyperbolic function in the denominator. However, as we move towards the corner ($x = a$, $y = b$), the forces N_x and N_y will be zero, while the shear force N_{xy} tends to infinity. The implication of this is very obvious as the membrane solution will not be valid near the corners of the shell. This is because, at the corners the membrane forces cannot carry the load and hence large transverse shearing forces will appear causing bending and twisting of the shell. Based on the above solution, Parme[3.2] has given tables, to compute the membrane forces directly, for different values of (f_1/f_2).

(c) Solution in terms of polynomials

If the shell is subjected to a continuous loading over its entire surface, such that the load can be expressed by means of simple polynomials, then a solution could be obtained in terms of polynomials. However, the solution could be obtained only for a certain type of boundary conditions. We will domenstrate the method of obtaining a solution in terms of polynomials for an all-round simply supported circular elliptic paraboloid. The differential equation for a circular elliptic paraboloid can be written as

$$\frac{\partial^2 \phi}{\partial x^2} + \frac{\partial^2 \phi}{\partial y^2} = -ZR \tag{3.28}$$

where $1/R = 2f/a^2$

If the shell is not shallow and is subjected to a vertical load of intensity q per unit area, then Eq. (3.28) will be

$$\frac{\partial^2 \phi}{\partial x^2} + \frac{\partial^2 \phi}{\partial y^2} = -qR\sqrt{1+p^2+q^2} = -qR\sqrt{1+\frac{x^2+y^2}{R^2}} \tag{a}$$

Expanding the loading term (right hand side of the above equation), using Binomial theorem and retaining only the first four terms, Eq. (a) can be written as

$$\frac{\partial^2 \phi}{\partial x^2} + \frac{\partial^2 \phi}{\partial y^2} = -qR\left[1 + \frac{1}{2R^2}(x^2+y^2) - \frac{1}{8R^4}(x^4+y^4) - \frac{1}{4R^4}x^2y^2\right] \tag{b}$$

The solution for ϕ in terms of polynomials can be written as:

$$\phi = A(x^2 + y^2) + B(x^2 y^2) + C(x^4 + y^4) + D(x^6 + y^6)$$

$$+ E(x^4 y^2 + x^2 y^4) + F(x^4 y^4) + G(x^2 y^6 + x^6 y^2) \quad \text{(c)}$$

where $A, B, C, \ldots, G$ are constants, so determined that the differential equation (b) and the boundary conditions are completely satisfied.

Substituting Eq. (c) in the differential equation (b), we get

$$(2A + 2By^2 + 12Cx^2 + 30Dx^4 + 12Ex^2y^2 + 2Ey^4 + 12Fx^2y^4$$

$$+ 2Gy^6 + 30Gx^4y^2) + (2A + 2Bx^2 + 12Cy^2$$

$$+ 30Dy^4 + 12Ex^2y^2 + 2Ex^4 + 12Fx^4y^2 + 2Gx^6 + 30Gx^2y^4)$$

$$= -qR\left[1 + \frac{1}{2R^2}(x^2 + y^2) - \frac{1}{8R^4}(x^4 + y^4) - \frac{1}{4R^4}x^2y^2\right] \quad \text{(d)}$$

By equating the coefficients of the variables with the same exponent, we get the following set of equations:

$$2A + 2A + qR = 0 \quad \text{(e)}$$

$$(x^2 + y^2)\left(2B + 12C + \frac{q}{2R}\right) = 0 \quad \text{(f)}$$

$$x^2y^2\left(12E + 12E - \frac{q}{4R^3}\right) = 0 \quad \text{(g)}$$

$$(x^4 + y^4)\left(30D + 2E - \frac{q}{8R^3}\right) = 0 \quad \text{(h)}$$

If the constants are so determined as to satisfy Eqs. (e)–(h), then the differential equation (b) will be completely satisfied. However, we have now only four equations involving seven unknown constants, viz. $A, B, C, \ldots, G$ and hence, we require three more additional equations to determine all the constants. These additional equations can now be obtained by using the following boundary conditions:

$$\text{at } x = \pm a, \ \overline{N}_x = 0$$

$$\text{at } y = \pm a, \ \overline{N}_y = 0$$

The expressions for the projected membrane forces can be obtained as

$$\overline{N}_x = 2A + 2Bx^2 + 12Cy^2 + 30Dy^4 + E(12x^2y^2 + 2x^4)$$
$$+ 12Fx^4y^2 + G(2x^6 + 30x^2y^4) \qquad \text{(i)}$$

$$\overline{N}_y = 2A + 2By^2 + 12Cx^2 + 30Dx^4 + E(12x^2y^2 + 2y^4)$$
$$+ 12Fx^2y^4 + G(2y^6 + 30x^4y^2) \qquad \text{(j)}$$

$$\overline{N}_{xy} = -4Bxy - 8E(x^3y + xy^3) - 16Fx^3y^3 - 12G(xy^5 + x^5y) \qquad \text{(k)}$$

Using the boundary condition that $x = \pm a$, $\overline{N}_x = 0$, we get

$$2A + 2Ba^2 + 2Ea^4 + 2Ga^6 = 0 \qquad \text{(l)}$$

$$y^2(12C + 12Ea^2 + 12Fa^4) = 0 \qquad \text{(m)}$$

$$y^4(30D + 30Ga^2) = 0 \qquad \text{(n)}$$

The boundary condition $\overline{N}_y = 0$ at $y = \pm a$ also results in the same set of equations as given in Eqs. (l)–(n). Hence, now we have seven equations, Eqs. (e)–(h) and (l)–(n), involving seven constants, from which the constants can be determined as :

$$A = \frac{-qR}{4}, \quad B = \frac{q}{4m^2R}\left(1 - \frac{m^4}{36}\right), \quad C = -\frac{q(1+m^2)}{24m^2R} + \frac{qm^2}{864R}$$

$$D = \frac{q}{288R^3}, \quad E = \frac{q}{96R^3}, \quad F = \left\{\frac{qR(1+m^2)}{24a^6} - \frac{5qm^2}{432a^4R}\right\},$$

$$G = -\frac{q}{288m^2R^5}$$

where $m = (a/R)$.

Substituting for $A, B, \ldots, G$ in Eqs. (i)–(k), the projected stress resultants can be determined as

$$\overline{N}_x = -\frac{qR}{2}\left[1 - \frac{x^2}{a^2}\left(1 - \frac{m^4}{36}\right) + \frac{y^2}{a^2}\left\{(1+m^2) - \frac{m^4}{36}\right\}\right.$$
$$- \frac{5m^4y^4}{24a^4} - \frac{m^4x^4}{24a^4} - \frac{m^4x^2y^2}{4a^4} - \frac{x^4y^2}{a^6}$$
$$\left.\times\left\{(1+m^2) - \frac{5m^4}{18}\right\} + \frac{m^4(x^6 + 15x^2y^4)}{72a^6}\right] \qquad \text{(o)}$$

$$\overline{N}_y = -\frac{qR}{2}\left[1-\frac{y^2}{a^2}\left(1-\frac{m^4}{36}\right)+\frac{x^2}{a^2}\left\{(1+m^2)-\frac{m^4}{36}\right\}\right.$$

$$-\frac{5m^4x^4}{24a^4}-\frac{m^4y^4}{24a^4}-\frac{m^4x^2y^2}{4a^4}-\frac{x^2y^4}{a^6}$$

$$\left.\times\left\{(1+m^2)-\frac{5m^4}{18}\right\}+\frac{m^4\,(y^6+15y^2x^4)}{72a^6}\right] \qquad \text{(p)}$$

$$\overline{N}_{xy} = -\,qR\left[\frac{xy}{a^2}\left(1-\frac{m^4}{36}\right)+\frac{m^4}{12a^4}\,(x^3y+xy^3)\right.$$

$$\left.+\left\{\frac{2}{3a^6}\,(1+m^2)-\frac{5m^4}{27a^6}\right\}x^3y^3-\frac{m^4}{24a^6}\,(xy^5+x^5y)\right] \qquad \text{(q)}$$

Generally, for most of the circular paraboloids, $f = (a/10)$ and hence, m will be equal to 0.2. In such cases, power equal to and greater than four for m can be safely neglected in the above expressions for membrane forces. Hence, we get the following approximate expressions for the projected membrane stress resultants:

$$\overline{N}_x = -\frac{qR}{2}\left[1-\frac{x^2}{a^2}+\frac{y^2}{a^2}\,(1+m^2)-\frac{x^4y^2}{a^6}\,(1+m^2)\right] \qquad \text{(r)}$$

$$\overline{N}_y = -\frac{qR}{2}\left[1-\frac{y^2}{a^2}+\frac{x^2}{a^2}\,(1+m^2)-\frac{x^2y^4}{a^6}\,(1+m^2)\right] \qquad \text{(s)}$$

$$\overline{N}_{xy} = -\frac{qRxy}{a^2}\left[1+\frac{2}{3}\,(1+m^2)\,\frac{(x^2y^2)}{a^4}\right] \qquad \text{(t)}$$

Now, the expressions for the actual stress resultants can be obtained as

$$N_x = -\sqrt{\frac{a^4+4f^2x^2}{a^4+4f^2y^2}}\left(\frac{qR}{2}\right)$$

$$\times\left[1-\frac{x^2}{a^2}+\frac{y^2}{a^2}\,(1+m^2)-\frac{x^4y^2}{a^6}\,(1+m^2)\right] \qquad \text{(3.29a)}$$

$$N_y = -\sqrt{\frac{a^4+4f^2y^2}{a^4+4f^2x^2}}\left(\frac{qR}{2}\right)$$

$$\times\left[1-\frac{y^2}{a^2}+\frac{x^2}{a^2}\,(1+m^2)-\frac{x^2y^4}{a^6}\,(1+m^2)\right] \qquad \text{(3.29b)}$$

$$N_{xy} = -\frac{qRxy}{a^2}\left[1+\frac{2\,(1+m^2)}{3a^4}\,(x^2y^2)\right] \qquad \text{(3.29c)}$$

(d) Solution using finite difference method

For a general support or loading condition, solution through trigonometric series or polynomials becomes rather difficult if not impossible. In such a case, one can resort to a numerical method. One such widely used numerical method is the finite difference method. We will illustrate here the application of this method to an all round simply supported elliptic paraboloid, subjected to a uniform vertical loading of intensity q. Following this, several problems of elliptic paraboloid of practical interest can be easily solved.

Instead of dealing with the differential equation in terms of the stress function ϕ, as was done in the earlier solutions, it will be more convenient here to solve the problem directly using equilibrium equations[3.4]. The equilibrium equations for an elliptic paraboloid can be written as

$$\frac{\partial \overline{N}_x}{\partial x} + \frac{\partial \overline{N}_{xy}}{\partial y} = 0 \tag{a}$$

$$\frac{\partial \overline{N}_y}{\partial y} + \frac{\partial \overline{N}_{xy}}{\partial x} = 0 \tag{b}$$

$$\frac{\overline{N}_x}{R_1} + \frac{\overline{N}_y}{R_2} = -\ q \tag{c}$$

where $\qquad \dfrac{1}{R_1} = \dfrac{2f_1}{a^2}$ and $\dfrac{1}{R_2} = \dfrac{2f_2}{b^2}$

Eliminating $\overline{N}_{xy}$ from Eqs. (a) and (b) above, we get

$$\frac{\partial^2 N_x}{\partial x^2} - \frac{\partial^2 N_y}{\partial y^2} = 0 \tag{d}$$

From Eq. (c),

$$\overline{N}_y = -\frac{R_2}{R_1} N_x - qR_2 \tag{e}$$

Substituting for N_y from Eq. (e) in Eq. (d), we get

$$\frac{1}{R_2}\frac{\partial^2 \overline{N}_x}{\partial x^2} + \frac{1}{R_1}\frac{\partial^2 \overline{N}_x}{\partial y^2} = -\ R_2 \frac{\partial^2 q}{\partial y^2} \tag{3.30}$$

Equation (3.30) is a partial differential equation of second order and for its solution, we need to specify two boundary conditions. Since the shell is simply supported on all the four edges, we can write the following boundary conditions:

for $\qquad x = \pm\ a,\ \overline{N}_x = 0$

for $\qquad y = \pm\ a,\ \overline{N}_y = 0$

We will solve the differential equation (3.30) here, by the method of differences. For this, the entire area of the shell is to be divided into a network of points having a mesh size Δx (in x-direction) by Δy (in the y-direction), as shown in Fig. 3.14. Using the standard finite difference, we may now write the difference form of Eq. (3.30) at any arbitrary point i, as

$$\frac{(\overline{N}_x)_{i-1} - 2\,(\overline{N}_x)_i + (\overline{N}_x)_{i+1}}{R_2\ (\Delta x)^2} + \frac{(\overline{N}_x)_{j-1} - 2\,(\overline{N}_x)_j + (\overline{N}_x)_{j+1}}{R_1\ (\Delta y)^2}$$

$$= -\ R_2\left[\frac{(q)_{j-1} - 2\,(q)_j + (q)_{j+1}}{(\Delta y)^2}\right] \tag{f}$$

Taking $(R_2 (\Delta x)^2) / (R_1 (\Delta y)^2) = 1$ and recognising the fact that in this example q is constant, Eq. (f) can now be reduced to the following form

$$(\overline{N}_x)_{i-1} + (\overline{N}_x)_{i+1} + (\overline{N}_x)_{j-1} + (\overline{N}_x)_{j+1} - 4(\overline{N}_x)_i = 0 \tag{3.31}$$

Equation of the above type can be formed for all inner points i of the network. If the shell is subjected to symmetrical loading, and has symmetric boundary conditions, as in the present example, then it is necessary to consider only one quadrant of the shell for formulating the finite difference equations.

We will write down the finite difference equations considering a quadrant of shell having a grid, as shown in Fig. 3.14. Further, using the boundary condition $\overline{N}_y = 0$ along $y = \pm b$ in Eq. (e), we can determine $\overline{N}_x$ along $y = \pm b$ as

$$\overline{N}_x = qR_1$$

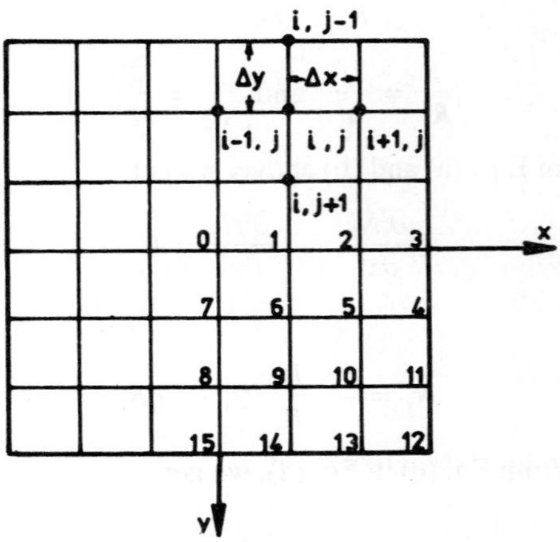

Fig. 3.14 Finite difference net

Applying Eq. (3.31) to the inner points 0 to 10, we get the following equations:

Point 0, $-4(\overline{N}_x)_0 + 2(\overline{N}_x)_1 + 2(\overline{N}_x)_7 = 0$

Point 1, $(\overline{N}_x)_2 + 2(\overline{N}_x)_6 + (\overline{N}_x)_0 - 4(\overline{N}_x)_1 = 0$

Point 2, $2(\overline{N}_x)_5 + (\overline{N}_x)_1 - 4(\overline{N}_x)_2 = 0$

Point 5, $(\overline{N}_x)_{10} + (\overline{N}_x)_6 + (\overline{N}_x)_2 - 4(\overline{N}_x)_5 = 0$

Point 6, $(\overline{N}_x)_5 + (\overline{N}_x)_9 + (\overline{N}_x)_7 + (\overline{N}_x)_1 - 4(\overline{N}_x)_6 = 0$

Point 7, $(\overline{N}_x)_8 + 2(\overline{N}_x)_6 + (\overline{N}_x)_0 - 4(\overline{N}_x)_7 = 0$

Point 8, $(\overline{N}_x)_7 + 2(\overline{N}_x)_9 + (\overline{N}_x)_{15} - 4(\overline{N}_x)_8 = 0$

Point 9, $(\overline{N}_x)_8 + (\overline{N}_x)_{14} + (\overline{N}_x)_{10} + (\overline{N}_x)_6 - 4(\overline{N}_x)_9 = 0$

Point 10, $(\overline{N}_x)_9 + (\overline{N}_x)_{13} + (\overline{N}_x)_5 - 4(\overline{N}_x)_{10} = 0$ (3.32)

It may be noted that while writing the above equations, the boundary condition that $\bar{N}_x = 0$ along $x = \pm\, a$ has been made use of, resulting in $(\bar{N}_x)_3 = (\bar{N}_x)_4 = (\bar{N}_x)_{11} = 0$. Further, in the above equations,

$$(\bar{N}_x)_{15} = (\bar{N}_x)_{14} = (\bar{N}_x)_{13} = -\ qR_1$$

Solving the above nine simultaneous equations, the value of $\bar{N}_x$ at all interior points can be determined. Using this, $\bar{N}_y$ at all interior points can be determined from Eq. (e).

The shear force $\bar{N}_{xy}$ at interior points can be determined, using the first equilibrium equation, namely

$$\frac{\partial \bar{N}_x}{\partial x} + \frac{\partial \bar{N}_{xy}}{\partial y} = 0$$

Referring to Fig. 3.15, the above equation can be written in the difference form as

$$\frac{(\bar{N}_x)_2 - (\bar{N}_x)_1}{2\Delta x} + \frac{(\bar{N}_{xy})_b - (\bar{N}_{xy})_e}{\Delta y} = 0$$

or

$$\frac{1}{2\Delta x}\left[\frac{(\bar{N}_x)_c + (\bar{N}_x)_d}{2} - \frac{(\bar{N}_x)_a + (\bar{N}_x)_f}{2}\right] + \frac{(\bar{N}_{xy})_b - (\bar{N}_{xy})_e}{\Delta y} = 0$$

from which $\bar{N}_{xy}$ at b can be determined from

$$(\bar{N}_{xy})_b = (\bar{N}_{xy})_e + \frac{\Delta y}{4\Delta x}\left[(\bar{N}_x)_a + (\bar{N}_x)_f - (\bar{N}_x)_c - (\bar{N}_x)_d\right]$$

Applying the above equation at point '6', for example (Fig. 3.14), we get

$$(\bar{N}_{xy})_6 = (\bar{N}_{xy})_1 + \frac{\Delta y}{4\Delta x}\left[(\bar{N}_x)_7 + (\bar{N}_x)_0 - (\bar{N}_x)_5 - (\bar{N}_x)_2\right] \qquad (3.33)$$

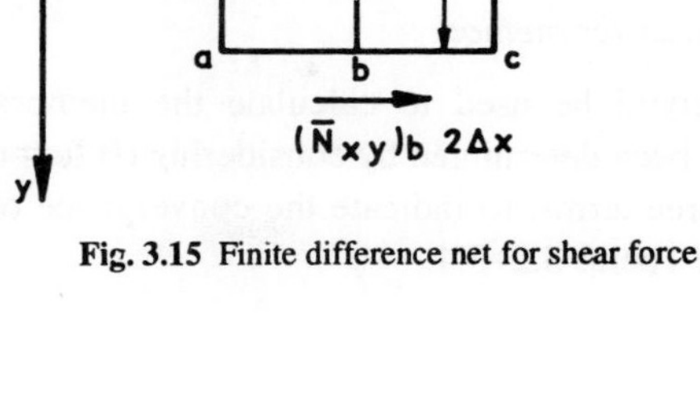

Fig. 3.15 Finite difference net for shear force

Since the shell is subjected to a symmetrical load, $(\overline{N}_{xy})_i = 0$. From the above equation, $\overline{N}_{xy}$ at point '6' can now easily be determined, as the value of $\overline{N}_x$ at all inner points has already been determined. By applying the above equation in a similar way at all 'i' interior points, $(\overline{N}_{xy})$ at all these points can be determined. As mentioned earlier, it may be noted that the membrane solution will not be valid at the corners.

Example 3.1

We will determine the membrane forces in an all-round simply supported elliptic paraboloid having plan dimensions 18 m by 24 m and thickness 6 cm. The rise of the elliptic paraboloid is $f_1 = f_2 = 1.2$ m. The shell will be subjected to uniform live load of 56 kg/m^2 in addition to its dead load.

In this example, $2a = 18\ m$, $2b = 24\ m$.

The radius of curvature will be

$$R_1 = \frac{a^2}{2f_1} = \frac{9^2}{2.4} = 33.75\ \text{m}$$

$$R_2 = \frac{b^2}{2f_2} = \frac{12^2}{2.4} = 60\ \text{m}$$

Loads

Dead load = 2400 × 0.06	=	144 kg/m^2
(assuming unit weight of concrete = 2400 kg/m^3)		
Live load	=	56 kg/m^2
Total load q	=	200 kg/m^2

We will determine the membrane forces in the elliptic paraboloid, using the following two methods:

(i) Single trigonometric series method,

(ii) Finite difference method.

The object of solving the problem using these two methods is to indicate the computational effort required in each case to get reasonably accurate results.

(i) Single trigonometric series method

Equations (3.25a–c) could be used to calculate the membrane forces. The membrane forces have been determined by considering (i) first term, (ii) first two terms, and (iii) first three terms, to indicate the convergence of the series. The results are presented in Tables 3.2–3.4.

Table 3.2 N_x force distribution in an elliptic paraboloid (kg/m)

x/a	No. of terms	y/b 0	0.33	0.67	1.0
0	$n = 1$	−3324	− 3766	− 5008	− 6618
	$n = 1, 3$	− 3376	− 3767	− 4957	− 6618
	$n = 1, 3, 5$	− 3374	− 3768	− 4956	− 6618
0.33	$n = 1$	− 2865	− 3371	− 4795	− 6664.5
	$n = 1, 3$	− 2993	− 3373	− 4668	− 6644.5
	$n = 1, 3, 5$	− 2984	− 3381	− 4664	− 6644.5
0.67	$n = 1$	− 1266	− 1996	− 4050	− 6723
	$n = 1, 3$	− 1881	− 2005	− 3440	− 6723
	$n = 1, 3, 5$	− 1780	− 2117	− 3372	− 6723
1.0	$n = 1$	0	0	0	0
	$n = 1, 3$	0	0	0	0
	$n = 1, 3, 5$	0	0	0	0

Table 3.3 N_y force distribution in an elliptic paraboloid (kg/m)

x/a	No. of terms	y/b 0	0.33	0.67	1.0
0	$n = 1$	− 6089	− 5300	− 3043	0
	$n = 1, 3$	− 5997	− 5299	− 3136	0
	$n = 1, 3, 5$	− 6000	− 5297	− 3137	0
0.33	$n = 1$	− 6899	− 6005	− 3448	0
	$n = 1, 3$	− 6673	− 6002	− 3676	0
	$n = 1, 3, 5$	− 6689	− 5988	− 3684	0
0.67	$n = 1$	− 9631	− 8384	− 4814	0
	$n = 1, 3$	− 8571	− 8368	− 5884	0
	$n = 1, 3, 5$	− 8796	− 8175	− 6003	0
1.0	$n = 1$	− 14762	− 12851	− 7379	0
	$n = 1, 3$	− 9841	− 12774	− 12344	0
	$n = 1, 3, 5$	− 12794	− 10251	− 13900	0

Table 3.4 N_{xy} force distribution in an elliptic paraboloid (kg/m)

x/a	No. of terms	y/b 0	0.33	0.67	1.0
0	$n = 1$	0	0	0	0
	$n = 1, 3$	0	0	0	0
	$n = 1, 3, 5$	0	0	0	0
0.33	$n = 1$	0	−1226	− 2149	− 2474
	$n = 1, 3$	0	−1070	− 2152	− 2630
	$n = 1, 3, 5$	0	−1077	− 2142	− 2642
0.67	$n = 1$	0	− 2846	− 4989	− 5744
	$n = 1, 3$	0	− 2040	− 5002	− 6549
	$n = 1, 3, 5$	0	− 2130	− 4885	− 6720
1.0	$n = 1$	0	− 5207	− 9129	− 10509
	$n = 1, 3$	0	− 1388	− 9189	− 14328
	$n = 1, 3, 5$	0	− 2596	− 7235	− 16620

From the above tables, it may be observed that reasonably accurate results could be obtained in respect of force N_x and N_y, by just taking the first term in the series. However, the convergence in respect of the force N_{xy} is not very good, particularly near the edges, even with the consideration of three terms in the series. Hence to obtain reasonably accurate results, it becomes necessary to consider more number of terms.

(b) Finite difference method

For solving the problem by finite difference method, a net, as indicated in Fig. 3.14, is considered. Hence, for the problem, $\Delta x = 3m$, $\Delta y = 4m$. First, making use of Eq. (3.32), $\overline{N}_x$ could be determined. Later, $\overline{N}_y$ and $\overline{N}_{xy}$ could be determined. Using these values, N_x, N_y and N_{xy} may be computed. The results are presented in Table 3.5.

Table 3.5 N_x, N_y and N_{xy} force distribution (kg/m)

Force	x/a	y/b			
		0	0.33	0.67	1.0
	0	- 3375	- 3765	- 4938	- 6750
N_x	0.33	- 2984	- 3365	- 4609	- 6750
	0.67	- 1811	- 2140	- 3775	- 6750
	1.0	0	0	0	0
	0	- 6000	- 5305	- 3221	0
N_y	0.33	- 6695	- 6000	- 3805	0
	0.67	- 8779	- 8995	- 6000	0
	1.0	- 12000	- 12000	- 12000	0
	0	0	0	0	0
N_{xy}	0.33	0	-1063	- 2120	- 2641
	0.67	0	- 2120	- 4781	- 8567
	1.0	0	- 2641	- 8567	-18281

Comparing the results from Table 3.5 with that obtained from single trigonometric series solution, it appears that the first term results of single trigonometric series are sufficiently accurate. Hence, in this particular case, it appears that the computational effort would be very small if single trigonometric series method is used.

3.5 MEMBRANE THEORY FOR ANTICLASTIC SHELLS

In anticlastic shells, we will consider here only the shells of translation. The commonly used shell surfaces for roof under this category are hyperbolic paraboloids (or hypar) and conoids. The surface of a hyperbolic paraboloid can be generated by moving a concave parabola (generatrix) against a convex parabola (directrix) or vice versa. The name hyperbolic paraboloid is derived from the fact that the vertical section (x or y = constant) will be a parabola and the horizontal section (z = constant) will be a hyperbola. Sometimes, a hyperbolic paraboloid of this type is referred as saddle shell. By suitable transformation of coordinates, a hyperbolic paraboloid with parabola as generatrix and directrix can be converted into a skew hyperbolic paraboloid with straight lines as generatrix and directrix. The surface of a conoid may be generated by moving a straight line (generatrix) along a plane curve at one end and a straight line at the opposite end (directrix). The plane-curve directrix can be either an ellipse or a parabola or an arc of a circle, and correspondingly the conoid is referred as elliptic or parabolic or circular conoid. In the following paragraphs, we will consider the analysis of hyperbolic paraboloid and conoid.

3.5.1 Hyperbolic Paraboloid whose Edges are Principal Parabolas

The equation of the middle surface of a hyperbolic paraboloid can be written as

$$z = \frac{x^2}{2R_1} - \frac{y^2}{2R_2} \tag{3.34}$$

where

$$\frac{1}{R_1} = \frac{2f_1}{a^2} \text{ and } \frac{1}{R_2} = \frac{2f_2}{b^2}$$

It may be seen that the above equation to the surface is similar to that of the elliptic paraboloid with a change in sign. This has a far reaching consequence, as the differential equation in this case will be of the hyperbolic type and solution obtained will have much restricted range of application, as will be shown later.

The slopes and curvatures of the surface of the hyperbolic paraboloid can be determined as

$$p = \frac{x}{R_1}, \quad q = \frac{-y}{R_2}, \quad r = \frac{1}{R_1}, \quad s = 0, \quad t = -\frac{1}{R_2}$$

3.5.1.1 Differential Equation

Substituting for r, s and t in Eq. (3.12), we get the governing membrane differential equation for an hyperbolic paraboloid as

$$-\frac{1}{R_2}\frac{\partial^2 \phi}{\partial x^2} + \frac{1}{R_1}\frac{\partial^2 \phi}{\partial y^2} = pX + qY - Z + r\int X\,dx + t\int Y\,dy \tag{a}$$

If we assume that the hypar is shallow and is subjected to vertical load only, then

$$X = Y = 0$$

and the above differential equation reduces to

$$\frac{1}{R_2}\frac{\partial^2 \phi}{\partial x^2} - \frac{1}{R_1}\frac{\partial^2 \phi}{\partial y^2} = Z \tag{3.35}$$

3.5.1.2 Solution

Solution for an hyperbolic paraboloid simply supported on all its four edges or simply supported along one pair of edges and free along the other pair can be obtained using trigonometric series. For an all-round simply supported hypar, the solution can be obtained using either a double or a single trigonometric series, while for the other case of support condition mentioned above, the solution can be obtained by using a single trigonometric series only. The procedure of obtaining the solution is identical to the one discussed for an elliptic paraboloid. However, in the case of hyperbolic paraboloid, it becomes necessary to examine the range of applicability of the membrane solution.

(a) Solution for an all-round simply supported hyperbolic paraboloid using double trigonometric series

The boundary conditions for an all-round simply supported hyperbolic paraboloid can be written as (Fig. 3.16)

along $x = \pm\, a,\ \overline{N}_x = 0$

along $y = \pm\, b,\ \overline{N}_y = 0$

A solution for ϕ in terms of double trigonometric series, satisfying the above boundary conditions, can be taken as

$$\phi = \sum_{m=1,3}^{\infty} \sum_{n=1,3}^{\infty} A_{mn} \cos \alpha_m x \cos \beta_n y \qquad \text{(a)}$$

where

$$\alpha_m = \frac{m\pi}{2a} \text{ and } \beta_n = \frac{n\pi}{2b}$$

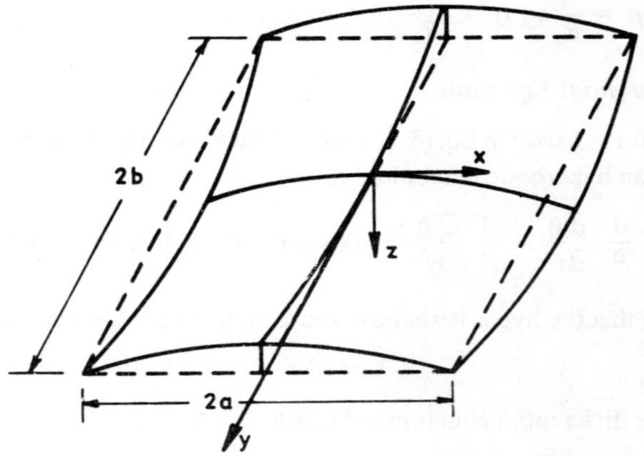

Fig. 3.16 - A hyperbolic paraboloid whose edges are principal parabolas

The load can also be expressed in terms of double trigonometric series as

$$Z = \sum_{m=1,3}^{\infty} \sum_{n=1,3}^{\infty} C_{mn} \cos \alpha_m x \cos \beta_n y \tag{b}$$

where C_{mn} can be determined from

$$C_{mn} = \frac{4}{ab} \int_{-a}^{+a} \int_{-b}^{+b} Z \cos \alpha_m x \cos \beta_n y \, dx \, dy$$

Substituting for ϕ and Z in the differential equation (3.35) from the above expressions, the constant A_{mn} can be determined as

$$A_{mn} = - \frac{C_{mn}}{\left(\dfrac{\alpha_m^2}{R_2} - \dfrac{\beta_n^2}{R_1} \right)} \tag{c}$$

Hence the solution can be written as

$$\phi = - \sum_{m=1,3}^{\infty} \sum_{n=1,3}^{\infty} \frac{C_{mn} \cos \alpha_m x \cos \beta_n y}{\left(\dfrac{\alpha_m^2}{R_2} - \dfrac{\beta_n^2}{R_1} \right)} \tag{3.36}$$

The actual membrane stress resultants can now be determined as

$$N_x = \frac{R_2}{R_1} \sqrt{\frac{R_1^2 + x^2}{R_2^2 + y^2}} \sum_{m=1,3}^{\infty} \sum_{n=1,3}^{\infty} \frac{C_{mn} \cos \alpha_m x \cos \beta_n y}{\left[\dfrac{1}{R_2} \left(\dfrac{\alpha_m}{\beta_n} \right)^2 - \dfrac{1}{R_1} \right]} \tag{3.37a}$$

$$N_y = \frac{R_1}{R_2} \sqrt{\frac{R_2^2 + y^2}{R_1^2 + x^2}} \sum_{m=1,3}^{\infty} \sum_{n=1,3}^{\infty} \frac{C_{mn} \alpha_m^2 \cos \alpha_m x \cos \beta_n y}{\beta_n^2 \left[\dfrac{1}{R_2} \left(\dfrac{\alpha_m}{\beta_n} \right)^2 - \dfrac{1}{R_1} \right]} \tag{3.37b}$$

$$N_{xy} = \sum_{m=1,3}^{\infty} \sum_{n=1,3}^{\infty} \frac{C_{mn} \alpha_m \sin \alpha_m x \sin \beta_n y}{\beta_n \left[\dfrac{1}{R_2} \left(\dfrac{\alpha_m}{\beta_n} \right)^2 - \dfrac{1}{R_1} \right]} \tag{3.37c}$$

As in the case of elliptic paraboloid, the series expression for the forces converges very slowly and requires the consideration of large number of terms for obtaining sufficiently accurate results. Apart from this, it is interesting to examine the range of applicability of the membrane solution obtained here. If, for given geometrical dimensions of the hyperbolic paraboloid, the following relation

$$\left(\frac{R_1}{R_2}\right)\left(\frac{\alpha_m}{\beta_n}\right)^2 = 1$$

exists, then we see that the denominator of Eqs. (3.37a–c) vanishes and hence, all the forces become infinite. From the physical point of view, this means that the saddle hyperbolic paraboloid is unable to support the loading corresponding to *m*, *n* harmonics entirely by developing membrane forces.

(b) Solution in terms of single trigonometric series

We will develop here, a solution for hyperbolic paraboloid shell, which is simply supported along one pair of edges ($y = \pm b$) and free along the other pair of edges ($x = \pm a$). The boundary conditions for this case can be written as (Fig. 3.16)

$$x = \pm a, \; \overline{N}_x = \overline{N}_{xy} = 0$$

$$y = \pm b, \; \overline{N}_y = 0$$

First, let us consider the homogeneous differential equation

$$\frac{1}{R_1}\frac{\partial^2\phi}{\partial y^2} - \frac{1}{R_2}\frac{\partial^2\phi}{\partial x^2} = 0 \tag{a}$$

The solution for the above equation may be taken in the form

$$\phi_0 = \sum_{n=1,3}^{\infty} f(x)\cos\beta_n y \tag{b}$$

The above assumed form of solution for ϕ satisfies the simply supported condition along $y = \pm b$, namely, $\overline{N}_y = 0$. Substituting Eq. (b) in Eq. (a) results in the following ordinary differential equation:

$$\frac{1}{R_2}\frac{d^2 f}{dx^2} + \frac{1}{R_1}\beta_n^2 f = 0 \tag{c}$$

the solution of which can be taken as

$$f = \left[A_n \cos\sqrt{\frac{R_2}{R_1}}\,\beta_n x + B_n \sin\sqrt{\frac{R_2}{R_1}}\,\beta_n x\right] \tag{d}$$

Hence, the solution for the homogeneous differential equation (a) can now be written as

$$\phi = \sum_{n=1,3}^{\infty}\left[A_n \cos\sqrt{\frac{R_2}{R_1}}\,\beta_n x + B_n \sin\sqrt{\frac{R_2}{R_1}}\,\beta_n x\right]\cos\beta_n y \tag{e}$$

The vertical loading acting on the shell can also be expressed in terms of trigonometric series as

$$Z = \sum_{n=1,3}^{\infty} C_n \cos \beta_n y \tag{f}$$

where C_n is determined from

$$C_n = \frac{2}{b} \int_{-b}^{+b} Z \cos \beta_n y \, dy$$

The particular integral can now be determined as

$$\phi_p = \sum_{n=1,3}^{\infty} \frac{C_n R_1}{\beta_n^2} \cos \beta_n y \tag{g}$$

Hence, the complete solution for ϕ can be written as

$$\phi = \phi_o + \phi_p = \sum_{n=1,3}^{\infty} \left[A_n \cos \sqrt{\frac{R_2}{R_1}}\, \beta_n x + B_n \sin \sqrt{\frac{R_2}{R_1}}\, \beta_n x + \frac{C_n R_1}{\beta_n^2} \right] \cos \beta_n y \tag{3.38}$$

Since, in the present case, the boundary conditions and loading are symmetrical with respect to both the x and y axes, the constant, $B_n = 0$.

Hence, for this problem ϕ can be taken as

$$\phi = \sum_{n=1,3}^{\infty} \left[A_n \cos \sqrt{\frac{R_2}{R_1}}\, \beta_n x + \frac{C_n R_1}{\beta_n^2} \right] \cos \beta_n y \tag{3.39}$$

The projected membrane stress resultants can be determined as

$$\overline{N}_x = -\sum_{n=1,3}^{\infty} \left[C_n R_1 + A_n \beta_n^2 \cos \sqrt{\frac{R_2}{R_1}}\, \beta_n x \right] \cos \beta_n y \tag{3.40a}$$

$$\overline{N}_y = -\sum_{n=1,3}^{\infty} A_n \left(\frac{R_2}{R_1} \right) \beta_n^2 \cos \sqrt{\frac{R_2}{R_1}}\, \beta_n x \Bigg] \cos \beta_n y \tag{3.40b}$$

$$\overline{N}_{xy} = -\sum_{n=1,3}^{\infty} A_n \beta_n^2 \sqrt{\frac{R_2}{R_1}} \sin \sqrt{\frac{R_2}{R_1}}\, \beta_n x \Bigg] \sin \beta_n y \tag{3.40c}$$

The constant A_n in the above expressions is determined from the boundary conditions along $x = \pm a$. Using the condition that $\overline{N}_x = 0$ along $x = \pm a$, we determine A_n as

$$A_n = \frac{C_n R_1}{\beta_n^2 \cos \sqrt{\frac{R_2}{R_1}}\, \beta_n a} \tag{h}$$

To satisfy the second condition $\overline{N}_{xy} = 0$ along $x = \pm a$, we should have

$$\sin \sqrt{\frac{R_2}{R_1}}\ \beta_n a = 0$$

or

$$\sqrt{\frac{R_2}{R_1}}\ \beta_n a = k\pi \ (k = 1, 2, \ldots)$$

Noting that n takes only odd values, we can write the above condition as

$$a \cdot \sqrt{\frac{R_2}{R_1}} = 2bk \tag{3.41}$$

Hence, to satisfy the condition that shear force $\overline{N}_{xy}$ should be zero along the edges $x = \pm a$, the above condition must be satisfied. In other words, membrane solution is possible only when the above condition is satisfied. As in the previous case, it is interesting to note here that the validity of membrane solution depends on the shell dimensions (a and b) as well as the rise f_1 and f_2. It is also possible to examine from physical consideration of the problem, whether a membrane state of stress could be achieved in the shell or not. This aspect has been discussed in great detail by Flugge[3.3] and we will highlight some points to support the above mathematical solution.

For the case of a vertical loading, viz. $Z = q$, we may assume that the shell carries the load like a series of arches. In such a case, we may write the following three possible particular solutions, which satisfy the differential equation (3.35).

$$\phi_p^{(1)} = -\frac{1}{2}\, qR_1 y^2\,,\ \phi_p^{(2)} = \frac{1}{2}\, qR_2 x^2\,,\ \phi_p^{(3)} = \frac{1}{4}\, q\,(R_2 x^2 - R_1 y^2) \tag{3.42}$$

The projected membrane stress resultants for the above three particular solutions can be determined as,

$$\overline{N}_x^{(1)} = -\,qR_1,\ \overline{N}_x^{(2)} = 0,\ \overline{N}_x^{(3)} = -\,qR_1$$

$$\overline{N}_y^{(1)} = 0,\ \overline{N}_y^{(2)} = qR_2,\ \overline{N}_y^{(3)} = qR_2$$

$$\overline{N}_{xy}^{(1)} = 0,\ \overline{N}_{xy}^{(2)} = 0,\ \overline{N}_{xy}^{(3)} = 0$$

The first particular solution indicates that the load will be carried by a series of arches in yz-plane and the membrane force $\overline{N}_x$ will be compressive. The second solution indicates that the load will be carried by a series of arches in xz-plane and the membrane force $\overline{N}_y$ will be tensile. The third solution indicates that both arch systems (in the xz- and yz-planes) act jointly in carrying the load. In all the three cases, forces will be left along the edges and these have to be suitably adjusted to satisfy the required boundary condition. This is what specifically is done in the mathematical solution, when the constants in the solution of the differential equation are so determined as to satisfy the boundary condition. Let us examine here, physically, that the forces applied at the edges, to satisfy the required boundary condition, will finally result in a membrane state of stress in the shell.

First, it can be shown that there are two families of straight lines on the paraboloid given by

$$y = x\sqrt{\frac{R_2}{R_1}}, \; y = -x\sqrt{\frac{R_2}{R_1}}$$

These are the generators of the surface and are often called as asymptotic lines. The projection of these lines on the *xy*-plane are called as characteristic lines and these make an angle $\pm\gamma$ with respect to *x*-axis (Fig. 3.17) such that

$$\tan\gamma = \sqrt{\frac{R_2}{R_1}}$$

If $R_2 = R_1$, the characteristic lines will be at right angles to each other. These lines may traverse the shell diagonally and end at the opposite corner. But in general, the generators from the corners will meet the opposite sides of the shell. For example, in Fig. 3.17, the line starting from the corner *B* intersects the side *AD*, while a line starting from the corner *A*, will intersect the side *BC*. The sides *AD* and *BC* are usually referred as principal sides, while the sides *AB* and *CD* are called as secondary sides. The characteristic lines have an unique property, in that a force applied at a point, say *E* (Fig. 3.17) will stress only the strip *EF* and requires a force of the same magnitude, but opposite in direction at the point *F* for maintaining equilibrium. This property could be made use of in removing some unwanted forces along an edge, so that the required boundary conditions can be satisfied. Using this procedure, we will show for the example considered here

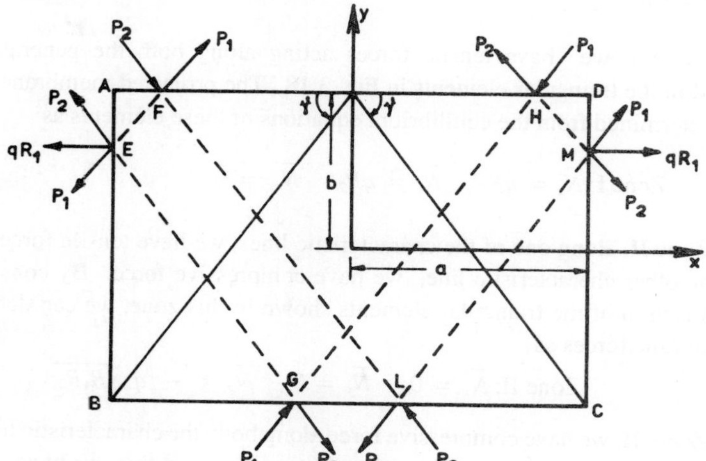

Fig. 3.17 Plan projection of hyperbolic paraboloid showing characteristic lines

that the edge forces obtained from the particular integral could be nullified by applying opposite forces along the edges *AB* and *CD*, thereby satisfying the free edge boundary conditions along these edges, which results in shear force along the other two edges *BC* and *AD*. Since these two edges are supported, the shear can be resisted by the diaphragms.

To illustrate the above point, let us choose the first particular solution given in Eq. (3.42). This solution yields along the edges *AB* and *CD*, a thrust $\overline{N}_x = -qR_1$. Since we want the sides *AB* and *CD* to be free, we apply a tensile force of the same magnitude, to nullify the thrust resulting from the particular solution. Now let us examine how this tensile force applied along the edges *AB* and *CD* gets transmitted to the edges *AD* and *BC*. For this, consider a point *E* on the edge *AB*, where a tensile force, qR_1 will be applied (Fig. 3.17). This force will now get resolved into two components P_1 and P_2 along the characteristic lines *EF* and *EG*. These forces (P_1 and P_2) will now appear on the edges *AD* and *BC*. To keep these edges free of thrust, we apply a compressive force of equal magnitude in the direction of the other characteristic lines, namely, *FL* and *GH*. This, however, will now leave shear at points *F*, *G*, *H* and *L*. Following this to the edge *CD*, we can show that the tensile forces applied along the edges *AB* and *CD* equilibrate along the two characteristic lines in such a way that the sides *AB* and *CD* will be free of forces, while along the edges *AD* and *BC*, it will yield shear. This is the condition we wanted to satisfy in the mathematical solution.

Using the above physical concept, we can determine the stress resultants $\overline{N}_x$, $\overline{N}_y$ and $\overline{N}_{xy}$ in the interior. For this, we will divide the shell into three zones (Fig. 3.18) and determine the stress resultants in each of these three zones from simple statics.

In Zone I, we have tensile forces acting along both the generators, as indicated in the triangular elements in Fig. 3.18. The projected membrane forces can be determined from the equilibrium equations of these elements as:

$$\text{Zone I: } \overline{N}_x = qR_1\,, \quad \overline{N}_y = qR_2\,, \quad \overline{N}_{xy} = 0$$

In Zone II, along one of the characteristic lines, we have tensile force, while along the other characteristic line, we have compressive force. By considering the equilibrium of the triangular elements shown in this zone, we can determine the membrane forces as

$$\text{Zone II: } \overline{N}_x = 0\,, \quad \overline{N}_y = 0\,, \quad \overline{N}_{xy} = -\,q\sqrt{R_1R_2}$$

In Zone III, we have compressive force along both the characteristic lines and considering the equilibrium of triangular element shown in this, we have

$$\text{Zone III: } \overline{N}_x = -qR_1\,, \quad \overline{N}_y = -qR_2\,, \quad \overline{N}_{xy} = 0$$

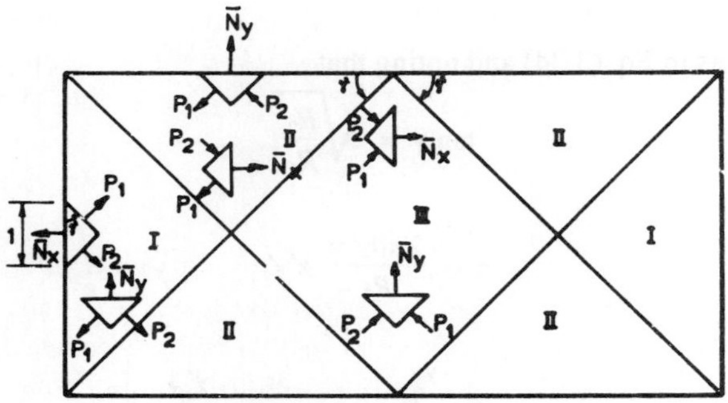

Fig. 3.18 Determination of stress resultants

Hence, the final forces in each of these zones could be obtained by adding the stress resultant obtained from the first particular solution. The final force distribution in each zone can be determined as follows:

Zone \ Force	$\bar{N}_x$	$\bar{N}_y$	$\bar{N}_{xy}$
I	0	qR_2	0
II	$-qR_1$	0	$-q\sqrt{R_1R_2}$
III	$-2qR_1$	$-qR_2$	0

The above force distribution shows severe discontinuities when one goes from Zone I to II and then onto Zone III. It is also worth noting that the magnitude of forces change abruptly as one moves from one zone to another. This is a general feature of all problems governed by hyperbolic type of differential equation and hence, for shells having negative gaussian curvature. It is necessary to examine in detail, the validity of the membrane solution, particularly for shells of negative gaussian curvature, for a shell of given dimensions and boundary conditions.

3.5.2.1 Hyperbolic Paraboloid Supported on Straight Line Generators

Hyperbolic paraboloid supported on straight generators are widely used for roofs. This particular shell falls under the category of doubly ruled surface in translational shells. From the constructional point of view, the form work for this type of shell will be much simpler, compared to hyperbolic paraboloid with parabola as generator. The equation for the surface of this type of shell can be obtained from Eq. (3.34) by suitable transformation of coordinates. For this, let us now choose the new $x'y'$-coordinate system along the direction of the two characteristic lines, which are inclined at an angle γ with the x-axis. We can now use the following equation to transform the original equation, in terms of xy-coordinate to a new $x'y'$-coordinate system (Fig. 3.19).

$$x = (x' + y')\cos\gamma$$

$$y = (x' - y') \sin \gamma \tag{a}$$

Substituting this in Eq. (3.34) and noting that

$$\tan \gamma = \sqrt{\frac{R_2}{R_1}}$$

we get

$$z = \frac{2 \sin^2 \gamma}{R_2} x'y' \tag{b}$$

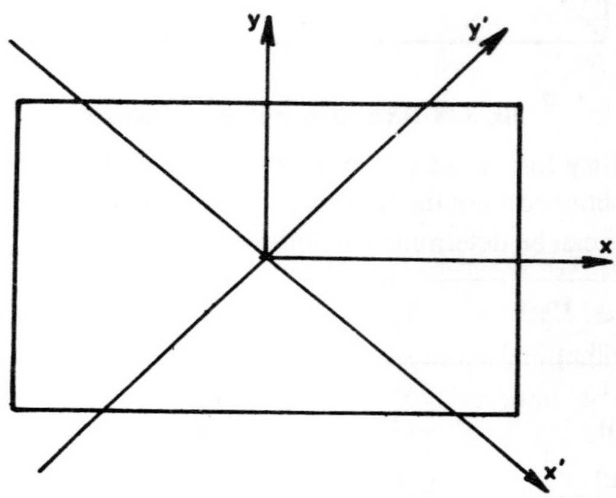

Fig. 3.19 Coordinate transformation

As a special case, if we consider that the characteristic lines are orthogonal, then the equation to the surface can be written as

$$z = \frac{x'y'}{C} \tag{c}$$

From the above equation, it is clear that the surface is formed by two sets of straight lines. A simple way of visualising physically, this surface, is to consider it as a warped surface, with one of the corners of the rectangle being raised or lowered by f, while the other three corners are at the same level (Fig. 3.20). The equation to the surface in terms of its physical dimension can now be written as

$$z = \left(\frac{f}{ab}\right) xy = \frac{xy}{c} \tag{3.43}$$

If we cut this hyperbolic paraboloid by a vertical plane, in general, we get a plane curve. If the angle between the vertical plane and xz-plane is not zero, then the curve will be a parabola. If the vertical plane and xz- or yz-plane are parallel, then the plane curve will be a straight line. Hence in a general case, the vertical section will result in a parabola and the horizontal section (z = constant) will result in a hyperbola. Hence, this type of shell is also called as hyperbolic paraboloid.

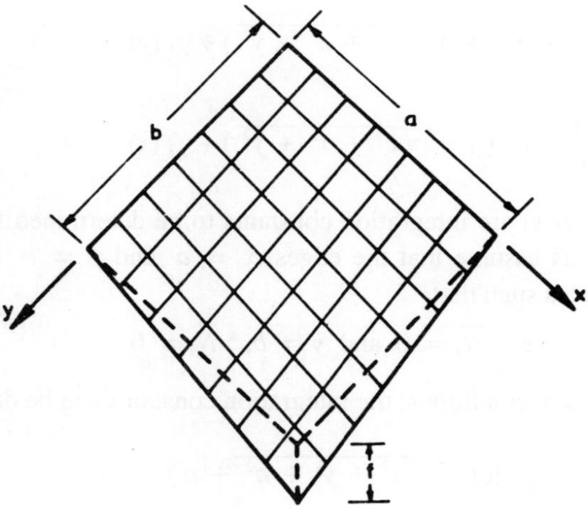

Fig. 3.20 Hyperbolic paraboloid with straight line generators

3.5.2.2 Differential Equation

The differential equation for a hyperbolic paraboloid, whose surface is defined by Eq. (3.43), can be obtained as

$$-\frac{2}{c}\frac{\partial^2 \phi}{\partial x\,\partial y} = -Z + pX + qY \tag{a}$$

If the shell is subjected to vertical load, only then the above differential equation reduces to

$$\frac{2}{c}\frac{\partial^2 \phi}{\partial x\,\partial y} = Z \tag{3.44}$$

3.5.2.3 Solution

Let us obtain the solution for a hyperbolic paraboloid, which is simply supported along its two adjacent edges. For a moment, let us assume that the shell could be deep. If q is the intensity of vertical load, then the load component Z can be determined as

$$Z = q\sqrt{1 + p^2 + q^2} = \frac{q}{c}\sqrt{c^2 + x^2 + y^2} \tag{b}$$

Equation (3.44) can now be written as

$$\frac{\partial^2 \phi}{\partial x\,\partial y} = -\overline{N}_{xy} = \frac{q}{2}\sqrt{c^2 + x^2 + y^2} \tag{3.45a}$$

The stress function ϕ can be determined by integrating the above equation and later, the membrane forces $\overline{N}_x$ and $\overline{N}_y$ could be determined. Alternatively, since $\overline{N}_{xy}$ is known (Eq. 3.45a), the other two membrane forces $\overline{N}_x$ and $\overline{N}_y$ can be determined by directly integrating the equilibrium equations (Eqs. 3.10a and 3.10b). We will follow the latter procedure and determine $\overline{N}_x$ and $\overline{N}_y$ as

$$\overline{N}_x = \frac{qy}{2} \log_e \left(x + \sqrt{c^2 + x^2 + y^2} \right) + f_1(y) \tag{c}$$

$$\overline{N}_y = \frac{qx}{2} \log_e \left(y + \sqrt{c^2 + x^2 + y^2} \right) + f_2(x) \tag{d}$$

where $f_1(y)$ and $f_2(x)$ are integration constants to be determined from boundary conditions. Let us assume that the edges, $x = a$ and $y = b$ (Fig. 3.20) are supported on gables such that,

$$x = a, \quad \overline{N}_x = 0 \text{ and } y = b, \quad \overline{N}_y = 0$$

Using the above conditions, the integration constants can be determined as

$$f_1(y) = -\frac{qy}{2} \log_e \left(\sqrt{c^2 + y^2 + a^2} + a \right) \tag{d}$$

$$f_2(x) = -\frac{qx}{2} \log_e \left(\sqrt{c^2 + y^2 + b^2} + b \right) \tag{f}$$

Substituting the above expressions for the constants and simplifying, we get $\overline{N}_x$ and $\overline{N}_y$ as

$$\overline{N}_x = \frac{qy}{2} \log_e \left(\frac{x + \sqrt{x^2 + y^2 + c^2}}{a + \sqrt{a^2 + c^2 + y^2}} \right) \tag{3.45b}$$

$$\overline{N}_y = \frac{qy}{2} \log_e \left(\frac{y + \sqrt{x^2 + y^2 + c^2}}{b + \sqrt{b^2 + c^2 + x^2}} \right) \tag{3.45c}$$

It must be noted in obtaining the solution here, that only boundary conditions along two adjacent edges ($x = 0, \ y = 0$ or $x = a, \ y = b$) can be accounted for. Hence, along the other two edges, we will obviously have forces which should be taken care of by providing a suitable support. Often, a hyperbolic paraboloid is used in different ways to form the roof structure. Some of the possibilities are shown in Fig. 3.21(a) to (d). These arrangements allow the designer to deal effectively with the forces appearing at the edge of the shell. For example, in the arrangement shown in Fig. 3.2(a), the edges *AB* and *CB* are supported on trusses such that the normal forces along these edges is zero. At the ridges *OA* and *OC*, edge members must be provided to take care of the forces obtained from the membrane analysis.

For a shallow hyperbolic paraboloid shell, p and q being small, their squares can be neglected. In such a case, we have the membrane forces as

$$\overline{N}_{xy} = -\frac{qc}{2}$$

$$\overline{N}_x = \overline{N}_y = 0 \tag{3.46}$$

Hence, when the shell becomes shallow, the entire load is resisted by developing a pure shear state of stress. Referring to the hyperbolic paraboloid shown in Fig. 3.21(a), the edge members along the gables as well as along the ridges have to be suitably designed to resist the shear. However, when the edge members are provided along the two ridges, the weight of these members has to be carried by the shell. This, however, is not possible because, the forces N_x and N_y needed along these edges cannot exist without disturbing the forces at the opposite edges (that is along the gable ends). Hence, it is necessary that the ridge beams are so designed that their weight is transferred to the gables. This can be done for a shell subjected to symmetric loading. The problem become much more complex when, for example, only one shell panel is loaded. For other types of shell roofs built from hyperbolic paraboloid, it is necessary to examine how the edge shear gets transferred to the support and if necessary, suitable edge members and ties have to be provided.

Example 3.2

Let us consider an inverted umbrella-type shell made up of four hyperbolic paraboloids, as shown in Fig. 3.21(b). The geometrical dimensions of a single hyperbolic paraboloid are length (a) = width (b) = 7m. Rise = 1.4m. Thickness of shell = 7cm. In addition to dead load, the shell is subjected to an uniform live load equal to 52 kg/m^2. The density of concrete is taken as 2400 kg/m^3.

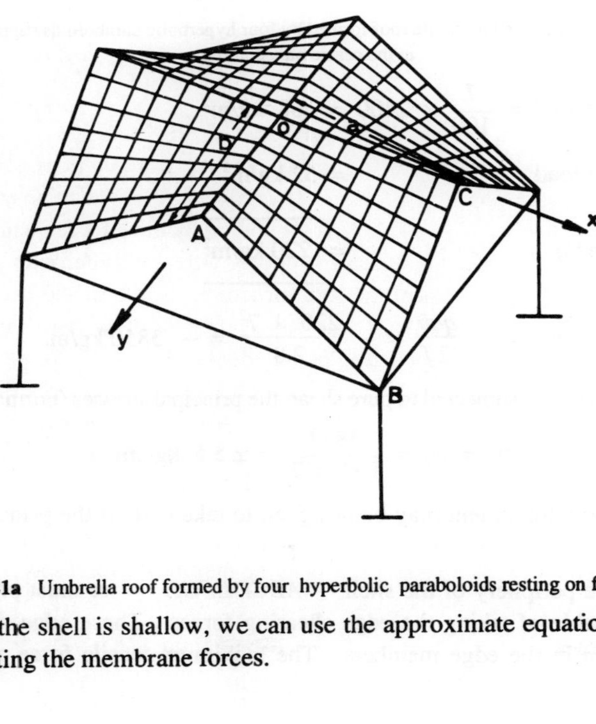

Fig. 3.21a Umbrella roof formed by four hyperbolic paraboloids resting on four trusses

Since the shell is shallow, we can use the approximate equations (Eq. 3.46) for calculating the membrane forces.

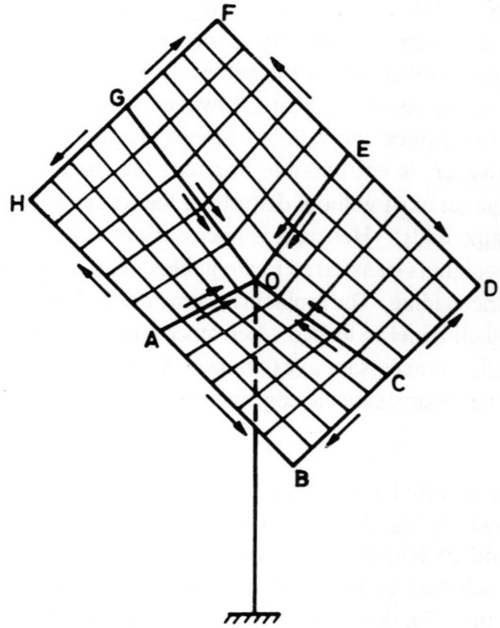

Fig. 3.21b Inverted umbrella roof formed by four hyperbolic paraboloids supported at the centre on a column

$$\text{Dead load} = \frac{7}{100} \times 2400 = 168 \text{ kg/m}^2$$

$$\text{Live load} = 52 \text{ kg/m}^2$$

$$\text{Total load } q = 220 \text{ kg/m}^2$$

$$\overline{N}_{xy} = -\frac{qab}{2f} = -\frac{220 \times 7^2}{2.8} = -3850 \text{ kg/m}$$

Since the shell is subjected to pure shear, the principal stresses (normal) would be

$$\sigma_1 = \sigma_2 = \frac{3850}{100 \times 7} = \pm 5.5 \text{ kg/cm}^2$$

Suitable reinforcement may be designed to take care of the principal tensile stress.

Along the periphery of the shell — *ABCDEFGH* — we must provide edge members capable of taking the edge shearing forces. These edge shear forces induce tension in the edge members. The maximum tensile force at *A* can be obtained as

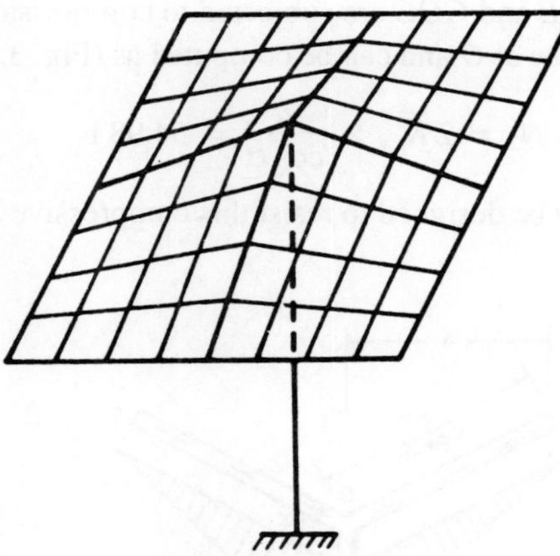

Fig. 3.21c Umbrella shell built of four hyperbolic paraboloids supported at the centre on a column

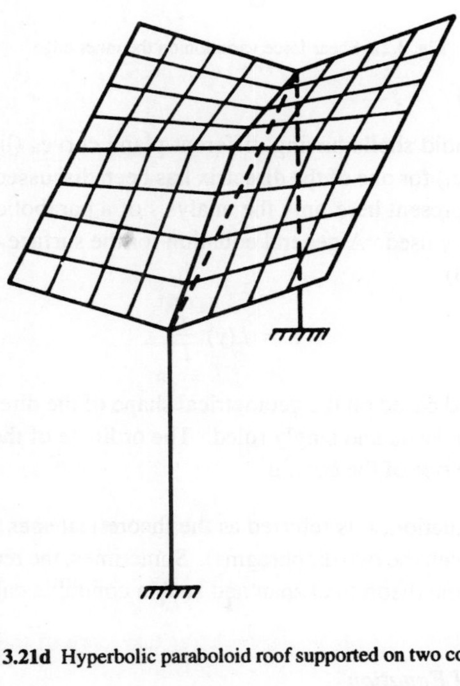

Fig. 3.21d Hyperbolic paraboloid roof supported on two columns

$$N_1 = \overline{N}_{xy} \times a = 3850 \times 7 = 26.95 \text{ t}$$

A suitable edge member may be designed to take care of this tensile force.

The inner edge *AOE* and *GOC* are subjected to compression. The maximum compressive force will be at *O* and can be computed as (Fig. 3.22).

$$N_2 = 2\,\overline{N}_{xy} \times \frac{a}{\cos\alpha} = 54.98 \text{ t}$$

A suitable member may be designed to resist this compressive force.

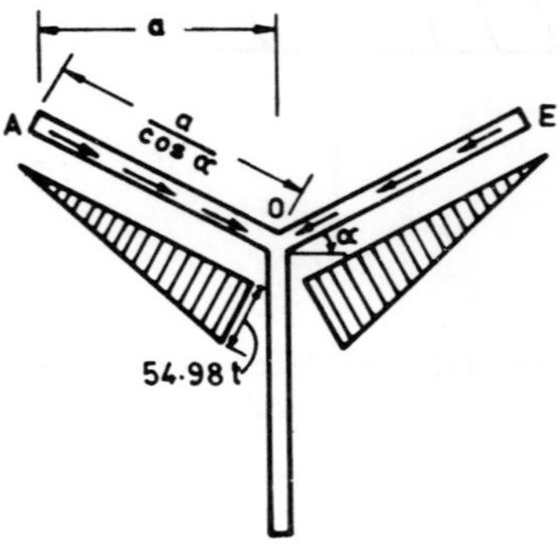

Fig. 3.22 Shear force variation on the inner edge

3.5.3 Conoid Shell

The analysis of conoid shells having different plane curves (like arc of a circle, parabola, ellipse, etc.) for one of the directrix has been discussed by Fischer [3.4] and Soare [3.5]. We will present here only the analysis of a parabolic conoid, which in practice is commonly used. A general equation for the surface of a conoid can be written as (Fig. 3.23).

$$z = f(y)\,\frac{x}{L}$$

where $f(y)$ is defined based on the geometrical shape of the directrix. The surface of the conoid is anticlastic and singly ruled. The ordinate of the directrix at $y = 0$ will be called as the rise of the conoid.

In the above equation, L is referred as the theoretical span, while l is the real span (distance between the two diaphragms). Sometimes, the real span of a conoid would be less than the theoretical span and such a conoid is called as a truncated conoid.

3.5.3.1 Differential Equation

The equation defining the surface of a parabolic conoid can be written as

$$z = -\frac{4f}{B^2}\left(\frac{B^2}{4} - y^2\right)\frac{x}{L} \tag{3.47}$$

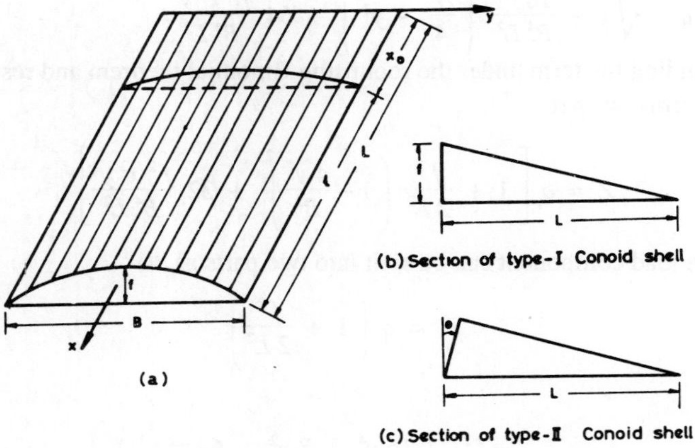

Fig. 3.23 Conoid shell

The slopes and curvatures can now be determined as

$$p = -\frac{4f}{B^2 L}\left(\frac{B^2}{4} - y^2\right), \quad q = \frac{8fxy}{B^2 L}$$

$$r = 0, \quad s = \frac{8fy}{B^2 L}, \quad t = \frac{8fx}{B^2 L}$$

The equilibrium equations for a conoid, in terms of the projected stress resultants, can be written as (Eqs. (3.10a–c))

$$\frac{\partial \bar{N}_x}{\partial x} + \frac{\partial \bar{N}_{xy}}{\partial y} + X = 0 \qquad \text{(a)}$$

$$\frac{\partial \bar{N}_y}{\partial y} + \frac{\partial \bar{N}_{xy}}{\partial x} + Y = 0 \qquad \text{(b)} \quad (3.48)$$

$$t\bar{N}_y + 2s\bar{N}_{xy} = pX + qY - Z \qquad \text{(c)}$$

and the differential equation in terms of the stress function ϕ can be obtained as (Eq. (3.12))

$$-2s\frac{\partial^2 \phi}{\partial x\,\partial y} + t\frac{\partial^2 \phi}{\partial x^2} = pX + qY + t\int Y\,dy - Z \qquad (3.49)$$

If the conoid is subjected to vertical loading only, of intensity q, then

$$X = Y = 0, \; Z = q\sqrt{1 + p^2 + q^2}$$

3.5.3.2 Solution

Substituting for p and q, the load component Z can be written as

$$Z = q \sqrt{1 + \frac{16 f^2}{B^4 L^2}\left(\frac{B^2}{4} - y^2\right)^2 + 64\,\frac{f^2 x^2 y^2}{B^4 L^2}} \qquad \text{(a)}$$

Expanding the term under the root using Binomial theorem and restricting to first two terms, we get

$$Z = q\left[1 + \frac{f^2}{2L^2}\left(1 - \frac{4y^2}{B^2}\right)^2 + 32\,\frac{f^2 x^2 y^2}{B^4 L^2}\right] \qquad \text{(b)}$$

The above load component can be split into two parts as

$$Z_1 = q\left(1 + \frac{f^2}{2L^2}\right) \qquad \text{(c)}$$

and

$$Z_2 = \frac{qf^2}{2L^2}\left(\frac{16y^4}{B^4} - \frac{8y^2}{B^2} + \frac{64x^2y^2}{B^4}\right)$$

$$= qa^2\left(\frac{y^4}{8} - \frac{B^2 y^2}{16} + \frac{x^2 y^2}{2}\right) \qquad \text{(d)}$$

where $a = 8\ f = B^2 L.$

The first part of the load component, namely, Z_1 is constant and could be conceived as an uniformly distributed load over the horizontal projection of the shell. We will have only this type of load, if we consider the conoid shell as shallow. The second part of the load component, namely Z_2, is a varying load. We will determine the solutions for these two components separately and later on superpose them. The solution to the first part of the load is very simple, as will be indicated later, while the solution to the second part of the load may conveniently be obtained using polynomials. We will assume that the conoid is supported in such a way that the normal forces, perpendicular to the diaphragms will be zero. Hence, the boundary conditions can be written as

$$\text{At } x = x_0,\ \overline{N}_x = 0$$

$$\text{At } x = L,\ \overline{N}_x = 0$$

It should be noted that the conoid shell is unsymmetrical, lengthwise and hence, we would have the above two boundary conditions. However, it is not possible to impose the condition that normal force $\overline{N}_y$ along $y = \pm B/2$ should also vanish simultaneously, with the above condition for the normal force $\overline{N}_x$.

Now, let us obtain the solution for the first part of load component Z_1. As mentioned earlier, this part of the load can be considered as uniform loading. Since the directrix of the conoid is a parabola, the uniform load will be the funicular loading on the shell. Hence, the shell, in this case, will behave as if it is an arch structure with linearly varying rise, and the load is wholly carried by the transverse arches. Because of this, the normal force $\overline{N}_x$ and shear force $\overline{N}_{xy}$ would be zero. Hence, the third equilibrium equation (Eq. (3.48)) will now reduce to

$$t\overline{N}_y = -p_0$$

where

$$p_0 = q\left(1 + \frac{f^2}{2L^2}\right)$$

or

$$\overline{N}_y = \frac{\partial^2 \phi}{\partial x^2} = -\frac{p_0}{a\,x} = -\frac{q}{a\,x}\left(1 + \frac{f^2}{2L^2}\right) \tag{e}$$

Integrating the above equation, we can determine the first part of the solution for the stress function as

$$\phi_1 = -\frac{qx}{a}\left[1 + \frac{1}{2}\left(\frac{f}{L}\right)^2\right](\log_e x - 1) \tag{3.50}$$

For obtaining the solution for the second part of the load component Z_2, let us consider the differential equation (3.49), which can now be written as

$$-2y\frac{\partial^2 \phi_2}{\partial x\,\partial y} + x\frac{\partial^2 \phi_2}{\partial x^2} = -qa\left(\frac{y^4}{8} - \frac{1}{16}B^2y^2 + \frac{x^2y^2}{2}\right) \tag{3.51}$$

The solution for ϕ_2 can now be taken in the following form:

$$\phi_2 = \sum A_{mn}\,(x^m - L^m)\,y^n \tag{f}$$

where m and n are unknown powers and are to be determined so as to satisfy the differential equation (3.51). Substituting the above expression for ϕ_2 in Eq. (3.51), we get

$$\sum A_{mn}\,[m(m - 2n - 1)]\,x^{m-1}y^n = -qa\left(\frac{y^4}{8} - \frac{B^2y^2}{16} + \frac{x^2y^2}{2}\right) \tag{g}$$

The values of A_{mn}, corresponding to each term of the right hand side of the above equation, can be determined as follows.

Let us consider the first term on the right hand side of Eq. (g), namely $-qay^4/8$. By equating indices of like powers on both sides, considering only this term on the right hand side, we get $m = 1$, and $n = 4$, from which A_{mn} can be determined as $qa/64$. Hence, the solution corresponding to the loading term $-qay^4/8$ will be

$$\frac{qa}{64}(x - L)y^4$$

Following the above procedure, the solution corresponding to the second and third loading terms can be determined as

$$-\frac{qa}{64}B^2y^2(x-L)\text{ and }\frac{qa}{12}(x^3-L^3)y^2$$

Hence, the complete solution for ϕ_2 can be written as

$$\phi_2 = qa\left[\frac{(x-L)y^4}{64} - \frac{B^2y^2}{64}(x-L) + \frac{y^2}{12}(x^3-L^3)\right] \quad (3.52)$$

The total solution for the stress function ϕ can now be written as

$$\phi = \phi_1 + \phi_2$$

$$= -\frac{qx}{a}\left[1+\frac{1}{2}\left(\frac{f}{L}\right)^2\right](\log_e x - 1) + qa$$

$$\times\left[\left(\frac{x-L}{64}\right)y^4 - \frac{B^2y^2}{64}(x-L) + \frac{y^2}{12}(x^3-L^3)\right] \quad (3.53)$$

The expressions for the projected stress resultants can be determined as

$$\overline{N}_x = qa\left[\frac{3y^2}{16}(x-L) - \frac{B^2}{32}(x-L) + \frac{1}{6}(x^3-L^3)\right] \quad (3.54a)$$

$$\overline{N}_y = \frac{qa}{2}xy^2 - \frac{q}{ax}\left[1+\frac{1}{2}\left(\frac{f}{L}\right)^2\right] \quad (3.54b)$$

$$\overline{N}_{xy} = -qa\left(\frac{y^3}{16} - \frac{yB^2}{32} + \frac{x^2y}{2}\right) \quad (3.54c)$$

The above solution satisfies the boundary condition that at $x = L$, $\overline{N}_x = 0$ and the symmetry condition that along $y = 0$, $\overline{N}_{xy} = 0$. However, it does not satisfy the boundary condition at $x = x_0$. If, on the other hand, a full conoid is used ($x_0 = 0$), then in such a case, the solution indicates that $\overline{N}_y$ becomes infinite. From a physical consideration, as one moves towards the straight line directrix (corresponding to $x = 0$), the surface also degenerates into a flat plate and hence, in this region, bending will be predominant. Hence, the membrane theory fails in this region. In order to overcome this difficulty and, as far as possible, to avoid, bending moments in the shell, truncated conoid is used in practice. As mentioned earlier, the above solution does not satisfy the specified boundary condition at the other edge, namely at $x = x_0$, $\overline{N}_x = 0$. We will now develop a supplementary solution, considering the shell to be subjected to a normal force of the same magnitude, but opposite in nature at $x = x_0$. When this solution is superposed on the previous solution, we would be able to satisfy the boundary conditions at the two ends.

We can determine $\overline{N}_x$ at $x = x_0$ from Eq. (3.54a) as

$$\overline{N}_x = qa \left[\frac{B^2}{32} (L - x_0) - \frac{1}{6} (L^3 - x_0^3) \right] - \frac{3\,aq}{16} (L - x_o) y^2 \qquad \text{(h)}$$

which can be put in the form

$$\overline{N}_x = A + Cy^2$$

where

$$A = qa \left[\frac{B^2}{32} (L - x_0) - \frac{1}{6} (L^3 - x_0^3) \right]$$

and

$$C = - \frac{3\,qa}{16} (L - x_0)$$

The supplementary solution should satisfy the equilibrium equation (3.48) or the differential equation (3.49) and the following boundary conditions:

$$\text{at } x = L, \ \overline{N}_x = 0$$

$$\text{at } x = x_0, \ \overline{N}_x = - A - Cy^2 \qquad \text{(i)}$$

To satisfy the above conditions, the following expression for $\overline{N}_x$ may be taken:

$$\overline{N}_x = - A \frac{L^n - x^n}{L^n - x_0^n} - Cy^2 \frac{L^m - x^m}{L^m - x_0^m} \qquad \text{(j)}$$

The unknown constants m and n in the above equation, as well as the forces $\overline{N}_{xy}$ and $\overline{N}_y$ may be obtained from the equilibrium equations (3.48).

Substituting for $\overline{N}_x$ (Eq. (j)), the above expression in the first equilibrium equation (3.48), we get

$$\frac{\partial \overline{N}_{xy}}{\partial y} = - n \frac{A x^{n-1}}{L^n - x_0^n} - mCy^2 \frac{x^{m-1}}{L^m - x_0^m} \qquad \text{(k)}$$

Integrating Eq. (k), we get $\overline{N}_{xy}$ as

$$\overline{N}_{xy} = - Any \frac{x^{n-1}}{L^n - x_0^n} - \frac{mCy^3}{3} \frac{x^{m-1}}{L^m - x_0^m} + f_1(x) \qquad \text{(l)}$$

From symmetry condition $\overline{N}_{xy} = 0$ along $y = 0$ and using this condition, it can be shown that $f_1(x) = 0$. Substituting the above expression for $\overline{N}_{xy}$ in the second equilibrium equation (3.48), we get

$$\frac{\partial \overline{N}_y}{\partial y} = An(n-1) y \frac{x^{n-2}}{L^n - x_0^n} + \frac{C}{3} m(m-1) y^3 \frac{x^{m-2}}{L^m - x_0^m}$$

which, after integration, gives

$$\overline{N}_y = \frac{A}{2}\, n\,(n-1)\,y^2\, \frac{x^{n-2}}{L^n - x_O^n} + \frac{C}{12}\, m\,(m-1)\,y^4\, \frac{x^{m-2}}{L^m - x_O^m} + f_2(x) \quad \text{(m)}$$

Substituting for $\overline{N}_y$ and $\overline{N}_{xy}$ in the third equilibrium equation (3 48c), we get

$$Any^2 \left(\frac{x^{n-1}}{L^n - x_0^n}\right)\left[\frac{n-1}{2} - 2\right] + \frac{C}{3}\, my^4\, \frac{x^{m-1}}{L^m - x_0^m} \times \left[\frac{m-1}{4} - 2\right] + xf_2(x) = 0 \quad \text{(n)}$$

Equation (n) can only be satisfied if the following conditions are satisfied :

$$\left[\frac{n-1}{2} - 2\right] = 0 \text{ which gives } n = 5$$

$$\left[\frac{m-1}{4} - 2\right] = 0 \text{ which gives } m = 9$$

and

$$f_2(x) = 0$$

Hence, the expression for projected stress resultants from the supplementary solution can be determined as

$$\overline{N}_x = -A\, \frac{L^5 - x^5}{L^5 - x_0^5} - Cy^2\, \frac{L^9 - x^9}{L^9 - x_0^9} \quad \text{(3.55a)}$$

$$\overline{N}_y = 10\,Ay^2\, \frac{x^3}{L^5 - x_0^5} - 6Cy^4\, \frac{x^7}{L^9 - x_0^9} \quad \text{(3.55b)}$$

$$\overline{N}_{xy} = 5Ay\, \frac{x^4}{L^5 - x_0^5} - 3Cy^3\, \frac{x^8}{L^9 - x_0^9} \quad \text{(3.55c)}$$

The total solution can now be written by superposing the two solutions given in Eqs. (3.54a–c) and Eqs. (3.55a–c). For easy computation of the forces, the final solution will be written in terms of non-dimensional parameters ξ and η, which are defined as

$$\xi = \frac{x}{L} \text{ and } \eta = \frac{2y}{B}$$

Hence, the final expressions for the projected stress resultants can be written as

$$\overline{N}_x = \frac{qf}{4B^2L}\left[B^2L\left(1 - \frac{3}{2}\eta^2\right)(1-\xi) - \frac{16}{3}L^3(1-\xi^3) - \left(\frac{1-\xi^5}{1-\xi_0^5}\right)\left\{B^2L(1-\xi_0) - \frac{16}{3}L^3(1-\xi_0^3)\right\} + \left(\frac{1-\xi^9}{1-\xi_0^9}\right)\left\{\frac{3}{2}B^2L(1-\xi_0)\eta^2\right\}\right] \quad \text{(3.56a)}$$

$$\overline{N}_y = -\frac{qB^2}{8f\xi}\left[1+\frac{f^2}{2L^2}-8f^2\frac{\xi^2\eta^2}{B^2}\right]+\frac{qf\eta^2}{8L}\left[\frac{5\xi^3}{L(1-\xi_0^5)}\right.$$

$$\left.\left\{B^2(1-\xi_0)-\frac{16}{3}L^2(1-\xi_0^3)\right\}-\frac{9B^2\eta^2\xi^7(1-\xi_0)}{2L(1-\xi_0^9)}\right] \quad (3.56b)$$

$$\overline{N}_{xy} = \frac{qf\eta}{8BL}\left[B^2\left(1-\frac{\eta^2}{2}\right)-16L^2\xi^2-\frac{5\xi^4}{1-\xi_0^5}\left\{B^2(1-\xi_0)\right.\right.$$

$$\left.\left.+\frac{16}{3}L^2(1-\xi_0^3)\right\}+\frac{9B^2\eta^2\xi^8}{2(1-\xi_0^9)}(1-\xi_0)\right] \quad (3.56c)$$

The actual stress resultants can be obtained from the following relation :

$$N_x = \overline{N}_x\sqrt{\frac{1+(f^2/L^2)(1-\eta^2)^2}{1+(16f^2/B^2)\xi^2\eta^2}}$$

$$N_y = \overline{N}_y\sqrt{\frac{1+(16f^2/B^2)\xi^2\eta^2}{1+(f^2/L^2)(1-\eta^2)^2}}$$

$$N_{xy} = \overline{N}_{xy}$$

While obtaining the above solution, no boundary condition was enforced along $y = \pm B/2$. Hence, the membrane solution will give certain stress resultants along these edges and if a support is provided to supply these stress resultants, the membrane solution will be valid. However, it is also possible to examine physically, whether a membrane solution is possible or not for a conoid, for a given loading and support conditions. This can be done in a similar way, as illustrated in the case of the hyperbolic paraboloid. But, it must be noted that a physical examination is not so simple in the case of a conoid as one of the characteristic line is not a straight line.

Example 3.3

A truncated parabolic conoid has the following geometrical dimensions and load

(a) Theoretical span (L) = 12 m

(b) Real span (l) = 8 m

(c) Width (b) = 20 m

(d) Rise (f) = 4.5 m

(e) Shell thickness = 10 cm

(f) Live load = 60 kg/m^2

Loading

$$\text{Dead load} = \frac{10}{100} \times 2400 = 240\ \text{kg/m}^2$$

$$\text{Live load} = 60\ \text{kg/m}^2$$

$$\text{Total load} = 300\ \text{kg/m}^2 \text{ or } 0.3\ \text{t/m}^2$$

$$x_0 = L - l = 4\text{m}$$

$$\xi_0 = \frac{x_0}{L} = \frac{4}{12} = 0.3333$$

Hence, the expressions for projected stress resultants can now be written as (Eqs. (3.56a–c)).

$$\overline{N}_x = 0.3375\,(1 - \xi)\left(1 - \frac{3}{2}\eta^2\right) - 0.648\,(1 - \xi^3) + 0.4006\,(1 - \xi^5) + 0.3375\,\eta^2\,(1 - \xi^9)$$

$$\overline{N}_y = \frac{1}{\xi}(-\,3.5676 + 1.35\,\eta^2\xi^2 - 2.7823\,\eta^2\xi^4 - 1.4063\,\eta^4\xi^2)$$

$$\overline{N}_{xy} = \eta\left[\left(1 - \frac{\eta^2}{2}\right)0.2813 - 1.62\xi^2 + 1.6694\,\xi^4 + 0.8438\,\eta^2\xi^8\right]$$

and the actual stress resultants can be obtained from

$$N_x = \overline{N}_x\sqrt{\frac{1 + 0.1406\,(1 - \eta^2)^2}{1 + 0.81\,\xi^2\eta^2}}$$

$$N_y = \overline{N}_y\sqrt{\frac{1 + 0.81\,\xi^2\eta^2}{1 + 0.1406\,(1 - \eta^2)^2}}$$

$$N_{xy} = \overline{N}_{xy}$$

The actual stress resultants at different points may be computed from the above equations and the values of the actual stress resultants are given in Tables 3.6–3.8.

Table 3.6 N_x force distribution (kg/m)

ξ	η				
	0	0.25	0.5	0.75	1.0
0.3333	0	0	0	0	0
0.5	–11	–5.4	10.7	35.3	66.8
0.6667	4.8	15.1	44.2	87	140.6
0.8333	24.4	35.9	67.7	113.3	168.2
1.0	0	0	0	0	0

Table 3.7 N_y force distribution (kg/m)

ξ	η				
	0	0.25	0.5	0.75	1.0
0.3333	−10017.8	−10104	−10340	−10623	−10812
0.5	− 6678.5	− 6752	− 6976.4	− 7246.7	− 7473.6
0.6667	− 5009	− 5096	− 5364	− 5773	− 6253
0.8333	− 4007	− 4136	− 4556	− 5301	− 6449
1.0	− 3339	− 3538	− 4239	− 5738	− 8623

Table 3.8 N_{xy} force distribution (kg/m)

ξ	η				
	0	0.25	0.5	0.75	1.0
0.3333	0	28.3	43.3	32.1	−18.6
0.5	0	− 7	− 27	− 72.5	− 156.7
0.6667	0	− 29	− 68	− 127	− 216.6
0.8333	0	− 8.7	− 12.3	− 5.3	17.3
1.0	0	93.9	253.3	544.7	1033.9

3.6 SUMMARY

In this chapter, we have first discussed the general membrane analysis of open cylindrical shells. It is shown that the membrane forces in a cylindrical shell can be determined by direct integration of equilibrium equations. It must be noted from the examples presented that while certain support conditions along the curved edges could be satisfied in the membrane analysis, boundary conditions along the straight edges cannot be accounted for. Hence, it must be said that in general, a membrane state of stress can exist in an open cylindrical shell only when the support provided along these edges can provide reactions as given by the membrane analysis. This is not always possibie and hence the shell will be subjected to bending near the straight edges. Based on this fact, one can say, in general, a membrane analysis is not valid for open cylindrical shells.

For the membrane analysis of a shell of double curvature, it is convenient to reduce the three equilibrium equations to a single differential equation by introducing a stress function. For each class of shell, it is shown that this differential equation can be solved by using classical or numerical methods. It is clearly brought out that the membrane state of stress is not always possible for anticlastic shell surface. However, for synclastic shells, the membrane theory can give reasonably good results. We will discuss this aspect later when we consider the bending analysis of doubly curved shells.

REFERENCES

3.1 Pucher, A., "*Uber den Spannungszustand in Gekrummten Flachen*", *Beton u Eisen*, Vol. 33, 1934, pp. 298–304.

3.2 Parme, A.L., "*Shells of double curvature*", Trans. ASCE, Vol. 123, 1958, pp. 989–1025.

3.3 Flugge, W., *Stresses in Shells*, Second edition, Springer-Verlag, Berlin, 1973.

3.4 Fischer, L., *Theory and Practice of Shell Structures*, Wilhelm Ernst and Sohn, Berlin-Munich, 1968.

3.5 Soare, M., *Application of Finite Difference Equations to Shell Analysis*, Pergamon Press, Oxford, 1967.

3.6 Pfluger, A., *Elementary Statics of Shells*, McGraw-Hill Book Co., New York, 1961.

3.7 Beles, A.A., and Soare, M.V., *Elliptic and Hyperbolic Paraboloidal Shells used in Construction* (Translated and edited by S.P. Christie), S.P. Christie and Partners, London, 1976.

3.8 Billington, D.P., *Thin Shell Concrete Structures*, McGraw-Hill Book Co., New York, 1982.

Chapter Four

Bending Analysis of Cylindrical Shells

4.1 INTRODUCTION

The membrane theory discussed earlier, gives a fair idea of the forces for certain dimensions of cylindrical shell only and even in this case, the membrane theory would be valid only for a portion of shell, far away from the edges. This fact could be recognised by looking to the membrane analysis, in which no boundary condition was enforced along the longitudinal edges. Hence, the membrane analysis would give forces along the longitudinal edges, wnich cannot be normally attained in practice by providing a suitable support. Any corrective force or displacement applied along these edges, so as to satisfy the actual support condition, would lead to bending of the shell. Hence, most of the cylindrical shell roof structures have to be analysed considering bending, to get a more realistic picture of force distribution in the shell. As mentioned earlier, a cylindrical shell could be either circular or noncircular, depending upon whether the plane curve is an arc of a circle or otherwise. The bending analysis of a circular cylindrical shell is somewhat simpler, compared to noncircular cylindrical shells. Further, a circular-cylindrical shell is widely used in practice as a roof structure. Because of these facts, we will restrict ourselves here to the detailed bending analysis of a circular-cylindrical shell.

Figure 4.1(a) shows a typical single-cylindrical shell roof. The longitudinal span (length) of the shell is denoted by L, the radius of the middle surface by R and the thickness by h. The half-angle subtended at the centre is called semicentral angle and is denoted by θ_0. Many times, cylindrical shells are provided with stiffening beams along the longitudinal edges (Fig. 4.1a) and these are called as edge-beams. The supporting members at the curved ends of the shell are called as traverses (Fig. 4.1a). The type of support at the traverse is of great importance to the mode of action of the shell structure. The traverses are normally intended to take large forces in their own plane, but can seldom resist a force normal to this

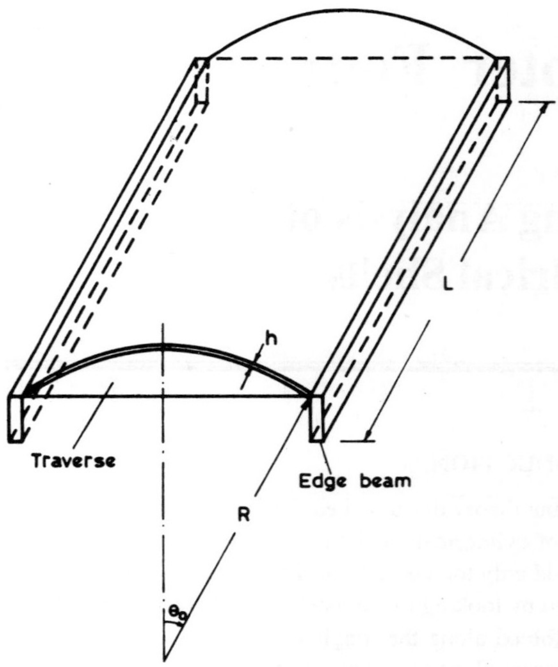

Fig. 4.1a Circular-cylindrical shell with edge-beam

plane. This type of support is often referred as simple support and a shell structure, which has only two traverses, is said to be simply supported. If the shell is supported on three or more traverses (Fig. 4.1b), then it is referred as a continuous shell. The traverse could be a solid wall, an arch rib or a bowstring girder. Often, several circular-cylindrical shells are placed side by side or one after another, connecting them along the longitudinal edge. Such a shell is called as a multiple cylindrical shell (Fig. 4.1c).

Circular-cylindrical shells are usually described as either long, intermediate or short, depending upon the ratio of the length (L) to radius (R) of the shell. A cylindrical shell can be called long, if the ratio (L/R) is greater than three and short, if this ratio is less than 0.5. If the ratio (L/R) of a given shell falls in between the above two limits, then such a shell is called as an intermediate shell. The object of this classification, principally, is to help the designer to determine whether a shell of particular dimensions is susceptible for an approximate method of analysis. For example, a short shell could be analysed using membrane theory, while a long shell can be analysed using a simple beam theory. We will discuss this aspect later through numerical examples.

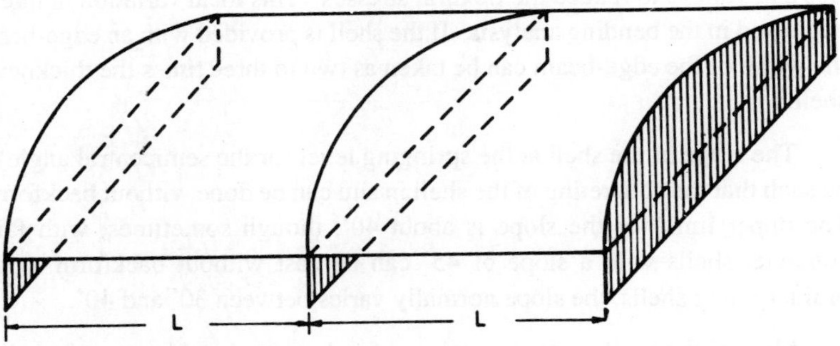

Fig. 4.1b Continuous circular-cylindrical shell

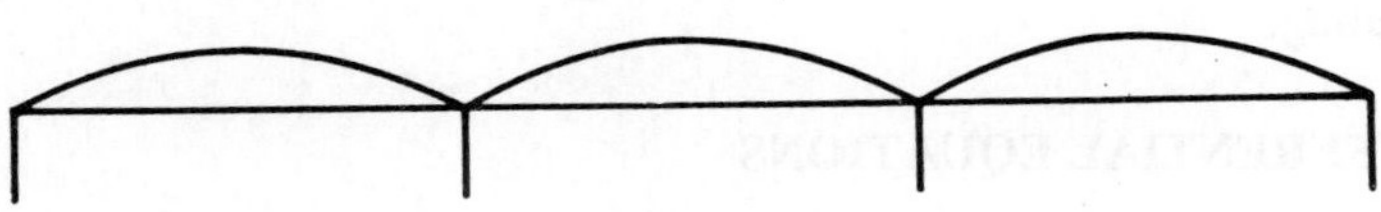

Fig. 4.1c Multiple cylindrical shell

4.2 SELECTION OF SHELL PARAMETERS

Bending analysis of a shell being a lengthy process, it is essential to start with properly chosen dimensions to avoid recalculation as far as possible. Some guidelines, which the designer may find useful, are available.

If a large rectangular area is to be covered with a cylindrical shell roof, then the aim will normally be to transfer the greater part of the load along the longer side. This can be done, for example, by using multiple cylindrical shell spanning along the shorter side. Alternatively, one can use a continuous short-shell, supported on tied arches spanning along the longer side. Cylindrical shells are normally provided with edge-beams along the longitudinal edges and practical limit for the longitudinal span for a shell, with a reinforced concrete edge-beam is about 30 m. For longer span, shells with prestressed edge-beam would be more economical.

The shell should always have the least possible thickness, as the self-weight of the shell itself will be a decisive factor in design. Short shells have a relatively small thickness, since the forces are small. For long shells, the recommended thickness is between 8 and 10 cm. For very long shells, the thickness will have to be decided based on the consideration of buckling. Also, in long shells having greater horizontal width, the transverse bending moment would be larger, thereby requiring greater thickness. Normally, the shell is thickened near the edge-beams, ribs and valleys to reduce the flexural stresses. This local variation in thickness is neglected in the bending analysis. If the shell is provided with an edge-beam, then the width of the edge-beam can be taken as two to three times the thickness of the shell.

The slope of the shell at the springing level (or the semicentral angle) should be such that the concreting of the shell in situ can be done without backform work. The upper limit for the slope is about 40°, though sometimes, with fairly dry concrete, shells with a slope of 45° can be cast without backform work. For ordinary long shells, the slope normally varies between 30° and 40°.

Most of the shell roofs are analysed for dead load and for a uniform live load or snow load. If the slope of a cylindrical shell at the springing level is less than 40°, then the wind load produces suction. Since the suction reduces the stresses in the shell produced by the dead weight, normally analysis of a shell for wind load is not carried out. However, shells which have large rise, have to be analysed for wind loading.

4.3 DIFFERENTIAL EQUATIONS

The governing differential equations for the bending analysis of a circular-cylindrical shell given by Flugge[4.1] will be presented here. These equations are often referred in the literature as exact differential equations. In view of the large number of available theories for a circular-cylindrical shell, it is considered appropriate here to first derive the exact equations so that a proper assessment regarding the various approximations considered in other theories could be made.

4.3.1 Equilibrium Equations

The middle surface of an element of a circular-cylindrical shell is described by (x, θ) coordinate system, where x is measured in the direction of the generatrix and θ is measured in the direction of the directrix.

Figure 4.2(a–c) shows the internal and external forces acting on the element of the shell. These forces and moments have to satisfy the six static equilibrium equations—three concerning the forces and the other three bending moments.

The condition of equilibrium for forces in the x-direction results in

$$\frac{\partial N_x}{\partial x}\, dx\, R\, d\theta + \frac{\partial N_{\theta x}}{R\, \partial\theta}\, R\, d\theta\, dx + XR\, d\theta\, dx = 0 \tag{a}$$

After dividing throughout by $R\, d\theta\, dx$, it reduces to

$$\frac{\partial N_x}{\partial x} + \frac{\partial N_{\theta x}}{R\, \partial\theta} + X = 0 \tag{4.1a}$$

In the y-direction, in addition to the forces in this direction, a contribution due to the transverse shear force Q_θ must be added. The two shear forces $Q_\theta\, dx$ and

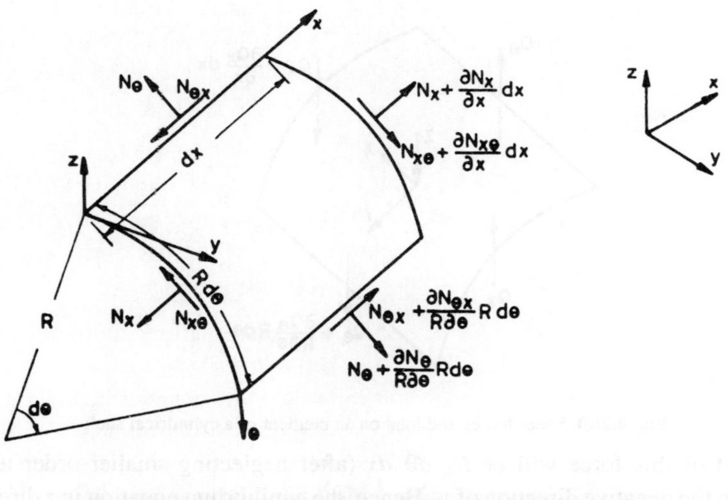

Fig. 4.2(a) Membrane forces on an element of a cylindrical shell

$\{Q_\theta + (\partial Q_\theta/R\,\partial\theta)\,R\,d\theta\}\,dx$ will have resultant (Fig. 4.3a) force $Q_\theta\,dx\,d\theta$ (after neglecting smaller order terms) directed in the decreasing direction of θ. Considering this component also, the equilibrium equation in the y-direction can now be written as

$$\frac{\partial N_\theta}{R\partial\theta} R\,d\theta\,dx + \frac{\partial N_{x\theta}}{\partial x} R\,d\theta\,dx - Q_\theta\,d\theta\,dx + YR\,d\theta\,dx = 0 \qquad \text{(b)}$$

which can be reduced to

$$\frac{\partial N_\theta}{R\partial\theta} + \frac{\partial N_{x\theta}}{\partial x} - \frac{Q_\theta}{R} + Y = 0 \qquad (4.1b)$$

In the radial direction, in addition to radial shear forces, the component of the force $N_\theta\,dx$ and $\{N_\theta + (\partial N_\theta/R\partial\theta)\,R\,d\theta\}\,dx$ should be included (Fig. 4.3b). The

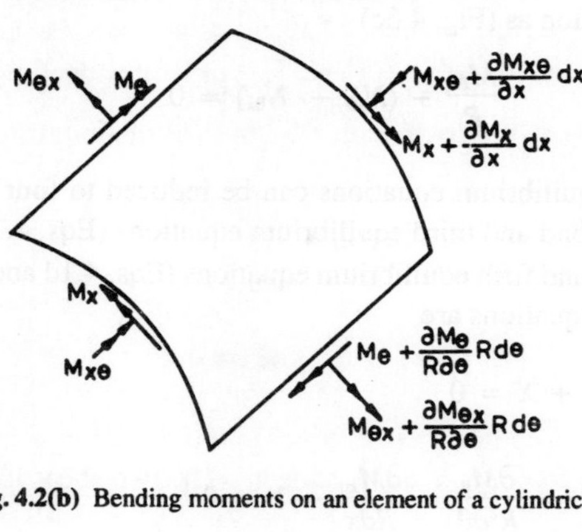

Fig. 4.2(b) Bending moments on an element of a cylindrical shell

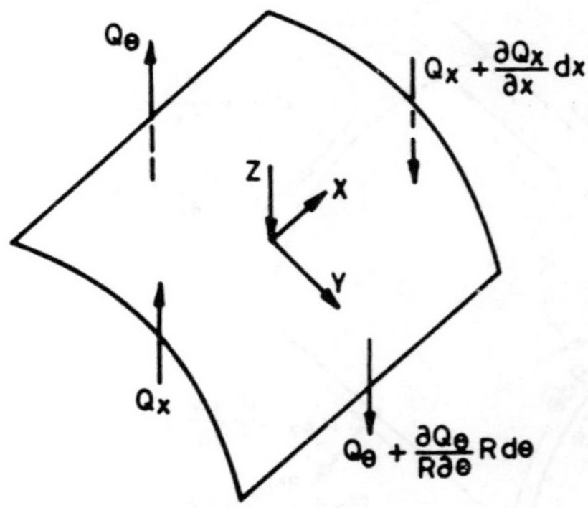

Fig. 4.2(c) Shear forces and load on an element of a cylindrical shell

resultant of this force will be $N_\theta\ d\theta\ dx$ (after neglecting smaller order terms) acting in the negative direction of z. Hence, the equilibrium equation in z direction can be written as

$$\frac{\partial Q_x}{\partial x} + \frac{\partial Q_\theta}{R\partial\theta} + \frac{N_\theta}{R} + Z = 0 \tag{4.1c}$$

The following moment equilibrium equations in x and y directions are obtained by including the couples caused by the two transverse shear forces Q_x and Q_θ to the moments in these two directions.

$$\frac{\partial M_x}{\partial x} + \frac{\partial M_{\theta x}}{R\partial\theta} - Q_x = 0 \tag{4.1d}$$

$$\frac{\partial M_\theta}{R\partial\theta} + \frac{\partial M_{x\theta}}{\partial x} - Q_\theta = 0 \tag{4.1e}$$

The last equilibrium equation is obtained by considering the moment equilibrium in the z-direction as (Fig. 4.3c)

$$\frac{M_{\theta x}}{R} + (N_{x\theta} - N_{\theta x}) = 0 \tag{4.1f}$$

The above six equilibrium equations can be reduced to four by eliminating Q_x and Q_θ in the second and third equilibrium equations (Eqs. 4.1b and 4.1c) by making use of fourth and fifth equilibrium equations (Eqs. 4.1d and 4.1e). Hence, the four equilibrium equations are

$$\frac{\partial N_x}{\partial x} + \frac{\partial N_{\theta x}}{R\partial\theta} + X = 0 \tag{4.2a}$$

$$\frac{\partial N_\theta}{R\partial\theta} + \frac{\partial N_{x\theta}}{\partial x} - \frac{\partial M_\theta}{R^2\partial\theta} - \frac{\partial M_{x\theta}}{R\partial x} + Y = 0 \tag{4.2b}$$

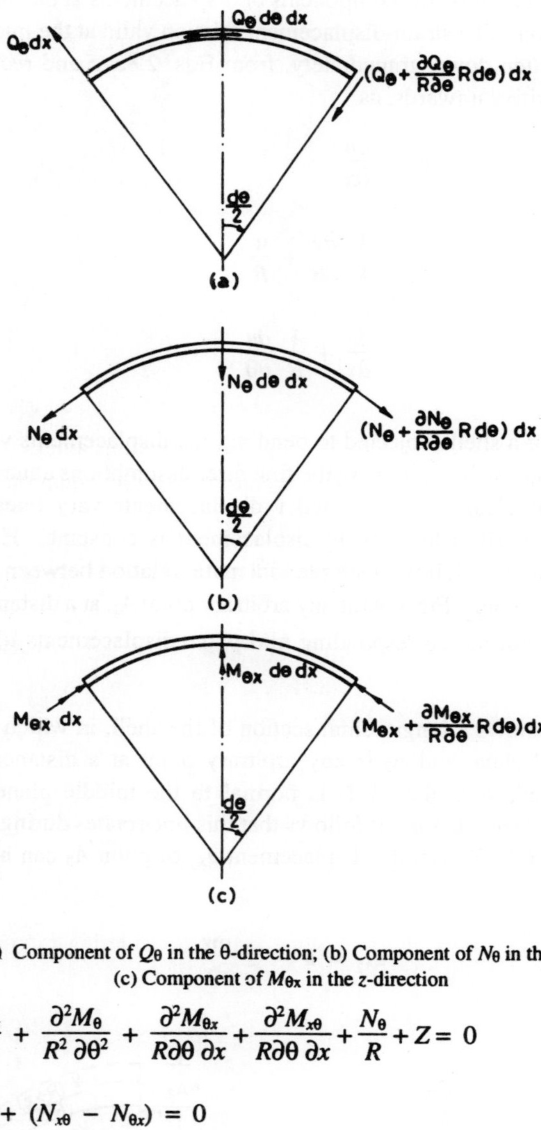

Fig. 4.3 (a) Component of Q_θ in the θ-direction; (b) Component of N_θ in the *z*-direction; (c) Component of $M_{\theta x}$ in the *z*-direction

$$\frac{\partial^2 M_x}{\partial x^2} + \frac{\partial^2 M_\theta}{R^2\,\partial\theta^2} + \frac{\partial^2 M_{\theta x}}{R\partial\theta\,\partial x} + \frac{\partial^2 M_{x\theta}}{R\partial\theta\,\partial x} + \frac{N_\theta}{R} + Z = 0 \tag{4.2c}$$

$$\frac{M_{\theta x}}{R} + (N_{x\theta} - N_{\theta x}) = 0 \tag{4.2d}$$

The above four equilibrium equations have eight unknown stress resultants and the problem is statically indeterminate internally. To obtain additional equations, it is necessary to consider the deformation of the shell.

4.3.2 Strain-Displacement Relationship

The strain-displacement relationship can be obtained purely from geometrical consideration by comparing the deformed shape of the shell element with the original. Let u, v and w be the components of displacements at the midplane in the x, θ and z direction. The strain-displacement relation valid at the mid-plane of the shell can be written down immediately, from Eqs. 2.8a–c and recognising that z-direction is positive upwards, as

$$\varepsilon_x = \frac{\partial u}{\partial x} \tag{4.3a}$$

$$\varepsilon_\theta = \frac{1}{R}\frac{\partial v}{\partial \theta} + \frac{w}{R} \tag{4.3b}$$

$$\gamma_{x\theta} = \frac{\partial v}{\partial x} + \frac{1}{R}\frac{\partial u}{\partial \theta} \tag{4.3c}$$

In the case of a shell subjected to bending, the displacements will vary over the thickness of the shell. Following the first three assumptions enumerated in Ch. 1 (Sec. 1.4), it is clear that the u and v displacements vary linearly over the thickness of the shell, while the w displacement is constant. Hence, it now becomes necessary to establish a simple kinematic relation between the displacements u_{A_2}, v_{A_2} and w_{A_2} (Fig. 4.4) at any arbitrary point A_2, at a distance z from the middle surface, with the corresponding mid-plane displacements u, v and w for that point.

Figure 4.4a shows a longitudinal section of the shell, in which A_1 is a point lying on the mid-plane and A_2 is any arbitrary point at a distance z from the mid-plane selected, such that A_1A_2 is normal to the middle plane. From the assumption of thin shell theory, it follows that this line rotates during deformation by an angle $(\partial w/\partial x)$. Hence, the displacement u_{A_2} of point A_2 can now be determined as

$$u_{A_2} = u - z\,\frac{\partial w}{\partial x} \tag{a}$$

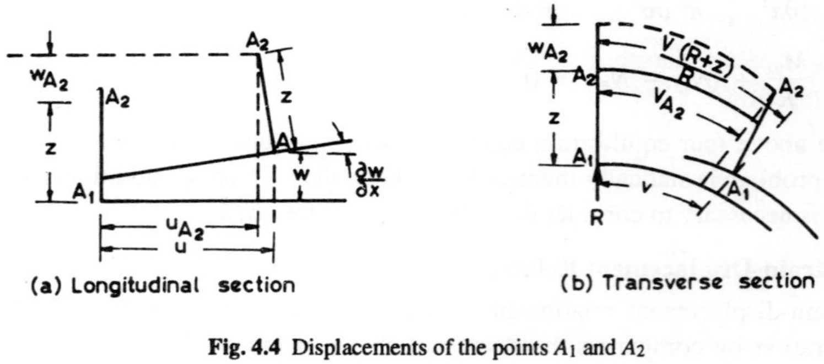

Fig. 4.4 Displacements of the points A_1 and A_2

To establish a similar relation for v_{A_2}, consider a transverse section of the shell as shown in Fig. 4.4b. The point A_2 is first displaced by $v\,(1 + z/R)$ and due to the rotation of the normal, it is further displaced by $(-\,z\ \partial w/R\partial\theta)$. Hence, the displacement

$$v_{A_2} = (1 + z/R)\,v - z\,\frac{\partial w}{R\partial\theta} \tag{b}$$

Since the shell does not suffer any deformation over its thickness (an assumption made in thin shell theory), the length A_1A_2 remains the same. However, due to the rotations $\partial w/\partial x$ and $\partial w/R\partial\theta$, there would be some change in the radial displacement. This can be shown to be very negligible and hence, we have $w = w_{A_2}$.

Now to determine the strains at any arbitrary point A_2 in terms of mid-plane displacements, first, the strain-displacement relation given in Eq. (4.3) is rewritten with the displacements u, v and w replaced by u_{A_2}, v_{A_2} and w_{A_2} and R by $(R + z)$ as

$$\varepsilon_x^{A2} = \frac{\partial u_{A_2}}{\partial x} \tag{c}$$

$$\varepsilon_\theta^{A2} = \frac{1}{R+z}\left(\frac{\partial v_{A_2}}{\partial\theta} + w_{A_2}\right) \tag{d}$$

$$\gamma_{x\theta}^{A2} = \frac{\partial v_{A_2}}{\partial x} + \frac{1}{R+z}\,\frac{\partial u_{A_2}}{\partial\theta} \tag{e}$$

In the above equations, u_{A_2} and v_{A_2} are replaced by the corresponding expressions given in Eqs. (a) and (b) and w_{A_2} is replaced by w to get the following strain-displacement relations:

$$\varepsilon_x^{A2} = \frac{\partial u}{\partial x} - z\,\frac{\partial^2 w}{\partial x^2} \tag{4.4a}$$

$$\varepsilon_\theta^{A2} = \frac{\partial v}{R\partial\theta} - \frac{1}{R}\left(\frac{z}{R+z}\right)\frac{\partial^2 w}{\partial\theta^2} + \frac{w}{R+z} \tag{4.4b}$$

$$\gamma_{x\theta}^{A2} = \frac{(R+z)}{R}\,\frac{\partial v}{\partial x} + \left(\frac{1}{R+z}\right)\frac{\partial u}{\partial\theta} - \frac{\partial^2 w}{\partial\theta\,\partial x}\left(\frac{z}{R} + \frac{z}{R+z}\right) \tag{4.4c}$$

4.3.3 Stress-Strain Relations

If σ_x and σ_θ are the normal stresses and $\tau_{x\theta}$ the shear stress in the shell, then following Hooke's law, the stress-strain relationship can be written as

$$\sigma_x = \frac{E}{1-\nu^2}\,(\varepsilon_x + \nu\,\varepsilon_\theta) \tag{4.5a}$$

$$\sigma_\theta = \frac{E}{1-\nu^2}\,(\varepsilon_\theta + \nu\,\varepsilon_x) \tag{4.5b}$$

$$\tau_{x\theta} = \frac{E}{2\,(1+\nu)}\,\gamma_{x\theta} \tag{4.5c}$$

The expressions for the stress resultants, in terms of the stresses, can be written using the general relation given in Ch. 1 (Sec. 1.6). For a circular-cylindrical shell, the following changes are to be made in this relation: y should be changed to θ, $R_1 = \infty$, $R_2 = R$.

We thus obtain the following expressions for the stress resultants:

$$
\begin{aligned}
N_x &= \int_{-h/2}^{+h/2} \sigma_x \left(1 + \frac{z}{R}\right) dz, & N_\theta &= \int_{-h/2}^{+h/2} \sigma_\theta \, dz \\
N_{x\theta} &= \int_{-h/2}^{+h/2} \tau_{x\theta} \left(1 + \frac{z}{R}\right) dz, & N_{\theta x} &= \int_{-h/2}^{+h/2} \tau_{\theta x} \, dz \\
M_x &= -\int_{-h/2}^{+h/2} \sigma_x \left(1 + \frac{z}{R}\right) z \, dz, & M_\theta &= -\int_{-h/2}^{+h/2} \sigma_\theta \, z \, dz \\
M_{x\theta} &= -\int_{-h/2}^{+h/2} \tau_{x\theta} \left(1 + \frac{z}{R}\right) z \, dz, & M_{\theta x} &= -\int_{-h/2}^{+h/2} \tau_{\theta x} \, z \, dz
\end{aligned}
\tag{4.6}
$$

4.3.4 Force-Displacement Relation

Substituting for strains in Eq. (4.5), the strain-displacement relation given in Eqs. (4.4a–c), we get the stress-displacement relation. These stress-displacement relations are then substituted in Eq. (4.6) and then the integration with respect to z is performed to get the force-displacement relations.

For example, for N_x, we have

$$N_x = \frac{E}{1-\nu^2} \int_{-h/2}^{+h/2} (\varepsilon_x + \nu\varepsilon_\theta) \left(\frac{R+z}{R}\right) dz \tag{a}$$

which, after integration, results in

$$N_x = \frac{Eh}{1-\nu^2} \left[\frac{\partial u}{\partial x} + \nu \left(\frac{\partial v}{R\,\partial\theta} + \frac{w}{R}\right)\right] - \frac{Eh^3}{12\,(1-\nu^2)} \frac{1}{R} \frac{\partial^2 w}{\partial x^2} \tag{b}$$

Denoting the extensional rigidity $(Eh/1-\nu^2)$ by K and flexural rigidity $[\,Eh^3/12\,(1-\nu^2)\,]$ by D, the above relation can be written as

$$N_x = K \left[\frac{\partial u}{\partial x} + \nu \left(\frac{\partial v}{R\,\partial\theta} + \frac{w}{R}\right)\right] - \frac{D}{R} \frac{\partial^2 w}{\partial x^2} \tag{c}$$

While it was possible to obtain the expression for N_x by simple integration, the expressions to some of the other stress resultants cannot be so easily obtained and needs explanation. For example, the expression for the stress resultant N_θ is determined from

$$N_\theta = \int_{-h/2}^{+h/2} \sigma_\theta \, dz = \frac{E}{1-\nu^2} \int_{-h/2}^{+h/2} (\varepsilon_\theta + \nu\,\varepsilon_x)\, dz \tag{d}$$

Substituting for ε_x and ε_θ from Eq. (4.4a–c), we get

$$N_\theta = \frac{E}{1-\nu^2}\int_{-h/2}^{+h/2}\left[\left\{\frac{\partial v}{R\,\partial\theta} - \frac{z}{R^2}\,(1+z/R)^{-1}\frac{\partial^2 w}{\partial\theta^2}\right.\right.$$

$$\left.\left. + \frac{w}{R}\,(1+z/R)^{-1}\right\} + \nu\left\{\frac{\partial u}{\partial x} - z\,\frac{\partial^2 w}{\partial x^2}\right\}\right]dz \tag{e}$$

while integrating the above expression, it is assumed that (z/R) is less than unity and $(1+z/R)^{-1}$ can be expanded as

$$(1+z/R)^{-1} \approx 1-(z/R)+(z/R)^2-(z/R)^3+(z/R)^4 \tag{f}$$

Substituting the above expression in Eq. (e) and neglecting terms higher than $(z/R)^3$, the following expression for N_θ is obtained:

$$N_\theta = K\left\{\left(\frac{\partial v}{R\partial\theta}+\frac{w}{R}\right)+\nu\frac{\partial u}{\partial x}\right\}+\left(\frac{D}{R}\right)\frac{\partial^2 w}{R^2\,\partial\theta^2}+\left(\frac{D}{R^3}\right)w \tag{g}$$

Following in a similar way, the force-displacement relation for the other forces and moments can be determined. The derivatives of the displacements in the force-displacement can later be classified as primary, secondary and tertiary, depending upon whether these derivatives are multiplied by terms like (h/R), $(h/R)^2$, etc. The force-displacement relation classified in the above mentioned form, is given in Table 4.1.

Table 4.1 Force-displacement relation

Force	Primary	Secondary	Tertiary
N_x	$K\left[\frac{\partial u}{\partial x}+\nu\left(\frac{\partial v}{R\partial\theta}+\frac{w}{R}\right)\right]$	$-\frac{D}{R}\frac{\partial^2 w}{\partial x^2}$	—
N_θ	$K\left[\left(\frac{\partial v}{R\partial\theta}+\frac{w}{R}\right)+\nu\frac{\partial u}{\partial x}\right]$	$\frac{D}{R}\frac{\partial^2 w}{R^2\,\partial\theta^2}$	$\frac{D}{R^3}\,w$
$N_{x\theta}$	$K\left(\frac{1-\nu}{2}\right)\left(\frac{\partial v}{\partial x}+\frac{\partial u}{R\partial\theta}\right)$	$-\left(\frac{1-\nu}{2}\right)\frac{D}{R}\frac{\partial^2 w}{R\,\partial\theta\,\partial x}$	$\left(\frac{1-\nu}{2}\right)\frac{D}{R^2}\frac{\partial v}{\partial x}$
$N_{\theta x}$	$K\left(\frac{1-\nu}{2}\right)\left(\frac{\partial v}{\partial x}+\frac{\partial u}{R\partial\theta}\right)$	$\left(\frac{1-\nu}{2}\right)\frac{D}{R}\frac{\partial^2 w}{R\partial\theta\,\partial x}$	$\left(\frac{1-\nu}{2}\right)\frac{D}{R^2}\frac{\partial u}{R\,\partial\theta}$
M_x	$D\left(\frac{\partial^2 w}{\partial x^2}+\nu\frac{\partial^2 w}{R^2\,\partial\theta^2}\right)$	$-\frac{D}{R}\left(\frac{\partial u}{\partial x}+\frac{\partial v}{R\,\partial\theta}\right)$	—
M_θ	$D\left(\frac{\partial^2 w}{R^2\,\partial\theta^2}+\nu\frac{\partial^2 w}{\partial x^2}\right)$	$\frac{D}{R^2}\,w$	—
$M_{x\theta}$	$D\,(1-\nu)\frac{\partial^2 w}{R\partial\theta\,\partial x}$	$-\frac{D}{R}\,(1-\nu)\frac{\partial v}{\partial x}$	—
$M_{\theta x}$	$D\,(1-\nu)\frac{\partial^2 w}{R\partial\theta\,\partial x}$	$-\frac{D\,(1-\nu)}{2R}\left(\frac{\partial v}{\partial x}-\frac{\partial u}{R\partial\theta}\right)$	—

It may be observed from Table 4.1 that in general, $N_{x\theta} \neq N_{\theta x}$ and $M_{x\theta} \neq M_{\theta x}$, even though $\tau_{x\theta} = \tau_{\theta x}$. However, in the force-displacement relation, if only the primary displacement components are considered, then $N_{x\theta} = N_{\theta x}$ and $M_{x\theta} = M_{\theta x}$.

In the above force-displacement relations, many times, the secondary and tertiary terms are not of much importance for the purpose of design. A detailed examination of the secondary and tertiary terms reveals that the membrane normal and shear forces are influenced by the change in curvature and twist, while the bending and twisting moments are influenced by the membrane strains and often, their contribution may be very small. From this, one may argue that the effect of secondary and tertiary terms are so small, that they can be safely neglected. Alternatively, one can say that the secondary and tertiary terms are multiplied by quantities like (h/R) and $(h/R)^2$, which are small and the derivatives of the displacements also being small, their product is so small that these terms can be safely neglected. Hence, the approximate force-displacement relations can be written as

$$N_x = K\left[\frac{\partial u}{\partial x} + \nu\left(\frac{\partial v}{R\partial\theta} + \frac{w}{R}\right)\right] \tag{4.7a}$$

$$N_\theta = K\left[\left(\frac{\partial v}{R\partial\theta} + \frac{w}{R}\right) + \nu\frac{\partial u}{\partial x}\right] \tag{4.7b}$$

$$N_{x\theta} = N_{\theta x} = K\frac{(1-\nu)}{2}\left(\frac{\partial v}{\partial x} + \frac{\partial u}{R\partial\theta}\right) \tag{4.7c}$$

$$M_x = D\left(\frac{\partial^2 w}{\partial x^2} + \nu\frac{\partial^2 w}{R^2\,\partial\theta^2}\right) \tag{4.7d}$$

$$M_\theta = D\left(\frac{\partial^2 w}{R^2\,\partial\theta^2} + \nu\frac{\partial^2 w}{\partial x^2}\right) \tag{4.7e}$$

$$M_{x\theta} = M_{\theta x} = D(1-\nu)\frac{\partial^2 w}{R\partial\theta\,\partial x} \tag{4.7f}$$

It must be noted that the above approximate force-displacement relation does not satisfy the fourth equilibrium equation (Eq. 4.2d).

4.3.5 Differential Equations in Terms of Displacements

Now we have four equilibrium equations (Eqs. 4.2a–d) and eight force-displacement relations (Table 4.1), giving altogether 12 equations, involving 11 unknowns (eight forces and three displacements). The one redundant equation is the last equilibrium equation (Eq. 4.2d), which will be automatically satisfied, when the force-displacement relation corresponding to forces $M_{\theta x}$, $N_{x\theta}$ and $N_{\theta x}$ is substituted in this equation. Hence, we are left with only 11 equations involving 11 unknowns. Instead of dealing with these 11 equations, it is preferable to reduce these to three equations in terms of displacements only. This can be done by substituting the force-displacement relation given in Table 4.1 in Eqs. (4.2 a–c), to get the following three differential equations in terms of the displacements u, v and w:

$$\frac{\partial^2 u}{\partial x^2} + \left(\frac{1-\nu}{2}\right)\frac{\partial^2 u}{R^2\partial\theta^2} + \left(\frac{1+\nu}{2}\right)\frac{\partial^2 v}{R\partial\theta\,\partial x} + \frac{\nu}{R}\frac{\partial w}{\partial x}$$

$$+ D'\left\{-R\frac{\partial^3 w}{\partial x^3} + \left(\frac{1-\nu}{2}\right)\frac{\partial^2 u}{R^2\partial\theta^2} + \left(\frac{1-\nu}{2}\right)\frac{\partial^3 w}{R\partial\theta^2\,\partial x}\right\} + \frac{X}{K} = 0 \quad (4.8a)$$

$$\frac{\partial^2 v}{R^2\partial\theta^2} + \left(\frac{1+\nu}{2}\right)\frac{\partial^2 u}{R\partial\theta\,\partial x} + \left(\frac{1-\nu}{2}\right)\frac{\partial^2 v}{\partial x^2} + \frac{1}{R^2}\frac{\partial w}{\partial\theta}$$

$$+ D'\left\{\frac{3\,(1-\nu)}{2}\frac{\partial^2 v}{\partial x^2} - \left(\frac{3-\nu}{2}\right)\frac{\partial^3 w}{\partial x^2\partial\theta}\right\} + \frac{Y}{K} = 0 \quad (4.8b)$$

$$\frac{\nu}{R}\frac{\partial u}{\partial x} + \frac{1}{R^2}\frac{\partial v}{\partial\theta} + \frac{w}{R^2} + D'\left\{\left(\frac{1-\nu}{2}\right)\frac{\partial^3 u}{R\partial\theta^2\,\partial x}\right.$$

$$- R\frac{\partial^3 u}{\partial x^3} - \left(\frac{3-\nu}{2}\right)\frac{\partial^3 v}{\partial\theta\partial x^2} + R^2\frac{\partial^4 w}{\partial x^4}$$

$$\left. + \frac{\partial^4 w}{R^2\partial\theta^4} + 2\frac{\partial^4 w}{\partial\theta^2\,\partial x^2} + 2\frac{\partial^2 w}{R^2\partial\theta^2} + \frac{w}{R^2}\right\} + \frac{Z}{K} = 0 \quad (4.8c)$$

where

$$D' = \frac{D}{KR^2} = \frac{h^2}{12R^2}$$

Equations (4.8a–c) are the exact differential equations for a circular-cylindrical shell. Instead of the exact differential equations, a set of simplified differential equations in terms of displacements, can be obtained by making use of the approximate force-displacement relations (Eq. 4.7). These equations will be

$$\frac{\partial^2 u}{\partial x^2} + \left(\frac{1-\nu}{2}\right)\frac{\partial^2 u}{R^2\partial\theta^2} + \left(\frac{1+\nu}{2}\right)\frac{\partial^2 v}{R\partial\theta\,\partial x} + \frac{\nu}{R}\frac{\partial w}{\partial x} + \frac{X}{K} = 0 \quad (4.9a)$$

$$\left(\frac{1+\nu}{2}\right)\frac{\partial^2 u}{R\,\partial\theta\,\partial x} + \frac{\partial^2 v}{R^2\partial\theta^2} + \left(\frac{1-\nu}{2}\right)\frac{\partial^2 v}{\partial x^2} + \frac{1}{R^2}\frac{\partial w}{\partial\theta}$$

$$- D'\left(\frac{\partial^3 w}{\partial\theta\,\partial x^2} + \frac{1}{R^2}\frac{\partial^3 w}{\partial\theta^3}\right) + \frac{Y}{K} = 0 \quad (4.9b)$$

$$\frac{\nu}{R}\frac{\partial u}{\partial x} + \frac{\partial v}{R^2\partial\theta} + \frac{w}{R^2} + D'\left\{R^2\frac{\partial^4 w}{\partial x^4} + 2\frac{\partial^4 w}{\partial\theta^2\,\partial x^2} + \frac{\partial^4 w}{R^2\partial\theta^4}\right\} + \frac{Z}{K} = 0 \quad (4.9c)$$

If we compare the above equations with the exact equations (Eqs. 4.8a–c), we notice that the terms without the factor D' are exactly the same, but there are considerable changes in terms multiplied by the factor D'. For example, the u and v terms multiplied by the factor D' in Eq. (4.8c) have completely disappeared in Eq. (4.9c), while terms involving higher derivatives in w are retained. Similarly, the terms multiplied by D' in Eq. (4.8a) have completely disappeared in Eq. (4.9a), while in Eq. (4.9b), the terms are quite different to the one compared to Eq. (4.8b). Perhaps, the terms multiplied by D' in Eq. (4.9b) have changed so much that it may be worth-while to consider whether they can be totally neglected. One can work back and find out what force would be neglected in the equilibrium equation, if these terms are neglected. It turns out that this term is due to Q_θ in the second equilibrium equation (Eq. 4.1b), and neglecting this term in effect, means neglecting Q_θ in the second equilibrium equation. This seems to be a valid point, as the magnitude of Q_θ for thin shells, is fairly small and could be neglected. As a result of these considerations, we now write the simplified differential equations for a circular-cylindrical shell in the following form:

$$\frac{\partial^2 u}{\partial x^2} + \left(\frac{1-\nu}{2}\right)\frac{\partial^2 u}{R^2\partial\theta^2} + \left(\frac{1+\nu}{2}\right)\frac{\partial^2 v}{R\,\partial\theta\,\partial x} + \nu\frac{\partial w}{R\partial x} + \frac{X}{K} = 0 \tag{4.10a}$$

$$\left(\frac{1+\nu}{2}\right)\frac{\partial^2 u}{R\partial\theta\partial x} + \frac{\partial^2 v}{R^2\partial\theta^2} + \left(\frac{1-\nu}{2}\right)\frac{\partial^2 v}{\partial x^2} + \frac{\partial w}{R^2\partial\theta} + \frac{Y}{K} = 0 \tag{4.10b}$$

$$\frac{\nu}{R}\frac{\partial u}{\partial x} + \frac{\partial v}{R^2\partial\theta} + \frac{w}{R^2} + D'R^2\,(\nabla^4 w) + \frac{Z}{K} = 0 \tag{4.10c}$$

where

$$\nabla^4 = \left(\frac{\partial^4}{\partial x^4} + 2\,\frac{\partial^4}{R^2\partial\theta^2\partial x^2} + \frac{\partial^4}{R^4\partial\theta^4}\right)$$

4.3.6 Differential Equation in Terms of Displacement *w*

For obtaining a practical solution to the cylindrical shell problem, we will consider here Flugge's approximate differential equations (Eqs. (4.10a–c)). Instead of dealing with three differential equations in terms of displacements u, v and w, it is preferable to reduce it to a single differential equation in terms of the displacement w. This can be done by eliminating u and v from Eq. (4.10c) using Eqs. (4.10a) and (4.10b). First we will eliminate u from Eqs. (4.10a) and (4.10b) and this will result in the following equation:

$$\nabla^4 v = -\;(2+\nu)\,\frac{\partial^3 w}{R^2\partial\theta\,\partial x^2} - \frac{\partial^3 w}{R^4\partial\theta^3} + \left(\frac{1+\nu}{1-\nu}\right)\frac{1}{K}\,\frac{\partial^2 X}{R\,\partial\theta\,\partial x}$$
$$-\left(\frac{2}{1-\nu}\right)\frac{1}{K}\,\frac{\partial^2 Y}{\partial x^2} - \frac{1}{K}\,\frac{\partial^2 Y}{R^2\partial\theta^2} \tag{4.11a}$$

In a similar way, eliminating v from the same two equations namely Eqs. (4.10a) and (4.10b), we get

$$\nabla^4 u = -\;\frac{\nu}{R}\,\frac{\partial^3 w}{\partial x^3} + \frac{\partial^3 w}{R^3\partial\theta^2\partial x} - \left(\frac{2}{1-\nu}\right)\frac{1}{K}$$
$$\times\left(\frac{\partial^2}{R^2\partial\theta^2} + \frac{1-\nu}{2}\,\frac{\partial^2}{\partial x^2}\right)X + \left(\frac{1+\nu}{1-\nu}\right)\frac{1}{K}\,\frac{\partial^2 Y}{R\,\partial\theta\,\partial x} \tag{4.11b}$$

Using Eqs. (4.11a) and (4.11b), Eqs. (4.10c) can now be obtained in terms of w as

$$\nabla^4\nabla^4 w + \frac{12\,(1-\nu^2)}{h^2R^2}\frac{\partial^4 w}{\partial x^4} = -\frac{\nabla^4 Z}{D}$$
$$-\frac{1}{DR}\frac{\partial}{\partial x}\left(\frac{\partial^2 X}{R^2\partial\theta^2} - \nu\frac{\partial^2 X}{\partial x^2}\right)$$
$$+\frac{1}{DR}\frac{\partial}{R\partial\theta}\left\{(2+\nu)\frac{\partial^2 Y}{\partial x^2} + \frac{\partial^2 Y}{R^2\partial\theta^2}\right\}$$

Multiplying the above equation by R^8 throughout, we get

$$R^8\nabla^8 w + \frac{12R^6\,(1-\nu^2)}{h^2}\frac{\partial^4 w}{\partial x^4} = -\frac{R^8}{D}\nabla^4 Z$$
$$-\frac{R^7}{D}\frac{\partial}{\partial x}\left(\frac{\partial^2 X}{R^2\partial\theta^2} - \nu\frac{\partial^2 X}{\partial x^2}\right)$$
$$+\frac{R^7}{D}\frac{\partial}{R\partial\theta}\left\{(2+\nu)\frac{\partial^2 Y}{\partial x^2} + \frac{\partial^2 Y}{R^2\partial\theta^2}\right\} \qquad (4.12)$$

In Eq. (4.12), if ν is taken as zero then we get the differential equation as given by Gibson[4.2]. It is also interesting to note that the homogeneous part of the differential equation (4.12) is identical to the one given in D-K-J (Donnell-Karman-Jenkins) theory[4.3–4.5]. As the above differential equation is in terms of w, it will be more appropriate to write the force-displacement relations in terms of w only. Consistent with the approximations made in deriving the differential equation, namely, only primary displacement components are considered and Q_θ is neglected in the second equilibrium equation, we can obtain the following expressions for forces in terms of w.

$$N_x = -DR\int\!\!\int \frac{\partial^2}{R^2\,\partial\theta^2}(\nabla^4 w)\,dx\,dx - \int\!\!\int \frac{\partial^2 Z}{R\partial\theta^2}\,dx\,dx$$
$$+\int\!\!\int \frac{\partial Y}{R\partial\theta}\,dx\,dx - \int X\,dx \qquad (4.13a)$$

$$N_\theta = -DR\,\nabla^4 w - ZR \qquad (4.13b)$$

$$N_{x\theta} = DR\int \frac{\partial}{R\partial\theta}(\nabla^4 w)\,dx + \int \frac{\partial Z}{\partial\theta}\,dx - \int Y\,dx \qquad (4.13c)$$

$$M_x = D\left(\frac{\partial^2 w}{\partial x^2} + \nu\frac{\partial^2 w}{R^2\,\partial\theta^2}\right) \qquad (4.13d)$$

$$M_\theta = D\left(\frac{\partial^2 w}{R^2\,\partial\theta^2} + \nu\frac{\partial^2 w}{\partial x^2}\right) \qquad (4.13e)$$

$$M_{x\theta} = D\,(1-\nu)\frac{\partial^2 w}{R\partial\theta\,\partial x} \qquad (4.13f)$$

$$Q_x = D\left(\frac{\partial^3 w}{\partial x^3} + \frac{\partial^3 w}{R^2\,\partial\theta^2\,\partial x}\right) \tag{4.13g}$$

$$Q_\theta = D\left(\frac{\partial^3 w}{R^3\partial\theta^3} + \frac{\partial^3 w}{R\,\partial\theta\,\partial x^2}\right) \tag{4.13h}$$

4.4 SOLUTION FOR A SIMPLY SUPPORTED CYLINDRICAL SHELL

Solution for a circular-cylindrical shell simply supported all-round, or one pair of edges simply supported and the other pair having any type of boundary conditions, can be developed using double (Navier type) or single (Levy type) trigonometric series. Since the latter type of solution is somewhat more general and many practical shell-roof problems can be solved using this solution, we will develop this solution in detail here.

4.4.1 Solution of the Differential Equation

The coordinate axes with the origin at the centre of the shell is shown in Fig. 4.5. According to this, $x = \pm L/2$ refers to the two curved ends while $\theta = \pm \theta_0$ refers to the straight edges. It is assumed here that the shell is supported on traverses along the two curved edges, which can take large forces in their own plane but cannot resist any load normal to their plane. As mentioned earlier, this type of support will be referred as simple support. To satisfy the above requirement at the traverses, the following boundary conditions may be enforced along the two curved ends.

$$\text{at } x = \pm\frac{L}{2},\; N_x = \varepsilon_\theta = M_x = w = 0 \tag{4.14}$$

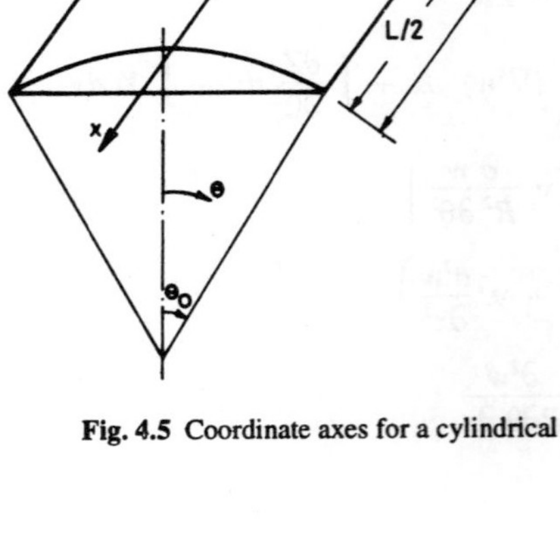

Fig. 4.5 Coordinate axes for a cylindrical shell

The solution of the differential equation (4.12) can be obtained as

$$w = w_0 + w_1$$

where w_0 is the solution for the homogeneous part of the differential equation (complementary function) and w_1 is the particular integral.

4.4.1.1 Complementary Function

The solution for the homogeneous part of the differential equation can be written as

$$w_0 = \sum_{m=1,3}^{\infty} A_m \, e^{\rho\theta} \cos \alpha_m x \qquad \text{(a)}$$

where

$$\alpha_m = \frac{m\pi}{L}$$

In the above equation, A_m is an arbitrary constant which will have in general, eight arbitrary values (since the differential equation is of eighth order). These values will be eventually determined from eight boundary conditions, four at each edge. It may also be observed that the above form for w_0 satisfies the boundary condition specified in Eq. (4.14). Substituting the above expression for w_0 in the homogeneous part of the differential equation, we get the following algebraic equation:

$$R^8 \left(\frac{\rho^2}{R^2} - \alpha_m^2 \right)^4 + \frac{12\,(1-\nu^2)\,R^6}{h^2}\,\alpha_m^4 = 0 \qquad \text{(b)}$$

The above equation being of eighth degree will have eight roots, and in this case, all the roots will be complex. The method of determining the roots of the above equation is given in Appendix – I. The eight roots of the above equation can be written as :

$$\rho_{1,2,3,4} = \pm\,\lambda\,(j \pm ik) = \pm\,(a \pm ib)$$

$$\rho_{5,6,7,8} = \pm\,\lambda\,(j_1 \pm ik_1) = \pm\,(a_1 \pm ib_1) \qquad \text{(c)}$$

where

$$\lambda = \sqrt[8]{3\,(1-\nu^2)}\;\sqrt{\alpha_m R}\;\sqrt[4]{\frac{R}{h}}$$

$$j = \sqrt{\frac{\sqrt{(1 + (1+\varepsilon)^2)} + (1+\varepsilon)}{2}}, \qquad k = \sqrt{\frac{\sqrt{(1 + (1+\varepsilon)^2)} - (1+\varepsilon)}{2}},$$

$$j_1 = \sqrt{\frac{\sqrt{(1 + (1-\varepsilon)^2)} - (1-\varepsilon)}{2}}, \qquad k_1 = \sqrt{\frac{\sqrt{(1 + (1-\varepsilon)^2)} + (1-\varepsilon)}{2}},$$

$$\varepsilon = \frac{1}{\sqrt[4]{3\,(1-\nu^2)}}\;\sqrt{\frac{h}{R}}\;(\alpha_m R)$$

Thus, the solution for w_0 can be written as

$$w_0 = \sum_{m=1,3}^{\infty} \left(A_1\, e^{\rho_1 \theta} + A_2\, e^{\rho_2 \theta} + \cdots + A_8\, e^{\rho_8 \theta} \right) \cos \alpha_m x \tag{d}$$

where A_1, A_2, ..., A_8 are the eight arbitrary complex constants. These arbitrary complex constants may be so chosen that the complete solution for w_0 is real and can be put in the following form:

$$\begin{aligned} w_0 = \sum_{m=1,3}^{\infty} & [(A_1 \cos b\theta + A_2 \sin b\theta)\, e^{a\theta} \\ & + (A_3 \cos b_1\theta + A_4 \sin b_1\theta)\, e^{a_1\theta} \\ & + (A_5 \cos b\theta + A_6 \sin b\theta)\, e^{-a\theta} \\ & + (A_7 \cos b_1\theta + A_8 \sin b_1\theta]\, e^{-a_1\theta}] \cos \alpha_m x \end{aligned} \tag{4.15}$$

In the above equation, the arbitrary constants A_1, A_2, ..., A_8 are real and are determined from the boundary conditions specified along the two straight edges of the shell ($\theta = \pm\, \theta_0$). The expressions for the stress resultants and displacements for the complementary function part may now be obtained from Eq. (4.15) using Eqs. (4.13a–h). It must be noted that the complementary function for certain forces and displacements will have even functions, while for certain other forces and displacements it will have odd functions. Hence a general expression for the force or displacement can be written as

$$\begin{aligned} F = \sum_{m=1,3}^{\infty} MF\ & [\{A_1\, \alpha_1 - A_2\, \alpha_2) \cos b\theta - (A_1\, \alpha_2 + A_2\, \alpha_1) \sin b\theta\}\, e^{a\theta} \\ & + \{(A_3\, \alpha_3 - A_4\alpha_4) \cos b_1\theta - (A_3\, \alpha_4 + A_4\, \alpha_3) \sin b_1\theta\}\, e^{a_1\theta} \\ & \pm \{(A_5\, \alpha_1 - A_6\, \alpha_2) \cos b\theta + (A_5\, \alpha_2 + A_6\, \alpha_1) \sin b\theta\}\, e^{-a\theta} \\ & \pm \{(A_7\, \alpha_3 - A_8\, \alpha_4) \cos b_1\theta + (A_7\, \alpha_4 + A_8\, \alpha_3) \sin b_1\, \theta\}\, e^{-a_1\theta}] \end{aligned} \tag{4.16}$$

where F denotes the force or displacement, MF the multiplying factor, α_1, α_2, α_3 and α_4 are the coefficients defined in Tables 4.2 and 4.3 and are taken from Gibson[4.2], for the various forces and displacements involving even or odd functions and A_1, A_2, …, A_8 are the eight arbitrary constants.

If the shell is subjected to symmetric load and has symmetrical boundary conditions along $\theta = \pm\, \theta_0$, then the constant $A_1 = A_5$, $A_2 = A_6$, $A_3 = A_7$ and $A_4 = A_8$, and Eq. (4.15) can be reduced to the form

$$\begin{aligned} w_0 = \sum_{m=1,3}^{\infty} & [A_1 \cosh a\theta \cos b\theta - A_2 \sinh a\theta \sin b\theta \\ & + A_3 \cosh a_1\theta \cos b_1\theta - A_4 \sinh a_1\theta \sin b_1\theta] \cos \alpha_m x \end{aligned} \tag{4.17}$$

The complementary function part for the shell forces and displacements involving even and odd functions can now be written as (Eq. 4.16).

$$\begin{aligned} F = \sum_{m=1,3}^{\infty} MF [& (A_1 \alpha_1 - A_2 \alpha_2) \cosh a\theta \cos b\theta \\ & - (A_1 \alpha_2 + A_2 \alpha_1) \sinh a\theta \sin b\theta \\ & + (A_3 \alpha_3 - A_4 \alpha_4) \cosh a_1 \theta \cos b_1\theta \\ & - (A_3 \alpha_4 + A_4 \alpha_3) \sinh a_1 \theta \sin b_1 \theta] \quad - \text{ (even function)} \end{aligned} \tag{4.18a}$$

and

$$\begin{aligned} F = \sum_{m=1,3}^{\infty} MF [& (A_1 \alpha_1 - A_2 \alpha_2) \sinh a\theta \cos b\theta \\ & - (A_1 \alpha_2 + A_2 \alpha_1) \cosh a\theta \sin b\theta \\ & + (A_3 \alpha_3 - A_4 \alpha_4) \sinh a_1 \theta \cos b_1\theta \\ & - (A_3 \alpha_4 + A_4 \alpha_3) \cosh a_1 \theta \sin b_1 \theta] - \text{ (odd function)} \end{aligned} \tag{4.18b}$$

where MF, α_1, α_2, α_3 and α_4 for the various shell forces and displacements can be obtained from the same Tables 4.2 and 4.3.

4.4.1.2 Particular Integral

The particular integral of Eq. (4.12) is determined depending upon the type of loading to which the shell is subjected. We will obtain the particular integral for the following three types of load:

(a) Dead load (g per unit area) acting on the curved surface of the shell.

(b) Uniformly distributed live load (q per unit area) acting on the horizontal projection of the shell.

(c) Radial load (p per unit area).

We will describe the procedure for obtaining the particular integral for dead load. Following this procedure, the particular integral for the other two types of load can be determined. To be of direct use with Eq. (4.15), the loading should be expressed in terms of Fourier series as

$$g = \sum_{m=1,3}^{\infty} E_m \cos \alpha_m x \tag{a}$$

where g is the dead load expressed in terms of Fourier series and E_m is the Fourier coefficient, which is determined from

$$E_m = \frac{2}{L} \int_{-L/2}^{+L/2} g \cos \alpha_m x \, dx \tag{b}$$

For the case of dead load g per unit area, E_m can be determined as

$$E_m = (-1)^{(m-1)/2} \frac{4g}{m\pi} \tag{c}$$

Table 4.2 Shell forces and displacements from complementary function (even)

$$F = MF \sum_{m=1,3}^{\infty} [\{(A_1\alpha_1 - A_2\alpha_2)\cos b\theta - (A_1\alpha_2 + A_2\alpha_1)\sin b\theta\} \times \exp(a\theta) + \{(A_3\alpha_3 - A_4\alpha_4)\cos b_1\theta - (A_3\alpha_4 + A_4\alpha_3)\sin b_1\theta\}$$
$$\times \exp(a_1\theta) + \{(A_5\alpha_1 - A_6\alpha_2)\cos b\theta + (A_5\alpha_2 + A_6\alpha_1)\sin b\theta\} \times \exp(-a\theta) + \{(A_7\alpha_3 - A_8\alpha_4)\cos b_1\theta + (A_7\alpha_4 + A_8\alpha_3)\sin b_1\theta\}$$
$$\times \exp(-a_1\theta)]$$

F	MF	α_1	α_2	α_3	α_4
N_x	$\dfrac{2DR\alpha_m^4}{\varepsilon^3}\cos\alpha_m x$	-1	$(1+\varepsilon)$	1	$(1-\varepsilon)$
N_θ	$-\dfrac{2DR\alpha_m^4}{\varepsilon^2}\cos\alpha_m x$	0	1	0	-1
M_x	$-D\alpha_m^2\cos\alpha_m x$	$\left[1-\dfrac{\nu\lambda^2(1+\varepsilon)}{\alpha_m^2R^2}\right]$	$-\dfrac{\nu\lambda^2}{\alpha_m^2R^2}$	$\left\{1-\dfrac{\nu\lambda^2(\varepsilon-1)}{\alpha_m^2R^2}\right\}$	$-\dfrac{\nu\lambda^2}{\alpha_m^2R^2}$
M_θ	$\dfrac{D}{R^2}\cos\alpha_m x$	$\{\lambda^2(1+\varepsilon)-\nu\alpha_m^2R^2\}$	λ^2	$\{\lambda^2(\varepsilon-1)-\nu\alpha_m^2R^2\}$	λ^2
Q_x	$\dfrac{-D\alpha_m^3\sin\alpha_m x}{\varepsilon}$	1	1	-1	1
u	$\dfrac{h^2R\alpha_m^3}{6(1-\nu^2)\varepsilon^3}\sin\alpha_m x$	-1	$\{1+\varepsilon(1+\nu)\}$	1	$\{1-\varepsilon(1+\nu)\}$
w	$\cos\alpha_m x$	1	0	1	0

Table 4.3 Shell forces and displacements from complementary function (odd)

$$F = \sum_{m=1,3}^{\infty} MF[\{A_1\alpha_1 - A_2\alpha_2)\cos b\theta - (A_1\alpha_2 + A_2\alpha_1)\sin b\theta\}\exp(a\theta) + \{(A_3\alpha_3 - A_4\alpha_4)\cos b_1\theta - (A_3\alpha_4 + A_4\alpha_3)\sin b_1\theta\}\exp(a_1\theta)$$
$$-\{(A_5\alpha_1 - A_6\alpha_2)\cos b\theta + (A_5\alpha_2 + A_6\alpha_1)\sin b\theta\}\exp(-a\theta) - \{(A_7\alpha_3 - A_8\alpha_4)\cos b_1\theta + (A_7\alpha_4 + A_8\alpha_3)\sin b_1\theta\}\exp(-a_1\theta)]$$

F	MF	α_1	α_2	α_3	α_4
$N_{x\theta}$	$\frac{2DR\alpha_m^4}{(\sqrt{\varepsilon})^5}\sin\alpha_m x$	$-k$	j	k_1	$-j_1$
$M_{x\theta}$	$\frac{-D(1-\nu)}{R}\alpha_m\sin\alpha_m x$	a	b	a_1	b_1
Q_θ	$\frac{D\alpha_m^3}{(\sqrt{\varepsilon})^3}\cos\alpha_m x$	$(j-k)$	$(j+k)$	$-(j_1+k_1)$	(j_1-k_1)
Q_θ	$\frac{D\alpha_m^3}{(\sqrt{\varepsilon})^3}\cos\alpha_m x$	$j\{1-\varepsilon(1-\nu)\}-k$	$j+k\{1-\varepsilon(1-\nu)\}$	$-k_1-j_1\{1+\varepsilon(1-\nu)\}$	$j_1-k_1\{1+\varepsilon(1-\nu)\}$
v	$-\frac{h^2R\alpha_m^3}{6(1-\nu^2)(\sqrt{\varepsilon})^7}\cos\alpha_m x$	$j+k\{1-\varepsilon(1+\nu)\}$	$k-j\{1-\varepsilon(1+\nu)\}$	$-j_1+k_1\{1+\varepsilon(1+\nu)\}$	$-k_1-j_1\{1+\varepsilon(1+\nu)\}$
β*	$\cos\alpha_m x$	$-\frac{a}{R}+\frac{(MF\alpha_1)v}{R}$	$-\frac{b}{R}+\frac{(MF\cdot\alpha_2)v}{R}$	$-\frac{a_1}{R}+\frac{(MF\cdot\alpha_3)v}{R}$	$-\frac{b_1}{R}+\frac{(MF\cdot\alpha_4)v}{R}$

*The coefficient α_1 for β for example will be

$$\alpha_1 = -\frac{a}{R} + \frac{h^2\alpha_m^3}{6(1-\nu^2)(\sqrt{\varepsilon})^7}[j+k\{1-\varepsilon(1+\nu)\}], \quad \left[\beta = \left(-\frac{\partial w}{R\partial\phi} + \frac{v}{R}\right)\right]$$

Hence, $$g' = \sum_{m=1,3}^{\infty} (-1)^{(m-1)/2} \frac{4g}{m\pi} \cos \alpha_m x \tag{d}$$

Next, the components of the dead load in the longitudinal (x), tangential (y) and radial (z) directions has to be determined. These components can be determined as (Fig. 4.6a)

$$X = 0,\ Y = g' \sin\theta,\ Z = g' \cos\theta \tag{e}$$

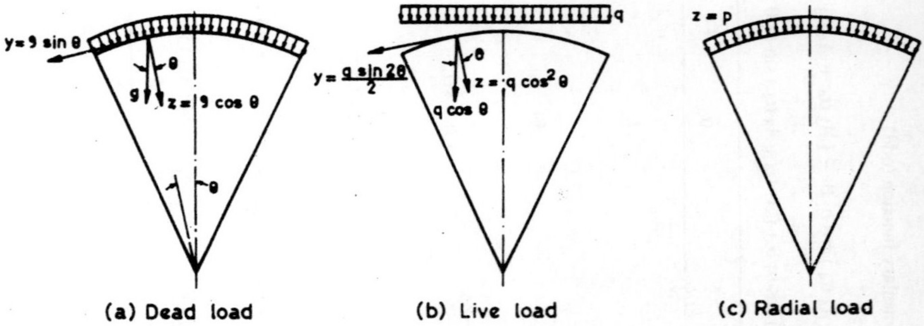

Fig. 4.6 Different types of loads and their components

Substituting for g' from Eq. (d), the load components can be obtained as

$$X = 0, Y = \sum_{m=1,3}^{\infty} (-1)^{(m-1)/2} \frac{4g}{m\pi} \cos \alpha_m x \sin\theta$$

$$Z = \sum_{m=1,3}^{\infty} (-1)^{(m-1)/2} \frac{4g}{m\pi} \cos \alpha_m x \cos\theta \tag{f}$$

Similarly, the components for the other two types of load can be determined and these are given in Table 4.4

Table 4.4 Components of the external load

Component of load	Type of load Dead load (Fig. 4.6a)	Live load (Fig. 4.6b)	Radial load (Fig. 4.6c)
X	0	0	0
Y	$(-1)^{(m-1)/2} \frac{4g}{m\pi}$ $\times \cos \alpha_m x \sin\theta$ $(m = 1, 3, 5, \ldots)$	$(-1)^{(m-1)/2} \frac{2q}{m\pi}$ $\times \cos \alpha_m x \sin 2\theta$ $(m = 1, 3, 5, \ldots)$	0
Z	$(-1)^{(m-1)/2} \frac{4g}{m\pi}$ $\times \cos \alpha_m x \cos\theta$ $(m = 1, 3, 5, \ldots)$	$(-1)^{(m-1)/2} \frac{4q}{m\pi}$ $\times \cos \alpha_m x \cos^2\theta$ $(m = 1, 3, 5, \ldots)$	$(-1)^{(m-1)/2} \frac{4p}{m\pi}$ $\times \cos \alpha_m x$ $(m = 1, 3, 5, \ldots)$

Now the particular integral of Eq. (4.12) can be taken as

$$w_1 = \sum_{m=1,3}^{\infty} CE_m \cos \alpha_m x \cos \theta$$

where C is a constant to be determined, such that the complete differential equation is satisfied.

By substituting the above expression as well as the components of the load (dead load) in Eq. (4.12), we can determine C as

$$C = -\frac{R^4}{D}\left[\frac{(\alpha_m R)^4 + (4+\nu)\,\alpha_m^2 R^2 + 2}{(\alpha_m^2 R^2 + 1)^4 + R^6(1-\nu^2)\,\alpha_m^4\left(\dfrac{12}{h^2}\right)}\right],$$

Hence the particular integral for the case of dead load can now be written as

$$w_1 = -\sum_{m=1,3}^{\infty} \frac{R^4}{D}\left[\frac{(\alpha_m R)^4 + (4+\nu)\,\alpha_m^2 R^2 + 2}{(\alpha_m^2 R^2 + 1)^4 + R^6(1-\nu^2)\,\alpha_m^4\left(\dfrac{12}{h^2}\right)}\right]$$

$$\times (-1)^{(m-1)/2}\,\frac{4g}{m\pi}\cos \alpha_m x \cos \theta \tag{4.19}$$

The particular integral for the forces and displacements can now be determined using Eq. (4.13a–h). In Table 4.5, the particular integral for the forces and displacements for three types of load is given.

Table 4.5 Particular integral

Force or displacement	Type of load		
	Dead load	Live load	Radial load
N_x	$-\dfrac{1}{\alpha_m^2 R}(H_3 + 2)\,g_1$	$-\dfrac{1}{\alpha_m^2 R}(4H_3' + 3)\,q_1$	0
N_θ	$-R(H_3 + 1)\,g_1$	$-R\left[H_3' + \dfrac{1}{2}\left(1 + \dfrac{1}{\cos 2\theta}\right)\right]q_1$	$-R(D\alpha_m^4 C_2 + 1)\,p_1$
$N_{x\theta}$	$-\dfrac{1}{\alpha_m}(H_3 + 2)\,g_2$	$-\left(2H_3' + \dfrac{3}{2}\right)q_2$	0
M_x	$-D\left(\alpha_m^2 + \dfrac{\nu}{R^2}\right)Cg_1$	$-D\left(\alpha_m^2 + \dfrac{4\nu}{R^2}\right)C_1 q_1$	$-D\alpha_m^2 C_2 p_1$
M_θ	$-D\left(\nu\alpha_m^2 + \dfrac{1}{R^2}\right)Cg_1$	$-D\left(\dfrac{4}{R^2} + \nu\alpha_m^2\right)C_1 q_1$	$-D\nu\alpha_m^2 C_2 p_1$

Table 4.5 (*Contd.*)

Force or displacement	Type of load		
	Dead load	Live load	Radial load
$M_{x\theta}$	$D(1-\nu)\left(\frac{\alpha_m}{R}\right)Cg_2$	$D(1-\nu)\left(\frac{2\alpha_m}{R}\right)C_1q_1$	0
Q_x	$D\left(\alpha_m^3+\frac{\alpha_m^2}{R}\right)Cg_3$	$D\left(\alpha_m^3+\frac{4\alpha_m}{R^2}\right)C_1q_3$	$D\alpha_m^3C_2p_2$
Q_θ	$D\left(\frac{\alpha_m^2}{R}+\frac{1}{R^3}\right)Cg_4$	$D\left(\frac{2\alpha_m^2}{R}+\frac{8}{R^3}\right)C_1q_4$	0
u	$\frac{1}{Eh\alpha_m}\left[-\frac{1}{\alpha_m^2R}(H_3+2)+\nu R(H_3+1)\right]g_3$	$\frac{1}{Eh\alpha_m}\left[-\frac{1}{\alpha_m^2R}(4H_3'+3)+\nu R\left\{H_3'+\frac{1}{2}\times\left(1+\frac{1}{\cos 2\theta}\right)\right\}\right]q_3$	$\frac{\nu R}{Eh}(D\alpha_m^4C_2+1)p_2$
v	$\frac{1}{Eh\alpha_m^2}\left[\nu(H_3+3)+(H_3+2)\left(2+\frac{1}{\alpha_m^2R^2}\right)\right]g_4$	$-\frac{2}{Eh\alpha_m}\left[-(4H_3'+3)\times\left\{\frac{1+\nu}{2}+\frac{1}{\alpha_m^3R}\right\}+\frac{\nu}{2\alpha_m}(2H_3'+1)+\frac{\nu}{2\alpha_m\cos 2\theta}\right]q_4$	0
w	Cg_1	C_1q_1	C_2p_1
β	$\frac{1}{R}(C+v^*)g_4$	$\frac{1}{R}(2C_1+v^*)q_4$	0

where

$$g_1=(-1)^{(m-1)/2}\frac{4g}{m\pi}\cos\alpha_mx\cos\theta,\quad g_2=(-1)^{(m-1)/2}\frac{4g}{m\pi}\sin\alpha_mx\sin\theta,$$

$$g_3=(-1)^{(m-1)/2}\frac{4g}{m\pi}\sin\alpha_mx\cos\theta,\quad g_4=(-1)^{(m-1)/2}\frac{4g}{m\pi}\cos\alpha_mx\sin\theta,$$

$$H_3=\frac{CD}{R^4}(\alpha_m^2R^2+1)^2$$

$$C=-\frac{R^4}{D}\left[\frac{(\alpha_mR)^4+(4+\nu)\alpha_m^2R^2+2}{(1+\alpha_m^2R^2)^4+R^6(1-\nu^2)\left(\frac{12\alpha_m^4}{h^2}\right)}\right],$$

$$q_1=(-1)^{(m-1)/2}\frac{4q}{m\pi}\cos\alpha_mx\cos 2\theta,\quad q_2=(-1)^{(m-1)/2}\frac{4q}{m\pi}\sin\alpha_mx\sin 2\theta,$$

$$q_3=(-1)^{(m-1)/2}\frac{4q}{m\pi}\sin\alpha_mx\cos 2\theta,\quad q_4=(-1)^{(m-1)/2}\frac{4q}{m\pi}\cos\alpha_mx\sin 2\theta,$$

$$H_3'=\frac{DC_1}{R^4}(\alpha_m^2R^2+4)^2$$

$$C_1 = -\frac{R^4}{D}\left[\frac{(\alpha_m^2 R^2+4)^2 + (2+\nu)\,\alpha_m^2 R^2 + 4}{(\alpha_m^2 R^2+4)^4 + R^6(1-\nu^2)\left(\dfrac{12\,\alpha_m^4}{h^2}\right)}\right],$$

$$p_1 = (-1)^{(m-1)/2}\frac{4p}{m\pi}\cos\alpha_m x, \quad p_2 = (-1)^{(m-1)/2}\frac{4p}{m\pi}\sin\alpha_m x,$$

$$C_2 = -\frac{1}{D\left[\alpha_m^4 + \dfrac{12(1-\nu^2)}{h^2 R^2}\right]}$$

v^* = particular integral of v without 'g' or 'q' term.

The complete solution of the differential equation (4.12) can now be obtained by adding the particular integral for w given in Table 4.5 (depending on the type of load) to the complementary function given in Eq. (4.15). The expression for forces and displacements may also be written down making use of Tables 4.2 or 4.3 and 4.5.

4.4.1.3 Boundary conditions

(a) Single cylindrical shell

The boundary conditions along the longitudinal edges ($\theta = \pm\,\theta_0$) of the shell depend on the method of supporting these edges. In general four conditions, either in terms of forces or displacements or a combination of forces and displacements, are to be specified at each edge. This will result in totally eight conditions for the two edges and the eight constants in Eq. (4.15) are determined using these eight conditions. On the other hand, if the shell is symmetrically loaded and has the same boundary conditions (same type of support) along the two edges, then in effect, only four conditions are specified. In such a case Eq. (4.17) is used and the four constants are determined from the four boundary conditions. We will describe below the boundary conditions for an edge depending upon the type of support provided along this edge.

(i) Edge free: Since the edge is free, all the forces and moments along the edge will be zero. For this case, the boundary condition may be specified as

$$\theta = \theta_0\,,\ M_\theta = Q'_\theta = N_\theta = N_{x\theta} = 0$$

where Q'_θ may be referred as the resultant shear and obtained in a similar way as is done in the theory of thin plates[4.6] (Kirchhoff 's condition) and is given by

$$Q'_\theta = \left(Q_\theta + \frac{\partial M_{x\theta}}{\partial x}\right)$$

(ii) Edge supported on unyielding wall: It is assumed that the wall restricts vertical and horizontal displacements of the shell edge but allows rotation. The vertical and horizontal displacements are determined by resolving v and w as

$$\Delta w = w\cos\theta_0 - v\sin\theta_0$$

$$\Delta H = w\sin\theta_0 + v\cos\theta_0$$

Hence the boundary condition in this case can be specified as

$$\theta = \theta_0 \,,\ \Delta w = \Delta H = M_\theta = N_{x\theta} = 0$$

(iii) Edge simply supported: It is assumed here that the edge is supported in such a way that the support takes large in-plane forces but cannot resist any force normal to its plane. The boundary condition for this case may be specified as

$$\theta = \theta_0 \,,\ N_\theta = \varepsilon_x = M_\theta = w = 0$$

(iv) Edge clamped: In this case, there will be complete restriction for the displacements and rotation, and hence the boundary condition can be specified as

$$\theta = \theta_0 \,,\ u = v = w = \frac{\partial w}{\partial \theta} = 0$$

(v) Edge supported on beam: In this case the edge of the shell is monolithically connected to the beam, such that the forces acting on the edge ($\theta = \theta_0$) of the shell namely N_θ, $N_{x\theta}$, M_θ, Q_θ and $M_{x\theta}$ gets transmitted onto the edge-beam. The direction of these forces and moments acting on the edge-beam will be opposite to that of the direction of forces on the edge of the shell (Fig. 4.7). These forces and moments will cause the edge-beam to displace longitudinally, laterally and vertically as well as twist. If u_b, v_b, w_b and β_b are the longitudinal, horizontal, vertical displacements and twist of the edge-beam respectively, then the boundary condition at the junction of shell edge and edge-beam can be specified as

$$\theta = \theta_0 \,,\ u_s = u_b \,,\ \Delta H_s = v_b \,,\ \Delta w_s = w_b \,,\ \beta_s = \beta_b$$

where subscript s stands for shell and b for beam. The horizontal and vertical displacement of the shell edge, viz. ΔH_s and Δw_s can be determined by using the same expression given in Sec. (ii) above. We will describe later the procedure for determining the edge-beam displacements, viz. u_b, v_b, w_b and β_b.

If the beam is torsionally stiff and cannot resist lateral thrust, then the above boundary conditions can be simplified as

$$\theta = \theta_0 \,,\ u_s = u_b \,,\ R_H = N_\theta \cos\theta_0 - Q'_\theta \sin\theta_0 = 0$$

$$\beta_s = 0 \,,\ \Delta w_s = w_b$$

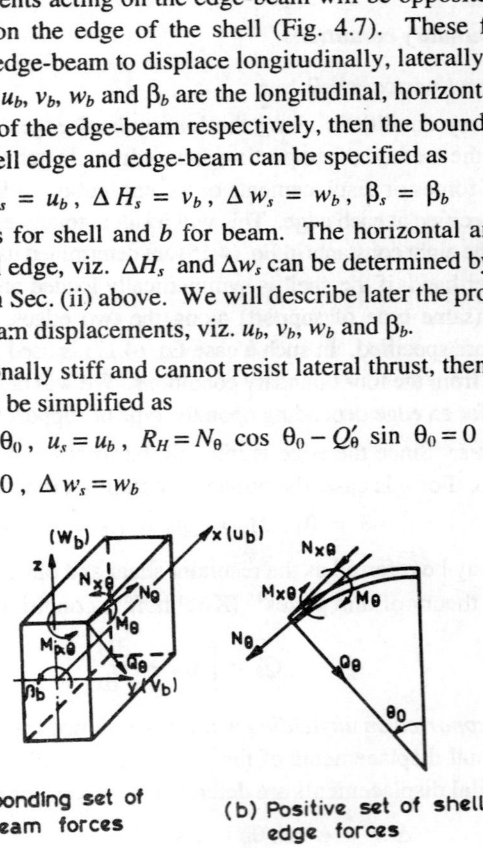

(a) Corresponding set of edge-beam forces

(b) Positive set of shell edge forces

Fig. 4.7 Shell edge-beam forces

(b) Multiple-cylindrical shell

(i) Multiple-cylindrical shell without edge-beam: We will for simplicity, consider here the case of a multishell having two cylindrical shells (Fig. 4.8). We will write down the boundary condition for edges *A*, *C* as well as for the common junction *B*. Let us assume that the edges *A* and *C* are free.

The boundary condition at the edge *A* can be written as

$$\theta = -\ \theta_1\,,\ N_\theta = N_{x\theta} = M_\theta = Q'_\theta = 0$$

where

$$Q'_\theta = \left(Q_\theta + \frac{\partial M_{x\theta}}{\partial x} \right)$$

At the junction *B*, we have to satisfy the condition of continuity for displacements and forces. Hence, the boundary condition can be written as

Shell 1	Shell 2		Shell 1	Shell 2
At $\theta = \theta_1$	At $\theta = -\theta_2$		At $\theta = \theta_1$	At $\theta = -\theta_2$
u_1	$= u_2$		$(N_\theta)_1$	$= (N_\theta)_2$
v_1	$= v_2$		$(N_{x\theta})_1$	$= (N_{x\theta})_2$
		and	$(M_\theta)_1$	$= (M_\theta)_2$
w_1	$= w_2$			
β_1	$= \beta_2$		$(Q'_\theta)_1$	$= (Q'_\theta)_2$

Finally, for the edge *C*, the boundary condition can be written as

$$\theta = \theta_2\,,\ N_\theta = N_{x\theta} = M_\theta = Q'_\theta = 0$$

Now if we write the solution for shell 1 and shell 2, since both the shells have asymmetrical boundary conditions, the solution for each of these shells would involve eight constants. By combining the solution for shell 1 and shell 2, we would have 16 constants and these are determined using the 16 boundary condi-

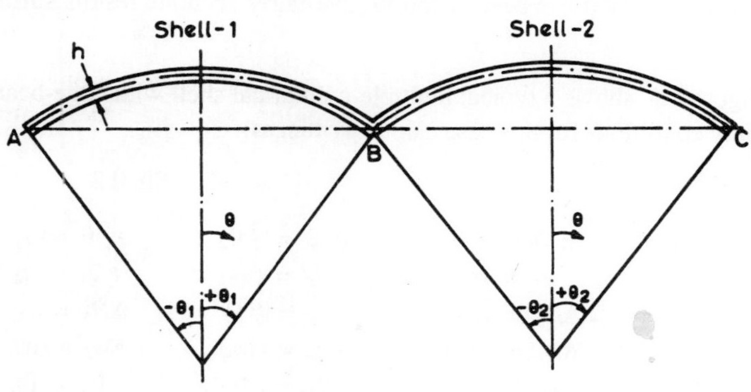

Fig. 4.8 A typical multishell unit

tions mentioned above. Hence, if a multicylindrical shell has n bays, in general $8n$ simultaneous equations are to be solved to determine the constants. On the other hand, if the multiple-cylindrical shell is symmetrical about the central line, we need to solve only $4n$ simultaneous equations. Even this would be an arduous task for a designer, if the multiple-cylindrical shell has a large number of bays. Alternatively, it is possible to do an approximate analysis by considering the exterior shell and one interior shell and then using modified boundary conditions. For the exterior shell, the boundary conditions along the exterior supported edge (for example A or C in the case discussed above) is specified by considering the shell as a single cylindrical shell. For the purpose of analysis, it will be assumed that the boundary conditions are symmetrical and hence we need to solve only four simultaneous equations. For the inner shell, we can write the following modified boundary conditions:

$$\theta = \pm\theta_0 \,,\; \Delta H = \Delta F = \frac{\partial N_{x\theta}}{\partial\theta} = \beta_s = 0$$

where ΔH is the horizontal displacement and ΔF is the vertical force and these can be determined from

$$\Delta H = v\cos\theta_0 + w\sin\theta_0$$

$$\Delta F = Q'_\theta\cos\theta_0 + N_\theta\sin\theta_0$$

Since the inner shell also has symmetric boundary conditions, we need to solve four simultaneous equations in this case also. Later on the forces can be computed independently for exterior shell and interior shell. Now for the exterior shell, the forces determined by using the boundary condition for the exterior shell are used for the left-half and the forces determined by using the boundary conditions for the inner shell are used for the right-half or vice versa. Hence by resorting to the approximate method, one needs to solve two sets of four simultaneous equations, irrespective of the number of bays in a multiple-cylindrical shell. This approximate method has been found to give fairly accurate results sufficient for the design.

Figure 4.9 shows a typical multiple-cylindrical shell with edge-beams. The boundary conditions for this case can be written as:

Shell 1		Shell 2	
at $\theta = -\theta_1$	at $\theta = +\theta_1$	at $\theta = -\theta_2$	at $\theta = +\theta_2$
$u_s = u_b$	$u_s = (u_b)^j$	$u_s = (u_b)^j$	$u_s = u_b$
$\Delta H_s = v_b$	$\Delta H_s = (v_b)^j$	$\Delta H_s = (v_b)^j$,	$\Delta H_s = v_b$
$\Delta w_s = w_b$	$\Delta w_s = (w_b)^j$	$\Delta w_s = (w_b)^j$	$\Delta w_s = w_b$
$\beta_s = \beta_b$	$\beta_s = (\beta_b)^j$	$\beta_s = (\beta_b)^j$	$\beta_s = \beta_b$

where subscript s and b stand for shell and beam and superscript j for junction.

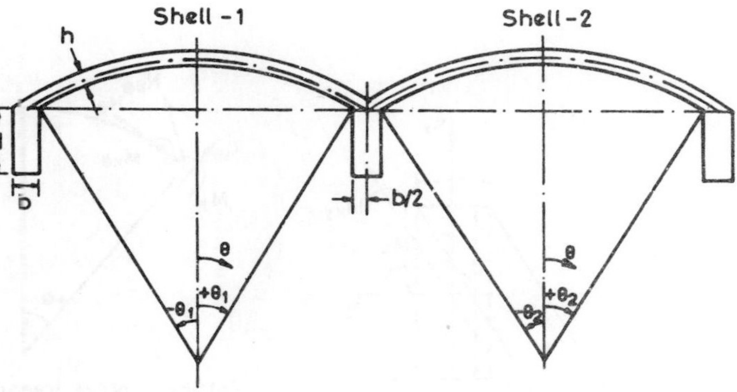

Fig. 4.9 Multiple cylindrical shell with edge-beam

In all there will be 16 constants (combining the constants of shell 1 and shell 2) and 16 conditions are specified above, using which all the constants can be determined. In order to reduce the computational effort, while analysing a multi-cylindrical shell with large number of bays, one can resort to the approximate method described earlier for a multicylindrical shell without edge-beam. The modified boundary condition for an inner shell with edge-beam can be written as

$$\theta = \pm\theta_0\,;\ \Delta H = \beta_s = 0$$

$$\Delta w_s = w_b$$

$$u_s = u_b$$

While calculating the displacements of the edge-beam, viz. w_b and u_b, only half the width of the beam is to be considered.

4.4.1.4 Edge-beam theory

It is assumed that when the shell forces get transmitted onto the edge-beam, they will cause an axial force, longitudinal and transverse bending as well as twist in the beam. The dimensions of the edge-beam normally used in practice are such that the beam can be considered as shallow. Figure 4.10a shows the internal forces acting on an element of the beam while Fig. 4.10b indicates the shell forces which get transmitted onto the beam as well as their direction when acting on the edge-beam. Figure 4.10c shows the displacements caused in the beam at the centre as well as at one corner *A* of the edge-beam due to these forces. We will now develop the edge-beam equations following Gibson[4.2].

First, we will write the equilibrium equations for the element acted upon by shell forces as shown in Fig. 4.10b. The weight of the beam per unit length can be taken as *g*. Now by summing up all the internal and external forces in the *x*-, *y*- and *z*-directions and equating them to zero, we get the following three equilibrium equations.

$$\frac{\partial T}{\partial x} - N_{x\theta} = 0 \tag{4.20a}$$

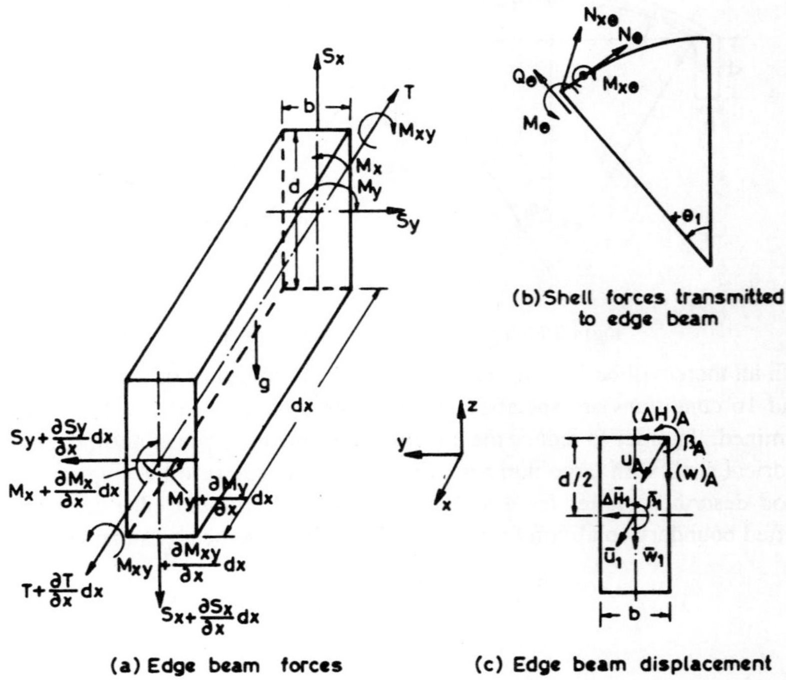

Fig. 4.10 Edge-beam forces and displacements

$$\frac{\partial S_x}{\partial x} - (Q_\theta \cos\theta_0 + N_\theta \sin\theta_0) + g = 0 \tag{4.20b}$$

$$\frac{\partial S_y}{\partial x} + (Q_\theta \sin\theta_0 - N_\theta \cos\theta_0) = 0 \tag{4.20c}$$

Similarly, summing up all the moments about x-, y- and z-directions and equating them to zero, we get the following three moment equilibrium equations.

$$\frac{\partial M_x}{\partial x} + N_{x\theta}\left(\frac{d}{2}\right) - M_{x\theta}\cos\theta_0 - S_x = 0 \tag{4.21a}$$

$$\frac{\partial M_y}{\partial x} - M_{x\theta}\sin\theta_0 - N_{x\theta}\left(\frac{b}{2}\right) + S_y = 0 \tag{4.21b}$$

$$\frac{\partial M_{xy}}{\partial x} + M_\theta + (Q_\theta\cos\theta_0 + N_\theta\sin\theta_0)\frac{b}{2}$$

$$+ (Q_\theta\sin\theta_0 - N_\theta\cos\theta_0)\frac{d}{2} = 0 \tag{4.21c}$$

Next we can write the force-displacement relation for the edge-beam following elementary strength of materials[4.7]:

$$T = AE \frac{\partial \bar{u}}{\partial x} \tag{4.22a}$$

$$M_x = EI_y \frac{\partial^2 \bar{w}}{\partial x^2} \tag{4.22b}$$

$$M_y = EI_z \frac{\partial^2 \bar{v}}{\partial x^2} \tag{4.22c}$$

$$\frac{\partial M_{xy}}{\partial x} = C \frac{\partial^2 \bar{\beta}}{\partial x^2} \tag{4.22d}$$

where,

A = cross-sectional area of the beam = $b \times$ d
I_y = moment of inertia about y-axis = $bd^3/12$
I_z = moment of inertia about z-axis = $db^3/12$
C = torsional rigidity = $G\alpha b^3 d$
G = shear modulus = $E/2\,(1 + \nu)$

and in general (for rectangular section),

$$\alpha = \left[\frac{1}{3} - 0.21 \frac{b}{d}\left(1 - \frac{b^4}{12\, d^4}\right)\right]$$

and for $\left(\frac{d}{b}\right) \geq 10,\ \alpha \approx \frac{1}{3}$

A simple kinematic relationship can be written relating the centroid displacements to the displacements at one corner of the edge-beam.

$$u_A = \bar{u} - \frac{d}{2}\frac{\partial \bar{w}}{\partial x} + \frac{b}{2}\frac{\partial \bar{v}}{\partial x} \tag{4.23a}$$

$$v_A = \bar{v} + \frac{d}{2}\bar{\beta} \tag{4.23b}$$

$$w_A = \bar{w} + \frac{b}{2}\bar{\beta} \tag{4.23c}$$

$$\beta_A = \bar{\beta} \tag{4.23d}$$

From the equilibrium Eqs. (4.20) and (4.21), we can obtain the following expressions for the edge-beam forces

$$M_x = \iint \left[Q'_\theta \cos\theta_0 + N_\theta \sin\theta_0 - \frac{\partial N_{x\theta}}{\partial x}\left(\frac{d}{2}\right) - g \right] dx\, dx \tag{4.24a}$$

$$M_y = \iint \left[Q'_\theta \sin\theta_0 - N_\theta \cos\theta_0 + \frac{\partial N_{x\theta}}{\partial x}\left(\frac{b}{2}\right)\right] dx\, dx \tag{4.24b}$$

$$M_{xy} = -\int \left[M_\theta + (Q_\theta \cos\theta_0 + N_\theta \sin\theta_0) \frac{b}{2} + (Q_\theta \sin\theta_0 - N_\theta \cos\theta_0) \frac{d}{2} \right] dx \quad (4.24c)$$

$$T = \int N_{x\theta}\, dx \quad (4.24d)$$

Using Eqs. (4.22) and (4.23) we can get the following expressions for the displacements at one corner of the edge-beam:

$$u_A = \int \left(\frac{T}{AE} - \frac{d}{2}\frac{M_x}{EI_y} + \frac{b}{2}\frac{M_y}{EI_z} \right) dx \quad (4.25a)$$

$$v_A = \int\int \frac{M_y}{EI_z}\, dx\, dx + \frac{1}{C}\left(\frac{d}{2}\right) \int M_{xy}\, dx \quad (4.25b)$$

$$w_A = \int\int \frac{M_x}{EI_y}\, dx\, dx + \frac{1}{C}\left(\frac{b}{2}\right) \int M_{xy}\, dx \quad (4.25c)$$

$$\beta_A = \frac{1}{C} \int M_{xy}\, dx \quad (4.25d)$$

On the other hand if the edge-beam is torsionally stiff and is incapable of taking lateral load, then the above edge-beam equations can be reduced to the following form:

$$M_x = \int\int \left[Q'_\theta \cos\theta_0 + N_\theta \sin\theta_0 - \left(\frac{d}{2}\right)\frac{\partial N_{x\theta}}{\partial x} - g \right] dx\, dx \quad (4.26a)$$

$$T = \int N_{x\theta}\, dx \quad (4.26b)$$

$$w_b = \int\int \frac{M_x}{EI_y}\, dx\, dx \quad (4.26c)$$

$$u_b = \int \left(\frac{T}{AE} - \frac{d}{2}\frac{M_x}{EI_y} \right) dx \quad (4.26d)$$

$$S_x = \int \{ (Q_\theta \cos\theta_0 + N_\theta \sin\theta_0) - g \}\, dx \quad (4.26e)$$

(In the above equation, w_b and u_b are the vertical and longitudinal displacements of the edge-beam at the top corner (Fig. 4.10c). The subscript b will be used hereafter to mean that the displacements refer to the edge-beam).

For convenience, the expressions for the edge-beam forces and displacements can be written in terms of shell forces. Since the solution for the shell problem has been obtained in terms of trigonometric series, it will be appropriate to express the dead weight of the beam also by trigonometric series. Hence the dead load can now be represented as

$$g = \sum_{m=1,3}^{\infty} (-1)^{(m-1)/2} \frac{4g}{m\pi} \cos \alpha_m x \text{ or}$$

$$g = \sum_{m=1,3}^{\infty} g' \cos \alpha_m x$$

where $g' = (-1)^{(m-1)/2} \dfrac{4g}{m\pi}$

Since the variation of the shell forces in the longitudinal direction (x-direction) is known, Eq. (4.26) can be integrated to obtain the edge-beam forces and displacements as

$$M_x = -\sum_{m=1,3}^{\infty} \frac{1}{\alpha_m^2} [\, Q'_\theta \cos \theta_0 + N_\theta \sin \theta_0 - \frac{\alpha_m d}{2} N_{x\theta} - g' \,] \cos \alpha_m x \tag{4.27a}$$

$$T = -\sum_{m=1,3}^{\infty} \frac{1}{\alpha_m} (N_{x\theta}) \cos \alpha_m x \tag{4.27b}$$

$$w_b = \frac{1}{EI_y} \sum_{m=1,3}^{\infty} \frac{1}{\alpha_m^4} [\, Q'_\theta \cos \theta_0 + N_\theta \sin \theta_0 - \frac{\alpha_m d}{2} N_{x\theta} - g' \,] \cos \alpha_m x \tag{4.27c}$$

$$u_b = -\sum_{m=1,3}^{\infty} \frac{1}{E\alpha_m^2} \left[\frac{N_{x\theta}}{bd} - \left\{ \frac{6}{\alpha_m bd^2} \left(Q'_\theta \cos \theta_0 + N_\theta \sin \theta_0 - \frac{\alpha_m d}{2} N_{x\theta} - g' \right) \right\} \right] \sin \alpha_m x \tag{4.27d}$$

$$S_x = \sum_{m=1,3}^{\infty} \frac{1}{\alpha_m} [\, Q'_\theta \cos \theta_0 + N_\theta \sin \theta_0 - g' \,] \sin \alpha_m x \tag{4.27e}$$

In the above, expressions for the shell forces Q'_θ, N_θ and $N_{x\theta}$ should be taken from Table 4.2 and 4.3 without the trigonometric series term.

If a prestressed edge-beam is used, then the edge-beam equations may be suitably modified as

$$w_b = -\frac{1}{EI_y} \sum_{m=1,3}^{\infty} \frac{1}{\alpha_m^2} (M_x - P_1 e) \cos \alpha_m x \tag{4.28a}$$

$$u_b = \sum_{m=1,3}^{\infty} \frac{1}{\alpha_m} \left[\frac{(T-P_1)}{AE} - \frac{d}{2} \left\{ \frac{M_x - P_1 e}{EI_y} \right\} \right] \sin \alpha_m x \tag{4.28b}$$

where P_1 is the prestressing force expressed in terms of trigonometric series and will be equal to $(-1)^{(m-1)/2}\,(4P/m\pi)$, P being the actual prestressing force, and e is the eccentricity of the prestressing force.

The final bending moment M_x' will be now equal to $(M_x - P_1 e)$ and the final axial force will be T' and equal to $(T - P_1)$ and M_x and T are same as given in Eq. (4.27).

4.4.2 Numerical Examples

Example 4.1

We will determine the forces in a simply supported cylindrical shell with the longitudinal edges free and having the following dimensions:

Length of the shell (L)	= 36 m
Radius of the shell (R)	= 9 m
Thickness of the shell (h)	= 0.075 m
Semicentral angle (θ_0)	= 40°

We will assume that the shell will be subjected to a live load of 70 kg/m² in addition to its own weight. We will assume the Poisson's ratio to be zero and consider only the first term in Fourier series for computing the forces.

(i) Loads

Dead load – 0.075 × 2400	= 180 kg/m²
Live load	= 70 kg/m²
Total load	= 250 kg/m²

It must be noted that though the dead load and live load would have different components in the *y*- and *z*-direction, for convenience, we can combine them and consider the total load as if it is a dead load. Though this procedure is not strictly correct, it simplifies the analysis and gives the magnitude of forces which are higher compared to the analysis made by considering the dead and live load components separately, as in Table 4.4. We will show this in the next example. Hence the load components are

$$Y = \frac{4}{\pi} \times 250 \times \cos \frac{\pi x}{L} \sin\theta = 318.31 \cos \frac{\pi x}{L} \sin\theta$$

$$Z = \frac{4}{\pi} \times 250 \times \cos \frac{\pi x}{L} \cos\theta = 318.31 \cos \frac{\pi x}{L} \cos\theta$$

(ii) Shell parameters

$$\lambda = \sqrt[8]{3}\ \sqrt{\frac{R\pi}{L}}\ \sqrt[4]{\frac{R}{h}} = 3.365$$

$$\varepsilon = \frac{1}{\sqrt[4]{3}}\ \sqrt{\frac{h}{R}}\left(\frac{R\pi}{L}\right) = 0.054477$$

(iii) Roots of the equation

$$j = \sqrt{\frac{\sqrt{1+(1+\varepsilon)^2}+(1+\varepsilon)}{2}} = 1.119759$$

$$k = \sqrt{\frac{\sqrt{1+(1+\varepsilon)^2}-(1+\varepsilon)}{2}} = 0.44652$$

$$j_1 = \sqrt{\frac{\sqrt{1+(1-\varepsilon)^2}-(1-\varepsilon)}{2}} = 0.46406$$

$$k_1 = \sqrt{\frac{\sqrt{1+(1-\varepsilon)^2}+(1-\varepsilon)}{2}} = 1.07744$$

$$a = \lambda j = 3.767989, \quad b = \lambda k = 1.502473$$

$$a_1 = \lambda j_1 = 1.561562, \quad b_1 = \lambda k_1 = 3.625586$$

(iv) Shell edge conditions and determination of constants: The boundary conditions to be specified for a shell with the longitudinal edges free has already been discussed earlier and these are

$$\theta = \theta_0 = 40^\circ, \ N_\theta = N_{x\theta} = M_\theta = Q'_\theta = 0$$

The expressions for the above forces can be written down by taking the complementary function part from the Tables 4.2 and 4.3 and the particular integral from Table 4.5. Using the above four conditions, the following four equations can be written down:

$$\begin{aligned}&-\frac{2DR(\pi/L)^4}{\varepsilon^2}\cos\frac{\pi x}{L}\\ &\times[-A_2\cosh a\theta_0\cos b\theta_0 - A_1\sinh a\theta_0\sin b\theta_0\\ &+A_4\cosh a_1\theta_0\cos b_1\theta_0 + A_3\sinh a_1\theta_0\sin b_1\theta_0]\\ &-R(H_3+1)g_1 = 0\end{aligned} \qquad \text{(a)}$$

$$\begin{aligned}&-\frac{2DR(\pi/L)^4}{(\sqrt{\varepsilon})^5}\sin\frac{\pi x}{L}\,[(-k\sinh a\theta_0\cosh b\theta_0\\ &-j\cosh a\theta_0\sin b\theta_0)A_1 + (-j\sinh a\theta_0\cos b\theta_0\\ &+k\cosh a\theta_0\sin b\theta_0)A_2 + (k_1\sinh a_1\theta_0\cos b_1\theta_0\\ &+j_1\cosh a_1\theta_0\sin b_1\theta_0)A_3 + (j_1\sinh a_1\theta_0\cos b_1\theta_0\\ &-k_1\cosh a_1\theta_0\sin b_1\theta_0)A_4] - \left(\frac{L}{\pi}\right)(H_3+2)g_2 = 0\end{aligned} \qquad \text{(b)}$$

$$\frac{D}{R^2} \cos \frac{\pi x}{L} \Big[A_1 \{ \lambda^2 (1+\varepsilon) \cosh a\theta_0 \cos b\theta_0$$

$$- \lambda^2 \sinh a\theta_0 \sin b\theta_0 \} + A_2 \{ -\lambda^2 \cosh a\theta_0 \cos b\theta_0$$

$$- \lambda^2 (1+\varepsilon) \sinh a\theta_0 \sin b\theta_0 \}$$

$$+ A_3 \{ \lambda^2 (\varepsilon - 1) \cosh a_1\theta_0 \cos b_1\theta_0 - \lambda^2 \sinh a_1\theta_0 \sin b_1\theta_0 \}$$

$$+ A_4 \{ -\lambda^2 \cosh a_1\theta_0 \cos b_1\theta_0$$

$$- \lambda^2 (\varepsilon - 1) \sinh a_1 \theta_0 \sin b_1\theta_0 \} \Big] - \frac{D}{R^2} C g_1 = 0 \qquad \text{(c)}$$

$$\frac{D (\pi/L)^3}{(\sqrt{\varepsilon})^3} \cos \frac{\pi x}{L} [\{ (j\overline{1-\varepsilon} - k) \sinh a\theta_0 \cos b\theta_0$$

$$- (j + k\overline{1-\varepsilon}) \cosh a\theta_0 \sin b\theta_0 \} A_1$$

$$+ \{ (j + k\overline{1-\varepsilon}) \sinh a\theta_0 \cos b\theta_0$$

$$- (j\overline{1-\varepsilon} - k) \cosh a\theta_0 \sin b\theta_0 \} A_2$$

$$+ \{ (-k_1 - j_1 \overline{1+\varepsilon}) \sinh a_1\theta_0 \cos b_1\theta_0$$

$$- (j_1 - k_1\overline{1+\varepsilon}) \cosh a_1\theta_0 \sin b_1\theta_0 \} A_3$$

$$+ \{ -(j_1 - k_1\overline{1+\varepsilon}) \sinh a_1\theta_0 \cos b_1\theta_0$$

$$- (-k_1 - j_1 \overline{1+\varepsilon}) \cosh a_1\theta_0 \sin b_1\theta_0 \} A_4]$$

$$+ D \left\{ \frac{2 (\pi/L)^2}{R} + \frac{1}{R^3} \right\} C g_4 = 0 \qquad \text{(d)}$$

where

$$g_1 = \frac{4}{\pi} g \cos \frac{\pi x}{L} \cos \theta$$

$$g_2 = \frac{4}{\pi} g \sin \frac{\pi x}{L} \sin \theta$$

$$g_4 = \frac{4}{\pi} g \cos \frac{\pi x}{L} \sin \theta$$

$$D = \frac{Eh^3}{12}$$

which yields the following four simultaneous equations after substituting the numerical values of the shell parameters and roots :

$$\begin{bmatrix} 2.1053845 & 1.2232055 & -0.266027 & 0.477118 \\ -12.521916 & -1.737918 & -1.091543 & -2.29693 \\ -0.324114 & -1.368437 & 0.073562 & 0.289582 \\ -0.37729 & -0.47089 & 0.121857 & 0.039742 \end{bmatrix} \begin{Bmatrix} A_1 \\ A_2 \\ A_3 \\ A_4 \end{Bmatrix}$$

$$= \begin{Bmatrix} 2194.1327 \\ 4688.7642 \\ -1.456112 \\ 0.303243 \end{Bmatrix} 1/D$$

Solving the above four simultaneous equations, we can determine the constants as

$$A_1 = \frac{-2025.0796}{D},\ A_2 = \frac{2085.7502}{D}$$

$$A_3 = \frac{-742.68816}{D},\ A_4 = \frac{7773.3888}{D}$$

The forces and moments at various points can now be calculated using the above values for the constants and using the expressions given in Tables 4.2, 4.3 and 4.5. The final values of all forces are given in Table 4.6.

It may be observed that the magnitudes of the forces Q_x, Q_θ, M_x and $M_{x\theta}$ are small and will produce very low stresses in the shell. However, the forces N_x, N_θ, $N_{x\theta}$ and M_θ are high and are to be considered in the design of a concrete shell. Further, it may be noted that the force N_x at the free edge of shell becomes tensile and has a large magnitude. To take care of this large tensile force in a concrete shell, reinforcements are to be provided. Since the shell is thin, all the steel cannot be provided at the edge. This difficulty can be overcome by providing an edge-beam. Further, by the introduction of the edge beam, the magnitude of forces and moments in the shell can be reduced. We will discuss this aspect later with an example.

Table 4.6 Shell forces and moments

	θ in degrees				
	0	10	20	30	40
$\frac{N_x}{\cos(\pi x/L)}$ kg/m	−62663.75	−56647.35	−30102.46	40421.99	188450.61
$\frac{N_\theta}{\cos(\pi x/L)}$ kg/m	−4864.82	−4328.34	−2844.1	−944.11	0
$\frac{N_{x\theta}}{\sin(\pi x/L)}$ kg/m	0	−8328.25	−14615.55	−14586.76	0
$\frac{M_x}{\cos(\pi x/L)}$ kg. m/m	22.25	36.69	75.79	129.24	186.7
$\frac{M_\theta}{\cos(\pi x/L)}$ kg. m/m	−1576.65	−1342.51	−763.93	−179.44	0
$\frac{M_{x\theta}}{\sin(\pi x/L)}$ kg. m/m	0	205.23	351.97	414.25	420.06
$\frac{Q_x}{\sin(\pi x/L)}$ kg./m	135.68	113.99	60.09	4.41	−16.27
$\frac{Q_\theta}{\cos(\pi x/L)}$ kg./m	0	320.51	476.18	354.46	0

Example 4.2

We will determine the forces in a simply supported cylindrical shell with the longitudinal edges free and having the following dimensions.

Length of the shell (L) = 19 m

Radius of the shell (R) = 9.5 m

Thickness of the shell (h) = 0.095 m

Semicentral angle (θ_0) = 40°

We will assume that the shell will be subjected to a uniform live load of 125 kg/m^2 in addition to its own weight (dead load 228 kg/m^2). As in the previous example, we will assume Poisson's ratio to be zero and consider only the first term in the Fourier series for the computation of the forces. We will compute the forces here for the following two cases:

(a) Considering dead and live loads separately.

(b) Dead load and live loads are combined and the components of the load are determined for the combined load as if it is a dead load (similar to the previous example).

For the first case, the particular integral for dead load and live load as given in Table 4.5 is taken. The procedure for determining the constants A_1, A_2, A_3 and A_4 and later on, forces is identical to that in the previous example. For the second case, we carry out the analysis as in the previous example. We will give here only the final results for these two cases (Tables 4.7, 4.8). Since, for the design of the shell, the forces N_x, N_θ, $N_{x\theta}$ and bending moment M_θ are considered, we will give the magnitudes of these forces and moment only for the above two cases.

It may be seen from Tables 4.7 and 4.8, that the combined load case gives higher forces compared to the case where dead and live loads are considered separately. Hence, for the purpose of design, it is adequate if the analysis is carried out by taking the total load, i.e. dead and live loads together.

Table 4.7 Shell forces and moment obtained by considering dead and live loads separately

θ	$\frac{N_\theta}{\cos(\pi x/L)}$ kg/m	$\frac{N_x}{\cos(\pi x/L)}$ kg/m	$\frac{N_{x\theta}}{\sin(\pi x/L)}$ kg/m	$\frac{M_\theta}{\cos(\pi x/L)}$ kg.m/m
0	− 5750.67	− 2909.49	0	− 1055.31
10	− 5624.5	− 12075.68	− 1679.82	− 953.08
20	− 4641.1	− 24067.39	− 7084.6	− 558.11
30	− 2064.98	− 3013.96	− 12396.69	− 70.67
40	0	115642.52	0	0

Table 4.8 Shell forces and moment obtained by considering both dead and live loads together

θ	$\frac{N_\theta}{\cos(\pi x/L)}$ kg/m	$\frac{N_x}{\cos(\pi x/L)}$ kg/m	$\frac{N_{x\theta}}{\sin(\pi x/L)}$ kg/m	$\frac{M_\theta}{\cos(\pi x/L)}$ kg.m/m
0	– 5841.79	– 2690.37	0	– 1159.43
10	– 5739.51	– 12482.65	– 1678.23	– 1019.14
20	– 4789.07	– 27041.28	– 7366.08	– 601.71
30	– 2156.19	– 3715.29	– 13113.01	– 81.42
40	0	123120.7	0	0

Example 4.3

We will determine the forces and moments in a simply supported shell having edge-beams along the longitudinal edges. In this example, we will show the extent of reduction in forces and moments that can be obtained by the introduction of the edge-beam. To show this, we will consider the same shell dimensions as in Ex. 4.1. Hence we have for this example, the following shell and edge-beam dimensions.

Shell dimensions:	Length (L) – 36 m
	Radius (R) – 9 m
	Thickness (h) – 0.075 m
	Semicentral angle (θ_0) – 40°
	Poisson's ratio (ν) – zero.
Edge-beam dimensions:	Width of edge-beam (b) – 0.25 m
	Depth of edge-beam (d) – 1.5 m

Load

For the shell, as before, the load will be 250 kg/m^2 (Ex. 4.1).

For the edge-beam, weight per metre run of edge-beam = 0.25 × 1.5 × 2400 = 900 kg/m.

Because the shell dimensions are the same as in Ex. 4.1, the shell parameter and roots will be same as computed in that example.

Shell-edge conditions and determination of constants

In this example, we will use the approximate boundary conditions at the longitudinal edge, as outlined earlier, namely

$$\text{at } \theta = \theta_0, \quad \beta = R_H = 0, \quad u_s = u_b, \ \Delta w_s = w_b$$

where

$$R_H = N_\theta \cos\theta_0 - Q'_\theta \sin\theta_0, \quad \Delta w_s = w\cos\theta_0 - v\sin\theta_0$$

The expressions for β, R_H, u_s and Δw_s can be obtained from Tables 4.2, 4.3 and 4.5 and only the final results in respect of these quantities will be presented here.

$$\beta = (-0.57992\ A_1 + 3.225844\ A_2 + 0.5573\ A_3 - 0.23231\ A_4) - \frac{0.863014}{D}$$

$$R_H = (1.8553346\, A_1 + 1.2397155\ A_2 - 0.28211\ A_3 + 0.33994\, A_4) - \frac{1680.6082}{D}$$

$$u_s = (-0.3395\ A_1 + 0.080412\ A_2 - 0.071845\ A_3 + 0.01825\ A_4) - \frac{38.21632}{D}$$

$$\Delta w_s = (3.5245025\ A_1 - 5.274706\, A_2 - 0.96647\, A_3 - 0.80205\, A_4) - \frac{148.97376}{D}$$

The edge-beam displacements can be determined using Eqs. (4.51(c) and (d)) as

$$u_b = (1.2171575\ A_1 + 0.32569\ A_2 + 0.0099335\, A_3 + 0.30333\, A_4) - \frac{1211.6841}{D}$$

$$w_b = (16.241539\, A_1 + 4.6493865\, A_2 - 0.053535\, A_3 + 4.202648\, A_4) - \frac{19395.083}{D}$$

Using the boundary conditions mentioned above, the following four simultaneous equations can be formulated.

$$\begin{bmatrix} -0.57992 & 3.225844 & 0.5573 & -0.23231 \\ 1.8553346 & 1.2397155 & -0.28211 & 0.33994 \\ -1.556664 & -0.24528 & -0.081778 & -0.28508 \\ -12.717037 & -9.9240925 & -0.91293 & -5.0047055 \end{bmatrix} \begin{Bmatrix} A_1 \\ A_2 \\ A_3 \\ A_4 \end{Bmatrix}$$

$$= \frac{1}{D} \begin{Bmatrix} 0.863014 \\ 1680.6082 \\ -1173.4678 \\ -19246.109 \end{Bmatrix}$$

Solving the above simultaneous equations, we can determine the constants as

$$A_1 = \frac{195.37141}{D}, \quad A_2 = \frac{257.94936}{D}$$

$$A_3 = \frac{-97.894302}{D}, \quad A_4 = \frac{2855.5168}{D}$$

The shell forces and moments can now be computed using the above values of constants and these are given in Table 4.9.

The edge-beam force and moment can also be calculated using the above value of the constants and Eqs. 4.27(a) and (b). The bending moment M_x can be determined as

$$\frac{M_x}{\cos\ \pi x/L} = 45946.52\ \text{kg.m/m}$$

The axial force T can be calculated as

$$\frac{T}{\cos \pi x/L} = 160835.5 \text{ kg./m}$$

Table 4.9 Shell forces and moments

	θ in degrees				
	0	10	20	30	40
$\frac{N_x}{\cos(\pi x/L)}$ kg/m	– 30369.84	– 30675.35	–29649.7	– 22553.33	– 4590.11
$\frac{N_\theta}{\cos(\pi x/L)}$ kg/m	– 3777.91	– 3535.46	– 2804.18	–1607.07	– 78.81
$\frac{N_{x\theta}}{\sin(\pi x/L)}$ kg/m	0	– 4180.16	– 8353.59	–12031.54	– 14035.55
$\frac{M_\theta}{\cos(\pi x/L)}$ kg.m/m	–391.6	–277.94	12.49	325.55	404.85
$\frac{M_x}{\cos(\pi x/L)}$ kg.m/m	0.43	3.93	12.36	20.52	22.92
$\frac{M_{x\theta}}{\sin(\pi x/L)}$ kg.m/m	0	48.41	67.96	43.79	–10.73
$\frac{Q_\theta}{\cos(\pi x/L)}$ kg/m	0	147.84	225.93	164.73	–93.93
$\frac{Q_x}{\sin(\pi x/L)}$ kg/m	34.17	23.95	–2.14	–30.17	–37.3

Bending moment in edge-beam (M_x) = 45946.52 kg.m
Axial force (T) = 160835.5 kg

Hence, the bending stress at the mid-span is determined as

$$\text{Maximum stress at top of edge-beam} = \frac{T}{bd} - \frac{6M_x}{bd^2}$$

$$= -61201.5 \text{ kg/m}^2$$

$$\text{Maximum stress at bottom of edge-beam} = \frac{T}{bd} + \frac{6M_x}{bd^2}$$

$$= 918990.8 \text{ kg/m}^2$$

A check on the numerical computation can be made by making use of the longitudinal stress continuity at the junction of the shell-edge and edge-beam.

$$\text{Longitudinal stress at the edge of shell} = \frac{N_x}{h} = -61201.47 \text{ kg/m}^2$$

Longitudinal stress at the top of edge-beam = – 61201.5 kg/m^2

Since there is perfect agreement both in magnitude and nature of the stress at the junction, it may be said that numerical computation has been verified.

The shell forces and moments obtained in this example can be compared with Ex. 4.1 (Table 4.6). One can immediately notice considerable reduction in the magnitudes of the forces when an edge-beam is provided.

Example 4.4

We will consider now an example of a simply supported cylindrical shell with prestressed edge-beams. To show the effect of prestressing force on the forces in the shell, we shall consider the same shell and edge-beam dimensions as in the previous example. We will take the magnitude of the prestressing force as 150,000 kg and eccentricity of prestressing force with respect to the centroid of the beam as 0.375 m. For solving this problem, we can proceed in an identical way as in the previous example except for the edge-beam displacement. We can now use Eqs. 4.28(a) and (b) instead of Eqs. 4.27(c) and (d) taken for the last example. The final forces are presented in Table 4.10.

Table 4.10 Shell forces and moments

	θ in degrees				
	0	10	20	30	40
$\frac{N_x}{\cos(\pi x/L)}$ kg/m	–25313.46	–25357.73	–24922.3	–22787.16	–18112.921
$\frac{N_\theta}{\cos(\pi x/L)}$ kg/m	–3287.97	–3093.55	–2509.07	–1540.78	–223.75
$\frac{N_{x\theta}}{\sin(\pi x/L)}$ kg/m	0	–3472.9	–6931.16	–10227.14	–13060.85
$\frac{M_\theta}{\cos(\pi x/L)}$ kg.m/m	–120.31	–67.82	50.08	112.69	–85.2
$\frac{M_x}{\cos(\pi x/L)}$ kg.m/m	1.4	2.44	4.65	6.00	5.64
$\frac{M_{x\theta}}{\sin(\pi x/L)}$ kg.m/m	0	14.03	15.48	2.70	–3.64
$\frac{Q'_\theta}{\cos(\pi x/L)}$ kg/m	0	65.11	77.4	–16.27	–266.65
$\frac{Q_x}{\sin(\pi x/L)}$ kg/m	10.41	5.74	–4.74	–10.33	6.97

Final bending moment in the edge-beam (M'_x) = 12311.24 kg.m
Final axial force (T^1) = – 41319.63 kg

The shell forces and moments obtained in this example can be compared with results of Exs. 4.1 and 4.3 (Tables 4.6 and 4.9). One could see that further reduction in the magnitude of the forces N_x, N_θ, $N_{x\theta}$ and M_θ can be achieved by providing prestressed edge-beam.

To bring out clearly the effect of reinforced and prestressed edge-beams on the forces in the shell, the variation of N_x, N_θ and M_θ forces at mid-span obtained in Ex. 4.1, 4.3 and 4.4, have been presented in Figs. 4.11a–c. It may be seen from Fig. 4.11a that the large tensile force which occurs at the edge of the shell having longitudinal edges free, can be completely eliminated by providing either a reinforced or prestressed concrete edge-beam. Further, by providing an edge-beam (either-reinforced or prestressed), the magnitude of N_θ can be considerably reduced as can be seen from Fig. 4.11b. From Fig. 4.11c, it may be observed that by providing an edge-beam, the transverse bending moment M_θ may be considerably reduced with the maximum value of negative and positive bending moment in the transverse direction being made almost equal. From the design point of

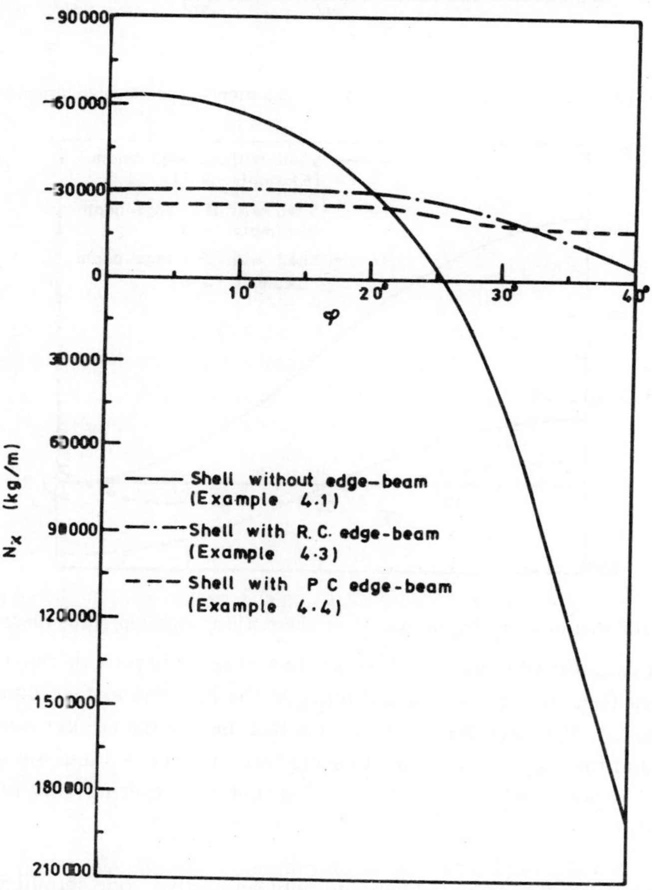

Fig. 4.11a Distribution of the force N_x at mid-span in a simply supported cylindrical shell

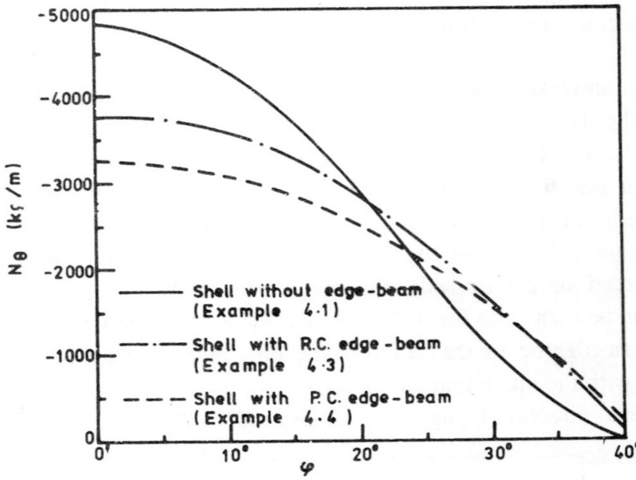

Fig. 4.11b Distribution of the force N_θ at mid-span in a simply supported cylindrical shell

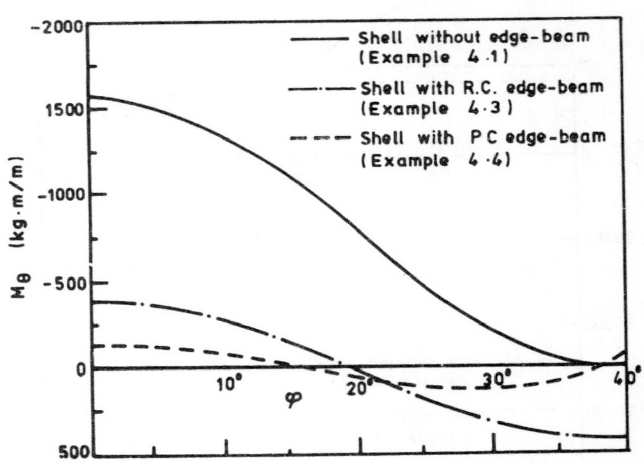

Fig. 4.11c Distribution of the bending moment M_θ at mid-span in a simply supported cylindrical shell

view, such a variation of moment is favourable as one could provide two layers of reinforcement (one at the top and the other at the bottom) to take care of the bending moment. It is also interesting to note that the assumed dimensions of the edge-beam and the magnitude of prestressing force in Exs. 4.3 and 4.4 are such that the shell is predominantly in compression thereby requiring only minimum reinforcement.

While the examples provided here are only suggestive, one should not draw a conclusion that always a prestressed edge-beam will reduce the forces in the shell considerably. It could be shown that the shell forces will reduce with increase in depth of the edge-beam. If one makes a parametric study of the variation of shell forces with edge-beam dimensions, one finds that there is an optimum dimension of the edge-beam for a given shell dimension, which will give minimum forces in the shell. Any further increase in depth or breadth of edge-beam beyond this will show an increasing trend for all shell forces. If the span of the shell is large (greater than 30 m), a reinforced concrete edge-beam becomes uneconomical and hence one may have to go in for prestressed edge-beam. Here also, one can make a parametric study of the variation of shell forces by keeping the edge-beam dimensions constant and varying the prestressing force or vice versa.

4.5 A BRIEF REVIEW OF EXISTING THEORIES FOR CYLINDRICAL SHELLS

Numerous investigators have presented different sets of equations for the analysis of circular-cylindrical shells. The purpose of this section is to briefly mention the various theories proposed for the cylindrical shells and to draw the attention of the reader to the applicability of these theories. Of the many theories available, the important and widely used ones are those given by Flugge[4.1], Gibson[4.2], D-K-J[4.3–4.5], Dischinger[4.8], Aas Jakobsen[4.9], Holand[4.10], Vlassov[4.11], Lundgren[4.12], ASCE manual[4.13], Finsterwalder[4.14] and Schorer[4.15]. The main object of these theories is to simplify the equations by making assumptions based on the behaviour of the shell. It is known that a long shell resists the external load predominantly through bending (similar to beam action), while a short shell resists the load predominantly by membrane action. Based on this fact, certain forces or displacements can be neglected while developing approximate equations for the analysis of long or short shells. Hence, it becomes necessary to carefully study the assumptions and approximations made in a particular theory before applying it to the analysis of a cylindrical shell of given dimensions.

In general, the approximations made in the various theories can be classified under one or more of the following heads:

(a) Neglecting the contribution of radial shear (Q_θ) in the second equilibrium equation.

(b) Neglecting some terms (which are small) in force-displacement relations.

(c) Neglecting some forces and deformations altogether.

(d) Neglecting the Poisson's ratio.

Flugge first presented the rigorous theory for the analysis of cylindrical shells and for assessing the applicability of the other theories, Flugge's equations have been taken as reference. Holand[4.10], McNamee[4.16], Moe[4.17], Sen[4.18], Jensen[4.19] and

Arya[4.20] have all made some comparison of various theories and have drawn conclusions on the applicability of the various theories for long, intermediate and short cylindrical shells.

The D-K-J theory (more often called as Donnell's theory in literature) has been used here to develop solution for a cylindrical shell roof, which is simply supported along the curved ends and can have any type of boundary conditions along the longitudinal edges. Some conclusions have been drawn regarding the accuracy of Donnell's theory earlier by Hoff[4.21] and Holand[4.10], who have compared the roots of the characteristic equation of Donnell's theory with those of Flugge's exact theory. The shell parameters considered for this comparison does not cover the ranges that are normally used in civil engineering practice. Hence, a comparison of the roots of the characteristic equation obtained from Flugge's and Donnell's theories are given here. For the Donnell's theory the characteristic equation given in Eq. (b) of Sec. 4.4.1.1 has been used while for Flugge's theory the characteristic equation was obtained using Eqs. 4.8a–c and assuming the same form for w_0 (Eq. (a) Sec. 4.4.1.1), as in Donnell's theory. The roots a, b, a_1 and b_1, obtained from these two theories have been given in Table 4.11. For long shells ($L/R > 3$), Schorer's theory which is much more simpler than Donnell's theory, has been found to give results adequate for the design. Hence the roots obtained from Schorer's theory (Eq. (b) Sec. 4.7.1.2) have also been compared with Donnell's and Flugge's theories only for long shells and these are given in Table 4.12. It may be seen from Table 4.11, that the roots given by Donnell's theory are almost the same as those given by Flugge's theory for $0.5 \leq L/R \leq 3$ and $50 \leq R/h \leq 200$ and hence Donnell's theory could be safely used for shell dimensions in the above range. Similarly the comparison of roots of Flugge's and Schorer's theories given in Table 4.12 indicate that Schorer's theory could be safely used for long shells ($L/R \geq 3$). It is also interesting to point out that Rish[4.22] has shown that roots of Schorer's equation are more accurate than those of Donnell's equation for very long shells.

4.6 APPROXIMATE METHODS

Two approximate methods, one for long and the other for a short circular-cylindrical shell can be used for the preliminary analysis. Normally, these methods are used to verify the assumed dimensions of the shell before proceeding with the rigorous analysis. The two approximate methods are (a) beam method for long shells (b) membrane analysis for short shells. As the latter method has already been discussed in detail in Ch. 3, only the beam method will be discussed here.

In the beam method, the shell is assumed to act as a beam of circular cross-section (open), spanning between the two traverses. Thus the longitudinal moment is determined as for a simply supported beam and longitudinal stresses are determined from the knowledge of the modulus of section.

Table 4.11 Comparison of roots of characteristic equation ($\nu = 0.3$)

R/h	*L/R*	Theory	Roots of characteristic equation *a*	*b*	a_1	b_1
50	0.5	Flugge	10.1967	2.7862	4.5687	6.2551
		Donnell	10.2175	2.7947	4.5901	6.2209
	1.0	Flugge	6.5363	2.1763	2.7542	5.1801
		Donnell	6.5687	2.1735	2.7785	5.1386
	2.0	Flugge	4.3533	1.6347	1.8043	3.9497
		Donnell	4.4017	1.6218	1.8329	3.8948
	3.0	Flugge	3.4662	1.3685	1.4317	3.3164
		Donnell	3.5265	1.3495	1.4641	3.2504
100	0.5	Flugge	11.4944	3.5058	4.9547	8.1500
		Donnell	11.5129	3.5076	4.9709	8.1238
	1.0	Flugge	7.5455	2.6716	3.1518	6.4024
		Donnell	7.5736	2.6660	3.1703	6.3689
	2.0	Flugge	5.1068	1.9740	2.1158	4.7670
		Donnell	5.1482	1.9610	2.1381	4.7218
	3.0	Flugge	4.0950	1.6410	1.6937	3.9688
		Donnell	4.1463	1.6232	1.7195	3.9142
200	0.5	Flugge	13.1213	4.3485	5.5448	10.2979
		Donnell	13.1375	4.3470	5.5569	10.2771
	1.0	Flugge	8.7792	3.2502	3.6516	7.8170
		Donnell	8.8034	3.2436	3.6657	7.7896
	2.0	Flugge	6.0139	2.3724	2.4912	5.7281
		Donnell	6.0492	2.3602	2.5090	5.6905
	3.0	Flugge	4.8473	1.9621	2.0063	4.7411
		Donnell	4.8908	1.9461	2.0270	4.6956

Let R be the radius of the cylindrical shell, θ_0 its semicentral angle, h the thickness and 0 its centre (Fig. 4.12).

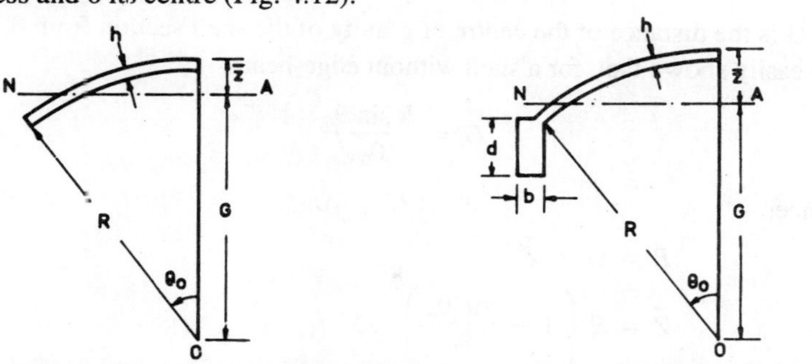

(a) Cylindrical shell (b) Cylindrical shell wit edge beam

Fig. 4.12 Circular cylindrical shell with and without edge beam

Table 4.12 Comparison of roots of characteristic equation ($\nu = 0$)

R/h	L/R	Theory	Roots of characteristic equation			
			a	b	a_1	b_1
50	4	Flugge	2.9894	1.2169	1.2318	2.9562
		Donnell	3.0584	1.1949	1.2684	2.8811
		Schorer	2.9703	1.2303	1.2303	2.9703
	6	Flugge	2.3880	1.0143	0.9821	2.4678
		Donnell	2.4733	0.9851	1.0250	2.3768
		Schorer	2.4252	1.0046	1.0046	2.4252
	8	Flugge	2.0327	0.8919	0.8345	2.1736
		Donnell	2.1316	0.8572	0.8832	2.0689
		Schorer	2.1003	0.8700	0.8700	2.1003
100	4	Flugge	3.5478	1.4535	1.4656	3.5198
		Donnell	3.6065	1.4330	1.4948	3.4575
		Schorer	3.5323	1.4631	1.4631	3.5323
	6	Flugge	2.8522	1.2045	1.1772	2.9192
		Donnell	2.9246	1.1781	1.2117	2.8434
		Schorer	2.8841	1.1946	1.1946	2.8841
	8	Flugge	2.4402	1.0549	1.0063	2.5585
		Donnell	2.5240	1.0238	1.0456	2.4713
		Schorer	2.4977	1.0346	1.0346	2.4977
200	4	Flugge	4.2134	1.7328	1.7429	4.1897
		Donnell	4.2631	1.7145	1.7664	4.1378
		Schorer	4.2006	1.7400	1.7400	4.2006
	6	Flugge	3.4026	1.4300	1.4069	3.4589
		Donnell	3.4639	1.4067	1.4350	3.3956
		Schorer	3.4298	1.4207	1.4207	3.4298
	8	Flugge	2.9216	1.2485	1.2074	3.0210
		Donnell	2.9924	1.2212	1.2396	2.9481
		Schorer	2.9703	1.2303	1.2303	2.9703

If G is the distance of the centre of gravity of the shell section from 0, then it can be easily shown that, for a shell without edge-beam,

$$G = \frac{R \sin \theta_0}{\theta_0} \tag{a}$$

and since,

$$R = G + \bar{Z}$$

$$\bar{Z} = R\left(1 - \frac{\sin \theta_0}{\theta_0}\right) \tag{4.29}$$

where $\bar{Z}$ is the distance of the neutral axis from the crown of the shell.

Moment of inertia I of the shell about the neutral axis (Fig. 4.12a) can be obtained as

$$I = 2hR^3 \left(\frac{\theta_0}{2} + \frac{\sin 2\theta_0}{4} - \frac{\sin^2 \theta_0}{\theta_0} \right) \tag{4.30}$$

If q is the load per unit area acting on the shell (including the self-weight), then the load per unit length p can be determined as

$$p = 2R\theta_0 q \tag{b}$$

$$\text{Maximum bending moment} = \frac{pL^2}{8} \tag{c}$$

where L is the span or length of the shell.

The longitudinal bending stress σ_x can be computed from

$$\sigma_x = \frac{Mz}{I} \tag{d}$$

and the longitudinal force per unit length from

$$N_x = \sigma_x h \tag{e}$$

Following this, the expressions for the longitudinal force N_x at crown and springing level can be written as

$$N_x \text{ at crown} = \frac{M}{I} \bar{Z} h \tag{4.31}$$

$$N_x \text{ at springing} = \frac{M}{I} [R(1 - \cos \theta_0) - \bar{Z}] h \tag{4.32}$$

If the shell has an edge-beam (Fig. 4.1b), then the above equations can be modified as follows. G the distance of the neutral axis from 0 will now be

$$G = \frac{\left[hR^2 \sin \theta_0 + \left\{ R \cos \theta_0 - \frac{d}{2} \right\} d.b \right]}{(Rh\theta_0 + bd)} \tag{4.33}$$

and

$$\bar{Z} = R - G$$

Moment of inertia I_0^s of shell about 0 is given by

$$I_0^s = 2\,hR^3 \left(\frac{\theta_0}{2} + \frac{\sin 2\theta_0}{4} \right) \tag{f}$$

and I_0^B the moment of inertia of the edge-beam about 0 will be

$$I_0^B = \frac{bd^3}{6} + 2\,bd \left(R \cos \theta_0 - \frac{d}{2} \right)^2 \tag{g}$$

If I_0 is the total moment of inertia about 0, then

$$I_0 = I_0^S + I_0^B \tag{h}$$

The moment of inertia of the cross-section about the neutral axis can then be computed from

$$I = I_0 - (2Rh\theta_0 + 2\,bd)\,G^2 \tag{4.34}$$

If q is the load per unit area acting on the shell (including self-weight) and w is the weight of the beam per unit length, then the load per unit length can be determined as

$$p = (2Rq\theta_0 + 2w) \tag{i}$$

$$\text{Maximum bending moment} = \frac{pL^2}{8} \tag{j}$$

The longitudinal force N_x per unit length can then be calculated from

$$N_x \text{ at crown} = -\frac{M}{I}\bar{Z}h \tag{4.35}$$

$$N_x \text{ at springing} = \frac{M}{I}(G - R\cos\theta_0)\,h \tag{4.36}$$

and the longitudinal stress at the bottom of the edge-beam as

$$\sigma = \frac{M}{I}[G - (R\cos\theta_0 - d)] \tag{4.37}$$

We will now consider two examples, one that of a long shell and the other that of a short shell to illustrate the applicability of the approximate methods, namely the beam method and membrane analysis for these two types of shells.

Example 4.5

For the beam method, we will consider the shell dimensions taken in Ex. 4.1. For this example, the following quantities can be immediately calculated.

$\bar{Z} = 0.7136$ m

$I = 0.37507$ m^4

p (load per metre run) = 3141.58 kg/m

Bending moment = 508936.76 kg.m

N_x at top = – 72622.92 kg/m

N_x at springing = 141664.61 kg/m

An exact analysis of the same shell (Ex. 4.1, Table 4.6) gives

N_x at top = – 62663.75 kg/m

N_x at springing = 188450.6 kg/m

A comparison of beam analysis results with those of exact analysis indicates that the beam method gives about 17% higher value for N_x at the top, while it underestimates by 22% the value of N_x at springing.

Example 4.6

We will consider a short shell to show that the application of membrane analysis, as an approximate method for the purpose of preliminary analysis. The dimensions of the shell are as follows :

Length of shell (L) = 3 m

Radius of shell (R) = 9 m

Thickness of shell (h) = 7.5 cm

Semicentral angle (θ_0) = 40°

Load (including dead load) = 250 kg/m²

The results of the bending analysis and membrane analysis are presented in Table 4.13.

Table 4.13 Comparison of shell forces obtained from bending and membrane analysis

θ	$\frac{N_\theta}{\cos(\pi x/L)}$ kg/m		$\frac{N_x}{\cos(\pi x/L)}$ kg/m		$\frac{N_{x\theta}}{\sin(\pi x/L)}$ kg/m	
	Bending	Membrane	Bending	Membrane	Bending	Membrane
0	–2678.6	–2864.8	–95.98	–64.5	0	0
10	–2630.95	–2821.28	63.69	–63.5	–61.16	–105.57
20	–2812.5	–2692.03	–93.9	–60.6	113.84	–207.92
30	–2589.29	–2480.99	–1571.4	–55.86	–1093.75	–303.97
40	0	–2194.56	8526.8	–49.41	0	–390.77

It may be observed from Table 4.13 that there is a good agreement between the membrane analysis and bending analysis results close to the crown of the shell but the difference between the two results is very large close to the springing due to the influence of the edge forces applied to satisfy the required boundary condition.

From the above two examples, it may be concluded that the beam method yields sufficiently accurate value for the longitudinal force N_x, adequate for preliminary design of long shells. Similarly, the membrane analysis yields forces which are sufficiently accurate in the central portion of the shell and could be used in the preliminary design of short shells.

4.7 SOLUTION FOR OTHER SUPPORT CONDITIONS

Solution for other support conditions like fixed or free, along the curved edge of a cylindrical shell cannot be so easily obtained as in the simply supported case. In most of the cases, the solution for the support condition other than simply supported is much more complicated. Pickett and Gopalacharyulu[4.23, 4.24] have suggested two methods namely the energy method and the multiple Fourier series method for the analysis of a circular-cylindrical shell clamped along all the four egdes. In the energy method, the displacements u, v and w are selected in the form of polynomials in x and θ, so as to satisfy all the boundary conditions. The total energy of the system is then determined and minimised. This results in a set of simultaneous equations for the unknown coefficients in the expression for displacements. In the multiple Fourier procedure, the solution for the differential equation in terms of radial displacement is obtained by considering the edge disturbances from the straight and curved edges separately. The two solutions are added to form the general solution to the problem. The constants occurring in the solution are then evaluated using the boundary conditions. This method has been applied to an all-around clamped cylindrical shell by Chandrashekhara and Chandrashekara[4.25]. It must be noted that this method of solution can also be applied for a cylindrical shell which is supported on beams along all the four edges as well as for the analysis of continuous cylindrical shells. For a cylindrical shell having a combination of simply supported and clamped conditions along the four edges, solution can be obtained using orthogonal functions. An all-round clamped cylindrical shell has been analysed using this method by Chandrashekhara and Chandrashekara[4.26]. The finite difference technique has also been applied to the solution of cylindrical shell problem by Chuang and Veletsos[4.27] who have indicated the necessity for considering higher order differences to get accurate results. Tottenham and Desayi[4.28] have presented the matrix progression method, which can be applied to a wide variety of shell problems. In all these approaches, Flugge's approximate differential equations have been used.

Schorer[4.15] has given a simple differential equation for the analysis of circular-cylindrical shells which is applicable only for long shells. Using this differential equation, Morice[4.29] has suggested a Levy type of solution for a cylindrical shell having clamped-clamped, clamped-supported and clamped-free boundary conditions along the curved edges using orthogonal functions. This solution is useful in some way for analysing a continuous cylindrical shell. Hence we will present here, first the basic equations as given by Schorer and develop solutions which are valid for the above types of support condition along the curved edges.

4.7.1 Schorer Theory for Long Circular-Cylindrical Shells

In addition to the assumptions made in the theory of thin shell, Schorer has made the following additional assumptions:

(a) The longitudinal bending amount M_x being small can be neglected.

(b) The twisting moment $M_{x\theta}$ being small can be neglected.

(c) The contribution of Q_θ in the second equilibrium equation is neglected.

(d) The transverse and shear strains being very small compared to longitudinal strain, can be neglected.

(e) Poisson's ratio is taken as zero.

Because of assumptions (a) and (b), the moment equilibrium condition (in x-direction results in $Q_x = 0$. With the above assumptions the equilibrium Eqs. (4.1a–f) will now reduce to

$$\frac{\partial N_x}{\partial x} + \frac{\partial N_{x\theta}}{R\,\partial\theta} + X = 0 \tag{4.38a}$$

$$\frac{\partial N_\theta}{R\,\partial\theta} + \frac{\partial N_{x\theta}}{\partial x} + Y = 0 \tag{4.38b}$$

$$\frac{\partial Q_\theta}{R\,\partial\theta} + \frac{N_\theta}{R} + Z = 0 \tag{4.38c}$$

$$\frac{\partial M_\theta}{R\,\partial\theta} - Q_\theta = 0 \tag{4.38d}$$

$$N_{x\theta} - N_{\theta x} = 0 \tag{4.38e}$$

We have five equilibrium equations involving six stress resultants, namely N_x, N_θ, $N_{x\theta}$, $N_{\theta x}$, M_θ and Q_θ and hence, the problem is statically indeterminate internally. Now additional equations are obtained by considering deformation. Because of the assumptions mentioned above, the strain-displacement relations (Eq. 4.3) can now be written as

$$\varepsilon_x = \frac{\partial u}{\partial x} \tag{4.39a}$$

$$\varepsilon_\theta = \frac{\partial v}{R\,\partial\theta} + \frac{w}{R} = 0 \tag{4.39b}$$

$$\gamma_{x\theta} = \frac{\partial u}{R\,\partial\theta} + \frac{\partial v}{\partial x} = 0 \tag{4.39c}$$

The force-displacement relation will now be

$$N_x = Eh\,\frac{\partial u}{\partial x} \tag{4.40a}$$

$$M_\theta = EI\,\frac{\partial^2 w}{R^2\,\partial\theta^2} \tag{4.40b}$$

where

$$I = \frac{h^3}{12}$$

4.7.1.1 Differential equation

Eliminating N_θ, $N_{x\theta}$ and Q_θ from Eqs. (4.38a–d), we get

$$\frac{\partial^4 M_\theta}{R^4\,\partial\theta^4} + \frac{1}{R}\,\frac{\partial^2 N_x}{\partial x^2} + \frac{1}{R}\left(\frac{\partial X}{\partial x} - \frac{\partial Y}{R\,\partial\theta}\right) + \frac{\partial^2 Z}{R^2\,\partial\theta^2} = 0 \tag{4.41}$$

From Eqs. (4.39b and c), we get

$$\frac{\partial^2 u}{R^2\,\partial\theta^2} = \frac{\partial w}{R\,\partial x}$$

Operating on Eq. (4.40a) by $\dfrac{\partial^4}{R^2\,\partial\theta^2\,\partial x^2}$, we get

$$\frac{\partial^4 N_x}{R^2\,\partial\theta^2\,\partial x^2} = Eh\,\frac{\partial^5 u}{R^2\,\partial\theta^2\,\partial x^3} = \frac{Eh}{R}\,\frac{\partial^4 w}{\partial x^4} \tag{4.42}$$

Operating on Eq. (4.41) by $\dfrac{\partial^2}{R^2\,\partial\theta^2}$, we get

$$\frac{\partial^6 M_\theta}{R^6\,\partial\theta^6} + \frac{1}{R}\,\frac{\partial^4 N_x}{R^2\,\partial\theta^2\,\partial x^2} = -\frac{1}{R}\left(\frac{\partial^3 X}{R^2\,\partial\theta^2\,\partial x} - \frac{\partial^3 Y}{R^3\,\partial\theta^3}\right) - \frac{\partial^4 Z}{R^4\,\partial\theta^4} \tag{4.43}$$

Substituting for the derivative of N_x, Eq. (4.42) and for M_θ, Eq. (4.40b), we get after simplification

$$\frac{\partial^8 w}{\partial\theta^8} + \frac{12R^6}{h^2}\,\frac{\partial^4 w}{\partial x^4} = -\frac{R^5}{EI}\,\frac{\partial^2}{\partial\theta^2}\left(\frac{\partial X}{\partial x} - \frac{\partial Y}{R\,\partial\theta}\right) - \frac{R^4}{EI}\,\frac{\partial^4 Z}{\partial\theta^4} \tag{4.44}$$

The forces can be determined from the following force-displacement relations:

$$N_x = -\frac{EI}{R^5}\iint \frac{\partial^6 w}{\partial\theta^6}\,dx\,dx - \int\!\!\int\left(\frac{\partial X}{\partial x} - \frac{\partial Y}{R\,\partial\theta}\right)dx\,dx$$
$$- \frac{1}{R}\iint \frac{\partial^2 Z}{\partial\theta^2}\,dx\,dx \tag{4.45a}$$

$$N_\theta = -\frac{EI}{R^3}\,\frac{\partial^4 w}{\partial\theta^4} - RZ \tag{4.45b}$$

$$N_{x\theta} = \frac{EI}{R^4}\int \frac{\partial^5 w}{\partial\theta^5}\,dx + \int \frac{\partial Z}{\partial\theta}\,dx - \int Y\,dx \tag{4.45c}$$

$$M_\theta = EI\,\frac{\partial^2 w}{R^2\,\partial\theta^2} \tag{4.45d}$$

$$Q_\theta = EI\,\frac{\partial^3 w}{R^3\,\partial\theta^3} \tag{4.45e}$$

The displacements u and v can be determined from

$$u = -\frac{I}{R^5 h}\iiint \frac{\partial^6 w}{\partial\theta^6}\,dx\,dx\,dx - \frac{1}{EhR}\iiint \frac{\partial^2 Z}{\partial\theta^2}\,dx\,dx\,dx$$
$$- \frac{1}{Eh}\iiint\left(\frac{\partial X}{\partial x} - \frac{\partial Y}{R\,\partial\theta}\right)dx\,dx\,dx \tag{4.46a}$$

$$v = \frac{I}{R^6 h} \iiiint \frac{\partial^7 w}{\partial \theta^7}\, dx\, dx\, dx\, dx + \frac{1}{EhR^2} \iiiint \frac{\partial^3 Z}{\partial \theta^3}\, dx\, dx\, dx\, dx + \frac{1}{EhR} \iiiint \left(\frac{\partial^2 X}{\partial \theta\, \partial x} - \frac{\partial^2 Y}{R\, \partial \theta^2} \right) dx\, dx\, dx\, dx \tag{4.46b}$$

4.7.1.2 Solution

The coordinate axes with the origin at one of the end of the shell is shown in Fig. 4.13. According to this, $x = 0$ and $x = L$ refers to the two curved ends, while $\theta = \pm \theta_0$ refers to the straight edges. The curved ends may have any one of the following types of support:

(a) $x = 0, x = L$, simply supported

(b) $x = 0, x = L$, clamped or fixed

(c) $x = 0$, clamped and $x = L$, simply supported

(d) $x = 0$, clamped and $x = L$, free

The following boundary conditions have to be satisfied for the above types of support

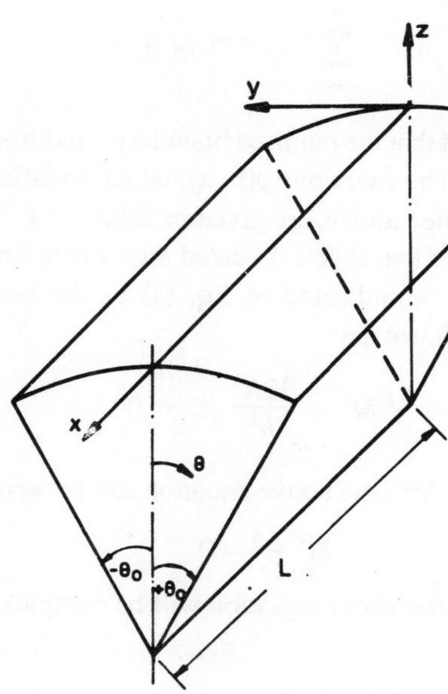

Fig. 4.13 Circular-cylindrical shell

(a) Simply supported edge

$$N_x = w = 0$$

The other boundary conditions, namely $\varepsilon_\theta = 0$ and $M_x = 0$ are not specified because these are assumed zero in Schorer theory.

(b) Clamped or fixed edge

$$u = v = w = \frac{\partial w}{\partial x} = 0$$

(c) Free edge

$$N_x = N_{x\theta} = Q_x = 0$$

The boundary condition $M_x = 0$ is not specified due to the same reason mentioned above.

For obtaining a Levy type of solution, the function in the x-direction should be so selected that the prescribed boundary conditions along the curved edges is automatically satisfied.

(a) Complementary function

The solution for the homogeneous part of the differential equation (4.44) can be taken in the form

$$w_0 = \sum_{n=1}^{\infty} A_n e^{M\gamma\theta} \phi(\beta_n x) \tag{a}$$

where $\phi(\beta_n x)$ is so selected that the required boundary conditions at $x = 0$ and $x = L$ are completely satisfied. The functions $\phi(\beta_n x)$, which satisfies the three types of support conditions mentioned above, are given in Table 4.14. The general property of the function $\phi(\beta_n x)$ is that it gets repeated after every fourth differentiation. Substituting the form for w indicated in Eq. (a) in the homogeneous part of differential equation (4.44), we get

$$\gamma^8 M^8 + \frac{12R^6}{h^2} \beta_n^4 = 0 \tag{b}$$

Defining $\gamma^8 = 3\beta_n^4 R^6/h^2$, the above equation can be written as

$$M^8 + 4 = 0$$

All the eight roots of the above equation will be complex and can be written in the form

$$M_{1,2,3,4} = \pm (j \pm ik)$$

$$M_{5,6,7,8} = \pm (k \pm ij)$$

Table 4.14 $\phi(\beta_n x)$ for different support conditions

Support condition	Simply supported at $x = 0, L$	Clamped at $x = 0$	Supported at $x = L$	Clamped at $x = 0$	Clamped at $x = L$	Clamped at $x = 0$	Free at $x = L$
$\phi\ (\beta_n x)$	$\sin \beta_n x$	$[(\cosh \beta_n x - \cos \beta_n x) - \alpha_n (\sinh \beta_n x - \sin \beta_n x)]$					
Characteristic equation	$\sin \beta_n L = 0$	$[(\cosh \beta_n L - \cos \beta_n L) - \alpha_n (\sinh \beta_n L - \sin \beta_n L)] = 0$ $[(\cosh \beta_n L + \cos \beta_n L) - \alpha_n (\sinh \beta_n L + \sin \beta_n L)] = 0$		$[(\cosh \beta_n L - \cos \beta_n L) - \alpha_n (\sinh \beta_n L - \sin \beta_n L)] = 0$ $[(\sinh \beta_n L + \sin \beta_n L) - \alpha_n (\cosh \beta_n L - \cos \beta_n L)] = 0$		$[(\cosh \beta_n L + \cos \beta_n L) - \alpha_n (\sinh \beta_n L + \sin \beta_n L)] = 0$ $[(\sinh \beta_n L - \sin \beta_n L) - \alpha_n (\cosh \beta_n L + \cos \beta_n L)] = 0$	
Roots	$\beta_n L = n\pi$ $(n = 1, 2, 3, \ldots)$	$\beta_n L$	α_n	$\beta_n L$	α_n	$\beta_n L$	$'\alpha_n$
		$n = 1$, 3.9266023	1.0007773	$n = 1$, 4.7300408	0.98250221	$n = 1$, 1.8751041	0.7340955
		$n = 2$, 7.06858275	1.00000144	$n = 2$, 7.8532046	1.00077731	$n = 2$, 4.69409113	1.01846644
		$n = 3$, 10.21017613	1.0	$n = 3$, 10.9956078	0.99996645	$n = 3$, 7.85475743	0.9992245
		$n = 4$, 13.35176578	1.0	$n = 4$, 14.1371655	1.00000145	$n = 4$, 10.99554074	1.00003355
		n = 5, 16.49336143	1.0	$n = 5$, 17.2787596	0.99999993	$n = 5$,14.13716839	0.99999855
		$n > 5$, $\dfrac{(4m + 1)\pi}{4}$	1.0	$n > 5$, $\dfrac{(2m + 1)\pi}{2}$	1.0	$n > 5$, $\dfrac{(2m - 1)\pi}{2}$	1.0

where

$$j = \sqrt{\frac{\sqrt{2} + 1}{2}} = 1.098684 \quad \text{and} \quad k = \sqrt{\frac{\sqrt{2} - 1}{2}} = 0.45508$$

It must be noted that the roots of Eq. (c) are independent of shell dimensions.

The solution for w_0 can now be written in the following form

$$\begin{aligned} w_0 = \sum_{n=1}^{\infty} & [A_1 \cosh j\gamma\theta \cos k\gamma\theta + A_2 \sinh j\gamma\theta \sin k\gamma\theta \\ & + A_3 \cosh k\gamma\theta \cos j\gamma\theta + A_4 \sinh k\gamma\theta \sin j\gamma\theta \\ & + A_5 \sinh j\gamma\theta \cos k\gamma\theta + A_6 \cosh j\gamma\theta \sin k\gamma\theta \\ & + A_7 \sinh k\gamma\theta \cos j\gamma\theta + A_8 \cosh k\gamma\theta \sin j\gamma\theta] \, \phi(\beta_n x) \end{aligned} \tag{4.47}$$

where $A_1, A_2, ..., A_8$ are constants to be determined from the boundary conditions. If the loading and boundary conditions are symmetrical about x, then the constants $A_5 = A_6 = A_7 = A_8 = 0$. On the other hand, if the loading is anti- symmetrical about x, then the constants $A_1 = A_2 = A_3 = A_4 = 0$. In either case, one has to determine only four constants from the four boundary conditions.

The expressions for stresses and displacements can be obtained from Eqs. (4.45–4.47), which involves either differentiating w odd or even number of times with respect to θ. In general, the shell forces and displacements in terms of even or odd functions of θ can be written in the form

$$\begin{aligned} F = MF \, [& (A_1 a_1 + A_2 b_1) \cosh j\gamma\theta \cos k\gamma\theta \\ & - (A_1 b_1 - A_2 a_1) \sinh j\gamma\theta \sin k\gamma\theta \\ & + (A_3 c_1 + A_4 d_1) \cosh k\gamma\theta \cos j\gamma\theta \\ & - (A_3 d_1 - A_4 c_1) \sinh k\gamma\theta \sin j\gamma\theta \\ & + (A_5 a_1 + A_6 b_1) \sinh j\gamma\theta \cos k\gamma\theta \\ & - (A_5 b_1 - A_6 a_1) \cosh j\gamma\theta \sin k\gamma\theta \\ & + (A_7 c_1 + A_8 d_1) \sinh k\gamma\theta \cos j\gamma\theta \\ & - (A_7 d_1 - A_8 c_1) \cosh k\gamma\theta \sin j\gamma\theta] \end{aligned}$$

and

$$\begin{aligned} F = MF \, [& (A_1 a_1 + A_2 b_1) \sinh j\gamma\theta \cos k\gamma\theta \\ & - (A_1 b_1 - A_2 a_1) \cosh j\gamma\theta \sin k\gamma\theta \\ & + (A_3 c_1 + A_4 d_1) \sinh k\gamma\theta \cos j\gamma\theta \\ & - (A_3 d_1 - A_4 c_1) \cosh k\gamma\theta \sin j\gamma\theta \\ & + (A_5 a_1 + A_6 b_1) \cosh j\gamma\theta \cos k\gamma\theta \\ & - (A_5 b_1 - A_6 a_1) \sinh j\gamma\theta \sin k\gamma\theta \\ & + (A_7 c_1 + A_8 d_1) \cosh k\gamma\theta \cos j\gamma\theta \\ & - (A_7 d_1 - A_8 c_1) \sinh k\gamma\theta \sin j\gamma\theta] \end{aligned}$$

where MF, a_1, b_1, c_1 and d_1 for the various shell forces and displacements are given in Tables 4.15 and 4.16.

Table 4.15 Shell forces and displacements from complementary function (even)

$$
\begin{aligned}
F = MF\,[&(A_1 a_1 + A_2 b_1)\cosh j\gamma\theta \cos k\gamma\theta - (A_1 b_1 - A_2 a_1)\sinh j\gamma\theta \sin k\gamma\theta \\
&+ (A_3 c_1 + A_4 d_1)\cosh k\gamma\theta \cos j\gamma\theta - (A_3 d_1 - A_4 c_1)\sinh k\gamma\theta \sin j\gamma\theta \\
&+ (A_5 a_1 + A_6 b_1)\sinh j\gamma\theta \cos k\gamma\theta - (A_5 b_1 - A_6 a_1)\cosh j\gamma\theta \sin k\gamma\theta \\
&+ (A_7 c_1 + A_8 d_1)\sinh k\gamma\theta \cos j\gamma\theta - (A_7 d_1 - A_8 c_1)\cosh k\gamma\theta \sin j\gamma\theta]
\end{aligned}
$$

Force or displacement	MF	a_1	b_1	c_1	d_1
N_x	$-\left(\dfrac{2EI\gamma^6}{R^5\beta_n^2}\right)\phi''(\beta_n x)$	-1	1	1	1
N_θ	$-\left(\dfrac{2EI\gamma^4}{R^3}\right)\phi(\beta_n x)$	0	1	0	-1
M_θ	$\left(\dfrac{EI\gamma^2}{R^2}\right)\phi(\beta_n x)$	1	1	-1	1
u	$-\dfrac{2I\gamma^6}{R^5 h\beta_n^3}\phi'(\beta_n x)$	-1	1	1	1
w	$\phi(\beta_n x)$	1	0	1	0

Note : $\dfrac{\partial}{\partial x}[\phi(\beta_n x)] = \phi'(\beta_n x)$, $\dfrac{\partial^2}{\partial x^2}[\phi(\beta_n x)] = \phi''(\beta_n x)$

Table 4.16 Shell forces and displacements from complementary function (odd)

$$
\begin{aligned}
F = MF\,[&(A_1 a_1 + A_2 b_1)\sinh j\gamma\theta \cos k\gamma\theta - (A_1 b_1 - A_2 a_1)\cosh j\gamma\theta \sin k\gamma\theta \\
&+ (A_3 c_1 + A_4 d_1)\sinh k\gamma\theta \cos j\gamma\theta - (A_3 d_1 - A_4 c_1)\cosh k\gamma\theta \sin j\gamma\theta \\
&+ (A_5 a_1 + A_6 b_1)\cosh j\gamma\theta \cos k\gamma\theta - (A_5 b_1 - A_6 a_1)\sinh j\gamma\theta \sin k\gamma\theta \\
&+ (A_7 c_1 + A_8 d_1)\cosh k\gamma\theta \cos j\gamma\theta - (A_7 d_1 - A_8 c_1)\sinh k\gamma\theta \sin j\gamma\theta]
\end{aligned}
$$

Force or displacement	MF	a_1	b_1	c_1	d_1
$N_{x\theta}$	$\dfrac{2EI\gamma^5}{R^4\beta_n}\phi'''(\beta_n x)$	$-k$	j	j	$-k$
Q_θ	$\left(\dfrac{EI\gamma^3}{R^3}\right)\phi(\beta_n x)$	$j-k$	$k+j$	$-(k+j)$	$-(j-k)$
β	$\dfrac{\gamma}{R}\phi(\beta_n x)$	j	k	k	j
v	$\dfrac{2I\gamma^7}{R^6 h\beta_n^4}\phi(\beta_n x)$	$-(k+j)$	$-(k-j)$	$(k-j)$	$(k+j)$

(b) Particular integral

The particular integral of Eq. (4.44) is determined depending upon the type of loading to which the shell is subjected to. We will obtain the particular integral for dead load only. Following this procedure, particular integral for other types of load can easily be obtained.

The dead load g per unit area can be expressed as

$$g = \sum_{n=1}^{\infty} K_n \, \phi(\beta_n x) \qquad \text{(a)}$$

where K_n is determined from orthogonality condition as

$$K_n = \frac{\int_0^L g\phi(\beta_n x)\, dx}{\int_0^L \phi^2 (\beta_n x)\, dx} \qquad \text{(b)}$$

In the above expression, $\phi(\beta_n x)$ is taken from Table 4.14 depending upon the support condition. The expression for K_n for the various support conditions is given in Table 4.17.

Table 4.17 Expressions for the coefficient K_n

	Support condition	K_n
(i)	Simply supported ($x = 0$ and L)	$\frac{4g}{\beta_n L}$ ($n = 1, 3, 5, \ldots$)
(ii)	Clamped-free ($x = 0, x = L$)	$\frac{2\alpha_n}{\beta_n L} g$
(iii)	Clamped-supported ($x = 0, x = L$)	$\frac{2g}{\beta_n L}\left[\frac{1 - \sinh \beta_n L \sin \beta_n L}{\sinh \beta_n L - \sin \beta_n L} + \alpha_n\right]$
(iv)	Clamped-clamped ($x = 0, x = L$)	$\frac{2g}{\beta_n L}\left[\frac{1 - \sinh \beta_n L \sin \beta_n L}{\sinh \beta_n L - \sin \beta_n L} + \alpha_n\right]$

For the case of dead load, the components of the load can be determined as

$$X = 0, \quad Y = g \sin \theta, \quad Z = g \cos \theta \qquad \text{(c)}$$

Since the load g is expressed in terms of the function $\phi(\beta_n x)$, the load components can now be written as

$$Y = \sum_{n=1}^{\infty} K_n \, \phi(\beta_n x) \sin \theta \qquad \text{(d)}$$

$$Z = \sum_{n=1}^{\infty} K_n \, \phi(\beta_n x) \cos \theta \qquad \text{(e)}$$

For these load components, the particular integral w_1 can be determined as

$$w_1 = \frac{2R^4}{EI} \sum_{n=1}^{\infty} CK_n \, \phi(\beta_n x) \cos \theta \qquad \text{(f)}$$

where

$$C = -\left[\frac{1}{1 + \dfrac{hR^6\ \beta_n^4}{I}}\right]$$

The particular integral for the above case of loading, for the various forces and displacements can be obtained as

$$N_x = \frac{2L^2}{R}\sum_{n=1}^{\infty}\left[\frac{1}{(\beta_n L)^2}(C+1)\right] K_n\,\phi''(\beta_n x)\cos\theta \tag{4.48a}$$

$$N_\theta = -R\sum_{n=1}^{\infty}(2C+1)\,K_n\cos\theta\phi(\beta_n x) \tag{4.28b}$$

$$N_{x\theta} = -2L\sum_{n=1}^{\infty}\frac{1}{\beta_n L}(C+1)\ K_n\,\phi'''(\beta_n x)\sin\theta \tag{4.48c}$$

$$M_\theta = -2R^2\sum_{n=1}^{\infty} CK_n\,\phi(\beta_n x)\cos\theta \tag{4.48d}$$

$$Q_\theta = 2R\sum_{n=1}^{\infty} CK_n\,\phi(\beta_n x)\sin\theta \tag{4.48e}$$

$$u = \frac{2}{EhR}\sum_{n=1}^{\infty}\left[\frac{1}{\beta_n^3}(C+1)\right]K_n\,\phi'(\beta_n x)\cos\theta \tag{4.48f}$$

$$v = \frac{2}{EhR^2}\sum_{n=1}^{\infty}\left[\frac{1}{\beta_n^4}(C+1)\right]K_n\,\phi(\beta_n x)\sin\theta \tag{4.48g}$$

$$w = \frac{2R^4}{EI}\sum_{n=1}^{\infty} CK_n\,\phi(\beta_n x)\cos\theta \tag{4.48h}$$

where,

$$\phi'(\beta_n x) = [(\sin\beta_n x + \sinh\beta_n x) - \alpha_n(\cosh\beta_n x - \cos\beta_n x)]$$

or

$$(\cos\beta_n x)$$

$$\phi''(\beta_n x) = [(\cosh\beta_n x + \cos\beta_n x) - \alpha_n(\sinh\beta_n x + \sin\beta_n x]$$

or

$$(-\sin\beta_n x)$$

$$\phi'''(\beta_n x) = [(\sinh\beta_n x - \sin\beta_n x) - \alpha_n(\cosh\beta_n x + \cos\beta_n x)]$$

or

$$(-\cos\beta_n x)$$

For a shell with edge beam, the forces and displacements in the edge beam in terms of shell forces can be obtained following edge beam theory discussed earlier (Section 4.4.1.4). The edge forces and displacements in terms of shell forces, following Eqn. 4.27, can be obtained as

$$M_x = \sum_{n=1}^{\infty} \frac{1}{\beta_n^2} [Q_\theta \cos\theta_0 + N_\theta \sin\theta_0 - \frac{\beta_n d}{2} N_{x\theta} - g'] \,\phi'''(\beta_n x) \tag{a}$$

$$T = \sum_{n=1}^{\infty} \frac{1}{\beta_n} N_{x\theta} \tag{b}$$

$$w_b = \frac{1}{EI_b} \sum_{n=1}^{\infty} \frac{1}{\beta_n^4} \left[Q_\theta \cos\theta_0 + N_\theta \sin\theta_0 - \frac{\beta_n d}{2} N_{x\theta} - g'\right] \phi(\beta_n x) \tag{c}$$

$$u_b = \frac{1}{E} \sum_{n=1}^{\infty} \frac{1}{\beta_n^2} \left[\frac{N_{x\theta}}{bd} - \frac{d}{2\beta_n I_b}\left\{(Q_\theta \cos\theta_0 + N_\theta \sin\theta_0 - g') - \frac{\beta_n d}{2} N_{x\theta}\right\}\right] \phi'(\beta_n x) \tag{d}$$

$$S_x = \sum_{n=1}^{\infty} \frac{1}{\beta_n} [Q_\theta \cos\theta_0 + N_\theta \sin\theta_0 - g'] \,\phi'(\beta_n x) \tag{e}$$

where

$$g' = \frac{\int_0^L g\phi(\beta_n x)\, dx}{\int_0^L \phi^2(\beta_n x)\, dx}$$

g – dead load of beam per unit length

and $I_b = bd^3/12$ (Moment of inertia of the beam)

Example 4.7

We will determine the forces in a simply supported cylindrical shell with longitudinal edges free and having the following dimensions:

Length of the shell (L) = 36 m

Radius of the shell (R) = 9 m

Thickness of the shell (h) = 0.075 m

Semicentral angle (θ_0) = 40°

We will assume that the shell will be subjected to a live load of 70 kg/m^2 in addition to its own weight. The forces have been computed by taking the first term in the series.

(i) Loads

Dead load – 0.075 × 2400	=	180 kg/m^2
Live load	=	70 kg/m^2
Total load	=	250 kg/m^2

The load components Y and Z can be determined as

$$Y = \frac{4}{\pi} \times 250 \times \sin\frac{\pi x}{L}\sin\theta = 318.31\sin\frac{\pi x}{L}\sin\theta$$

$$Z = \frac{4}{\pi} \times 250 \times \sin\frac{\pi x}{L}\cos\theta = 318.31\sin\frac{\pi x}{L}\cos\theta$$

(ii) Shell Parameters

$$\gamma = \sqrt[8]{3}\sqrt{\left(\frac{\pi R}{L}\right)}\sqrt[4]{\frac{R}{h}} = 3.365$$

$$j = 1.098684,\ k = 0.45508$$

(iii) Shell Edge Conditions and Determinations of Constants: The boundary conditions to be specified for a shell with the longitudinal edges free have already been discussed earlier. In this case, the boundary conditions can be written as

$$\theta = \theta_0 = 40°,\ N_\theta = N_{x\theta} = M_\theta = Q_\theta = 0$$

(It must be noted that in Schorer's theory, $M_{x\theta}$ is taken as zero and hence instead of specifying $Q'_\theta = 0$, it is specified here that $Q_\theta = 0$).

Using the above boundary conditions, the following four equations can be written down:

$$-\frac{2EI\gamma^4}{R^3}\sin\frac{\pi x}{L}[-A_1\sinh j\gamma\theta_0\sin k\gamma\theta_0 + A_2\cosh j\gamma\theta_0\cos k\gamma\theta_0 + A_3\sinh k\gamma\theta_0\sin j\gamma\theta_0 - A_4\cosh k\gamma\theta_0\cos j\gamma\theta_0] - \frac{4gR}{\pi}(2C+1)\cos\theta_0\sin\frac{\pi x}{L} = 0 \quad \text{(i)}$$

$$-\frac{2EI\gamma^5}{R^4(\pi/L)}\cos\frac{\pi x}{L}[A_1\{-k\sinh j\gamma\theta_0\cos k\gamma\theta_0 - j\cosh j\gamma\theta_0\sin k\gamma\theta_0\} + A_2\{j\sinh j\gamma\theta_0\cos k\gamma\theta_0 - k\cosh j\gamma\theta_0\sin k\gamma\theta_0\} + A_3\{j\sinh k\gamma\theta_0\cos j\gamma\theta_0 + k\cosh k\gamma\theta_0\sin j\gamma\theta_0\} + A_4\{-k\sinh k\gamma\theta_0\cos j\gamma\theta_0 + j\cosh k\gamma\theta_0\sin j\gamma\theta_0\}] + \frac{8gL}{\pi^2}(C+1)\cos\frac{\pi x}{L}\sin\theta_0 = 0 \quad \text{(ii)}$$

$$\frac{EI\gamma^2}{R^2} \sin \frac{\pi x}{L} [A_1 \{\cosh j\gamma\theta_0 \cos k\gamma\theta_0$$
$$- \sinh j\gamma\theta_0 \sin k\gamma\theta_0\} + A_2 \{\cosh j\gamma\theta_0 \cos k\gamma\theta_0$$
$$+ \sinh j\gamma\theta_0 \sin k\gamma\theta_0\} + A_3 \{- \cosh k\gamma\theta_0 \cos j\gamma\theta_0$$
$$- \sinh k\gamma\theta_0 \sin j\gamma\theta_0\} + A_4 \{\cosh k\gamma\theta_0 \cos j\gamma\theta_0$$
$$- \sinh k\gamma\theta_0 \sin j\gamma\theta_0\}]$$
$$- \frac{8gR^2}{\pi} C \sin \frac{\pi x}{L} \cos \theta_0 = 0 \qquad \text{(iii)}$$

$$\frac{EI\gamma^3}{R^3} \sin \frac{\pi x}{L} [A_1 \{(j-k) \sinh j\gamma\theta_0 \cos k\gamma\theta_0$$
$$- (k+j) \cosh j\gamma\theta_0 \sin k\gamma\theta_0\}$$
$$+ A_2 \{ (k+j) \sinh j\gamma\theta_0 \cos k\gamma\theta_0$$
$$+ (j-k) \cosh j\gamma\theta_0 \sin k\gamma\theta_0\}$$
$$+ A_3 \{ - (k+j) \sinh k\gamma\theta_0 \cos j\gamma\theta_0$$
$$+ (j-k) \cosh k\gamma\theta_0 \sin j\gamma\theta_0\}$$
$$+ A_4 \{- (j-k) \sinh k\gamma\theta_0 \cos j\gamma\theta_0$$
$$- (k+j) \cosh k\gamma\theta_0 \sin j\gamma\theta_0\}]$$
$$+ \frac{8gR}{\pi} C \sin \frac{\pi x}{L} \sin \theta_0 = 0 \qquad \text{(iv)}$$

The above four equations will result in the following four simultaneous equations in terms of the constants A_1, A_2, A_3 and A_4

$$\begin{bmatrix} -2.02536 & 1.12375 & 0.24026 & 0.485 \\ 11.80979 & -1.23491 & 1.20792 & -2.17939 \\ 0.35832 & -1.25153 & -0.09727 & 0.28823 \\ 0.36675 & -0.45241 & -0.11748 & 0.03369 \end{bmatrix} \begin{Bmatrix} A_1 \\ A_2 \\ A_3 \\ A_4 \end{Bmatrix} = \frac{1}{EI} \begin{Bmatrix} -2194.4886 \\ -4689.1439 \\ 0.60077 \\ -0.05601 \end{Bmatrix}$$

Solving the above four simultaneous equations, the constants can be determined as

$$A_1 = -\frac{2235.4672}{EI}, \quad A_2 = -\frac{2570.7236}{EI},$$

$$A_3 = \frac{573.35034}{EI}, \quad A_4 = -\frac{8187.6352}{EI}$$

The forces can now be determined at various points using the above values for the constants, in the expressions given in Tables 4.16 and 4.17. The final values of the forces are given in Table 4.18. It may be observed that the forces obtained using Schorer theory here are very close to the one obtained by using Donnell's theory (Table 4.6) for the same dimensions and loading on the shell. Hence, it may be concluded that Schorer's theory gives reliable results for shells whose (*L/R*) ratio is equal to or greater than 3.

Table 4.18 Shell forces and moments in a simply supported cylindrical shell

θ in degress	$\frac{N_x}{\sin(\pi x/L)}$ kg/m	$\frac{N_\theta}{\sin(\pi x/L)}$ kg/m	$\frac{N_{x\theta}}{\cos(\pi x/L)}$ kg/m	$\frac{M_\theta}{\sin(\pi x/L)}$ kg.m/m	$\frac{Q_\theta}{\sin(\pi x/L)}$ kg/m
0	- 60615.46	- 4840.41	0	- 1895.77	0
10	- 55912.56	- 4320.99	- 8109.8	- 1635.22	316.97
20	- 31864.76	- 2865.59	- 14471.89	- 984.73	473.37
30	38724.9	- 965.26	- 14735.54	- 295.23	354.76
40	193803.11	0	0	0	0

Example 4.8

We will determine the shell forces and moments in a simply supported cylindrical shell having edge beams along the longitudinal edges. We will use the same shell and edge beam dimensions as used in Example 4.3. These are:

Shell dimensions :	Length (*L*)	=	36 m
	Radius (*R*)	=	9 m
	Thickness (*h*)	=	0.075 m
	Semicentral angle (θ_0)	=	40°
Edge beam dimensions:	Width (*b*)	=	0.25 m
	Depth (*d*)	=	1.5 m

Only the first term in the series is considered for computation.

(i) Loads: For shell, a uniform load (including dead load) of 250 kg/m² is taken. For beam, the dead weight has been taken as 900 kg/m.

The load components *Y* and *Z* can be determined as (same as in Example 4.7).

$$Y = 318.31 \sin\frac{\pi x}{L} \sin\theta \text{ kg/m}^2$$

$$Z = 318.31 \sin\frac{\pi x}{L} \cos\theta \text{ kg/m}^2$$

The dead weight of the beam is taken as

$$g' = \frac{4}{\pi} g = \frac{4}{\pi} \times 900 = 1145.9 \text{ kg/m}$$

(ii) Shell parameters:

$$\gamma = \sqrt[8]{3}\,\sqrt{\frac{\pi R}{L}}\,\sqrt[4]{\frac{R}{h}} = 3.365$$

$$j = 1.098684, \quad k = 0.45508$$

(iii) Shell edge conditions and determination of constants: The approximate boundary conditions for a single cylindrical shell with edge beams discussed earlier and used in Example 4.3 are used here. These are

$$\theta = \pm\,\theta_0 = \pm\,40, \quad R_H = \beta = 0, \quad u_s = u_b, \quad \Delta w_s = w_b$$

where $R_H = N_\theta \cos\theta_0 - Q_\theta \sin\theta_0$, $\Delta w_s = w\cos\theta_0 - v\sin\theta_0$

(instead of Q'_θ, Q_θ is used here in the expression for R_H as $M_{x\theta}$ is taken as zero in Schorer's theory)

The expressions for R_H, β, u and Δw_s can be obtained using Tables 4.15 and 4.16 and the particular integrals given later (Eqn. 4.48). Since the shell is simply supported and only the first term is considered in computation

$$\phi(\beta_n x) = \sin\frac{\pi x}{L} \text{ and } \beta_n = \pi/L$$

The four equations, for the force and displacements mentioned above, can be obtained as (since the boundary conditions, along the longitudinal edges, are symmetrical, the constants A_5, A_6, A_7 and A_8 would be zero)

$$R_H = 1.7875\,A_1 - 1.1516A_2 - 0.25956\,A_3 - 0.34988\,A_4 - \frac{1681}{EI}$$

$$\beta = -\,0.81945\,A_1 + 7.8366\,A_2 - 1.4462\,A_3 - 0.80154\,A_4 + \frac{12.135}{EI}$$

$$u_s = \left(0.8832\,A_1 + 0.25287\,A_2 + 0.20341\,A_3 + 0.068641\,A_4 + \frac{108.71}{EI}\right) \times 10^4$$

$$\Delta w_s = 3.27415\,A_1 + 5.08112\,A_2 - 0.99473\,A_3 + 0.73792\,A_4 - \frac{63.525}{EI}$$

The edge beam displacements can be determined using Eqs. 4.74(c) and (d) as

$$u_b = \left(-\,3.2928\,A_1 + 0.77612\,A_2 - 0.065757\,A_3 + 0.847061\,A_4 - \frac{3446.62}{EI}\right) \times 10^4$$

$$w_b = 15.4657\,A_1 - 3.93653\,A_2 + 0.12607\,A_3 - 4.1402\,A_4 + \frac{19394.81}{EI}$$

Using the boundary conditions mentioned above, the following four simultaneous equations can be obtained.

$$\begin{bmatrix} 0.81945 & 7.8366 & -1.4462 & -0.80154 \\ 1.7875 & -1.1516 & -0.25956 & -0.34988 \\ 4.176 & -0.52322 & 0.26917 & -0.77842 \\ -12.192 & 9.0176 & -1.1207 & 4.878 \end{bmatrix} \begin{Bmatrix} A_1 \\ A_2 \\ A_3 \\ A_4 \end{Bmatrix} = \frac{1}{EI} \begin{Bmatrix} -12.135 \\ 1681 \\ 3337.9 \\ -19332 \end{Bmatrix}$$

Solving the above simultaneous equations, we can determine the constants as

$$A_1 = \frac{224.22}{EI}, \quad A_2 = \frac{-\ 285.69}{EI},$$
$$A_3 = \frac{160.13}{EI}, \quad A_4 = \frac{-\ 2837.7}{EI},$$

The shell and edge beam forces can now be computed, using the above constants and expressions given in Tables 4.15 and 4.16 and Eqs. (4.48) and (4.49a,b), and are given in Table 4.19.

Table 4.19 **Shell forces and moments in a simply supported cylindrical shell with edge beam**

θ in degrees	$\frac{N_x}{\sin(\pi x/L)}$ kg/m	$\frac{N_\theta}{\sin(\pi x/L)}$ kg/m	$\frac{N_{x\theta}}{\cos(\pi x/L)}$ kg/m	$\frac{M_\theta}{\sin(\pi x/L)}$ kg.m/m	$\frac{Q_\theta}{\sin(\pi x/L)}$ kg/m
0	− 29868.8	− 3762.4	0	− 426.9	0
10	− 30391.5	− 3524.3	− 4121.7	− 308.3	145.4
20	− 29831.1	− 2802.3	− 8287.6	− 6.04	222.2
30	− 23013.2	− 1611.3	− 12014.4	317.4	161.1
40	− 4731.4	− 81.5	− 14067.9	396.2	− 97.1

Bending moment in the edge beam (M_x) = 46215.8 kg.m
Axial force in the edge beam (T) = 161,206

It may be observed that the shell forces obtained using Schorer's theory are in close agreement with the one obtained using Donnell's theory (Table 4.9) thus further proving the applicability of Schorer's theory for long shells with edge beams.

Example 4.9

We will determine the forces in an all-round clamped shell, having the same dimensions and subjected to the same loading as in the previous example.

(a) Loads

The total load acting on the shell (including dead load) is 250 kg/m^2. The load components Y and Z can be determined as

$$Y = 2g \sum_{n=1}^{\infty} \frac{1}{\beta_n L} \left(\frac{1 - \sinh \beta_n L \sin \beta_n L}{\sinh \beta_n L - \sin \beta_n L} + \alpha_n \right) \sin \theta\, \phi(\beta_n x)$$

$$Z = 2g \sum_{n=1}^{\infty} \frac{1}{\beta_n L} \left(\frac{1 - \sinh \beta_n L \sin \beta_n L}{\sinh \beta_n L - \sin \beta_n L} + \alpha_n \right) \cos \theta \, \phi(\beta_n x)$$

Taking $n = 1$, the load components can be determined as

$$Y = 207.7154 \sin \theta \, \phi(\beta_1 x)$$

$$Z = 207.7154 \cos \theta \, \phi(\beta_1 x)$$

(b) Shell Parameters

$$\gamma = \sqrt[8]{3} \sqrt{\beta_n L} \sqrt{\frac{R}{L}} \sqrt[4]{\frac{R}{h}} = 4.12893$$

$$j = 1.098684, \quad k = 0.45508$$

(c) Shell Edge Conditions and Determination of Constants

In this case, the longitudinal edges of the shell are clamped and hence the boundary condition can be written as

$$\theta = \theta_0 = 40^\circ , \quad u = v = w = \frac{\partial w}{R \, \partial \theta} = 0$$

Using the above boundary conditions, following four equations can be written down:

$$- \frac{2 I \gamma^6}{R^5 h \beta_n^3} \phi'(\beta_n x) \left[(- A_1 + A_2) \cosh j\gamma\theta_0 \cos k\gamma\theta_0 - (A_1 + A_2) \sinh j\gamma\theta_0 \sin k\gamma\theta_0 + (A_3 + A_4) \cosh k\gamma\theta_0 \cos j\gamma\theta_0 - (A_3 - A_4) \sinh k\gamma\theta_0 \sin j\gamma\theta_0 \right] + \frac{2}{EhR} \left[\frac{1}{\beta_n^3} (C + 1) \right] K_n \phi'(\beta_n x) \cos \theta_0 = 0$$

which results in the equation

$$- 14300.99 \, A_1 - 8293.665 \, A_2 - 1920.45 \, A_3 - 2006.753 \, A_4 = \frac{207855}{EI} \quad \text{(i)}$$

$$\frac{2 I \gamma^7}{R^6 h \beta_n^4} \phi(\beta_n x) [\{ A_1 (- k - j) + A_2 (- k + j) \} \sinh j\gamma\theta_0 \cos k\gamma\theta_0 - \{ A_1 (- k + j) + A_2 (k + j) \} \cosh j\gamma\theta_0 \sin k\gamma\theta_0 + \{ A_3 (k - j) + A_4 (k + j) \} \sinh k\gamma\theta_0 \cos j\gamma\theta_0 - \{ A_3 (k + j) - A_4 (k - j) \} \cosh k\gamma\theta_0 \sin j\gamma\theta_0] + \frac{2}{EhR^2} \left[\frac{1}{\beta_n^4} (C + 1) \right] K_n \phi(\beta_n x) \sin \theta_0 = 0$$

which results in the equation

$$41715.75\ A_1 + 54782.98\ A_2 - \ 4086.489\ A_3\ +\ 9099.917\ A_4\ = \frac{147492.2}{EI} \quad \text{(ii)}$$

$$\begin{aligned}&\phi(\beta_n x)\,[A_1 \cosh j\gamma\theta_0 \cos k\gamma\theta_0 + A_2 \sinh j\gamma\theta_0 \sin k\gamma\theta_0\\&\quad + A_3 \cosh k\gamma\theta_0 \cos j\gamma\theta_0 + A_4 \sinh k\gamma\theta_0 \sin j\gamma\theta_0\,]\\&\quad + \frac{2R^4}{EI}\ CK_n\phi(\beta_n\, x)\cos\theta_0 \ = \ 0\end{aligned}$$

which results in the equation

$$3.04477\ A_1 + 11.45194\ A_2 - \ 1.990475\ A_3\ -\ 0.0437423\ A_4\ = \frac{6.179566}{EI} \quad \text{(iii)}$$

$$\begin{aligned}&\frac{\gamma}{R}\,\phi\,(\beta_n\, x)\,[\,(A_1 j + A_2 k)\ \sinh j\gamma\theta_0 \cos k\gamma\theta_0\\&\quad - (A_1 k - A_2 j)\cosh j\gamma\theta_0 \sin\ k\gamma\theta_0\\&\quad + (A_3 k + A_4 j)\sinh k\gamma\theta_0 \cos j\gamma\theta_0\\&\quad - (A_3 j - A_4 k)\cosh k\gamma\theta_0 \sin j\gamma\theta_0\,]\\&\quad - \frac{2R^3}{EI}\ CK_n\phi\,(\beta_n x)\sin\theta_0\ = \ 0\end{aligned}$$

which results in the equation

$$\begin{aligned}&-\ 0.8702004\ A_1\ + 6.426248\ A_2 - \ 0.3338648\ A_3\ -\ 0.8781371\ A_4\\&= \frac{-\ 0.5761413}{EI}\end{aligned} \quad \text{(iv)}$$

Solving Eqs. (i)–(iv), we get

$$A_1\ = \frac{-\ 39.61038}{EI}, \qquad A_2\ = \frac{11.99367}{EI},$$

$$A_3\ = \frac{2.52393}{EI}, \qquad A_4\ = \frac{126.71914}{EI},$$

Using the above values of the constants A_1, A_2, A_3 and A_4, the shell forces can be determined by making use of Tables 4.16 and 4.17 and these are given in Table 4.20.

Table 4.20 Shell forces and moments in an all-round clamped cylindrical shell at midspan ($x = L/2$)

θ in degrees	N_x kg/m	N_θ kg/m	M_θ kg.m/m	Q_θ kg/m
0	– 1113.23	– 2823.64	32.44	0
10	– 860.86	– 2839.01	13.89	– 21.86
20	– 353.68	– 2896.56	– 24.93	– 22.0
30	– 41.14	– 3018.18	– 31.09	24.06
40	0	– 3214.26	88.91	142.94

Example 4.10

As a general application of the Schorer's theory, we will determine the forces and moments in a simply supported butterfly shell having one of the longitudinal edge free and the other connected to an edge beam as shown in Fig. 4.14. The shell and edge beam dimensions are:

Shell:

Radius (R) = 9 m,

Length (L) = 36 m,

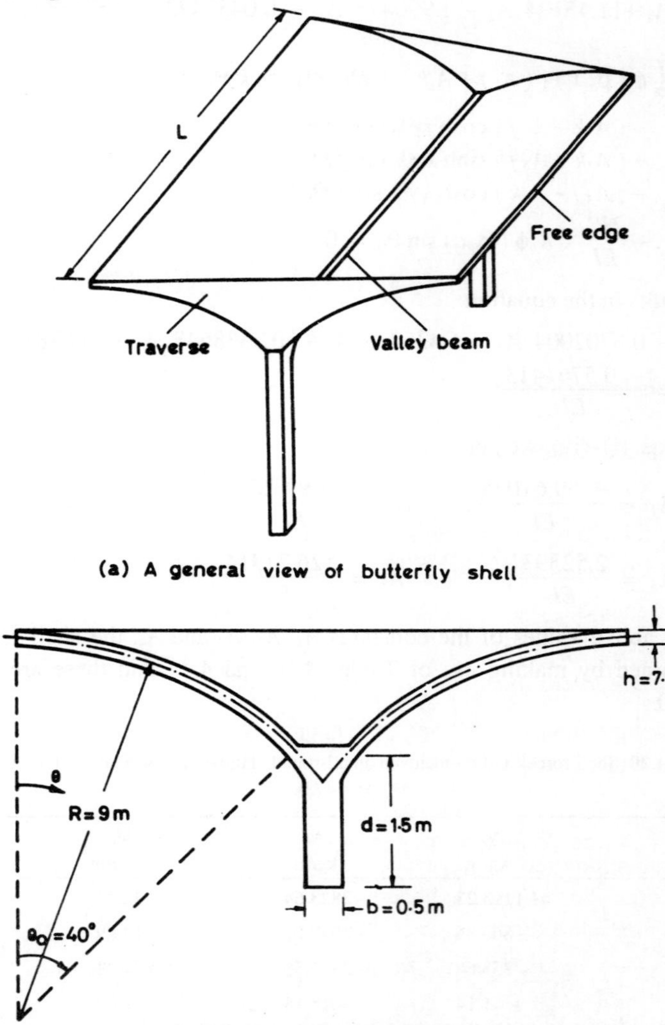

(a) A general view of butterfly shell

(b) Cross section

Fig. 4.14

Thickness (h) = 0.075 m

Angle subtended at the centre = 40°

Beam:

Width = 0.5 m

Depth = 1.5 m

The forces have been computed by taking only the first term in the series.

Loads:

The load on the shell (including the dead load) is taken as 250 kg/m^2.

The self weight of edge beam is taken as 1800 kg/m.

The load components Y and Z can be computed as

$$Y = 318.31 \sin \frac{\pi x}{L} \sin \theta$$

$$Z = 318.31 \sin \frac{\pi x}{L} \cos \theta$$

The dead weight of the beam g' can be computed as

$$g' = \frac{4}{\pi} \times 1800 = 2291.83$$

Shell parameters:

$$\gamma = \sqrt[8]{3} \sqrt{\frac{\pi R}{L}} \sqrt[4]{\frac{R}{h}} = 3.365$$

$$j = 1.098684, \; k = 0.4550899$$

Shell edge conditions and determination of constants:

Since the longitudinal edge at the crown (Fig. 4.14) is free, the following boundary conditions have to be satisfied along this edge.

$$\theta = 0, \; N_\theta = N_{x\theta} = M_\theta = Q_\theta = 0$$

The other longitudinal edge beam is connected to common edge beam and the boundary conditions along this edge is taken similar to that of inner shell with edge beam of a multiple cylindrical shell (Sec. 4.4.1.3). These conditions can be written as

$$\theta = \theta_0 = 40^\circ, \; \Delta H = \beta = 0, \; \Delta w_s = w_b, \; u_s = u_b$$

where $\Delta H = w \sin \theta_0 + v \cos \theta_0$

While calculating the displacements of the edge beam, namely w_b and u_b, only half the width and dead weight of beam has to be considered ($b = 0.25$ m, $g' = 1145.92$ kg/m in the present example).

Using Tables 4.16 and 4.17 and the particular integral given in Eqs. (4.48), the equations for the shell forces and displacements used in the above boundary conditions can be obtained as:

Along $\theta = 0$,

$$N_\theta = -\ 0.35174\,A_2 + 0.35174\,A_4 - \frac{2864.7}{EI}$$

$$N_{x\theta} = -\ 0.68582\,A_5 + 1.6557\,A_6 + 1.6557\,A_7 - 0.68582\,A_8$$

$$M_\theta = 0.13979\,A_1 + 0.13979\,A_2 - 0.13979\,A_3 + 0.13979\,A_4 + \frac{0.78425}{EI}$$

$$Q_\theta = 0.033638\,A_5 + 0.081209\,A_6 - 0.081209\,A_7 - 0.033638\,A_8$$

Along $\theta = 40°$:

$$\begin{aligned}\Delta H = {} & 1.0683\,A_1 + 2.9025\,A_2 - 0.95965\,A_3 + 0.1832\,A_4 \\ & + 1.0433\,A_5 + 2.9596\,A_6 - 0.7192\,A_7 + 0.26248\,A_8\end{aligned}$$

$$\begin{aligned}\beta = {} & 0.81945\,A_1 + 7.8366\,A_2 - 1.4462\,A_3 - 0.8015\,A_4 + 0.88965\,A_5 \\ & + 7.7802\,A_6 - 1.378\,A_7 - 1.2041\,A_8 + \frac{12.135}{EI}\end{aligned}$$

$$\begin{aligned}\Delta w_s = {} & 3.27415\,A_1 + 5.08112\,A_2 - 0.99473\,A_3 + 0.73792\,A_4 \\ & + 3.24758\,A_5 + 5.11993\,A_6 - 0.816913\,A_7 + 0.90968\,A_8 \\ & - \frac{63.525}{EI}\end{aligned}$$

$$\begin{aligned}u_s = \Big(& 0.8832\,A_1 + 0.25287\,A_2 + 0.20341\,A_3 + 0.068641\,A_4 \\ & + 0.88616\,A_5 + 0.2630\,A_6 + 0.19273\,A_7 + 0.021949\,A_8 \\ & + \frac{108.71}{EI}\Big) \times 10^4\end{aligned}$$

The equations corresponding to edge beam displacements can be obtained, using Eqs. 4.74c and d, as

$$\begin{aligned}u_b = \Big(& -\ 3.2928\,A_1 + 0.776122\,A_2 - 0.065757\,A_3 + 0.84706\,A_4 \\ & - 3.31316\,A_5 + 0.776847\,A_6 - 0.105979\,A_7 + 0.696889\,A_8 \\ & - \frac{3446.153}{EI}\Big) \times 10^4\end{aligned}$$

$$w_b = 15.4657\,A_1 - 3.93653\,A_2 + 0.12607\,A_3 - 4.14012\,A_4 + 15.5905\,A_5 - 3.92042\,A_6 + 0.22787\,A_7 - 3.352819\,A_8 + \frac{19394.82}{EI}$$

Using the boundary conditions, the eight simultaneous equations are obtained (page 208), solving which the constants $A_1, A_2, ..., A_8$ can be determined. The shell and edge beam forces can then be computed and these are given in Table 4.21.

Table 4.21 Shell forces in a butterfly shell

θ in degrees	$\frac{N_x}{\sin(\pi x/L)}$ kg/m	$\frac{N_\theta}{\sin(\pi x/L)}$ kg/m	$\frac{N_{x\theta}}{\cos(\pi x/L)}$ kg/m	$\frac{M_\theta}{\sin(\pi x/L)}$ kg.m/m	$\frac{Q_\theta}{\sin(\pi x/L)}$ kg/m
0	174316	0	0	0	0
10	- 26565	- 914.6	8145.75	- 346.63	- 434.36
20	- 86311.7	- 1636.5	- 840.7	- 1257.1	- 676.89
30	- 65130	- 944	- 11840.6	- 2471.3	- 883.2
40	- 8837.4	844	- 17133.7	- 4130.8	- 1274

Edge beam moment (M_x) – 60123.66 kg.m
Axial force in edge beam (T) – 196337.46 kg.

4.8 DESIGN OF REINFORCEMENTS

We will very briefly describe the principle of designing the reinforcements for a cylindrical shell with or without edge-beam. The principle of designing the reinforcements in the shell and edge-beam follows the well established procedures used in the design of reinforced concrete members. Though in the shell we have eight forces, as mentioned earlier, only the four predominant forces, namely N_x, N_θ, $N_{x\theta}$ and M_θ need be considered for the design of reinforcement in the shell. The reinforcement in the edge-beam is designed to resist the longitudinal stress, direct and bending, and the vertical shear S.

The shell reinforcement can be further divided into three groups, namely (a) longitudinal reinforcement to resist the force N_x, (b) transverse reinforcement to resist the forces N_θ and M_θ, (c) diagonal reinforcement to resist the combined effect of the forces N_x, N_θ and $N_{x\theta}$. The design of longitudinal and transverse reinforcement is simple and straightforward. The diagonal reinforcement is to be designed to resist principal tension caused by the combination of N_x, N_θ and $N_{x\theta}$. The principal forces can be calculated from

$$N_{1,2} = \left\{\frac{N_x + N_\theta}{2}\right\} \pm \sqrt{\frac{(N_x - N_\theta)^2}{2} + N_{x\theta}^2}$$

Matrix of eight simultaneous equations

$$\begin{bmatrix} 0 & -0.35714 & 0 & 0.35714 & 0 & 0 & 0 & 0 \\ 0 & 0 & 0 & 0 & -0.68582 & 1.6557 & 1.6557 & -0.6858 \\ 0.13979 & 0.13979 & -0.13979 & 0.13979 & 0 & 0 & 0 & 0 \\ 0 & 0 & 0 & 0 & 0.033638 & -0.081209 & -0.081209 & -0.033638 \\ -12.192 & 9.0176 & -1.1207 & 4.878 & -12.343 & 9.0404 & -1.0448 & 4.2624 \\ 0.4176 & -0.052322 & 0.026917 & -0.077842 & 0.41993 & -0.05138 & 0.02987 & -0.067494 \\ 1.0683 & 2.9025 & -0.95969 & 0.1832 & 1.0433 & 2.9596 & -0.7192 & 0.26248 \\ 0.81945 & 7.8366 & -1.4462 & -0.80154 & 0.88965 & 7.7802 & -1.378 & -1.2041 \end{bmatrix} \begin{Bmatrix} A_1 \\ A_2 \\ A_3 \\ A_4 \\ A_5 \\ A_6 \\ A_7 \\ A_8 \end{Bmatrix} = \frac{1}{EI} \begin{Bmatrix} 0.28647 \times 10^4 \\ 0 \\ -0.78425 \\ 0 \\ -0.19332 \times 10^5 \\ 0.33379 \times 10^3 \\ 0 \\ -12.135 \end{Bmatrix}$$

Solving the above simultaneous equations the constants can be determined as

$$A_1 = \frac{-0.30237 \times 10^5}{EI} \qquad A_5 = \frac{0.31007 \times 10^5}{EI}$$

$$A_2 = \frac{0.30356 \times 10^4}{EI} \qquad A_6 = \frac{-0.47424 \times 10^4}{EI}$$

$$A_3 = \frac{-0.16016 \times 10^5}{EI} \qquad A_7 = \frac{0.12844 \times 10^5}{EI}$$

$$A_4 = \frac{0.1118 \times 10^5}{EI} \qquad A_8 = \frac{-0.11449 \times 10^5}{EI}$$

The direction of principal forces can be determined from

$$\tan 2\theta = \frac{2N_{x\theta}}{N_x - N_\theta}$$

For a simply supported cylindrical shell at the support, both N_x and N_θ would be zero and only $N_{x\theta}$ will be existing. Hence the principal forces, at the support, will be equal to $\pm N_{x\theta}$ and the direction of this principal force will be 45°. Since one of the principal forces is tensile and acts at an angle of 45°, this force is often referred as diagonal tension. The reinforcement to resist this tension can be determined directly by dividing the force by the safe stress in steel. We will illustrate the procedure of designing reinforcement through an example discussed earlier, for which the forces are given in Table 4.9.

The reinforcement detailing is normally outlined in relevant standards for shell structures[4.30]. According to the Indian Standards Specification, the maximum spacing of reinforcement in any direction of the body of the shell is limited to five times the thickness of the shell. The area of unreinforced panel, according to this standard, should be limited to 15 times the square of the thickness. Wherever nominal steel is adequate it should be limited to 0.15 percent of the cross-sectional area.

Example 4.11

We will briefly illustrate the design of reinforcement for the example of a cylindrical shell with an edge-beam, the result of which for particular dimensions and loading are given in Table 4.9.

(a) Shell Reinforcement

(i) Longitudinal reinforcement: Since the N_x force is compressive throughout, no reinforcement is required in the longitudinal direction. However, a nominal reinforcement of 8 mm diameter bars at 20 cm c/c in the longitudinal direction may be provided.

(ii) Transverse reinforcement: First let us consider the force N_θ. This being compressive throughout, no reinforcement is required.

The maximum value of positive bending moment M_θ is 404.85 kg.m/m. Assuming a cover of 2.5 cm, the effective depth = 5 cm. Hence, area of steel required will be

$$A_{st} = \frac{404.85 \times 100}{1400 \times 0.87 \times 5} = 6.65 \text{ cm}^2/\text{m}$$

(Assuming safe stress in steel = 1400 kg/cm^2)

Hence, provide 10 mm bars at 10 cm c/c at the bottom. Since the maximum value of negative bending moment is close to 400 kg.m/m, the same reinforcement as determined above could be provided at the top. Hence, to take care of both

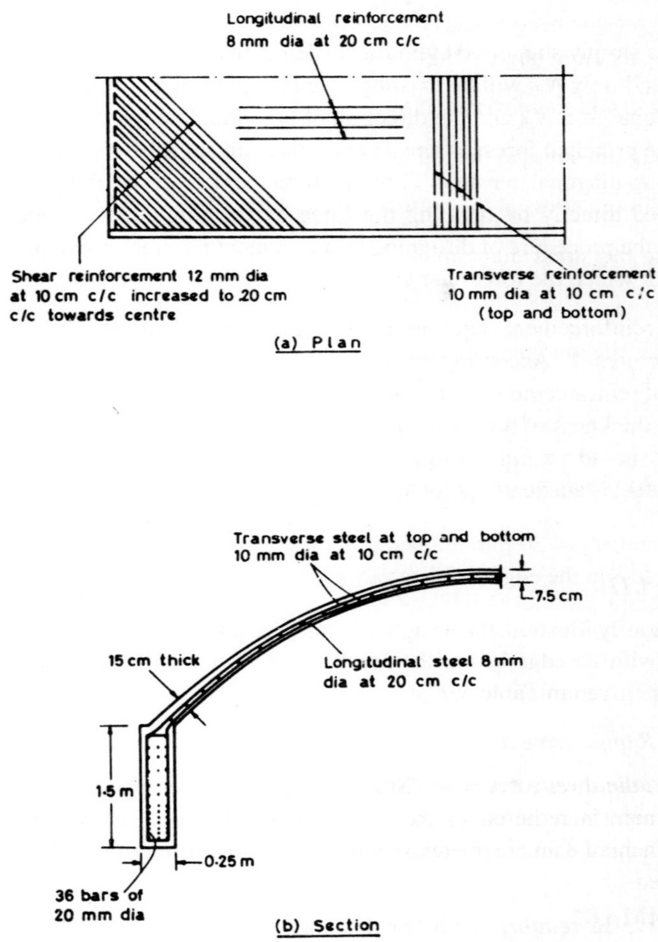

Fig. 4.15 Plan and section of a cylindrical shell with Edge-beam showing reinforcement

positive and negative moments, provide two layers (one at the top and the other at the bottom) of steel of 10 mm diameter at 10 cm c/c.

(iii) Diagonal reinforcement: At the support, as is indicated earlier, the principal tension will be equal to the magnitude of $N_{x\theta}$. The maximum value of $N_{x\theta}$ at the support is 14035 kg/m.

$$A_{st} = \frac{14035}{1400} = 10.03 \text{ cm}^2/\text{m}$$

Provide 12 mm diameter bars at a spacing of 10 cm c/c. The principal tension at quarter span and $\theta = 40°$ will be 7843 kg/m. Hence in this region, 12 mm diameter bars at a spacing of 20 cm c/c may be provided. After quarter span, the principal tension becomes very small and hence, theoretically no diagonal reinforcement is required beyond this region.

(b) Edge-Beam Reinforcement

Maximum stress at the top of edge-beam = – 61201.5 kg/m^2

Maximum stress at the bottom of edge-beam = 918990.8 kg/m^2

From the stress diagram we can determine the depth of the tensile zone as 1.407 m.

$$\text{Hence the total tensile force} = \frac{918990}{2} \times 1.41 \times 0.25$$

$$= 161971.98 \text{ kg}$$

$$\text{Area of steel} = \frac{161971.98}{1400} = 115.7 \text{ cm}^2$$

Provide 36 bars of 20 mm diameter in three vertical rows in the edge-beam. The shear force S in the edge-beam is calculated from

$$S = \frac{L}{\pi} \left(Q_\theta \cos \theta_0 + N_\theta \sin \theta_0 - g \right)$$

which for this example works out as

$$S = 14536 \text{ kg}$$

Since the shear force is very small, a nominal two legged 8 mm diameter shear reinforcement may be provided at 40 cm c/c. The reinforcement details for the shell and edge-beam are shown in Figs. 4.15(a) and (b).

4.9 SUMMARY

In this chapter, first the basic equations for the bending of an open cylindrical shell has been presented. Exact differential equations in terms of the three displacements as given by Flugge have been presented later. Approximate differential equations in terms of displacements have been obtained by making certain approximations in the force-displacement relations as well as in the differential equations. The three approximate differential equations have been reduced to a single differential equation of eighth order in terms of displacement w. A Levy type of solution satisfying the simply supported condition along the curved edge has been presented. It is emphasized that in the case of long cylindrical shells, edge-beams become necessary. Hence, necessary equations have been developed to analyse cylindrical shells with edge-beams. It is shown through examples that short shells may be approximately analysed using membrane theory, while long shells may be analysed using simple beam theory. It is also shown that bending analysis of long cylindrical shells can be made using Schorer theory. It is also demonstrated that by using Schorer theory for long shells, it is possible to obtain a Levy type of solution for support conditions other than simple support along the curved edges. Finally, a brief description for designing and detailing the reinforcement for a cylindrical shell with edge-beams is presented.

REFERENCES

4.1 Flugge, W., *Stresses in Shells*, Second edition, Springer Verlag, 1973.

4.2 Gibson, J.E., *The Design of Shell Roofs,* E. and F.N. Spon Ltd., London, 1968.

4.3 Donnell, L.H., *Stability of Thin Walled Tubes under Torsion*, NACA Rep. No. 479, Washington, D.C., 1933.

4.4 Von Karman, T., and H.S. Tsien, 'The buckling of thin cylindrical shells under axial compression', *Jl. of Aeronautical Sciences,* Vol. 8, 1941, pp. 305–312.

4.5 Jenkins, R.S., *Theory and Design of Cylindrical Shell Structures*, The O.N. Arup group of consulting engineers, Bulletin No. 1. 1947.

4.6 Timoshenko, S., and W. Krieger, *Theory of Plates and Shells*, Second edition, McGraw-Hill, 1959.

4.7 Timoshenko, S. '*Strength of materials*', Part - 1, Affiliated East West Press Pvt. Ltd., New Delhi, 1965.

4.8 Dischinger, F., Die Strenge Theorie der Kreiszylinder-schale in Ihrer Anwendung auf die Zeiss-Dywidag-Schalen, *Beton u Eisen*, Vol. 34, 1935, pp. 257–264 and pp. 283–294.

4.9 Aas-Jakobsen, A., Uber das Randstorungs Problem an Krieszylinder Schalen, *Bauingenieur*, Vol. 20, 1939, pp. 395–405.

4.10 Holand, I., *Design of Circular Cylindrical Shells*, Oslo University Press, Oslo, 1957.

4.11 Vlassov, V.S., *Basic Differential Equations in General Theory of Elastic Shells* (Translated from Russian) NACA Tech. Mem. 1241, 1951.

4.12 Lundgren, H., *Cylindrical Shells*, The Danish Technical Press, Copenhagen, 1949.

4.13 'Design of Cylindrical Concrete Shell Roofs' *ASCE Manual of Engineering Practice*, No. 31, New York, 1952.

4.14 Finsterwalder, W., Die theorie der zylindrischen Schalen gewolbe system Zeiss-Dywideg und ihre anwendung auf die Grossmarkthalle in

Budapest, *Int. Association of Bridge and Structural Engineering, Vol.* 1, 1932, pp. 127–132.

4.15 Schorer, H., 'Line load action on thin cylindrical shells', *Trans., ASCE,* Vol. 61, 1935, pp. 281–316.

4.16 McNamee, J.J., 'Existing methods for the analysis of concrete shell roofs', Proc. of the Symposium on Concrete Shell Roof Construction held in July 1952, Cement and Concrete Association, London, 1954, pp. 45–78.

4.17 Moe, J., 'On the theory of cylindrical shells', Publications of Int. Association of Bridge and Structural Engineering, Vol. 13, 1953, pp. 283–296.

4.18 Sen, B., 'On a few existing methods for design of cylindrical shell roofs', Proc. of Seminar on Shell Structures, Bengal Engineering College Shibpur Jan. 1962-Indian Industries, Oxford Book and Stationary Co., Calcutta, Vol. 5, No. 3, paper No. 12.

4.19 Jensen, O., 'Methods for analysis of concrete shell roofs', Proc. of the Second Symposium on Concrete Shell Roof Construction, Oslo, 1957, p. 111.

4.20 Arya, A.S., 'Elastic theories of cylindrical shells', Proc. of the Seminar on Shell Structures, Bengal Engineering College, Shibput, Jan. 1962-Indian Industries, Oxford Book and Stationary Co., Calcutta, Vol. 5, No. 3, Paper No. 3.

4.21 Hoff, N.J., 'The accuracy of Donnell's equations', *Jl. of Appl. Mech., Trans.* ASME, Vol. 22, 1955, pp. 329–334.

4.22 Raphel Foner Rish, 'The analysis of cylindrical shell roofs with post tensioned edge beams', *Int. Jl. of Solids and Structures,* Vol. 10, 1974, pp. 1035–1052.

4.23 Pickett, G. and B. Gopalacharyulu, 'Clamped cylindrical shell panel (By energy method)', Proc. of the Seminar on Shell Structures, Bengal Engineering College, Shibpur, Jan. 1962-Indian Industries, Oxford Book and Stationary Co., Calcutta, Vol. 5, No. 3, Paper No. 8.

4.24 Pickett, G., and B. Gopalacharyulu, 'Clamped cylindrical shell panel (By Fourier method)', Proc. of the Seminar on Shell Structures, Bengal Engineering Collage, Shibpur, Jan. 1962-Indian Industries, Oxford Book and Stationary Co., Calcutta, Vol. 5, No. 3, Paper No. 7.

4.25 Chandrashekhara, K., and S. Chandrashekara, 'Analysis of clamped circular cylindrical shell panels', *Acta Technica,* Tomus 74(3–4), 1973, pp. 337–363.

4.26 Chandrashekhara, K., and S. Chandrashekara, 'Analysis of clamped circular cylindrical shells using basic functions', *Bull. IASS*, No. 49, June 1972, pp. 43–57.

4.27 Chuang, K.P., and A.S. Veletsos, 'A Study of two approximate methods of analysing cylindrical shell roofs', Civil Engineering Studies, Structural Research Series, No. 258, University of Illinois, Oct. 1962.

4.28 Tottenham, H., and J.R. Desai, 'Approximate Solutions in the Shell Theory of Arch Dams', Int. Symposium on Theory of Arch dams, Southampton University, Pergamon Press, pp. 193–237.

4.29 Morice, P.B., 'An approximate solution for the problem of longitudinally continuous shell', *Magazine of Concrete Research,* Vol. 9, 1957, pp. 95–104.

4.30 'Code of Practice for Construction of Reinforced Concrete Shell Roofs' - IS: 2204-1962, Indian Standard Institution, 1972.

Chapter Five

Bending Analysis of Symmetrically Loaded Shells of Revolution

5.1 INTRODUCTION

In the membrane analysis of symmetrically loaded shells of revolution, it was shown that the membrane analysis of these shells is normally inadequate, as in most of the cases bending of shell cannot be avoided. This happens because the boundary conditions, derived from the type of support provided for these shells, cannot be completely satisfied by the membrane solution. Further, the bending of shell occurs in the region of discontinuous loads, sudden change in thickness or of curvature of the shell. These regions are often referred as lines of distortion and it can be shown that in the case of symmetrically loaded shells of revolution, the bending will be confined to a very small zone near the lines of distortion. From this point of view, the bending analysis of symmetrically loaded shells of revolution can be made much simpler compared to that of the bending analysis of an arbitrary shell surface.

The analysis of shells of revolution can be done in two parts. The first part concerns determining the membrane forces and displacements due to external load using the membrane theory. This part of the analysis will be referred as primary analysis and has been discussed in detail in Chapter 2. The second part concerns with the corrective analysis, in which suitable edge forces or displacements are applied along the edges of the shell, taking into account the edge forces and displacements derived from the membrane analysis, so as to satisfy the required boundary conditions. This part of the analysis will be referred as secondary analysis and will be discussed here in detail. The superposition of the secondary solution over the primary gives the complete solution for a given problem.

5.2 GENERAL THEORY OF A SYMMETRICALLY LOADED SHELLS OF REVOLUTION

It is assumed that the deformation caused by the symmetrical loading of the shell is such that both bending and membrane stretching occurs simultaneously and both these actions must be considered. The general procedure adopted is to first obtain the equilibrium equations by considering an element of the shell and if the equilibrium equations are not sufficient, next the deformation of the shell has to be considered. Figure 5.1 shows the element of a shell with the internal forces. As mentioned earlier, no external loads will be considered here as the basic equations and solution for a symmetrically loaded shell of revolution subjected to either edge forces or displacements will be developed here. It should be noted that because of rotational symmetry, the membrane shear force $N_{\theta\phi}$, transverse shear force Q_θ, the twisting moment $M_{\theta\phi}$ and the displacement u in a direction tangent to the circle of latitude would be zero. For the same reason the bending moment M_θ and the membrane force N_θ will be constant. Considering the internal forces shown in Fig. 5.1, a set of equilibrium equations can now be derived.

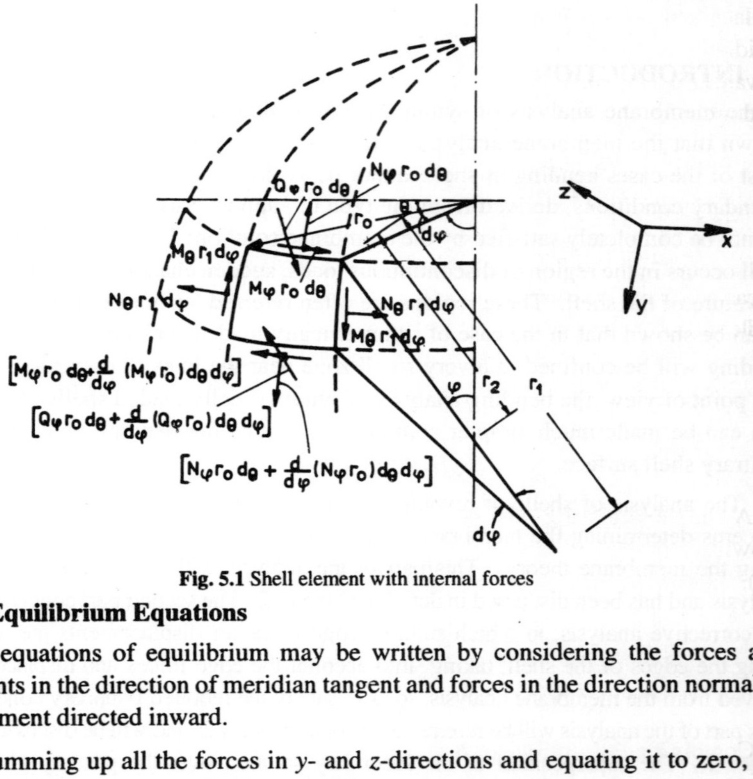

Fig. 5.1 Shell element with internal forces

5.2.1 Equilibrium Equations

Three equations of equilibrium may be written by considering the forces and moments in the direction of meridian tangent and forces in the direction normal to the element directed inward.

Summing up all the forces in y- and z-directions and equating it to zero, we get the following two equilibrium equations.

$$\frac{d}{d\phi}(N_\phi r_o) - N_\theta r_1 \cos\phi + Q_\phi r_o = 0 \tag{5.1a}$$

$$N_\phi r_o + N_\theta r_1 \sin\phi - \frac{d}{d\phi}(Q_\phi r_o) = 0 \tag{5.1b}$$

It may be seen that the above two equations are substantially the same as Eqs. (2.38a) and (2.38b) obtained from the membrane theory but they do contain in addition, the contribution due to radial shear force Q_ϕ. Considering the moment equilibrium in the y-direction, we get

$$\frac{d}{d\phi}(M_\phi r_o) - M_\theta r_1 \cos\phi + Q_\phi r_o r_1 = 0 \tag{5.1c}$$

Now we have three equilibrium equations involving five unknown forces and it is not possible to determine all the five forces uniquely from these three equations. Hence additional relationships have to be established by considering the deformation of the shell.

5.2.2 Strain-Displacement Relationship

For a symmetrically loaded shell of revolution, we need to consider only two displacement components, namely v-the displacement component along the meridian direction and w-the displacement component along the normal directed outward. First the strain-displacement relation in terms of middle plane displacements v and w can be obtained. These have already been given in Eq. (2.39a and 2.39b).

$$\varepsilon_\phi = \frac{dv}{r_1\, d\phi} + \frac{w}{r_1} \tag{5.2a}$$

$$\varepsilon_\theta = \frac{v}{r_2}\cot\phi + \frac{w}{r_2} \tag{5.2b}$$

We can next write the strain-displacement relation at any point A at a distance z from the middle surface, by replacing v and w by v_A and w_A and r_1 and r_2 by $r_1 + z$ and $r_2 + z$, as

$$\varepsilon_\phi = \frac{dv_A}{(r_1 + z)\, d\phi} + \frac{w_A}{r_1 + z} \tag{5.3a}$$

$$\varepsilon_\theta = \frac{v_A}{r_2 + z}\cot\phi + \frac{w_A}{r_2 + z} \tag{5.3b}$$

A simple kinematic relation can be established between v and w, v_A and w_A, following a procedure identical to the one discussed for a cylindrical shell (Fig. 4.4a). Following this, it can be shown that

$$v_A = \left(\frac{r_1 + z}{r_1}\right) v - \frac{z}{r_1}\frac{dw}{d\phi} \tag{5.4a}$$

$$w = w_A \tag{5.4b}$$

Combining Eqs. (5.3) and (5.4), we can get the following strain-displacement relation at point A at a distance z from the middle surface in terms of mid-plane displacements v and w:

$$\varepsilon_\phi = \frac{dv}{r_1\, d\phi} - \frac{z}{r_1(r_1 + z)}\frac{d^2w}{d\phi^2} + \frac{w}{r_1 + z} \tag{5.5a}$$

$$\varepsilon_\theta = \frac{(r_1 + z)}{r_1(r_2 + z)} v\cot\phi - \frac{z}{r_1(r_2 + z)}\frac{dw}{d\phi}\cot\phi + \frac{w}{r_2 + z} \tag{5.5b}$$

5.2.3 Stress-Strain Relation

If σ_ϕ and σ_θ are the normal stresses, then using Hooke's law, the following stress-strain relationship can be written

$$\sigma_\phi = \frac{E}{1 - \nu^2} (\varepsilon_\phi + \nu \, \varepsilon_\theta) \tag{5.6a}$$

$$\sigma_\theta = \frac{E}{1 - \nu^2} (\varepsilon_\theta + \nu \, \varepsilon_\phi) \tag{5.6b}$$

The expressions for the stress resultants in terms of the stresses can be written using the general relation given in Chapter 1. For a shell of revolution, the following changes are to be made in this direction:

x should be changed to θ and y to ϕ

$R_1 = r_2, R_2 = r_1$

We thus obtain the following expressions for the stress resultants:

$$N_\phi = \int_{-h/2}^{+h/2} \sigma_\phi \left(1 + \frac{z}{r_2}\right) dz \tag{5.7a}$$

$$N_\theta = \int_{-h/2}^{+h/2} \sigma_\theta \left(1 + \frac{z}{r_1}\right) dz \tag{5.7b}$$

$$M_\phi = -\int_{-h/2}^{+h/2} \sigma_\phi \left(1 + \frac{z}{r_2}\right) z \, dz \tag{5.7c}$$

$$M_\theta = -\int_{-h/2}^{+h/2} \sigma_\theta \left(1 + \frac{z}{r_1}\right) z \, dz \tag{5.7d}$$

5.2.4 Force-Displacement Relation

Substituting for strains in Eqs. (5.6), the strain-displacement relation given in Eq. (5.5), we get the stress-displacement relations. These stress-displacement relations are then substituted in Eq. (5.7) and after integration, we get the following force-displacement relations:

$$N_\phi = K \left[\frac{dv}{r_1 \, d\phi} + \frac{w}{r_1} + \frac{\nu}{r_2} (v \cot \phi + w) \right] + D \left[\frac{r_2 - r_1}{r_1^3 \, r_2} \left(\frac{d^2 w}{d\phi^2} + w \right) \right] \tag{5.8a}$$

$$N_\theta = K \left[\frac{1}{r_2} \{ v \cot \phi + w \} + \frac{\nu}{r_1} \left\{ \frac{dv}{d\phi} + w \right\} \right] + \frac{D}{r_1 \, r_2} \left(\frac{r_2 - r_1}{r^2} \right) \left[\frac{v}{r_1} \left(\frac{r_2 - r_1}{r_2} \right) \cot \phi - \frac{dw}{r_1 \, d\phi} \cot \phi - \frac{w}{r_2} \right] \tag{5.8b}$$

$$M_\phi = -\frac{D}{r_1}\left[\left\{-\frac{d^2w}{r_1\,d\phi^2} + \frac{1}{r_1}\frac{dv}{d\phi} + \frac{r_2 - r_1}{r_1 r_2}\left(-w - \frac{dv}{d\phi}\right)\right\}\right.$$

$$\left. + \frac{\nu}{r_2}\cot\phi\left(v - \frac{dw}{d\phi}\right)\right] \tag{5.8c}$$

$$M_\theta = -\frac{D}{r_1}\left[\left\{\left(-\frac{dw}{d\phi} + v\right)\frac{\cot\phi}{r_2} + \frac{v\cot\phi + w}{r_2}\left(\frac{r_2 - r_1}{r_2}\right)\right\}\right.$$

$$\left. + \frac{\nu}{r_1}\left(-\frac{d^2w}{d\phi^2} + \frac{dv}{d\phi}\right)\right] \tag{5.8d}$$

Now we have three equilibrium equations (Eqs. (5.1a–c)) and four force-displacement relations (Eqs. 5.8(a)–(d)) making altogether seven equations involving seven unknowns, viz. five forces N_ϕ, N_θ, M_ϕ, M_θ, Q_ϕ and two displacements v and w. Hence, we have as many number of equations as the unknowns and the problem can be solved using these equations.

5.2.5 Spherical Shell

5.2.5.1 Differential equation

We will now develop the bending theory for a spherical shell of constant thickness and subjected to edge loading only. The basic equations for a spherical shell can be obtained from the general equations derived earlier by using the following identity.

$$r_1 = r_2 = a, \quad r_o = a \sin\phi$$

where a is radius of the middle surface.

Hence, the equilibrium equations for a spherical shell can now be written down following Eqs. (5.1a–c), as

$$\frac{d}{d\phi}(N_\phi \sin\phi) - N_\theta \cos\phi + Q_\phi \sin\phi = 0 \tag{5.9a}$$

$$N_\phi \sin\phi + N_\theta \sin\phi - \frac{d}{d\phi}(Q_\phi \sin\phi) = 0 \tag{5.9b}$$

$$\frac{d}{d\phi}(M_\phi \sin\phi) - M_\theta \cos\phi + Q_\phi a \sin\phi = 0 \tag{5.9c}$$

The force-displacement relations can be written following Eq. (5.8) as :

$$N_\phi = \frac{K}{a}\left[\frac{dv}{d\phi} + w + \nu(v\cot\phi + w)\right] \tag{5.10a}$$

$$N_\theta = \frac{K}{a}\left[(v\cot\phi + w) + \nu\left(\frac{dv}{d\phi} + w\right)\right] \tag{5.10b}$$

$$M_\phi = -\frac{D}{a^2}\left[-\frac{d^2w}{d\phi^2} + \frac{dv}{d\phi} + \nu\cot\phi\left(v - \frac{dw}{d\phi}\right)\right] \qquad (5.10c)$$

$$M_\theta = -\frac{D}{a^2}\left[\left(-\frac{dw}{d\phi} + v\right)\cot\phi + \nu\left(-\frac{d^2w}{d\phi^2} + \frac{dv}{d\phi}\right)\right] \qquad (5.10d)$$

The last two equations suggest that an auxiliary variable defined as

$$\chi = \frac{1}{a}\left(-\frac{dw}{d\phi} + v\right) \qquad (5.11)$$

could be introduced which represents the angle by which the meridian element rotates during deformation. With the introduction of the above variable, the moment relations (Eqs. 5.10(c) and (d)) can be written as

$$M_\phi = -\frac{D}{a}\left[\frac{d\chi}{d\phi} + \nu\chi\cot\phi\right] \qquad (5.12a)$$

$$M_\theta = -\frac{D}{a}\left[\chi\cot\phi + \nu\frac{d\chi}{d\phi}\right] \qquad (5.12b)$$

With the introduction of the new variable χ, we have now eight equations and eight unknowns, namely the five stress resultants N_ϕ, N_θ, M_ϕ, M_θ and Q_ϕ and three displacements v, w and χ. We will now reduce these eight equations to a pair of equations in Q_ϕ and χ.

First substituting Eq. (5.12 a, b) in Eq. (5.9c), we get

$$\frac{d^2\chi}{d\phi^2} + \cot\phi\frac{d\chi}{d\phi} - (\cot^2\phi + \nu)\chi = \frac{Q_\phi a^2}{D} \qquad (5.13)$$

From Eq. (5 12a, b), we get

$$\frac{dv}{d\phi} + w = \frac{a}{K(1-\nu^2)}(N_\phi - \nu N_\theta)$$

$$v\cot\phi + w = \frac{a}{K(1-\nu^2)}(N_\theta - \nu N_\phi)$$

Differentiating with respect to ϕ, the second of the above equation, we get

$$\frac{dv}{d\phi}\cot\phi - \frac{v}{\sin^2\phi} + \frac{dw}{d\phi} = \frac{a}{K(1-\nu^2)}\left(\frac{dN_\theta}{d\phi} - \nu\frac{dN_\phi}{d\phi}\right)$$

Using the above three relations together with Eq. (5.11), we get

$$\chi = -\frac{1}{K(1-\nu^2)}\left[\left(\frac{dN_\theta}{d\phi} - \nu\frac{dN_\phi}{d\phi}\right) + (1+\nu)\cot\phi\,(N_\theta - N_\phi)\right] \qquad (5.14)$$

Using the first two equilibrium equations, viz. Eq. (5.9a, b), N_θ, N_ϕ can be determined as

$$N_\phi = Q_\phi \cot\phi + \frac{c}{\sin^2\phi} \tag{5.15a}$$

$$N_\theta = \frac{dQ_\phi}{d\phi} - \frac{c}{\sin^2\phi} \tag{5.15b}$$

Using Eq. (5.15), and the derivatives of N_ϕ and N_θ with respect to ϕ in Eq. (5.16) we get the following equation:

$$\frac{d^2Q_\phi}{d\phi^2} + \frac{dQ_\phi}{d\phi}\cot\phi - Q_\phi\,(\cot^2\phi - \nu) = -K\chi\,(1 - \nu^2) \tag{5.16}$$

Equations (5.13) and (5.16) are a pair of second order ordinary differential equations in terms of χ and Q_ϕ. It is possible to eliminate either χ or Q_ϕ from these two equations resulting in a fourth order differential equation in terms of any one variable. This equation would be of Bessel type and the solution would be in terms of Bessel functions. However, it is possible to simplify these two equations, such that the solution to these equations can be obtained in a simple form. The simplification is made based on the fact that the bending stresses in shells of revolution are generally confined to a narrow zone near the boundaries and dampen quickly as one moves away from the boundaries. An approximate theory of dealing with the edge effect of this type was suggested by Geckler[5.1]. According to this theory, the edge effect is represented by a function of the type $e^{\lambda\phi}$ (λ being large), and since the edge effect dies out rapidly, only the highest derivative in the differential equation needs to be retained. This approximation has been found to be reasonably valid for $\phi > 20°$. By making this approximation, Eqs. (5.13) and (5.16) can now be written as

$$\frac{d^2\chi}{d\phi^2} = \frac{Q_\phi\, a^2}{D} \tag{5.17a}$$

$$\frac{d^2Q_\phi}{d\phi^2} = -\,K\chi\,(1 - \nu^2) \tag{5.17b}$$

Eliminating χ from the above equations, we get the following fourth order differential equation in terms of Q_ϕ as

$$\frac{d^4Q_\phi}{d\phi^4} + 4k^4\,Q_\phi = 0 \tag{5.18}$$

where

$$k^4 = \frac{3\,(1 - \nu^2)\,a^2}{h^2}$$

Consistent with the approximation made in deriving the above differential equation, we can use the following relation to determine the forces and displacements:

$$N_\phi = Q_\phi \cot \phi \tag{5.19a}$$

$$N_\theta = \frac{dQ_\phi}{d\phi} \tag{5.19b}$$

$$M_\phi = - \frac{D}{a}\left(\frac{d\chi}{d\phi}\right) \tag{5.19c}$$

$$M_\theta = M_\phi - \frac{D}{a} \nu \, (\chi \cot \phi) \tag{5.19d}$$

Horizontal displacement

$$\Delta H = \frac{a \sin \phi}{Eh} (N_\theta - \nu N_\phi) \tag{5.19e}$$

Rotation

$$\beta = - \frac{1}{K(1-\nu^2)} \frac{d^2 Q_\phi}{d\phi^2} \tag{5.19f}$$

5.2.5.2 Solution

The differential equation (5.18) is a fourth order ordinary differential equation with constant coefficient. A similar type of equation is also obtained for the bending of a beam on elastic foundation and the solution of this equation has been discussed in detail elsewhere[5.6]. Following this, the solution for Q_ϕ can be written as

$$Q_\phi = (C_1 e^{k\phi} \cos k\phi + C_2 e^{k\phi} \sin k\phi + C_3 e^{-k\phi} \cos k\phi + C_4 e^{-k\phi} \sin k\phi) \tag{5.20}$$

in which C_1, C_2, C_3 and C_4 are constants to be determined from the boundary conditions. The above solution could be used to determine the bending stresses in a spherical shell, with or without opening at the crown. First, let us examine the solution for a spherical shell (without opening at the crown) subject to edge loads, namely a bending moment and a horizontal force as shown in Fig. 5.2.

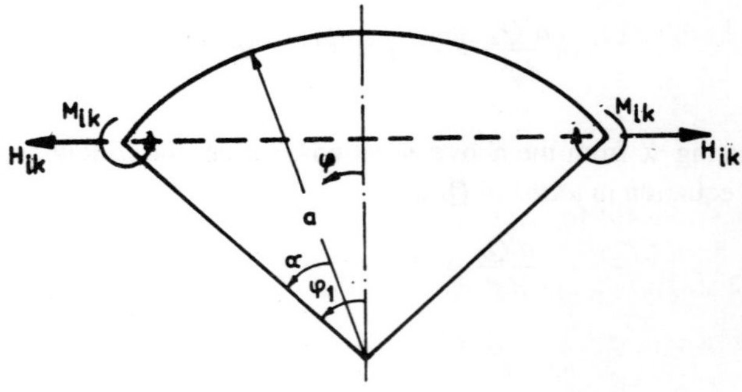

Fig. 5.2 Spherical shell subjected to edge loading

The terms involving constants C_3 and C_4 in the above solution must be discarded in this case, as these terms indicate that the edge disturbance dies away as we approach the edge, while actually the edge disturbance originates at the edge. Hence, the solution for this problem can be written as

$$Q_\phi = C_1 e^{k\phi} \cos k\phi + C_2 e^{k\phi} \sin k\phi \qquad (5.21)$$

Since it is more convenient to work from the edge, the above equation can be rewritten in terms of α (Fig. 5.2) as

$$Q_\phi = C_1 e^{-k\alpha} \cos k\alpha + C_2 e^{-k\alpha} \sin k\alpha \qquad (5.22)$$

where $\alpha = \phi_1 - \phi$.

The constants C_1 and C_2 are determined from the boundary conditions specified at the edge ($\alpha = 0$).

Expressions for forces and displacements can now be obtained using Eqs. (5.19a–f) (by changing $d\phi$ to $-\ d\alpha$) as

$$N_\phi = \cot \phi \, [C_1 F_{17}(\alpha) + C_2 F_{18}(\alpha)] \qquad (5.23a)$$

$$N_\theta = k\,[C_1 F_{19}(\alpha) - C_2 F_{20}(\alpha)] \qquad (5.23b)$$

$$M_\phi = -\frac{a}{2K}[C_1 F_{20}(\alpha) + C_2 F_{19}(\alpha)] \qquad (5.23c)$$

$$\Delta H = \frac{ak}{Eh} \sin \phi \, [C_1 F_{19}(\alpha) - C_2 F_{20}(\alpha)] \qquad (5.23d)$$

$$\beta = -\frac{2k^2}{Eh}[C_1 F_{18}(\alpha) - C_2 F_{17}(\alpha)] \qquad (5.23e)$$

where $F_{17}(\alpha)$, $F_{18}(\alpha)$, $\cdots$, $F_{20}(\alpha)$ have been defined in Table 5.3.

For convenience, we can obtain the expressions for forces and displacements separately for the two-edge loading, viz. bending moment M_{ik} and a horizontal force H_{ik}. When only a bending moment M_{ik} is acting, the boundary conditions can be written as

$$\alpha = 0,\ M_\phi = -\ M_{ik},\ Q_\phi = 0$$

Using the above boundary conditions, the constants C_1 and C_2 can be determined as

$$C_1 = 0,\ C_2 = M_{ik}\left(\frac{2k}{a}\right)$$

The expressions for forces and displacements can now be obtained using the above constants in Eq. (5.23) and these are given in Table 5.1. The F functions appearing in this table are defined in Table 5.3.

Similarly, when only the horizontal force H_{ik} is acting, the boundary conditions may be written as

$$\alpha = 0,\ M_\phi = 0,\ Q_\phi = H_{ik} \sin \phi_1$$

Using the above boundary conditions, the constants C_1 and C_2 can be determined as

$$C_1 = H_{ik} \sin \phi_1, \; C_2 = - H_{ik} \sin \phi_1$$

The expressions for forces and displacements may now be obtained using the above constants in Eq. (5.23) and these are given in Table 5.1.

For a spherical shell with an opening at the crown, the solution for Q_ϕ may be taken in the form given in Eq. (5.20). However, it will be more convenient to write the solution in terms of hyperbolic and trigonometric functions rather than exponential and trigonometric functions. Hence, Eq. (5.20) can now be rewritten as

$$Q_\phi = (C_1 \cosh k\alpha \cos k\alpha + C_2 \cosh k\alpha \sin k\alpha + C_3 \sinh k\alpha \cos k\alpha + C_4 \sinh k\alpha \sin k\alpha) \quad (5.24)$$

where $C_1, \ldots, C_4$ are constants to be determined from the boundary conditions.

As an example, let us consider a spherical shell acted upon by a horizontal force H_{ik} at the bottom edge as shown in Fig. 5.3.
The boundary conditions can be written as

$$\alpha = 0 \; (\phi = \phi_1), \; M_\phi = 0, \; Q_\phi = H_{ik} \sin \phi_1$$
$$\alpha = \alpha_0 \; (\phi = \phi_1 - \phi_2), \; M_\phi = 0, \; Q_\phi = 0$$

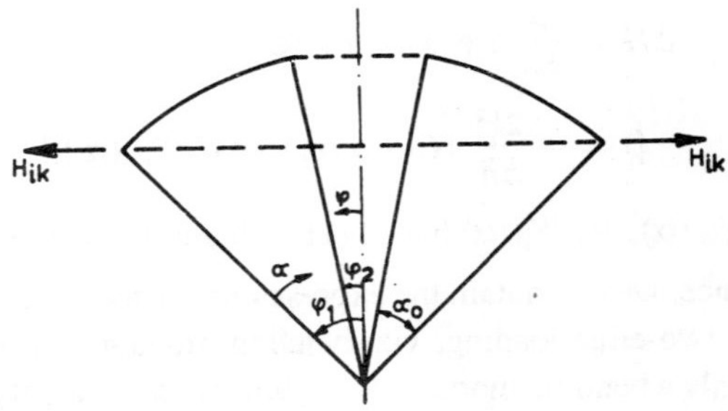

Fig. 5.3 Open spherical shell subjected to a horizontal force at the bottom edge

Using the above boundary conditions, the constants can be determined as

$$C_1 = H_{ik} \sin \phi_1, \; C_2 = - H_{ik} \sin \phi_1 \frac{F_4}{F_1}$$

$$C_3 = - H_{ik} \sin \phi_1 \frac{F_4}{F_1}, \; C_4 = H_{ik} \sin \phi_1 \frac{F_2}{F_1}$$

where the functions F_1, F_2 and F_4 are defined in Table 5.3.

Substituting for the constants in Eq. (5.24) and using Eq. (5.19), the expressions for forces and displacements may be obtained. The expressions for forces and displacements for different edge loadings have been given by Hampe[5.2] and these are presented in Tables 5.2a and b. The F functions appearing in these tables are defined in Table 5.3.

Table 5.1 Forces and displacements in a spherical shell due to edge loading

Force or displacement	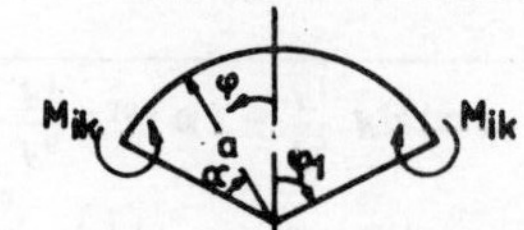	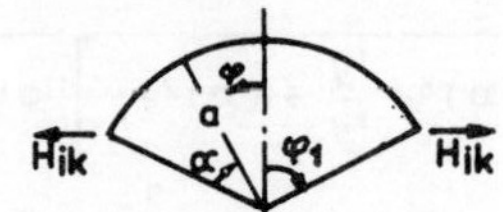
N_ϕ	$M_{ik}\,\dfrac{2\,k\cot\phi}{a}\,F_{18}(\alpha)$	$H_{ik}\,\sin\phi_1\cot\phi\,F_{20}(\alpha)$
N_θ	$-\,M_{ik}\,\dfrac{2\,k^2}{a}\,F_{20}(\alpha)$	$H_{ik}\,2\,k\sin\phi_1\,F_{17}(\alpha)$
M_ϕ	$-\,M_{ik}\,F_{19}(\alpha)$	$H_{ik}\,\dfrac{a\sin\phi_1}{k}\,F_{18}(\alpha)$
M_θ	$-\,M_{ik}\left[\dfrac{\cot\phi}{k}\,F_{17}(\alpha)+\nu\,F_{19}(\alpha)\right]$	$H_{ik}\,\dfrac{a\sin\phi_1}{2\,k}\left[\dfrac{\cot\phi}{k}\,F_{19}(\alpha)+2\,\nu\,F_{18}(\alpha)\right]$
Q_ϕ	$M_{ik}\,\dfrac{2\,k}{a}\,F_{18}(\alpha)$	$H_{ik}\,\sin\phi_1\,F_{20}(\alpha)$
ΔH	$-\,M_{ik}\,\dfrac{2\,k\sin\phi}{Eh}\,[\,k\,F_{20}(\alpha)+\nu\cot\phi\,F_{18}(\alpha)]$	$H_{ik}\,\dfrac{2\,a\,k}{Eh}\,\sin\phi_1\left[\sin\phi\,F_{17}(\alpha)-\dfrac{\nu}{2\,k}\cos\phi\,F_{20}(\alpha)\right]$
β	$M_{ik}\,\dfrac{4\,k^3}{Eha}\,F_{17}(\alpha)$	$-\,H_{ik}\,\dfrac{2\,k^2}{Eh}\,\sin\phi_1\,F_{19}(\alpha)$

$k=\sqrt[4]{3\,(1-\nu^2)\,a^2/h^2}$

Table 5.2a Forces and displacements in an open spherical shell due to edge loading (F functions are defined in Table 5.3)

Force or displacement	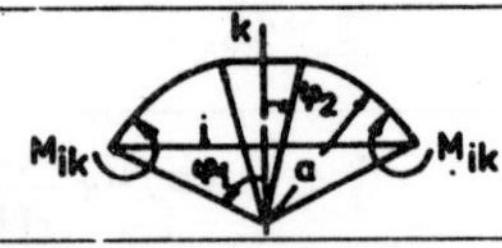	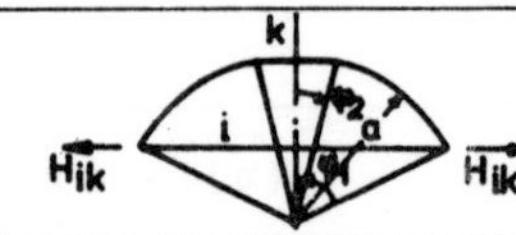
N_ϕ	$M_{ik}\left[\frac{2k\cot\phi}{a}\left\{\frac{F_6}{F_1}F_{15}(\alpha)+\frac{F_5}{F_1}F_{16}(\alpha)-\frac{F_3}{F_1}F_8(\alpha)\right\}\right]$	$H_{ik}\left[\sin\phi_1\cot\phi\left\{F_7(\alpha)-\frac{F_4}{F_1}F_{10}(\alpha)+\frac{F_2}{F_1}F_8(\alpha)\right\}\right]$
N_θ	$-M_{ik}\left[\frac{2k^2}{a}\left\{\frac{F_6}{F_1}F_{14}(\alpha)+\frac{F_5}{F_1}F_{13}(\alpha)-\frac{F_3}{F_1}F_{10}(\alpha)\right\}\right]$	$-H_{ik}\left[k\sin\phi_1\left\{-F_9(\alpha)-\frac{2F_4}{F_1}F_7(\alpha)+\frac{F_2}{F_1}F_{10}(\alpha)\right\}\right]$
Q_ϕ	$M_{ik}\left[\frac{2k}{a}\left\{\frac{F_6}{F_1}F_{15}(\alpha)+\frac{F_5}{F_1}F_{16}(\alpha)-\frac{F_3}{F_1}F_8(\alpha)\right\}\right]$	$H_{ik}\left[\sin\phi_1\left\{F_7(\alpha)-\frac{F_4}{F_1}F_{10}(\alpha)+\frac{F_2}{F_1}F_8(\alpha)\right\}\right]$
M_ϕ	$-M_{ik}\left[\frac{F_6}{F_1}F_{13}(\alpha)-\frac{F_5}{F_1}F_{14}(\alpha)+\frac{F_3}{F_1}F_9(\alpha)\right]$	$-H_{ik}\left[\frac{a}{2k}\sin\phi_1\left\{-F_{10}(\alpha)+\frac{2F_4}{F_1}F_8(\alpha)-\frac{F_2}{F_1}F_9(\alpha)\right\}\right]$
M_θ	$M_{ik}\left\{\frac{F_6}{F_1}\left[\frac{\cot\phi}{k}F_{16}(\alpha)-\nu F_{13}(\alpha)\right]-\frac{F_5}{F_1}\left[\frac{\cot\phi}{k}F_{15}(\alpha)-\nu F_{14}(\alpha)\right]-\frac{F_3}{F_1}\left[\frac{\cot\phi}{k}F_7(\alpha)+\nu F_9(\alpha)\right]\right\}$	$H_{ik}\left[\frac{a}{2k}\sin\phi_1\left\{-\left(\frac{\cot\phi}{k}F_8(\alpha)-\nu F_{10}(\alpha)\right)+\frac{F_4}{F_1}\left(\frac{\cot\phi}{k}F_9(\alpha)-2\nu F_8(\alpha)\right)+\frac{F_2}{F_1}\left(\frac{\cot\phi}{k}F_7(\alpha)+\nu F_9(\alpha)\right)\right\}\right]$
ΔH	$-M_{ik}\left[\frac{2k^2}{Eh}\sin\phi\left\{\frac{F_6}{F_1}F_{14}(\alpha)+\frac{F_5}{F_1}F_{13}(\alpha)-\frac{F_3}{F_1}F_{10}(\alpha)\right\}\right]$	$-H_{ik}\left\{\frac{ak}{Eh}\sin\phi\sin\phi_1\left[-F_9(\alpha)-\frac{2F_4}{F_1}F_7(\alpha)+\frac{F_2}{F_1}F_{10}(\alpha)\right]\right\}$
β	$-M_{ik}\left[\frac{4k^3}{Eha}\left\{\frac{F_6}{F_1}F_{16}(\alpha)-\frac{F_5}{F_1}F_{15}(\alpha)-\frac{F_3}{F_1}F_7(\alpha)\right\}\right]$	$-H_{ik}\left\{\frac{2k^2}{Eh}\sin\phi_1\left[-F_8(\alpha)+\frac{F_4}{F_1}F_9(\alpha)+\frac{F_2}{F_1}F_7(\alpha)\right]\right\}$

$k = \sqrt[4]{3(1-\nu^2)a^2/h^2}$

(It may be noted that in the expression for ΔH, the effect of N_ϕ is neglected which is equivalent to neglecting Q_ϕ known to be very small for thin shells).

Table 5.2b Forces and displacements in an open spherical shell due to edge loading (*F* functions are defined in Table 5.3)

Force or displacement	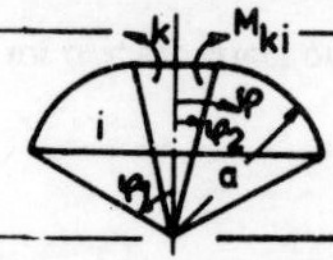	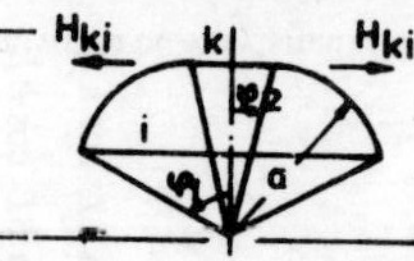
N_ϕ	$M_{ki}\left[\frac{2k}{a}\cot\phi\left\{\frac{F_8}{F_1}F_{10}(\alpha)-\frac{F_{10}}{F_1}F_8(\alpha)\right\}\right]$	$H_{ki}\left[\cot\phi\sin\phi_2\left\{\frac{F_9}{F_1}F_{10}(\alpha)-2\frac{F_8}{F_1}F_8(\alpha)\right\}\right]$
N_θ	$M_{ki}\left[\frac{2k^2}{a}\left\{-2\frac{F_8}{F_1}F_7(\alpha)+\frac{F_{10}}{F_1}F_{10}(\alpha)\right\}\right]$	$H_{ki}\left[2k\sin\phi_2\left\{-\frac{F_9}{F_1}F_7(\alpha)+\frac{F_8}{F_1}F_{10}(\alpha)\right\}\right]$
Q_ϕ	$-M_{ki}\left[\frac{2k}{a}\left\{-\frac{F_8}{F_1}F_{10}(\alpha)+\frac{F_{10}}{F_1}F_8(\alpha)\right\}\right]$	$H_{ki}\left[\sin\phi_2\left\{\frac{F_9}{F_1}F_{10}(\alpha)-2\frac{F_8}{F_1}F_8(\alpha)\right\}\right]$
M_ϕ	$M_{ki}\left[2\frac{F_8}{F_1}F_8(\alpha)-\frac{F_{10}}{F_1}F_9(\alpha)\right]$	$H_{ki}\left[\frac{a\sin\phi_2}{k}\left\{\frac{F_9}{F_1}F_8(\alpha)-\frac{F_8}{F_1}F_9(\alpha)\right\}\right]$
M_θ	$-M_{ki}\left[\frac{F_8}{F_1}\left\{\frac{\cot\phi}{k}F_9(\alpha)-2\nu F_8(\alpha)\right\}+\frac{F_{10}}{F_1}\left\{\frac{\cot\phi}{k}F_7(\alpha)+\nu F_9(\alpha)\right\}\right]$	$H_{ki}\left[\frac{a}{2k}\sin\phi_2\left\{\frac{F_9}{F_1}\left(-\frac{\cot\phi}{k}F_9(\alpha)+2\nu F_8(\alpha)\right)-2\frac{F_8}{F_1}\left(\frac{\cot\phi}{k}F_7(\alpha)+\nu F_9(\alpha)\right)\right\}\right]$
ΔH	$M_{ki}\left[\frac{2k^2}{Eh}\sin\phi\left\{-2\frac{F_8}{F_1}F_7(\alpha)+\frac{F_{10}}{F_1}F_{10}(\alpha)\right\}\right]$	$-H_{ki}\left[\frac{2ak}{Eh}\sin\phi_2\left\{\frac{F_9}{F_1}F_7(\alpha)-\frac{F_8}{F_1}F_{10}(\alpha)\right\}\right]$
β	$M_{ki}\left[\frac{4k^3}{Eha}\left\{\frac{F_8}{F_1}F_9(\alpha)+\frac{F_{10}}{F_1}F_7(\alpha)\right\}\right]$	$H_{ki}\left[\frac{2\sin\phi_2 k^2}{Eh}\left\{\frac{F_9}{F_1}F_9(\alpha)+\frac{2F_8}{F_1}F_7(\alpha)\right\}\right]$

$k=\sqrt[4]{3(1-\nu^2)a^2/h^2}$

Table 5.3 Definition of F function

i	$F_i(\xi)$	F_i
1.	$\sinh^2 kL\xi - \sin^2 kL\xi$	$\sinh^2 kL - \sin^2 kL$
2.	$\sinh^2 kL\xi + \sin^2 kL\xi$	$\sinh^2 kL + \sin^2 kL$
3.	$\sinh kL\xi \cosh kL\xi + \sin kL\xi \cos kL\xi$	$\sinh kL \cosh kL + \sin kL \cos kL$
4.	$\sinh kL\xi \cosh kL\xi - \sin kL\xi \cos kL\xi$	$\sinh kL \cosh kL - \sin kL \cos kL$
5.	$\sin^2 kL\xi$	$\sin^2 kL$
6.	$\sinh^2 kL\xi$	$\sinh^2 kL$
7.	$\cosh kL\xi \cos kL\xi$	$\cosh kL \cos kL$
8.	$\sinh kL\xi \sin kL\xi$	$\sinh kL \sin kL$
9.	$\cosh kL\xi \sin kL\xi - \sinh kL\xi \cos kL\xi$	$\cosh kL \sin kL - \sinh kL \cos kL$
10.	$\cosh kL\xi \sin kL\xi + \sinh kL\xi \cos kL\xi$	$\cosh kL \sin kL + \sinh kL \cos kL$
11.	$\sin kL\xi \cos kL\xi$	$\sin kL \cos kL$
12.	$\sinh kL\xi \cosh kL\xi$	$\sinh kL \cosh kL$
13.	$\cosh kL\xi \cos kL\xi - \sinh kL\xi \sin kL\xi$	$\cosh kL \cos kL - \sinh kL \sin kL$
14.	$\cosh kL\xi \cos kL\xi + \sinh kL\xi \sin kL\xi$	$\cosh kL \cos kL + \sinh kL \sin kL$
15.	$\cosh kL\xi \sin kL\xi$	$\cosh kL \sin kL$
16.	$\sinh kL\xi \cos kL\xi$	$\sinh kL \cos kL$
17.	$e^{-kL\xi} \cos kL\xi$	$e^{-kL} \cos kL$
18.	$e^{-kL\xi} \sin kL\xi$	$e^{-kL} \sin kL$
19.	$e^{-kL\xi}(\cos kL\xi + \sin kL\xi)$	$e^{-kL}(\cos kL + \sin kL)$
20.	$e^{-kL\xi}(\cos kL\xi - \sin kL\xi)$	$e^{-kL}(\cos kL - \sin kL)$

For spherical shell, $L\xi = \alpha_o(\alpha/\alpha_o)$,

$$k = \sqrt[4]{3(1-\nu^2)(a/h)^2}$$

For conical shell, $\xi = \dfrac{\bar{x}}{L}$, $k = \dfrac{\sqrt[4]{3(1-\nu^2)}}{\sqrt{h\,x_m \cot\alpha_o}}$

For cylindrical shell, $\xi = \dfrac{x}{L}$, $k = \dfrac{\sqrt[4]{3(1-\nu^2)}}{\sqrt{ah}}$

Example 5.1

A concrete spherical dome of radius 28.25 m is supported as shown in Fig. 5.4 and is subjected to a load corresponding to its own weight. The thickness of the shell is 10 cm and the semi-central angle is 28°. It is required to determine the forces in the shell. Poisson's ratio may be taken as 0.15 and the unit weight of concrete as 2400 kg/m^3.

Since the edge of the shell is fixed, there would be no horizontal displacement and rotation at the edge.

(a) Primary analysis

Dead load = 0.1 × 2400 = 240 kg/m^2

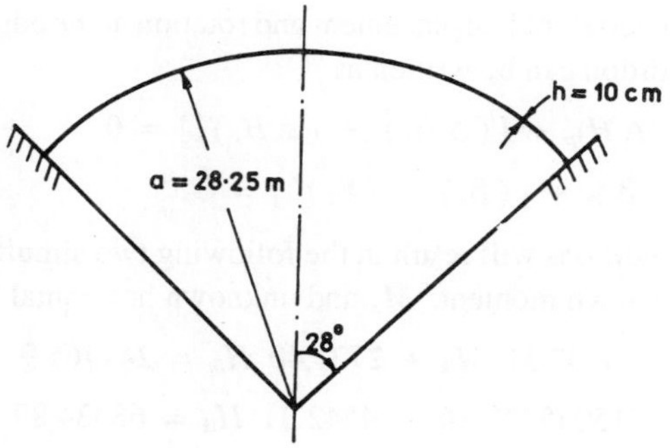

Fig. 5.4 Spherical dome fixed at the periphery

The horizontal displacement and rotation at the edge of shell ($\phi_1 = 28°$) can be determined using Table 2.4a as

$$(\Delta H)_p = \frac{ga^2}{Eh} \sin\phi_1 \left[-\cos\phi_1 + \frac{1+\nu}{\sin^2\phi_1}(1-\cos\phi_1) \right]$$

$$= -\frac{244765.9}{E}$$

$$(\beta)_p = -\frac{ga}{Eh}(2+\nu)\sin\phi_1 = -\frac{68434.87}{E}$$

(b) Secondary analysis

The horizontal displacement and rotation determined from the primary analysis can now be nullified by applying a moment and a horizontal force along this edge. These forces to start with are not known and the displacements caused by the application of these forces at the edge of the shell can be determined using Table 5.1.

$$k = \sqrt[4]{3(1-\nu^2)\frac{a^2}{h^2}} = 21.99$$

$(\Delta H)'_s$ due to moment M_{ik} at the edge ($\alpha = 0$) is determined from

$$(\Delta H)'_s = -\frac{M_{ik}}{Eh}(2k^2 \sin\phi_1) = -\left(\frac{4542.31}{E}\right) M_{ik}$$

Similarly, $(\Delta H_s)''$ due to horizontal force H_{ik} at the edge ($\alpha = 0$) is determined from

$$(\Delta H_s)'' = \frac{H_{ik}}{Eh}[a\sin\phi_1 / 2k\sin\phi_1 - \nu\cos\phi_1 /] = \left(\frac{2721.40}{E}\right) H_{ik}$$

The rotation $(\beta_s)'$ due to M_{ik} at the edge ($\alpha = 0$) can be determined from

$$(\beta_s)' = M_{ik}\left(\frac{4k^3}{Eah}\right) = \left(\frac{15065.99}{E}\right) M_{ik}$$

The rotation $(\beta_s)''$ due to H_{ik} at the edge ($\alpha = 0$) can be determined from

$$(\beta_s)'' = -H_{ik}\left(\frac{2k^2\sin\phi_1}{Eh}\right) = -H_{ik}\left(\frac{4542.31}{E}\right)$$

Now the total horizontal displacement and rotation at the edge should be equal to zero. This condition can be written as

$$(\Delta H)_p + [(\Delta H_s)' + (\Delta H_s)''] = 0$$

$$(\beta)_p + [(\beta_s)' + (\beta_s)''] = 0$$

The above conditions will result in the following two simultaneous equations in terms of the unknown moment, M_{ik} and unknown horizontal force, H_{ik}

$$-4542.31\ M_{ik} + 2721.40\ H_{ik} = 244765.9 \quad \text{(a)}$$

$$15065.99\ M_{ik} - 4542.31\ H_{ik} = 68434.87 \quad \text{(b)}$$

Solving the above two equations, we get

$$M_{ik} = 63.73\ \text{kg.m/m},\ H_{ik} = 196.31\ \text{kg/m}$$

The final forces can be determined by superposing the results of primary and secondary analysis. For the computation of forces in primary analysis, Table 2.4a can be used, while for the computation of forces in secondary analysis, Table 5.1 can be made use of.

Table 5.4 Variation of membrane force N_ϕ (t/m) in the dome

Force	α in deg						
	0	1	2	5	10	20	28
Membrane (due to dead load)	−3.6	−3.58	−3.57	−3.53	−3.47	−3.4	−3.39
Due to M_{ik}	0	0.05	0.07	0.032	0	0	0
Due to H_{ik}	0.18	0.07	0	−0.04	0	0	0
Final N_ϕ	−3.42	−3.46	−3.50	−3.502	−3.47	−3.4	−3.39

Table 5.5 Variation of membrane force N_θ (t/m) in the dome

Force	α in deg						
	0	1	2	5	10	20	28
Membrane	−2.38	−2.45	−2.53	−2.71	−2.97	−3.3	−3.39
Due to M_{ik}	−2.18	−0.82	−0.025	0.41	0	0	0
Due to H_{ik}	4.05	2.56	1.35	−0.20	−0.07	0	0
Final N_θ	−0.51	−0.71	−1.205	−2.50	−3.04	−3.3	−3.39

Table 5.6 Variation of bending moment M_ϕ t/m.m

Force	α in deg						
	0	1	2	5	10	20	28
Due to M_{ik}	−0.064	−0.056	−0.042	−0.006	0	0	0
Due to H_{ik}	0	0.030	0.038	0.016	−0.001	0	0
Final M_ϕ	−0.064	−0.026	−0.004	0.010	−0.001	0	0

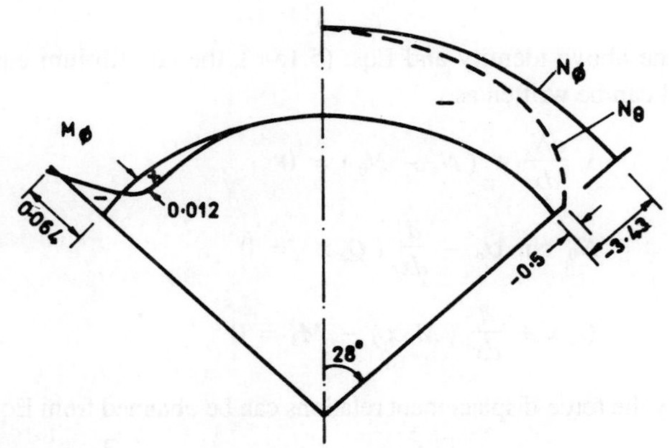

Fig. 5.5 Variation of forces in a spherical dome

5.2.6 Conical Shell

5.2.6.1 Differential equations

The equations of equilibrium (5.1a-c) and the force-displacement relations (5.8) have been given earlier in terms of spherical coordinates. Since for a cone $\phi = \alpha$ is a constant, it will be convenient to refer to the inclined length coordinate x (Fig. 5.6). Hence, for this new coordinate system, we have the following identity:

$$\phi \rightarrow x, \; \frac{d}{r_1\, d\phi}(\ldots) = \frac{d}{dx}(\ldots), \; \text{angle}\ \phi = \alpha_o, \; r_1 = \infty$$

$$r_2 = x \cot \alpha_o, \; r_o = x \cos \alpha_o$$

and displacement v to be changed to u.

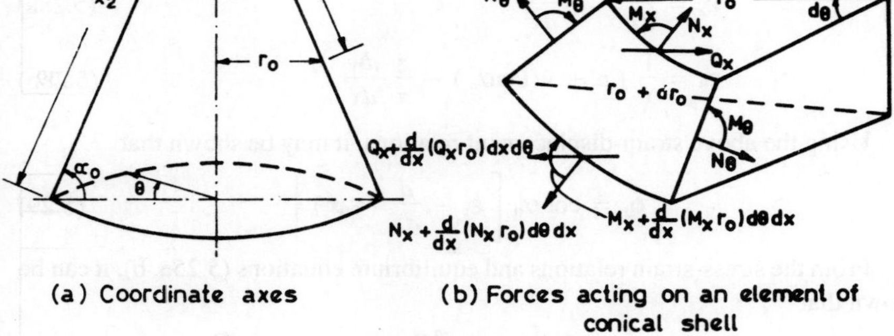

Fig. 5.6 Conical shell

Using the above identity and Eqs. (5.1a-c), the equilibrium equations for a conical shell can be written as

$$x \frac{dN_x}{dx} + (N_x - N_\theta) = 0 \tag{5.25a}$$

$$N_\theta \tan \alpha_o - \frac{d}{dx}(Q_x x) = 0 \tag{5.25b}$$

$$Q_x x + \frac{d}{dx}(M_x x) - M_\theta = 0 \tag{5.25c}$$

Similarly the force-displacement relations can be obtained from Eq. (5.8) as

$$N_x = K\left[\frac{du}{dx} + \frac{\nu}{x}(u + w \tan \alpha_o)\right] \tag{5.26a}$$

$$N_\theta = K\left[\frac{1}{x}(u + w \tan \alpha_o) + \nu \frac{du}{dx}\right] \tag{5.26b}$$

$$M_x = D\left[\frac{d^2w}{dx^2} + \frac{\nu}{x}\frac{dw}{dx}\right] \tag{5.26c}$$

$$M_\theta = D\left[\frac{1}{x}\frac{dw}{dx} + \nu \frac{d^2w}{dx^2}\right] \tag{5.26d}$$

Now the third equilibrium equation (5.25c), using the force-displacement relation (Eq. 5.26c, d), can be written as,

$$\phi_x'' + \frac{1}{x}\phi_x' - \frac{1}{x^2}\phi_x = \frac{Q_x}{D} \tag{5.27}$$

where

$$\phi_x = -\frac{dw}{dx}$$

The strain-displacement relations for a conical shell can be obtained, from Eq. (5.25), as

$$\varepsilon_x = \frac{du}{dx} - z\frac{d^2w}{dx^2} \tag{5.28a}$$

$$\varepsilon_\theta = \frac{1}{x}(u + w \tan\alpha_o) - \frac{z}{x}\frac{dw}{dx} \tag{5.28b}$$

Using the above strain-displacement relations, it may be shown that

$$\phi_x = \cot \alpha_0 \left[\varepsilon_x - \frac{d}{dx}(\varepsilon_\theta x)\right] \tag{5.29}$$

From the stress-strain relations and equilibrium equations (5.25a, b), it can be shown that

$$\left[\varepsilon_x - \frac{d}{dx}(\varepsilon_\theta x)\right] = \frac{1}{Eh}\left[-x^2 \frac{d^2Q_x}{dx^2}\cot \alpha_o - 3x\frac{dQ_x}{dx}\cot \alpha_o\right] \tag{5.30}$$

Hence from Eqs. (5.29) and (5.30), we get

$$\frac{d^2Q_x}{dx^2} + \frac{3}{x}\frac{dQ_x}{dx} = -\frac{Eh\tan^2\alpha_o}{x^2}\phi_x \tag{5.31}$$

Now we will introduce a new variable U defined by

$$U = Q_x x$$

Equation (5.31) can now be rewritten in terms of the new variable U as

$$\frac{d^2U}{dx^2} + \frac{1}{x}\frac{dU}{dx} - \frac{U}{x^2} = -\frac{Eh\tan^2\alpha_o}{x}\phi_x \tag{5.32}$$

Now we have two simultaneous differential Eqs. (5.27) and (5.32) and these can be written in the operator form by introducing the differential operator defined as

$$L(\ldots) = x(\ldots)'' + (\ldots)' - \frac{1}{x}(\ldots)$$

where $\quad (\ldots)' = \dfrac{d}{dx}(\ldots)$ and $(\ldots)'' = \dfrac{d^2}{dx^2}(\ldots)$

Equations (5.27) and (5.32) can now be written as

$$L(\phi_x) = \frac{U}{D} \tag{5.33a}$$

$$L(U) = -Eh\tan^2\alpha_0\,\phi_x \tag{5.33b}$$

Eliminating U from the above equations, we get

$$LL(\phi_x) + \frac{Eh\tan^2\alpha_o}{D}\phi_x = 0 \tag{5.34}$$

Alternatively eliminating ϕ_x from Eq. (5.33), we get

$$LL(U) + \frac{Eh\tan^2\alpha_o}{D}U = 0 \tag{5.35}$$

or

$$LL(U) + \lambda^4 U = 0$$

where

$$\lambda^4 = \frac{Eh\tan^2\alpha_o}{D} = \frac{12(1-\nu^2)\tan^2\alpha_o}{h^2}$$

Equation (5.35) may be written in either of the following forms:

$$L[L(U) + i\lambda^2(U)] - i\lambda^2[L(U) + i\lambda^2 U] = 0$$

$$L[L(U) - i\lambda^2(U)] + i\lambda^2[L(U) - i\lambda^2 U] = 0$$

which shows that the solution of the two second-order equations

$$L(U) \pm i\lambda^2(U) = 0 \tag{5.36 a, b}$$

satisfy Eq. (5.35). The solution of this equation has a complex form as there is a factor i in the second term. The solutions are conjugate complex and it will be sufficient to solve one of the equations, for example, Eq. (5.36a), and then use the real and imaginary parts of this solution separately, as solutions of the fourth order equation (5.35).

Equation (5.36a) resembles Bessel's equation and we can recast the equation to the Bessel's type by a simple transformation of the independent variable. For this purpose, we introduce a new variable defined as

$$\eta = 2\lambda\sqrt{ix} = \alpha\sqrt{i} \text{ and } \alpha = (2\lambda\sqrt{x})$$

with

$$\frac{d}{dx}(\dots) = \frac{2\lambda^2 i}{\eta}\frac{d}{d\eta}(\dots)$$

$$\frac{d^2}{dx^2}(\dots) = -\frac{4\lambda^4}{\eta^2}\left[\frac{d^2}{d\eta^2}(\dots) - \frac{1}{\eta}\frac{d}{d\eta}(\dots)\right]$$

Equation (5.36a) in terms of the new variable η can now be obtained as

$$\frac{d^2U}{d\eta^2} + \frac{1}{\eta}\frac{dU}{d\eta} + \left(1 - \frac{4}{\eta^2}\right)U = 0 \tag{5.37}$$

The solution of the above equation will be in terms of Bessel functions of second order with complex arguments and can be written as

$$U = Q_x x = C_1 J_2(\alpha\sqrt{i}) + C_2 J_2(\alpha\sqrt{-i}) + C_3 H_2(\alpha\sqrt{i}) + C_4 H_2(\alpha\sqrt{-i}) \tag{5.38}$$

Hampe[5.2] has expressed the above solution in terms of G functions involving the real variable α by using the relation

$$J_2(\alpha\sqrt{i}) = G_9(\alpha) + iG_{10}(\alpha),$$

$$J_2(\alpha\sqrt{-i}) = G_9(\alpha) - iG_{10}(\alpha)$$

$$H_2(\alpha\sqrt{i}) = G_{11}(\alpha) + iG_{12}(\alpha),$$

$$H_2(\alpha\sqrt{-i}) = G_{11}(\alpha) - iG_{12}(\alpha)$$

where the G functions and their first derivatives are related to the Kelvin functions and their first derivatives as follows :

$$G_1 = ber\ \alpha,\ G_2 = -\ bei\ \alpha,$$

$$G_3 = -\frac{2}{\pi}\ kei\ \alpha,\ G_4 = -\frac{2}{\pi}\ ker\ \alpha$$

$$G_1' = ber'\ \alpha,\ G_2 = -bei'\ \alpha,$$

$$G_3' = -\frac{2}{\pi}\ kei'\ \alpha,\ G_4' = -\frac{2}{\pi}\ ker'\ \alpha$$

$$G_9 = -\frac{2}{\alpha} G_2' - G_1, \; G_{10} = -\frac{2}{\alpha} G_1' - G_2,$$

$$G_{11} = -\frac{2}{\alpha} G_4' - G_3, \; G_{12} = \frac{2}{\alpha} G_3' - G_4$$

where prime denotes differentiation with respect to α.

Hence solution given in Eq. (5.38) can be rewritten in terms of G functions as

$$Q_x = \frac{1}{x} [C_1 G_9 (\alpha) + C_2 G_{10} (\alpha) + C_3 G_{11} (\alpha) + C_4 G_{12} (\alpha)] \tag{5.39}$$

The forces and displacements can be determined as

$$N_x = Q_x \cot \alpha_o = \frac{\cot \alpha_o}{x} [C_1 G_9 (\alpha) + C_2 G_{10} (\alpha) + C_3 G_{11} (\alpha) + C_4 G_{12} (\alpha)] \tag{5.40}$$

$$N_\theta = \frac{d}{dx} (Q_x x) \cot \alpha_o = \frac{\lambda \cot \alpha_o}{\sqrt{x}} [C_1 G_9' (\alpha) + C_2 G_{10}'(\alpha) + C_3 G_{11}'(\alpha) + C_4 G_{12}'(\alpha)] \tag{5.41}$$

Using Eq. (5.32), the rotation can be determined as (see Hampe[5.2])

$$\beta = \phi_x = -\frac{\lambda^2}{Eh \tan^2 \alpha_o} [C_1 G_{10} (\alpha) - C_2 G_9 (\alpha) + C_3 G_{12} (\alpha) - C_4 G_{11} (\alpha)] \tag{5.42}$$

$$\begin{aligned} M_x &= -D \left(\frac{d\phi_x}{dx} + \frac{\nu}{x} \phi_x \right) \\ &= \frac{1}{\lambda^2 x} [C_1 \{\lambda \sqrt{x} G_{10}'(\alpha) + \nu G_{10} (\alpha)\} \\ &\quad - C_2 \{\lambda \sqrt{x} G_9' (\alpha) + \nu G_9 (\alpha)\} \\ &\quad + C_3 \{\lambda \sqrt{x} G_{12}'(\alpha) + \nu G_{12} (\alpha)\} \\ &\quad - C_4 \{\lambda \sqrt{x} G_{11}'(\alpha) + \nu G_{11} (\alpha) \}] \end{aligned} \tag{5.43}$$

$$\begin{aligned} M_\theta &= -D \left(\frac{\phi_x}{x} + \nu \frac{d\phi_x}{dx} \right) \\ &= \frac{1}{\lambda^2 x} [C_1 \{\nu\lambda \sqrt{x} G_{10}'(\alpha) + G_{10} (\alpha)\} \\ &\quad - C_2 \{\nu\lambda \sqrt{x} G_9' (\alpha) + G_9 (\alpha)\} \\ &\quad + C_3 \{\nu\lambda \sqrt{x} G_{12}'(\alpha) + \dot{G}_{12} (\alpha)\} \\ &\quad - C_4 \{\nu\lambda \sqrt{x} G_{11}'(\alpha) + G_{11} (\alpha)\}] \end{aligned} \tag{5.44}$$

The horizontal displacement ΔH is given by

$$\Delta H = r_o \varepsilon_\theta = \frac{r_o}{Eh} (N_\theta - \nu N_x)$$

$$= \frac{\cos^2 \alpha_o}{Eh \sin \alpha_o} [C_1 \{\lambda \sqrt{x}\ G_9'(\alpha) - \nu G_9(\alpha)\}$$

$$+ C_2 \{\lambda \sqrt{x}\ G_{10}'(\alpha) - \nu G_{10}(\alpha)\}$$

$$+ C_3 \{\lambda \sqrt{x}\ G_{11}'(\alpha) - \nu G_{11}(\alpha)\}$$

$$+ C_4 \{\lambda \sqrt{x}\ G_{12}'(\alpha) - \nu G_{12}(\alpha)\}] \tag{5.45}$$

where

$$G_9' = \frac{2}{\alpha} G_1 - G_1' + \frac{4}{\alpha^2} G_2',$$

$$G_{10}' = \frac{2}{\alpha} G_2 - G_2' + \frac{4}{\alpha^2} G_1',$$

$$G_{11}' = \frac{2}{\alpha} G_3 + \frac{4}{\alpha^2} G_4' - G_3',$$

$$G_{12}' = \frac{2}{\alpha} G_4 - \frac{4}{\alpha^2} G_3' - G_4'$$

Equations (5.39) – (5.45) represent the exact solution for the various forces and displacements in a conical shell of constant thickness and subjected to edge loading. The constants C_1, C_2, C_3 and C_4 are determined from four boundary conditions specified at the two edges (i.e. two boundary conditions at each edge).

For a conical shell with an apex (i.e. a complete conical shell) the forces and displacements at the apex (i.e. at $\alpha = x = 0$) must be finite. As $G_{11}(\alpha)$ and $G_{12}(\alpha)$ as well as their derivatives are infinite for $\alpha = 0$, to satisfy the above condition, the constants C_3 and C_4 must vanish. For a truncated conical shell in general, all the four constants need to be considered. However, for a long truncated conical shell, the two edge effects do not interact and hence each edge may be considered independently. Hence, for the case of an edge loading applied at the smaller end of the frustum of a cone, the constants C_1 and C_2 are neglected. This is because the edge forces decay with distance and functions associated with the constants C_1 and C_2, namely $G_9(\alpha)$ and $G_{10}(\alpha)$ as well as their derivatives increase exponentially with α. Similarly, when the larger end is considered independently, for an edge loading applied at this end of the cone, the constants C_3 and C_4 are neglected.

For the purpose of illustration, let us consider a truncated conical shell subjected to an edge loading as shown in Fig. 5.7.

The boundary conditions for the edge loading shown in Fig. 5.7 can be written as

$$x = x_1 \ (\alpha = \alpha_1),\ M_x = 0,\ Q_x = -H_{ki} \sin \alpha_o$$

$$x = x_2 \ (\alpha = \alpha_2),\ M_x = 0,\ Q_x = 0$$

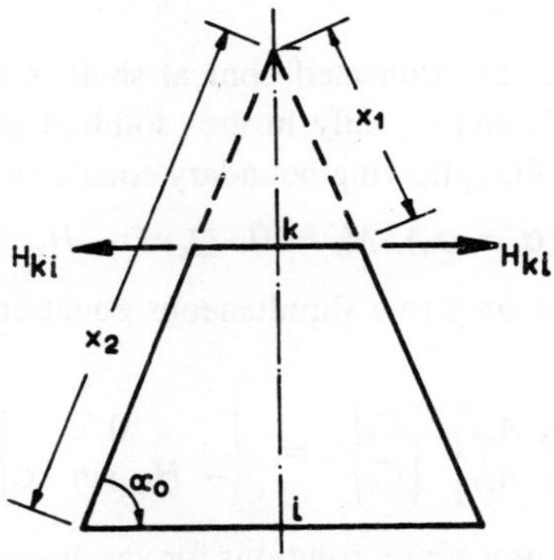

Fig. 5.7 Truncated conical shell subjected to horizontal force at the smaller end

Using the expressions for M_x and Q_x given in Eqs. (5.39) and (5.43) and the boundary conditions, we get the following four simultaneous equations:

$$\begin{bmatrix} A_{11} & A_{12} & A_{13} & A_{14} \\ A_{21} & A_{22} & A_{23} & A_{24} \\ A_{31} & A_{32} & A_{33} & A_{34} \\ A_{41} & A_{42} & A_{43} & A_{44} \end{bmatrix} \begin{Bmatrix} C_1 \\ C_2 \\ C_3 \\ C_4 \end{Bmatrix} = \begin{Bmatrix} 0 \\ -H_{ki} \sin \alpha_o \\ 0 \\ 0 \end{Bmatrix} \tag{5.46}$$

where

$$A_{m1} = \frac{1}{\lambda^2 x_n} [\lambda \sqrt{x_n}\; G'_{10}(\alpha_n) + \nu\, G_{10}(\alpha_n)]$$

$$A_{m2} = \frac{-1}{\lambda^2 x_n} [\lambda \sqrt{x_n}\; G'_9(\alpha_n) + \nu\, G_9(\alpha_n)]$$

$$A_{m3} = \frac{1}{\lambda^2 x_n} [\lambda \sqrt{x_n}\; G'_{12}(\alpha_n) + \nu\, G_{12}(\alpha_n)]$$

$$A_{m4} = \frac{-1}{\lambda^2 x_n} [\lambda \sqrt{x_n}\; G'_{11}(\alpha_n) + \nu\, G_{11}(\alpha_n)]$$

$$A_{l1} = \frac{1}{x_n} G_9(\alpha_n),\; A_{l2} = \frac{1}{x_n} G_{10}(\alpha_n)$$

$$A_{l3} = \frac{1}{x_n} G_{11}(\alpha_n),\; A_{l4} = \frac{1}{x_n} G_{12}(\alpha_n)$$

and

$m = 1, \quad n = 1$

$m = 2, \quad n = 2$

$l = 3, \quad n = 1$

$l = 4, \quad n = 2$

The constants C_1 to C_4 can now be determined by solving Eq. (5.46) and then the forces and displacements can be determined using Eqs. (5.40) – (5.45).

If on the other hand, the truncated conical shell is long, then we need to consider the constants C_3 and C_4 only in the solution and these constants are determined by enforcing the following boundary condition at the small end:

$$x = x_1 \ (\alpha = \alpha_1), \ M_x = 0, \ Q_x = - H_{ki} \sin \alpha_o$$

Hence, we will now have only two simultaneous equations and Eq. (5.46) now reduces to

$$\begin{bmatrix} A_{13} & A_{14} \\ A_{23} & A_{24} \end{bmatrix} \begin{Bmatrix} C_3 \\ C_4 \end{Bmatrix} = \begin{Bmatrix} 0 \\ - H_{ki} \sin \alpha_o \end{Bmatrix} \qquad (5.47)$$

Following the above procedure, solutions for various edge loadings for a long truncated conical shell can be obtained and these have been given by Hampe[5.2] and are presented in Tables 5.7 and 5.8. The solution given in Table 5.8 for a truncated conical shell subjected to the edge loadings at the larger end can also be used for a long complete conical shell. Tables giving the value of G functions for a wide range of α values are available (see for example Hampe[5.2], Vol. 4). However, G functions can also be computed by using Kelvin functions and tables giving the values of Kelvin functions and their first derivative for a wide range of α values are available (see for example Lowell[5.7]). For convenience, a table of G functions and their first derivative, covering a range $0 \leq \alpha \leq 10$ is given in Appendix II. For $\alpha > 10$, the G functions may be computed with sufficient accuracy using the asymptotic expressions which are also given in Appendix-II.

Example 5.2

To illustrate the use of the above solution, consider a concrete conical shell hinged at the bottom and having dimensions as shown in Fig. 5.8. We will determine the membrane forces and bending moment in the shell due to its own weight and assuming that the Poisson's ratio as zero. (Density of concrete – 2400 kg/m^3).

Dead load $g = 0.1 \times 2400 = 240$ kg/m^2

Since the bottom end is hinged, no horizontal displacement can occur.

(a) Primary analysis

The membrane forces and the horizontal displacement at the bottom end can be computed using Table 2.2a.

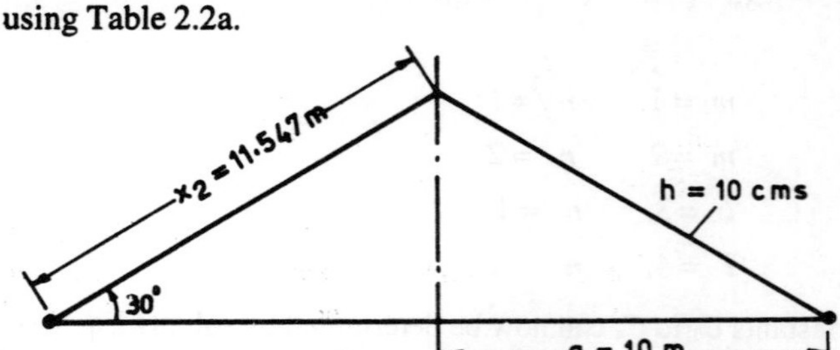

Fig. 5.8

Table 5.7 Forces and displacements in a truncated conical shell due to edge loadings at the smaller end

Force or displacement		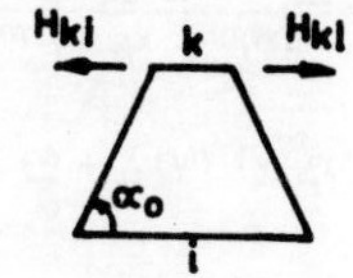
N_x	$M_{ki} \dfrac{x_1 \lambda^2 \cot \alpha_0}{x N_{M_{ki}}} [G_{12} G_{11}(\alpha) - G_{11} G_{12}(\alpha)]$	$- H_{ki} \dfrac{x_1 \cos \alpha_0}{x N_{H_{ki}}} [\{\lambda \sqrt{x_1} G'_{11} + \nu G_{11}\} G_{11}(\alpha) + \{\lambda \sqrt{x_1} G'_{12} + \nu G_{12}(\alpha)\} G_{12}(\alpha)]$
N_θ	$M_{ki} \dfrac{x_1 \lambda^3 \cot \alpha_o}{\sqrt{x} N_{M_{ki}}} [G_{12} G'_{11}(\alpha) - G_{11} G'_{12}(\alpha)]$	$- H_{ki} \dfrac{\lambda x_1 \cos \alpha_o}{\sqrt{x} N_{H_{ki}}} [\{\lambda \sqrt{x_1} G'_{11} + \nu G_{11}\} G'_{11}(\alpha) + \{\lambda \sqrt{x_1} G'_{12} + \nu G_{12}\} G'_{12}(\alpha)]$
M_x	$\dfrac{M_{ki}\, x_1}{x N_{M_{ki}}} [G_{12} \{\lambda \sqrt{x} G'_{12}(\alpha) + \nu G_{12}(\alpha)\}$ $+ G_{11} \{\lambda \sqrt{x} G'_{1}(\alpha) + \nu G_{11}(\alpha)\}]$	$- H_{ki} \dfrac{x_1 \sin \alpha_0}{x \lambda^2 N_{H_{ki}}} [(\lambda \sqrt{x_1} G'_{11} + \nu G_{11}) \{\lambda \sqrt{x} G'_{12}(\alpha) + \nu G_{12}(\alpha)\}$ $- (\lambda \sqrt{x_1} G'_{12} + \nu G_{12}) \{\lambda \sqrt{x} G'_{11}(\alpha) + \nu G_{11}(\alpha)\}]$
M_θ	$\dfrac{M_{ki}\, x_1}{x N_{M_{ki}}} [G_{12} \{\nu\lambda \sqrt{x} G'_{12}(\alpha) + G_{12}(\alpha)\}$ $+ G_{11} \{\nu\lambda \sqrt{x} G'_{11}(\alpha) + G_{11}(\alpha)\}]$	$- H_{ki} \dfrac{x_1 \sin \alpha_0}{\lambda^2 x N_{H_{ki}}} [(\lambda \sqrt{x_1} G'_{11} + \nu G_{11}) \{\nu\lambda \sqrt{x} G'_{12}(\alpha) + G_{12}(\alpha)\}$ $- (\lambda \sqrt{x_1} G'_{12} + \nu G_{12}) \{\nu\lambda \sqrt{x} G'_{11}(\alpha) + G_{11}(\alpha)\}]$
β	$- \dfrac{M_{ki}\, x_1}{D N_{M_{ki}}} [G_{12} G_{12}(\alpha) + G_{11} G_{11}(\alpha)]$	$H_{ki} \dfrac{x_1 \sin \alpha_0}{\lambda^2 D N_{H_{ki}}} [(\lambda \sqrt{x_1} G'_{11} + \nu G_{11}) G_{12}(\alpha) - (\lambda \sqrt{x_1} G'_{12} + \nu G_{12}) G_{11}(\alpha)]$
ΔH	$M_{ki} \dfrac{x_1 \sin \alpha_0}{D \lambda^2 N_{M_{ki}}} [G_{12} \{\lambda \sqrt{x} G'_{11}(\alpha) - \nu G_{11}(\alpha)\}$ $- G_{11} \{\lambda \sqrt{x} G'_{12}(\alpha) - \nu G_{12}(\alpha)\}]$	$- H_{ki} \dfrac{x_1 \sin^2 \alpha_0}{D \lambda^4 N_{H_{ki}}} [(\lambda \sqrt{x_1} G'_{11} + \nu G_{11}) \{\lambda \sqrt{x} G'_{11}(\alpha) - \nu G_{11}(\alpha)\}$ $+ (\lambda \sqrt{x_1} G'_{12} + \nu G_{12}) \{\lambda \sqrt{x} G'_{12}(\alpha) - \nu G_{12}(\alpha)\}]$

where $N_{M_{ki}} = \lambda \sqrt{x_1} (G_{11} G'_{11} + G_{12} G'_{12}) + \nu (G_{11}^2 + G_{12}^2)$, $N_{H_{ki}} = \lambda \sqrt{x_1} (G_{12} G'_{12} + G_{11} G'_{11}) + \nu (G_{12}^2 + G_{11}^2)$, $G_{11} = G_{11}(\alpha_1)$, $G_{12} = G_{12}(\alpha_1)$, etc.

Table 5.8 Forces and displacements in a truncated conical shell due to edge loadings at the end

Force or Displacement	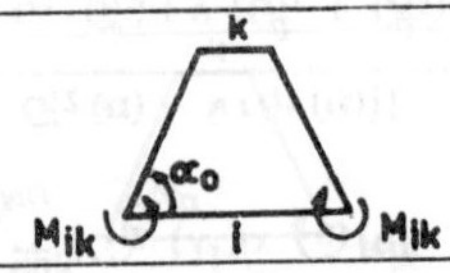	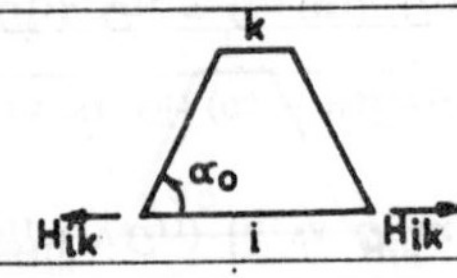
N_x	$M_{ik} \dfrac{x_2 \lambda^2}{N_{M_{ik}} x} \cot \alpha_o \, [- G_{10} G_9(\alpha) + G_9 G_{10}(\alpha)]$	$H_{ik} \dfrac{x_2 \cos \alpha_o}{x N_{H_{ik}}} [(\lambda \sqrt{x_2}\, G_9' + \nu G_9)\, G_9(\alpha)$ $+ (\lambda \sqrt{x_2}\, G_{10}' + \nu G_{10})\, G_{10}(\alpha)]$
N_θ	$M_{ik} \dfrac{x_2 \lambda^3}{\sqrt{x} N_{M_{ik}}} \cot \alpha_o \, [- G_{10} G_9'(\alpha) + G_9 G_{10}'(\alpha)]$	$H_{ik} \dfrac{\lambda x_2 \cos \alpha_o}{\sqrt{x} N_{H_{ik}}} [(\lambda \sqrt{x_2}\, G_9' + \nu G_9)\, G_9'(\alpha)$ $+ (\lambda \sqrt{x_2}\, G_{10}' + \nu G_{10})\, G_{10}'(\alpha)]$
M_x	$- M_{ik} \dfrac{x_2}{x N_{M_{ik}}} [G_{10} \{\lambda \sqrt{x}\, G_{10}'(\alpha) + \nu G_{10}(\alpha)\}$ $+ G_9 \{\lambda \sqrt{x}\, G_9'(\alpha) + \nu G_9(\alpha)\}]$	$H_{ik} \dfrac{x_2 \sin \alpha_o}{x \lambda^2 N_{H_{ik}}} [(\lambda \sqrt{x_2}\, G_9' + \nu G_9)\, \{\lambda \sqrt{x}\, G_{10}'(\alpha) + \nu G_{10}(\alpha)\}$ $- (\lambda \sqrt{x_2}\, G_{10}' + \nu G_{10})\, \{\lambda \sqrt{x}\, G_9'(\alpha) + \nu G_9(\alpha)\}]$
M_θ	$- M_{ik} \dfrac{x_2}{x N_{M_{ik}}} [G_{10} \{\nu\lambda \sqrt{x}\, G_{10}'(\alpha) + G_{10}(\alpha)\}$ $+ G_9 \{\nu\lambda \sqrt{x}\, G_9'(\alpha) + G_9(\alpha)\}]$	$H_{ik} \dfrac{x_2 \sin \alpha_o}{\lambda^2 x N_{H_{ik}}} [(\lambda \sqrt{x_2}\, G_9' + \nu G_9)\, \{\nu\lambda \sqrt{x}\, G_{10}'(\alpha) + G_{10}(\alpha)\}$ $- (\lambda \sqrt{x_2}\, G_{10}' + \nu G_{10})\, \{\nu\lambda \sqrt{x}\, G_9'(\alpha) + G_9(\alpha)\}]$
β	$M_{ik} \dfrac{x_2}{D N_{M_{ik}}} [G_{10} G_{10}(\alpha) + G_9 G_9(\alpha)]$	$- H_{ik} \dfrac{x_2 \sin \alpha_o}{\lambda^2 D N_{H_{ik}}} [(\lambda \sqrt{x_2}\, G_9' + \nu G_9)\, G_{10}(\alpha) - (\lambda \sqrt{x_2}\, G_{10}' + \nu G_{10})\, G_9(\alpha)]$
ΔH	$- M_{ik} \dfrac{x_2 \sin \alpha_o}{D \lambda^2 N_{M_{ik}}} [G_{10} \{\lambda \sqrt{x}\, G_9'(\alpha) - \nu G_9(\alpha)\}$ $- G_9 \{\lambda \sqrt{x}\, G_{10}'(\alpha) - \nu G_{10}(\alpha)\}]$	$H_{ik} \dfrac{x_2 \sin^2 \alpha_o}{D \lambda^4 N_{H_{ik}}} [(\lambda \sqrt{x_2}\, G_9' + \nu G_9)\, \{\lambda \sqrt{x}\, G_9'(\alpha) - \nu G_9(\alpha)\}$ $+ (\lambda \sqrt{x_2}\, G_{10}' + \nu G_{10})\, \{\lambda \sqrt{x}\, G_{10}'(\alpha) - \nu G_{10}(\alpha)\}]$

where $N_{M_{ik}} = \lambda \sqrt{x_2}\, (G_{10} G_{10}' + G_9 G_9') + \nu\, (G_9^2 + G_{10}^2)$, $N_{H_{ik}} = \lambda \sqrt{x_2}\, (G_{10} G_{10}' + G_9 G_9') + \nu\, (G_9^2 + G_{10}^2)$, $G_9 = G_9(\alpha_2)$, $G_{10} = G_{10}(\alpha_2)$, etc.

The membrane forces are

$$N_x = -\frac{gx}{2\sin\alpha_o}$$

$$N_\theta = -\frac{g\,x\cos^2\alpha_o}{\sin\alpha_o}$$

The horizontal displacement at the bottom end can be computed as

$$\Delta H_{ik} = -\frac{gx_2^2\cot\alpha_o\cos^2\alpha_o}{Eh} = -\frac{415703.61}{E}$$

(b) Secondary analysis

$$\lambda = \sqrt[4]{\frac{12(1-\nu^2)\tan^2\alpha_o}{h^2}} = 4.472136$$

$$\alpha = 2\lambda\sqrt{x_2} = 30.3934$$

From Table 5.8,

$$\Delta H_{ik} = \frac{H_{ik}\lambda^2 x_2^2 \sin^2\alpha_o}{D\lambda^4 N_{H_{ik}}}\left[(G_9')^2 + (G_{10}')^2\right]$$

$$\text{and } N_{H_{ik}} = \lambda\sqrt{x_2}\,(G_{10}G_{10}' + G_9G_9')$$

Values of G functions are taken from Hampe[5.2] and are given in Appendix - II. Alternatively from the tables of ber, bei, ker and kei function, G functions can be computed using the relation given earlier.

for $\alpha = 30.3934 \approx 30.4$, the G functions can be obtained as

$$G_1 = -0.98825\times10^8,\quad G_1' = -0.15588\times10^9$$

$$G_2 = -0.12155\times10^9,\quad G_2' = -0.16017\times10^8$$

Now the functions G_9, G_9', G_{10} and G_{10}' are computed using the following relation

$$G_9 = -\frac{2}{\alpha}G_2' - G_1 = 0.99879\times10^8$$

$$G_9' = \frac{2}{\alpha}G_1 - G_1' + \frac{4}{\alpha^2}G_2' = 1.493076\times10^8$$

$$G_{10} = \frac{2}{\alpha}G_1' - G_2 = 1.112925\times10^8$$

$$G_{10}' = \frac{2}{\alpha}G_2 - G_2' + \frac{4}{\alpha^2}G_1' = 0.0734362\times10^8$$

Using the above G functions, $N_{H_{ik}}$ and ΔH_{ik} may be computed as

$$N_{H_{ik}} = \sqrt{x_2}\,(G_{10}G_{10}' + G_9G_9') = 23.904379\times10^{16}$$

$$\Delta H_{ik} = \frac{1869.67}{E}H_{ik}$$

Now, the total horizontal displacement at the bottom edge ($x = x_2$) must be equal to zero. This condition can be written as

$$(\Delta H)_{mem} + (\Delta H_{ik})_{H_{ik}} = 0$$

which gives

$$\frac{1869.67}{E} H_{ik} - \frac{415703.61}{E} = 0$$

from which H_{ik} may be obtained as

$$H_{ik} = 222.34 \text{ kg/m.}$$

Due to the above H_{ik}, the membrane forces N_x, N_θ and bending mement M_x are determined from

$$N_x = \frac{H_{ik} \lambda \sqrt{x_2^3} \cos \alpha_o}{x N_{H_{ik}}} [G_9' G_9(\alpha) + G_{10}' G_{10}(\alpha)]$$

$$N_\theta = \frac{H_{ik} \lambda^2 \sqrt{x_2^3} \cos \alpha_o}{\sqrt{x} N_{H_{ik}}} [G_9' G_9'(\alpha) + G_{10}' G_{10}'(\alpha)]$$

$$M_x = \frac{H_{ik} \sqrt{x_2^3} \sin \alpha_0}{\sqrt{x} N_{H_{ik}}} [G_9' G_{10}'(\alpha) - G_{10}' G_9'(\alpha)]$$

The membrane forces obtained from the above expression are superposed on those obtained from the membrane analysis, to get the final membrane forces. These are given in Table 5.9. Fig. 5.9 shows the distribution of these forces over the inclined length of the shell.

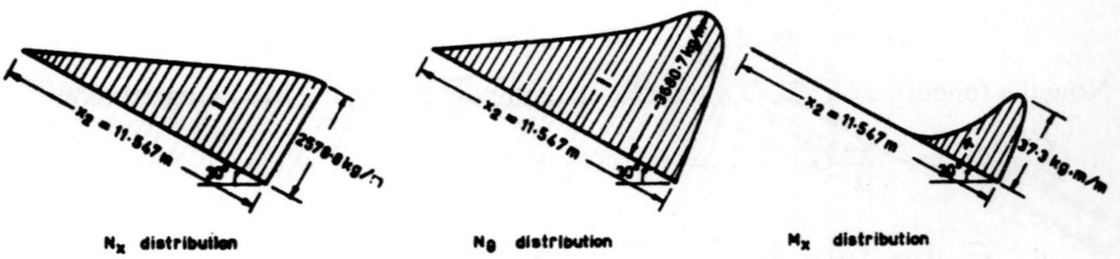

Fig. 5.9

5.2.6.2 Approximate solution for a conical shell

The exact solution for the bending analysis of a conical shell as given above is rather involved. Further, the solution is not easily amenable to design engineers even though tables for Kelvin functions are available. Various attempts have been made to obtain approximate solutions either by simplifying the differential equation or by using simple asymptotic expansion for the Bessel's function in the exact solution. The Geckler approximation, which has been used earlier for spherical shells, provides a method of simplifying the exact differential equation to a form

Table 5.9 Distribution of N_x (kg/m), N_θ (kg/m) and M_x (kg.m/m) in a conical shell

$\frac{x_2}{x}$	N_x (kg/m)			N_θ (kg/m)			M_x (kg.m/m)
	Primary	Secondary	Final	Primary	Secondary	Final	Final
1	−2771.28	192.5	−2578.8	−4157	4157	0	0
0.975							25.63
0.95							36.94
0.9	−2494.15	29.77	−2464.38	−3741	486	−3255	37.31
0.8	−2217.02	−39.59	−2256.61	−3325.6	−355.1	−3680.7	11.51
0.7	−1939.9	−6.24	−1946.14	−2910	−144	−3054	2.02
0.5	−1385.6	0.14	−1385.46	−2078.5	−12.5	−2091	–
0.25	−692.8	–	−692.8	−1039.25	–	−1039.25	–
0	0	–	0	0	–	0	–

similar to the differential equation of a beam on elastic foundation. As mentioned earlier, in the Geckler approximation only the highest derivative in the differential equation which contributes more to the bending effect is retained. It is suggested that the approximate solution so obtained should be used for $\alpha_o \geq 40°$. However, one can get an estimate of the error in the final results for $\alpha_o < 40°$ by comparing the results of this approximate solution with the results of the exact solution given above

Following the above approximation, only the highest derivative in the operator

$$L(\dots) = x(\dots)'' + (\dots)' - \frac{1}{x}(\dots)$$

is to be retained. Thus we have

$$L_1(\dots) = x(\dots)''$$

from which

$$\begin{aligned} L_1 L_1(\dots) &= x[x(\dots)'']'' \\ &= x[(\dots)'' + x(\dots)''']' \end{aligned}$$

Again, retaining the highest derivative in the above operator, we have

$$L_1 L_1(\dots) = x^2(\dots)''''$$

Making use of the above simplification, Eq. (5.35) can now be simplified as

$$\frac{d^4 Q_x}{dx^4} + \frac{\lambda^4}{x^2} Q_x = 0$$

or

$$\frac{d^4 Q_x}{dx^4} + 4k^4 Q_x = 0 \tag{5.48}$$

For k = constant, the above differential equation is similar to that of the beam on elastic foundation. In the above equation, k is given by

$$k = \sqrt[4]{\frac{\lambda^4}{4x^2}} = \frac{\sqrt[4]{3(1-\nu^2)}}{\sqrt{hx \cot \alpha_o}}$$

and is a function of x. To make k constant for a given shell, the above relation can be written

$$k = \frac{\sqrt[4]{3(1-\nu^2)}}{\sqrt{hx_m \cot \alpha_o}}$$

where x_m is an average value of x.

Consistent with the approximation made in the differential equation, the force and displacements are determined using the following relation:

$$N_x = Q_x \cot\alpha_o \tag{5.49a}$$

$$N_\theta = \left(\frac{dQ_x}{dx}\right)(x_m \cot \alpha_o) \tag{5.49b}$$

$$\beta = \phi_x = -\left(\frac{d^2Q_x}{dx^2}\right)\left(\frac{x_m^2}{Eh \tan^2 \alpha_o}\right) \tag{5.49c}$$

$$\Delta H = \frac{r}{Eh}(N_\theta - \nu N_x) = \frac{r}{Eh}(x_m \cot \alpha_o)\frac{dQ_x}{dx} \tag{5.49d}$$

$$M_x = D\frac{d^2w}{dx^2} = -D\frac{d\phi_x}{dx} \tag{5.49e}$$

$$M_\theta = -D\nu\frac{d\phi_x}{dx} = \nu M_x \tag{5.49f}$$

It should be noted that in the expression for ΔH (Eq. 5.49d), the effect of Q_x is neglected as this would be small for a thin shell. This according to Eq. (5.49a) means that the effect of N_x in Eq. (5.49d) can be neglected.

For a truncated conical shell, shifting the origin from the apex to the small end of the frustum, we get a new coordinate (Fig. 5.10)

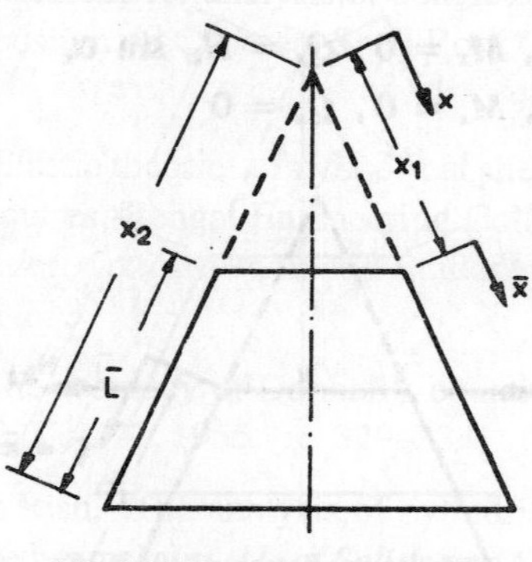

Fig. 5.10 Truncated conical shell

$$\bar{x} = x - x_1$$

and

$$x_m = \frac{x_1 + x_2}{2}$$

where x_1 and x_2 are respectively the distances of the small and large ends of the conical frustum from the apex.

The solution for the differential Eq. (5.48) can now be written as

$$Q_x(\bar{x}) = C_1F_7(\xi) + C_2F_{15}(\xi) + C_3F_{16}(\xi) + C_4F_8(\xi) \tag{5.50}$$

where $\xi = \bar{x}/\bar{L}$ and $F_i(\xi) = F_i(k\bar{L}\xi) = F_i(k\bar{x})$ and are defined in Table 5.3.

Using the solution given in Eqs. (5.50), and Eq. (5.49), the following expressions for forces and displacements may be obtained:

$$N_x = [\,C_1F_7(\xi) + C_2F_{15}(\xi) + C_3F_{16}(\xi) + C_4F_8(\xi)\,] \cot\alpha_o \tag{5.51a}$$

$$N_\theta = kx_m \cot\alpha_o [\,-C_1F_9(\xi) + C_2F_{14}(\xi) + C_3F_{13}(\xi) + C_4F_{10}(\xi)\,] \tag{5.51b}$$

$$M_x = \frac{1}{2k} [-C_1F_{10}(\xi) + C_2F_{13}(\xi) - C_3F_{14}(\xi) - C_4F_9(\xi)\,] \tag{5.51c}$$

$$M_\theta = \frac{\nu}{2k} [-C_1F_{10}(\xi) + C_2F_{13}(\xi) - C_3F_{14}(\xi) - C_4F_9(\xi)\,] \tag{5.51d}$$

$$\beta = \frac{1}{2Dk^2} [\,C_1F_8(\xi) - C_2F_{16}(\xi) + C_3F_{15}(\xi) - C_4F_7(\xi)\,] \tag{5.51e}$$

$$\Delta H = \frac{\sin\alpha_o}{4Dk^3} [\,-C_1F_9(\xi) + C_2F_{14}(\xi) + C_3F_{13}(\xi) + C_4F_{10}(\xi)\,] \tag{5.51f}$$

The constants C_1 to C_4 are determined from the boundary conditions.

As an example, consider a truncated conical shell subjected to a horizontal force at the short end as shown in Fig. 5.11. The boundary conditions can be written as

$$\xi = 0,\ M_x = 0,\ Q_x = H_{ki} \sin\alpha_o$$
$$\xi = 1,\ M_x = 0,\ Q_x = 0$$

Fig. 5.11 Truncated conical shell with a horizontal force at the smaller end

Using the above boundary conditions, the following four equations can be set up to determine the constants C_1 to C_4

$$\begin{bmatrix} 0 & 1 & -1 & 0 \\ 1 & 0 & 0 & 0 \\ -F_{10} & F_{13} & -F_{14} & -F_9 \\ F_7 & F_{15} & F_{10} & F_8 \end{bmatrix} \begin{Bmatrix} C_1 \\ C_2 \\ C_3 \\ C_4 \end{Bmatrix} = \begin{Bmatrix} 0 \\ H_{ki}\sin\alpha_o \\ 0 \\ 0 \end{Bmatrix} \tag{5.52}$$

Solving the above equations, the constants C_1 to C_4 can be determined. In Tables 5.10 and 5.11 (Ref. 5.2, 5.3), expressions for forces and displacements in a truncated conical shell subjected to different edge loadings are given.

A conical shell water tower is shown in Fig. 5.12.

Fig. 5.12 A conical shell water tower of capacity 450,000 litres on a circular cylindrical shaft (courtesy H.K. Nanjundaswamy, Consulting and Construction Engineer, Bangalore)

Example 5.3

A truncated conical shell water tank has a radius of 1.25 m at the bottom and a radius of 5.5m at the top (Fig. 5.13). The thickness of the shell is 15 cms and the base angle $\alpha_o = 40^\circ$. It is assumed that the bottom end of the conical shell is fixed. It is required to determine the membrane forces and bending moment in the shell due to dead load and water load, considering the tank is full. Poisson's ratio has been assumed to be zero and the unit weight of concrete has been taken as 2500 kg/m^3. We will use the approximate solution to solve this problem.

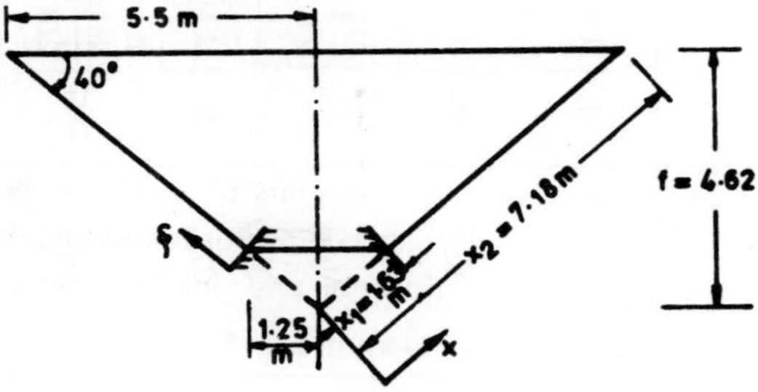

Fig. 5.13

Table 5.10 Forces and displacements in a truncated conical shell due to edge loading

Force or displacement	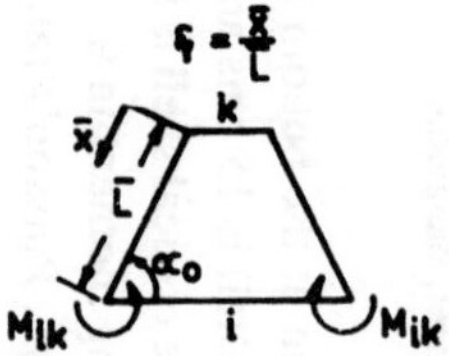 	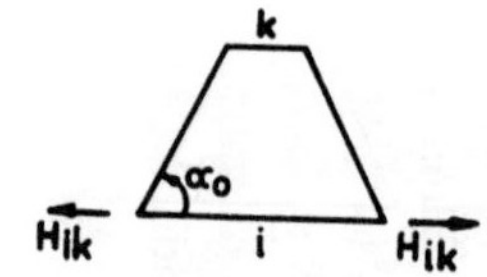
N_x	$M_{ik}\left[2k\cot\alpha_o\left\{\frac{F_8}{F_2}F_{10}(\xi)-\frac{F_{10}}{F_1}F_8(\xi)\right\}\right]$	$H_{ik}\left[\cos\alpha_o\left\{-\frac{F_9}{F_1}F_{10}(\xi)+\frac{2F_8}{F_1}F_8(\xi)\right\}\right]$
N_θ	$M_{ik}\left[2k^2x_m\cot\alpha_o\left\{\frac{2F_8}{F_1}F_7(\xi)-\frac{F_{10}}{F_1}F_{10}(\xi)\right\}\right]$	$H_{ik}\left[2x_mk\cos\alpha_o\left\{-\frac{F_9}{F_1}F_7(\xi)+\frac{F_8}{F_1}F_{10}(\xi)\right\}\right]$
M_x	$-M_{ik}\left[\frac{2F_8}{F_1}F_8(\xi)-\frac{F_{10}}{F_1}F_9(\xi)\right]$	$H_{ik}\left[\frac{\sin\alpha_o}{k}\left\{\frac{F_9}{F_1}F_8(\xi)-\frac{F_8}{F_1}F_9(\xi)\right\}\right]$
Q_x	$M_{ik}\left[2k\left\{\frac{F_8}{F_1}F_{10}(\xi)-\frac{F_{10}}{F_1}F_8(\xi)\right\}\right]$	$H_{ik}\left[\sin\alpha_o\left\{-\frac{F_9}{F_1}F_{10}(\xi)+\frac{2F_8}{F_1}F_8(\xi)\right\}\right]$
ΔH	$M_{ik}\left[\frac{\sin\alpha_o}{2Dk^2}\left\{\frac{2F_8}{F_1}F_7(\xi)-\frac{F_{10}}{F_1}F_{10}(\xi)\right\}\right]$	$H_{ik}\left[\frac{\sin^2\alpha_o}{2Dk^3}\left\{-\frac{F_9}{F_1}F_7(\xi)+\frac{F_8}{F_1}F_{10}(\xi)\right\}\right]$
β	$M_{ik}\left[\frac{1}{Dk}\left\{\frac{F_8}{F_1}F_9(\xi)+\frac{F_{10}}{F_1}F_7(\xi)\right\}\right]$	$-H_{ik}\left[\frac{\sin\alpha_o}{2Dk^2}\left\{\frac{F_9}{F_1}F_9(\xi)+\frac{2F_8}{F_1}F_7(\xi)\right\}\right]$

Table 5.11 Forces and displacements in a truncated conical shell due to edge loading

Force or dispiacement	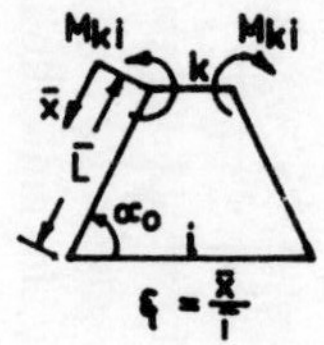	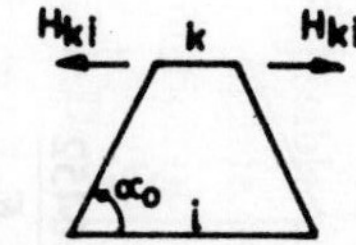
N_x	$M_{ki}\left[2k\cot\alpha_o\left\{\frac{F_6}{F_1}F_{15}(\xi)+\frac{F_5}{F_1}F_{16}(\xi)-\frac{F_3}{F_1}F_8(\xi)\right\}\right]$	$-H_{ki}\cos\alpha_o\left[F_7(\xi)-\frac{F_4}{F_1}F_{10}(\xi)+\frac{F_2}{F_1}F_8(\xi)\right]$
N_θ	$M_{ki}\left[2k^2x_m\cot\alpha_o\left\{\frac{F_6}{F_1}F_{14}(\xi)+\frac{F_5}{F_1}F_{13}(\xi)-\frac{F_3}{F_1}F_{10}(\xi)\right\}\right]$	$H_{ki}\left[x_mk\cos\alpha_o\left\{F_9(\xi)+\frac{2F_4}{F_1}F_7(\xi)-\frac{F_2}{F_1}F_{10}(\xi)\right\}\right]$
M_x	$M_{ki}\left[\frac{F_6}{F_1}F_{13}(\xi)-\frac{F_5}{F_1}F_{14}(\xi)+\frac{F_3}{F_1}F_9(\xi)\right]$	$H_{ki}\left[\frac{\sin\alpha_o}{2k}\left\{F_{10}(\xi)-\frac{2F_4}{F_1}F_8(\xi)+\frac{F_2}{F_1}F_9(\xi)\right\}\right]$
Q_x	$M_{ki}\left[2k\left\{\frac{F_6}{F_1}F_{15}(\xi)+\frac{F_5}{F_1}F_{16}(\xi)-\frac{F_3}{F_1}F_8(\xi)\right\}\right]$	$-H_{ki}\left[\sin\alpha_o\left\{F_7(\xi)-\frac{F_4}{F_1}F_{10}(\xi)+\frac{F_2}{F_1}F_8(\xi)\right\}\right]$
ΔH	$M_{ki}\left[\frac{\sin\alpha_o}{2Dk^2}\left\{\frac{F_6}{F_1}F_{14}(\xi)+\frac{F_5}{F_1}F_{13}(\xi)-\frac{F_3}{F_1}F_{10}(\xi)\right\}\right]$	$H_{ki}\left[\frac{\sin^2\alpha_o}{4Dk^3}\left\{F_9(\xi)+\frac{2F_4}{F_1}F_7(\xi)-\frac{F_2}{F_1}F_{10}(\xi)\right\}\right]$
β	$-\frac{M_{ki}}{Dk}\left[\frac{F_6}{F_1}F_{16}(\xi)-\frac{F_5}{F_1}F_{15}(\xi)-\frac{F_3}{F_1}F_7(\xi)\right]$	$H_{ki}\left[\frac{\sin\alpha_o}{2Dk^2}\left\{-F_8(\xi)+\frac{F_4}{F_1}F_9(\xi)+\frac{F_2}{F_1}F_7(\xi)\right\}\right]$

Since the bottom end ($x = x_1$) is assumed to be fixed, no displacement can occur at this end.

(a) Primary analysis

The membrane horizontal displacement and rotation due to dead and water loads are first determined using Table 2.3b. Since for the membrane analysis, the shell is to be considered as supported at bottom ($x = x_1$), the expressions given in Table 2.3b are to be used.

Dead load.

$$g = 2500 \times 0.15 = 0.375 \text{ t/m}^2$$

$$\Delta H_{ik} = \frac{g x_1^2 \cot \alpha_o}{2Eh}\left[2\cos^2 \alpha_o - \nu\left(1 - \frac{x_2^2}{x_1^2}\right)\right] = \frac{4.6452}{E}$$

$$\beta_{ik} = \frac{g x_1 \cos \alpha_o}{2Eh \sin^2 \alpha_o}\left[2\cos^2 \alpha_o (2+\nu) - 1 - 2\nu + \frac{x_2^2}{x_1^2}\right] = \frac{78.3872}{E}$$

Water load.

$$\Delta H_{ik} = \frac{\gamma x_1^2 \cos^2 \alpha_o}{Eh}\left[\nu\left\{\frac{x_1}{3}\left(1 - \frac{x_2^3}{x_1^3}\right) - \frac{f}{2\sin \alpha_o}\left(1 - \frac{x_2^2}{x_1^2}\right)\right\} + \frac{f}{\sin \alpha_o} - x_1\right] = \frac{57.7653}{E}$$

$$\beta_{ik} = \frac{\gamma x_1 \cos^2 \alpha_o}{Eh \sin \alpha_o}\left[\frac{f}{2\sin \alpha_o}\left(3 + \frac{x_2^2}{x_1^2}\right) - \frac{x_1}{3}\left(8 + \frac{x_2^3}{x_1^3}\right)\right] = \frac{294.8977}{E}$$

The total horizontal displacement and rotation due to dead and water loads will then be

$$(\Delta H_{ik})_m = \frac{4.6452}{E} + \frac{57.7653}{E} = \frac{62.4105}{E}$$

$$(\beta_{ik})_m = \frac{78.3872}{E} + \frac{294.8977}{E} = \frac{373.2849}{E}$$

Secondary analysis:

$$k = \frac{\sqrt[4]{3(1 - \nu^2)}}{\sqrt{h x_m \cot \alpha_o}} \quad \text{and} \quad x_m = (x_1 + x_2)/2$$

$$k = 1.483\ m^{-1} \quad \bar{L} = x_2 - x_1 = 5.55\text{m}$$

$$k\bar{L} = 8.23065$$

The horizontal displacement and rotation due to the application of the moment M_{ki} and horizontal force H_{ki} at the bottom end ($x = x_1$) can be determined using Table 5.11.

$$\Delta H_{ki} = M_{ki}\left[\frac{\sin \alpha_o}{2Dk^2}\left\{\frac{F_6}{F_1} F_{14}(\xi) + \frac{F_5}{F_1} F_{13}(\xi) - \frac{F_3}{F_1} F_{10}(\xi)\right\}\right]$$

$$+ H_{ki}\left[\frac{\sin^2\alpha_o}{4Dk^3}\left\{F_9(\xi) + \frac{2F_4}{F_1}F_7(\xi) - \frac{F_2}{F_1}F_{10}(\xi)\right\}\right]$$

$$\beta_{ki} = -M_{ki}\left[\frac{F_6}{F_1}F_{16}(\xi) - \frac{F_5}{F_1}F_{15}(\xi) - \frac{F_3}{F_1}F_7(\xi)\right]$$

$$+ H_{ki}\left[\frac{\sin^2\alpha_o}{2Dk^3}\left\{-F_8(\xi) + \frac{F_4}{F_1}F_9(\xi) - \frac{F_2}{F_1}F_7(\xi)\right\}\right]$$

for $k\bar{L} = 8.23$, $\frac{F_6}{F_1} \approx 1$, $\frac{F_5}{F_1} \approx 0$, $\frac{F_3}{F_1} \approx 1$

The bottom end ($x = x_1$) corresponds to $\xi = 0$ and hence

$$F_7(\xi) = 1,\ F_8(\xi) = 0,\ F_9(\xi) = 0,\ F_{10}(\xi) = 0$$

$$F_{13}(\xi) = 1,\ F_{14}(\xi) = 1,\ F_{15}(\xi) = 0,\ F_{16}(\xi) = 0$$

Using the above values of function in ΔH_{ki} and β_{ki} we get

$$\Delta H_{ki} = \frac{1}{2Dk^3}(k\sin\alpha_o M_{ki} + \sin^2\alpha_0 H_{ki})$$

$$= \frac{544.935}{E}(0.953255\,M_{ki} + 0.413176\,H_{ki})$$

$$\beta_{ki} = \frac{1}{2Dk^2}(2k\,M_{ki} + \sin\alpha_o H_{ki})$$

$$= \frac{808.1391}{E}(2.966\,M_{ki} + 0.642788\,H_{ki})$$

Since the bottom end is fixed, the total horizontal displacement and rotation should be zero. This can be written as

$$(\Delta H_{ik})_m + (\Delta H_{ki}) = 0$$

$$(\beta_{ik})_m + (\beta_{ki}) = 0$$

The above condition results in the following two equations

$$\begin{bmatrix} 0.953255, & 0.413176 \\ 2.966, & 0.642788 \end{bmatrix}\begin{Bmatrix} M_{ki} \\ H_{ki} \end{Bmatrix} = \begin{Bmatrix} -0.114528 \\ -0.461907 \end{Bmatrix}$$

Solving the above simultaneous equations, we get

$$M_{ki} = -0.191 \text{ t.m/m},\quad H_{ki} = 0.164 \text{ t/m}$$

The membrane forces and bending mement developed in the shell due to the above edge forces can be determined from Table 5.11. The final membrane forces are obtained by adding the results obtained from membrane analysis (Table 2.3b). The results are given in Tables 5.12 - 5.14.

Table 5.12 N_x(t/m) distribution

ξ	x in m	Membrane dead load	Membrane water load	due to M_{ki}	due to H_{ki}	Total
0	1.63	−8.75	−70.09	0	−0.13	−78.97
0.2	2.74	−4.69	−33	−0.13	0.03	−37.79
0.4	3.85	−2.78	−16.88	0	0	−19.66
0.6	4.96	−1.59	−8.08	0	0	−9.67
0.8	6.07	−0.71	−2.92	0	0	−3.63
1.0	7.18	0	0	0	0	0

Table 5.13 N_θ(t/m) distribution

ξ	x in m	Membrane dead load	Membrane water load	due to M_{ki}	due to H_{ki}	Total
0	1.63	0.56	6.93	−4.41	1.64	4.72
0.2	2.74	0.94	9.32	0.91	−0.02	11.15
0.4	3.85	1.32	9.82	0.14	−0.06	11.22
0.6	4.96	1.7	8.44	−0.04	0	10.1
0.8	6.07	2.08	5.16	0	0	7.24
1.0	7.18	2.46	0	0	0	2.46

Table 5.14 M_x (t.m/m) distribution

ξ	x in m	Due to M_{ki}	Due to H_{ki}	Total
0	1.63	−0.191	0	−0.191
0.1	2.185	−0.118	0.023	−0.095
0.2	2.74	−0.034	0.014	−0.02
0.4	3.85	0.008	0	0.008
0.6	4.96	0.001	0	0.001
0.8	6.07	0	0	0
1.0	7.18	0	0	0

5.2.7 Cylindrical shell

5.2.7.1 Differential equation

We will use x-coordinate in the length direction and θ-coordinate in the circumferential direction. The equilibrium Eqs. (5.1a–c) and the force-displacement relation (5.8) can now be reduced for a cylindrical shell by making use of the following identity:

$$\phi \rightarrow x, \ \frac{d}{r_1\, d\phi}(\dots) = \frac{d}{dx}(\dots), \quad r_1 = \infty, \ r_2 = r_o = a, \ \phi = 90^\circ$$

Figure 5.14 shows an element of the cylindrical shell with the internal forces acting on it, when it is subjected to an axisymmetric edge loading. The equilibrium equations can be obtained as

$$\frac{dN_x}{dx} = 0 \tag{5.53a}$$

$$\frac{dQ_x}{dx} + \frac{N_\theta}{a} = 0 \tag{5.53b}$$

$$\frac{dM_x}{dx} - Q_x = 0 \tag{5.53c}$$

[Note that the direction of Q_x is opposite to the one considered in Eqs. (5.1a–c)].

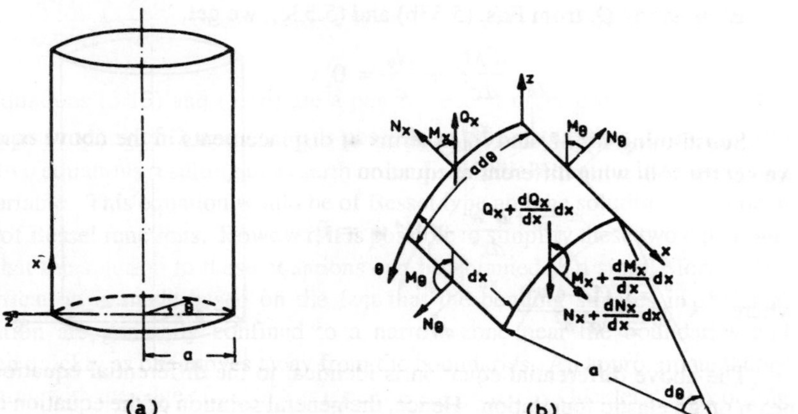

Fig.5.14 Internal forces in a cylindrical shell

The first equilibrium equation indicates that force N_x is constant and for convenience this force can be assumed to be zero. If it is likely to be different from zero, then the stress and displacements corresponding to this constant force can be computed and superposed. Considering the last two equations (Eqs. (5.53a) and (5.53b)), we find that there are three unknown quantities namely N_θ, M_x and Q_x. Since there are only two equations involving three unknowns, it becomes necessary to consider the deformation of the shell.

The force-displacement relation given earlier in Eq. (5.8) can now be reduced for a cylindrical shell as:

$$N_x = K\left(\frac{du}{dx} + \nu\,\frac{w}{a}\right) \tag{5.54a}$$

$$N_\theta = K\left(\frac{w}{a} + \nu\,\frac{du}{dx}\right) \tag{5.54b}$$

$$M_x = D \frac{d^2w}{dx^2} \tag{5.54c}$$

Since N_x has been assumed to be zero, Eq. (5.54a) gives the following relationship between u and w

$$\frac{du}{dx} = -\nu \left(\frac{w}{a}\right)$$

Substituting the above relation in Eq. (5.54b), we get

$$N_\theta = \frac{Ehw}{a}$$

Eliminating Q_x from Eqs. (5.53b) and (5.53c), we get

$$\frac{d^2M_x}{dx^2} + \frac{N_\theta}{a} = 0$$

Substituting for M_x and N_θ in terms of displacements in the above equation, we get the following differential equation

$$\frac{d^4w}{dx^4} + 4k^4 w = 0 \tag{5.55}$$

where $k^4 = \dfrac{3\,(1 - \nu^2)}{a^2 h^2}$

The above differential equation is identical to the differential equation of a beam on an elastic foundation. Hence, the general solution of the equation can be written as

$$w = e^{-kL\xi}\,(C_1 \cos kL\xi + C_2 \sin kL\xi) + e^{kL\xi}\,(C_3 \cos kL\xi + C_4 \sin kL\xi) \tag{5.56a}$$

or in terms of hyperbolic functions, the solution can be written as

$$w = C_1F_7(\xi) + C_2F_{15}(\xi) + C_3F_{16}(\xi) + C_4F_8(\xi) \tag{5.56b}$$

where $\xi = x/L$ and functions $F_7(\xi)$, $F_8(\xi)$, etc. are defined in Table 5.3. The constants $C_1, C_2, \ldots C_4$ are determined by using the boundary conditions.

As an example, let us consider a cylindrical shell subjected to an edge moment at $\xi = 0$ as shown in Fig. 5.15. For this case, the boundary conditions can be written as

$$\xi = 0,\ M_x = -M_{ik},\ Q_x = 0$$

$$\xi = 1,\ M_x = 0,\ Q_x = 0$$

Using the above boundary conditions, the constants, C_1 to C_4 can be determined as

$$C_1 = -\frac{M_{ik}}{2Dk^2}\,\frac{F_2}{F_1} \tag{5.57a}$$

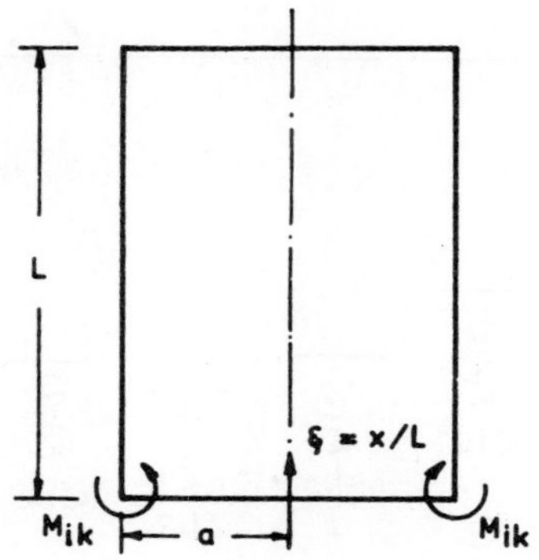

Fig. 5.15 Cylindrical shell subjected to moment at the edge

$$C_2 = C_3 = \frac{M_{ik}}{2Dk^2}\frac{F_3}{F_1} \tag{5.57b}$$

$$C_4 = -\frac{M_{ik}}{2Dk^2} \tag{5.57c}$$

Using the above values for the constants, the forces and displacements, for this case, can be determined as

$$N_\theta = M_{ik}\left[2k^2 a\left\{-\frac{F_2}{F_1}F_7(\xi) + \frac{F_3}{F_1}F_{10}(\xi) - F_8(\xi)\right\}\right] \tag{5.58a}$$

$$M_x = M_{ik}\left[\left\{\frac{F_2}{F_1}F_8(\xi) - \frac{F_3}{F_1}F_9(\xi) - F_7(\xi)\right\}\right] \tag{5.58b}$$

$$Q_x = -M_{ik}\left[k\left\{\frac{F_2}{F_1}F_{10}(\xi) - \frac{2F_3}{F_1}F_8(\xi) + F_9(\xi)\right\}\right] \tag{5.58c}$$

$$\Delta H = \frac{M_{ik}}{2Dk^2}\left[-\frac{F_2}{F_1}F_7(\xi) + \frac{F_3}{F_1}F_{10}(\xi) - F_8(\xi)\right] \tag{5.58d}$$

$$\beta = \frac{M_{ik}}{2Dk}\left[\frac{F_2}{F_1}F_9(\xi) + \frac{2F_3}{F_1}F_7(\xi) - F_{10}(\xi)\right] \tag{5.58e}$$

The expressions for forces and displacements for several cases of edge loadings as given by Baker et al[5.3] are given in Tables 5.15 and 5.16.

Example 5.4

A circular water tank has a radius of 12 m thickness 16 cm and height 5 m but filled with water partially upto 2 m, as shown in Fig. 5.16. It is assumed that the wall is fixed at the base and free at top. It is required to determine the membrane force and bending moment in the wall. Poisson's ratio may be taken as 1/6.

Table 5.15 Forces and displacements in a cylindrical shell due to edge loading

Force or displacement	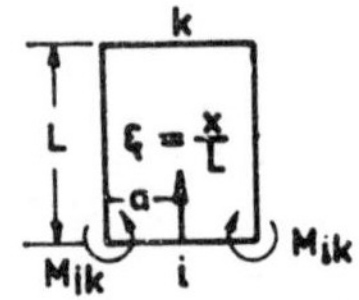	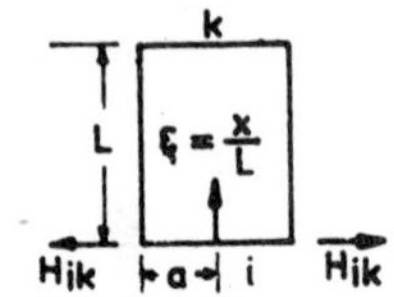
N_θ	$M_{ik}\left[2k^2a\left\{-\frac{F_2}{F_1}F_7(\xi)+\frac{F_3}{F_1}F_{10}(\xi)-F_8(\xi)\right\}\right]$	$H_{ik}\left[2ka\left\{\frac{F_4}{F_1}F_7(\xi)-\frac{F_5}{F_1}F_{15}(\xi)-\frac{F_6}{F_1}F_{16}(\xi)\right\}\right]$
M_x	$M_{ik}\left[\frac{F_2}{F_1}F_8(\xi)-\frac{F_3}{F_1}F_9(\xi)-F_7(\xi)\right]$	$\frac{H_{ik}}{k}\left[-\frac{F_4}{F_1}F_8(\xi)-\frac{F_5}{F_1}F_{16}(\xi)+\frac{F_6}{F_1}F_{15}(\xi)\right]$
Q_x	$-kM_{ik}\left[\frac{F_2}{F_1}F_{10}(\xi)-\frac{2F_3}{F_1}F_8(\xi)+F_9(\xi)\right]$	$-H_{ik}\left[\frac{F_4}{F_1}F_{10}(\xi)+\frac{F_5}{F_1}F_{13}(\xi)-\frac{F_6}{F_1}F_{14}(\xi)\right]$
ΔH	$\frac{M_{ik}}{2Dk^2}\left[-\frac{F_2}{F_1}F_7(\xi)+\frac{F_3}{F_1}F_{10}(\xi)-F_8(\xi)\right]$	$\frac{H_{ik}}{2Dk^3}\left[\frac{F_4}{F_1}F_7(\xi)-\frac{F_5}{F_1}F_{15}(\xi)-\frac{F_6}{F_1}F_{16}(\xi)\right]$
β	$\frac{M_{ik}}{2Dk}\left[\frac{F_2}{F_1}F_9(\xi)+\frac{2F_3}{F_1}F_7(\xi)-F_{10}(\xi)\right]$	$-\frac{H_{ik}}{2Dk^2}\left[\frac{F_4}{F_1}F_9(\xi)+\frac{F_5}{F_1}F_{14}(\xi)+\frac{F_6}{F_1}F_{13}(\xi)\right]$

Table 5.16 Forces and displacements in a cylindrical shell due to edge loading

Force or displacement	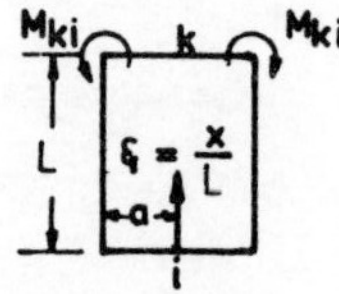	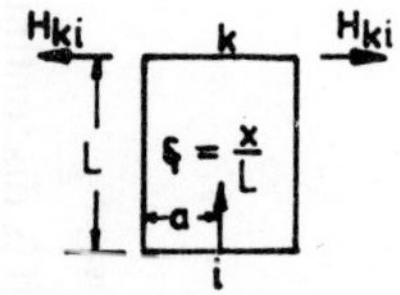
N_θ	$M_{ki}\,2k^2 a\left[-\dfrac{2F_8}{F_1}F_7(\xi)+\dfrac{F_{10}}{F_1}F_{10}(\xi)\right]$	$H_{ki}\,2k\,a\left[-\dfrac{F_9}{F_1}F_7(\xi)+\dfrac{F_8}{F_1}F_{10}(\xi)\right]$
M_x	$M_{ki}\left[\dfrac{2F_8}{F_1}F_8(\xi)-\dfrac{F_{10}}{F_1}F_9(\xi)\right]$	$\dfrac{H_{ki}}{k}\left[\dfrac{F_9}{F_1}F_8(\xi)-\dfrac{F_8}{F_1}F_9(\xi)\right]$
Q_x	$-M_{ki}\,k\left[\dfrac{2F_8}{F_1}F_{10}(\xi)-\dfrac{2F_{10}}{F_1}F_8(\xi)\right]$	$H_{ki}\left[\dfrac{F_9}{F_1}F_{10}(\xi)-\dfrac{2F_8}{F_1}F_8(\xi)\right]$
ΔH	$\dfrac{M_{ki}}{2Dk^2}\left[-\dfrac{2F_8}{F_1}F_7(\xi)+\dfrac{F_{10}}{F_1}F_{10}(\xi)\right]$	$\dfrac{H_{ki}}{2Dk^3}\left[-\dfrac{F_9}{F_1}F_7(\xi)+\dfrac{F_8}{F_1}F_{10}(\xi)\right]$
β	$\dfrac{M_{ki}}{2Dk}\left[\dfrac{2F_8}{F_1}F_9(\xi)+\dfrac{2F_{10}}{F_1}F_7(\xi)\right]$	$\dfrac{H_{ki}}{2Dk^2}\left[\dfrac{F_9}{F_1}F_9(\xi)+\dfrac{2F_8}{F_1}F_7(\xi)\right]$

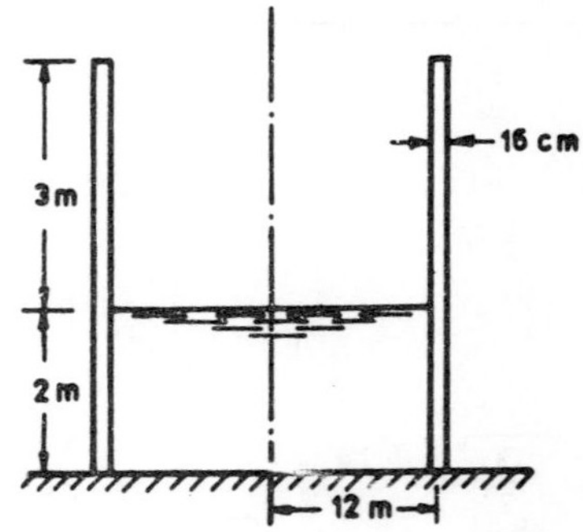

Fig. 5.16 Circular water tank partially filled with water

Since the water load acting on the cylindrical shell wall is discontinuous, the problem cannot be solved directly. To solve this problem, the shell is to be cut, at the point of discontinuity of the load, into two parts as shown in Fig. 5.17 and each part is analysed (both primary and secondary analysis) separately. The unknown forces along the cut are determined by using the continuity conditions.

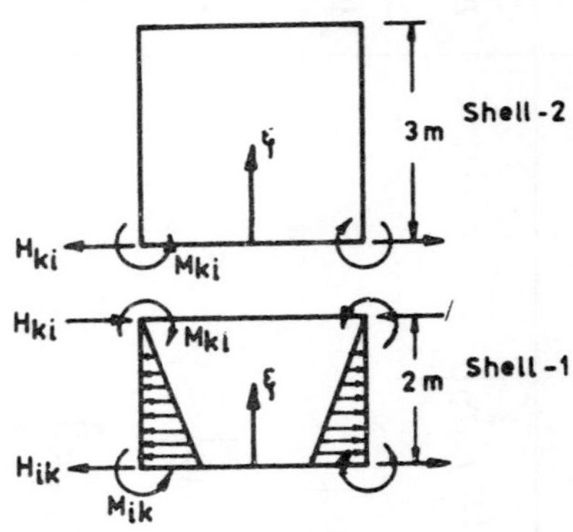

Fig. 5.17

Shell – 1 (Lower shell)

(a) Primary analysis:

The horizontal displacement and rotation at top and bottom due to water load can be determined by using Table 2.1

$$\xi = 0, \quad (\Delta H_{ik})_m = \frac{\gamma L a^2}{Eh} = \frac{1000 \times 2 \times 144}{E \times 0.16} = \frac{1.8 \times 10^6}{E}$$

$$(\beta_{ik})_m = -\frac{\gamma a^2}{Eh} = -\frac{1000 \times 144}{E \times 0.16} = -\frac{0.9 \times 10^6}{E}$$

$$\xi = 1, \quad (\Delta H_{ki})_m = 0$$

$$(\beta_{ki})_m = -\frac{\gamma a^2}{Eh} = -\frac{0.9 \times 10^6}{E}$$

(b) Secondary analysis:

Using Tables 5.15 and 5.16, the horizontal displacement and rotation at bottom and top of the shell due to moment and horizontal force viz., M_{ik}, M_{ki} and H_{ik}, H_{ki} (Fig. 5.17) can be determined as follows:

$$k = \frac{\sqrt[4]{3\,(1 - \nu^2)}}{\sqrt{ah}} = 0.9434 \text{ m}^{-1}$$

$$kL = 1.8868$$

$$\xi = 0,\ \Delta H_{ik} = \frac{M_{ik}}{2Dk^2}\left(-\frac{F_2}{F_1}\right) + \frac{H_{ik}}{2Dk^3}\left(\frac{F_4}{F_1}\right)$$

$$- \frac{M_{ki}}{2Dk^2}\left(-\frac{2F_8}{F_1}\right) - \frac{H_{ki}}{2Dk^3}\left(-\frac{F_9}{F_1}\right)$$

$$\beta_{ik} = \frac{M_{ik}}{2Dk}\left(\frac{2F_3}{F_1}\right) - \frac{H_{ik}}{2Dk^2}\left(\frac{F_5}{F_1} + \frac{F_6}{F_1}\right)$$

$$- \frac{M_{ki}}{2Dk}\left(\frac{2F_{10}}{F_1}\right) - \frac{H_{ki}}{2Dk^2}\left(\frac{2F_8}{F_1}\right)$$

$$\xi = 1,\ (\Delta H_{ki})_1 = \frac{M_{ik}}{2Dk^2}\left[-\frac{F_2F_7 + F_3F_{10}}{F_1} - F_8\right]$$

$$+ \frac{H_{ik}}{2Dk^3}\left[\frac{F_4F_7 - F_5F_{15} - F_6F_{16}}{F_1}\right]$$

$$- \frac{M_{ki}}{2Dk^2}\left[-\frac{2F_8F_7 + F_{10}^2}{F_1}\right]$$

$$- \frac{H_{ki}}{2Dk^3}\left[-\frac{F_9F_7 + F_8F_{10}}{F_1}\right]$$

$$(\beta_{ki})_1 = \frac{M_{ik}}{2Dk}\left[-\frac{F_2F_9 + 2F_3F_7}{F_1} - F_{10}\right]$$

$$- \frac{H_{ik}}{2Dk^2}\left[\frac{F_4F_9 + F_5F_{14} + F_6F_{13}}{F_1}\right]$$

$$- \frac{M_{ki}}{2Dk}\left[\frac{2F_8F_9 + 2F_{10}F_7}{F_1}\right]$$

$$- \frac{H_{ki}}{2Dk^2}\left[\frac{F_9^2 + 2F_7F_8}{F_1}\right]$$

where functions 'F' are determined using Table 5.3 for $kL = 1.8868$.

Shell – 2 (Top shell)

(a) Secondary analysis:

$$kL = 2.8293$$

The horizontal displacement and rotation at the bottom of shell–2, due to horizontal force and moment can be determined from Table 5.15 as

$$\xi = 0,\ (\Delta H_{ki})_2 = \frac{M_{ki}}{2Dk^2}\left(-\frac{\overline{F}_2}{\overline{F}_1}\right) + \frac{H_{ki}}{2Dk^3}\left(\frac{\overline{F}_4}{\overline{F}_1}\right)$$

$$(\beta_{ki})_2 = \frac{M_{ki}}{2Dk}\left(\frac{2\overline{F}_3}{\overline{F}_1}\right) - \frac{H_{ki}}{2Dk^2}\left(\frac{\overline{F}_5}{\overline{F}_1} + \frac{\overline{F}_6}{\overline{F}_1}\right)$$

where functions '$\overline{F}$' are determined using Table 5.3 for $kL = 2.8293$.

Boundary and Continuity Conditions:

Since the lower shell (Shell–1) is fixed at the bottom end, no displacements can occur along this end. This means that the total horizontal displacement and rotation at this end must be zero. Hence, for shell–1,

at $\xi = 0$, $\quad (\Delta H_{ik})_m + (\Delta H_{ik})_{M_{ik}} + (\Delta H_{ik})_{M_{ki}} + (\Delta H_{ik})_{H_{ik}} + (\Delta H_{ik})_{H_{ki}} = 0$

and $\quad (\beta_{ik})_m + (\beta_{ik})_{M_{ik}} + (\beta_{ik})_{M_{ki}} + (\beta_{ik})_{H_{ik}} + (\beta_{ik})_{H_{ki}} = 0$

The above two boundary conditions will result in the following two simultaneous equations:

$$-\frac{M_{ik}}{2Dk^2}\left(\frac{F_2}{F_1}\right) + \frac{H_{ik}}{2Dk^3}\left(\frac{F_4}{F_1}\right) + \frac{M_{ki}}{2Dk^2}\left(\frac{2F_8}{F_1}\right) + \frac{H_{ki}}{2Dk^3}\left(\frac{F_9}{F_1}\right) + \frac{1.8\times 10^6}{E} = 0 \qquad (1)$$

$$\frac{M_{ik}}{2Dk}\left(\frac{2F_3}{F_1}\right) - \frac{H_{ik}}{2Dk^2}\left(\frac{F_5 + F_6}{F_1}\right) - \frac{M_{ki}}{2Dk}\left(\frac{2F_{10}}{F_1}\right) - \frac{H_{ki}}{2Dk^2}\left(\frac{2F_8}{F_1}\right) - \frac{0.9\times 10^6}{E} = 0 \qquad (2)$$

The following continuity conditions have to be used along the cut.

Total horizontal displacement of shell–1 at $\xi = 1$ must be equal to the total horizontal displacement of shell–2 at $\xi = 0$. Total rotation of shell–1 at $\xi = 1$ must be equal to the total rotation of shell–2 at $\xi = 0$. The above continuity conditions will result in the following two simultaneous equations:

$$\frac{M_{ik}}{2Dk^2}\left(\frac{2F_8}{F_1}\right) + \frac{H_{ik}}{2Dk^3}\left(-\frac{F_9}{F_1}\right) - \frac{M_{ki}}{2Dk^2}\left(\frac{F_2}{F_1}\right) - \frac{H_{ki}}{2Dk^3}\left(\frac{F_4}{F_1}\right) = -\frac{M_{ki}}{2D}\left(\frac{\overline{F}_2}{\overline{F}_1}\right) + \frac{H_{ki}}{2Dk^3}\left(\frac{\overline{F}_4}{\overline{F}_1}\right) \qquad (3)$$

$$\frac{M_{ik}}{2Dk}\left(\frac{2F_{10}}{F_1}\right) - \frac{H_{ik}}{2Dk^2}\left(-\frac{2F_8}{F_1}\right) - \frac{M_{ki}}{2Dk}\left(\frac{2F_3}{F_1}\right)$$
$$- \frac{H_{ki}}{2Dk^2}\left(\frac{F_2}{F_1}\right) - \frac{0.9 \times 10^6}{E} = \frac{M_{ki}}{2Dk}\left(\frac{2\bar{F}_3}{\bar{\bar{F}}_1}\right)$$
$$- \frac{H_{ki}}{2Dk^2}\left(\frac{\bar{F}_2}{\bar{\bar{F}}_1}\right) \tag{4}$$

For $kL = 1.89$, the following ratios of the functions can be computed as,

$$\frac{F_2}{F_1} = 1.18864, \ \frac{F_3}{F_1} = 1.11426, \ \frac{F_4}{F_1} = 1.1766$$

$$\frac{F_8}{F_1} = 0.3213, \ \frac{F_9}{F_1} = 0.4425, \ \frac{F_{10}}{F_1} = 0.2301$$

For $kL = 2.83$,

$$\frac{\bar{F}_2}{\bar{\bar{F}}_1} = 1.00264, \ \frac{\bar{F}_3}{\bar{\bar{F}}_1} = 1.00422, \ \frac{\bar{F}_4}{\bar{\bar{F}}_1} = 1.01243$$

Using the above values of the ratios of functions in Eqs. (1–4), the following four simultaneous equations can be obtained.

$$\begin{bmatrix} -1.12101, & 1.1766, & 0.60604, & 0.41732 \\ 2.10172 & -1.18864, & -0.43401, & -0.6426 \\ 0.60604 & -0.4425, & -0.17542, & -2.18902 \\ 0.43401, & -0.6426, & -3.9959, & -0.186 \end{bmatrix} \begin{Bmatrix} M_{ik} \\ H_{ik} \\ M_{ki} \\ H_{ki} \end{Bmatrix} = \begin{Bmatrix} -1060.33 \\ 562.15 \\ 0 \\ 562.15 \end{Bmatrix}$$

Solving the above simultaneous equations, we get

$$M_{ik} = -\ 496.13 \text{ kg.m/m}$$
$$H_{ik} = -\ 1433.49 \text{ kg/m}$$
$$M_{ki} = 30.49 \text{ kg.m/m}$$
$$H_{ki} = 15.995 \text{ kg/m}$$

Following the sign convention for bending moment (moment, which causes tensile stresses in inner fibres is positive) and directions marked in Fig. 5.17, the signs for the bending moments would be

$$M_{ik} = 496.13 \text{ kg.m/m}$$
$$M_{ki} = -\ 30.49 \text{ kg.m/m.}$$

The final membrane forces N_θ can be determined by superposing on the membrane N_θ, the effect of M_{ik}, H_{ik}, M_{ki} and H_{ki} which could be computed using Tables 5.15 and 5.16. Similarly, the bending moment M_x can be determined, by superposing the effect of M_{ik}, H_{ik}, M_{ki} and H_{ki}, by using Tables 5.15 and 5.16. The final results are given in Tables 5.17 and 5.18. The distribution of N_θ and M_x in the cylindrical shell wall is shown in Fig. 5.18.

Table 5.17 Distribution of N_θ (kg/m) in the cylindrical tank

	ξ	Membrane	Due to M_{ik}	Due to H_{ik}	Due to M_{ki}	Due to H_{ki}	Total
	0	24,000	12,611	–38,491	420.8	1527.4	68.2 (≈0)
	0.2	19,200	5,165	–24,279	305	683.7	1074.7
Shell–1	0.4	14,400	298.2	–12,047	171.7	–215.1	2607.8
(Lower	0.6	9,600	–2,794	–2,042	–18.3	–1268.5	3477.2
shell)	0.8	4,800	–4,964	6,493	–317.4	–2556.5	3455.1
	1.0	0	–6,847	14,506	–775	–4053	2831
	0	—	—	—	–652.6	3483.1	2830.5
Shell–2	0.2	—	—	—	–112.4	1686	1573.6
(Top	0.4	—	—	—	105.4	493	598.4
shell)	0.6	—	—	—	140.7	–106.2	34.5
	0.8	—	—	—	102.6	–364.6	–262.0
	1.0	—	—	—	47.5	–514.8	–467.3

Table 5.18 Distribution of moment M_x (kg. m/m)

	ξ	Due to M_{ik}	Due to H_{ik}	Due to M_{ki}	Due to H_{ki}	Total
	0	496.1	0	0	0	496.1
	0.2	430.2	– 353.1	– 2.5	– 8.3	66.3
	0.4	292.5	– 380.1	– 9.1	– 25.7	– 122.4
Shell-1	0.6	148.9	– 243.9	– 17.9	– 40	– 152.9
	0.8	41.5	– 78.9	– 26.4	– 37.2	– 101
	1.0	0	0	– 30.5	0	– 30.5
	0	—	—	– 30.5	0	– 30.5
	0.2	—	—	– 23.9	48.5	24.6
	0.4	—	—	– 13.1	44.7	31.6
Shell-2	0.6	—	—	– 5	24.7	19.7
	0.8	—	—	– 1	7	6
	1.0	—	—	0	0	0

5.2.7.2 Long cylindrical shell

If the dimensions of a cylindrical shell are such that $kL > \pi$, then the shell may be called long (infinite). In such a shell the forces or displacement applied at one end will have no effect at the other end. This means the effect of forces applied along

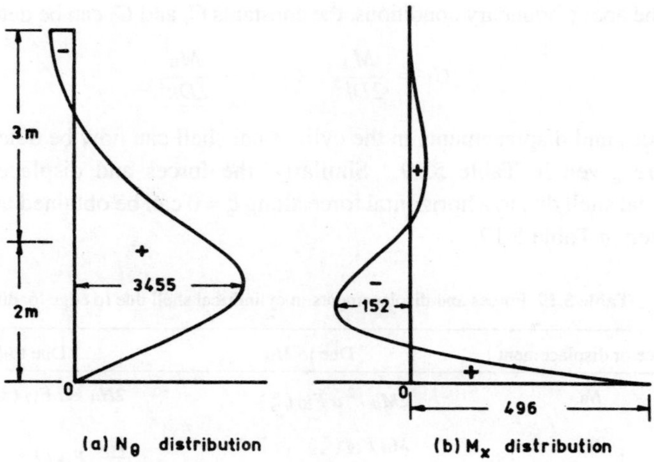

Fig. 5.18

an edge die out quickly as we move away from the edge. Such shells are often referred as semi-infinite shells (Fig. 5.19). For such shells, a simpler solution can be obtained by considering the boundary conditions at one end only. To satisfy the requirement that the edge effect should die out, the constants C_3 and C_4 in the solution given in Eq. (5.56a) should be taken as zero. Hence, the solution of the differential equation (5.55) can be taken as

$$w = e^{-kL\xi}\ (C_1 \cos kL\,\xi + C_2 \sin kL\,\xi)$$

or (5.59)

$$w = C_1 F_{17}(\xi) + C_2 F_{18}(\xi)$$

where the functions $F_{17}(\xi)$ and $F_{18}(\xi)$ are defined in Table 5.3. The constants C_1 and C_2 are determined by using the boundary conditions at $\xi = 0$.

As an example, consider a long cylindrical shell subjected to bending moment M_{ik} (Fig. 5.19), the boundary conditions for this problem can be written as

$$\xi = 0,\ M_x = M_{ik},\ Q_x = 0$$

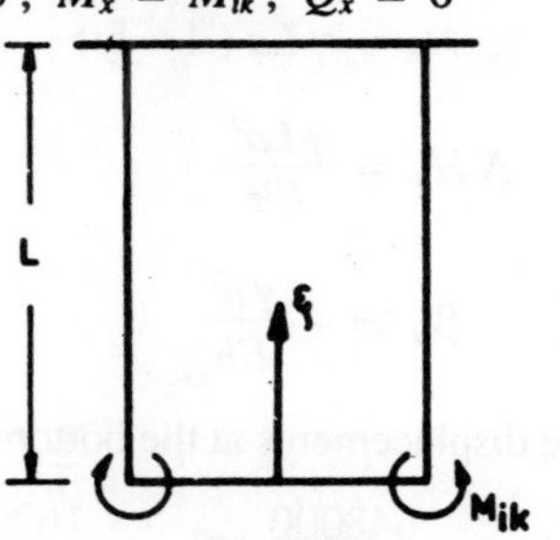

Fig. 5.19

Using the above boundary conditions, the constants C_1 and C_2 can be determined as

$$C_1 = \frac{M_{ik}}{2Dk^2},\ C_2 = -\frac{M_{ik}}{2Dk^2} \tag{5.60}$$

The forces and displacements in the cylindrical shell can now be determined and these are given in Table 5.19. Similarly, the forces and displacements in a cylindrical shell due to a horizontal force along $\xi = 0$ can be obtained and these are also given in Table 5.19.

Table 5.19 Forces and displacements in cylindrical shell due to edge loading

Force or displacement	Due to M_{ik}	Due to H_{ik}
N_θ	$2M_{ik}\, k^2\, a\, F_{20}(\xi)$	$2H_{ik}\, k\, a\, F_{17}(\xi)$
M_x	$M_{ik}\, F_{19}(\xi)$	$\frac{H_{ik}}{k} F_{18}(\xi)$
Q_x	$2M_{ik}\, k\, F_{18}(\xi)$	$-H_{ik}\, F_{20}(\xi)$
ΔH	$\frac{M_{ik}}{2Dk^2} F_{20}(\xi)$	$\frac{H_{ik}}{2Dk^3} F_{17}(\xi)$
β	$-\frac{M_{ik}}{Dk} F_{17}(\xi)$	$-\frac{H_{ik}}{2Dk^2} F_{19}(\xi)$

Example 5.5

A circular water tank has a diameter of 9 m, thickness 12.5 cm and height 4 m. The wall is monolithic with the base at the bottom, such that it may be considered as fixed, while the top of the wall is free. It is required to determine the membrane force and bending moment in the wall. Take Poisson's ratio as zero.

It should be noted that from the support condition specified above, there will be no displacement of the wall at the bottom ($\xi = 0$).

(a) Primary analysis

The membrane force and displacements at the bottom edge due to the hydrostatic loading can be determined, using Table 2.1, as

$$N_\theta = \gamma La(1-\xi)$$

$$\Delta H_{ik} = \frac{\gamma La^2}{Eh}$$

$$\beta_{ik} = -\frac{\gamma a^2}{Eh}$$

For the present example, the displacements at the bottom edge can be determined as

$$\Delta H_{ik} = \frac{648000}{E},\ \beta_{ik} = \frac{162000}{E}$$

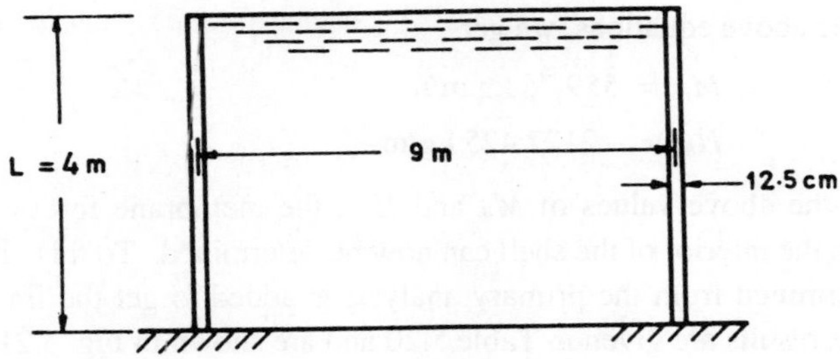

Fig. 5.20 Circular water tank

(b) Secondary analysis

$$k^4 = \frac{3(1-\nu^2)}{a^2h^2} = 9.48$$

$$k = 1.75\text{m}^{-1}, \; kL = 7.02$$

Since $kL > 3$, the cylindrical shell can be considered as infinite, which means the bottom edge and top edge effects may be considered independently. The membrane analysis does satisfy the top edge free condition. However at the bottom, to nullify the membrane displacements–horizontal displacement and rotation– an unknown bending moment M_{ik} and horizontal force H_{ik} should be applied, such that the total horizontal displacement and rotation at the bottom edge is made zero.

First we will determine the horizontal displacement and rotation at the bottom edge due to horizontal force H_{ik} and bending moment M_{ik} using Table 5.19.

$$\Delta H \text{ due to } M_{ik} = \frac{M_{ik}}{2Dk^2} = \frac{992.25}{E} M_{ik}$$

$$\Delta H \text{ due to } H_{ik} = \frac{H_{ik}}{2Dk^3} = \frac{567}{E} H_{ik}$$

$$\beta \text{ due to } M_{ik} = \frac{-M_{ik}}{2Dk} = \frac{-3472.28}{E} M_{ik}$$

$$\beta \text{ due to } H_{ik} = -\frac{H_{ik}}{2Dk^2} = -\frac{992.25}{E} H_{ik}$$

The total horizontal displacement and rotation at the bottom edge must be equal to zero. This condition can be written as

$$(\Delta H)_{\text{mem}} + [(\Delta H)_{M_{ik}} + (\Delta H)_{H_{ik}}] = 0$$

$$(\beta)_{\text{mem}} + [(\beta)_{M_{ik}} + (\beta)_{H_{ik}}] = 0$$

After substituting for ΔH and β in the above equations, we get the following two equations in terms of M_{ik} and H_{ik}

$$1.75\, M_{ik} + H_{ik} = -1142.85$$

$$-3.5\, M_{ik} - H_{ik} = 163.265$$

Solving the above equations, we get

$$M_{ik} = 559.76 \text{ kg.m/m},$$
$$H_{ik} = -2122.425 \text{ kg/m}$$

With the above values of M_{ik} and H_{ik}, the membrane forces and bending moment in the interior of the shell can now be determined. To this. the membrane force determined from the primary analysis is added to get the final membrane force. The results are given in Table 5.20 and are shown in Fig. 5.21.

Table 5.20 Distribution of N_θ (kg/m) and M_x (kg.m/m) in cylindrical tank

	N_θ (kg/m)			
ξ	Primary	Secondary	Final	M_x kg.m/m
0	18000	−18000	0	559.76
0.05	17100	−15633.5	1466.5	211.96
0.1	16200	−11748.9	4451.6	2.82
0.15	15300	−7785.6	7514.4	−101.31
0.25	13500	−2052.5	11447.5	−128.73
0.5	9000	668.7	9668.7	−8.57
0.75	4500	19.6	4519.6	4.26
1.0	0	−41.2	−41.2	0

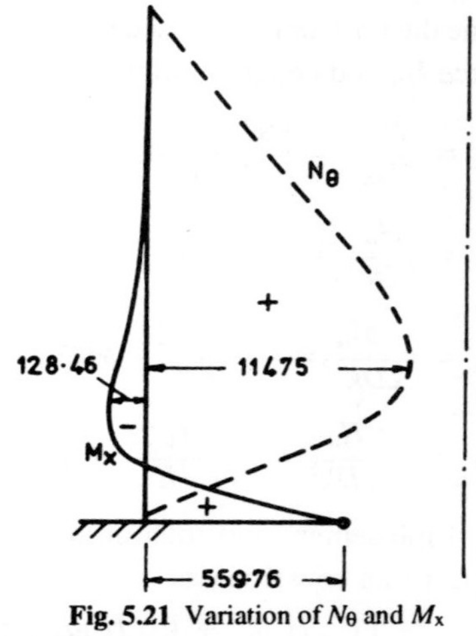

Fig. 5.21 Variation of N_θ and M_x

5.3 MULTISHELL STRUCTURE

As mentioned earlier, thin shells of revolution subjected to axisymmetric load are used in water tanks, silos, pressure vessels, etc. and normally contain combinations of shells having different geometry like spherical shell, circular-cylindrical shell or conical shell. Consequently, a geometrical discontinuity exists at the junction of each of these shell elements when these shells are used in combination.

Normally, the analysis of multishell structures is carried out by separating each of the shell elements and the continuity at the junction is later established through continuity conditions. The analysis of simple shell elements like spherical, conical or cylindrical shell can be carried out by using the solutions developed earlier. We will illustrate the use of these solutions in the analysis of a multishell structure through an example.

Let us consider a cylindrical tank with a spherical dome roof as shown in Fig. 5.22. In this example, let us assume that the cylindrical tank will be subjected to water pressure, while the spherical dome is subjected to dead and live load. First, the stresses and displacements at the junction (1) are determined separately for the spherical shell and cylindrical shell using the membrane analysis (primary analysis). Let δ_c and β_c be the horizontal displacement and rotation of the cylindrical shell, at the junction (1), due to water load obtained from the membrane analysis. Similarly, let δ_d and β_d be the horizontal displacement and rotation of the dome at the junction (1) due to dead and live load obtained from membrane analysis. Since the two shells are separated at the junction and analysed independently, we find at the junction.

$$\delta_c \neq \delta_d \text{ and } \beta_c \neq \beta_d$$

Hence, there exists a discontinuity in horizontal displacement equal to $(\delta_c - \delta_d)$ and in rotation equal to $(\beta_c - \beta_d)$. To close this gap, unknown forces H and M will be introduced at the junction (Fig. 5.22c) and the magnitude of these forces is determined by making use of the continuity conditions at the junction. Let the horizontal displacement and rotation at the junction due to unit horizontal force and moment for the cylindrical shell be δ_H^c, β_H^c, δ_M^c and β_M^c.

Similarly, the horizontal displacement and rotation of the dome at the junction due to unit horizontal force and moment be δ_H^d, β_H^d. δ_M^d and β_M^d. Hence, to close

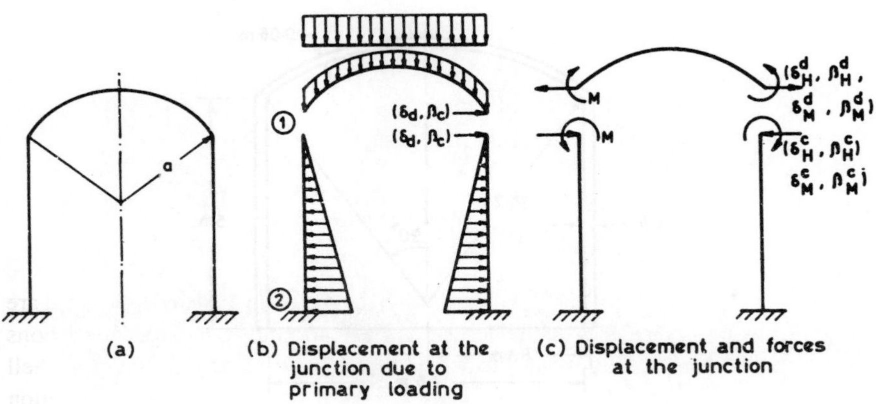

Fig. 5.22 Cylindrical tank with a spherical shell roof

the gap or to establish the continuity of displacements, the following conditions are to be satisfied.

$$\delta_d + \delta^d_H H + \delta^d_M M = \delta_c + \delta^c_H H + \delta^c_M M$$

$$\beta_d + \beta^d_H H + \beta^d_M M = \beta_c + \beta^c_H H + \beta^c_M M$$

The above condition will result in two simultaneous equations in terms of two unknown forces H and M, solving which the two forces can be determined. Following this example, it may be said that at each junction it is possible to set up two simultaneous equations in terms of the two unknown forces at the junction, provided that the forces acting at the other end of the shell (joint 2 in Fig. 5.22b) has no effect on the displacements at the junction (joint 1 in Fig. 5.22b). On the other hand, if the shell dimensions are such that the forces or displacements applied at another edge affect the forces and displacements at the junction, then it is necessary to consider the effect of the forces or displacement acting at the other edge while computing the displacements at the junction. In such a case, we would have two equations at each junction involving in general four unknown forces. Hence, if we have n junctions, then we will have to solve 2 n simultaneous equations to determine the unknown forces at all the n junctions.

Example 5.6

It is required to determine the forces in the cylindrical tank and spherical dome roof having dimensions as shown in Fig. 5.23. The cylindrical tank portion is used to store water while the dome roof will be subjected to a uniform live load of 75 kg/m^2 in addition to its own weight. The Poisson's ratio is taken as zero.

First, the spherical and cylindrical shells are separated at the common junction. The horizontal displacement and rotation, due to loads, at the edge of the spherical shell and top edge of cylindrical shell are determined from the membrane analysis. This part of the analysis, as mentioned earlier is called as the primary analysis.

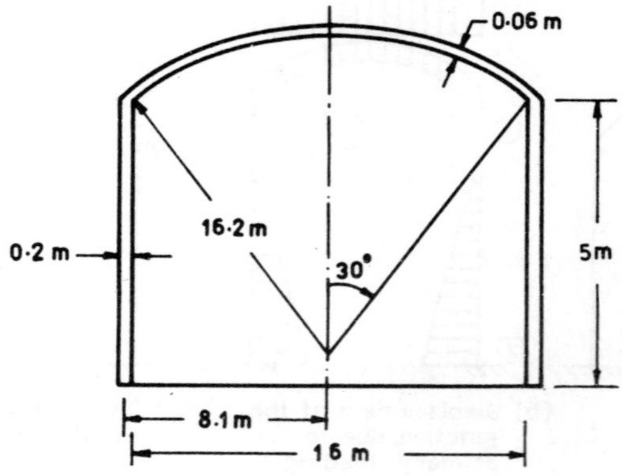

Fig. 5.23 Cylindrical tank with a spherical dome roof

(a) Primary analysis

(i) Spherical dome

Dead load of the shell (g) = $0.06 \times 2400 = 144$ kg/m^2

Live load on the shell (p) = 75 kg/m^2

The horizontal displacement and rotation due to the above two loads can be determined from Table 2.4c as

$$(\Delta H)_{\text{due to } g} = \frac{ga^2 \sin \phi_1}{Eh}\left(-\cos \phi_1 + \frac{1}{1 + \cos \phi_1}\right) = -\frac{103966.24}{E}$$

$$(\Delta H)_{\text{due to } p} = \frac{pa^2 \sin \phi_1}{Eh}\left(-\cos^2 \phi_1 + \frac{1}{2}\right) = -\frac{41006.25}{E}$$

$$\text{Total } (\Delta H) = -\frac{144972.49}{E}$$

$$(\beta)_{\text{due to } g} = -\frac{ga}{Eh}(2 \sin \phi_1) = -\frac{38880}{E}$$

$$(\beta)_{\text{due to } p} = -\frac{pa}{2Eh}(3 \sin 2\phi_1) = -\frac{26304.75}{E}$$

$$\text{Total } (\beta) = -\frac{65184.75}{E}$$

The membrane analysis leaves the membrane force N_ϕ at the edge whose magnitude can be determined as

$$(N_\phi)_{\text{due to } g} = -\frac{ga}{1 + \cos \phi_1} = -1250.16 \text{ kg/m}$$

$$(N_\phi)_{\text{due to } p} = -\frac{pa}{2} = -607.5 \text{ kg/m}$$

$$(N_\phi)_{\text{total}} = -1857.66 \text{ kg/m}$$

The horizontal component of this force can be determined as

$$H' = N_\phi \cos \phi_1 = -1608.73 \text{ kg/m}$$

This horizontal force can be nullified by applying a force of the same magnitude but of opposite nature. The displacements caused due to the application of this horizontal force can be determined in the secondary analysis.

(ii) Cylindrical shell

From Table 2.1,

$$(\Delta H)_{\text{due to water load}} = 0$$

$$(\beta)_{\text{due to water load}} = -\frac{\gamma a^2}{Eh} = -\frac{328050}{E}$$

(b) Secondary analysis

(i) Spherical shell

First, a horizontal force H' of magnitude 1608.73 kg/m is applied at the edge of shell to nullify the horizontal component of N_ϕ obtained from the membrane analysis. Next, a horizontal force H and a bending moment M is applied as shown in Fig. 5.24. The displacements caused by these forces at the edge are computed using the expressions given in Table 5.1.

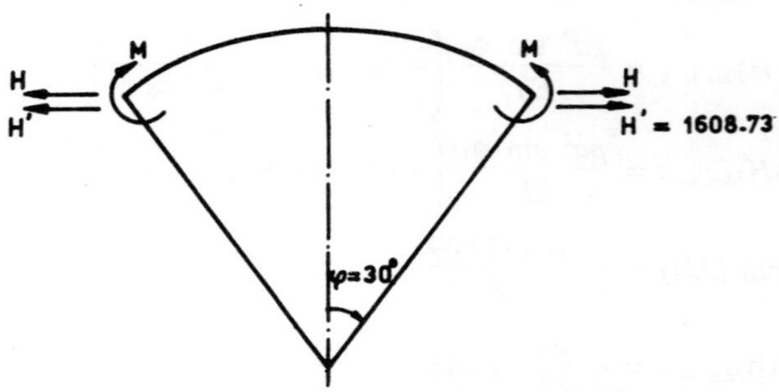

Fig. 5.24 Spherical shell roof with edge force

$$k = \sqrt[4]{3\left(\frac{a}{h}\right)^2} = \sqrt[4]{3\left(\frac{16.2}{0.06}\right)^2} = 21.625$$

$$(\Delta H)_{\text{due to } H'} = \frac{H'}{Eh}\,(2ka \sin^2 \phi_1) = \frac{4696486.1}{E}$$

$$(\Delta H)_{\text{due to } H} = \frac{H}{Eh}\,(2ka \sin^2 \phi_1) = \frac{2919.375}{E}\,H$$

$$(\Delta H)_{\text{due to } M} = \frac{M}{Eh}\,(2k^2 \sin \phi_1) = \frac{7794}{E}\,M$$

$$(\beta)_{\text{due to } H'} = -\frac{H'}{Eh}\,(2k^2 \sin \phi_1) = -\frac{12538441}{E}$$

$$(\beta)_{\text{due to } H} = -\frac{H}{Eh}\,(2k^2 \sin \phi_1) = -\frac{7794}{E}\,H$$

$$(\beta)_{\text{due to } M} = -\frac{M}{Eh}\left(\frac{4k^3}{a}\right) = -\frac{41616}{E}\,M$$

(ii) Cylindrical shell

At the top edge of the cylindrical shell, a horizontal force H and a bending moment M is applied (whose direction is opposite to that on the spherical shell), as shown in Fig. 5.25. The displacements caused due to these forces at the top edge can be computed using expressions given in Table 5.16.

$$k = \sqrt[4]{\frac{3\,(1 - \nu^2)}{a^2\,h^2}} = \sqrt[4]{\frac{3}{8.1^2 \times 0.2^2}} = 1.034 \text{ m}^{-1}$$

$$kL = 5.17$$

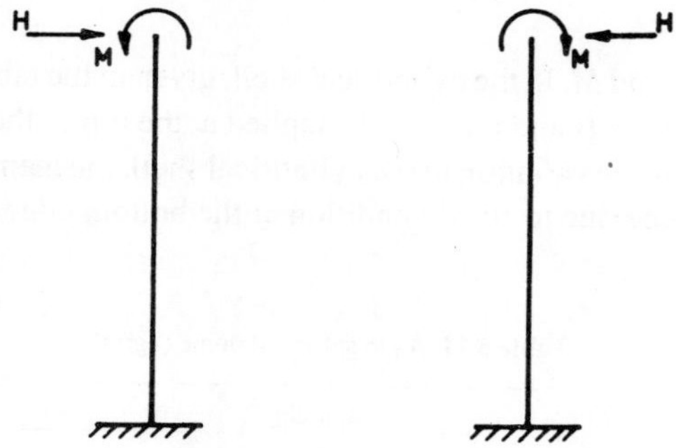

Fig. 5.25 Cylindrical shell with edge forces

Since $kL > 3$, the effect of the forces acting at the bottom edge, on the displacements at the top edge, need not be considered.

$$(\Delta H)_{\text{due to } H} = -\frac{2a^2 k}{Eh}\left(\frac{F_4}{F_1}\right) H = -\frac{678.4}{E} H$$

$$(\Delta H)_{\text{due to } M} = \frac{2a^2 k^2}{Eh}\left(\frac{F_2}{F_1}\right) M = \frac{701.47}{E} M$$

$$(\beta)_{\text{due to } H} = -\frac{2a^2 k^2}{Eh}\left(\frac{F_2}{F_1}\right) H = -\frac{701.47}{E} H$$

$$(\beta)_{\text{due to } M} = \frac{2a^2 k^3}{Eh}\left(\frac{2F_3}{F_1}\right) M = 1450.64\ M$$

Now to determine the horizontal force H and the moment M, the following continuity conditions are to be used.

$$[(\Delta H)_{\text{mem}} + (\Delta H)_{\text{due to } H_1} + (\Delta H)_{\text{due to } H} + (\Delta H)_{\text{due to } M}]_{\text{dome}}$$
$$= [(\Delta H)_{\text{mem}} + (\Delta H)_{\text{due to } H} + (\Delta H)_{\text{due to } M}]_{\text{Cyl}}$$

and

$$[(\beta)_{\text{mem}} + (\beta)_{\text{due to } H_1} + (\beta)_{\text{due to } H} + (\beta)_{\text{due to } M}]_{\text{dome}}$$
$$= [(\beta)_{\text{mem}} + (\beta)_{\text{due to } H} + (\beta)_{\text{due to } M}]_{\text{Cyl}}$$

The above two conditions will result in the following simultaneous equations

$$4551554 = -3597.8\ H - 7092.53\ M \quad (1)$$

$$-12275341 = 7092.53\ H + 43066\ M \quad (2)$$

Solving the above two equations, we get

$$M = -113.56 \text{ kg.m/m}$$

$$H = -1041.16 \text{ kg/m}$$

The final forces in the spherical dome and cylindrical shell can now be computed and these are given in Tables 5.21 – 5.26.

The forces N_θ and M_x in the cylindrical shell, given in the tables below, are due to the horizontal force H and moment M applied at the top of the cylindrical shell. To get at the final force variation in the cylindrical shell, the membrane part as well as the effect of force due to fixed condition at the bottom edge of the shell are to be added.

Table 5.21 N_ϕ **in spherical dome (kg/m)**

	ϕ in deg							
	30	27.5	25	22.5	20	15	10	0
Due to dead load	– 1250.2	– 1236.2	– 1223.7	– 1212.5	– 1202.7	– 1186.6	– 1175.3	– 1166.4
Due to live load	– 607.5	– 607.5	– 607.5	– 607.5	– 607.5	– 607.5	– 607.5	– 607.5
Due to H	695	–47	– 116.2	– 50.8	– 3.8	5.1	– 5.6	0
Due to M	0	183.5	93.5	13.2	– 11.3	– 2.3	—	—
ΣN_ϕ	– 1162.7	– 1707.2	– 1853.9	– 1857.6	– 1825.3	– 1791.3	– 1788.4	– 1773.9

Table 5.22 N_θ **in spherical dome (kg/m)**

	ϕ in deg							
	30	27.5	25	22.5	20	15	10	0
Due to dead load	– 770	– 832.9	– 890.4	– 942.7	– 989.5	– 1066.6	– 1122	– 1166.4
Due to live load	–455.6	– 477.97	– 499	– 518.55	– 536.44	– 566.8	–589.18	– 607.5
Due to H	12272.2	2807.8	– 579.2	– 688.5	– 227.4	34.7	1.94	0
Due to M	– 6556.2	566.6	1252.6	486.8	32.5	– 31.8	2	0
ΣN_θ	4490.4	2063.5	– 716.1	– 1662.9	– 1720.8	– 1630	– 1707.3	– 1773.9

Table 5.23 M_ϕ **in spherical dome (kg.m/m)**

	ϕ in deg							
	30	27.5	25	22.5	20	15	10	0
Due to H	0	66.99	30.57	3.83	– 2.88	–0.43	—	—
Due to M	– 113.56	– 61.79	– 10.97	4.33	3.66	0	0	0
ΣM_ϕ	– 113.56	5.2	19.6	8.16	0.78	– 0.43		

Table 5.24 M_θ **in spherical dome (kg.m/m)**

	ϕ in deg							
	30	27.5	25	22.5	20	15	10	0
Due to H	–9.83	–5.13	–1.01	0.45	0.44	—	—	—
Due to M	–9.09	–2.31	0.53	0.29	0.26	—	—	—
ΣM_θ	– 18.92	– 7.44	– 0.48	0.74	0.7	—	—	—

Table 5.25 N_θ in cylindrical shell (kg/m)

$\xi = x/L$	N_θ in kg/m		Total
	Due to *H*	Due to *M*	
1	– 1966.9	17740.9	15474
0.95	– 1080.4	13023.5	11943.1
0.9	– 440	9042.8	8602.8
0.8	243.5	3170.9	3414.4
0.7	409.3	68.9	478.2
0.6	338.4	– 1062.2	– 723.8
0.5	206.1	– 1134.5	– 928.4
0.4	99.9	– 806.8	– 706.9
0.3	23.6	– 432.2	– 409.6
0.2	– 12.25	– 138.8	– 151.1
0.1	—	—	—
0	—	—	—

Table 5.26 M_x in cylindrical shell (kg.m/m)

$\xi = x/L$	M_x in kg.m/m		Total
	Due to *H*	Due to *M*	
1	0	– 113.56	– 113.56
0.95	198.75	– 107.2	91.55
0.9	296.73	– 92.3	204.43
0.8	307.52	– 55.3	252.22
0.7	213.22	– 24.5	188.72
0.6	110.16	– 5.8	104.36
0.5	40.29	2.7	42.99
0.4	2.9	4.75	7.65
0.3	– 9.7	3.8	– 5.9
0.2	– 8.65	2.01	– 6.64
0.1	– 3.15	0.56	– 2.59
0	—	—	—

5.4 CIRCULAR RINGS

Multishell structures built of shells of revolution of different geometries are often provided with a ring beam at the junctions for effectively transmitting the forces from one shell to the other. The ring dimensions normally used are such that the ring may be assumed thin. The forces which get transmitted to a ring beam, are shown in Fig. 5.26. The stresses and deformation in the ring due to these forces can be determined from theory of structures.

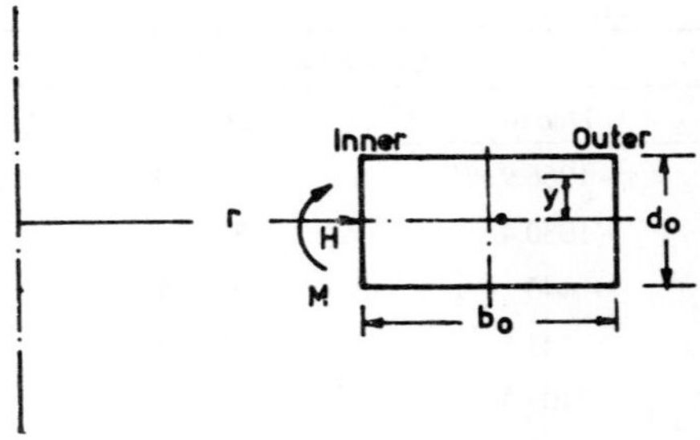

Fig. 5.26 Forces acting on a ring beam

The horizontal displacement due to the horizontal force H and bending moment M can be determined as

$$(\Delta H)_1 = \frac{r^2}{Eb_0\ d_0} H,\ (\Delta H)_2 = \frac{12\ r^2\ y}{Eb_0\ d_0^3} M$$

The rotation of the ring beam can be determined from

$$(\beta) = \frac{12\ r^2}{Eb_0\ d_0^3} M$$

Example 5.7

We will consider the example of a cylindrical tank having a spherical dome roof with a ring beam provided at the junction of a spherical dome and a cylindrical shell. The dimensions of the dome, ring beam and cylindrical shell are shown in Fig. 5.27. The dome will be subjected to a live load of 75 kg/m^2 in addition to its own weight. The Poisson's ratio is taken as zero.

Geometrical data

(a)	Dome :	Radius	=	60.05 m
		Thickness	=	0.1 m
		Semicentral angle	=	30°
(b)	Ring beam :	Width	=	1.5 m
		Depth	=	0.6 m
		Radius	=	30.75 m
(c)	Cylindrical shell :	Radius	=	30.15 m
		Thickness	=	0.3 m
		Height	=	8 m

(i) Primary analysis

(a) Dome

Dead load (g) = 240 kg/m^2

Live load (p) = 75 kg/m^2

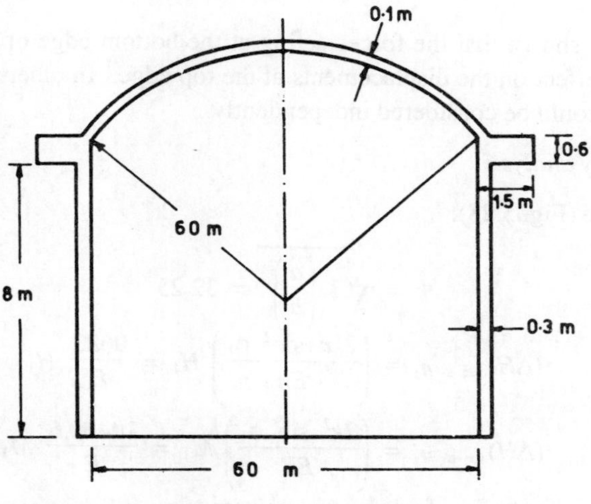

Fig. 5.27 Cylindrical water tank with a dome roof and ring beam

$$(\Delta H)_{\text{due to } g} = \frac{ga^2}{Eh} \sin \phi_1 \left(-\cos \phi_1 + \frac{1}{1 + \cos \phi_1} \right)$$

$$= -\frac{1428385}{E}$$

$$(\Delta H)_{\text{due to } p} = \frac{pa^2 \sin \phi_1}{Eh} \left(-\cos^2 \phi_1 + \frac{1}{2} \right)$$

$$= -\frac{338062}{E}$$

$$(\Delta H)_{\text{Total}} = -\frac{1766447}{E}$$

$$(\beta)_{\text{due to } g} = -\frac{2ga \sin \phi_1}{Eh} = -\frac{144120}{E}$$

$$(\beta)_{\text{due to } p} = -\frac{3pa \sin 2\phi_1}{2Eh} = -\frac{585037}{E}$$

$$(\beta)_{\text{Total}} = -\frac{202623.7}{E}$$

$$N_\phi = -\frac{ga}{1 + \cos \phi_1} - \frac{pa}{2} = -9975.375 \text{ kg/m}$$

Horizontal component of $N_\phi = N_\phi \cos \phi_1 = -8638.67$ kg/m

(b) Cylindrical shell

$$(\Delta H)_{\text{due to water load at top}} = 0$$

$$(\beta)_{\text{due to water load at top}} = -\frac{\gamma a^2}{Eh} = -\frac{3030075}{E}$$

It can be shown that the forces acting at the bottom edge of the cylindrical shell has no effect on the displacements at the top edge. In other words, the two edge effects could be considered independently.

(ii) Secondary analysis

(a) Dome (Fig. 5.28):

$$k = \sqrt[4]{3\left(\frac{a}{h}\right)^2} = 32.25$$

$$(\Delta H)_{\text{due to } H_1} = \left(\frac{2ka\ \sin^2\ \phi_1}{Eh}\right) H_1 = \frac{9683}{E} H_1$$

$$(\Delta H)_{\text{due to } M_1} = \left(\frac{2k^2\ \sin\ \phi_1}{Eh}\right) M_1 = \frac{10400.6}{E} M_1$$

$$(\beta)_{\text{due to } H_1} = -\left(\frac{2k^2\ \sin\ \phi_1}{Eh}\right) H_1 = -\frac{10400.6}{E} H_1$$

$$(\beta)_{\text{due to } M_1} = -\left(\frac{4k^3}{aEh}\right) M_1 = \frac{-22342.7}{E} M_1$$

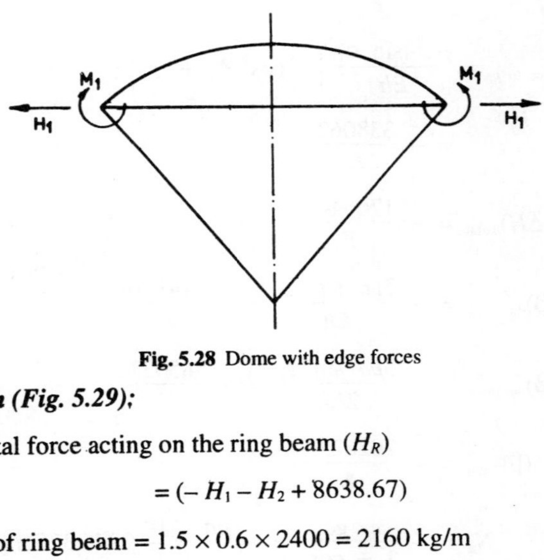

Fig. 5.28 Dome with edge forces

(b) Ring beam (Fig. 5.29);

Total horizontal force acting on the ring beam (H_R)

$$= (-H_1 - H_2 + 8638.67)$$

Dead weight of ring beam = $1.5 \times 0.6 \times 2400 = 2160$ kg/m

Vertical component of N_ϕ = $N_\phi\ \sin\ \phi_1 = 4987.69$ kg

Moment due to vertical forces = $-2160 \times 0.6 + 4987.69 \times 0.15$

$$= -547.85 \text{ kg.m}$$

Moment due to horizontal forces

$$= H_1 \times 0.3 - H_2 \times 0.3 - 8638.67 \times 0.3 = 0.3\ (H_1 - H_2) - 2591.61$$

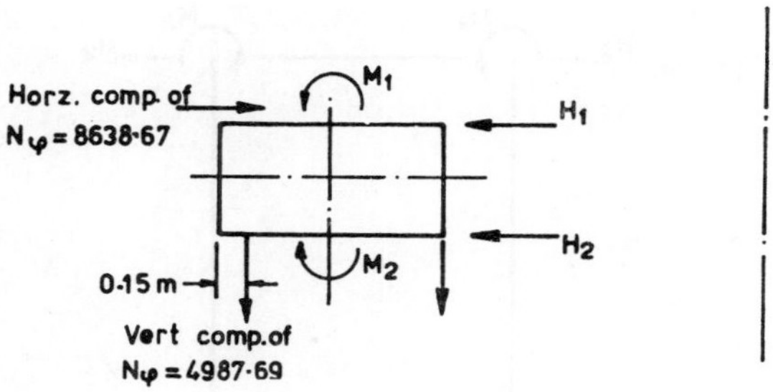

Fig. 5.29 Forces on the ring beam

$$\text{Total moment } (M_R) = -3139.46 + 0.3\ (H_1 - H_2) + (M_2 - M_1)$$

$$(\Delta H)_{\text{Ring beam}} = \frac{r^2}{E h_o\, b_o}\left(H_R \pm \frac{6M_R}{h_o}\right)$$

$$(\Delta H)_R = \frac{30.75^2}{E \times 0.6 \times 1.5}\Big[(-H_1 - H_2 + 8638.67) \pm \frac{6}{0.6}\left\{-3139.46 + (M_2 - M_1) + 0.3\ (H_1 - H_2)\right\}\Big]$$

$$(\beta)_R = \frac{12 M_R r^2}{E b_o h_o^3} = -\frac{12 \times 30.75^2}{E \times 0.6^3 \times 1.5}[-M_1 + M_2 + 0.3\,(H_1 - H_2) - 3139.46]$$

$$(\Delta H)_R^{\text{top}} = (-4202.5\ H_1 + 2101.25\ H_2 + 10506.25\ M_1 - 10506.25\ M_2 + 42059849)\ \frac{1}{E}$$

$$(\Delta H)_R^{\text{bottom}} = (2101.25\ H_1 - 4202.5\ H_2 - 10506.25\ M_1 + 10506.25\ M_2 - 23907843)\ \frac{1}{E}$$

$$(\beta)_R = (35020.83\ M_1 - 35020.83\ M_2 - 10506.25\ H_1 + 10506.25\ H_2 + 109910000)\ \frac{1}{E}$$

(c) Cylindrical shell (Fig. 5.30):

$$k = \sqrt[4]{\frac{3}{a^2\ h^2}}, \quad k = 0.4376\ \text{m}^{-1}$$

$$(\Delta H)_{\text{due to } H_2} = \left(\frac{2a^2\ k}{Eh}\right)\left(\frac{F_4}{F_1}\right) H_2 = \frac{2651.9}{E}\ H_2$$

$$(\Delta H)_{\text{due to } M_2} = \left(\frac{2a^2\ k^2}{Eh}\right)\left(\frac{F_2}{F_1}\right) M_2 = \frac{1160.5}{E}\ M_2$$

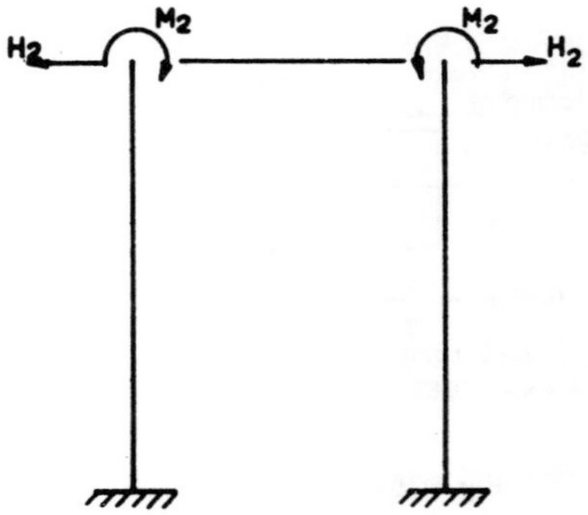

Fig. 5.30 Cylindrical shell with edge forces

$$(\beta)_{\text{due to } H_2} = \left(\frac{2a^2\,k^2}{Eh}\right)\left(\frac{F_2}{F_1}\right) H_2 = \frac{1160.5}{E}\,H_2$$

$$(\beta)_{\text{due to } M_2} = \left(\frac{2a^3\,k^3}{Eh}\right)\left(\frac{2F_3}{F_1}\right) M_2 = \frac{1015.67}{E}\,M_2$$

(iii) Continuity conditions

(a) $(\Delta H)_{\text{dome}} = (\Delta H)_R^{\text{top}}$

The above condition will give the following equation

$$H_1 - 0.151327\,H_2 + 0.007609\,M_1 + 0.756635\,M_2 = 3156.26 \qquad (1)$$

(b) $(\beta)_{\text{dome}} = (\beta)_R$

The above condition will give the following equation

$$0.010056H_1 - H_2 - 5.459943M_1 + 3.33333M_2 = 10480.68 \qquad (2)$$

(c) $(\Delta H)_R^{\text{bottom}} = (\Delta H)_{\text{Cyl}}$

The above condition will give the following equation

$$0.2H_1 - 0.652412H_2 - M_1 + 0.889542M_2 = 2275.58 \qquad (3)$$

(d) $(\beta)_R = (\beta)_{\text{Cyl}}$

The above condition will give the following equation

$$-0.291545H_1 + 0.259341H_2 + 0.971816\,M_1 - M_2 = -3134.05 \qquad (4)$$

Now we have four equations involving the four unknowns H_1, H_2, M_1 and M_2 solving which, we can determine these four forces. The forces can be obtained as

$$H_1 = 1713.43 \text{ kg/m}, \quad H_2 = 1241.41 \text{ kg/m}$$

$$M_1 = -833.12 \text{ kg. m/m}, \quad M_2 = 2146.81 \text{ kg. m/m}$$

The final forces in the dome and cylindrical shell can now be computed by superposing the effect of the above forces on the membrane forces and the results are presented in Tables 5.27 - 5.31.

Table 5.27 Variation of N_ϕ in dome (kg/m)

ϕ	N_ϕ (kg/m)			Total N_ϕ
in degrees	Membrane	Due to H_1	Due to M_1	
0	−9975.35	1483.82	0	−8491.53
2.5	−9889.4	−331.91	218.15	−10003.16
5	−9812.07	−139.68	17.44	−9934.31
7.5	−9742.91	12.46	−11.69	−9742.14
10	−9681.89	11.86	−1.92	−9671.95
15	−9582.87	−0.95	0.16	−9583.66
20	−9513.06	0	0	−9513.06
30	−9457.88	0	0	−9457.88

Table 5.28 Variation of N_θ in dome (kg/m)

ϕ	N_θ (kg/m)			Total N_θ
in degrees	Membrane	Due to H_1	Due to M_1	
0	−6446.12	55257.95	−21935.55	26876.28
2.5	−6917.57	2203.41	4423.98	−290.28
5	−7351.07	−3136.5	1667.81	−8819.76
7.5	−7746.32	−382.3	−132.16	−8260.78
10	−8101.4	157.52	−110.5	−8054.38
15	−8690.57	−6.61	6.55	−8690.63
20	−9115.72	0.18	−0.34	−9115.88
30	−9457.88	0	0	−9457.88

Table 5.29 Variation of M_ϕ in dome (kg.m/m)

ϕ	M_ϕ (kg.m/m)		Total M_ϕ
in degrees	Due to H_1	Due to M_1	
0	0	−833.12	−833.12
2.5	385.34	−234.47	150.87
5	30.8	31.24	62.04
7.5	−20.64	16.55	−4.09
10	−3.49	−0.54	−4.03
15	0.28	0	0.28
20	0	0	0
30	0	0	0

Table 5.30 Variation of N_θ in cylindrical portion (kg/m)

	N_θ (kg/m)			
ξ	Due to Membrane	Due to M_2	Due to H_2	Total
1	0	25794.82	29207.50	55002
0.95	12060	17714.63	24041.98	58816.61
0.90	24120	11106.03	19161.46	54387.46
0.80	48240	2113.00	10883.00	61236
0.70	72360	−3083.30	4881.51	74153.2
0.60	96480	−5062.73	1044.63	92461.9
0.50	120600	−7122.83	−1717.14	111760
0.40	144720	−4363.92	−1949.39	138406.7
0.30	168840	−3102.93	−2103.68	163633.40
0.20	192960	−1731.88	−1852.76	189375.36
0.10	217080	−362.76	−1437.92	215279.32
0	241200	991.57	−982.72	241208.85

Table 5.31 Variation of M_x in cylindrical portion (kg.m/m)

	M_x (kg.m/m)		
ξ	Due to M_2	Due to H_2	Total M_x
1	2118.90	55.46	2174.36
0.95	2077.63	415.48	2493.11
0.90	1923.30	646.18	2569.48
0.80	1519.42	828.19	2347.61
0.70	1049.50	773.92	1823.42
0.60	640.84	613.53	1254.37
0.50	335.79	427.26	763.05
0.40	139.73	261.47	401.20
0.30	34.76	135.91	170.67
0.20	−3.73	54.47	50.74
0.10	−5.62	12.03	6.41
0	0	0	0

It must be noted that the variation of forces in the cylindrical shell, given in Tables 5.30 and 5.31, have been obtained by considering only the effect of edge forces applied at the top of the cylindrical shell and load, since the cylindrical shell is long. However, to get the complete distribution of forces in the cylindrical shell, it is necessary to superpose on these results, the effect of the bottom edge.

5.5 GENERAL METHOD OF ANALYSIS OF SHELL OF REVOLUTION

Shells of revolution made up of short shell segments having constant material properties and thickness, and whose lengths are not necessarily equal, can be analysed using a finite element method [5.4]. Since for a shell element subjected to edge loading the displacements could be computed in terms of edge loads, it is possible to write down an exact flexibility matrix for each shell element. The finite element method as developed here facilitates in solving large class of problems like shells of revolution of variable thickness, shells of revolution subjected to discontinuous axisymmetric loads and multi-shells, in which shells of revolution of different geometries are used. For solving the problem of shell of revolution of variable thickness using this method, it is necessary to divide the shell into small segments of constant thickness, such that the assembled shell will have step variation in thickness. This step variation in thickness may be made very small by suitably selecting the number of elements, such that the assembly of these elements would closely approximate a shell of variable thickness. We will describe here, the method with reference to short cylindrical shell segments, but this could be generalised for other types of shells of revolution as well, including multishell structures.

Let us consider ith and $(i+1)$th segments of the assembly of cylindrical shells. For the ith and (i+1)th element, the edge loadings are indicated in Fig. 5.31. For the ith element the total horizontal displacement and rotation at edge (i) can be written as

$$\begin{Bmatrix} \delta_{i,i} \\ \beta_{i,i} \end{Bmatrix} = \begin{bmatrix} \delta^{M_{i-1}}_{i,i}, & \delta^{H_{i-1}}_{i,i}, & \delta^{M_i}_{i,i}, & \delta^{H_i}_{i,i} \\ \beta^{M_{i-1}}_{i,i}, & \beta^{H_{i-1}}_{i,i}, & \beta^{M_i}_{i,i}, & \beta^{H_i}_{i,i} \end{bmatrix} \begin{Bmatrix} M_{i-1} \\ H_{i-1} \\ M_i \\ H_i \end{Bmatrix} + \begin{Bmatrix} \delta^p_{i,i} \\ \beta^p_{i,i} \end{Bmatrix} \tag{5.59}$$

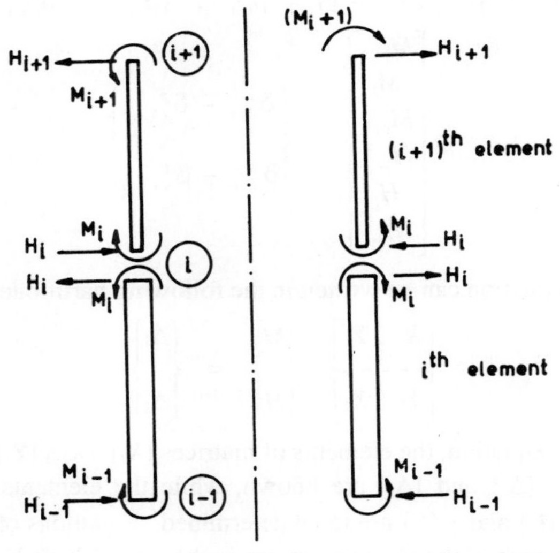

Fig. 5.31 Typical cylindrical shell element subjected to edge loads

where $\delta_{i,i}^{M_{i-1}}, \ldots, \delta_{i,i}^{H_i}$ and $\beta_{i,i}^{M_{i-1}}, \ldots, \beta_{i,i}^{H_i}$ are the flexibility coefficients due to unit edge loadings M and H acting at the edges (i) and (i–1) and $\delta_{i,i}^{p}$ and $\beta_{i,i}^{p}$ are the horizontal displacement and rotation of element (i) at the edge (i) due to primary loading.

Similarly for (i+1)th element, the total horizontal displacement and rotation at edge (i) can be written as

$$\begin{Bmatrix} \delta_{i+1,i} \\ \beta_{i+1,i} \end{Bmatrix} = \begin{bmatrix} \delta_{i+1,i}^{M_i}, & \delta_{i+1,i}^{H_i}, & \delta_{i+1,i}^{M_{i+1}}, & \delta_{i+1,i}^{H_{i+1}} \\ \beta_{i+1,i}^{M_i}, & \beta_{i+1,i}^{H_i}, & \beta_{i+1,i}^{M_{i+1}}, & \beta_{i+1,i}^{H_{i+1}} \end{bmatrix} \begin{Bmatrix} M_i \\ H_i \\ M_{i+1} \\ M_{i+1} \end{Bmatrix} + \begin{Bmatrix} \delta_{i+1,i}^{p} \\ \beta_{i+1,i}^{p} \end{Bmatrix} \tag{5.60}$$

where $\delta_{i+1,i}^{M_i}, \ldots; \delta_{i+1,i}^{H_{i+1}}$ and $\beta_{i+1,i}^{M_i}, \ldots, \beta_{i+1,i}^{H_{i+1}}$ are the flexibility coefficients due to unit edge loadings M and H acting at the edges (i) and (i+1) and $\delta_{i+1,i}^{p}$ and $\beta_{i+1,i}^{p}$ are the horizontal displacement and rotation of element (i+1) at the edge i due to primary loading.

Now the horizontal displacement and rotation at the joint i must be continuous, and hence

$$\begin{Bmatrix} \delta_{i,i} \\ \beta_{i,i} \end{Bmatrix} = \begin{Bmatrix} \delta_{i+1,i} \\ \beta_{i+1,i} \end{Bmatrix} \tag{5.61}$$

Making use of Eqs. (5.59) and (5.60) and the above continuity condition, we get

$$\left[\begin{array}{ccc|ccc} \delta_{i,i}^{M_{i-1}}, & \{\delta_{i,i}^{M_i} - \delta_{i+1,i}^{M_i}\}, & \delta_{i+1,i}^{M_{i+1}} & \delta_{i,i}^{H_{i-1}}, & \{\delta_{i,i}^{H_i} - \delta_{i+1,i}^{H_i}\}, & \delta_{i+1,i}^{H_{i+1}} \\ \hline \beta_{i,i}^{M_{i-1}}, & \{\beta_{i,i}^{M_i} - \beta_{i+1,i}^{M_i}\}, & \beta_{i+1,i}^{M_{i+1}} & \beta_{i,i}^{H_{i-1}}, & \{\beta_{i,i}^{H_i} - \beta_{i+1,i}^{H_i}\}, & \beta_{i+1,i}^{H_{i+1}} \end{array}\right]$$

$$\times \begin{bmatrix} M_{i-1} \\ M_i \\ M_{i+1} \\ H_{i-1} \\ H_i \\ H_{i+1} \end{bmatrix} = \begin{Bmatrix} \delta_{i,i}^{p} - \delta_{i+1,i}^{p} \\ \beta_{i,i}^{p} - \beta_{i+1,i}^{p} \end{Bmatrix} \tag{5.62}$$

The above equation can be written in the following partitioned matrix form:

$$\left[\begin{array}{c|c} X_1 & Y_1 \\ \hline Y_2 & X_2 \end{array}\right] \begin{Bmatrix} M \\ H \end{Bmatrix} = \begin{Bmatrix} \Delta_1 \\ \Delta_2 \end{Bmatrix} \tag{5.63}$$

In the above equation, the elements of matrices [X_1], [X_2], [Y_1], [Y_2] as well as column matrices [Δ_1] and [Δ_2] are known, while the elements in the column matrices, viz. { M } and { H } are to be determined. Equations of the above type can be written at each of the (N–1) junctions in the assembly of N segments. This leads to 4 (N–1) equations involving 4N unknown forces and moments. Additional equations can now be obtained by considering the boundary conditions at the edges of the first and last elements in the assembly.

The system of equations (5.63) can be solved for $[M]$ and $[H]$ as follows:

First, by carrying out the matrix multiplication in Eq. (5.63), we obtain the following two matrix equations:

$$[X_1]\ [M\ ] + [Y_1]\ [H\ ] = [\Delta_1] \tag{5.64a}$$

$$[Y_2]\ [M\ ] + [X_2]\ [H\ ] = [\Delta_2\ ] \tag{5.64b}$$

Multiplying Eq. (5.64a) by $[X_1]^{-1}$, we get

$$[M\ ] = [X_1]^{-1}\ \{[\Delta_1] - [Y_1]\ [H\ ]\ \} \tag{5.65}$$

Substituting Eqs. (5.65) in Eq. (5.64b), we get

$$\{\ [X_2] - [Y_2]\ [Y_1]\ [X_1]^{-1}\ \}\ [H] = \{\ [\Delta_2] - [Y_2]\ [X_1]^{-1}\ [\Delta_1]\ \} \tag{5.66}$$

from which we can determine $[H]$ as

$$[H] = \{\ [X_2] - [Y_2]\ [Y_1]\ [X_1]^{-1}\ \}^{-1}\ \{\ [\Delta_2] - [Y_2]\ [X_1]^{-1}\ [\Delta_1]\ \} \tag{5.67}$$

Once $[H]$ is determined, $[M]$ can be determined using Eq. (5.65). With this, the corrective forces and moments at the joints would be known. The final forces and moment in the shell element can then be calculated by superposing the effect of the corrective forces at the edges over the membrane forces. We will illustrate the application of this method through an example.

Example 5.8

Let us consider a cylindrical tank with stepwise variation in thickness, fixed at the bottom and free at top, and subjected to hydrostatic loading. The dimensions of the tank are given in Fig. 5.32.

(a) Primary analysis

From the membrane analysis, first the displacements are computed at joint 1 of element 2 and element 1 as well as at joint 0 of element 1 due to hydrostatic loading.

(i) Displacement at joint 0

$$\delta^p_{1,o} = \frac{\gamma a^2}{Eh_1}(L_1 + L_2) = \frac{1000 \times 9 \times 10^2}{E \times 0.25} = \frac{36 \times 10^5}{E}$$

$$\beta^p_{1,o} = -\frac{\gamma a^2}{Eh_1} = -\frac{1000 \times 10^2}{E \times 0.25} = \frac{-4 \times 10^5}{E}$$

(ii) Displacement at joint 1 of element 1

$$\delta^p_{1,1} = \frac{\gamma L_2 a^2}{Eh_1} = \frac{1000 \times 4 \times 10^2}{E \times 0.15} = \frac{26.67 \times 10^5}{E}$$

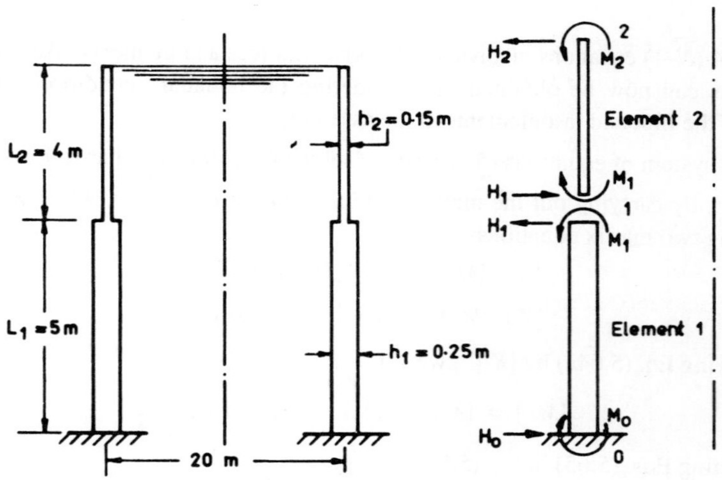

Fig. 5.32 Cylindrical water tank with step variation in thickness

$$\beta^p_{1,1} = -\frac{\gamma a^2}{Eh_1} = \frac{-1000 \times 10^2}{E \times 0.15} = \frac{-4 \times 10^5}{E}$$

(iii) Displacement at joint 1 of element 2

$$\delta^p_{2,1} = \frac{\gamma L_2 a^2}{Eh_2} = \frac{1000 \times 4 \times 10^2}{E \times 0.15} = \frac{26.67 \times 10^5}{E}$$

$$\beta^p_{2,1} = -\frac{\gamma a^2}{Eh_2} = \frac{-1000 \times 10^2}{E \times 0.15} = \frac{-6.67 \times 10^5}{E}$$

(b) Secondary analysis

The total horizontal displacement and rotation of element 1 at joint 0 can be determined from Eq. (5.59) as

$$\begin{Bmatrix} \delta_{1,0} \\ \beta_{1,0} \end{Bmatrix} = \begin{bmatrix} \delta^{M_0}_{1,0}\ , & \delta^{H_0}_{1,0}\ , & \delta^{M_1}_{1,0}\ , & \delta^{H_1}_{1,0} \\ \beta^{M_0}_{1,0}\ , & \beta^{H_0}_{1,0}\ , & \beta^{M_1}_{1,0}\ , & \beta^{H_1}_{1,0} \end{bmatrix} \begin{Bmatrix} M_0 \\ H_0 \\ M_1 \\ H_1 \end{Bmatrix} + \begin{Bmatrix} \delta^p_{1,o} \\ \beta^p_{1,0} \end{Bmatrix} \quad \text{(a)}$$

and for element 1 to joint 1

$$\begin{Bmatrix} \delta_{1,1} \\ \beta_{1,1} \end{Bmatrix} = \begin{bmatrix} \delta^{M_0}_{1,1}\ , & \delta^{H_0}_{1,1}\ , & \delta^{M_1}_{1,1}\ , & \delta^{H_1}_{1,1} \\ \beta^{M_0}_{1,1}\ , & \beta^{H_0}_{1,1}\ , & \beta^{M_1}_{1,1}\ , & \beta^{H_1}_{1,1} \end{bmatrix} \begin{Bmatrix} M_0 \\ H_0 \\ M_1 \\ H_1 \end{Bmatrix} + \begin{Bmatrix} \delta^p_{1,1} \\ \beta^p_{1,1} \end{Bmatrix} \quad \text{(b)}$$

Similarly for element 2 at joint 1, we have

$$\begin{Bmatrix} \delta_{2,1} \\ \\ \beta_{2,1} \end{Bmatrix} = \begin{bmatrix} \delta^{M_1}_{2,1}, & \delta^{H_1}_{2,1}, & \delta^{M_2}_{2,1}, & \delta^{H_2}_{2,1} \\ \\ \beta^{M_1}_{2,1}, & \beta^{H_1}_{2,1}, & \beta^{M_2}_{2,1}, & \beta^{H_2}_{2,1} \end{bmatrix} \begin{Bmatrix} M_1 \\ H_1 \\ M_2 \\ H_2 \end{Bmatrix} + \begin{Bmatrix} \delta^{p}_{2,1} \\ \\ \beta^{p}_{2,1} \end{Bmatrix} \tag{c}$$

and for element 2 at joint 2

$$\begin{Bmatrix} \delta_{2,2} \\ \\ \beta_{2,2} \end{Bmatrix} = \begin{bmatrix} \delta^{M_1}_{2,2}, & \delta^{H_1}_{2,2}, & \delta^{M_2}_{2,2}, & \delta^{H_2}_{2,2} \\ \\ \beta^{M_1}_{2,2}, & \beta^{H_1}_{2,2}, & \beta^{M_2}_{2,2}, & \beta^{H_2}_{2,2} \end{bmatrix} \begin{Bmatrix} M_1 \\ H_1 \\ M_2 \\ H_2 \end{Bmatrix} + \begin{Bmatrix} \delta^{p}_{2,2} \\ \\ \beta^{p}_{2,2} \end{Bmatrix} \tag{d}$$

Now we have to satisfy the following boundary and continuity conditions:

at joint 0, $\delta_{1,o} = \beta_{1,0} = 0$

at joint 2, $M_2 = H_2 = 0$

at joint 1, $\delta_{1,1} = \delta_{2,1}$, $\beta_{1,1} = \beta_{2,1}$

Using the boundary conditions, Eqs. (a), (c) and (d) can be written as

$$\begin{Bmatrix} 0 \\ 0 \end{Bmatrix} = \begin{bmatrix} \delta^{M_0}_{1,0}, & \delta^{H_0}_{1,0}, & \delta^{M_1}_{1,0}, & \delta^{H_1}_{1,0} \\ \beta^{M_0}_{1,0}, & \beta^{H_0}_{1,0}, & \beta^{M_1}_{1,0}, & \beta^{H_1}_{1,0} \end{bmatrix} \begin{Bmatrix} M_0 \\ H_0 \\ M_1 \\ H_1 \end{Bmatrix} + \begin{Bmatrix} \delta^{p}_{1,0} \\ \beta^{p}_{1,0} \end{Bmatrix} \tag{e}$$

$$\begin{Bmatrix} \delta_{2,1} \\ \beta_{2,1} \end{Bmatrix} = \begin{bmatrix} \delta^{M_1}_{2,1}, & \delta^{H_1}_{2,1} \\ \beta^{M_1}_{2,1}, & \beta^{H_1}_{2,1} \end{bmatrix} \begin{Bmatrix} M_1 \\ H_1 \end{Bmatrix} + \begin{Bmatrix} \delta^{p}_{2,1} \\ \beta^{p}_{2,1} \end{Bmatrix} \tag{f}$$

$$\begin{Bmatrix} \delta_{2,2} \\ \beta_{2,2} \end{Bmatrix} = \begin{bmatrix} \delta^{M_1}_{2,2}, & \delta^{H_1}_{2,2} \\ \beta^{M_1}_{2,2}, & \beta^{H_1}_{2,2} \end{bmatrix} \begin{Bmatrix} M_1 \\ H_1 \end{Bmatrix} + \begin{Bmatrix} \delta^{p}_{2,2} \\ \beta^{p}_{2,2} \end{Bmatrix} \tag{g}$$

Further, the continuity condition results in

$$\left[\begin{array}{cc|cc} \left(\delta^{H_1}_{1,1} - \delta^{H_1}_{2,1}\right), & \delta^{H_o}_{1,1} & \left(\delta^{M_1}_{1,1} - \delta^{M_1}_{2,1}\right), & \delta^{M_o}_{1,1} \\ \delta^{H_1}_{1,o}, & \delta^{H_o}_{1,o} & \delta^{M_1}_{1,o}, & \delta^{M_o}_{1,o} \\ \hline \left(\beta^{H_1}_{1,1} - \beta^{H_1}_{2,1}\right), & \beta^{H_o}_{1,1} & \left(\beta^{M_1}_{1,1} - \beta^{M_1}_{2,1}\right), & \beta^{M_o}_{1,1} \\ \beta^{H_1}_{1,o}, & \beta^{H_o}_{1,o} & \beta^{M_1}_{1,o}, & \beta^{M_o}_{1,o} \end{array}\right] \begin{Bmatrix} H_1 \\ H_o \\ M_1 \\ M_o \end{Bmatrix} = \begin{Bmatrix} \delta^{p}_{2,1} - \delta^{p}_{1,1} \\ \delta^{p}_{1,o} \\ \beta^{p}_{2,1} - \beta^{p}_{1,1} \\ \beta^{p}_{1,o} \end{Bmatrix} \tag{h}$$

The above matrix can be partitioned and written as

$$\begin{bmatrix} A_1 & \vdots & B_1 \\ \cdots & & \cdots \\ B_2 & \vdots & A_2 \end{bmatrix} \begin{Bmatrix} F_1 \\ \\ F_2 \end{Bmatrix} = \begin{Bmatrix} \Delta_1 \\ \\ \Delta_2 \end{Bmatrix}$$

The coefficients in the matrix $[A_1]$, $[B_1]$, $[B_2]$ and $[A_2]$ can be determined using Tables 5.15 and 5.16 by using suitable signs for the forces and displacements. From this the matrix $[A_I]$, $[B_I]$, $[A_2]$ and $[B_2]$ can be determined as

$$[A_1] = \begin{bmatrix} \left(\dfrac{2a^2k_1}{Eh_1} + \dfrac{2a^2 k_2}{Eh_2}\right) & 0 \\ 0 & -\dfrac{2a^2k_2}{Eh_2} \end{bmatrix} = \frac{1}{E}\begin{bmatrix} 2098.93 & 0 \\ 0 & -665.6 \end{bmatrix}$$

$$[B_1] = \begin{bmatrix} \left(\dfrac{2a^2k_1^2}{Eh_1} - \dfrac{2a^2k_2^2}{Eh_2}\right) & 0 \\ 0 & -\dfrac{2a^2k_2^2}{Eh_2} \end{bmatrix} = \frac{1}{E}\begin{bmatrix} 987.05 & 0 \\ 0 & -553.78 \end{bmatrix}$$

$$[A_2] = \begin{bmatrix} \left(\dfrac{4a^2k_1^3}{Eh_1} + \dfrac{4a^2k_2^3}{Eh_2}\right) & 0 \\ 0 & -\dfrac{4a^2k_2^3}{Eh_2} \end{bmatrix} = \frac{1}{E}\begin{bmatrix} 4234.28 & 0 \\ 0 & -921.5 \end{bmatrix}$$

$$[B_2] = \begin{bmatrix} \left(\dfrac{2a^2k_1^2}{Eh_1} - \dfrac{2a^2k_2^2}{Eh_2}\right) & \bar{0} \\ 0 & -\dfrac{2a^2k_2^3}{Eh_2} \end{bmatrix} = \frac{1}{E}\begin{bmatrix} 987.05 & 0 \\ 0 & -553.78 \end{bmatrix}$$

$$[\Delta_1] = \frac{10^5}{E}\begin{bmatrix} 10.67 \\ 36 \end{bmatrix}, \quad [\Delta_2] = \frac{10^5}{E}\begin{bmatrix} -2.67 \\ -4 \end{bmatrix}$$

Using Eq. (5.67), $[F_2]$ can be obtained as

$$[F_2] = \{[A_2] - [B_2][A_1]^{-1}[B_1]\}^{-1}\{[\Delta_2] - [B_2][A_1]^{-1}[A_1]\}$$

from which $[F_2]$ can be determined as

$$[F_2] = \begin{bmatrix} M_1 \\ M_o \end{bmatrix} = \begin{bmatrix} -62.32 \\ -5632.56 \end{bmatrix} \text{kg. m / m}$$

Hence $\quad M_o = -5632.56$ kg . m / m

and

$$M_1 = -\ 62.32\ \text{kg . m / m}$$

Now using Eq. (5.65), $[F_1]$ can be obtained from

$$[F_1] = [A_1]^{-1} \{ [\Delta_1] - [B_1]\ [F_2] \}$$

which gives

$$[F_1] = \begin{bmatrix} H_1 \\ H_o \end{bmatrix} = \begin{bmatrix} 537.5 \\ 10095 \end{bmatrix} \text{kg/m}$$

Hence,

$H_o = 10095$ kg/m

$H_1 = 537.5$ kg/m

The final membrane force N_θ and the bending moment M_x may be determined by superposing the force N_θ obtained from the membrane analysis on the force and moment obtained from the bending analysis due to the above edge loads.

5.6 SUMMARY

In this chapter, bending analysis of shells of revolution, like spherical, conical and cylindrical shells, subjected to axisymmetric edge loads has been discussed in detail. It is indicated that the exact solution of basic equations is rather difficult and the solution would be in a form not normally amenable to a design engineer. In literature, two approximate methods are available — the first based on asymptotic integration and the second based on Geckler's approximation. No attempts have been made here to discuss the asymptotic method, since the solution in this method would be in terms of Bessel's functions and ordinarily not convenient for use in design office. The Geckler's approximation reduces the differential equation of the bending problem of a shell of revolution, similar to the one for a beam on elastic foundation. The solution for this equation can be written in a simple form and influence coefficients for shells subject to different types of edge loads could easily be obtained. Further, in practice, shells of revolution of varying thickness either singly or in combination with other shapes (multishells) are used. An exact solution for this type of problem is rather difficult. An approximate finite element method is presented here, which could be used to solve the problem of shells of variable thickness including multishell structures.

REFERENCES

5.1 Geckler, *'Uber die Festigkeit Achsensymmetrischer Schalen'*, Forschungsarb Ingwes, Berlin Heft, 276, 1926.

5.2 Hampe, E., *Statik-Rotationsymmetrischer Flachentragwerke, Band 3 and 4*, VEB Verlag Fur Bauwesen, Berlin, 1963.

5.3 Baker, E.H., L. Kovalevsky and F.L. Rish, *Structural Analysis of shells*, McGraw-Hill, 1972.

5.4 Kraus, H., *Thin Elastic Shells*, John Wiley and Sons, New York, 1967.

5.5 Flugge, W., *Stresses in Shells*, 2nd edition, Springer-Verlag, Berlin, 1973.

5.6 Hetenyi, M., *Beams on elastic foundations*, University of Michigan Press, Ann Arbor, 1946.

5.7 Lowell, H.H., Tables of Bessel-Kelvin functions ber, bei, ker, kei and their derivatives for the argument range 0 (0.01) 107.50, NASA TR R-32, 1959.

Chapter Six

Bending Analysis of Shells of Revolution Subjected to Asymmetric Load

6.1 INTRODUCTION

In the previous chapter, we have discussed the bending analysis of shells of revolution subjected to axisymmetric loads. However, often, shells of revolution like cylindrical and conical shells are subjected to asymmetric loads when they are used as shafts for overhead tanks, chimney stacks and for foundation of tall structures. We will discuss in this chapter, the bending analysis of cylindrical and conical shells of revolution subjected to asymmetric load. The solution will be presented by considering either the three simultaneous differential equations in terms of displacements u, v and w, or a single differential equation in terms of displacement w. For shells of revolution, the displacements and the stress resultants will be periodic in the circumferential direction (θ-direction) and hence, can be expanded in terms of Fourier series. By using the Fourier series expansion in the θ-direction, the partial differential equation/s (three in the first case or one in the second case) are reduced to ordinary differential equations in the axial coordinate (x-direction), the solution of which could be obtained by using any standard procedure. If a general load in the circumferential direction is expanded by a cosine series, the zeroth terms in the expansion also needs to be considered. The solution corresponding to zeroth term in the expansion is a special case in which the shell variable would be independent of θ (axisymmetric) and has been discussed in the previous chapter. Hence, the solution corresponding to zeroth term of the expansion will not be considered here.

6.2 CYLINDRICAL SHELL

The basic equations which describe the bending behaviour of a circular cylindrical shell has been discussed in detail in Chapter 4. We have discussed the exact differential equations in terms of displacements as given by Flugge[6.1] and later, it has been shown that by making some approximations, simplified differential equations corresponding to Donnell's[6.2] and Schorer's[6.3] theories could be obtained. We will consider here Donnell's and Schorer's theories for developing solutions for a cylindrical shell of revolution with various support conditions in the longitudinal direction. Further, we will also show through examples that for certain dimensions of cylindrical shell, these theories give results adequate for design.

6.2.1 Solution for Simply Supported Cylindrical Shell

Let us consider a simply supported cylindrical shell of revolution of radius 'a' and length 'L' subjected to a load which is symmetrical about $\theta = 0$ (Fig. 6.1). For such a case, a simple solution in terms of double trigonometric series could be obtained. Hence, the displacements can be taken in the form

$$u = \sum_{m=1}^{\infty} \sum_{n=1}^{\infty} A_{mn} \cos m\theta \cos \alpha_n x \tag{6.1a}$$

$$v = \sum_{m=1}^{\infty} \sum_{n=1}^{\infty} B_{mn} \sin m\theta \sin \alpha_n x \tag{6.1b}$$

$$w = \sum_{m=1}^{\infty} \sum_{n=1}^{\infty} C_{mn} \cos m\theta \sin \alpha_n x \tag{6.1c}$$

where $\alpha_n = \left(\dfrac{n\pi}{L}\right)$

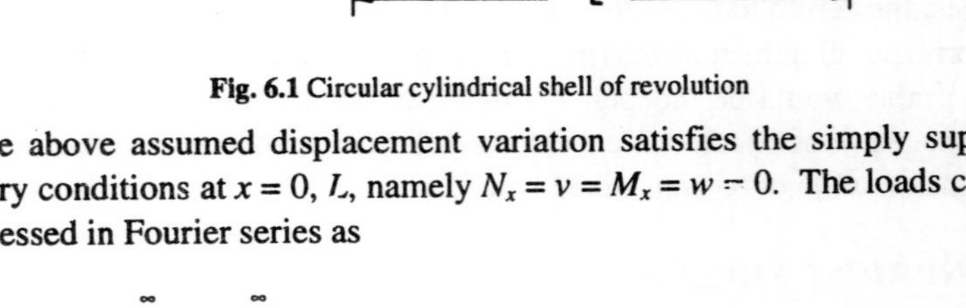

Fig. 6.1 Circular cylindrical shell of revolution

The above assumed displacement variation satisfies the simply supported boundary conditions at $x = 0, L$, namely $N_x = v = M_x = w = 0$. The loads can also be expressed in Fourier series as

$$X = \sum_{m=1}^{\infty} \sum_{n=1}^{\infty} (p_x)_{mn} \cos m\theta \cos \alpha_n x \tag{6.2a}$$

$$Y = \sum_{m=1}^{\infty} \sum_{n=1}^{\infty} (p_y)_{mn} \sin m\theta \sin \alpha_n x \tag{6.2b}$$

$$Z = \sum_{m=1}^{\infty} \sum_{n=1}^{\infty} (p_z)_{mn} \cos m\theta \sin \alpha_n x \tag{6.2c}$$

Introducing Eqns. (6.1) and (6.2) in Eqn. (4.10 a–c), we get the following three algebraic equations

$$\begin{bmatrix} -\left\{\alpha_n^2 + \left(\dfrac{1-\nu}{2}\right)\dfrac{m^2}{a^2}\right\}, & \left(\dfrac{1+\nu}{2}\right)\left(\dfrac{m\,\alpha_n}{a}\right), & \dfrac{\nu\,\alpha_n}{a} \\ \left(\dfrac{1+\nu}{2}\right)\dfrac{m\,\alpha_n}{a}, & -\left\{\left(\dfrac{1-\nu}{2}\right)\alpha_n^2 + \dfrac{m^2}{a^2}\right\}, & -\dfrac{m}{a^2} \\ -\dfrac{\nu\,\alpha_n}{a}, & \dfrac{m}{a^2}, & \dfrac{1}{a^2}\{1 + D'(\alpha_n^2 a^2 + m^2)^2\} \end{bmatrix} \begin{Bmatrix} A_{mn} \\ B_{mn} \\ C_{mn} \end{Bmatrix}$$

$$= \frac{-1}{K} \begin{Bmatrix} (p_x)_{mn} \\ (p_y)_{mn} \\ (p_z)_{mn} \end{Bmatrix}$$

Solving the above equation, the constants A_{mn}, B_{mn} and C_{mn} can be determined. The stress resultants can then be obtained by substituting Eq. (6.2) in the force-displacement relation given in Eq. (4.7).

Alternatively, a direct solution to the above problem can be obtained using the differential equation in terms of w (Eq. 4.12). Introducing (6.1c) and (6.2) in Eqn. (4.12), we can determine C_{mn} as

$$C_{mn} = \frac{-\,a^4 [\,(\alpha_n^2 a^2 + m^2)^2 (p_z)_{mn} + \{\,(2+\nu)\,\alpha_n^2 a^2 m + m^3\,\}(p_y)_{mn} + \alpha_n a\,\{\,m^2 - \nu\,\alpha_n^2 a^2\,\}(p_x)_{mn}\,]}{D\left[(\alpha_n^2 a^2 + m^2)^4 + \dfrac{12 a^6 (1-\nu^2)}{h^2}\,\alpha_n^4\right]} \tag{6.4a}$$

Now A_{mn} and B_{mn} can be determined by substituting Eqs. (6.2a) and (6.2b) in Eqs. (4.11a, b) as

$$A_{mn} = \frac{1}{(\alpha_n^2 a^2 + m^2)^2}\left[(\nu\,\alpha_n^2 a^2 - m^2)\,\alpha_n a\, C_{mn} + \left(\frac{2}{1-\nu}\right)\frac{(p_x)_{mn}}{K}\,a^2 \left\{m^2 + \left(\frac{1-\nu}{2}\right)\alpha_n^2 a^2\right\} + \left(\frac{1+\nu}{1-\nu}\right)\frac{(p_y)_{mn}}{K}\,a^2\,(m\alpha_n a)\right] \tag{6.4b}$$

$$B_{mn} = \frac{1}{(\alpha_n^2 a^2 + m^2)} \Big[- \{ (2+\nu)\alpha_n^2 a^2 + m^2 \} \; m \, C_{mn}$$
$$+ \left(\frac{1+\nu}{1-\nu}\right) \frac{(p_x)_{mn}}{K} \, a^2 \, (m\,\alpha_n a)$$
$$+ \left\{ \left(\frac{2}{1-\nu}\right) \alpha_n^2 a^2 + m^2 \right\} \frac{(p_y)_{mn}}{K} \, a^2 \Big] \qquad (6.4c)$$

The stress resultants can then be obtained by using Eq. (4.7) as,

$$N_x = \frac{K}{a} \left[-\alpha_n a A_{mn} + \nu (m B_{mn} + C_{mn}) \right] \cos m\theta \sin \alpha_n x \qquad (a)$$

$$N_\theta = \frac{K}{a} \left[(m B_{mn} + C_{mn}) - \nu \alpha_n a A_{mn}) \right] \cos m\theta \sin \alpha_n x \qquad (b)$$

$$N_{x\theta} = \frac{K(1-\nu)}{2a} \left[\alpha_n a B_{mn} - m A_{mn} \right] \sin m\theta \cos \alpha_n x \qquad (c)$$

$$M_x = -\frac{D}{a^2} \left[(\alpha_n^2 a^2 + \nu m^2) C_{mn} \right] \cos m\theta \sin \alpha_n x \qquad (d)$$

$$M_\theta = -\frac{D}{a^2} \left[(m^2 + \nu \alpha_n^2 a^2) C_{mn} \right] \cos m\theta \sin \alpha_n x \qquad (e)$$

$$M_{x\theta} = \frac{-D(1-\nu)}{a^2} \left[(m\alpha_n a) C_{mn} \right] \sin m\theta \cos \alpha_n x \qquad (f)$$

$$Q_x = -\frac{D}{a^3} \left[(\alpha_n a (\alpha_n^2 a^2 + m^2)) C_{mn} \right] \cos m\theta \cos \alpha_n x \qquad (g)$$

$$Q_\theta = \frac{D}{a^3} \left[m (m^2 + \alpha_n^2 a^2) C_{mn} \right] \sin m\theta \sin \alpha_n x \qquad (h)$$

As an example, let us consider a cylindrical shell having the dimensions $(h/a) = 0.1$ and $(L/a) = \pi$. The shell is subjected to a load whose components are

$$X = 0, \quad Y = p \sin m\theta \sin \frac{n\pi x}{L}, \quad Z = p \cos m\theta \sin \frac{n\pi x}{L}$$

We will assume the Poisson's ratio zero and first consider a load corresponding to $m = n = 1$. The constants C_{11}, A_{11} and B_{11} can be directly determined from Eq. (6.4a-c) as

$$C_{11} = -6.9079 \frac{pa^2}{Eh}, \quad A_{11} = 1.977 \frac{pa^2}{Eh}, \quad B_{11} = 5.931 \frac{pa^2}{Eh}.$$

The results of displacements and forces for this example is given in Table 6.1. Flugge[6.1] has solved this problem using the exact differential equation in terms of displacements (Eq. 4.8a-c) and these results are also given in the table for comparison. This problem can also be solved using membrane theory. The membrane stress resultants can be computed by substituting the above load components in Eq. (2.9a-c). The integration constants in Eq. (2.9b, c) are determined by using the boundary condition that at $x = 0, L$ $N_x = 0$. We can also determine the membrane

displacements using Eq. (2.10a-c) and the integration constants in these equations are determined by using the boundary condition that at $x = 0, L$, $v = 0$. The results or the membrane analysis are also included in Table 6.1 for comparison.

Table 6.1 Variation of displacements and forces in a simply supported cylindrical shell ($m = n = 1$)

Displacement/force	Bending theory		Membrane theory
	Flugge	Donnell	
$\dfrac{u}{\cos\theta\cos\frac{\pi x}{L}}$	$1.987\dfrac{pa^2}{Eh}$	$1.977\dfrac{pa^2}{Eh}$	$2\dfrac{pa^2}{Eh}$
$\dfrac{v}{\sin\theta\sin\frac{\pi x}{L}}$	$5.968\dfrac{pa^2}{Eh}$	$5.931\dfrac{pa^2}{Eh}$	$6\dfrac{pa^2}{Eh}$
$\dfrac{w}{\cos\theta\sin\frac{\pi x}{L}}$	$-6.957\dfrac{pa^2}{Eh}$	$-6.908\dfrac{pa^2}{Eh}$	$-7\dfrac{pa^2}{Eh}$
$\dfrac{N_x}{\cos\theta\sin\frac{\pi x}{L}}$	$-1.993\,pa$	$-1.977\,pa$	$-2\,pa$
$\dfrac{N_\theta}{\cos\theta\sin\frac{\pi x}{L}}$	$-0.989\,pa$	$-0.977\,pa$	$-pa$
$\dfrac{N_{x\theta}}{\sin\theta\cos\frac{\pi x}{L}}$	$1.990\,pa$	$1.977\,pa$	$2\,pa$
$\dfrac{N_{\theta x}}{\sin\theta\cos\frac{\pi x}{L}}$	$1.993\,pa$	$1.977\,pa$	$2\,pa$
$\dfrac{M_x}{\cos\theta\sin\frac{\pi x}{L}}$	$0.00744\,pa^2$	$0.00576\,pa^2$	—
$\dfrac{M_\theta}{\cos\theta\sin\frac{\pi x}{L}}$	0	$0.00576\,pa^2$	—
$\dfrac{M_{x\theta}}{\sin\theta\cos\frac{\pi x}{L}}$	$0.000823\,pa^2$	$0.00576\,pa^2$	—
$\dfrac{M_{\theta x}}{\sin\theta\cos\frac{\pi x}{L}}$	$0.00248\,pa^2$	$0.00576\,pa^2$	—
$\dfrac{Q_x}{\cos\theta\cos\frac{\pi x}{L}}$	$0.00994\,pa$	$0.0115\,pa$	—
$\dfrac{Q_\theta}{\sin\theta\sin\frac{\pi x}{L}}$	$-0.000823\,pa$	$-0.0115\,pa$	—

It may be seen from Table 6.1 that the Donnell's theory predicts displacements and stress resultants (except bending moments) very close to Flugge's exact theory. It is also interesting to note that the membrane theory gives displacements and stress resultants which are very close to the bending theory. This good agreement between the membrane and bending theories is due to the fact that a smooth variation of the load is considered in this example. However, if a highly discontinuous load is considered to be acting on the shell, then it is unlikely that the membrane theory would be acceptable. To bring out this point, we will consider the following load components acting on the shell

$$X = 0\,,\; Y = p\ \sin 10\,\theta \sin 10\,\frac{\pi x}{L}\,,\quad Z = p\ \cos 10\,\theta \sin 10\,\frac{\pi x}{L}$$

(The above Y and Z components of load correspond to $m = n = 10$ in the expression for loads given in Eq. 6.2).

The above load components correspond to alternative positive and negative load both in the longitudinal and circumferential direction acting over a strip width of $L/10$ and $\pi/10$ respectively. For the above load components, the displacements and stress resultants have been computed using Flugge's, Donnell's and membrane theories and these are given in Table 6.2. It may be observed from this table that the membrane theory results are no where near the results of bending theory. Further, since the load is rapidly varying, the shell will be subjected to bending and the membrane stress resultants will be somewhat insignificant. This example clearly brings out the point that for rapidly varying loads in the longitudinal or transverse direction, the membrane theory will not give acceptable results. It may also be observed from this table that there is an excellent agreement between the results (including the bending and twisting moments) of Flugge and Donnell theories, while in the earlier example ($m = n = 1$) some discrepancy in the magnitude of bending and twisting moments, as given by the two theories, was noted. The reason for this will be discussed later when we develop a general solution using Donnell's theory to deal with any type of boundary conditions along the edge x = constant.

It may be emphasized here that the solution given above is for a load which is symmetrical about the horizontal diametric plane i.e. $\theta = 0$ (Fig. 6.1). However, for load which is antisymmetrical about the plane $\theta = 0$, a solution can be obtained following the same procedure, but replacing $\cos n\theta$ and $\sin n\theta$ in Eqs. (6.1) and (6.2) by $\sin n\theta$ and $\cos n\theta$. Hence, by suitable combination of the symmetric and antisymmetric solutions, it is possible to handle any general unsymmetrical load.

6.2.2 General Solution for a Cylindrical Shell of Revolution[6.2]

In the previous section, we have discussed a solution for cylindrical shell of revolution, which is simply supported along the curved edges (x = constant), by using double trigonometric series. Though this solution is very much restricted in

Table 6.2 Variation of displacements and forces in a simply supported cylindrical shell ($m = 10$ $n = 10$)

Displacement/force	Bending theory		Membrane theory
	Flugge	Donnell	
$\dfrac{u}{\cos 10\theta \cos \dfrac{10\pi x}{L}}$	$0.0033 \dfrac{pa^2}{Eh}$	$0.0033 \dfrac{pa^2}{Eh}$	$0.11 \dfrac{pa^2}{Eh}$
$\dfrac{v}{\sin 10\theta \sin \dfrac{10\pi x}{L}}$	$0.0102 \dfrac{pa^2}{Eh}$	$0.0099 \dfrac{pa^2}{Eh}$	$0.33 \dfrac{pa^2}{Eh}$
$\dfrac{w}{\cos 10\theta \sin \dfrac{10\pi x}{L}}$	$-0.0326 \dfrac{pa^2}{Eh}$	$-0.0320 \dfrac{pa^2}{Eh}$	$-4.3 \dfrac{pa^2}{Eh}$
$\dfrac{N_x}{\cos 10\theta \sin \dfrac{10\pi x}{L}}$	$-0.0358\, pa$	$-0.0330\, pa$	$-1.1\, pa$
$\dfrac{N_\theta}{\cos 10\theta \sin \dfrac{10\pi x}{L}}$	$0.0722\, pa$	$0.067\, pa$	$-\, pa$
$\dfrac{N_{x\theta}}{\sin 10\theta \cos \dfrac{10\pi x}{L}}$	$0.0332\, pa$	$0.033\, pa$	$1.1\, pa$
$\dfrac{N_{\theta x}}{\sin 10\theta \cos \dfrac{10\pi x}{L}}$	$0.0358\, pa$	$0.033\, pa$	$1.1\, pa$
$\dfrac{M_x}{\cos 10\theta \sin \dfrac{10\pi x}{L}}$	$0.0027\, pa^2$	$0.0027\, pa^2$	—
$\dfrac{M_\theta}{\cos 10\theta \sin \dfrac{10\pi x}{L}}$	$0.0027\, pa^2$	$0.0027\, pa^2$	—
$\dfrac{M_{x\theta}}{\sin 10\theta \cos \dfrac{10\pi x}{L}}$	$0.0026\, pa^2$	$0.0027\, pa^2$	—
$\dfrac{M_{\theta x}}{\sin 10\theta \cos \dfrac{10\pi x}{L}}$	$0.0027\, pa^2$	$0.0027\, pa^2$	—
$\dfrac{Q_x}{\cos 10\theta \cos \dfrac{10\pi x}{L}}$	$0.054\, pa$	$0.0533\, pa$	—
$\dfrac{Q_\theta}{\sin 10\theta \sin \dfrac{10\pi x}{L}}$	$-0.0532\, pa$	$-0.0533\, pa$	—

its application so far as the support condition is concerned, the solution can deal with any type of load, including discontinuous load, in the longitudinal and circumferential direction. However, for highly discontinuous loads and very thin shells, the series converges very slowly, thus requiring the consideration of large number of terms in the series to get sufficiently accurate results. Since the stresses, strains and displacements are periodic functions of θ with the period 2π, they can be expressed in terms of Fourier series. Hence, by taking the displacements in terms of Fourier series, the partial differential equations are reduced to ordinary differential equations with constant coefficients whose solution could be obtained using a standard procedure [6.4]. Following this approach, we will now develop a solution using Donnell's theory. By introducing the following non-dimensional variables

$$\bar{u} = u/R\,,\ \bar{v} = v/R\,,\ \bar{w} = w/R \text{ and } \bar{x} = x/R$$

Eqs. (4.11a, b and 4.12) can be written in non-dimensional form as

$$\nabla^4 \bar{u} = -\nu \frac{\partial^3 \bar{w}}{\partial \bar{x}^3} + \frac{\partial^3 \bar{w}}{\partial \theta^2 \partial \bar{x}} - \frac{R}{K}\left\{\frac{2}{1-\nu}\frac{\partial^2 X}{\partial \theta^2} + \frac{\partial^2 X}{\partial \bar{x}^2} - \left(\frac{1+\nu}{1-\nu}\right)\frac{\partial^2 Y}{\partial \theta \partial \bar{x}}\right\} \tag{6.6a}$$

$$\nabla^4 \bar{v} = -(2+\nu)\frac{\partial^3 \bar{w}}{\partial \theta \partial \bar{x}^2} - \frac{\partial^3 \bar{w}}{\partial \theta^3} + \frac{R}{K}\left\{\left(\frac{1+\nu}{1-\nu}\right)\frac{\partial^2 X}{\partial \theta \partial \bar{x}} - \frac{2}{1-\nu}\frac{\partial^2 Y}{\partial \bar{x}^2} - \frac{\partial^2 Y}{\partial \theta^2}\right\} \tag{6.6b}$$

$$\nabla^8 \bar{w} + 4\lambda^4 \frac{\partial^4 \bar{w}}{\partial \bar{x}^4} = -\frac{R^3}{D}\left[\nabla^4 Z + \frac{\partial}{\partial \bar{x}}\left(\frac{\partial^2 X}{\partial \theta^2} - \nu \frac{\partial^2 X}{\partial \bar{x}^2}\right) - \frac{\partial}{\partial \theta}\left\{(2+\nu)\frac{\partial^2 Y}{\partial \bar{x}^2} + \frac{\partial^2 Y}{\partial \theta^2}\right\}\right] \tag{6.6c}$$

where $\lambda^4 = 3(1-\nu^2)\left(\dfrac{R}{h}\right)^2$,

$$\nabla^4 = \left(\frac{\partial^4}{\partial \bar{x}^4} + 2\frac{\partial^4}{\partial \bar{x}^2 \partial \theta^2} + \frac{\partial^4}{\partial \theta^4}\right)$$

The force-displacement relations, given in Eq. (4.7a-c), in terms of non-dimensional variables can be written as

$$N_x = K\left[\frac{\partial \bar{u}}{\partial \bar{x}} + \nu\left(\frac{\partial \bar{v}}{\partial \theta} + \bar{w}\right)\right] \tag{6.7a}$$

$$N_\theta = K\left[\left(\frac{\partial \bar{v}}{\partial \theta} + \bar{w}\right) + \nu \frac{\partial \bar{u}}{\partial \bar{x}}\right] \tag{6.7b}$$

$$N_{x\theta} = N_{\theta x} = \frac{K(1-\nu)}{2}\left[\frac{\partial \bar{v}}{\partial \bar{x}} + \frac{\partial \bar{u}}{\partial \theta}\right] \tag{6.7c}$$

$$M_x = \frac{D}{R}\left[\frac{\partial^2 \bar{w}}{\partial \bar{x}^2} + \nu \frac{\partial^2 \bar{w}}{\partial \theta^2}\right] \tag{6.7d}$$

$$M_\theta = \frac{D}{R}\left[\frac{\partial^2 \overline{w}}{\partial \theta^2} + \nu \frac{\partial^2 \overline{w}}{\partial \overline{x}^2}\right] \tag{6.7e}$$

$$M_{x\theta} = M_{\theta x} = D(1-\nu)\frac{\partial^2 \overline{w}}{\partial \overline{x}\,\partial \theta} \tag{6.7f}$$

The solution of the differential equation (6.6c) is obtained as

$$\overline{w} = \overline{w}_0 + \overline{w}_1$$

where $\overline{w}_0$ is the solution of the homogeneous part of the differential equation (complementary function) and $\overline{w}_1$ is the particular integral.

6.2.2.1 Complementary function

The homogeneous part of the differential equation (6.6c) is

$$\nabla^8 \overline{w} + 4\lambda^4 \frac{\partial^4 \overline{w}}{\partial \overline{x}^4} = 0 \tag{6.8}$$

The solution for the above differential equation in general may be taken as

$$\overline{w}_0 = \sum_{m=1}^{\infty} (A_m \cos m\theta + B_m \sin m\theta)\, e^{\rho \overline{x}} \tag{6.9a}$$

In the above form of solution, the cosine series is taken for load symmetrical about $\theta = 0$ and sine series for load antisymmetrical about $\theta = 0$ (Fig. 6.1). For illustrating the development of the solution, we will consider only the cosine series in Eq. (6.9a). Solution by taking sine series can be developed in a similar way and by suitably combining these two solutions, it is possible to handle any general load in the circumferential direction. Hence $\overline{w}_0$ is taken as

$$\overline{w}_0 = \sum_{m=1}^{\infty} A_m\, e^{\rho \overline{x}} \cos m\theta \tag{6.9b}$$

Substituting the above form of $\overline{w}_0$ in Eq. (6.8), we get the following characteristic equation

$$(\rho^2 - m^2)^4 + 4\lambda^4 \rho^4 = 0 \tag{6.10}$$

The above equation will have eight roots and all the roots will be complex. The eight complex roots in general can be written as

$$\rho_{1,2,3,4} = \pm(c \pm id)$$
$$\rho_{5,6,7,8} = \pm(c_1 \pm id_1) \tag{6.11}$$

where c, c_1 and d, d_1 are the real and imaginary part of roots of Eq. (6.10). A method of determining the real and imaginary part of the roots is given in Appendix-I and are shown to be related as

$$c = \frac{1}{2}\left[\Omega + \lambda + \frac{m^2}{\Omega}\right],\quad d = \frac{1}{2}\left(\Omega - \lambda - \frac{m^2}{\Omega}\right)$$

$$c_1 = \frac{1}{2}\left[\Omega - \lambda + \frac{m^2}{\Omega}\right],\ d_1 = \frac{1}{2}\left[\Omega + \lambda - \frac{m^2}{\Omega}\right]$$

$$\text{where} \quad \Omega = \left[-\frac{\lambda^2}{2} + \left\{\left(\frac{\lambda^2}{2}\right)^2 + m^4\right\}^{\frac{1}{2}}\right]^{\frac{1}{2}}$$

Before we write the solution of the differential equation (6.8), it is worthwhile to discuss the accuracy of Donnell's theory. Hoff[6.5], who has studied the accuracy of Donnell's equation, has determined error in the roots for different harmonics (m) and shell parameter. He concludes that Donnell's and Flugge's equations should yield the same results within engineering accuracy when m is sufficiently large. We will reexamine this conclusion here. For this, as a first stage, we can compare the roots of the characteristic equation of Donnell's and Flugge's theories. For Flugge's theory we will consider Eqs. (4.8a-c) and the homogeneous part of these equations can be rewritten in terms of the nondimensional variables as follows:

$$\frac{\partial^2 \bar{u}}{\partial \bar{x}^2} + \left(\frac{1-\nu}{2}\right)\frac{\partial^2 \bar{u}}{\partial \theta^2} + \left(\frac{1+\nu}{2}\right)\frac{\partial^2 \bar{v}}{\partial \theta\, \partial \bar{x}} + \nu\frac{\partial \bar{w}}{\partial \bar{x}}$$
$$+ D'\left\{-\frac{\partial^3 \bar{w}}{\partial \bar{x}^3} + \left(\frac{1-\nu}{2}\right)\frac{\partial^2 \bar{u}}{\partial \theta^2} + \left(\frac{1-\nu}{2}\right)\frac{\partial^3 \bar{w}}{\partial \theta^2\, \partial \bar{x}}\right\} = 0 \quad (6.12a)$$

$$\frac{\partial^2 \bar{v}}{\partial \theta^2} + \left(\frac{1+\nu}{2}\right)\frac{\partial^2 \bar{u}}{\partial \theta\, \partial \bar{x}} + \left(\frac{1-\nu}{2}\right)\frac{\partial^2 \bar{v}}{\partial \bar{x}^2} + \frac{\partial \bar{w}}{\partial \theta}$$
$$+ D'\left\{\frac{3(1-\nu)}{2}\frac{\partial^2 \bar{v}}{\partial \bar{x}^2} - \left(\frac{3-\nu}{2}\right)\frac{\partial^3 \bar{w}}{\partial \bar{x}^2\, \partial \theta}\right\} = 0 \quad (6.12b)$$

$$\nu\frac{\partial \bar{u}}{\partial \bar{x}} + \frac{\partial \bar{v}}{\partial \theta} + \bar{w} + D'\left\{\left(\frac{1-\nu}{2}\right)\frac{\partial^3 \bar{u}}{\partial \theta^2 \partial \bar{x}} - \frac{\partial^3 \bar{u}}{\partial \bar{x}^3}\right.$$
$$- \left(\frac{3-\nu}{2}\right)\frac{\partial^3 \bar{v}}{\partial \theta\, \partial \bar{x}^2} + \frac{\partial^4 \bar{w}}{\partial \bar{x}^4} + \frac{\partial^4 \bar{w}}{\partial \theta^4}$$
$$\left. + 2\frac{\partial^4 \bar{w}}{\partial \bar{x}^2\, \partial \theta^2} + 2\frac{\partial^2 \bar{w}}{\partial \theta^2} + \bar{w}\right\} = 0 \quad (6.12c)$$

The non-dimensionalised displacements are then taken in the following form

$$\bar{u} = \sum_{m=1}^{\infty} A\, e^{\rho \bar{x}} \cos m\theta$$

$$\bar{v} = \sum_{m=1}^{\infty} B\, e^{\rho \bar{x}} \sin m\theta \quad (6.13)$$

$$\bar{w} = \sum_{m=1}^{\infty} C\, e^{\rho \bar{x}} \cos m\theta$$

Introducing the above form of displacements in Eq. (6.12a-c), we get three algebraic equations in terms of *A*, *B* and *C*. For a nontrivial solution, the determinant of these equations should be zero resulting in the following eighth degree polynomial equation in ρ.

$$
\begin{aligned}
&(1+3D')(1-D')\rho^8 - \left[4\left\{1+\frac{11-3\nu}{8}D'\right.\right.\\
&\left.\left.+\,9\left(\frac{1-\nu}{8}\right)(D')^2\right\}m^2 - 2\nu(1+3D')\right]\rho^6\\
&+\left[\left(\frac{1-\nu^2}{D'}+1\right)(1+3D') - 6\left(1+\frac{2-\nu+\nu^2}{2}D'\right)m^2\right.\\
&\left.+\,6\left\{1+\left(\frac{2-\nu}{2}\right)D' - \frac{(\nu D')^2}{6}\right\}m^4\right]\rho^4 - m^2(m^2-1)\\
&\left[4m^2\left\{1+\left(\frac{7-3\nu}{8}\right)D' + 3\left(\frac{1-\nu}{8}\right)(D')^2\right\}\right.\\
&\left.-\left\{2(2-\nu)+\frac{7(1-\nu)}{2}D' + 3\left(\frac{1-\nu}{2}\right)(D')^2\right\}\right]\rho^2\\
&+\,m^4(m^2-1)^2(1+D') = 0
\end{aligned}
\qquad (6.14)
$$

The roots of the above equation can be determined by using any standard numerical procedure. In Table 6.3, the roots of the above characteristic equation (Flugge's theory) have been compared with those given by Eqn. (6.11) (Donnell's theory) for different values of (R/h) and m. It may be seen from this table that there is a large difference in the second set of roots, corresponding to $\pm(c_1 \pm id_1)$, for $m = 1$ between Flugge and Donnell theories while for $m > 1$, there is a good agreement in the roots given by the two theories. This is the reason why we got different magnitude for moments by Flugge and Donnell theories in the earlier example of a simply supported cylindrical shell for $m = 1$ while there was an excellent agreement between the results obtained from the two theories for $m = 10$. Hence, it may be concluded that except for the error involved in the first harmonic, Donnell's theory gives acceptable results.

The solution of Eq. (6.8) can now be written as

$$
\begin{aligned}
\overline{w}_0 = \sum_{m=1}^{\infty} &[(A_1 \cos d\overline{x} + A_2 \sin d\overline{x})\, e^{-c\overline{x}}\\
&+ (A_3 \cos d_1\overline{x} + A_4 \sin d_1\overline{x})\, e^{-c_1\overline{x}}\\
&+ (A_5 \cos d\overline{x} + A_6 \sin d\overline{x})\, e^{c\overline{x}}\\
&+ (A_7 \cos d_1\overline{x} + A_8 \sin d_1\overline{x})\, e^{c_1\overline{x}}] \cos m\theta
\end{aligned}
\qquad (6.15)
$$

Table 6.3 Comparison of roots of characteristic equation for $\nu = 0.3$ ($\overline{w}_0 = Ae^{\rho\overline{x}} \cos m\theta$)

			Roots			
R/h	*m*	Theory	*c*	*d*	c_1	d_1
50	1	Flugge	9.1360	9.0425	0	0
		Donnell	9.1445	9.0345	0.0553	0.0547
	2	Flugge	9.3045	8.8813	0.1940	0.1868
		Donnell	9.3143	8.8747	0.2251	0.2145
	3	Flugge	9.5964	8.6275	0.4871	0.4417
		Donnell	9.6080	8.6236	0.5188	0.4656
	8	Flugge	12.9037	6.9925	3.7951	2.0774
		Donnell	12.9164	7.0116	3.8272	2.0776
100	1	Flugge	12.8871	12.8210	0	0
		Donnell	12.8931	12.8153	0.0390	0.0388
	2	Flugge	13.0051	12.7056	0.1360	0.1334
		Donnell	13.0115	12.7004	0.1574	0.1537
	3	Flugge	13.2060	12.5184	0.3377	0.3215
		Donnell	13.2131	12.5140	0.3591	0.3401
	8	Flugge	15.5955	10.9215	2.7278	1.9189
		Donnell	15.6059	10.9272	2.7518	1.9268
150	1	Flugge	15.7700	15.7160	0	0
		Donnell	15.7748	15.7113	0.0318	0.0317
	2	Flugge	15.8659	15.6214	0.1107	0.1093
		Donnell	15.8710	15.6170	0.1280	0.1260
	3	Flugge	16.0283	15.4665	0.2738	0.2649
		Donnell	16.0338	15.4625	0.2908	0.2805
	8	Flugge	17.9497	14.0128	2.1956	1.7190
		Donnell	17.9579	14.0144	2.2149	1.7285
200	1	Flugge	18.2018	18.1550	0	0
		Donnell	18.2059	18.1509	0.0275	0.0275
	2	Flugge	18.2848	18.0730	0.0957	0.0948
		Donnell	18.2891	18.0691	0.1107	0.1093
	3	Flugge	18.4246	17.9379	0.2362	0.2304
		Donnell	18.4292	17.9343	0.2508	0.2441
	8	Flugge	20.0641	16.6121	1.8760	1.5566
		Donnell	20.0708	16.6121	1.8924	1.5663

In the above equation, the constants $A_1, A_2, A_3, \ldots A_8$ are determined from the boundary conditions along the two curved edges, $\overline{x}$ = constant. The expressions for stress resultants and displacements can be obtained using Eq. (6.7) and the general expression, depending up on even or odd functions, for the force or displacement can be written as

$$F = \sum_{m=1}^{\infty} MF \; [\, \{ (A_1\alpha_1 - A_2\alpha_2) \cos d\bar{x}$$

$$+ (A_1\alpha_2 + A_2\alpha_1) \sin d\bar{x}\} \, e^{-c\bar{x}}$$

$$+ \{(A_3\alpha_3 - A_4\alpha_4) \cos d_1 \bar{x} + (A_3\alpha_4 + A_4\alpha_3) \sin d_1 \bar{x}\} \, e^{-c_1\bar{x}}$$

$$\pm \{(A_5\alpha_1 - A_6\alpha_2) \cos d\bar{x} - (A_5\alpha_2 + A_6\alpha_1) \sin d\bar{x}\} \, e^{c\bar{x}}$$

$$\pm \{(A_7\alpha_3 - A_8\alpha_4) \cos d_1 \bar{x} - (A_7\alpha_4 + A_8\alpha_3) \sin d_1 \bar{x}\} \, e^{c_1\bar{x}} \quad (6.16)$$

Where F denotes force or displacement, MF – the multiplying factor, α_1, α_2, α_3 and α_4 are coefficients given in Tables 6.4 and 6.5 and A_1, A_2 ,..., A_8 are the eight arbitrary constants.

6.2.2.2 Particular integral

The particular integral of the differential equation (6.6c) can be determined once the components of the load acting on the shell are known. We will restrict ourselves here to obtain the particular integral for a load which has only a Z-component (radial load) and X and Y components are zero.

Let the Z component of the loading be expressed in terms of Fourier series as

$$Z = \sum_{m=1}^{\infty} Z_m \cos m\theta \quad (6.17)$$

where,

$$Z_m = \frac{1}{\pi} \int_0^{2\pi} Z(\theta) \cos m\theta \, d\theta$$

Now the particular integral of Eq. (6.6c) can be taken as

$$\bar{w}_1 = \sum_{m=1}^{\infty} C Z_m \cos m\theta \quad (a)$$

where C is constant so determined to satisfy the complete differential equation (6.6c). By introducing (6.17) and (a) in Eq. (6.6c), we get

$$C = -\frac{R^3}{Dm^4}$$

Hence, the particular integral for the load considered here is

$$\bar{w}_1 = -\frac{R^3}{D} \sum_{m=1}^{\infty} \frac{Z_m}{m^4} \cos m\theta \quad (6.18)$$

The particular integral for forces and displacements can now be determined from (6.6b, c) and (6.7) as

$$N_x = N_\theta = N_{x\theta} = M_{x\theta} = Q_x = \bar{u} = 0 \quad (6.19a)$$

$$M_x = \nu R^2 \sum_{m=1}^{\infty} \frac{Z_m}{m^2} \cos m\theta \quad (6.19b)$$

Table 6.4 Shell forces and displacements from complementary function (even)

$$F = \Sigma\, MF\, [\{(A_1\alpha_1 - A_2\alpha_2)\cos d\bar{x} + (A_1\alpha_2 + A_7\alpha_1)\sin d\bar{x}\}\, e^{-c\bar{x}} + \{(A_3\alpha_3 - A_4\alpha_4)\cos d_1\bar{x} + (A_3\alpha_4 + A_4\alpha_3)\sin d_1\bar{x}\} e^{-c_1\bar{x}}$$
$$+ \{(A_5\alpha_1 - A_6\alpha_2)\cos d\bar{x} - (A_5\alpha_2 + A_6\alpha_1)\sin d\bar{x}\}\, e^{c\bar{x}} + \{(A_7\alpha_3 - A_8\alpha_4)\cos d_1\bar{x} - (A_7\alpha_4 + A_8\alpha_3)\sin d_1\bar{x}\}\, e^{c_1\bar{x}}$$

Force or displacement	MF	α_1	α_2	α_3	α_4
N_x	$\frac{Ehm^2}{2\lambda^2}\cos m\theta$	0	–1	0	–1
N_θ	$\frac{Eh}{2\lambda^2}\cos m\theta$	$-2cd$	$(c^2 - d^2)$	$-2c_1d_1$	$(c_1^2 - d_1^2)$
M_x	$\frac{D}{R}\cos m\theta$	$-(\nu m^2 - c^2 + d^2)$	$2cd$	$-(\nu m^2 - c_1^2 + d_1^2)$	$2c_1d_1$
M_θ	$\frac{D\cos m\theta}{R}$	$-\{m^2 - \nu(c^2 - d^2)\}$	$2\nu cd$	$-\{m^2 - \nu(c_1^2 - d_1^2)\}$	$2\nu c_1d_1$
Q_θ	$\frac{D\sin m\theta}{R}$	$-\{m(c^2 - d^2) - m^3\}$	$-2mcd$	$-\{m(c_1^2 - d_1^2) - m^3\}$	$-2mc_1d_1$
$\bar{v}$	$\frac{m\sin m\theta}{2\lambda^2}$	$-\frac{2m^2\, cd}{(c^2 + d^2)^2}$	$-\frac{m^2(c^2 - d^2)}{(c^2 + d^2)^2} + (2 + \nu)$	$-\frac{2m^2\, c_1d_1}{(c_1^2 + d_1^2)^2}$	$-\frac{m^2(c_1^2 - d_1^2)}{(c_1^2 + d_1^2)^2} + (2 + \nu)$
$\bar{w}$	$\cos m\theta$	1	0	1	0

Table 6.5 Shell forces and displacements from complementary function (odd)

$$F = \Sigma\, MF\ [\{(A_1\alpha_1 - A_2\alpha_2)\cos d\bar{x} + (A_1\alpha_2 + A_2\alpha_1)\sin d\bar{x}\}\, e^{-c\bar{x}} + \{(A_3\alpha_3 - A_4\alpha_4)\cos d_1\bar{x} + (A_3\alpha_4 + A_4\alpha_3)\sin d_1\bar{x}\}\, e^{-c_1\bar{x}}$$
$$+ \{(A_5\alpha_1 - A_6\alpha_2)\cos d\bar{x} - (A_5\alpha_2 + A_6\alpha_1)\sin d\bar{x}\}\, e^{c\bar{x}} - \{(A_7\alpha_3 - A_8\alpha_4)\cos d_1\bar{x} - (A_7\alpha_4 + A_8\alpha_3)\sin d_1\bar{x}\}\, e^{c_1\bar{x}}$$

Force or displacement	MF	α_1	α_2	α_3	α_4
$N_{x\theta}$	$\dfrac{Ehm}{2\lambda^2}\sin m\theta$	d	$-c$	d_1	$-c_1$
$M_{x\theta}$	$\dfrac{mD(1-\nu)}{R}\sin m\theta$	c	d	c_1	d_1
Q'_x	$\dfrac{-D}{R^2}\cos m\theta$	$\{c^3 - 3cd^2 - cm^2(2-\nu)\}$	$-\{d^3 - 3c^2 d + dm^2(2-\nu)\}$	$-\{c_1^3 - 3c_1 d_1^2 - c_1 m^2(2-\nu)\}$	$-\{d_1^3 - 3c_1^2 d_1 + (2-\nu)m^2 d_1\}$
$\bar{u}$	$\dfrac{\cos m\theta}{2\lambda^2}$	$\left(\dfrac{m^2}{c^2+d^2} - \nu\right)d$	$\left(\dfrac{m^2}{c^2+d^2} + \nu\right)c$	$\left(\dfrac{m^2}{c_1^2+d_1^2} - \nu\right)d_1$	$\left(\dfrac{m^2}{c_1^2+d_1^2} + \nu\right)c_1$

$$M_\theta = R^2 \sum_{m=1}^{\infty} \frac{Z_m}{m^2} \cos m\theta \tag{6.19c}$$

$$Q_\theta = -R \sum_{m=1}^{\infty} \frac{Z_m}{m} \sin m\theta \tag{6.19d}$$

$$\overline{v} = \frac{R^3}{D} \sum_{m=1}^{\infty} \frac{Z_m}{m^5} \sin m\theta \tag{6.19e}$$

The complete solution of the differential equation (6.6c) can now be obtained by adding the particular integral given in Eq. (6.18) to the complementary function given in (6.15). Similarly, the complete expressions for the forces and displacements may be obtained by adding the particular integral given in (6.19) to complementary function given in Tables 6.4 and 6.5.

It must be noted that while this solution can deal with any load continuous or discontinuous in the circumferential direction which is symmetric with respect to $\theta = 0$, it cannot handle discontinuous loads in the longitudinal direction (x-direction) directly. To overcome this difficulty Chandrashekhara and Srinivas[6.6] have reformulated the solution using transfer matrix approach and have shown that this can handle any arbitrary loading as well as shell of variable thickness.

6.2.2.3 Boundary conditions:

The boundary conditions along the edge $\overline{x}$ = constant depend on the type of support provided along this edge. In general, four boundary conditions either in terms of forces or displacements or a combination of forces and displacements can be specified at each edge. Considering the two edges of the shell totally, eight conditions can be specified using which all the eight constants in the solution (Eq. 6.15) can be determined. We will give below the boundary conditions for an edge $\overline{x}$ = constant depending upon the type of support provided along this edge.

(i) Edge simply supported:

It is assumed that the support provided is such that it can take large in-plane forces, but cannot resist any force normal to its plane. The boundary conditions for such a type of support can be written as

$$\overline{x} = \text{constant}, \; N_x = \overline{v} = M_x = \overline{w} = 0$$

(ii) Edge clamped or fixed:

In this case, at the support, all the displacements and rotation will be prevented and hence, the boundary condition can be specified as

$$\overline{x} = \text{const.}, \; \overline{u} = \overline{v} = \overline{w} = \frac{\partial \overline{w}}{\partial \overline{x}} = 0$$

(iii) Edge free:

For a free edge, all the forces acting normal to the edge must be zero. Hence the boundary conditions can be specified as

$$\bar{x} = \text{const.},\ N_x = N_{x\theta} = M_x = Q'_x = 0$$

where Q'_x is the resultant shear and is given by

$$Q'_x = \left(Q_x + \frac{\partial M_{x\theta}}{R\,\partial\theta} \right).$$

Example 6.1

We will illustrate the application of the above solution by considering an example of a cantilever cylindrical shell, of length 'L' and radius 'R', subjected to wind loading. This problem has been solved by Gopalacharyulu and Johns[6.7] using the above solution. The variation of wind load p_1 has been taken as

$$p_1 = p_0 \sum_{m=0,\,1}^{6} a_m \cos m\theta$$

where, p_0 – wind pressure and a_m are constants determined from a wind tunnel test as (Section 2.5.1.1 b)

$$a_0 = -\ 0.387,\ a_1 = 0.338,\ a_2 = 0.533,\ a_3 = 0.471$$

$$a_4 = 0.166,\ a_5 = -\ 0.066,\ a_6 = -\ 0.055$$

It must be noted that $m = 0$, in the above variation of wind load, corresponds to uniform pressure (axisymmetric) acting on the cylindrical shell and the solution for this type of problem has already been discussed in Chapter 5. We will discuss here the solution for the case $m \geq 1$. The boundary condition for the cantilever cylindrical shell can be written as (Fig. 6.2)

$$\bar{x} = 0,\ \bar{u} = \bar{v} = \bar{w} = \frac{\partial \bar{w}}{\partial \bar{x}} = 0$$

$$\bar{x} = L/R,\ N_x = N_{x\theta} = M_x = Q'_x = 0$$

The wind load acting normal to cylindrical surface will have only Z component and this is taken as

$$Z = \sum_{m=1}^{\infty} Z_m \cos m\theta = p_0 \sum_{m=1}^{\infty} a_m \cos m\theta$$

and hence, $Z_m = a_m\, p_0 \qquad (m = 1,\ 2,\ \ldots 6)$

$$Z_m = 0 \qquad (m > 6)$$

Using the above boundary conditions, and taking the complementary function for the corresponding forces and displacements from Tables 6.4 and 6.5 and the

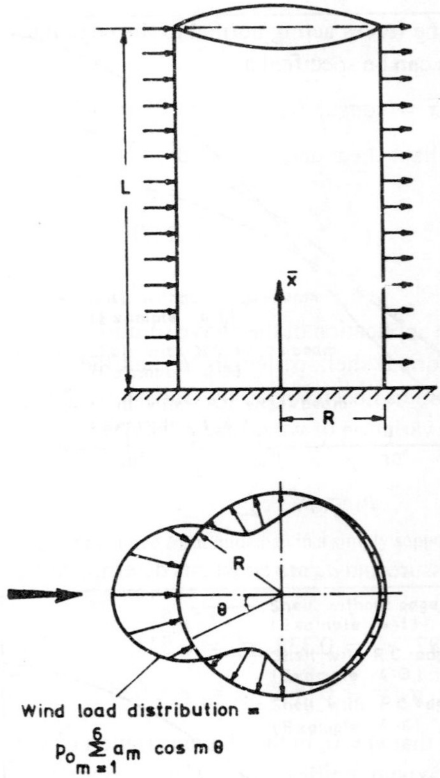

Fig. 6.2 Cantilever cylindrical shell subjected to wind load

particular integral from (6.19), the following eight simultaneous equations can be formulated. These simultaneous equations can be written in a compact form as

$$\sum_{j=1}^{8} b_{ij} A_j = k_i \qquad (i = 1,\ 2,\ \ldots 8)$$

where,

$$b_{11} = -\, b_{15} = -\left(\frac{m^2}{c^2 + d^2} - \nu\right) d,$$

$$b_{12} = -\, b_{16} = \left(\frac{m^2}{c^2 + d^2} + \nu\right) c$$

$$b_{13} = -\, b_{17} = -\left(\frac{m^2}{c_1^2 + d_1^2} - \nu\right) d_1,$$

$$b_{14} = -\, b_{18} = \left(\frac{m^2}{c_1^2 + d_1^2} + \nu\right) c_1$$

$$k_1 = 0$$

$$b_{21} = b_{25} = \frac{2m^2\,cd}{(c^2 + d^2)^2},$$

$$b_{22} = b_{26} = -\left\{\frac{m^2\,(c^2 - d^2)}{(c^2 + d^2)^2} - (2 + \nu)\right\}$$

$$b_{23} = b_{27} = \frac{2m^2\,c_1\,d_1}{(c_1^2 + d_1^2)^2},$$

$$b_{24} = b_{28} = -\left\{\frac{m^2\,(c_1^2 - d_1^2)}{(c_1^2 + d_1^2)^2} - (2 + \nu)\right\}$$

$$k_2 = -\frac{2p_0\,R^3\,\lambda^2\,a_n}{Dm^6}$$

$$b_{31} = b_{33} = b_{35} = b_{37} = 1,$$

$$b_{32} = b_{34} = b_{36} = b_{38} = 0$$

$$k_3 = \frac{p_0\,R^3\,a_n}{n^4\,D}$$

$$b_{41} = -b_{45} = -c, \quad b_{42} = -b_{46} = d,$$

$$b_{43} = -b_{47} = -c_1,$$

$$b_{44} = -\,b_{48} = d_1, \quad k_4 = 0$$

$$b_{51} = F1, \quad b_{52} = -E1, \quad b_{53} = F2,$$

$$b_{54} = -\,E2, \quad b_{55} = -F3$$

$$b_{56} = -\,E3, \quad b_{57} = -\,F4, \quad b_{58} = -E4$$

$$b_{61} = (cF1 - dE1), \quad b_{62} = -(cE1 + dF1),$$

$$b_{63} = (c_1\,F2 - d_1\,E2)$$

$$b_{64} = (c_1\,E2 + d_1\,F2), \quad b_{65} = (cF3 + dE3),$$

$$b_{66} = (cE3 - dF3)$$

$$b_{67} = (d_1\,E4 - c_1\,F4), \quad b_{68} = (c_1\,E4 + d_1\,F4)$$

$$b_{71} = [-(\nu n^2 - c^2 + d^2)\,E1 + 2cd\,F1],$$

$$b_{72} = -[2cd\,E1 + (\nu n^2 - c^2 + d^2)\,F1]$$

$$b_{73} = [-(\nu n^2 - c^2 + d^2)\,E2 + 2c_1\,d_1\,F2],$$

$$b_{74} = -[2c_1\,d_1\,E2 + (\nu n^2 - c_1^2 + d_1^2)\,F2]$$

$$b_{75} = -[(\nu n^2 - c^2 + d^2)\,E3 + 2cd\,F3],$$

$$b_{76} = [-2cd\,F3 + (\nu n^2 - c^2 + d^2)\,F3],$$

$$b_{77} = -[(\nu n^2 - c_1^2 + d_1^2)\,E4 + 2c_1 d_1\,F4]$$

$$b_{78} = [-2c_1 d_1\,E4 + (\nu n^2 - c_1^2 + d_1^2)\,F4],$$

$$k_7 = -\frac{\nu R^3 p_0 a_n}{n^2 D}$$

$$b_{81} = [\{c^3 - 3cd^2 - cn^2(2-\nu)\}\ E1 - \{d^3 - 3c^2 d + dn^2(2-\nu)\}\ F1]$$

$$b_{82} = [\{d^3 - 3c^2 d + dn^2(2-\nu)\}\ E1 - \{c^3 - 3cd^2 + cn^2(2-\nu)\}\ F1]$$

$$b_{83} = -[\{c_1^3 - 3c_1 d_1^2 - c_1 n^2(2-\nu)\}\ E2 + \{d_1^3 - 3c_1^2 d_1 - d_1 n^2(2-\nu)\}\ F2]$$

$$b_{84} = [\{d_1^3 - 3c_1^2 d_1 + d_1 n^2(2-\nu)\}\ E2 - \{c_1^3 - 3c_1 d_1^2 - c_1 n^2(2-\nu)\}\ F2]$$

$$b_{85} = [\{c^3 - 3cd^2 - cn^2(2-\nu)\}\ E3 - \{d^3 - 3c^2 d + dn^2(2-\nu)\}\ F3]$$

$$b_{86} = -[\{d^3 - 3c^2 d + dn^2(2-\nu)\}\ E3 + \{c^3 - 3cd^2 - cn^2(2-\nu)\}\ F3]$$

$$b_{87} = [\{c_1^3 - 3c_1 d_1^2 - c_1 n^2(2-\nu)\}\ E4 - \{d_1^3 - 3c_1^2 d_1 + d_1 n^2(2-\nu)\}\ F4]$$

$$b_{88} = -[\{d_1^3 - 3c_1^2 d_1 + d_1 n^2(2-\nu)\}\ E4 + \{c_1^3 - 3c_1 d_1^2 - c_1 n^2(2-\nu)\}\ F4]$$

$$k_8 = 0$$

and

$$E1 = \frac{\cos dL}{R}\, e^{-(cL/R)}, \qquad E2 = \frac{\cos d_1 L}{R}\, e^{-(c_1 L/R)}$$

$$E3 = \frac{\cos dL}{R}\, e^{(cL/R)}, \qquad E4 = \frac{\cos d_1 L}{R}\, e^{(c_1 L/R)}$$

$$F1 = \frac{\sin dL}{R}\, e^{-(cL/R)}, \qquad F2 = \frac{\sin d_1 L}{R}\, e^{-(c_1 L/R)}$$

$$F3 = \frac{\sin dL}{R}\, e^{(cL/R)}, \qquad F4 = \frac{\sin d_1 L}{R}\, e^{(c_1 L/R)}$$

By solving the above simultaneous equations, the constants A_1, A_2, ... A_8 are determined for each harmonic i.e. from $n = 1$ to 6. The stress resultants and displacements are then computed for each harmonic and summed up for the six harmonics. Some typical results are presented in Figs. 6.3 and 6.4, for $(L/R) = 1$, $(R/h) = 100$ and $\nu = 0.3$. Fig. 6.3 shows the variations of nondimensionalised stress

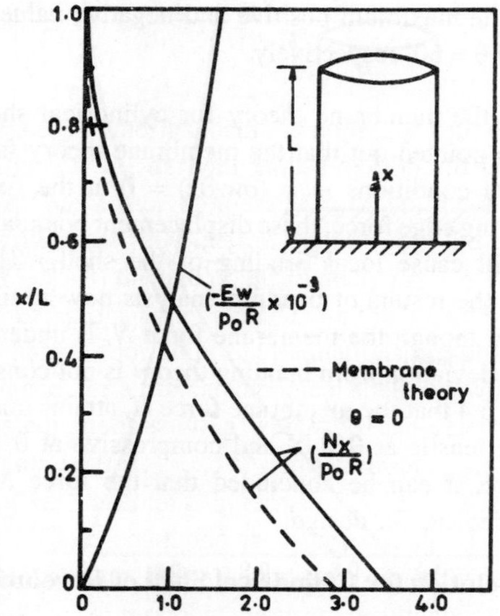

Fig. 6.3 Distribution of membrane force N_x and displacement w along the length of the shell

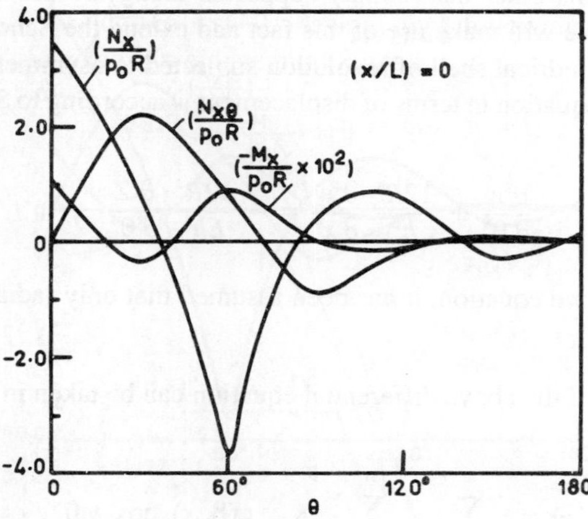

Fig. 6.4 Distribution of membrane forces N_x and $N_{x\theta}$ and bending moment M_x along the fixed edge

resultant (N_x) and radial displacement (w) over the length of the shell ($\theta = 0°$). In this figure, the N_x variation obtained from membrane theory also has been incorporated for comparison. It may be seen from this figure that the membrane theory underestimates the magnitude of max. N_x (along the fixed edge) by about 18%. Fig. 6.4 shows the variation of stress resultants N_x, $N_{x\theta}$ and M_x along the fixed edge. It may be seen from this figure that the magnitude of M_x is fairly small at the fixed edge. Further, the maximum positive and negative values of the force N_x occur along $\theta = 0°$ and $\theta = 60°$ respectively.

While discussing the membrane theory for cylindrical shell of revolution (Section 2.5.1), it was pointed out that the membrane theory fails to satisfy the displacement boundary conditions $w = (\partial w/\partial x) = 0$ at the fixed end. It was indicated that by applying edge force, these displacement boundary conditions can be satisfied which will cause local bending of the shell. This point can be reexamined here with the results of bending analysis now available. It may be seen from Fig. 6.3 that though the membrane force N_x is underestimated by the membrane theory, the deviation from bending theory is not considerable. It may be observed from Fig. 6.4 that the membrane force N_x attains maximum values at $\theta = 0°$ and $60°$, being tensile at $\theta = 0°$ and compressive at $\theta = 60°$. From the comparison made here, it can be concluded that the force N_x obtained from membrane theory is adequate for design.

6.2.3 Approximate Solution for Cylindrical Shell of Revolution

It has been shown in Section 4.7 that Schorer's[6.3] theory, which is an approximate bending theory for long shells, gives acceptable results for long cylindrical shell panels. It has also been shown in this section that it is possible to deal with boundary conditions other than simply supported along the curved ends using Schorer theory. We will make use of this fact and extend the Schorer theory for the analysis of cylindrical shell of revolution subjected to asymmetric load. The basic differential equation in terms of displacement w according to Schorer theory (Eq. 4.44) is

$$\frac{\partial^8 w}{\partial \theta^8} + \frac{12R^6}{h^2}\frac{\partial^4 w}{\partial x^4} = -\frac{12R^4}{Eh^3}\frac{\partial^4 Z}{\partial \theta^4} \tag{6.20}$$

(In writing the above equation, it has been assumed that only radial load will be acting on the shell).

The solution of the above differential equation can be taken in the following form:

$$w = \sum_{m=1}^{\infty} \sum_{n=1}^{\infty} K_{mn}\ \phi(\beta_n x)\ \cos\ m\theta \tag{6.21a}$$

where $\phi(\beta_n x)$ is selected from Table 4.14 depending on the support condition at $x = 0$ and L.

The radial load acting on the shell can also be expressed as

$$Z = \sum_{m=1}^{\infty} \sum_{n=1}^{\infty} Z_{mn}\ \phi(\beta_n x)\ \cos\ m\theta \tag{6.21b}$$

where Z_{mn} is determined from the orthogonality condition as

$$Z_{mn_i} = \frac{\int_0^L \int_0^{2\pi} Z\ \phi(\beta_n x)\ \cos m\theta\ dx\ d\theta}{\frac{\pi}{2} \int_0^L \phi^2\ (\beta_n x) dx} \tag{6.21c}$$

Introducing (6.21a and b) in (6.20), we can find K_{mn} as

$$K_{mn} = \frac{-12R^4\ m^4\ Z_{mn}}{Eh^3 \left(m^8 + \dfrac{12R^6\ \beta_n^4}{h^2} \right)}$$

Hence, the expression for w can be written as

$$\frac{Ew}{h} = -12 \left(\frac{R}{h} \right)^4 \sum_{m=1}^{\infty} \sum_{n=1}^{\infty} \frac{m^4\ Z_{mn}}{\left\{ m^8 + 12 \left(\dfrac{R}{h} \right)^2 \left(\dfrac{R}{L} \right)^4 (\beta_n L)^4 \right\}} \tag{6.22}$$

The stress resultants and displacements can now be determined from Eqs. (4.45 and 4.46) together with Eq. (6.22).

Example 6.2

To illustrate the application of the above solution, let us consider a long cantilever cylindrical shell subjected to wind load as in Example 6.1. This problem has been solved by Chandrashekhara[6.8] using Schorer theory and the above method of solution. For this example, the function $\phi(\beta_n x)$ is taken as

$$\phi(\beta_n x) = [(\cosh \beta_n x - \cos \beta_n x) - \alpha_n (\sinh \beta_n x - \sin \beta_n x)]$$

where $\beta_n L$ and α_n are determined from the following characteristic equations.

$$(\cosh \beta_n L + \cos \beta_n L) - \alpha_n (\sinh \beta_n L + \sin \beta_n L) = 0$$
$$(\sinh \beta_n L - \sin \beta_n L) - \alpha_n (\cosh \beta_n L + \cos \beta_n L) = 0$$

The values of $\beta_n L$ and α_n, satisfying the above equations are given in Table 4.14. It may be verified that the above function satisfies the fixed end boundary conditions at the bottom viz. $x = 0, u = v = w = (\partial w / \partial x) = 0$ and the free boundary conditions at the top viz. $x = L$, $N_x = N_{x\theta} = 0$. The other two free boundary conditions, namely Q_x and M_x are not specified here because these forces are neglected in Schorer's theory (see assumptions in Section 4.7.1.).

As in the previous example, the wind load is taken as

$$Z = p_0 \sum_{m=1}^{6} a_m \cos m\theta$$

where $a_1, a_2, a_3, \ldots, a_6$ have the same values as in the previous example. For the above load component Z_{mn}, can be determined from Eq. (6.21c) as

$$Z_{mn} = a_m \, \psi(\beta_n L) \, p_0 \qquad (m = 1,2,\cdots,6 \quad n = 1,2,\cdots\infty)$$

$$\text{where } \psi(\beta_n L) = \frac{1}{\beta_n L} [(\sinh \beta_n L - \sin \beta_n L) - \alpha_n (\cosh \beta_n L + \cos \beta_n L) + 2\alpha_n]$$

Substituting for Z_{mn}, the above expression in Eq. (6.22), we obtain w as

$$w = -24 \left(\frac{p_0 R}{E}\right)\left(\frac{R}{h}\right)^3 \sum_{m=1}^{6} \sum_{n=1}^{\infty} \frac{a_m m^4 (\beta_n L) \, \phi(\beta_n x) \cos m\theta}{\left\{m^8 + 12\left(\frac{R}{h}\right)^2 \left(\frac{R}{L}\right)^4 (\beta_n L)^4\right\}} \tag{6.23}$$

The expression for the nondimensionalised stress resultants can be obtained as

$$\left(\frac{N_x}{p_0 R}\right) = 2\left(\frac{L}{R}\right)^2 \sum_{m=1}^{6} \sum_{n=1}^{\infty} \left\{-\frac{m^{10}}{A_{mn}} + m^2\right\} \frac{a_m (\beta_n L) \, \phi_1(\beta_n x) \cos m\theta}{(\beta_n L)^2} \tag{6.24a}$$

$$\left(\frac{N_\theta}{p_0 R}\right) = 2 \sum_{m=1}^{6} \sum_{n=1}^{\infty} \left(\frac{m^8}{A_{mn}} - 1\right) a_m (\beta_n L) \, \phi(\beta_n x) \cos m\theta \tag{6.24b}$$

$$\left(\frac{N_{x\theta}}{p_0 R}\right) = 2\left(\frac{L}{R}\right) \sum_{m=1}^{6} \sum_{n=1}^{\infty} \left(\frac{m^9}{A_{mn}} - m\right) \frac{a_m (\beta_n L) \, \phi_2(\beta_n x) \sin m\theta}{(\beta_n L)} \tag{6.24c}$$

$$\left(\frac{M_\theta}{p_0 R^2}\right) = 2 \sum_{m=1}^{6} \sum_{n=1}^{\infty} \frac{a_m m^6 (\beta_n L) \, \phi(\beta_n x) \cos m\theta}{A_{mn}} \tag{6.24d}$$

$$\left(\frac{Q_\theta}{p_0 R}\right) = -2 \sum_{m=1}^{6} \sum_{n=1}^{\infty} \frac{a_m m^7 (\beta_n L) \, \phi(\beta_n x) \cos m\theta}{A_{mn}} \tag{6.24e}$$

where

$$A_{mn} = \left[m^8 + 12\left(\frac{R}{h}\right)^2 \left(\frac{R}{L}\right)^4 (\beta_n L)^4\right]$$

$$\phi_1(\beta_n x) = [(\cosh \beta_n x + \cos \beta_n x) - \alpha_n (\sinh \beta_n x + \sin \beta_n x)]$$

$$\phi_2(\beta_n x) = [(\sinh \beta_n x - \sin \beta_n x) - \alpha_n (\cosh \beta_n x + \cos \beta_n x)]$$

It may be seen that unlike in the previous example, the stress resultants can be directly determined from the above expression. For the type of load considered here, it is adequate if first five terms in the *n*-series are considered[6.8]. Some typical results are presented in Figs. 6.5 and 6.6 for $L/R = 3$, $R/h = 100$. To assess the accuracy, these results have been compared with the results obtained from the previous solution using Donnell's theory. It can be seen from Figs. 6.5 and 6.6 that the agreement between Schorer's theory and Donnell's theory results is excellent indicating that Schorer's theory could be safely used for long shells ($L/R > 3$). Further, in Fig. 6.5, the variation of the bending moment M_x along the fixed end obtained from Donnell's theory has been given. It may be seen that the magnitude of M_x is fairly small and confirms the assumption made in Schorer's theory.

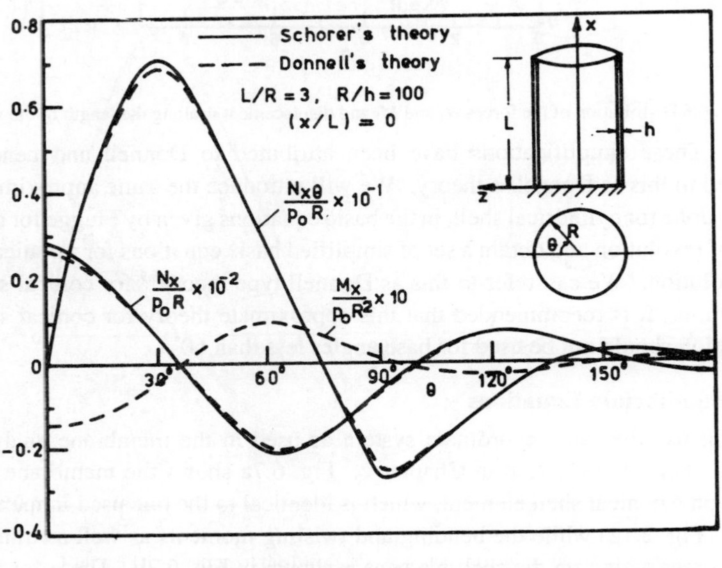

Fig. 6.5 Distribution of the forces N_x, $N_{x\theta}$ and M_x along the fixed edge

6.3 CONICAL SHELL OF REVOLUTION

Flugge[6.1] has given the basic equations for the bending analysis of a conical shell of revolution. These equations, when specialised for the case of a cylindrical shell (by making the base angle tend to 90°) the equations corresponding to the bending of a cylindrical shell are obtained (Eq. 4.8 a–c). These equations have been referred as the exact equations for the bending analysis of a cylindrical shell. Hence, the basic equations given by Flugge for a conical shell of revolution can also be referred as the exact equations. As noted earlier, these equations have complex form and rather difficult to handle. Hence, we introduced some simplification and obtain a set of simpler equations (Eq. 4.9 a–c) for cylindrical

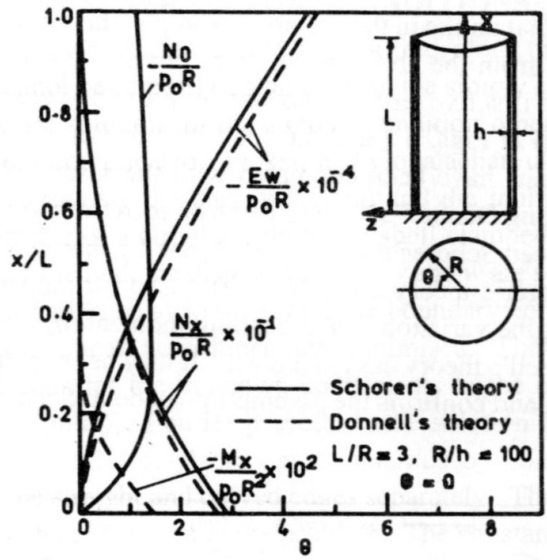

Fig. 6.6 Distribution of the forces N_x and M_x and displacement w along the length of the shell

shell. These simplifications have been attributed to Donnell and hence, we referred to this as Donnell's theory. We will introduce the same approximations, as was done for cylindrical shell, in the basic equations given by Flugge for conical shell of revolution and obtain a set of simplified basic equations for a conical shell of revolution. We can refer to this as Donnell type theory[6.9] for conical shell of revolution. It is recommended that this approximate theory for conical shell of revolution should not be used for base angles less than 60°.

6.3.1 Equilibrium Equations

We will use the same coordinate system as used in the membrane analysis of conical shell of revolution in Chapter 2. Fig. 6.7a shows the membrane forces acting on a conical shell element, which is identical to the one used in membrane theory (Fig. 2.12) while the bending and twisting moments as well as transverse shear forces acting on the shell element is shown in Fig. 6.7b. These forces and moments have to satisfy the six equations of equilibrium — three for the force components in the direction of external load components X, Y and Z and three for the moments with respect to the three reference axes.

The first three force equilibrium equations can be obtained as

$$\frac{\partial}{\partial x}(xN_x) + \frac{\partial N_{\theta x}}{\partial \theta}\sec\alpha - N_\theta = -Xx \tag{6.25a}$$

$$\frac{\partial}{\partial x}(xN_{x\theta}) + \frac{\partial N_\theta}{\partial \theta}\sec\alpha + N_{\theta x} = -Yx \tag{6.25b}$$

$$N_\theta \tan\alpha + \frac{\partial Q_\theta}{\partial \theta}\sec\alpha + \frac{\partial}{\partial x}(xQ_x) = Zx \tag{6.25c}$$

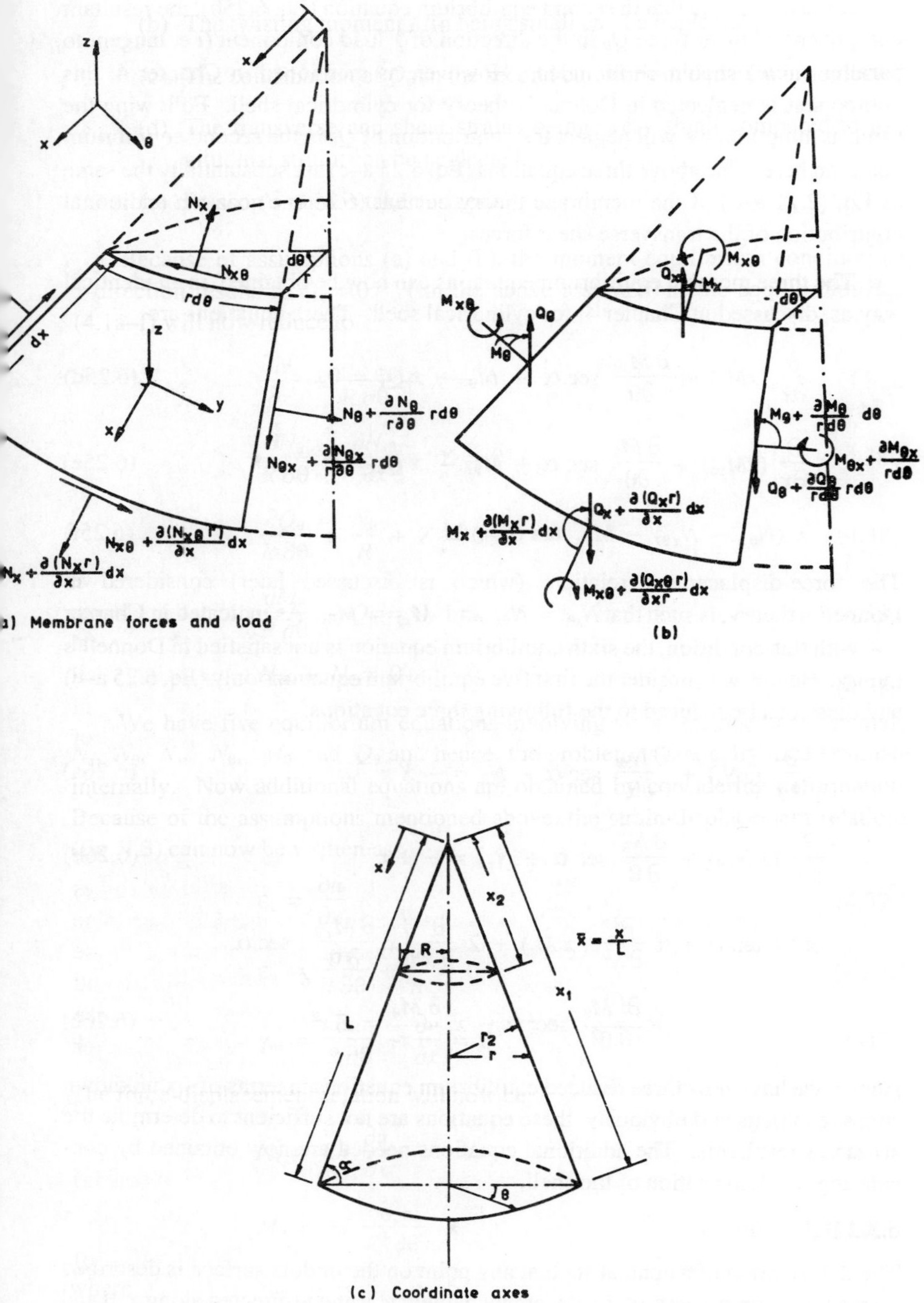

Fig. 6.7 Internal forces and load acting on an element of a conical shell with coordinate axes

It must be noted that in second equilibrium equation (Eq. 6.25b), the resultant component of shear force Q_θ in the direction of Y load component (i.e. tangent to parallel circle) should be included. However, as mentioned in Chapter 4, this component is neglected in Donnell's theory for cylindrical shell. Following the same assumption, we will neglect the contribution of Q_θ in the second equilibrium equation here. The above three equations (Eq. 6.25 a–c) are substantially the same as Eq. (2.21 a–c) of the membrane theory but Eq. (6.25 a–c) contain additional contribution of the transverse shear forces.

The three moment equilibrium equations can now be obtained, in an identical way as, discussed in Chapter 4, for cylindrical shell. These equations are

$$\frac{\partial}{\partial x}(xM_x) + \frac{\partial M_{x\theta}}{\partial \theta}\sec\alpha - M_\theta - xQ_x = 0 \tag{6.25d}$$

$$\frac{\partial}{\partial x}(xM_{x\theta}) + \frac{\partial M_\theta}{\partial \theta}\sec\alpha + M_{\theta x} - xQ_\theta = 0 \tag{6.25e}$$

$$x(N_{\theta x} - N_{x\theta}) - M_{\theta x}\tan\alpha = 0 \tag{6.25f}$$

The force-displacement relation, (which is discussed later) considered in Donnell's theory, is such that $N_{x\theta} = N_{\theta x}$ and $M_{x\theta} = M_{\theta x}$. As indicated in Chapter – 4, with this condition, the sixth equilibrium equation is not satisfied in Donnell's theory. Hence, we consider the first five equilibrium equations only (Eq. 6.25 a–e) and these can be reduced to the following three equations:

$$\frac{\partial}{\partial x}(xN_x) + \frac{\partial N_{x\theta}}{\partial \theta}\sec\alpha - N_\theta = -Xx \tag{6.26a}$$

$$\frac{\partial}{\partial x}(xN_{x\theta}) + \frac{\partial N_\theta}{\partial \theta}\sec\alpha + N_{x\theta} = -Yx \tag{6.26b}$$

$$xN_\theta\tan\alpha + x\frac{\partial^2}{\partial x^2}(xM_x) + 2\frac{\partial}{\partial x}\left(x\frac{\partial M_{x\theta}}{\partial \theta}\right)\sec\alpha + \frac{\partial^2 M_\theta}{\partial \theta^2}\sec^2\alpha - x\frac{\partial M_\theta}{\partial x} = Zx^2 \tag{6.26c}$$

Hence, we have now three reduced equilibrium equations in terms of six unknown stress resultants and obviously, these equations are not sufficient to determine the six stress resultants. The additional equations needed are now obtained by considering the deformation of the shell.

6.3.2 Deformation

The deformation of a conical shell at any point on the middle surface is described by the three components of displacement namely u, v and w directed along x, θ and z directions respectively. For a thin shell, it is possible to establish a geometrical relationship between the displacement at any arbitrary point (over the thickness of the shell) to corresponding displacement at the middle surface of the shell. It has been illustrated how this relationship can be obtained for a cylindrical shell in Section 4.3.2. Following the same procedure for the conical shell, a strain-displacement relation valid anywhere over the thickness of the shell can be obtained. Using this with the stress-strain relation (Eq. 4.5) and the stress-resultant expression (Eq. 4.6, where R is to be changed to r_2), the general force-displacement relation for a conical shell can be obtained. These general force-displacement relations have been given by Flugge[6.1] and looks as complicated as the one we have derived for the cylindrical shell (Table 4.1). In general, these force-displacement relations show that the change of curvature will influence the membrane normal and shearing forces and the middle surface strains influence the moments. However, in Donnell's theory, these are assumed to be of minor importance and are neglected. Further, while writing down the strain-displacement relation and the expressions for stress resultants, it is assumed in Donnell's theory that z/r_2 is very small and hence, $r_2 + z \approx r_2$. These approximations result in a much simpler force-displacement relations similar to the one we have for cylindrical shell (Eq. 4.7). Hence, the approximate force-displacement relations can be obtained as:

$$N_x = K\left[\frac{\partial u}{\partial x} + \frac{\nu}{x}\left(\frac{1}{\cos\alpha}\frac{\partial v}{\partial \theta} + u + w\tan\alpha\right)\right] \tag{6.27a}$$

$$N_\theta = K\left[\frac{1}{x}\left(\frac{1}{\cos\alpha}\frac{\partial v}{\partial \theta} + u + w\tan\alpha\right) + \nu\frac{\partial u}{\partial x}\right] \tag{6.27b}$$

$$N_{x\theta} = N_{\theta x} = \frac{K(1-\nu)}{2}\left[\frac{\partial v}{\partial x} - \frac{v}{x} + \frac{1}{x\cos\alpha}\frac{\partial u}{\partial \theta}\right] \tag{6.27c}$$

$$M_x = D\left[\frac{\partial^2 w}{\partial x^2} + \nu\left(\frac{1}{x^2\cos^2\alpha}\frac{\partial^2 w}{\partial \theta^2} + \frac{\partial w}{x\partial x}\right)\right] \tag{6.27d}$$

$$M_\theta = D\left[\left(\frac{1}{x^2\cos^2\alpha}\frac{\partial^2 w}{\partial \theta^2} + \frac{1}{x}\frac{\partial w}{\partial x}\right) + \nu\frac{\partial^2 w}{\partial x^2}\right] \tag{6.27e}$$

$$M_{x\theta} = M_{\theta x} = \frac{D(1-\nu)}{x\cos\alpha}\left(\frac{\partial^2 w}{\partial\theta\,\partial x} - \frac{\partial w}{x\partial\theta}\right) \tag{6.27f}$$

Substituting the above force-displacement relations in Eq. (6.26), we get the following equilibrium equations in terms of displacements:

$$\frac{\partial^2 u}{\partial x^2} + \frac{1}{x}\frac{\partial u}{\partial x} - \frac{u}{x^2} + \frac{1-\nu}{2x^2\cos^2\alpha}\frac{\partial^2 u}{\partial \theta^2} + \frac{1+\nu}{2x\cos\alpha}\frac{\partial^2 v}{\partial x\,\partial\theta}$$

$$-\left(\frac{3-\nu}{2x^2\cos\alpha}\right)\frac{\partial v}{\partial \theta} + \frac{\nu\tan\alpha}{x}\frac{\partial w}{\partial x} - \frac{w}{x^2}\tan\alpha = -\frac{X}{K} \tag{6.28a}$$

$$\left(\frac{1+\nu}{2\,x\cos\alpha}\right)\frac{\partial^2 u}{\partial x\,\partial\theta}+\left(\frac{3-\nu}{2}\right)\frac{1}{x^2\cos\alpha}\frac{\partial u}{\partial\theta}$$

$$+\left(\frac{1-\nu}{2}\right)\frac{\partial^2 v}{d\,x^2}+\left(\frac{1-\nu}{2x}\right)\frac{\partial v}{\partial x}$$

$$-\left(\frac{1-\nu}{2}\right)\frac{v}{x^2}+\frac{1}{x^2\cos^2\alpha}\frac{\partial^2 v}{\partial\theta^2}+\frac{\sin\alpha}{x^2\cos^2\alpha}\frac{\partial w}{\partial\theta}=-\frac{Y}{K} \quad (6.28b)$$

$$K\tan\alpha\left[\frac{1}{x^2}\left(\frac{1}{\cos\alpha}\frac{\partial v}{\partial\theta}+u+w\tan\alpha\right)+\frac{\nu}{x}\frac{\partial u}{\partial x}\right]$$

$$+D\left[\frac{\partial^4 w}{\partial x^4}+\frac{2}{x}\frac{\partial^3 w}{\partial x^3}-\frac{1}{x^2}\frac{\partial^2 w}{\partial x^2}+\frac{1}{x^3}\frac{\partial w}{\partial x}\right.$$

$$+\frac{2}{x^2\cos^2\alpha}\frac{\partial^4 w}{\partial\theta^2\,\partial x^2}+\frac{1}{x^4\cos^4\alpha}\frac{\partial^4 w}{\partial\theta^4}$$

$$\left.+\frac{4}{x^4\cos^2\alpha}\frac{\partial^2 w}{\partial\theta^2}-\frac{2}{x^3\cos^2\alpha}\frac{\partial^3 w}{\partial x\,\partial\theta^2}\right]=Z \quad (6.28c)$$

The above three simultaneous partial differential equations in terms of displacements *u, v* and *w* form the basic differential equations for the bending of a conical shell. These equations as well as the force-displacement relations (Eq. 6.27) can be specialised for the case of a cylindrical shell by making $\alpha \to 90^\circ$ and $x\cos\alpha \to R$. It can be seen that these reduced equations would be same as those given by Donnell's theory for cylindrical shell (Eqs. 4.10). Hence, we can refer to above approximate equations as Donnell type theory for conical shell.

6.3.3 Solution

As was done for cylindrical shell of revolution (Section 6.2.2), the displacements can be taken in terms of Fourier series in the circumferential direction as

$$u=\sum_{m=1}^{\infty} u_m(x)\cos m\theta$$

$$v=\sum_{m=1}^{\infty} v_m(x)\sin m\theta \quad (6.29)$$

$$w=\sum_{m=1}^{\infty} w_m(x)\cos m\theta$$

Introducing the above form of displacements in Eq. (6.28), we obtain three ordinary differential equations, with variable coefficients, in u_m, v_m and w_m. The solution of these equations may be obtained by using asymptotic method of solution[6.10] or Frobenius method[6.11, 6.12]. However, neither of these methods have been found useful for obtaining the numerical results[6.13] It appears that any attempt to get an analytical solution to these differential equations involves tedious manipulations many times resulting in only an approximate solution. With the availability of large digital computer nowadays, it is more profitable to attempt a numerical solution of the ordinary differential equations. Budiansky and Radkowski[6.14] have suggested the finite difference method for the solution of these ordinary differential equations and have emphasised the generality of this approach to deal with any arbitrary shell of revolution subjected to asymmetric load. Instead of dealing with two second order and one fourth order ordinary differential equations in u_m, v_m and w_m they suggest the use of four ordinary differential equations with respect to x, each of second order, in u_m, v_m, w_m and M_m, which is more attractive from the numerical analysis point of view. This approach has been used by Chandrashekhara and Karekar[6.15] to study the bending behaviour of truncated conical shell of revolution subjected to asymmetric loads. We will describe this procedure in somewhat detail and later on illustrate its application to a truncated conical shell.

For obtaining four differential equations, we will retain the first two differential equations (Eq. 6.28a, b) as it is and split the third equation (Eq. 6.28c) by introducing a new variable M_x, namely the bending moment. This is achieved by considering the equilibrium equation (Eq. 6.26c) in which M_x is retained and M_θ is replaced by using the following relation:

$$M_\theta = D(1-\nu^2)\left(\frac{1}{x^2\cos^2\alpha}\frac{\partial^2 w}{\partial\theta^2} + \frac{1}{x}\frac{\partial w}{\partial x}\right) + \nu M_x$$

Hence, Eq. (6.28c) can now be written as

$$\begin{aligned} &K\tan\alpha\left[\frac{1}{x^2}\left(\frac{1}{\cos\alpha}\frac{\partial v}{\partial\theta} + u + w\tan\alpha\right) + \frac{\nu}{x}\frac{\partial u}{\partial x}\right] + \frac{\partial^2 M_x}{\partial x^2} \\ &+ \left(\frac{2-\nu}{x}\right)\frac{\partial M_x}{\partial x} + \frac{\nu}{x^2\cos^2\alpha}\frac{\partial^2 M_x}{\partial\theta^2} \\ &+ D\left[\frac{1-\nu^2}{x^4\cos^4\alpha}\frac{\partial^4 w}{\partial\theta^4} + \frac{2(1-\nu)}{x^2\cos^2\alpha}\right. \\ &\left\{\frac{\partial^4 w}{\partial x^2\partial\theta^2} + \frac{(2+\nu)}{x^2}\frac{\partial^2 w}{\partial\theta^2} - \frac{1}{x}\frac{\partial^3 w}{\partial x\partial\theta^2}\right\} \\ &\left. - \frac{1-\nu^2}{x^2}\left(\frac{\partial^2 w}{\partial x^2} - \frac{1}{x}\frac{\partial w}{\partial x}\right)\right] = Z \end{aligned} \tag{6.30a}$$

and the fourth equation

$$M_x - D\left[\frac{\partial^2 w}{\partial x^2} + \nu\left(\frac{1}{x^2\cos^2\alpha}\frac{\partial^2 w}{\partial\theta^2} + \frac{1}{x}\frac{\partial w}{\partial x}\right)\right] = 0 \tag{6.30b}$$

For carrying out the numerical anaylsis, it is more convenient to nondimensionalise the above differential equations (Eq. 6.28 a, b and Eq. 6.30 a, b) by introducing the following nondimensional variables:

$$\bar{x} = x/L\,,\ \bar{u} = \frac{E\,u}{p\,R}\,,\ \bar{v} = \frac{E\,v}{p\,R}\,,\ \bar{w} = \frac{E\,w}{p\,R}\,,\ \overline{M}_x = \frac{M_x}{p\,R^2}$$

where L is the inclined length of complete or truncated conical shell, p is the load per unit area, R is the radius (at the bottom end for complete conical shell or at the top or smaller end for a truncated conical shell). The nondimensional form of Eqs. (6.28 a,b) and Eqs. (6.30 a,b) can now be written as

$$\frac{\partial^2 \bar{u}}{\partial \bar{x}^2} + \frac{1}{\bar{x}}\frac{\partial \bar{u}}{\partial \bar{x}} - \frac{\bar{u}}{\bar{x}^2} + \frac{1-\nu}{2\bar{x}^2\cos^2\alpha}\frac{\partial^2 \bar{u}}{\partial \theta^2} + \left(\frac{1+\nu}{2\bar{x}\cos\alpha}\right)$$

$$\frac{\partial^2 \bar{v}}{\partial \bar{x}\,\partial\theta} - \frac{3-\nu}{2\bar{x}^2\cos\alpha}\frac{\partial \bar{v}}{\partial \theta} + \frac{\nu\tan\alpha}{\bar{x}}\frac{\partial \bar{w}}{\partial \bar{x}} - \frac{\tan\alpha}{\bar{x}^2}\,\bar{w}$$

$$= -\left(\frac{L}{h}\right)\left(\frac{L}{R}\right)\frac{X(1-\nu^2)}{p} \tag{6.31a}$$

$$\frac{1+\nu}{2\bar{x}\cos\alpha}\frac{\partial^2 \bar{u}}{\partial \bar{x}\,\partial\theta} + \frac{3-\nu}{2\bar{x}^2\cos\alpha}\frac{\partial \bar{u}}{\partial \theta} + \frac{1-\nu}{2}\frac{\partial^2 \bar{v}}{\partial \bar{x}^2}$$

$$+ \frac{1-\nu}{2\bar{x}}\frac{\partial \bar{v}}{\partial \bar{x}} - \frac{1-\nu}{2}\frac{\bar{v}}{\bar{x}^2} + \frac{1}{\bar{x}^2\cos^2\alpha}\frac{\partial^2 \bar{v}}{\partial \theta^2} + \frac{\sin\alpha}{\bar{x}^2\cos^2\alpha}\frac{\partial \bar{w}}{\partial \theta}$$

$$= -\left(\frac{L}{h}\right)\left(\frac{L}{R}\right)\frac{Y(1-\nu^2)}{p} \tag{6.31b}$$

$$\left(\frac{h}{L}\right)\left(\frac{\tan\alpha}{1-\nu^2}\right)\left[\frac{1}{\bar{x}^2}\left(\frac{1}{\cos\alpha}\frac{\partial \bar{v}}{\partial \theta} + \bar{u} + \bar{w}\tan\alpha\right) + \frac{\nu}{\bar{x}}\frac{\partial \bar{u}}{\partial \bar{x}}\right]$$

$$+ \left(\frac{R}{L}\right)\frac{\partial^2 \overline{M}_x}{\partial \bar{x}^2} + (2-\nu)\left(\frac{R}{L}\right)\frac{1}{\bar{x}}\frac{\partial \overline{M}_x}{\partial \bar{x}}$$

$$+ \left(\frac{\nu R}{L}\right)\frac{1}{\bar{x}^2\cos^2\alpha}\frac{\partial^2 \overline{M}_x}{\partial \theta^2}$$

$$+ \frac{1}{12}\left(\frac{h}{L}\right)^3\left[\frac{1}{\bar{x}^4\cos^4\alpha}\frac{\partial^4 \bar{w}}{\partial \theta^4} + \frac{2}{(1+\nu)\,\bar{x}^2\cos^2\alpha}\right.$$

$$\left\{\frac{\partial^4 \bar{w}}{\partial\theta^2\,\partial \bar{x}^2} + \frac{(2+\nu)}{\bar{x}^2}\frac{\partial^2 \bar{w}}{\partial \theta^2} - \frac{1}{\bar{x}}\frac{\partial^3 \bar{w}}{\partial \bar{x}\,\partial\theta^2}\right\} - \frac{1}{\bar{x}^2}$$

$$\left.\left(\frac{\partial^2 \bar{w}}{\partial \bar{x}^2} - \frac{1}{\bar{x}}\frac{\partial \bar{w}}{\partial \bar{x}}\right)\right] = \left(\frac{L}{R}\right)\left(\frac{Z}{p}\right) \tag{6.31c}$$

$$\overline{M}_x - \left(\frac{h}{L}\right)^3 \left(\frac{L}{R}\right) \frac{1}{12\,(1-\nu^2)}$$

$$\left[\frac{\partial^2 \overline{w}}{\partial \overline{x}^2} + \nu \left\{\frac{1}{\overline{x}^2 \cos^2 \alpha} \frac{\partial^2 \overline{w}}{\partial \theta^2} + \frac{1}{\overline{x}} \frac{\partial \overline{w}}{\partial \overline{x}}\right\}\right] = 0 \qquad (6.31d)$$

The nondimensionalised displacements and bending moment are expanded in terms of Fourier series in the circumferential direction as

$$\overline{u} = \sum_{m=1}^{\infty} \overline{u}_m \cos m\theta$$

$$\overline{v} = \sum_{m=1}^{\infty} \overline{v}_m \sin m\theta \qquad (6.32)$$

$$\overline{w} = \sum_{m=1}^{\infty} \overline{w}_m \cos m\theta$$

$$\overline{M}_x = \sum_{m=1}^{\infty} \overline{M}_m \cos m\theta$$

Similarly, the external load components acting on the shell can be expanded in terms of Fourier series as

$$X = \sum_{m=1}^{\infty} X_m \cos m\theta$$

$$Y = \sum_{m=1}^{\infty} Y_m \sin m\theta$$

$$Z = \sum_{m=1}^{\infty} Z_m \cos m\theta \qquad (6.33)$$

where, X_m, Y_m and Z_m can be determined once the load components are known or given by using the orthogonality condition.

Introducing Eqs. (6.32) and (6.33) in Eq. (6.31), we get the following ordinary differential equations

$$\frac{d^2 \overline{u}_m}{d\overline{x}^2} + \frac{1}{\overline{x}} \frac{d\overline{u}_m}{d\overline{x}} - \frac{\overline{u}_m}{\overline{x}^2} - \frac{m^2 (1-\nu)}{2\overline{x}^2 \cos^2 \alpha}\, \overline{u}_m$$

$$+ \frac{m\,(1+\nu)}{2\overline{x} \cos \alpha} \frac{d\overline{v}_m}{d\overline{x}} - \frac{m\,(3-\nu)}{2\overline{x}^2 \cos \alpha}\, \overline{v}_m + \frac{\nu \tan \alpha}{\overline{x}} \frac{d\overline{w}_m}{d\overline{x}}$$

$$- \frac{\tan \alpha}{\overline{x}^2}\, \overline{w}_m = -\left(\frac{L}{h}\right)\left(\frac{L}{R}\right) \frac{X_m\,(1-\nu^2)}{p} \qquad (6.34a)$$

$$-\frac{m(1+\nu)}{2\bar{x}\cos\alpha}\frac{d\bar{u}_m}{d\bar{x}}-\frac{m(3-\nu)}{2\bar{x}^2\cos\alpha}\bar{u}_m+\left(\frac{1-\nu}{2}\right)\frac{d^2\bar{v}_m}{d\bar{x}^2}$$

$$+\left(\frac{1-\nu}{2}\right)\frac{d\bar{v}_m}{d\bar{x}}-\left(\frac{1-\nu}{2}\right)\frac{\bar{v}_m}{\bar{x}^2}-\frac{m^2}{\bar{x}^2\cos^2\alpha}\bar{v}_m$$

$$-\frac{m\sin\alpha}{\bar{x}^2\cos^2\alpha}\bar{w}_m=-\left(\frac{L}{h}\right)\left(\frac{L}{R}\right)\frac{Y_m(l-\nu^2)}{p} \tag{6.34b}$$

$$\left(\frac{h}{L}\right)\frac{\tan\alpha}{1-\nu^2}\left[\frac{1}{\bar{x}^2}\left(\frac{m\bar{v}_m}{\cos\alpha}+\bar{u}_m+\bar{w}_m\tan\alpha\right)+\frac{\nu}{\bar{x}}\frac{d\bar{u}_m}{d\bar{x}}\right]$$

$$+\left(\frac{R}{L}\right)\frac{d^2\bar{M}_m}{d\bar{x}^2}+(2-\nu)\left(\frac{R}{L}\right)\frac{1}{\bar{x}}\frac{d\bar{M}_m}{d\bar{x}}-\nu\left(\frac{R}{L}\right)$$

$$\frac{m^2}{\bar{x}^2\cos^2\alpha}\bar{M}_m+\frac{1}{12}\left(\frac{h}{L}\right)^3\left[\frac{m^4\bar{w}_m}{\bar{x}^4\cos^4\alpha}+\frac{2}{(1+\nu)\bar{x}^2\cos^2\alpha}\right.$$

$$\left\{-\frac{m^2 d^2\bar{w}_m}{d\bar{x}^2}-\frac{(2+\nu)m^2}{\bar{x}^2}\bar{w}_m+\frac{m^2}{\bar{x}}\frac{d\bar{w}_m}{d\bar{x}}\right\}$$

$$\left.-\frac{1}{\bar{x}^2}\left(\frac{d^2\bar{w}_m}{d\bar{x}^2}-\frac{1}{\bar{x}}\frac{d\bar{w}_m}{d\bar{x}}\right)\right]=\left(\frac{Z_m}{p}\right)\left(\frac{L}{R}\right) \tag{6.34c}$$

$$\bar{M}_m-\left(\frac{h}{L}\right)^3\left(\frac{R}{L}\right)\frac{1}{12(1-\nu^2)}$$

$$\left[\frac{d^2\bar{w}_m}{d\bar{x}^2}+\nu\left\{\frac{-m^2}{\bar{x}^2\cos^2\alpha}\bar{w}_m+\frac{1}{\bar{x}}\frac{d\bar{w}_m}{d\bar{x}}\right\}\right] \tag{6.34d}$$

The above four second-order ordinary differential equations can be written in the matrix form as

$$[E]\frac{d^2\bar{z}}{d\bar{x}^2}+[F]\frac{d\bar{z}}{d\bar{x}}+[G]\bar{z}=C \tag{6.35}$$

$$\text{where } \bar{z}=\begin{Bmatrix}\bar{u}_m\\ \bar{v}_m\\ \bar{w}_m\\ \bar{M}_m\end{Bmatrix},\quad C=\begin{Bmatrix}-X_m\\ -Y_m\\ \dfrac{Z_m}{1-\nu^2}\left(\dfrac{h}{L}\right)\\ 0\end{Bmatrix}\left(\frac{L}{h}\right)\left(\frac{L}{R}\right)\left(\frac{1-\nu^2}{p}\right)$$

$[E]$, $[F]$ and $[G]$ are 4×4 coefficient matrix whose elements can be obtained from Eq. (6.34). Now, the four ordinary differential equations (Eq. 6.35) are expanded, using the finite difference method[6.16], at all interior points that is $\bar{x}_i$ for $1\le i\le N-1$. At the end points (for a truncated conical shell) $i=0, N$ the relevant equations are obtained from the boundary conditions.

6.3.4 Boundary Conditions

The boundary conditions along the edge $\bar{x}$ = constant can be specified once the type of support that is provided along this edge is known. In general, the support may be such that the boundary conditions can be specified either in terms of displacements alone, or force alone, or a combination of forces and displacements. If the boundary conditions are in terms of displacements, then these could be directly combined with Eq. (6.35) since the difference equations involve displacements as unknowns. On the other hand, if the boundary conditions are in terms of forces, these are to be retranslated in terms of displacements using the foree-displacement relations. We will discuss below, the three types of boundary conditions that are normally used

(i) Fixed edge:

The boundary conditions for a fixed edge can be written as

$$\bar{x} = \text{const}\,,\ \bar{u}_m = \bar{v}_m = \bar{w}_m = \frac{d\bar{w}_m}{d\bar{x}} = 0 \qquad (6.36)$$

The first three conditions mentioned above can be directly used in the finite difference equations, while the last condition is expanded, using the central difference at a nodal point 'O' (Fig. 6.8) on the edge of the shell as

$$\frac{d\bar{w}_m}{d\bar{x}} = \frac{(\bar{w}_m)_1 - (\bar{w}_m)_{-1}}{2\Delta\bar{x}} = 0$$

or $$(\bar{w}_m)_1 = (\bar{w}_m)_{-1}$$

where subscript '1' and '–1' corresponds to the nodal point in the interior of the shell and fictitious point outside the boundary of the shell with an interval of $2\Delta\bar{x}$ respectively.

(ii) Simply supported edge:

The boundary conditions for the simply supported edge can be written as

$$\bar{x} = const.,\ (\bar{N}_x)_m = \bar{v}_m = (\bar{M}_x)_m = \bar{w}_m = 0 \qquad (6.37)$$

The second and the fourth condition mentioned above being in terms of displacements they could be directly used along with Eq. (6.35). The first and the third condition have to be rewritten using the force-displacement relation given in Eq. (6.25) as

$$(\bar{N}_x)_m = 0,\quad \left[\frac{d\bar{u}_m}{d\bar{x}} + \frac{\nu}{\bar{x}}\left(\frac{m\bar{v}_m}{\cos\alpha} + \bar{u}_m + \bar{w}_m\tan\alpha\right)\right] = 0 \qquad (6.37a)$$

$$(\bar{M}_x)_m = 0,\quad \left[\frac{d^2\bar{w}_m}{d\bar{x}^2} + \nu\left(\frac{-m^2\bar{w}_m}{\bar{x}^2\cos^2\alpha} + \frac{d\bar{w}_m}{\bar{x}\,d\bar{x}}\right)\right] = 0$$

where, $\overline{N}_x$ and $\overline{M}_x$ are nondimensional stress resultants and equal to $(N_x)/(pR)$ and $(M_x)/(pR^2)$ respectively. The derivatives in the above equations are expanded at a nodal point on the boundary using the central difference.

(iii) Free edge

The free edge boundary conditions are

$$\bar{x} = const., \ (\overline{N}_x)_m = (\overline{N}_{x\theta})_m = (\overline{M}_x)_m = (\overline{Q}'_x)_m = 0 \tag{6.38}$$

where $\overline{N}_x$, $\overline{N}_{x\theta}$, $\overline{M}_x$ and $\overline{Q}'_x$ are nondimensional stress resultants and are equal to N_x/pR, $N_{x\theta}/pR$, M_x/pR^2 and Q'_x/pR respectively and Q'_x is the resultant shear (Kirchoff's shear) and is given by

$$Q'_x = \left(Q_x + \frac{\partial M_{x\theta}}{\bar{x}\cos\alpha\,\partial\theta}\right)$$

The above boundary conditions can now be written in terms of displacements using the force-displacement (Eq. 6.35) relation as

$$\left.\begin{aligned}
&(\overline{N}_x)_m = 0, \left[\frac{d\bar{u}_m}{d\bar{x}} + \frac{\nu}{\bar{x}}\left(\bar{u}_m + \frac{m\bar{v}_m}{\cos\alpha} + \bar{w}_m\tan\alpha\right)\right] = 0 \\
&(\overline{N}_{x\theta})_m = 0, \left[\frac{d\bar{v}_m}{d\bar{x}} - \frac{\bar{v}_m}{\bar{x}} - \frac{m\bar{u}_m}{\bar{x}\cos\alpha}\right] = 0 \\
&(\overline{M}_x)_m = 0, \left[\frac{d^2\bar{w}_m}{d\bar{x}^2} + \nu\left(-\frac{m^2\bar{w}_m}{\bar{x}^2\cos^2\alpha} + \frac{d\bar{w}_m}{d\bar{x}}\right)\right] = 0 \\
&(\overline{Q}'_x)_m = 0, -\frac{1}{12}\left(\frac{h}{L}\right)^3\frac{1}{\bar{x}^2}\left\{1 + \frac{2m^2}{(1+\nu)\cos^2\alpha}\right\}\frac{d\bar{w}_m}{d\bar{x}} \\
&\quad + \frac{m^2}{12\bar{x}^3\cos^2\alpha}\left(\frac{h}{L}\right)^3\left\{\frac{2}{1+\nu} + 1\right\}\bar{w}_m + \left(\frac{R}{L}\right)\frac{d\overline{M}_m}{d\bar{x}} \\
&\quad + \left(\frac{1-\nu}{\bar{x}}\right)\left(\frac{R}{L}\right)\overline{M}_m = 0
\end{aligned}\right\} \tag{6.38a}$$

Again, all the derivatives appearing in the above equations are expanded at a nodal point on the boundary using the central difference.

6.3.5 Numerical Analysis

The first step in the finite difference method is to divide the generator into N finite subintervals. (Fig. 6.8). The governing differential equations are then approximated by using central difference[6.16] for the first and second derivatives of the variable $\bar{z}$ with respect to $\bar{x}$ at any point 'i' as

$$\left(\frac{d\bar{z}}{d\bar{x}}\right)_i = \frac{\bar{z}_{i+1} - \bar{z}_{i-1}}{2\Delta\bar{x}} \tag{a}$$

$$\left(\frac{d^2 \bar{z}}{d\bar{x}^2}\right) = \frac{\bar{z}_{i+1} - 2\bar{z}_i + \bar{z}_{i-1}}{(\Delta \bar{x})^2} \tag{b}$$

For convenience, the mesh spacing is normally kept constant. By using the above approximation for the derivatives in Eq. 6.35, difference equations at any *i*–th point along the generator of the shell can be obtained. These difference equations are written at all interior points of the shell that is at all $\bar{x}_i$ for $1 \leq i \leq N-1$. At the end points, namely $i = 0, N$ (for a truncated conical shell) the relevant equations are obtained from the boundary conditions specified at each edge and hence, four additional equations are obtained at the each end points $i = 0, N$. Hence, for a truncated conical shell, we will have altogether 4 $(N + 1)$ simultaneous equations solving which we can determine $\bar{u}_m$, $\bar{v}_m$, $\bar{w}_m$ and $\bar{M}_m$ at all nodal points $i = 0, 1, 2, \ldots N$. For determining the stress resultants, first, the nondimensional displacements in terms of Fourier series (Eq. 6.32) are introduced in Eq. 6.27. These equations are later expanded in difference form at all nodal points. Substituting the already determined values of displacements $\bar{u}_m$, $\bar{v}_m$ and $\bar{w}_m$ in these expressions, the stress resultants can be determined.

Example 6.3

To illustrate the application of the above method of solution, let us consider a truncated cantilever conical shell having the following nondimensional parameters and subjected to wind loading (Fig. 6.8).

$$\frac{L}{R} = 1.0, \quad \frac{R}{h} = 100, \quad \alpha = 60°, \quad \nu = 0$$

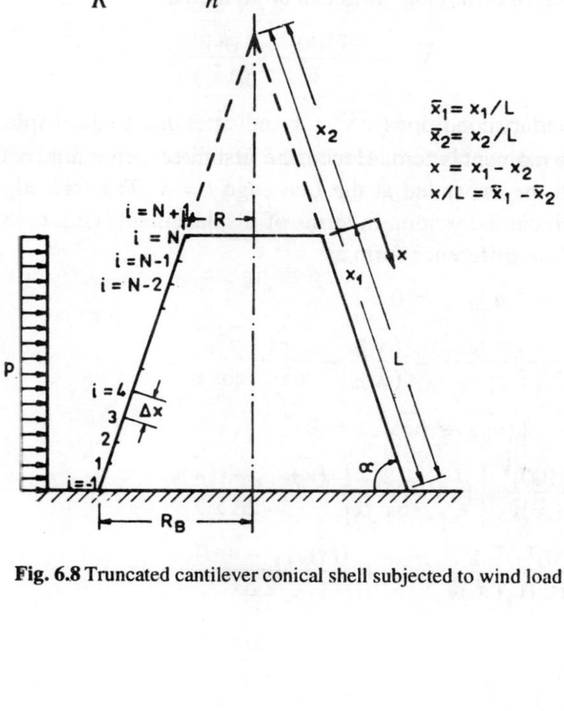

Fig. 6.8 Truncated cantilever conical shell subjected to wind load

The load components for the wind loading would be

$$X = Y = 0, \quad Z = -\,p\cos\theta\ \sin\alpha$$

For the above load components

$$X_m = Y_m = 0, \quad Z_m = \begin{cases} -p\sin\alpha & \text{for } m = 1 \\ 0 & \text{for } m > 1 \end{cases}$$

In this particular example, we need to consider only the first harmonic ($m = 1$) and henceforth, we will drop the suffix m in all the expressions. It is assumed that the bottom or larger end of truncated conical shell is fixed and smaller or top end is free. The following boundary conditions can then be written down in this case.

$$\bar{x} = \bar{x}_1, \quad \bar{u} = \bar{v} = \bar{w} = \frac{d\bar{w}}{d\bar{x}} = 0$$

$$\bar{x} = \bar{x}_2\,, \ \bar{N}_x = \bar{N}_{x\theta} = \bar{M}_x = \bar{Q}'_x = 0$$

At the fixed edge $i = 0$ ($\bar{x} = \bar{x}_1$), the only unknown is moment $\bar{M}$ which implies that only the fourth equation viz. Eq. 6.34d need to be expanded in the difference form. While expanding this equation, we make use of the following relationship

$$(\bar{w})_0 = 0, \quad (\bar{w})_1 = (\bar{w})_{-1}$$

$$\left(\text{resulting from the condition, } \frac{d\bar{w}}{d\bar{x}} = 0\right)$$

Hence, Eq. (6.34d) in difference form can be written as

$$\bar{M} = \frac{(100)^3}{6}\ \frac{(\bar{w})_1}{(\Delta\bar{x})^2} \tag{a}$$

The free boundary conditions at $\bar{x} = \bar{x}_2$ indicates that all the displacements are permitted and the moment is zero. Hence, the first three differential equations (Eq. 6.34 a–c) need to be expanded at the free edge $i = N$. The free edge boundary conditions, which can be written in terms of displacements (Eq. 6.38a), are now expanded at $i = N$ in difference form as

$$(\bar{u})_{N+1} - (\bar{u})_{N-1} = 0 \tag{b}$$

$$\frac{(\bar{v})_{N+1} - (\bar{v})_{N-1}}{2\Delta\bar{x}} - \frac{(\bar{v})_N}{(\bar{x})_N} - \frac{m\,(\bar{u})_N}{(\bar{x})_N\cos\alpha} = 0 \tag{c}$$

$$(\bar{w})_{N-1} - 2\,(\bar{w})_N + (\bar{w})_{N+1} = 0 \tag{d}$$

$$-\frac{1}{12}\,\frac{(100)^3}{(\bar{x})_N^2}\left\{1 + \frac{2}{\cos^2\alpha}\right\}\frac{(\bar{w})_{N+1} - (\bar{w})_{N-1}}{2\Delta\bar{x}}$$

$$+\ \frac{(100)^3}{4\cos^2\alpha}\,\frac{1}{(\bar{x})_N^3}\,(\bar{w})_N + \frac{(\bar{M})_{N+1} - (\bar{M})_{N-1}}{2\,\Delta\bar{x}} = 0 \tag{e}$$

Eq. (6.35) when expanded in difference form at any arbitrary point say $i = 3$

$$[E]\left\{\frac{\bar{z}_2 - 2\bar{z}_3 + \bar{z}_4}{(\Delta\bar{x})^2}\right\} + [F].\left\{\frac{\bar{z}_2 - \bar{z}_4}{2\Delta\bar{x}}\right\} + [G]\,\bar{z}_3 = c_3$$

where for example $\bar{z}_2$ is

$$\bar{z}_2 = \begin{Bmatrix}(\bar{u})_2\\(\bar{v})_2\\(\bar{w})_2\\(\bar{M})_2\end{Bmatrix}, \quad c_3 = \begin{Bmatrix}0\\0\\-1\\0\end{Bmatrix}\sin\alpha$$

and $[E]$, $[F]$ and $[G]$ are (4×4) matrices whose coefficients, as mentioned earlier, can be obtained from Eq. (6.34).

We can now expand Eq. (6.35) at all interior points, using the above difference form, to get $4\,(N-1)$ algebraic equations.

Next, we expand Eq. (6.35 a–c) at the free edge ($i = N$) to get an additional three algebraic equations. Further, we get from the fixed boundary condition (Eq. a) one equation and from the free boundary conditions (Eq. b–e) four more equations. Adding up all these, totally, we get $4\,(N+1)$ simultaneous equations solving which the displacements $\bar{u}$, $\bar{v}$, $\bar{w}$ and $\bar{M}$ at all nodal points are determined.

The accuracy of the finite difference solution depends on the number of subintervals into which the generator of the shell is divided. For a very coarse mesh (i.e. small number of nodal points), the total number of equations to be solved will be less, but, in such a case, the approximation of the derivatives made in terms of difference form normally results in a large error and hence, the final results would not be acceptable. However, a finer mesh (i.e. large number of nodal points) could reduce the errors for the derivatives considerably, but it increases the number of simultaneous equations to be solved enormously. Hence, it becomes necessary to work out the optimum mesh size which results in less number of simultaneous equations, but at the same time, the error in the approximation of the derivatives also is kept at a low level. This can be done by carrying out a convergence study of the results with decrease in mesh size (increasing the number of nodal points). A typical result of such a study is presented in Table 6.6.

Table 6.6 Convergence study for the displacement $\bar{u}$

		No. of nodal points		
$\bar{x}$	Displacement	5	10	20
$\bar{x}_2$	$\bar{u}$	12.4408	11.9240	11.8022

The results presented in the above table indicate that in this case, the displacement $\bar{u}$ is monotonically decreasing as the mesh becomes finer and finer. It may be seen from this that the difference in the value of displacement between 10 and 20 nodal points is small. However, if more accurate value of displacement is required, then it is necessary to consider still finer mesh size. From the engineering design point of view, the above convergence study shows that sufficiently accurate results can be obtained by just taking 10 nodal points. Hence, some of the results presented, for this example, have been obtained by taking 10 nodal points along the generator of the shell.

Some typical results of the membrane forces, bending moment and radial displacement are presented in Figs. 6.9 a–c. In Figs. 6.9a and c the results of membrane analysis (Section 2.5.2.1) have also been included for comparison. It may be seen from these figures that the membrane theory results are in good agreement with the bending theory results except for over a region of 20% of the length of the shell from the fixed edge. This point has also been mentioned earlier in the membrane analysis of truncated conical shell subjected to wind load. From Fig. 6.9b, it may be observed that the bending moment decreases rapidly as one moves away from the fixed edge and becomes negligible at a distance of about 20% of the length of the shell from the fixed edge. If an approximate method could be developed to predict this localised longitudinal bending moment, then, for purpose of design, this can be used along with the membrane theory. Such a procedure completely eliminates the cumbersome bending analysis. Keeping this point in view, an approximate analysis may be carried out by making use of an equivalent cylindrical shell concept[6.15]. The dimensions of equivalent cylindrical shell can be worked out based on the dimensions of the truncated conical shell. It is suggested that the equivalent radius of cylindrical shell may be taken as

$$R_e = \frac{R + R_B}{2 \sin \alpha}$$

and the inclined length of the conical shell can be taken as the length of the cylindrical shell. The thickness of equivalent cylindrical shell will be same as that of the conical shell. It has been shown that if an equivalent cylindrical shell analysis of a conical shell is done for the same loading and boundary conditions, the longitudinal bending moment obtained for an equivalent cylindrical shell is very close to that of the relative conical shell for $\alpha \geq 75^\circ$. However, for $\alpha < 75^\circ$, the deviation is considerable and hence, an equivalent cylindrical shell analysis is not recommended for conical shell, whose base angle is less than 75°.

Alternatively, for this example, one can carry out the membrane analysis first and find out the radial displacement and slope at the fixed edge. This radial displacement and slope is nullified by applying equal and opposite radial displacement and slope at this edge so as to satisfy the fixed boundary conditions. This latter problem may be termed as secondary problem in which the shell will be subjected to end displacement only. The rigorous bending analysis can be carried out in a small region of fixed edge (about 20% of the length in the present case)

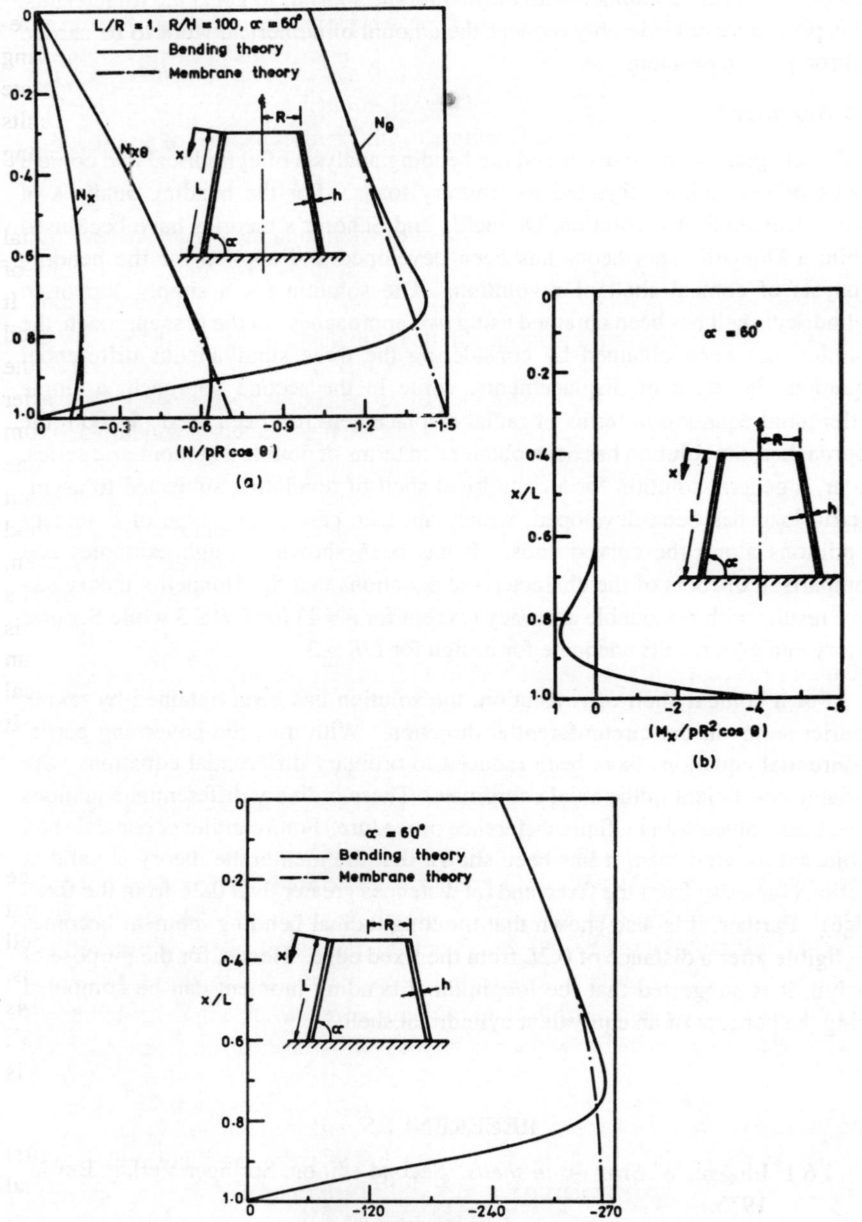

Fig. 6.9 Distribution of membrane forces, bending moment and radial displacement along the length of the truncated conical shell

and the results are combined with the membrane analysis to get at the final results. This procedure considerably reduces the amount of numerical work to be carried out for a given problem.

6.4 Summary

In this chapter, we have discussed the bending analysis of cylindrical and conical shells of revolution subjected to arbitrary loads. For the bending analysis of cylindrical shell of revolution, Donnell's and Schorer's theories have been used while a Donnell type theory has been developed and applied for the bending analysis of conical shell of revolution. The solution for a simply supported cylindrical shell has been obtained using two approaches. In the first approach, the solution has been obtained by considering the three simultaneous differential equations in terms of displacements, while in the second approach, a single differential equation in terms of radial displacement has been used. In both the approaches, the solution has been obtained in terms of double trigonometric series. Later, a general solution for a cylindrical shell of revolution subjected to asymmetric load has been developed, which can take care of any type of boundary conditions along the curved ends. It has been shown through examples and comparison of roots of the characteristic equations that the Donnell's theory can give results with reasonable accuracy (except for $n = 1$) for $L/R \leq 3$ while Schorer theory can give results adequate for design for $L/R > 3$.

For a conical shell of revolution, the solution has been obtained by taking Fourier series in the circumferential direction. With this, the governing partial differential equations have been reduced to ordinary differential equations with variable coefficient in the axial coordinate. These ordinary differential equations have been solved using a finite difference procedure. For a cantilever conical shell subjected to wind load, it has been shown that the membrane theory is valid at sections far away from the fixed end (at distances greater than $0.2L$ from the fixed edge). Further, it is also shown that the longitudinal bending moment becomes negligible after a distance of $0.2L$ from the fixed edge. Hence, for the purpose of design, it is suggested that the longitudinal bending moment can be computed using the concept of an equivalent cylindrical shell.

REFERENCES

6.1 Flugge, W. *Stresses in shells*. Second edition, Springer Verlag, Berlin, 1973.

6.2 Donnell, L.H. *Stability of thin walled tubes under torsion*, NACA Rep. No. 479. Washington D.C. 1933.

6.3 Schorer, H. Line load action on thin cylindrical shells. *Trans. ASCE*, Vol. 61, 1935, pp. 281–316.

6.4 Hoff, N.J. Boundary value problems of the thin walled circular cylinder. *Jl. of Applied Mech., Trans.* ASME, 1954, pp. 343–350.

6.5 Hoff, N.J. The accuracy of Donnell's equations. *Jl. of Applied Mechanics, Trans.* ASME, Vol. 22, 1955, pp. 329-334.

6.6 Chandrashekhara, K. and Srinivas, M.K. Bending analysis of cylindrical shells through transfer matrix approach. *Bulletin International Association of Shell and Spatial Structures,* Vol. 31, No. 104, 1990, pp. 123–130.

6.7 Gopalacharyulu, S. and Johns, D.J. Cantilever cylindrical shell under assumed wind pressure. *Jl. of Engineering Mechanics Div.,* ASCE. Vol. 99, 1973, pp. 943–956.

6.8 Chandrashekhara, K. Analysis of long cantilever cylindrical shell subjected to wind loading. *Jl. of Engineering Mechanics,* ASCE, Vol.115, No. 9, 1989, pp. 2101–2105.

6.9 Seide, P. A Donnell type theory for asymmetrical bending and buckling of thin conical shells. *Jl. of Applied Mechanics, Trans.* ASME, Vol. 24, 1957, pp. 547–552.

6.10 Love, A.E.H. *Treatise on mathematical theory of elasticity,* Dover Publication, New York, Fourth edition, 1944.

6.11 Hoff, N.J. Thin circular conical shells under arbitrary loads. *Jl. of Applied Mechanics, Trans.* ASME, Vol. 22, No. 4, 1955, pp. 557–562.

6.12 Wilson, B. Asymmetrical bending of conical shells. *Jl. of Engineering Mechanics Div.,* ASCE, Vol. 86, No. EM3, 1960, pp. 119–139.

6.13 Pohle, F.V. Discussion on 'Thin circular conical shells under arbitrary loads'. *Jl. of Appl. Mech., Trans.* ASME, Vol. 23, No. 2, 1956, p. 322.

6.14 Budiansky, B. and Radkowski, P.P. 'Numerical analysis of unsymmetrical bending of shells of revolution'. *AIAA Jl.*, Vol. 1, No. 8, 1963, pp. 1833–1842.

6.15 Chandrashekhara, K. and Meghal S. Karekar. 'Bending analysis of a truncated conical shell subjected to asymmetric load'. *Thin-walled structures,* Vol. 13, No. 4, 1992, pp. 299-318.

6.16 Salvadori, M.G. and Baron, M.L. *Numerical methods in engineering.* Prentice Hall (India), 1966.

Chapter Seven

Bending Analysis of Shallow Doubly Curved Shell

7.1 INTRODUCTION

A shell may be called shallow when its rise is small compared with its plan dimensions. Vlassov[7.1] has suggested that a shell may be called as shallow when the ratio of the rise to the shorter side is less than 0.2. In shells of this kind, the middle surface does not deviate considerably from a plane. Hence, it is possible to make certain approximations on the geometrical properties of the surface which finally leads to a simplified bending theory. Apart from the usual assumptions made in the theory of thin elastic shells, the following additional assumptions are made in the shallow shell theory:

(a) The slopes $\partial z / \partial x$ and $\partial z / \partial y$ are fairly small and hence their products or squares and higher powers can be neglected. It follows from this that the distance between any two points on the surface can be approximated by its projected length (a result which could be obtained from the first quadratic form of the surface).

(b) The Gauss curvature of undeformed middle surface being very small, can be taken as zero.

(c) The derivatives of r, s and t may be neglected, which means the principal curvatures of the shell remain constant.

Based on the above assumptions, we will now derive the basic equations for the bending analysis of doubly curved shell.

7.2 EQUILIBRIUM EQUATIONS

Figure 7.1 shows an element of a doubly curved shell with all the forces and moments acting on it. Following an identical procedure presented for cylindrical shells in Ch. 4, we can derive the equilibrium equations for a doubly curved shell. However, it is important to note that the contribution of the shear forces Q_x and Q_y

in the first and second equilibrium equations is neglected on the assumption that these quantities are small compared to the variation of N_x, N_y and N_{xy}. Further, while deriving the equilibrium equations, we will assume $N_{xy} = N_{yx}$ and $M_{xy} = -M_{yx}$ and because of this assumption, the sixth equilibrium equation would not exist. Hence, we would have only five equilibrium equations, namely three force equilibrium equations and two moment equilibrium equations.

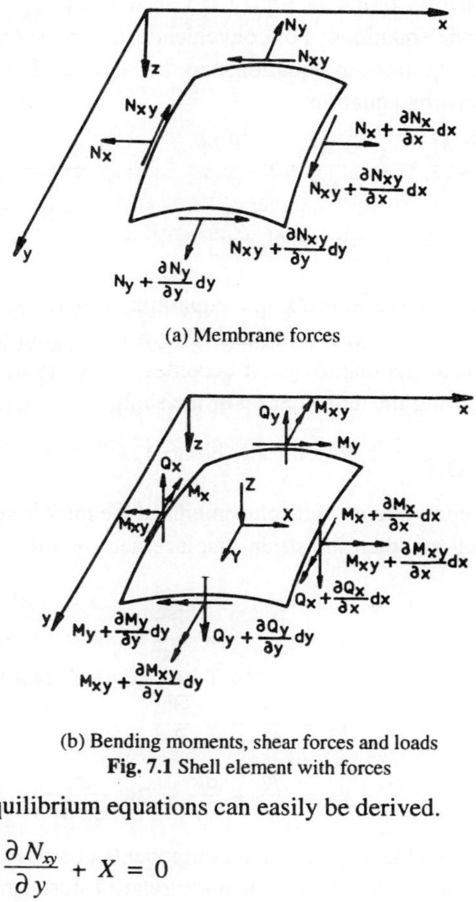

(a) Membrane forces

(b) Bending moments, shear forces and loads

Fig. 7.1 Shell element with forces

The following equilibrium equations can easily be derived.

$$\frac{\partial N_x}{\partial x} + \frac{\partial N_{xy}}{\partial y} + X = 0 \tag{7.1a}$$

$$\frac{\partial N_y}{\partial y} + \frac{\partial N_{xy}}{\partial x} + Y = 0 \tag{7.1b}$$

$$\frac{\partial Q_x}{\partial x} + \frac{\partial Q_y}{\partial y} + N_x \frac{\partial^2 z}{\partial x^2} + 2 N_{xy} \frac{\partial^2 z}{\partial x \partial y}$$

$$+ N_y \frac{\partial^2 z}{\partial y^2} + Z = 0 \tag{7.1c}$$

$$\frac{\partial M_x}{\partial x} - \frac{\partial M_{xy}}{\partial y} - Q_x = 0 \tag{7.1d}$$

$$\frac{\partial M_x}{\partial y} - \frac{\partial M_{xy}}{\partial x} - Q_y = 0 \tag{7.1e}$$

If the shell degenerates into a plate, then the last three terms in Eq. (7.1c) as well as Eqs. (7.1a & b) vanish. On the other hand, if the bending of shell is not there, then the first two terms in Eq. (7.1c) as well as Eqs. (7.1d, e) vanish, resulting in membrane equations. For convenience, the transverse shear forces Q_x and Q_y in the third equilibrium equation may be replaced using Eqs. (7.1d, e), resulting in the following equation:

$$\frac{\partial^2 M_x}{\partial x^2} - 2\frac{\partial^2 M_{xy}}{\partial x \partial y} + \frac{\partial^2 M_y}{\partial y^2} + N_x \frac{\partial^2 z}{\partial x^2}$$

$$+ 2N_{xy}\frac{\partial^2 z}{\partial x \partial y} + N_y \frac{\partial^2 z}{\partial y^2} + Z = 0 \tag{7.1f}$$

Hence, we now have three equilibrium equations (7.1 a, b, f), involving six unknowns, namely N_x, N_y, N_{xy}, M_x, M_y and M_{xy}. Since we do not have as many number of equations as the unknowns, it becomes necessary to derive additional equations by considering the deformation of the shell.

7.3 DEFORMATION

If u, v and w are the components of displacements at the middle surface of the shell in x-, y- and z-directions, then the strain-displacement relation can be written as (Eq. 2.7)

$$\varepsilon_x = \frac{\partial u}{\partial x} - w\frac{\partial^2 z}{\partial x^2} \tag{7.2a}$$

$$\varepsilon_y = \frac{\partial v}{\partial y} - w\frac{\partial^2 z}{\partial y^2} \tag{7.2b}$$

$$\gamma_{xy} = \frac{\partial v}{\partial x} + \frac{\partial u}{\partial y} - 2w\frac{\partial^2 z}{\partial x \partial y} \tag{7.2c}$$

Let u_A, v_A and w_A be the displacement components at a point A at a distance $\bar{z}$ from the middle surface. A simple kinematic relationship can be obtained between displacements at this point and the mid-plane displacement. For this, consider a section of a shell with the plane y = constant (Fig. 7.2).

It must be noted that the normal $\bar{z}$ deviates from the vertical plane by a small angle, but for our purpose here, we will assume that the actual distance A_0A and $\bar{z}$ are the same. It can be seen easily from the figure that

$$u_A = u - \bar{z}\frac{\partial w}{\partial x}$$

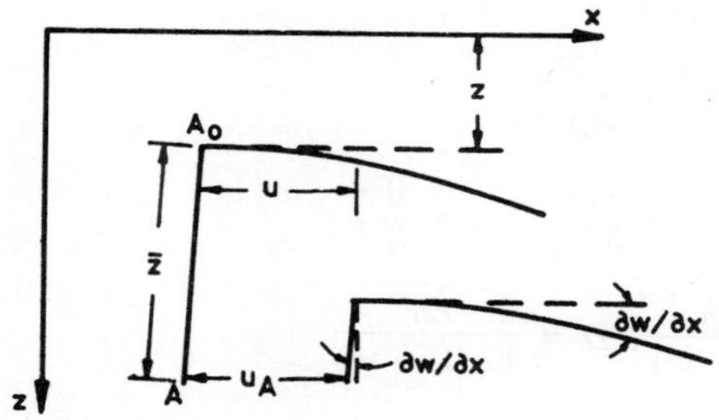

Fig. 7.2 Displacement of a shell element

Similarly, by taking a section in *yz*-plane, we can show

$$v_A = v - \bar{z}\,\frac{\partial w}{\partial y}$$

Since the shell is thin, $w_A = w$.

Rewriting the strain-displacement relations (Eq. 7.2) in terms of the displacement components at *A* and substituting the above relation for displacement at *A* in terms of mid-plane displacements, we get the following strain-displacement relations:

$$\varepsilon_x = \frac{\partial u}{\partial x} - \bar{z}\,\frac{\partial^2 w}{\partial x^2} - w\,\frac{\partial^2 z}{\partial x^2} \tag{7.3a}$$

$$\varepsilon_y = \frac{\partial v}{\partial y} - \bar{z}\,\frac{\partial^2 w}{\partial y^2} - w\,\frac{\partial^2 z}{\partial y^2} \tag{7.3b}$$

$$\gamma_{xy} = \frac{\partial u}{\partial y} + \frac{\partial v}{\partial x} - 2\bar{z}\,\frac{\partial^2 w}{\partial x\,\partial y} - 2w\,\frac{\partial^2 z}{\partial x\,\partial y} \tag{7.3c}$$

By making use of the stress-strain relationship and the expressions for the stress resultants (where *z* must be replaced by $\bar{z}$) and neglecting terms containing $(\bar{z}/R)$ compared to unity, we get the following force-displacement relations:

$$N_x = K\left[\frac{\partial u}{\partial x} + \nu\,\frac{\partial v}{\partial y} - (r + \nu t)\,w\right] \tag{7.4a}$$

$$N_y = K\left[\frac{\partial v}{\partial y} + \nu\,\frac{\partial u}{\partial x} - (t + \nu r)\,w\right] \tag{7.4b}$$

$$N_{xy} = \frac{K(1-\nu)}{2}\left[\frac{\partial v}{\partial x} + \frac{\partial u}{\partial y} - 2\,sw\right] \tag{7.4c}$$

$$M_x = -\,D\left(\frac{\partial^2 w}{\partial x^2} + \nu\,\frac{\partial^2 w}{\partial y^2}\right) \tag{7.4d}$$

$$M_y = - D\left(\frac{\partial^2 w}{\partial y^2} + \nu\frac{\partial^2 w}{\partial x^2}\right) \tag{7.4e}$$

$$M_{xy} = D(1 - \nu)\frac{\partial^2 w}{\partial x \partial y} \tag{7.4f}$$

$$\text{where } r = \frac{\partial^2 z}{\partial x^2}, \ s = \frac{\partial^2 z}{\partial x \partial y}, \ t = \frac{\partial^2 z}{\partial y^2}$$

$$K = \frac{Eh}{(1 - \nu^2)}, \ D = \frac{Eh^3}{12(1 - \nu^2)}$$

We have now three equilibrium Eqs. (7.1 a, c and f) and six force-displacement relations involving totally nine unknowns (six forces and three displacements). Hence, we have now as many number of equations as the unknowns are and a solution to a doubly curved shell problem can be obtained by solving these equations.

7.4 DIFFERENTIAL EQUATIONS

If the shell is supported in such a way that the boundary conditions are in terms of displacements, then it is preferable to have the governing differential equations in terms of displacements. By substituting the force-displacement relations (Eq. 7.4) in the equilibrium equations (Eq. 7.1 a, b, f), we get the following three simultaneous differential equations in terms of displacements:

$$\frac{\partial^2 u}{\partial x^2} + \left(\frac{1-\nu}{2}\right)\frac{\partial^2 u}{\partial y^2} + \left(\frac{1+\nu}{2}\right)\frac{\partial^2 v}{\partial x \partial y} - \frac{\partial}{\partial x}\{(r + \nu t)w\}$$
$$- \frac{\partial}{\partial y}\{(1-\nu)sw\} + \frac{X(1-\nu^2)}{Eh} = 0 \tag{7.5a}$$

$$\frac{\partial^2 v}{\partial y^2} + \left(\frac{1-\nu}{2}\right)\frac{\partial^2 v}{\partial x^2} + \left(\frac{1+\nu}{2}\right)\frac{\partial^2 u}{\partial x \partial y} - \frac{\partial}{\partial y}\{(t + \nu r)w\}$$
$$- \frac{\partial}{\partial x}\{(1-\nu)sw\} + \frac{Y(1-\nu^2)}{Eh} = 0 \tag{7.5b}$$

$$(r + t\nu)\frac{\partial u}{\partial x} + (r\nu + t)\frac{\partial v}{\partial y} - \{r^2 + 2\nu rt + t^2 + 2s^2(1-\nu)\}w$$
$$+ s(1-\nu)\left(\frac{\partial u}{\partial y} + \frac{\partial v}{\partial x}\right) - \frac{h^2}{12}\nabla^4 w + \frac{Z(1-\nu^2)}{Eh} = 0 \tag{7.5c}$$

For r and t constant and $s = 0$, the above equations reduce to

$$\frac{\partial^2 u}{\partial x^2} + \left(\frac{1-\nu}{2}\right)\frac{\partial^2 u}{\partial y^2} + \left(\frac{1+\nu}{2}\right)\frac{\partial^2 v}{\partial x \partial y} - (r + \nu t)\frac{\partial w}{\partial x}$$
$$+ \frac{X(1-\nu^2)}{Eh} = 0 \tag{7.6a}$$

$$\frac{\partial^2 v}{\partial y^2} + \left(\frac{1-\nu}{2}\right)\frac{\partial^2 v}{\partial x^2} + \left(\frac{1+\nu}{2}\right)\frac{\partial^2 u}{\partial x\,\partial y} - (t+\nu r)\frac{\partial w}{\partial y}$$

$$+ \frac{Y(1-\nu^2)}{Eh} = 0 \tag{7.6b}$$

$$(r+\nu t)\frac{\partial u}{\partial x} + (r\nu + t)\frac{\partial v}{\partial y} - (r^2 + 2\nu rt + t^2)\,w - \frac{h^2}{12}\nabla^4 w$$

$$+ \frac{Z(1-\nu^2)}{Eh} = 0 \tag{7.6c}$$

If ν is taken as zero, then the above equations can be further simplified as

$$\frac{\partial^2 u}{\partial x^2} + \frac{1}{2}\frac{\partial^2 u}{\partial y^2} + \frac{1}{2}\frac{\partial^2 v}{\partial x\,\partial y} - r\frac{\partial w}{\partial x} + \frac{X}{Eh} = 0 \tag{7.7a}$$

$$\frac{\partial^2 v}{\partial y^2} + \frac{1}{2}\frac{\partial^2 v}{\partial x^2} + \frac{1}{2}\frac{\partial^2 u}{\partial x\,\partial y} - t\frac{\partial w}{\partial y} + \frac{Y}{Eh} = 0 \tag{7.7b}$$

$$r\frac{\partial u}{\partial x} + t\frac{\partial v}{\partial y} - (r^2 + t^2)\,w - \frac{h^2}{12}\nabla^4 w + \frac{Z}{Eh} = 0 \tag{7.7c}$$

If, on the other hand, the boundary conditions are in terms of displacements and forces, as for example, in a simply supported condition, then it is preferable to have differential equations in terms of force and displacement. For this, we introduce now a stress function ϕ such that

$$N_x = \frac{\partial^2 \phi}{\partial y^2} - \int X\,dx \tag{7.8a}$$

$$N_y = \frac{\partial^2 \phi}{\partial x^2} - \int Y\,dy \tag{7.8b}$$

$$N_{xy} = -\frac{\partial^2 \phi}{\partial x\,\partial y} \tag{7.8c}$$

From the strain-displacement relations given earlier (Eq. 7.3), the following relation can be derived

$$\frac{\partial^2 \varepsilon_x}{\partial y^2} + \frac{\partial^2 \varepsilon_y}{\partial x^2} - \frac{\partial^2 \gamma_{xy}}{\partial x\,\partial y} = -\left(r\frac{\partial^2 w}{\partial y^2} - 2s\frac{\partial^2 w}{\partial x\,\partial y} + t\frac{\partial^2 w}{\partial x^2}\right) \tag{7.9}$$

Making use of the stress-strain relation in the above equation along with Eq. (7.8), the above equation can be written as

$$\nabla^4 \phi + Eh\,\nabla_k^2 w = \frac{\partial^2}{\partial y^2}\int X\,dx$$

$$+ \frac{\partial^2}{\partial x^2}\int Y\,dy - \nu\frac{\partial X}{\partial x} - \nu\frac{\partial Y}{\partial y} \tag{7.10}$$

A second equation can be obtained, starting from Eq. (7.1f) and using Eqs. (7.4 d, f) and Eq. (7.8), as

$$D\nabla^4 w - \nabla_k^2 \phi = Z - \frac{\partial^2 z}{\partial x^2}\int X\,dx - \frac{\partial^2 z}{\partial y^2}\int Y\,dy \tag{7.11}$$

where $\nabla^4 = \nabla^2\nabla^2$ and $\nabla^2 = \left(\frac{\partial^2}{\partial x^2} + \frac{\partial^2}{\partial y^2}\right)$

$$\nabla_k^2 = \left(r\frac{\partial^2}{\partial y^2} - 2s\frac{\partial^2}{\partial x\,\partial y} + t\frac{\partial^2}{\partial x^2}\right)$$

If the shell is subjected to vertical load only, then $X = Y = 0$ and Eqs. (7.10) and (7.11) reduce to

$$\nabla^4\phi + Eh\,\nabla_k^2 w = 0 \tag{7.12a}$$

$$\nabla^4 w - \frac{1}{D}\nabla_k^2\phi = \frac{Z}{D} \tag{7.12b}$$

It must be recognised that the first differential equation (Fq. 7.12a) is a statement of compatibility of deformation, while the second equation (Eq. 7.12b) is that of equilibrium. It is interesting to note that if the membrane action is negligible, the above equations degenerate to the well known plate bending equation ($\nabla^4 w = Z/D$). On the other hand, if the bending is negligible and we have a pure membrane state, then the equation reduces to governing differential equation of the membrane theory (Eq. 3.30).

Sometimes, it is advantageous to have a single differential equation in terms of w and this can be obtained by eliminating ϕ from Eqs. (7.12a, b). Hence, we get the following eighth order equation in terms of w as

$$D\,\nabla^8 w + Eh\,\nabla_k^4 w = \nabla^4 Z \tag{7.13}$$

Once the solution for the above differential equation is obtained, the forces and displacements can be determined by using the following expressions (in which the Poisson's ratio is taken as zero).

$$\nabla^4 w = \frac{1}{D}\nabla_k^2\phi$$

$$N_x = \frac{\partial^2\phi}{\partial y^2},\ N_y = \frac{\partial^2\phi}{\partial x^2},\ N_{xy} = -\frac{\partial^2\phi}{\partial x\,\partial y}$$

$$M_x = -D\frac{\partial^2 w}{\partial x^2},\ M_y = -D\frac{\partial^2 w}{\partial y^2},\ M_{xy} = D\frac{\partial^2 w}{\partial x\,\partial y} \tag{7.14}$$

$$Q_x = -D\frac{\partial}{\partial x}(\nabla^2 w),\ Q_y = -D\frac{\partial}{\partial y}(\nabla^2 w)$$

$$u = \int\left[\frac{1}{Eh}\frac{\partial^2\phi}{\partial y^2} + wr\right]dx,\ v = \int\left[\frac{1}{Eh}\frac{\partial^2\phi}{\partial x^2} + wt\right]dy$$

7.5 BOUNDARY CONDITIONS

The solution of Eqs. (7.7), (7.12) or (7.13) would have finally eight arbitrary constants, which have to be determined from the boundary conditions. As we have seen in the cylindrical shells, at each edge, we can specify four conditions — two of which correspond to the membrane part and the other two to the bending part. In general, several combinations of these conditions are possible. However, we will examine here only the boundary conditions corresponding to some of the common types of supports provided along the edge of the shell.

(a) Simply Supported Edge

Considering an edge normal to the x-direction and assuming that this edge will be simply supported, we can write the following boundary conditions:

$$N_x = \varepsilon_y = w = M_x = 0$$

The first two conditions come from the membrane effect while the last two from the bending effect. The first condition means that the support provided is such that it is incapable of resisting any force normal to its plane. The second condition states that the strain along the edge shall be zero. Alternatively, making use of the stress-strain relationship (membrane) and the condition $N_x = 0$, it can be shown that $N_y = 0$ if $\varepsilon_y = 0$. Sometimes, instead of specifying the condition $\varepsilon_y = 0$ it is possible to state that $v = 0$, as along the edge $\partial v/\partial y = 0$. The last two conditions $w = M_x = 0$ are the well known conditions used for a simply supported plate subjected to bending. It is necessary here only to ensure that the support provided along the edge is infinitely rigid such that $w = 0$.

(b) Clamped Edge

A clamped edge, in the strictest sense, means, no displacement can take place along the edge. Hence, the boundary condition corresponding to this edge can be written as (x = constant)

$$u = v = w = \frac{\partial w}{\partial x} = 0$$

Again, in the above conditions, the first two correspond to the membrane part and last two to the bending part.

(c) Free Edge

Along a free edge, no force can exist and hence, the boundary conditions can be written as

$$N_x = N_{xy} = M_x = Q'_x = 0$$

where Q'_x is the resultant shear.

7.6 SOLUTION

A brief survey on the available solutions for a doubly curved shell reveals that attempts have been made by various investigators to obtain solutions for doubly curved shells with various support conditions adopting different methods of solution. A Navier type solution, using double trigonometric series, can be obtained for an all-round simply supported elliptic or hyperbolic paraboloid.

To deal with somewhat more general support conditions, a Levy type solution[7.2,7.3] has been developed for elliptic and hyperbolic paraboloids, in which one pair of edges are simply supported and the other pair can have any type of boundary conditions. A series solution[7.4] has also been given for an elliptic paraboloid supported on edge-beams along all the four edges. Solution[7.5] for an hyperbolic paraboloid clamped along the four edges has been given using orthogonal functions, which can be extended to other types of doubly curved shells having clamped boundary conditions or a combination of simply supported and clamped boundary conditions. Matrix progression method[7.6,7.7] based on variational calculus has been used to solve several doubly curved shell problems having different support conditions. Most of these solutions, which are of classical type, sometimes cannot be used in the analysis of doubly curved shells as the type of support used in practice, are such that these solutions cannot satisfy the support conditions. Such problems can be effectively handled by the numerical methods like finite difference method. Several problems of practical interest have been solved by using the numerical methods[7.8-7.14] and the results are presented in many cases in a form useful for design. A detailed explanation and discussion of many of the methods of solutions mentioned may be found in the book by Beles and Soare[7.15]. In the following paragraphs, we will present some of the classical solutions which are useful in the analysis and design of doubly curved shells.

7.6.1 All-round Simply Supported Doubly Curved Shell

A Navier type of solution in terms of double trigonometric series can be obtained for an all-round simply supported elliptic or hyperbolic paraboloid. The surface of the shell can be defined by

$$z = \frac{y^2}{2r_y} \pm \frac{x^2}{2r_x}$$

The plan of the shell would be a rectangle and the boundaries will be principal parabolas. The radius of curvature r_x can be varied in such a way that the rise of the parabola in x-direction passes through a series of both positive and negative values. By this, we can obtain a whole range of elliptic paraboloid shells with increasing rise, cylindrical shell with zero rise and hyperbolic paraboloidal shell with increasing sag respectively. Figures 7.3a, b show an elliptic and hyperbolic paraboloid on rectangular plan having dimensions $2a \times 2b$.

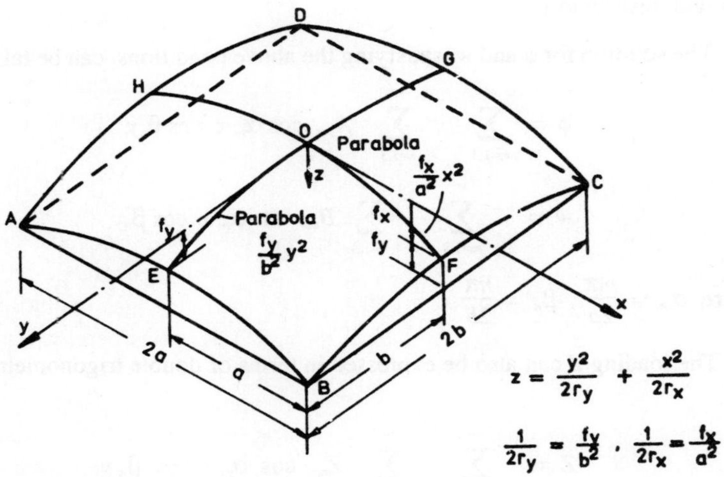

(a) Elliptic Paraboloid

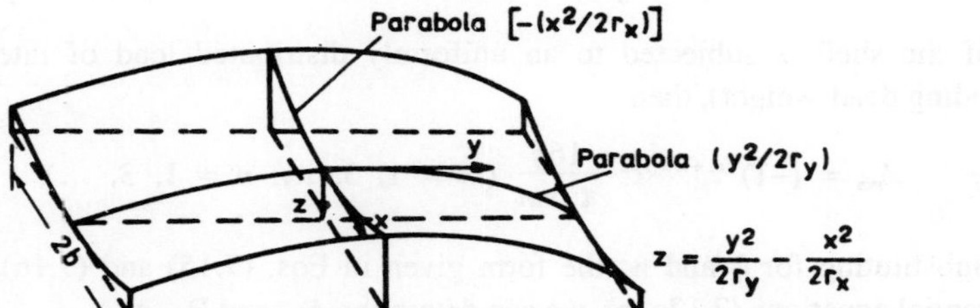

(b) Hyperbolic paraboloid

Fig. 7.3 Elliptical and hyperbolic paraboloids

The boundary conditions for an all-round simply supported doubly curved shell (Fig. 7.3) can be written as

$$x = \pm\, a,\; N_x = \varepsilon_y = w = M_x = 0$$

$$y = \pm\, b,\; N_y = \varepsilon_x = w = M_y = 0$$

The above conditions can also be written in terms of ϕ and w as

$$x = \pm\, a,\; \phi = \phi'' = w = w'' = 0$$

$$y = \pm b, \; \phi = \phi^{\circ\circ} = w = w^{\circ\circ} = 0$$

where (...)′ denotes differentiation with respect to x and (...)$^{\circ}$ denotes differentiation with respect to y.

The solution for ϕ and w, satisfying the above conditions, can be taken as

$$\phi = \sum_{m=1,3}^{\infty} \sum_{n=1,3}^{\infty} A_{mn} \cos \alpha_m x \cos \beta_n y$$

$$w = \sum_{m=1,3}^{\infty} \sum_{n=1,3}^{\infty} B_{mn} \cos \alpha_m x \cos \beta_n y \tag{7.15}$$

where $\alpha_m = \dfrac{m\pi}{2a}, \; \beta_n = \dfrac{n\pi}{2b}$

The loading Z can also be expressed in terms of double trigonometric series as

$$Z = \sum_{m=1,3}^{\infty} \sum_{n=1,3}^{\infty} Z_{mn} \cos \alpha_m x \cos \beta_n y \tag{7.16}$$

where Z_{mn} is determined by making use of orthogonality condition as

$$Z_{mn} = \frac{4}{ab} \int_0^a \int_0^b Z \cos \alpha_m x \cos \beta_n y \, dx \, dy$$

and if the shell is subjected to an uniformly distributed load of intensity q (including dead-weight), then

$$Z_{mn} = (-1)^{(m+n-1)/2} \frac{16q}{\pi^2 mn} \quad (m = 1, 3, \ldots, n = 1, 3, \ldots)$$

Substituting for ϕ and w, the form given in Eqs. (7.15) and (7.16), in the differential equations (7.12a, b), we can determine A_{mn} and B_{mn} as

$$A_{mn} = \frac{Z_{mn}\left(\pm \dfrac{\alpha_m^2}{r_y} + \dfrac{\beta_n^2}{r_x}\right)}{\left[\dfrac{h^2}{12(1-\nu^2)}(\alpha_m^2 + \beta_n^2)^4 + \left(\pm \dfrac{\alpha_m^2}{r_y} + \dfrac{\beta_n^2}{r_x}\right)\right]} \tag{7.17a}$$

$$B_{mn} = \frac{Z_{mn}(\alpha_m^2 + \beta_n^2)^2}{Eh\left[\dfrac{h^2}{12(1-\nu^2)}(\alpha_m^2 + \beta_n^2)^4 + \left(\pm \dfrac{\alpha_m^2}{r_y} + \dfrac{\beta_n^2}{r_x}\right)\right]} \tag{7.17b}$$

In the above expressions, positive sign for α_m^2/r_y is to be used for elliptic paraboloid and a negative sign for hyperbolic paraboloid.

If $r_x = r_y = \infty$, then the shell degenerates into a plate and A_{mn} and B_{mn} reduce to

$$A_{mn} = 0$$

$$B_{mn} = \frac{Z_{mn}}{D\,(\alpha_m^2 + \beta_n^2)^2}$$

It is interesting to note that the expression for B_{mn} is identical to the one obtained in plate theory for an all-round simply supported rectangular plate using a Navier type solution.

It may be noted that the convergence of the series in this solution is very slow. Hence, one has to consider large number of terms to get reasonably accurate results. Doganoff[7.16] while solving the problem of paraboloid of revolution, appeared to have considered 256 harmonics for forces and 2304 harmonics for moments. This computational effort, however, may not cause much problem if the computations are done on a digital computer while the calculations could be done only by considering first few terms if hand computation is resorted to. In such a case, one may end up with erroneous results. Hence, to overcome this difficulty, Flugge and Conrad[7.17] have suggested a procedure to accelerate the convergence by separating the plate and curvature effects. This can be done by rewriting B_{mn} as

$$B_{mn} = \frac{Z_{mn}}{D}\left[\frac{1}{(\alpha_m^2+\beta_n^2)^2} - \frac{\frac{12\,(1-\nu^2)}{h^2}\left(\pm\frac{\alpha_m^2}{r_y}+\frac{\beta_n^2}{r_x}\right)^2}{(\alpha_m^2+\beta_n^2)^2\left\{(\alpha_m^2+\beta_n^2)^4+\frac{12\,(1-\nu^2)}{h^2}\left(\pm\frac{\alpha_m^2}{r_y}+\frac{\beta_n^2}{r_x}\right)\right\}}\right] \tag{7.18}$$

In the above expression, the first part represents the plate effect, which converges slowly and the second part corresponds to the curvature effect, which converges rapidly. It is possible to replace the plate effect by a rapidly converging series or use a converged numerical value for the moments available from plate analysis. The expressions for forces and moments can now be written as

$$N_x = -\sum_{m=1,3}^{\infty}\sum_{n=1,3}^{\infty} \beta_n^2\, A_{mn} \cos\alpha_m x \cos\beta_n y \tag{7.19a}$$

$$N_y = -\sum_{m=1,3}^{\infty}\sum_{n=1,3}^{\infty} \alpha_m^2\, A_{mn} \cos\alpha_m x \cos\beta_n y \tag{7.19b}$$

$$N_{xy} = -\sum_{m=1,3}^{\infty}\sum_{n=1,3}^{\infty} \alpha_m \beta_n A_{mn} \sin\alpha_m x \sin\beta_n y \tag{7.19c}$$

$$M_x = D\sum_{m=1,3}^{\infty}\sum_{n=1,3}^{\infty} (\alpha_m^2 + \nu\beta_n^2)\, B_{mn} \cos\alpha_m x \cos\beta_n y \tag{7.19d}$$

$$M_y = D \sum_{m=1,3}^{\infty} \sum_{n=1,3}^{\infty} (\nu \alpha_m^2 + \beta_n^2) B_{mn} \cos \alpha_m x \cos \beta_n y \tag{7.19e}$$

$$M_{xy} = D(1 - \nu) \sum_{m=1,3}^{\infty} \sum_{n=1,3}^{\infty} \alpha_m \beta_n B_{mn} \sin \alpha_m x \sin \beta_n y \tag{7.19f}$$

$$Q_x = -D \sum_{m=1,3}^{\infty} \sum_{n=1,3}^{\infty} \alpha_m (\alpha_m^2 + \beta_n^2) B_{mn} \sin \alpha_m x \cos \beta_n y \tag{7.19g}$$

$$Q_y = -D \sum_{m=1,3}^{\infty} \sum_{n=1,3}^{\infty} \beta_n (\alpha_m^2 + \beta_n^2) B_{mn} \cos \alpha_m x \sin \beta_n y \tag{7.19h}$$

where A_{mn} and B_{mn} are given in Eqs. (7.17a) and (7.18).

7.6.2 Solution Through Single Trigonometric Series (Levy Type of Solution)

A Levy type of solution will be developed here following Bouma[7.2] and this will be applied to a shell whose surface is defined by the equation

$$z = \frac{x^2}{2r_x} + \frac{y^2}{2r_y} \tag{a}$$

in which $r_x = \pm R_1$ and $r_y = R_2$. By taking r_x and r_y in this form, the solution for both elliptic paraboloid and hyperbolic paraboloid can be obtained. Let us now consider the eighth order differential equation in terms of w (Eq. 7.13):

$$D\nabla^8 w + Eh \nabla_k^4 w = \nabla^4 Z \tag{b}$$

A solution for the homogeneous part of the above differential equation may be taken in the following form:

$$w = \sum_{n=1,3}^{\infty} e^{My} \cos \alpha_n x \tag{c}$$

where $\alpha_n = \dfrac{n\pi}{2a}$

It must be noted that the above form for w satisfies the simply supported boundary condition, viz. $N_x = \varepsilon_y = w = M_x = 0$ along $x = \pm a$

Substituting this solution in the differential equation, we obtain the following algebraic equation:

$$(M^2 - \alpha_n^2)^4 + \frac{12}{h^2}\left(\frac{\alpha_n^2}{r_y} - \frac{M^2}{r_x}\right)^2 = 0 \tag{d}$$

The above equation will have eight complex roots which can be written in the form

$$M_{1,2,3,4} = \pm (m_1 \pm i n_1)$$
$$M_{5,6,7,8} = \pm (m_2 \pm i n_2)$$

For values $R_1 > R_2$, the real and imaginary part can be determined as

$$m_1 = \sqrt{\left[\sqrt{(\alpha_n^2 + \gamma_1)^2 + (-(\sqrt{3}/hr_x) + \gamma_2)^2} + (\alpha_n^2 + \gamma_1)\right]/2}$$

$$n_1 = \sqrt{\left[\sqrt{(\alpha_n^2 + \gamma_1)^2 + (-(\sqrt{3}/hr_x) + \gamma_2)^2} - (\alpha_n^2 + \gamma_1)\right]/2}$$

$$m_2 = \sqrt{\left[\sqrt{(\alpha_n^2 - \gamma_1)^2 + (-(\sqrt{3}/hr_x) - \gamma_2)^2} + (\alpha_n^2 - \gamma_1)\right]/2}$$

$$n_2 = \sqrt{\left[\sqrt{(\alpha_n^2 - \gamma_1)^2 + (-(\sqrt{3}/hr_x) - \gamma_2)^2} - (\alpha_n^2 - \gamma_1)\right]/2}$$

where $$\gamma_1 = \sqrt{\left[\sqrt{(9/h^4 r_x^4) + (12\alpha_n^4/h^2 r_x^2 r_y^2)(-r_x + r_y)^2} - (3/h^2 r_x^2)\right]/2}$$

$$\gamma_2 = \sqrt{\left[\sqrt{(9/h^4 r_x^4) + (12\alpha_n^4/h^2 r_x^2 r_y^2)(-r_x + r_y)^2} + (3/h^2 r_x^2)\right]/2}$$

The solution of the homogeneous equation can now be written as

$$\begin{aligned} w = \sum_{n=1,3}^{\infty} & [(a_n \cos n_1 y + b_n \sin n_1 y)e^{-m_1 y} + (c_n \cos n_1 y + d_n \sin n_1 y)e^{m_1 y} \\ & + (e_n \cos n_2 y + f_n \sin n_2 y)e^{-m_2 y} \\ & + (g_n \cos n_2 y + h_n \sin n_2 y)e^{m_2 y}] \cos \alpha_n x \end{aligned} \quad (7.20a)$$

or alternatively, in the following form

$$\begin{aligned} w = \sum_{n=1,3}^{\infty} & [a_n \cosh m_1 y \cos n_1 y + b_n \sinh m_1 y \cos n_1 y \\ & + c_n \cosh m_1 y \sin n_1 y + d_n \sinh m_1 y \sin n_1 y \\ & + e_n \cosh m_2 y \cos n_2 y + f_n \sinh m_2 y \cos n_2 y \\ & + g_n \cosh m_2 y \sin n_2 y + h_r \sinh m_2 y \sin n_2 y] \cos \alpha_n x \end{aligned} \quad (7.20b)$$

To determine the membrane forces, an expression for ϕ must be first obtained. This can be obtained by using the Eq (7.12b) as

$$\begin{aligned} \phi = \frac{2D\sqrt{3}}{h} & [e^{-m_1 y}(b_n \sin n_1 y - a_n \cos n_1 y) + e^{m_1 y}(-d_n \cos n_1 y \\ & + c_n \sin n_1 y) + e^{-m_2 y}(-f_n \cos n_2 y + e_n \sin n_2 y) \\ & + e^{m_2 y}(h_n \cos n_2 y - g_n \sin n_2 y)] \cos \alpha_n x \end{aligned} \quad (7.21)$$

Alternatively, the expressions for ϕ can be obtained in terms of products of hyperbolic and trigonometric functions using Eqs. (7.20b) and (7.12b).

The expressions for the forces and displacements can now be obtained using the relations given in Eq. (7.14) and are given in Tables 7.1 and 7.2.

On the other hand, if the loading and the boundary conditions are symmetrical then it is preferable to use the solution given in Eq. (7.20b). Because of symmetry, the constants e_n, f_n, g_n and h_n are zero and the solution can be written in the following form:

Complementary function (even)

$$\begin{aligned} F = MF\ [&\{(a_nB_1 + b_nB_2) \cosh m_1y \cos n_1y \\ &- (a_nB_2 - b_nB_1) \sinh m_1y \sin n_1y\} \\ &+ \{(c_nB_3 + d_nB_4) \cosh m_2y \cos n_2y \\ &- (c_nB_4 - d_nB_3) \sinh m_2y \sin n_2y\}] \end{aligned} \tag{7.22}$$

Complementary function (odd)

$$\begin{aligned} F = MF\ [&\{(a_nB_1 + b_nB_2) \sinh m_1y \cos n_1y \\ &- (a_nB_2 - b_nB_1) \cosh n_1y \sin n_1y\} \\ &+ \{(c_nB_3 + d_nB_4) \sinh m_2y \cos n_2y \\ &- (c_nB_4 - d_nB_3) \cosh m_2y \sin n_2y\}] \end{aligned} \tag{7.23}$$

where B_1, B_2, B_3 and B_4 will have the same values for the various forces and displacements as given in Tables 7.1 and 7.2.

The particular integral for Eq. (7.13) can now be determined. The load component in the z-direction can be expressed in terms of trigonometric series as

$$Z = \sum_{n=1.3}^{\infty} K_n \cos \alpha_n x$$

and K_n is determined from the orthogonality condition as

$$K_n = \frac{2}{a} \int_0^a Z \cos \alpha_n x \, dx$$

Table 7.1 Shell coefficients of the complementary function (even)

$$\begin{aligned} F = MF\ [\{ (a_nB_1 + b_nB_2) \cos n_1y - (a_nB_2 - b_nB_1) \sin n_1y\} \exp (m_1y) \\ + \{(c_nB_3 + d_nB_4) \cos n_2y - (c_nB_4 - d_nB_3) \sin n_2y\} \exp (m_2y) \\ + \{(e_nB_1 - f_nB_2) \cos n_1y + (e_nB_2 + f_nB_1) \sin n_1y\} \exp (-m_1y) \\ + \{(g_nB_3 - h_nB_4) \cos n_2y + (g_nB_4 + h_nB_3) \sin n_2y\} \exp (-m_2y)] \end{aligned}$$

Force or displacement	MF	B_1	B_2	B_3	B_4
N_x	$\frac{2D\sqrt{3}}{h} \cos \alpha_n x$	$2m_1n_1$	$-(m_1^2 - n_1^2)$	$-2m_2n_2$	$(m_2^2 - n_2^2)$
N_y	$\frac{2D\alpha_n^2\sqrt{3}}{h} \cos \alpha_n x$	0	1	0	−1
M_x	$D\alpha_n^2 \cos \alpha_n x$	1	0	1	0
M_y	$D \cos \alpha_n x$	$-(m_1^2 - n_1^2)$	$-2m_1n_1$	$-(m_2^2 - n_2^2)$	$-2m_2n_2$
$\overline{Q}_x$	$D\alpha_n \sin \alpha_n x$	$2(m_1^2 - n_1^2) - \alpha_n^2$	$4m_1n_1$	$2(m_2^2 - n_2^2) - \alpha_n^2$	$4m_2n_2$
u	$\frac{h\sqrt{3}}{6\alpha_n} \sin \alpha_n x$	$2\left(m_1n_1 + \frac{\sqrt{3}}{hr_x}\right)$	$-(m_1^2 - n_1^2)$	$-2\left(m_2n_2 - \frac{\sqrt{3}}{hr_x}\right)$	$(m_2^2 - n_2^2)$
w	$\cos \alpha_n x$	1	0	1	0

Table 7.2 Shell coefficients of complementary functiion (odd)

$$F = MF[\ \{ (a_n B_1 + b_n B_2) \cos n_1 y - (a_n B_2 - b_n B_1) \sin n_1 y \} \exp(m_1 y)$$
$$+ \{ (c_n B_3 + d_n B_4) \cos n_2 y - (c_n B_4 - d_n B_3) \sin n_2 y \} \exp(m_2 y)$$
$$- \{ (e_n B_1 - f_n B_2) \cos n_1 y + (e_n B_2 + f_n B_1) \sin n_1 y \} \exp(-m_1 y)$$
$$- \{ (g_n B_3 - h_n B_4) \cos n_2 y + (g_n B_4 + h_n B_3) \sin n_2 y \} \exp(-m_2 y)\ ]$$

Force or displacement	MF	B_1	B_2	B_3	B_4
N_{xy}	$\frac{2D\alpha_n\sqrt{3}}{h}\sin\alpha_n x$	n_1	$-m_1$	$-n_2$	m_2
$\overline{Q}_y$	$D\cos\alpha_n x$	$-P_1$	Q_1	$-P_2$	Q_2
v	$\frac{h\sqrt{3}}{6\alpha_n^2}\cos\alpha_n x$	$\left(-Q_1 + \frac{2m_1\sqrt{3}}{hr_x}\right)$	$\left(-P_1 + \frac{2n_1\sqrt{3}}{hr_x}\right)$	$\left(Q_2 + \frac{2m_2\sqrt{3}}{hr_x}\right)$	$\left(P_2 + \frac{2n_2\sqrt{3}}{hr_x}\right)$
θ	$\cos\alpha_n x$	m_1	n_1	m_2	n_2

where

$P_1 = m_1^3 - 3m_1n_1^2 - 2\alpha_n^2 m_1$, $P_2 = m_2^3 - 3m_2n_2^2 - 2\alpha_n^2 m_2$,

$Q_1 = n_1^3 - 3m_1^2 n_1 + 2\alpha_n^2 n_1$, $Q_2 = n_2^3 - 3m_2^2 n_2 + 2\alpha_n^2 n_2$,

If the shell is subjected to an uniformly distributed load of intensity q per unit area (including dead-weight), then K_n can be determined as

$$K_n = (-1)^{(n-1)/2}\left(\frac{4}{n\pi}\right) q$$

The particular integral, satisfying Eq. (7.13), can be determined as

$$w_p = \frac{1}{D}\sum_{n=1,3}^{\infty} \frac{1}{\left(\alpha_n^4 + \dfrac{12}{h^2 r_y^2}\right)} K_n \cos \alpha_n x$$

The particular integral part for ϕ can also be determined as

$$\phi_p = \frac{12}{h^2 r_y} \sum_{n=1,3}^{\infty} \frac{1}{\alpha_n^2 \left(\alpha_n^4 + \dfrac{12}{h^2 r_y^2}\right)} K_n \cos \alpha_n x \tag{7.24}$$

The particular integral part for the forces can be determined as

$$N_x = 0,\ N_y = -\sum_{n=1,3}^{\infty} C_1\, \alpha_n^2 K_n \cos \alpha_n x$$

$$N_{xy} = 0,\ M_x = D \sum_{n=1,3}^{\infty} \alpha_n^2 C K_n \cos \alpha_n x$$

$$M_y = 0,\ \overline{Q}_x = -D \sum_{n=1,3}^{\infty} \alpha_n^3 C K_n \sin \alpha_n x$$

$$\overline{Q}_y = 0$$

where $$C = \frac{1}{D}\frac{1}{\left(\alpha_n^4 + \dfrac{12}{h^2 r_y^2}\right)}$$

$$C_1 = \frac{12}{h^2 r_y \alpha_n^2}\frac{1}{\left(\alpha_n^4 + \dfrac{12}{r_y^2 h^2}\right)}$$

Example 7.1

Let us determine the forces in an elliptic paraboloid which is simply supported along one pair of edges ($x = \pm a$) and free along the other pair ($y = \pm b$). The dimensions and loading acting on the shell are as given below:

$2a = 18$ m, $2b = 9$ m, $r_x = R_1 = 105.5$ m, $r_y = R_2 = 9$ m

$h = 0.75$ m, load = 250 kg/m^2 (including dead-load)

We will determine first the forces considering the first term in the series and later compare the results obtained by considering one, two and three terms in the series.

(a) Roots of the equation: $(n = 1)$

$$\gamma_1 = \sqrt{\left[\sqrt{(9/h^4 r_x^4) + (12\,\alpha_n^4/h^2 r_x^2 r_y^2)\,(-r_x + r_y)^2} - (3/h^2 r_x^2)\right]/2} = 0.227$$

$$\gamma_2 = \sqrt{\left[\sqrt{(9/h^4 r_x^4) + (12\,\alpha_n^4/h^2 r_x^2 r_y^2)\,(-r_x + r_y)^2} + (3/h^2 r_x^2)\right]/2} = 0.315$$

$$m_1 = \sqrt{\left[\sqrt{(\alpha_n^2 + \gamma_1)^2 + (-\sqrt{3}/hr_x + \gamma_2)^2} + (\alpha_n^2 + \gamma_1)\right]/2} = 0.516$$

$$n_1 = \sqrt{\left[\sqrt{(\alpha_n^2 + \gamma_1)^2 + (-\sqrt{3}/hr_x + \gamma_2)^2} - (\alpha_n^2 + \gamma_1)\right]/2} = 0.093$$

$$m_2 = \sqrt{\left[\sqrt{(\alpha_n^2 - \gamma_1)^2 + (-\sqrt{3}/hr_x - \gamma_2)^2} + (\alpha_n^2 - \gamma_1)\right]/2} = 0.432$$

$$n_2 = \sqrt{\left[\sqrt{(\alpha_n^2 - \gamma_1)^2 + (-\sqrt{3}/hr_x - \gamma_2)^2} - (\alpha_n^2 - \gamma_1)\right]/2} = 0.619$$

(b) Boundary conditions:

$$y = \pm\, b \;(\pm\, 4.5\, m),\; N_y = N_{xy} = M_y = \overline{Q}_y = 0$$

(c) Formulation of simultaneous equations and solution:

Since the boundary conditions and loading are symmetrical with respect to x and y axes, it is convenient to select the solution in the form given in Eqs. (7.22) and (7.23). Hence, referring to Table 7.1 and taking the particular integral from Eq. (7.25), the expression for N_y can be written as

$$N_y = \frac{2D\,\alpha_n^2\,\sqrt{3}}{h}\cos\alpha_n x\;[b\cosh m_1 b\cos n_1 b - a\sinh m_1 b\sin n_1 b$$
$$- d\cosh m_2 b\cos n_2 b + c\sinh m_2 b\sin n_2 b]$$
$$- \alpha_n^2\, C_1 K_n\cos\alpha_n x = 0$$

which will result in the following equation:

$$-\,2.89458\,a + 6.604461b + 1.683268\,c + 4.691892\,d = \frac{2864.688}{D} \qquad \text{(a)}$$

Referring to Table 7.2 and taking the particular integral from Eq. (7.25), the expression for N_{xy} can be written as

$$\frac{2D\,\alpha_n\sqrt{3}}{h}\sin\alpha_n x\ [(an_1 - bm_1)\sinh m_1 b\cos n_1 b - (-am_1 - bn_1)$$
$$\times\cosh m_1 b\sin n_1 b + (-cn_2 + dm_2)\sinh m_2 b\cos n_2 b$$
$$-(cm_2 + dn_2)\times\cosh m_2 b\sin n_2 b] = 0$$

which results in the following equation

$$12.186075a - 17.564845b + 11.622946c - 17.354413d = 0 \qquad \text{(b)}$$

Referring to Table 7.1 and using the particular integral given in Eq. (7.25), the expression for M_y can be written as

$$D\cos\alpha_n x\ [\{-a\ (m_1^2 - n_1^2) - 2m_1 n_1 b\}\cosh m_1 b\cos n_1 b$$
$$-\{-a\ (2m_1 n_1) + b\ (m_1^2 - n_1^2)\}\sinh m_1 b\sin n_1 b$$
$$+\{-c\ (m_2^2 - n_2^2) - (2m_2 n_2)\, d\}\cosh m_2 b\cos n_2 b$$
$$-\{c\ (-2m_2 n_2) + d\ (m_2^2 - n_2^2)\}\sinh m_2 b\sin n_2 b] = 0$$

which results in the following equation:

$$-1.009533\,a - 0.981432b - 0.015784\,c + 2.016072\,d = 0 \qquad \text{(c)}$$

Similarly, referring to Table 7.2 and using the particular integral given in Eq. (7.25), the expression for $\overline{Q}_y$ can be written as

$$D\cos\alpha_n x\ [(-aP_1 + bQ_1)\sinh m_1 b\cos n_1 b - (aQ_1 + bP_1)$$
$$\times\cosh m_1 b\sin n_1 b + (-cP_2 + dQ_2)\sinh m_2 b\cos n_2 b$$
$$-(cQ_2 + dP_2)\cosh m_2 b\sin n_2 b] = 0$$

which results in the following equation

$$-0.282235\,a - 0.506692\,b - 1.323969\,c + 0.778904\,d = 0 \qquad \text{(d)}$$

Solving the above four simultaneous equations (Eqs. a-d), we get

$$a = \frac{2803.5093}{D},\quad b = \frac{458.4468}{D}$$

$$c = \frac{184.95361}{D},\quad d = \frac{1628.458}{D}$$

The forces and moments throughout the transverse section of the shell may now be computed using the above values for the constants in the expressions for forces and moments given in Tables 7.1 and 7.2 and adding the particular integral given in Eq. (7.25). The forces and moments are given in Table 7.3.

Table 7.3 Shell forces and moments (n = 1)

$\frac{y}{b}$	$\frac{N_x}{\cos \alpha_n x}$ kg/m	$\frac{N_y}{\cos \alpha_n x}$ kg/m	$\frac{N_{xy}}{\sin \alpha_n x}$ kg/m	$\frac{M_x}{\cos \alpha_n x}$ kg.m/m	$\frac{M_y}{\cos \alpha_n x}$ kg.m/m	$\frac{\overline{Q}_x}{\sin \alpha_n x}$ kg/m	$\frac{\overline{Q}_y}{\cos \alpha_n x}$ kg/m
0	– 12300	– 4510	0	91.4	– 1600	542	0
0.2	– 16600	– 4350	– 2170	111	– 1510	509	280
0.4	– 24400	– 3770	– 5410	167	– 1240	403	584
0.6	– 20900	– 2610	– 9260	254	– 763	222	836
0.8	18400	– 1010	– 10100	359	– 207	9.6	707
1.0	1,24,000	0	0	471	0	–82.1	0

The results can be obtained in a similar way by considering the second (n = 3), third (n = 5) and fourth (n = 7) harmonics. Comparing the results of the first two, three and four terms with that of one term results, it is possible to draw some conclusions regarding the convergence of the series. The results of one, two, three and four terms are given below in respect of the forces N_x, N_y and N_{xy} and the moment M_y.

Table 7.4 (N_x) kg/m, at x = 0

$\frac{y}{b}$	n = 1	n = 1,3	n = 1,3,5	n = 1,3,5,7
0	– 12 300	– 13 200	– 13 000	– 13 100
0.2	– 16 600	– 16 900	– 16 800	– 16 900
0.4	– 24 400	– 23 400	– 23 500	– 23 500
0.6	– 20 900	– 18 500	– 19 000	– 18 900
0.8	18 400	19 100	18 800	18 900
1.0	1 24 000	1 14 000	1 17 000	1 16 000

Table 7.5 (N_y) kg/m, at x = 0

$\frac{y}{b}$	n = 1	n = 1,3	n = 1;3;5	n = 1,3,5,7
0	– 4510	– 3520	– 4060	– 3650
0.2	– 4350	– 3270	– 3850	– 3470
0.4	– 3770	– 2550	– 3220	– 2790
0.6	– 2610	– 1480	– 2150	– 1720
0.8	– 1010	– 441	– 821	– 556
1.0	0	0	0	0

Table 7.6 (N_{xy}) kg/m, at $x = a$

$\frac{y}{b}$	$n = 1$	$n = 1,3$	$n = 1,3,5$	$n = 1,3,5,7$
0	0	0	0	0
0.2	– 2170	– 2490	– 2390	– 2420
0.4	– 5410	– 5600	– 5500	– 5530
0.6	– 9260	– 8590	– 8740	– 8690
0.8	– 10 100	– 8510	– 9080	– 8820
1.0	0	0	0	0

Table 7.7 (M_y) kg.m/m, at $x = 0$

$\frac{y}{b}$	$n = 1$	$n = 1,3$	$n = 1,3,5$	$n = 1,3,5,7$
0	– 1600	– 1580	– 1580	– 1580
0.2	– 1510	– 1490	– 1490	– 1490
0.4	– 1240	– 1200	– 1210	– 1210
0.6	– 763	– 733	– 740	– 738
0.8	– 207	– 205	– 205	– 205
1.0	0	0	0	0

From Tables 7.4–7.7, it may be seen that results obtained by considering the first term in the series is adequate for the design.

Example 7.2

As a second example, we will determine the forces in an hyperbolic paraboloid which is simply supported along one pair of edges ($x = \pm\ a$) and free along the other pair ($y = \pm\, b$). The dimensions and loading acting on the shell are identical to the previous example, except that the radius of curvature r_x is taken as negative. For convenience, we will repeat the data here: $2a$ = 18 m, $2b$ = 9 m, $r_x = R_1$ = – 105.5 m, $r_y = R_2$ = 9 m, h = 0.075 m, load = 220 kg/m^2 (including dead-load). We will determine the forces here considering only the first term in the series (n = 1).

(a) Roots of the equation (n = 1):

$$\gamma_1 = \sqrt{\left[\sqrt{(9/h^4 r_x^4) + (12\,\alpha_n^4/h^2 r_x^2 r_y^2)\,(-r_x + r_y)^2} - (3/h^2 r_x^2)\right]/2} = 0.253$$

$$\gamma_2 = \sqrt{\left[\sqrt{(9/h^4 r_x^4) + (12\,\alpha_n^4/h^2 r_x^2 r_y^2)\,(-r_x + r_y)^2} + (3/h^2 r_x^2)\right]/2} = 0.335$$

$$m_1 = \sqrt{\left[\sqrt{(\alpha_n^2 + \gamma_1)^2 + (-\sqrt{3}/hr_x + \gamma_2)^2} + (\alpha_n^2 + \gamma_1)\right]/2} = 0.673$$

$$n_1 = \sqrt{\left[\sqrt{(\alpha_n^2 + \gamma_1)^2 + (-\sqrt{3}/hr_x + \gamma_2)^2} - (\alpha_n^2 + \gamma_1)\right]/2} = 0.411$$

$$m_2 = \sqrt{\left[\sqrt{(\alpha_n^2 - \gamma_1)^2 + (-\sqrt{3}/hr_x - \gamma_2)^2} + (\alpha_n^2 - \gamma_1)\right]/2} = 0.119$$

$$n_2 = \sqrt{\left[\sqrt{(\alpha_n^2 - \gamma_1)^2 + (-\sqrt{3}/hr_x - \gamma_2)^2} - (\alpha_n^2 - \gamma_1)\right]/2} = 0.487$$

(b) Boundary conditions

$$y = \pm\, b\ (\pm\ 4.5\ m),\ N_y = N_{xy} = M_y = \overline{Q}_y = 0$$

(c) Formulation of simultaneous equations and solution

Following the previous example, the following four simultaneous equations can be obtained

$$\begin{bmatrix} -13.943065 & -4.031907 & 0.643087 & 0.937975 \\ 44.564306 & 48.491979 & 0.385814 & -3.976633 \\ 6.300823 & -1.225865 & -0.095613 & 0.179167 \\ 4.401934 & 2.09866 & -0.145558 & 0.043603 \end{bmatrix} \begin{bmatrix} a \\ b \\ c \\ d \end{bmatrix} = \begin{bmatrix} \frac{2864.688}{D} \\ 0 \\ 0 \\ 0 \end{bmatrix}$$

Solving the above simultaneous equations, we get

$$a = \frac{11.043436}{D},\ b = \frac{124.4527}{D},\ c = \frac{2698.4449}{D},\ d = \frac{1903.1679}{D}$$

The forces and moments throughout the transverse section of the shell may now be computed, using the above value for the constants and these are given in Table 7.8.

Table 7.8 Forces and moments in a hyperbolic paraboloid ($n = 1$)

$\frac{y}{b}$	$\frac{N_x}{\cos\alpha_n x}$ kg/m	$\frac{N_y}{\cos\alpha_n x}$ kg/m	$\frac{N_{xy}}{\sin\alpha_n x}$ kg/m	$\frac{M_x}{\cos\alpha_n x}$ kg.m/m	$\frac{M_y}{\cos\alpha_n x}$ kg.m/m	$\frac{\overline{Q}_x}{\sin\alpha_n x}$ kg/m	$\frac{\overline{Q}_y}{\cos\alpha_n x}$ kg/m
0	− 35400	− 5370	0	82.9	309	− 122	0
0.2	− 30900	− 4940	− 5320	79.1	294	− 116	− 51.1
0.4	− 17800	− 3770	− 9260	68.2	244	− 97	− 109
0.6	3530	− 2170	− 10500	51.3	155	− 63.1	− 161
0.8	32200	− 682	− 7750	30.6	45.3	− 21.1	− 159
1.0	67600	0	0	8.67	0	− 1.45	0

7.6.3 Solution Using Orthogonal Functions

We have shown earlier that the solution for an all-round simply supported shell can be obtained using double trigonometric series. Such a simple approach is not possible, for example, for a shell clamped along all the four edges. However, it is possible to express the displacements by means of a set of orthogonal functions satisfying the boundary conditions exactly. The differential equations (in terms of displacements) are then satisfied using the orthogonal property of these functions, resulting in a set of three infinite simultaneous equations. The solution of these equations gives the undetermined coefficients in the series, using which the forces and displacements in the shell can be computed. This method has been applied to a hyperbolic paraboloid shell with straight line generators by Iyengar and Srinivasan[7.5]. The solution as given by them will be described in some detail, as it is possible to solve doubly curved shell problem involving a combination of simply supported and clamped boundary conditions, by choosing appropriate functions, using this method.

The surface of the hyperbolic paraboloid is defined by (Fig. 7.4)

$$z = kxy$$

where $k = (c/ab)$.

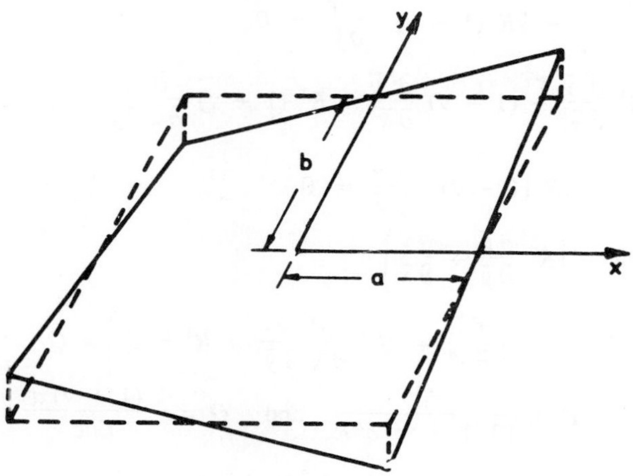

Fig. 7.4 Hyperbolic paraboloid with straight line generators

For this surface, it is obvious that $r = t = 0$ and $s = k$. Since we are dealing with clamped boundary, the boundary conditions will be in terms of displacements and hence it is preferable to use the differential equation in terms of displacements.

The differential equation in terms of the displacements for the hyperbolic paraboloid, can be written following Eq. (7.5) as

$$\frac{\partial^2 u}{\partial x^2} + \left(\frac{1-\nu}{2}\right)\frac{\partial^2 u}{\partial y^2} + \left(\frac{1+\nu}{2}\right)\frac{\partial^2 v}{\partial x \partial y} - (1-\nu)\,k\,\frac{\partial w}{\partial y} = 0 \qquad (7.24a)$$

$$\frac{\partial^2 v}{\partial y^2} + \left(\frac{1-\nu}{2}\right)\frac{\partial^2 v}{\partial x^2} + \left(\frac{1+\nu}{2}\right)\frac{\partial^2 u}{\partial x \partial y} - (1-\nu)\,k\,\frac{\partial w}{\partial x} = 0 \qquad (7.24b)$$

$$- 2k^2(1-\nu)\,w + k(1-\nu)\left(\frac{\partial u}{\partial y} + \frac{\partial v}{\partial x}\right)$$

$$- \frac{h^2}{12}\nabla^4 w + \frac{Z}{Eh}(1-\nu^2) = 0 \qquad (7.24c)$$

(while writing the above equations, it is assumed that the shell is subjected to a loading in the z-direction only and hence $X = Y = 0$).

The above differential equations may be nondimensionalised, by introducing the following new variables.

$$\bar{x} = (x/a),\ \bar{y} = (y/b),\ \bar{u} = (u/a),\ \bar{v} = (v/b),\ \bar{w} = wk \text{ and } R = (a/b)$$

as

$$2\frac{\partial^2 \bar{u}}{\partial \bar{x}^2} + (1-\nu)R^2\frac{\partial^2 \bar{u}}{\partial \bar{y}^2} + (1+\nu)\frac{\partial^2 \bar{v}}{\partial \bar{x}\,\partial \bar{y}}$$

$$- 2R(1-\nu)\frac{\partial \bar{w}}{\partial \bar{y}} = 0 \qquad (7.25a)$$

$$2R^2\frac{\partial^2 \bar{v}}{\partial \bar{y}^2} + (1-\nu)\frac{\partial^2 \bar{v}}{\partial \bar{x}^2} + R^2(1+\nu)\frac{\partial^2 \bar{u}}{\partial \bar{x}\,\partial \bar{y}}$$

$$- 2R(1-\nu)\frac{\partial \bar{w}}{\partial \bar{x}} = 0 \qquad (7.25b)$$

$$2R\bar{w} - \left(R^2\frac{\partial \bar{u}}{\partial \bar{y}} + \frac{\partial \bar{v}}{\partial \bar{x}}\right)$$

$$+ P\left(\frac{\partial^4 \bar{w}}{\partial \bar{x}^4} + 2R^2\frac{\partial^4 \bar{w}}{\partial \bar{x}^2\,\partial \bar{y}^2} + R^4\frac{\partial^4 \bar{w}}{\partial \bar{y}^4}\right) = Q \qquad (7.25c)$$

where $$P = \frac{h^2}{12(1-\nu^2)c^2 R} \quad \text{and} \quad Q = \frac{Z(1+\nu)a^2}{Ehc}$$

The boundary conditions for the clamped edge are

$$x = \pm 1,\ \bar{u} = \bar{v} = \bar{w} = \frac{\partial \bar{w}}{\partial \bar{x}} = 0$$

$$(7.26)$$

$$y = \pm 1,\ \bar{u} = \bar{v} = \bar{w} = \frac{\partial \bar{w}}{\partial \bar{y}} = 0$$

The expressions for the displacements can be taken as

$$\bar{u} = \sum_{m=1}^{\infty} \sum_{n=1}^{\infty} A_{mn} \bar{X}_m (\bar{x}) \psi_n (\bar{y})$$

$$\bar{v} = \sum_{m=1}^{\infty} \sum_{n=1}^{\infty} B_{mn} \phi_m (\bar{x}) \bar{Y}_n (\bar{y}) \qquad (7.27)$$

$$\bar{w} = \sum_{m=1}^{\infty} \sum_{n=1}^{\infty} C_{mn} X_m (\bar{x}) Y_n (\bar{y})$$

Since the loading considered here is symmetrical with respect to both x and y axes, the expressions for the displacements should have the following property:

$\bar{u}$ = (even functions in $\bar{x}$) (odd functions in $\bar{y}$)

$\bar{v}$ = (odd functions in $\bar{x}$) (even functions in $\bar{y}$)

$\bar{w}$ = (even functions in $\bar{x}$) (even functions in $\bar{y}$)

To satisfy the boundary conditions specified in Eq. (7.26) as well as the above property, the functions in Eq. (7.27) can be taken as

$$\bar{X}_m = \cos \left(\frac{2m-1}{2}\right) \pi \bar{x}$$

$$\bar{Y}_n = \cos \left(\frac{2n-1}{2}\right) \pi \bar{y}$$

$$\phi_m = \sin m \pi \bar{x}, \quad \psi_n = \sin n \pi \bar{y} \qquad (7.28)$$

$$X_m = \left(\frac{\cosh \lambda_m \bar{x}}{\cosh \lambda_m} - \frac{\cos \lambda_m \bar{x}}{\cos \lambda_m}\right),$$

$$Y_n = \left(\frac{\cosh \lambda_n \bar{y}}{\cosh \lambda_n} - \frac{\cos \lambda_n \bar{y}}{\cos \lambda_n}\right)$$

where λ_m and λ_n are determined from the transcendental equations

$$\tanh \lambda_m + \tan \lambda_m = 0$$

$$\tanh \lambda_n + \tan \lambda_n = 0$$

and the value of λ_m and λ_n are given below:

m or n	λ_m or λ_n
1	2.36504
2	5.49760
3	8.63910
4	11.78060
5	14.92210
$m \geq 5$	$\left(\frac{4m-1}{4}\right)\pi$

Substituting Eq. (7.27) in Eqs. (7.25 a–c), we get

$$\sum_{m=1}^{\infty} \sum_{n=1}^{\infty} [B_{mn}(1+\nu)\phi_m' \overline{Y}^{\circ}_n + 2A_{mn} \overline{X}_m'' \psi_n + (1-\nu)R^2 A_{mn} \overline{X}_m \psi_n^{\circ\circ} - 2R(1-\nu)C_{mn} X_m Y_n^{\circ}] = 0 \quad (7.29a)$$

$$\sum_{m=1}^{\infty} \sum_{n=1}^{\infty} [R^2(1+\nu) A_{mn} \overline{X}_m' \psi_n^{\circ} + 2R^2 B_{mn} \phi_n \overline{Y}_n^{\circ\circ} + (1-\nu)B_{mn} \phi''_{mn} \overline{Y}_n - 2R(1-\nu) C_{mn} X'_m Y_n] = 0 \quad (7.29b)$$

$$\sum_{m=1}^{\infty} \sum_{n=1}^{\infty} [2RC_{mn} X_m Y_n - R^2 A_{mn} \overline{X}_m \psi_n^{\circ} - B_{mn} \phi_m' \overline{Y}_n + P\{C_{mn} X_m'''' Y_n + 2R^2 C_{mn} X_m'' Y_n^{\circ\circ} + R^4 C_{mn} X_m Y_n^{\circ\circ\circ\circ}\}] = Q \quad (7.29c)$$

where $(\cdots)' = \dfrac{\partial}{\partial \overline{x}}$, $(\cdots)^{\circ} = \dfrac{\partial}{\partial y}$.

Since the functions are orthogonal in the interval – 1 to + 1, the various expressions and their derivatives in the above equations can be expressed as follows:

$$X_m = \sum_{i=1}^{\infty} M_i^m X_i, \qquad Y_n = \sum_{j=1}^{\infty} \overline{M_j^n}\, \overline{Y}_j, \qquad X'_m = \lambda_m \sum_{i=1}^{\infty} K_i^m \phi_i$$

$$Y_n^{\circ} = \lambda_n \sum_{j=1}^{\infty} \overline{K_j^n} \psi_j, \qquad X_m'' = \lambda_m^2 \sum_{i=1}^{\infty} F_i^{\circ\circ} X_i, \qquad Y_n^{\circ\circ} = \lambda_n^2 \sum_{j=1}^{\infty} \overline{F_j^n} Y_j$$

$$\overline{X}_m = \sum_{i=1}^{\infty} S_i^m X_i, \qquad \overline{Y}_n = \sum_{j=1}^{\infty} S_j^n Y_j, \qquad \overline{X}'_m = -(s\pi)_m \sum_{i=1}^{\infty} P_i^m \phi_i$$

$$Y_n^{\circ} = -(s\pi)_n \sum_{j=1}^{\infty} \overline{P_j^n} \psi_j, \qquad \phi'_m = m\pi \sum_{i=1}^{\infty} E_i^m X_i, \qquad \psi_n^{\circ} = n\pi \sum_{j=1}^{\infty} \overline{E_j^n} Y_j$$

$$\phi'_m = m\pi \sum_{i=1}^{\infty} R_i^m \overline{X}_i, \qquad \psi^{\circ}_n = n\pi \sum_{j=1}^{\infty} \overline{R_j^n} \overline{Y}_j$$

where $(s\pi)_m = \left(\dfrac{2m-1}{2}\right)\pi$.

The various coefficients M_i^m, K_i^m, etc. in the above expressions can easily be determined using the tables given by Felgar[7.18] as

$$M_i^m = \frac{4(-1)^i (s\pi)_i \lambda_m^2}{(s\pi)_i^4 - \lambda_m^4}, \quad K_i^m = \frac{4(-1)^{i+1} (i\pi) \lambda_m^2 \tanh \lambda_m}{\lambda_m^4 - (i\pi)^4}$$

$$F_i^m = \frac{4\lambda_i^2}{\lambda_m^4 - \lambda_i^4} (\lambda_m \tanh \lambda_m - \lambda_i \tanh \lambda_i) \text{ when } i \neq m$$

$$= \frac{1}{2}\left(\frac{1}{\cosh^2 \lambda_m} - \frac{1}{\cos^2 \lambda_m}\right) + \frac{\tanh \lambda_m}{m} \text{ when } i = m$$

$$S_i^m = \frac{2(-1)^m (s\pi)_m \lambda_i^2}{(s\pi)_m^4 - \lambda_i^4}, \quad P_i^m = -\frac{2(-1)^{m+i} (i\pi)}{(s\pi)_m^2 - (i\pi)^2}$$

$$E_i^m = \frac{2(-1)^m \lambda_i^3 \tanh \lambda_i}{\lambda_i^4 - (m\pi)^4}, \quad R_i^m = \frac{2(-1)^{m+i} (s\pi)_i}{(m\pi)^2 - (s\pi)_i^2}$$

The coefficients M_j^m, K_j^m, etc. can be obtained by changing i to j in the above expressions.

The loading term Q can also be expressed in terms of orthogonal functions as

$$Q = \sum_{m=1}^{\infty} \sum_{n=1}^{\infty} q_{mn} X_m Y_n$$

where q_{mn} is determined from

$$q_{mn} = \frac{\int_{-1}^{+1} \int_{-1}^{+1} Q X_m Y_n \, d\bar{x} \, d\bar{y}}{\int_{-1}^{+1} \int_{-1}^{+1} X_m^2 Y_n^2 \, d\bar{x} \, d\bar{y}}$$

and for the case of uniformly distributed load (including dead-load) of intensity p per unit area, q_{mn} can be determined as

$$q_{mn} = 4Q \frac{\tanh \lambda_m \tan \lambda_n}{\lambda_m \lambda_n}$$

where

$$Q = \frac{p(1 + \nu) a^2}{Ehc}$$

Substituting Eq. (7.30) in, for example, Eq. (7.29a), we get

$$\sum_{m=1}^{\infty} \sum_{n=1}^{\infty} \left[-B_{mn} (1 + \nu) m\pi \sum_{i=1}^{\infty} R_i^m \bar{X}_i (s\pi)_n \sum_{j=1}^{\infty} \bar{P}_j^n \psi_j \right.$$

$$- 2A_{mn} (s\pi)_m^2 \bar{X}_m \psi_n - A_{mn} R^2 (1 - \nu) (n\pi)^2 \bar{X}_m \psi_n$$

$$\left. - 2C_{mn} R (1 - \nu) \sum_{i=1}^{\infty} M_i^m \bar{X}_i \lambda_n \sum_{j=1}^{\infty} \bar{K}_j^n \psi_j \right] = 0 \tag{7.31}$$

which can be written as

$$\sum_{m=1}^{\infty} \sum_{n=1}^{\infty} \left[A_{mn} \xi_1 + \sum_{i=1}^{\infty} \sum_{j=1}^{\infty} (B_{ij} \xi_2 + C_{ij} \xi_3) \right] \bar{X}_m \psi_n = 0 \tag{7.32a}$$

Similarly, Eqs. (7.29b and c) can be reduced to the following form, after using Eq. (7.30) and simplification:

$$\sum_{m=1}^{\infty} \sum_{n=1}^{\infty} \left[\sum_{i=1}^{\infty} \sum_{j=1}^{\infty} A_{ij}\, \xi_4 + B_{mn}\, \xi_5 + \sum_{i=1}^{\infty} \sum_{j=1}^{\infty} C_{ij}\, \xi_6 \right] \phi_m\, \overline{Y}_n = 0 \tag{7.32b}$$

$$\sum_{m=1}^{\infty} \sum_{n=1}^{\infty} \left[\sum_{i=1}^{\infty} \sum_{j=1}^{\infty} (A_{ij}\, \xi_7 + B_{ij}\, \xi_8 + C_{ij}\, \xi_9) + C_{mn}\, \xi_{10} \right] X_m\, Y_n = \sum_{m=1}^{\infty} \sum_{n=1}^{\infty} q_{mn}\, X_m\, Y_n \tag{7.32c}$$

where

$$\xi_1 = -\left[2(s\pi)_m^2 + (1-\nu)\, R^2 (n\pi)^2\right], \qquad \xi_2 = -(1+\nu)\,(i\pi)\,(s\pi)_j\, R_m^i\, \overline{P}_n^j$$

$$\xi_3 = -2(1-\nu)\, R\lambda_j\, M_m^i\, \overline{K}_n^j, \qquad \xi_4 = -(1+\nu)\, R^2 (s\pi)_i\, (j\pi)\, Q_m^i\, \overline{R}_n^j$$

$$\xi_5 = -\left[2R^2 (s\pi)_n^2 + (1-\nu)\,(m\pi)^2\right], \qquad \xi_6 = -2R(1+\nu)\lambda_i\, K_m^i\, \overline{M}_n^j$$

$$\xi_7 = -R^2 (j\pi)\, S_m^i\, \overline{E}_m^j, \qquad \xi_8 = -i\pi\, E_m^i\, \overline{S}_n^j$$

$$\xi_9 = 2R^2 P \lambda_i^2 \lambda_j^2 . F_m^i\, \overline{F}_n^j, \qquad \xi_{10} = 2R + P(\lambda_m^4 + R^4 \lambda_n^4)$$

Equations (7.32a-c) can now be wirtten as

$$A_{mn}\, \xi_1 + \sum_{i=1}^{\infty} \sum_{j=1}^{\infty} (B_{ij}\, \xi_2 + C_{ij}\, \xi_3) = 0 \tag{7.33a}$$

$$\sum_{i=1}^{\infty} \sum_{j=1}^{\infty} (A_{ij}\, \xi_4 + C_{ij}\, \xi_6) + B_{mn}\, \xi_5 = 0 \tag{7.33b}$$

$$\sum_{i=1}^{\infty} \sum_{j=1}^{\infty} (A_{ij}\, \xi_7 + B_{ij}\, \xi_8 + C_{ij}\, \xi_9) + C_{mn}\, \xi_{10} = q_{mn} \tag{7.33c}$$

Hence, the solution results in three sets of infinite simultaneous equations. However, in practice, only a finite number of terms are considered resulting in $3mn$ simultaneous equations solving which the constants A_{mn}, B_{mn}, and C_{mn} are determined. The stress resultants can then be determined by using the force-displacement relations given in Eq. (7.4) together with the expressions for the displacements given in Eq. (7.27). Iyengar and Srinivasan[7.5] have illustrated the application of the method through a numerical example of a hypar subjected to uniformly distributed load. It has been shown that sufficiently accurate results could be obtained by considering three terms in each series. This method of approach can easily be extended to other types of doubly curved shells having simply supported or clamped boundary conditions.

7.7 SIMPLIFIED METHOD FOR DETERMINING BOUNDARY EFFECT[7.15]

It has been indicated earlier that the membrane theory provides a reasonable picture of state of stress at points far away from certain lines called alteration lines. According to Goldenveizer[7.19] the alteration lines are:

(a) the edges of shell,

(b) lines of discontinuity of load,

(c) lines along which the middle surface of the shell is discontinuous,

(d) lines along which the shell thickness or rigidity is abruptly changed.

Goldenveizer states that to have pure membrane state of stress in a shell, it is essential that

(i) the alteration lines should not be closely spaced,

(ii) no alteration lines should be tangent to an asymptotic line of middle surface.

It should be noted that in shells whose Gauss curvature is positive (synclastic shells), the asymptotic lines are imaginary and hence, the second condition mentioned above is fulfilled. Hence, for synclastic shells, the application of membrane theory is valid. However, in the case of shells whose Gauss curvature is zero (developable shells) or negative (anticlastic shells), the perturbations from the boundary propagate along the asymptotic lines and hence, in these types of shells, the application of membrane theory should be carefully examined.

With the existence of alteration lines, it becomes necessary to study the effect of forces or displacements applied along a boundary, since this effect can get transmitted into the interior of the shell. This may be called as a simple boundary effect and an approximate method may be developed to study this effect. The final state of stress in a shell can then be determined by superposing on the membrane state of stress, the perturbation stresses obtained from the simple boundary effect. An approach to determine the simple boundary effect as given by Beles and Soare[7.15] will be presented here.

To develop the necessary equations to determine the simple boundary effect, let us consider a boundary of the shell x = constant (Fig. 7.5). If the alteration line coincides with the coordinate line y (x = constant), then the force N_y will be predominant while the other forces, namely N_x and N_{xy} will be small and can be neglected. Similarly, the bending moment M_x and the shear force Q_x will be predominant and the other bending moment (M_y), twisting moment (M_{xy}) and shear force (Q_y), being small, can be neglected. Amongst the displacement, it will be assumed that only the displacement w will be predominant and the displacements

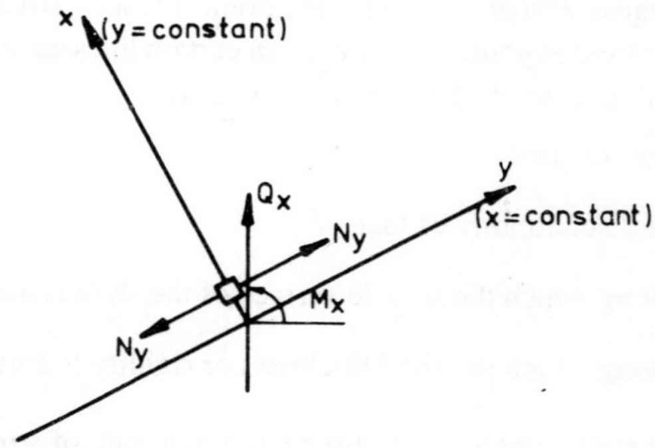

Fig. 7.5 Line of alteration x = constant

u and v may be neglected. With these assumptions, the equilibrium Eqs. (7.1a–e) and force-displacement relations (Eq. 7.4) will now reduce to

$$\frac{\partial Q_x}{\partial x} + t N_y = 0 \tag{7.34a}$$

$$\frac{\partial M_x}{\partial x} - Q_x = 0 \tag{7.34b}$$

$$N_y = - Ehtw \tag{7.34c}$$

$$M_x = - D \frac{\partial^2 w}{\partial x^2} \tag{7.34d}$$

Using the above equations, we can now derive the following differential equation in terms of displacement w as

$$\frac{\partial^4 w}{\partial x^4} + \left\{ \frac{12 (1 - \nu^2) t^2}{h^2} \right\} w = 0 \tag{7.35}$$

If, for a shallow translational shell, t is constant, then the above equation can be put in the following form:

$$\frac{\partial^4 w}{\partial x^4} + \frac{4 \lambda^4}{a^4} w = 0 \tag{7.36}$$

where $\lambda = \sqrt[4]{3 (1 - \nu^2)} \quad \sqrt{(t/h)}\ a$

Following the same simplifying assumptions made here, Zerna[7.20] also has derived an equation similar to Eq. (7.36), in which λ in general is assumed as a variable.

The general solution of Eq. (7.36) can be written as

$$w = e^{-(\lambda x)/a}\left(A\cos\frac{\lambda x}{a} + B\sin\frac{\lambda x}{a}\right) + e^{(\lambda x)/a}\left(C\cos\frac{\lambda x}{a} + D\sin\frac{\lambda x}{a}\right) \tag{7.37}$$

where *A, B, C* and *D* are constants.

Now we will assume that the boundary effect dampens rapidly as we move away from the boundary. With this assumption, it becomes necessary only to retain the first two constants in Eq. (7.37) and hence, the solution can be written as

$$w = e^{-(\lambda x)/a}\left(A\cos\frac{\lambda x}{a} + B\sin\frac{\lambda x}{a}\right) \tag{7.38}$$

Using the above solution, we can now determine the boundary perturbation for different cases of support conditions.

For example, for a simple support (or hinged support), we can determine the simple boundary effect as follows. If w_o is the displacement along the boundary ($x = 0$) determined from the membrane analysis, then we enforce the following conditions along the edge ($x = 0$) to determine the constants *A* and *B* in the solution given above:

$$\text{at } x = 0,\ w + w_0 = 0,\ M_x = 0$$

Using the above conditions, the constants *A* and *B* may be determined. The force N_y and bending moment M_x will now be superposed on the results obtained from the membrane analysis, to get the final forces in the shell.

Similarly, if the edge is clamped or fixed, we use the following conditions to determine the constants.

$$\text{at } x = 0,\ \frac{dw}{dx} + \frac{dw_0}{dx} = 0,\ w + w_0 = 0$$

where dw_0/dx and w_0 are the slope and displacement determined from the membrane analysis.

Though there is no conclusive evidence to show the reliability of this approximate solution for anticlastic shells, in general, it has been shown[7.15] that the method gives reasonably good results for a paraboloid of revolution.

7.8 SUMMARY

In this chapter, we have first derived the basic equations for the bending analysis of doubly curved shell, assuming the shell to be shallow. It is shown that Navier and Levy type of solutions could be obtained for the differential equation satisfying certain particular types of boundary conditions. Finally, a simple method of determining the boundary effect is presented, which the designers may find very useful. By using this method along with membrane theory, several practical problems can be solved easily.

REFERENCES

7.1 Vlassov, V.Z., *General Theory of Shells and Its Applications in Engineering* (translated from Russian), National Aeronautics and Space Administration, N 64-1983, Washington D.C., April, 1964.

7.2 Bouma, A.L., 'Some applications of the bending theory regarding doubly curved shells', *Proc. of the Symposium on the Theory of Thin Elastic Shells,* Edited by W.T. Koiter, North-Holland Publishing Co., Amsterdam, 1960, pp. 202-234.

7.3 Apeland, K. and E.P. Popov, 'Analysis of bending stresses in translational shells', *Proc. of the Colloquium on Simplified Calculation Methods of Shell Structures*, Brussels, edited by A. Paduart and R. Dutron, Sept. 1961, North-Holland Publishing Co., Amsterdam, 1962, pp. 9–25.

7.4 Keshava Rao, M.N. and S.P. Sharma, 'Analysis of shallow elliptic paraboloidal shell with edge-beams', *The Indian Concrete Jl.*, Vol. 39, 1965, pp. 7–14.

7.5 Sundara Raja Iyengar, K.T. and R.S. Srinivasan, 'Bending analysis of hyperbolic paraboloid shells', *The Structural Engineer,* Vol. 12, 1968, pp. 397–401.

7.6 Jenkins, R.S. and H. Tottenham, 'The solution of shell problems by the matrix progression method', *Proc. of the World Conference on Shell Structures,* California, Oct. 1962, National Academy of Sciences — National Research Council, Publication No. 1187, Washington D.C. 1964, pp. 563–580.

7.7 Chetty, S.M.K. and H. Tottenham, 'An investigation into the bending analysis of hyperbolic paraboloid shells', *The Indian Concrete Jl.*, Vol. 38, 1964, pp 248–258.

7.8 Das Gupta, N.C., 'Using finite difference equations to find the stresses in hypar shells', *Civil Engg. and Public Works Review*, Vol. 56, Feb. 1961, pp. 199–201.

7.9 Keshava Rao, M.N. and S.P. Sharma, 'Application of the methods of finite differences for the analysis of a conoid shell using bending theory', *The Indian Concrete Jl.*, Vol. 36, No. 3, 1962,pp. 84-92.

7.10 Soare, M.A., 'A numerical approach to the bending theory of hypar shells', *The Indian Concrete Jl.*, Vol. 40, No. 2 and 3, 1966, pp. 63-70 and pp. 113-119.

7.11 Russel, R.R. and K.H. Gerstle, 'Bending of hyperbolic paraboloid structures', *Jl. of the Structural Div., Proc. ASCE,* Vol. 93, ST3, 1967, pp. 181–199.

7.12 Russel, R.R. and K.H. Gerstle, 'Bending of hyperbolic paraboloids supported on four corners', *Jl. of the Structural Div., Proc. ASCE,* Vol. 94, 1968, pp. 995–1010.

7.13 Crool, J.G.A. and J.C. Scrivener, 'Convergence of hyper finite difference solutions', *Jl. of the Structural Div., Proc. ASCE, Vol. 95, ST-5, 1969, pp. 809–830.*

7.14 Hedgren, A.W. and D.P. Billington, 'Numerical analysis of translational shell roofs', *Jl. of the Structural Div., Proc. ASCE, Vol. 92, ST-1, 1966, pp. 223–244.*

7.15 Beles, A.A. and M. Soare, '*Elliptic and Hyperbolic Paraboloidal Shell Used in Construction*', S.P. Christie and Partners, London, 1976.

7.16 Doganoff, I. 'Betrochtungen iiber die Berechungs Verfahren Rechteckiger Kugel-Calotten *Proc. of the Colloquium on Simplified Calculation Methods of Shell Structures,* Brussels, Edited by A. Paduart and R. Dutran, Brussels, Sept. 1961, North Holland Publishing Co., Amsterdam, 1962, pp 176–190.

7.17 Flugge, W. and D.A. Conrad, 'A note on the calculation of shallow shells', *Jl. of Appl. Mech., Trans. ASME,* Vol. 4, 1959,pp. 683–685.

7.18 Felgar, R.P., '*Formulas for integrals Containing Characteristic Functions of a Vibrating Beam*', Univ. of Texas Circular No. 14, 1950.

7.19 Goldenveizer, A.L., '*Theory of Thin Elastic Shells*', Pergamon Press, New York, 1961.

7.20 Zerna, W., 'Berechung von Translationsschalen', *Osterreichisches Ingenieur-Archiv.,* Vol. 7, 1953, pp. 181–187.

Chapter Eight

Analysis of Folded Plates

8.1 INTRODUCTION

A folded plate structure is composed of a series of thin plates monolithic along their common longitudinal edges and supported by transverse diaphragms, frames or columns (Fig. 8.1). Figure 8.2 defines the various elements of a typical folded plate structure. A folded plate may be prismatic or non-prismatic. A prismatic folded plate consists of rectangular plate elements each of constant width and thickness while a nonprismatic folded plate is characterised by its variable plate width along the span. Folded plate structures with more than two plates meeting at a common longitudinal joint are known as complex folded plate structures. The edge plates of the folded plate structure are often made thicker than the interior plates, thereby strengthening the longitudinal boundaries. Sometimes, the thicker edge plates are placed vertically downwards forming projecting beams. Such edge plates are referred to as edge-beams. Several typical cross-sections of folded plates are shown in Fig. 8.3. Folded plates may find application as roof structures, coal bunkers, cooling towers, water tanks, stair cases, boxgirder bridges, etc.

The structural action of folded plates is similar to that of shells. However, folded plates consume little more material compared to for example, cylindrical shells. But the extra cost on the materials is offset in the form work. In addition, because of their inherent stiffness, larger spans may be obtained with folded plates without an increase in material requirement.

8.2 FOLDED PLATE BEHAVIOUR

For a clear understanding of the behaviour of a folded plate structure, it is necessary to know its structural action. In the course of discussing the structural action, some terminologies will be introduced which are commonly used in the analysis of folded plates.

Although the behaviour of a folded plate is three-dimensional, it can be analysed as a two-dimensional structure, since in practice, the thickness of the

Fig. 8.1 A folded plate water tank of capacity 1,00,000 litres supported on a folded plate shaft. (*Architects*: Civil Engineering Division, ISRO, Bangalore) (*Courtesy*: Sri H.K. Nanjundaswamy, Consulting and Construction Engineer, Bangalore).

plate is very small in comparison with its other two dimensions. Figure 8.4 shows an element taken from the folded plate. The element is subjected to a general system of external loading, defined by the three components *X, Y* and *Z* corresponding to *x*-, *y*- and *z*-directions respectively. The internal forces developed in resisting the external loads can be conveniently divided into two separate actions, namely slab action and plate action. These two actions are shown separately in Figs. 8.5(a) and (b).

For small displacements, the slab action supports the *Z*-component of the external load while the plate action takes care of the in-plane load components *X* and *Y* of

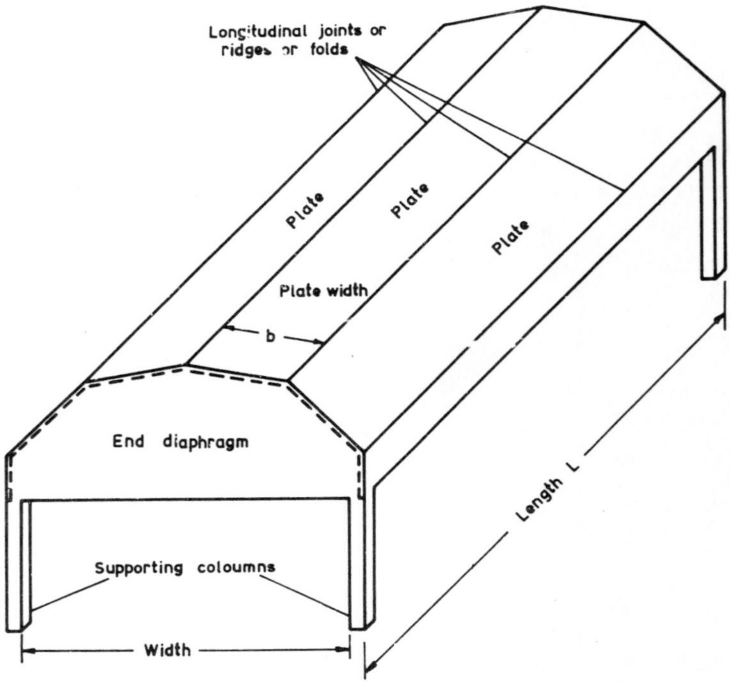

Fig. 8.2 Elements of a folded plate structure

the external load. The slab action deals with the bending of the individual plates out of their plane, that is, the plate acts as a two-way slab continuous over junctions. The plate action involves primarily the displacements and stresses in the plane of the plate and is identical to a deep beam action. It should be noted that the slab and plate actions are not independent but they interact at the folds or junctions of the plates.

8.3 SELECTION OF DIMENSIONS OF FOLDED PLATES

A fundamental difference between cylindrical shells and folded plate structures is that the transverse moments are small in the former (for symmetrical distributed loads), while it is the governing factor in the latter. If folded plates have to compete with shells in respect of economy, their thickness and reinforcement should be within certain limits.

The problem of selection of dimensions is generally viewed from three angles:

(a) Consumption of materials (steel and concrete)

(b) Ease of construction

(c) Aesthetic appeal

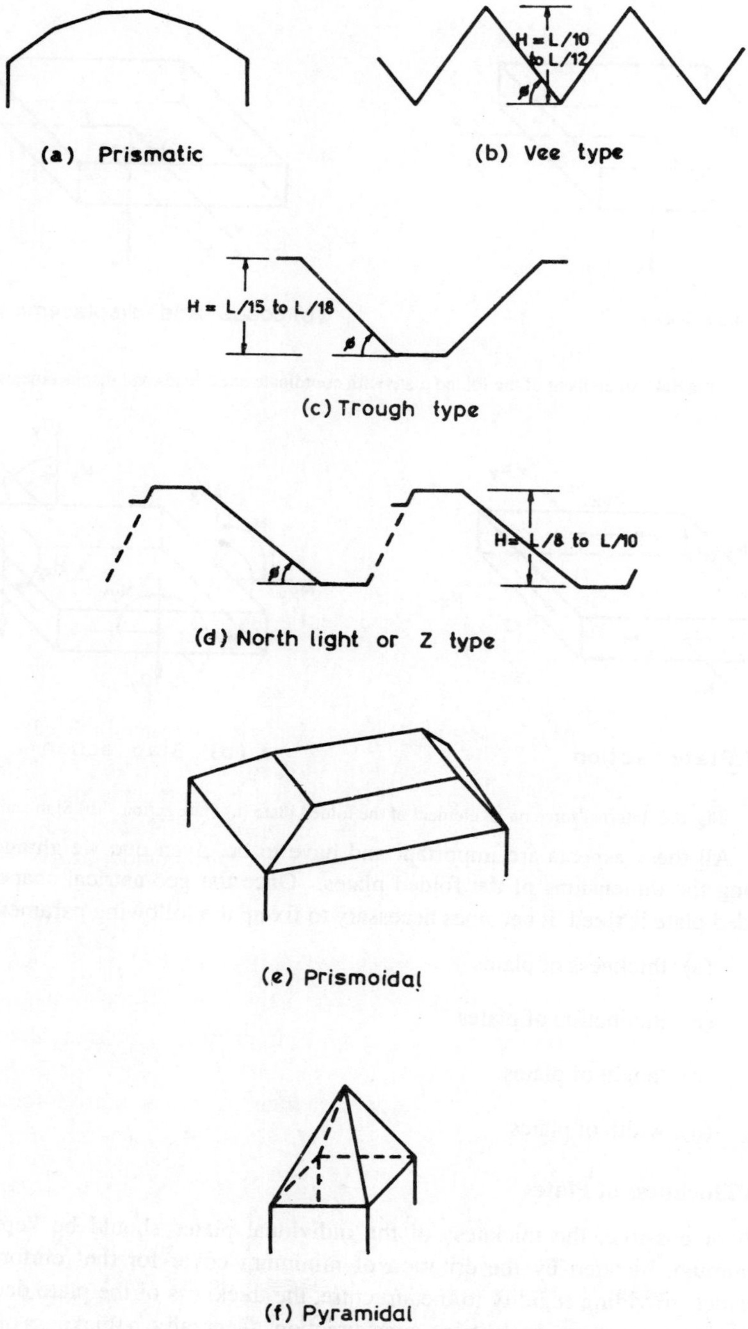

Fig. 8.3 Types of folded plates

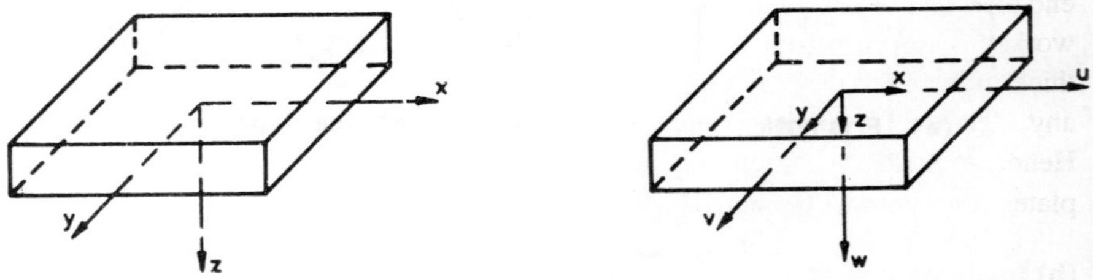

(a) Axes (b) Loads and displacements

Fig.8.4 An element of the folded plate with coordinate axes, loads and displacements

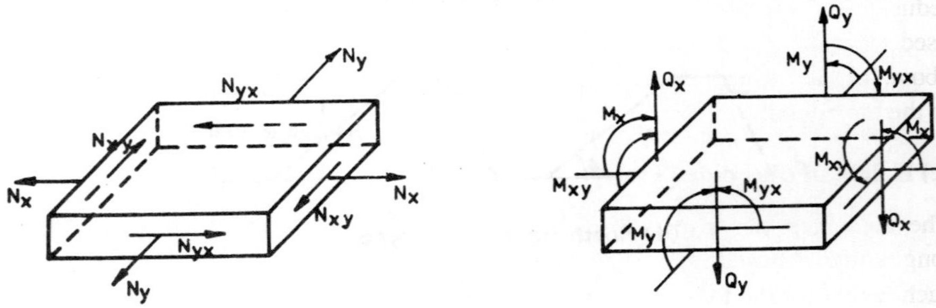

(a) Plate action (b) Slab action

Fig. 8.5 Internal force on an element of the folded plate (a) Plate action (b) Slab action

All these aspects are important and have to be given due weightage while fixing the dimensions of the folded plates. Once the geometrical shape of the folded plate is fixed, it becomes necessary to fix up the following parameters:

(a) thickness of plates

(b) inclination of plates

(c) height of plates

(d) width of plates

(a) Thickness of Plates

Where possible, the thickness of the individual plates should be kept at the minimum, dictated by the criterion of minimum cover for the reinforcement. Besides providing regidity to the structure, the thickness of the plate decides its moment of resistance in the transverse direction. Generally, a thickness of 8 cm is a practical minimum for cast-in-situ concrete plates. In the case of vee and trough type folded plates, the end plates are thicker than the interior plates, as normally, these plates have to resist higher transverse moments than the interior plates. If the end plate can be considered as a cantilever, the thickness of end plate can easily be worked out even before starting the analysis. Where the end plates become too thick, tapering of the plates can also be considered. It should be remembered that any increase in thickness increases the dead-weight and thereby the stresses. Hence, to make the structure economical, one has to use minimum thickness for plates consistent with practical and transverse moment consideration.

(b) Inclination of Plates

Plates should not have slopes more than 45° to the horizontal to avoid the use of backform work while concreting. At the same time, the larger the inclination, greater will be the structural depth and hence the inclination should not be unduly reduced. In precast construction, plates having inclination more than 45° can be used. From the aesthetic point of view, a slope below 35° would be too flat and above 45°, too steep. Hence, it is advisable to keep the slope between 40° to 45° to the horizontal.

(c) Height of the Folded Plate

The guiding principle in the selection of the height of the folded plate is the longitudinal stress at top and bottom of the folded plate. It is necessary to have such height for the folded plate, so that the longitudinal stresses are very near to the permissible stresses in concrete. The height of the folded plate varies from shape to shape to satisfy the above mentioned criteria. On solving a large number of folded plate structures of different shapes and span, the following guidelines have been arrived at for the height of the folded plate:

(i) Trough shape $L/15$ to $L/18$

(ii) Vee shape $L/10$ to $L/12$

(iii) North light $L/8$ to $L/10$

where L is the span of the folded plate.

(d) Width of Plate

Once the height and inclination of plate and bay width are fixed, the rest of the dimensions get automatically fixed. However, while fixing the width of horizontal plate, it should be remembered that the width of the plate has a direct influence on the stress it carries. For example, if the width of plate is too small, the section modulus for such a plate being less, results in very high stress. Further, if two adjoining plates are too much of unequal length, then the transverse moment increases. As a general rule, the horizontal projection of inclined plates should be made approximately equal to the width of the horizontal plates.

8.4 METHODS OF ANALYSIS

The first paper on folded plate theory was presented by Ehlers[8.1] in 1920. Ehlers in his analysis assumed the plates as hinged to each other along their common junction, so that sliding in the longitudinal direction is prevented. Since then, numerous contributions to the analysis of folded plates may be found in the literature. A fairly extensive bibliography on the folded plate analysis up to 1963 may be found in a report prepared by the ASCE Task Committee on folded plate construction[8.2].

In general, all the existing methods of analysis of folded plate structure may be broadly classified under the following three categories:

(a) Elasticity method

(b) Ordinary folded plate theory

(c) Beam method

The following basic assumptions are common to all the above three categories:

(i) The material is homogeneous and linearly elastic.

(ii) The displacements are very small in comparison with the overall configuration of the structure.

(iii) The principle of superposition is valid.

(iv) Longitudinal joints are fully monolithic with slab acting continuous through the joints.

(v) Each supporting diaphragm is infinitely stiff parallel to its own plane but is perfectly flexible normal to the plane.

8.4.1 Elasticity Method

Goldberg and Leve[8.3] have developed a solution for the stresses in a folded plate by combining the equations of classical plate theory for loads normal to the plane of plate (slab action) and the elasticity equations defining the plane stress problem for loads in the plane of the plates (plate action). The solution has been obtained using Fourier series and is applicable only for simply supported folded plate. The method is particularly useful in analysing short folded plate structures such as in bunkers, where the individual plates have a small length to width ratio (normally less than 5) and is given in detail here.

The method involves, in first determining the fixed edge forces along the longitudinal edges of each plate and these fixed edge forces are later modified or corrected by considering the effect of joint displacements.

It is visualised that there would be four displacements at each point of joint. These edge displacements are (Fig. 8.6):

(a) Rotations θ_i and θ_j about the longitudinal axis along the edges *i* and *j* respectively. The corresponding transverse moments per unit length are M_i and M_j. They are positive counterclockwise looking towards the origin of the plate.

(b) Displacements w_i and w_j along the edges normal to the plane of the plate. The corresponding shear forces per unit length are V_i and V_j. They are positive if they tend to turn the plate cross-section clockwise, looking towards the origin of the plate.

(c) Displacements u_i and u_j along and parallel to the plate edges, the corresponding membrane shear forces per unit length are S_i and S_j. They are positive when acting towards the origin of the plate.

(d) Displacements v_i and v_j in the plane of the plate and normal to the edges. The corresponding transverse membrane forces per unit length are N_i and N_j. They are positive if they produce tension in the plate.

It is assumed that the edge displacement and edge forces can be expanded into Fourier series. The relationship between the edge forces and edge displacements are established by a semi-inverse technique, in which an arbitrary harmonic of one of the displacements is applied to one edge and the resulting homogeneous boundary value problem is solved for the displacements within the plate. These displacements define the resulting internal forces in the plate and in particular, they establish the relationship between the edge forces and edge displacements. Using these relationships, four equilibrium conditions at each of the internal joint and four boundary conditions for each of the longitudinal boundaries are written,

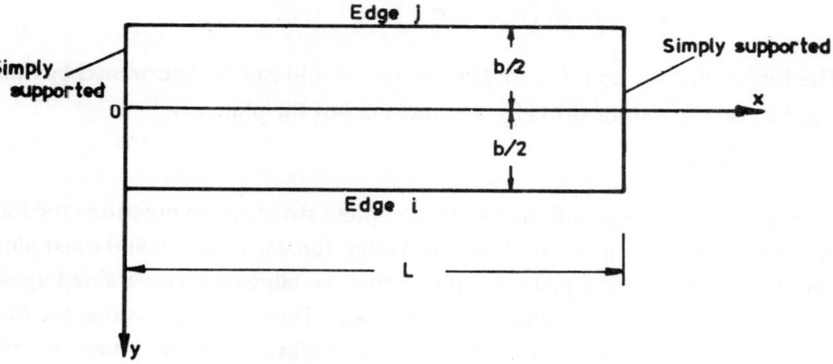

Fig. 8.6 A local coordinate system for an individual plate.

which result in $4n$ simultaneous equations (where n is the number of plates) and these equations are solved to determine the unknown displacements. The joint as well as internal forces are then obtained by using these known displacements.

8.4.1.1 Basic equations

The governing differential equation for a laterally loaded plate (slab action) is

$$\nabla^4 w = q/D \tag{8.1}$$

The moments and shear forces in the plate can be determined from

$$M_x = -D\left(\frac{\partial^2 w}{\partial x^2} + \nu\,\frac{\partial^2 w}{\partial y^2}\right),\quad M_y = -D\left(\frac{\partial^2 w}{\partial y^2} + \nu\,\frac{\partial^2 w}{\partial x^2}\right)$$

$$M_{xy} = -D\,(1-\nu)\,\frac{\partial^2 w}{\partial x\,\partial y} \tag{8.2}$$

$$Q_x = -D\frac{\partial}{\partial x}\nabla^2 w,\quad Q_y = -D\frac{\partial}{\partial y}\nabla^2 w$$

where D is the flexural rigidity of the plate.

The governing differential equations for a plate in a plane state of stress and loaded in its own plane (plate action) in terms of displacements are

$$\frac{\partial^2 u}{\partial x^2} + \frac{\partial^2 u}{\partial y^2} + \left(\frac{1+\nu}{1-\nu}\right)\frac{\partial}{\partial x}\left(\frac{\partial u}{\partial x} + \frac{\partial v}{\partial y}\right) = 0$$

$$\frac{\partial^2 v}{\partial x^2} + \frac{\partial^2 v}{\partial y^2} + \left(\frac{1+\nu}{1-\nu}\right)\frac{\partial}{\partial y}\left(\frac{\partial u}{\partial x} + \frac{\partial v}{\partial y}\right) = 0 \tag{8.3}$$

The stresses can be determined from

$$\sigma_x = \frac{E}{1-\nu^2}\left(\frac{\partial u}{\partial x} + \nu\,\frac{\partial v}{\partial y}\right);\quad \sigma_y = \frac{E}{1-\nu^2}\left(\frac{\partial v}{\partial y} + \nu\,\frac{\partial u}{\partial x}\right)$$

$$\tau_{xy} = \frac{E}{2\,(1+\nu)}\left(\frac{\partial u}{\partial y} + \frac{\partial v}{\partial x}\right) \tag{8.4}$$

The forces N_x, N_y and N_{xy} are per unit length and can be determined by multiplying the corresponding stress by the thickness of the plate (d).

8.4.1.2 Solution

Before deriving the equations for the complete structure, expressions for forces in individual plate are derived. The fixed edge forces, which would exist along the longitudinal edges of a plate, assuming that the edges are constrained against all displacements, due to loading are first given. Then the expressions for forces in individual plate resulting from various edge displacements are given. Combining these two, equations for the complete structure are obtained by considering the equilibrium at each joint.

(a) Fixed edge forces for a loaded plate

(i) Uniform load normal to the plate

The boundary conditions are (Fig. 8.6)

$$w = \frac{\partial^2 w}{\partial x^2} = 0 \text{ for } x = 0 \text{ and } x = L$$

$$w = \frac{\partial w}{\partial y} = 0 \text{ for } y = \pm (b/2) \tag{8.5}$$

The expression for the deflection w of a thin plate subjected to a lateral load of intensity q, satisfying the above boundary conditions, is

$$w = \left(\frac{4q}{D}\right) \frac{L^4}{n^5 \pi^5} \{\lambda_3 [S_1(y) - (1 + k_c) C(y)] + 1\} \sin \frac{n\pi x}{L} \tag{8.6}$$

(for simplicity, the summation signs are not shown). The resulting internal forces for this case are

$$M_{xF} = 4q (1 - \nu) \frac{L^2}{n^3 \pi^3} \sin \frac{n \pi x}{L}$$

$$\left\{\lambda_3 [S_1(y) - (\mu_3 + k_c) C(y)] + \frac{1}{1 - \nu}\right\} \tag{8.7}$$

$$M_{yF} = \frac{-4q (1 - \nu) L^2}{n^3 \pi^3} \sin \frac{n \pi x}{L}$$

$$\left\{\lambda_3 [S_1(y) + (\mu_3 - k_c) C(y)] - \frac{\nu}{1 - \nu}\right\} \tag{8.8}$$

$$Q_{xF} = \frac{-4qL}{n^2 \pi^2} \cos \frac{n\pi x}{L} [2 \lambda_3 C(y) - 1] \tag{8.9}$$

$$Q_{yF} = \frac{-8 q L}{n^2 \pi^2} \sin \frac{n \pi x}{L} \lambda_3 S(y) \tag{8.10}$$

$$M_{yxF} = M_{xyF} = -4q (1 - \nu) \left(\frac{L^2}{n^3 \pi^3}\right)$$

$$\cos \frac{n \pi x}{L} \lambda_3 [C_1(y) - k_c S(y)] \tag{8.11}$$

The fixed edge forces are

$$M_{Fij} = -M_{Fji} = 4q \frac{L^2}{n^3 \pi^3} \sin \frac{n \pi x}{L} [2\lambda_3 \cosh \alpha - 1] \tag{8.12}$$

$$V_{Fij} = V_{Fji} = \frac{8qL}{n^2 \pi^2} \sin \frac{n \pi x}{L} \lambda_3 \sinh \alpha \tag{8.13}$$

$\left(\text{where } V_{Fij} \text{ is determined from } V_y = Q_y + \frac{\partial M_{yx}}{\partial x}\right)$.

(ii) Uniform load in the plane of the plate

The boundary conditions are (Fig.8.6)

$$\sigma_x = v = 0 \quad \text{for } x = 0 \text{ and } x = L$$

$$u = v = 0 \quad \text{for } y = \pm(b/2) \tag{8.14}$$

The load term is introduced in the differential equations in terms of displacement, by considering the load as a constant body force.

The expressions for the in-plane displacements u and v, when an in plane load of intensity p is acting in the y-direction, can be obtained as

$$u = \frac{4pd}{D_2}\frac{L^2}{n^3\pi^3}\lambda_6\,[C_1(y) - k_c\,S(y)]\cos\frac{n\pi x}{L} \tag{8.15}$$

$$v = \frac{4pd}{D_2}\frac{L^2}{n^3\pi^3}\{\lambda_6\,[S_1(y) - (\mu + k_c)C(y)] + 1\}\sin\frac{n\pi x}{L} \tag{8.16}$$

The resulting internal forces for this case are

$$N_{xF} = \frac{-8pdL}{n^2\pi^2}\sin\frac{n\pi x}{L}\lambda_6\,[C_1(y) - (k_c - \mu_4)\,S(y)] \tag{8.17}$$

$$N_{yF} = \frac{8pdL}{n^2\pi^2}\sin\frac{n\pi x}{L}\lambda_6\,[C_1(y) - (k_c + \mu_5)\,S(y)] \tag{8.18}$$

$$N_{xyF} = N_{yxF} = \frac{4pdL}{(n\pi)^2}\{2\lambda_6\,[S_1(y)$$

$$- (k_c + \mu_6)\,C(y)] + 1\}\cos\frac{n\pi x}{L} \tag{8.19}$$

The fixed edge forces are

$$N_{Fij} = N_{Fji} = \frac{-8pdL}{n^2\pi^2}\mu_5\,(\lambda_6\sinh\alpha)\sin\frac{n\pi x}{L} \tag{8.20}$$

$$S_{Fij} = -S_{Fji} = \frac{-4pdL}{n^2\pi^2}[2\lambda_6\,\mu_5\cosh\alpha - 1]\cos\frac{n\pi x}{L} \tag{8.21}$$

(b) Edge forces due to displacements

Expressions for the internal forces resulting from the various generalized edge displacements are given below. As explained earlier there are in total four displacements, two normal to the plane of the plate and the other two in the plane of the plate. For the determination of internal forces due to edge displacement normal to the plane plate, plate theory has to be used, while for the displacements in the plane of the plate, two-dimensional elasticity theory is to be used.

(i) Displacements normal to plate

1. Due to rotations θ_i and θ_j of edges *i* and *j*

The boundary conditions are (Fig. 8.5)

$$w = \frac{\partial^2 w}{\partial x^2} = 0 \text{ for } x = 0 \text{ and } L$$

$$w = 0 \text{ for } y = \pm\, b/2$$

and

$$\left(\frac{\partial w}{\partial y}\right)_{y=b/2} = \theta_i(x) = \bar{\theta}_i \sin\frac{n\pi x}{L}$$

$$\left(\frac{\partial w}{\partial y}\right)_{y=-b/2} = \theta_j(x) = \bar{\theta}_j \sin\frac{n\pi x}{L} \tag{8.22}$$

The solution for the displacement *w*, satisfying the above boundary conditions can be written as

$$\begin{aligned} w = \frac{1}{2} s_{-1}(x) \,[\, & \bar{\theta}_i \,\{\lambda_1 (s_1(y) - k_t\, C(y)) \\ & - \lambda_2 (C_1(y) - k_c\, S(y))\} \\ & - \bar{\theta}_j \,\{\lambda_1 (S_1(y) - k_t\, C(y)) + \lambda_2 (C_1(y) - k_c\, S(y))\}\,] \end{aligned} \tag{8.23}$$

The internal forces can be determined as

$$\begin{aligned} M_x = D_1 s_1(x) \,[\, & \bar{\theta}_i \,\{\lambda_1 (S_1(y) - (\mu_2 + k_t)\, C(y)) \\ & - \lambda_2 (C_1(y) - (\mu_2 + k_c)\, S(y))\} \\ & - \bar{\theta}_j \,\{\lambda_1 (S_1(y) - (\mu_2 + k_t)\, C(y)) + \lambda_2 (C_1(y) \\ & - (\mu_2 + k_c)\, S(y))\}] \end{aligned} \tag{8.24}$$

$$\begin{aligned} M_y = D_1 s_1(x) \,[\, & \bar{\theta}_i \,\{- \lambda_1 (S_1(y) + (\mu_1 - k_t)\, C(y)) \\ & + \lambda_2 (C_1(y) + (\mu_1 - k_c)\, S(y))\} \\ & + \bar{\theta}_j \,\{\lambda_1 (S_1(y) + (\mu_1 - k_t)\, C(y)) \\ & + \lambda_2 (C_1(y) + (\mu_1 - k_c)\, S(y))\}\,] \end{aligned} \tag{8.25}$$

$$\begin{aligned} Q_x = D c_2(x) \,\{ & \bar{\theta}_i \,(- \lambda_1\, C(y) + \lambda_2\, S(y)) \\ & + \bar{\theta}_j \,(\lambda_1\, C(y) + \lambda_2\, S(y))\} \end{aligned} \tag{8.26}$$

$$\begin{aligned} Q_y = D s_2(x) \,\{ & \bar{\theta}_i \,(- \lambda_1\, S(y) + \lambda_2\, C(y)) \\ & + \bar{\theta}_j \,(\lambda_1\, S(y) + \lambda_2\, C(y))\} \end{aligned} \tag{8.27}$$

$$M_{xy} = M_{yx} = D_1 c_1(x)\ [\bar{\theta}_i\ \{-\lambda_1\ (C_1(y) + (1 - k_t)\ S(y)) + \lambda_2\ (S_1(y) + (1 - k_c)\ C(y))\} + \bar{\theta}_j\ \{\lambda_1\ (C_1(y) + (1 - k_t)\ S(y)) + \lambda_2\ (S_1(y) + (1 - k_c)\ C(y))\}] \tag{8.28}$$

2. Due to displacements w_i and w_j of the edges i and j

The boundary conditions are (Fig. 8.6)

$$w = \frac{\partial^2 w}{\partial x^2} = 0 \quad \text{for} \quad x = 0 \text{ and } L$$

$$\frac{\partial w}{\partial y} = 0 \quad \text{for} \quad y = \pm\ b/2$$

$$(w)_{y=b/2} = w_i(x) = \bar{w}_i \sin \frac{n\pi x}{L}$$

$$(w)_{y=-b/2} = w_j(x) = \bar{w}_j \sin \frac{n\pi x}{L} \tag{8.29}$$

The solution for the displacement w satisfying the above boundary conditions can be written as

$$w = \frac{1}{2} s(x)\ [-\bar{w}_i\ \{\lambda_3\ (S_1(y) - (1 + k_c)\ C(y)) - \lambda_4\ (C_1(y) - (1 + k_t)\ S(y))\} - \bar{w}_j\ \{\lambda_3\ (S_1(y) - (1 + k_c)\ C(y)) + \lambda_4\ (C_1(y) - (1 + k_t)\ S(y))\}] \tag{8.30}$$

The internal forces are

$$M_x = D_1 s_2(x)\ [-\bar{w}_i\ \{\lambda_3\ (S_1(y) - (\mu_3 + k_c)\ C(y)) - \lambda_4\ (C_1(y) - (\mu_3 + k_t)\ S(y))\} - \bar{w}_j\ \{\lambda_3\ (S_1(y) - (\mu_3 + k_c)\ C(y)) + \lambda_4\ (C_1(y) - (\mu_3 + k_t)\ S(y))\}] \tag{8.31}$$

$$M_y = D_1 s_2(x)\ [-\bar{w}_i\ \{-\lambda_3(S_1(y) + (\mu_3 - k_c)\ C(y)) + \lambda_4(C_1(y) + (\mu_3 - k_t)\ S(y))\} + \bar{w}_j\ \{\lambda_3\ (S_1(y) + (\mu_3 - k_c)\ C(y)) + \lambda_4\ (C_1(y) + (\mu_3 - k_t)\ S(y))\}] \tag{8.32}$$

$$Q_x = D c_3(x)\ \{-\bar{w}_i\ (-\lambda_3\ C(y) + \lambda_4\ S(y)) + \bar{w}_j\ (\lambda_3\ C(y) + \lambda_4\ S(y))\} \tag{8.33}$$

$$Q_y = D s_3(x)\ \{-\bar{w}_i\ (-\lambda_3\ S(y) + \lambda_4\ C(y)) + \bar{w}_j\ (\lambda_3\ S(y) + \lambda_4\ C(y))\} \tag{8.34}$$

$$M_{xy} = M_{yx} = D_1 c_2(x) [-\overline{w}_i \{-\lambda_3(C_1(y) + k_c S(y)) + \lambda_4 (S_1(y) - k_t C(y))\} + \overline{w}_j \{\lambda_3(C_1(y) - k_c S(y)) + \lambda_4 (S_1(y) - k_t C(y))\}] \quad (8.35)$$

(ii) Displacements in the plane of plate

1. Due to displacements v_i and v_j in the plane of the plate and normal to edges i and j.

The boundary conditions for this case are (Fig. 8.6)

$$\sigma_x = v = 0 \text{ for } x = 0 \text{ and } L$$

$$u = 0 \text{ for } y = \pm b/2$$

$$(v)_{y=b/2} = v_i(x) = \overline{v}_i \sin \frac{n\pi x}{L}$$

$$(v)_{y=-b/2} = v_j(x) = \overline{v}_j \sin \frac{n\pi x}{L} \quad (8.36)$$

Based on two-dimensional elasticity theory, the solutions for in-plane displacements u and v can be obtained as

$$u = \frac{1}{2} c(x) [\overline{v}_i \{\lambda_5 (S_1(y) - k_t C(y)) - \lambda_6 (C_1(y) - k_c S(y))\} - \overline{v}_j \{\lambda_5 (S_1(y) - k_t C(y)) + \lambda_6 (C_1(y) - k_c S(y))\}] \quad (8.37)$$

$$v = \frac{1}{2} s(x) [\overline{v}_i \{\lambda_5 (C_1(y) - (\mu + k_t) S(y)) - \lambda_6 (S_1(y) - (\mu + k_c) C(y))\} - \overline{v}_j \{\lambda_5 (C_1(y) - (\mu + k_t) S(y)) + \lambda_6 (S_1(y) - (\mu + k_c) C(y))\}]$$

The expressions for the internal forces can be obtained as

$$N_x = D_2 s_1(x) [\overline{v}_i \{-\lambda_5 (S_1(y) + (\mu_4 - k_t) C(y)) + \lambda_6 (C_1(y) + (\mu_4 - k_c) S(y))\} + \overline{v}_j \{\lambda_5 (S_1(y) + (\mu_4 - k_t) C(y)) + \lambda_6 (C_1(y) + (\mu_4 - k_c) S(y))\}] \quad (8.38)$$

$$N_y = D_2 s_1(x) [\overline{v}_i \{\lambda_5 (S_1(y) - (\mu_5 + k_t) C(y)) - \lambda_6 (C_1(y) - (\mu_5 + k_c) S(y))\} - \overline{v}_j \{\lambda_5 (S_1(y) - (\mu_5 + k_t) C(y)) + \lambda_6 (C_1(y) - (\mu_5 + k_c) S(y))\}] \quad (8.39)$$

$$N_{xy} = N_{yx} = D_2 c_1(x) \, [\bar{v}_i \, \{\lambda_5 \, (C_1(y) - (\mu_6 + k_t) \, S(y)) - \lambda_6 \, (S_1(y) - (\mu_6 + k_c) \, C(y))\} - \bar{v}_j \, \{\lambda_5 \, (C_1(y) - (\mu_6 + k_t) \, S(y)) + \lambda_6 \, (S_1(y) - (\mu_6 + k_c) \, C(y))\}] \quad (8.40)$$

2. Due to displacements u_i and u_j along edges i and j

The boundary conditions are

$$\sigma_x = v = 0 \text{ for } x = 0 \text{ and } L \text{ (Fig. 8.6)}$$

$$(u)_{y=b/2} = u_i(x) = \bar{u}_i \cos \frac{n \pi x}{L}$$

$$(u)_{y=-b/2} = u_j(x) = \bar{u}_j \cos \frac{n \pi x}{L} \quad (8.41)$$

$$u = \frac{1}{2} c(x) \, [-\bar{u}_i \, \{\lambda_7 (S_1(y) + (\mu - k_c) \, C(y)) - \lambda_8 (C_1(y) + (\mu - k_t) \, S(y))\} - \bar{u}_j \, \{\lambda_7 (S_1(y) + (\mu - k_c) \, C(y)) + \lambda_8 (C_1(y) + (\mu - k_t) \, S(y))\}] \quad (8.42)$$

$$v = \frac{1}{2} s(x) \, [-\bar{u}_i \, \{\lambda_7 \, (C_1(y) - k_c S(y)) - \lambda_8 \, (S_1(y) - k_t \, C(y))\} - \bar{u}_j \, \{\lambda_7 \, (C_1(y) - k_c S(y)) + \lambda_8 (S_1(y) - k_t C(y))\}] \quad (8.43)$$

The equations for internal forces are

$$N_x = D_2 s_1(x) \, [\bar{u}_i \, \{\lambda_7 (S_1(y) + (\mu_7 - k_c) \, C(y)) - \lambda_8 (C_1(y) + (\mu_7 - k_t) \, S(y))\} + \bar{u}_j \, \{\lambda_7 (S_1(y) + (\mu_7 - k_c) \, C(y)) + \lambda_8 \, (C_1(y) + (\mu_7 - k_t) \, S(y))\}] \quad (8.44)$$

$$N_y = D_2 s_1(x) \, [-\bar{u}_i \, \{\lambda_7 (S_1(y) + (\mu_6 - k_c) \, C(y)) - \lambda_8 \, (C_1(y) + (\mu_6 - k_t) \, S(y))\} - \bar{u}_j \, \{\lambda_7 (S_1(y) + (\mu_6 - k_c) \, C(y)) + \lambda_8 \, (C_1(y) + (\mu_6 - k_t) \, S(y))\}] \quad (8.45)$$

$$N_{xy} = D_2 c_1(x) \, [-\bar{u}_i \, \{\lambda_7 \, (C_1(y) + (\mu_5 - k_c) \, S(y)) - \lambda_8 \, (S_1(y) + (\mu_5 - k_t) \, C(y))\} - \bar{u}_j \, \{\lambda_7 \, (C_1(y) + (\mu_5 - k_c) \, S(y)) + \lambda_8 \, (S_1(y) + (\mu_5 - k_t) \, C(y))\}] \quad (8.46)$$

where

$$\alpha = \frac{n\pi b}{2L},\ s(x) = \sin\frac{n\pi x}{L},\ s_{-1}(x) = \frac{L}{n\pi}\sin\frac{n\pi x}{L}$$

$$s_1(x) = \frac{n\pi}{L}\sin\frac{n\pi x}{L},\ s_2(x) = \frac{n^2\pi^2}{L^2}\sin\frac{n\pi x}{L},$$

$$s_3(x) = \frac{n^3\pi^3}{L^3}\sin\frac{n\pi x}{L},\ c(x) = \cos\frac{n\pi x}{L},\ c_1(x) = \frac{n\pi}{L}\cos\frac{n\pi x}{L}$$

$$c_2(x) = \frac{n^2\pi^2}{L^2}\cos\frac{n\pi x}{L},\ c_3(x) = \frac{n^3\pi^3}{L^3}\cos\frac{n\pi x}{L},$$

$$\lambda_1 = (\alpha \operatorname{sech}\alpha + \sinh\alpha)^{-1},\ \lambda_2 = (\alpha \operatorname{cosech}\alpha - \cosh\alpha)^{-1},$$

$$\lambda_3 = (\alpha \operatorname{cosech}\alpha + \cosh\alpha)^{-1},\ \lambda_4 = (\alpha \operatorname{sech}\alpha - \sinh\alpha)^{-1},$$

$$\lambda_5 = (\alpha \operatorname{sech}\alpha - \mu\sinh\alpha)^{-1},\ \lambda_6 = (\alpha \operatorname{cosech}\alpha + \mu\cosh\alpha)^{-1},$$

$$\lambda_7 = (\alpha \operatorname{cosech}\alpha - \mu\cosh\alpha)^{-1},\ \lambda_8 = (\alpha \operatorname{sech}\alpha + \mu\sinh\alpha)^{-1}$$

$$S(y) = \sinh\frac{n\pi y}{L},\ C(y) = \cosh\frac{n\pi y}{L},\ S_1(y) = \frac{n\pi y}{L}\sinh\frac{n\pi y}{L},$$

$$C_1(y) = \frac{n\pi y}{L}\cosh\frac{n\pi y}{L},\ k_t = \alpha\tanh\alpha,\ k_c = \alpha\coth\alpha\ .$$

$$\mu = \left(\frac{3-\nu}{1+\nu}\right),\ \mu_1 = \left(\frac{2}{1-\nu}\right),\ \mu_2 = \left(\frac{2\nu}{1-\nu}\right),\ \mu_3 = \left(\frac{1+\nu}{1-\nu}\right),$$

$$\mu_4 = \left(\frac{2\nu}{1+\nu}\right),\ \mu_5 = \left(\frac{2}{1+\nu}\right),\ \mu_6 = \left(\frac{1-\nu}{1+\nu}\right),\ \mu_7 = \left(\frac{3+\nu}{1+\nu}\right),$$

$$D = \frac{Ed^3}{12(1-\nu^2)},\ D_1 = \frac{Ed^3}{24(1+\nu)},\ D_2 = \frac{Ed}{2(1+\nu)}$$

(c) *Joint force equations*

By combining the fixed edge forces and forces due to edge displacements, the expression for forces acting at the joint can be obtained. These are

$$M_{ij} = M_{Fij} + \frac{Ed^3}{12\ (1-\nu^2)}\frac{n}{L}\sin\frac{n\pi x}{L}$$

$$[C_1\bar{\theta}_i + C_2\bar{\theta}_j - C_3\bar{w}_i + C_4\bar{w}_j] \tag{8.47}$$

$$V_{ij} = V_{Fij} + \frac{Ed^3}{12\ (1-\nu^2)}\left(\frac{n}{L}\right)^2\sin\frac{n\pi x}{L}$$

$$[C_5\bar{\theta}_i + C_6\bar{\theta}_j - C_7\bar{w}_i + C_8\bar{w}_j] \tag{8.48}$$

$$N_{ij} = N_{Fij} + \frac{Ed}{(1 + \nu)^2} (n / L) \sin \frac{n \pi x}{L}$$
$$[- C_9 \overline{v}_i + C_{10} \overline{v}_j - C_{11} \overline{u}_i + C_{12} \overline{u}_j] \tag{8.49}$$

$$S_{ij} = S_{Fij} + \frac{Ed}{(1 + \nu)^2} (n / L) \cos \frac{n\pi x}{L}$$
$$[- C_{13} \overline{v}_i - C_{14} \overline{v}_j - C_{15} \overline{u}_i + C_{16} \overline{u}_j] \tag{8.50}$$

and

$$M_{ji} = M_{Fji} + \frac{Ed^3}{12 (1 - \nu^2)} (n/L) \sin \frac{n\pi x}{L}$$
$$[C_1 \overline{\theta}_j + C_2 \overline{\theta}_i + C_3 \overline{w}_j - C_4 \overline{w}_i] \tag{8.51}$$

$$V_{ji} = V_{Fji} + \frac{Ed^3}{12 (1 - \nu^2)} (n/L)^2 \sin \frac{n\pi x}{L}$$
$$[- C_5 \overline{\theta}_j - C_6 \overline{\theta}_i - C_7 \overline{w}_j + C_8 \overline{w}_i] \tag{8.52}$$

$$N_{ji} = N_{Fji} + \frac{Ed}{(1 + \nu)^2} (n/L) \sin \frac{n\pi x}{L}$$
$$[- C_9 \overline{v}_j + C_{10} \overline{v}_i + C_{11} \overline{u}_j - C_{12} \overline{u}_i] \tag{8.53}$$

$$S_{ji} = S_{Fji} + \frac{Ed}{(1 + \nu)^2} (n/L) \cos \frac{n\pi x}{L}$$
$$[C_{13} \overline{v}_j + C_{14} \overline{v}_i - C_{15} \overline{u}_j + C_{16} \overline{u}_i] \tag{8.54}$$

where

$$C_3 = (n/L)\, C_3^*,\ C_4 = (n/L)\, C_4^*,\ C_7 = (n/L)\, C_7^*,\ C_8 = (n/L)\, C_8^*$$

and

$$C_1 = \pi\, [\lambda_1 \cosh \alpha - \lambda_2 \sinh \alpha]$$

$$C_2 = - \pi\, [\lambda_1 \cosh \alpha + \lambda_2 \sinh \alpha]$$

$$C_3^* = C_5 = \pi^2\, [\lambda_3 \cosh \alpha - \lambda_4 \sinh \alpha - (1 - \nu)]$$

$$C_4^* = C_6 = -\pi^2\, [\lambda_3 \cosh \alpha + \lambda_4 \sinh \alpha]$$

$$C_7^* = \pi^3\, [\lambda_3 \sinh \alpha - \lambda_4 \cosh \alpha]$$

$$C_8^* = -\pi^3\, [\lambda_3 \sinh \alpha + \lambda_4 \cosh \alpha]$$

$$C_9 = \pi\, [- \lambda_5 \cosh \alpha + \lambda_6 \sinh \alpha]$$

$$C_{10} = -\pi\,[\lambda_5 \cosh\alpha + \lambda_6 \sinh\alpha]$$

$$C_{11} = C_{13} = \pi\,[\lambda_7 \cosh\alpha - \lambda_8 \sinh\alpha + (1 + \nu)]$$

$$C_{12} = C_{14} = -\pi\,[\lambda_7 \cosh\alpha + \lambda_8 \sinh\alpha]$$

$$C_{15} = \pi\,[-\lambda_7 \sinh\alpha + \lambda_8 \cosh\alpha]$$

$$C_{16} = \pi\,[\lambda_7 \sinh\alpha + \lambda_8 \cosh\alpha]$$

The directions of the corresponding joint forces and joint displacements of the two plates meeting at a joint do not, in general, have a common orientation. To facilitate the writing of the joint equilibrium equations, it is convenient to refer to the same set of axes for both the plates at a joint. To accomplish this, the displacements and forces in the (y, z) directions at each edge are transformed to the (ξ, η) directions. If a joint i with preceding joint j and following joint h is considered, then the joint displacements and forces can be transformed using the following equations. Referring to Fig. 8.7, the joint displacement transformation equations can be obtained as

$$\begin{aligned} \overline{w}_{ij} &= \overline{\eta}_i \cos\phi_{ij} - \overline{\xi}_i \sin\phi_{ij} \\ \overline{w}_{ih} &= \overline{\eta}_i \cos\phi_{ih} - \overline{\xi}_i \sin\phi_{ih} \\ \overline{v}_{ij} &= -\overline{\eta}_i \sin\phi_{ij} - \overline{\xi}_i \cos\phi_{ij} \\ \overline{v}_{ih} &= -\overline{\eta}_i \sin\phi_{ih} - \overline{\xi}_i \cos\phi_{ih} \end{aligned} \tag{8.55}$$

From Fig. 8.7, the joint force transformation equations are

$$\begin{aligned} F_{\eta ij} &= V_{ij} \cos\phi_{ij} - N_{ij} \sin\phi_{ij} \\ F_{\eta ih} &= V_{ih} \cos\phi_{ih} - N_{ih} \sin\phi_{ih} \\ F_{\xi ij} &= -V_{ij} \sin\phi_{ij} - N_{ij} \cos\phi_{ij} \end{aligned}$$

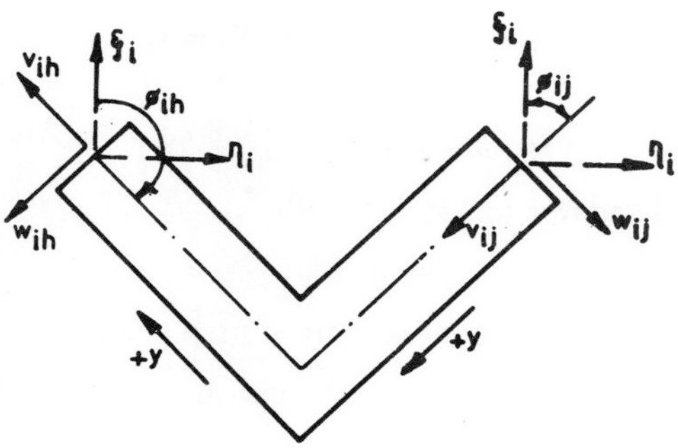

Joint i

Fig. 8.7 A global coordinate system (a) Transformation of joint displacement

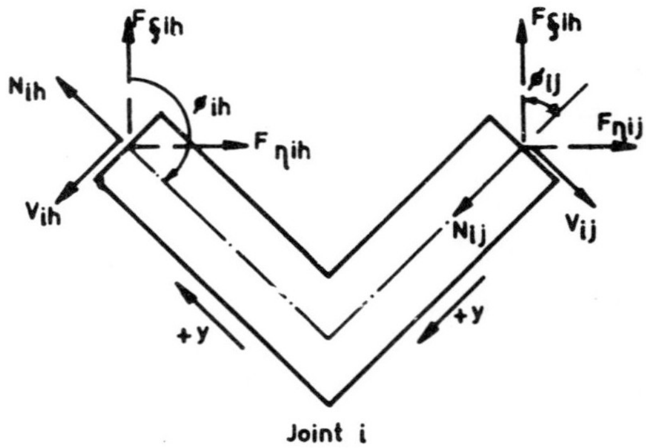

Fig. 8.7 A global coordinate system (b) Transformation of joint forces

$$F_{\xi ih} = -V_{ih}\sin\phi_{ih} - N_{ih}\cos\phi_{ih} \tag{8.56}$$

It should be noted that the above transformations which are given for span *i–h* are also applicable for span *i–j* at joint *j*.

At each joint of the folded plate structure, it is only necessary to write four equilibrium equations, since compatibility is automatically satisfied. Considering joint *i*, the joint equilibrium equations can be written as

$$M_{ij} + M_{ih} = 0; \quad F_{\eta_{ij}} + F_{\eta_{ih}} = 0$$
$$F_{\xi ij} + F_{\xi ih} = 0; \quad S_{ij} + S_{ih} = 0 \tag{8.57}$$

In writing down the above equilibrium equations at each joint, the transformed displacements are substituted into the joint force equations and the transformed forces in the equilibrium equations.

For a boundary edge or extreme edge *i* followed by joint *j*, the following boundary conditions may be written depending upon how the edge is supported.

If the edge is free,

$$M_{ij} = F_{\eta ij} = F_{\xi ij} = S_{ij} = 0 \tag{8.58}$$

If the edge is fixed,

$$\theta_{ij} = \eta_{ij} = \xi_{ij} = u_{ij} = 0 \tag{8.59}$$

If the edge is pinned and free to slide,

$$\eta_{ij} = \xi_{ij} = 0, \; M_{ij} = S_{ij} = 0 \tag{8.60}$$

If the edge is pinned and completely restrained from sliding,

$$\eta_{ij} = \xi_{ij} = u_{ij} = 0 \text{ and } M_{ij} = 0 \tag{8.61}$$

Once the joint equilibrium equations are written, these equations can then be solved to determine the unknown displacements. After determining the displacements, the forces can be computed by back substitution. It should be noted that the method involves solution of $4n$ simultaneous equations for each harmonic (where n is the number of joints).

In order to facilitate easy computations on the digital computer using the above method, Goldberg et al[8.4] have suggested the formulation of the equation in matrix form. Following the same theoretical approach of two-way slab action and deep beam effect of plates, Mast[8.5] has developed an iteration method which considerably reduces the computational effort and could be adopted both for manual computation as well as for use on the digital computer.

Solutions for folded plates with different support (other than simply supported) conditions can be obtained using Fourier series but the solution will not be in as simple a form as for the simply supported case. Goldberg et al.[8.6] have suggested a finite-difference method to solve the plate and slab equations and this method is more general as it can be applied to folded plate having any type of support conditions and loading. These methods, although general, are tedious and require considerable computational effort.

Reiss and Yitzhak[8.7] have developed a simple method for the analysis of short folded plates. The method essentially consists of treating slab action and plate action as two-dimensional. The slab action is treated as a two-way continuous system and the plate action is treated as a deep beam with in-plane loads coming from the reaction of the slab system. The two-way continuous slab analysis is done in the same way as the Hardy-cross method for a continuous beam. First, each slab is considered separately as built along the joints and fixed end moments are computed. Next, the moment difference at each joint is distributed according to the stiffness of the adjoining slabs. The distributed moments multiplied by a carry-over factor are then transferred to the next joint. The procedure is continued till the joint moment for the two adjoining slabs are the same. After the moments are balanced for all joints, the reaction at each joint is determined. The reactions of the slab are assumed to vary according to sine curve and are resolved into coplanar plate forces. The stresses and displacements are then computed by considering the beam as a deep beam. To achieve continuity at the joints, edge shear at each joint is applied and for balancing the stresses at a common joint, a stress distribution procedure has been suggested. This part of the analysis assumes that there is no joint displacement. However, the influence of joint displacement on slab action only is considered. For convenience, tables have been given for determining the moments due to slab action and stresses and displacements due to plate action for several ratios of width to length of the plate.

8.4.2 Ordinary Folded Plate Theory

The analysis of folded plate, based on ordinary folded plate theory, assumes that both the slab and plate action are one-dimensional. This means that the longitudinal plate action is governed by beam theory and the transverse slab action is that of a continuous one-way slab. The assumptions implied by the adoption of beam theory for plate action are:

(a) Longitudinal stress in each plate vary linearly across the width, but the transverse rate of variation of stress may be different in the various plates.

(b) Membrane shearing stresses in each plate have negligible effect on the deflection of the structure.

(c) Normal stress in each plate in the transverse direction is included in equilibrium considerations but have negligible effect on the deflection of the structure.

The assumptions implied by the adoption of one-way slab are:

(d) Slab bending is essentially a one-way phenomenon occurring in the transverse direction. The effect of longitudinal bending is negligible.

(e) Individual plates possess negligible torsional resistance. Torsional stresses due to twisting of the plates as well as deflections due to these stresses may be ignored.

(f) Radial shearing stresses (normal to the slab) have negligible effect on the deflection of the structure.

The limitations, which the preceding assumptions impose, are those customarily associated with beam theory and one-way slab action. Assumptions (a) and (b) do not introduce any substantial inaccuracies for plate-length to width ratios of more than three for longitudinal stress and more than five for shear deformation. This means that if the span-length to plate-width ratio is greater than five, then beam theory can be safely used for the analysis of plate action. Assumptions (d), (e) and (f) arising out of the one-way slab theory are sufficiently accurate for length to width ratios greater than three and width to thickness ratios greater than 10.

Ordinary folded plate theory can be further classified under the following two heads:

(a) Folded plate theory neglecting relative joint displacements.

(b) Folded plate theory considering the relative joint displacements.

Winter and Pei[8.8] suggested a method of analysing folded plates neglecting relative joint displacements. In addition to the assumptions already mentioned, they made a further assumption that the changes in transverse bending moment and in longitudinal stress due to relative joint displacement are negligible in comparison with the values of these moments and stresses computed on the basis of no relative joint displacements. The relative magnitude of the corrections needed to take account of the relative displacements is actually dependent on the longitudinal and transverse rigidities of the component plates — slabs as well as on the shape of the structure. In view of the large number of independent parameters involved, it is difficult to evaluate systematically, the necessary corrections. Several studies made using more rigorous methods as well as the experimental results, confirmed that in general, the necessary corrections are not negligible. Hence, folded plate theory neglecting relative joint displacement must be considered as unsatisfactory for a general case. However, this method may be safely used only where previous analysis by more rigorous theory has shown that the effects of relative joint displacements are negligible.

In the theory of folded plate considering joint displacements, the overall basic assumptions and the general assumptions of ordinary folded plate theory, both of which have already been described, are used. However, in contrast with the previous method, this theory takes into account the effect of relative joint displacements on the transverse moments and longitudinal stresses. Several practical methods based on these assumptions are available, out of which only two methods, one suggested by Whitney et al.[8.9] and the other one by Simpson[8.10] will be described here.

8.4.2.1 Whitney's method of analysis

Whitney et al.[8.9] have developed a method of analysis for a simply supported folded plate. The load acting on the folded plate is expressed by means of Fourier series, which satisfies the simply supported boundary condition for the plate action. It is suggested that for design purpose, only the first term in the series need be considered. A step-by-step procedure of Whitney's method of analysis is given below:

(a) Replace the uniform load $\bar{p}_n$ by their first Fourier components. The uniform load is expressed by means of Fourier series as (taking the origin at one support).

$$\bar{p}_n = \sum_{n=1,2}^{\infty} a_n \sin \frac{n\pi x}{L} \tag{8.62}$$

and

$$a_n = (4\,\bar{p}_n / n\pi) \text{ for } n = 1,3,\ldots$$

Hence,

$$p_n = \sum_{n=1,3}^{\infty} \frac{4\,\bar{p}_n}{n\pi} \cdot \sin \frac{n\pi x}{L} \tag{8.63}$$

Considering only the first term in the series,

$$p_n = \frac{4\,\bar{p}_n}{\pi} \sin \frac{\pi x}{L}$$

(b) From the uniform load, arrive at the corresponding ridge loads P_n. To determine the ridge loads, first the plates are considered to be hinged at the joints. Loads such as P_n (Fig. 8.8) applied at the ridges where adjacent plates meet, are known as ridge loads. Considering a unit length of the folded plate (at mid-span)

$$P_1 = p_1 b_1 + \frac{1}{2} p_2 b_2 , \quad P_2 = \frac{1}{2} p_2 b_2 + \frac{1}{2} p_3 b_3 , \ldots$$

$$P_n = \frac{1}{2} (p_n b_n + p_{n+1} b_{n+1}) . \tag{8.64}$$

It is assumed that the first plate is a cantilever while arriving at the above equation.

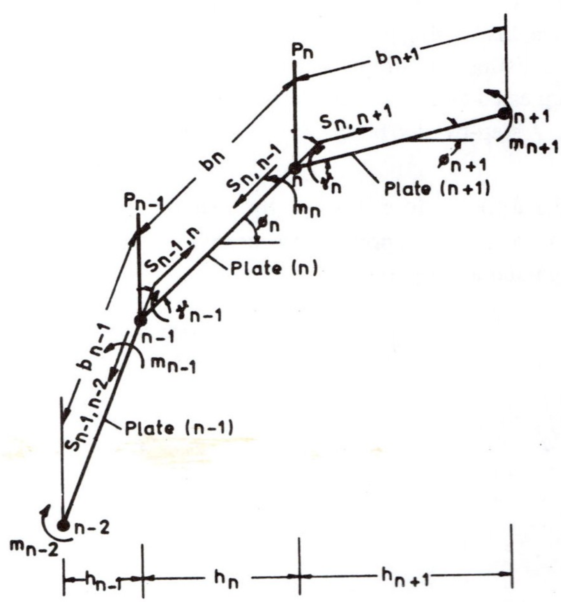

Fig. 8.8 Plate loads due to ridge loads

(c) Resolve the ridge loads and arrive at the plate loads at each joint. The plate loads are designated by $S_{n,n-1}$ (Fig. 8.8) where the first subscript n stands for the joint at which the load acts and the second subscript $(n-1)$ indicates the joint towards which the plate load is directed. Thus the plate load $S_{n,n-1}$ is directed from n to $n-1$ at ridge n, if it is positive. It is clear that the net plate load carried by the nth plate is $(S_{n,n-1} - S_{n-1,n})$.

The plate loads can be determined from the triangle of forces as

$$S_{n,n-1} = \frac{P_n \cos \phi_{n+1}}{\sin \gamma_n} \tag{8.65}$$

$$S_{n,n+1} = \frac{P_n \cos \phi_n}{\sin \gamma_n} \tag{8.66}$$

The following convention is to be observed in measuring the angles ϕ and γ. The angle ϕ is measured from each plate, pointing towards the higher order joint, to a horizontal reference line pointing to the right in a clockwise direction (Fig. 8.9) and the angle γ clockwise from the extended direction of the previous plate to the next, as indicated in Fig. 8.9.

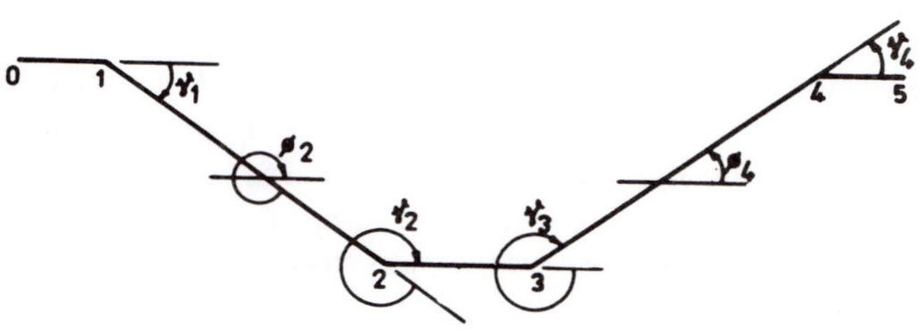

Fig. 8.9 Conventions for measuring angle between plates and horizontal

(d) In order to establish continuity at the joints, apply transverse moments m_n whose magnitudes are not known (Fig. 8.8). Due to the application of the transverse moments m_n, m_{n+1}, ... at the joints, the additional ridge loads may be computed from

$$\Delta P_n = \frac{m_{n+1} - m_n}{h_{n+1}} - \frac{m_n - m_{n-1}}{h_n} \tag{8.67}$$

(e) The above additional ridge loads ΔP_n will result in plate loads $\Delta S_{n,\,n-1}$ which can be determined from

$$\Delta S_{n,\,n-1} = \frac{\Delta P_n \cos \phi_{n+1}}{\sin \gamma_n} \tag{8.68}$$

$$\Delta S_{n,n+1} = \frac{\Delta P_n \cos \phi_n}{\sin \gamma_n} \tag{8.69}$$

(f) Compute the net plate loads R_n on the plate. For example, the plate load on the nth plate is determined as

$$R_n = (S_{n,n-1} - S_{n-1,n}) + (\Delta S_{n,n-1} - \Delta S_{n-1,n}) \tag{8.70}$$

These plate loads will involve the unknown transverse moments at the joints.

(g) The longitudinal bending moment (due to plate action) due to the resultant plate load is then computed. For example, for an nth plate, the bending moment is determined as

$$M_{o,n} = (L/\pi)^2 R_n \tag{8.71}$$

The bending stress computed for two adjacent plates at joint n from the longitudinal bending moment normally, is not the same, as the plates cannot deflect independently. Since the joints are monolithic, the bending of the plates in their own plane would introduce shear force along the joints. These edge shear forces should be of such magnitude that compatibility of the longitudinal bending stress will exist at a common joint. These edge shears can be determined in the following way.

Consider two adjacent plates (n) and ($n + 1$) subjected to moments $M_{o,n}$ and $M_{o,n+1}$ due to plate action (Fig. 8.10). If the plates were independent, they would develop different fibre stresses f_n and f_{n+1} at the joint n. Due to the joint being monolithic, edge shear forces T_{n-1}, T_n and T_{n+1} would exist at joint ($n - 1$), n and ($n + 1$) respectively. These edge shear forces are related to the corresponding edge shear stresses as

$$T_{n-1} = -\int_0^x t_{n-1}\, dx \tag{8.72}$$

$$T_n = -\int_0^x t_n\, dx \tag{8.73}$$

$$T_{n+1} = -\int_0^x t_{n+1}\, dx \tag{8.74}$$

Referring to Fig. 8.10, the fibre stress at B of plate ($n + 1$) is given by

$$\frac{M_{o,n+1}}{Z_{n+1}} + \frac{T_n b_{n+1}}{2 Z_{n+1}} + \frac{T_n}{A_{n+1}} - \frac{T_{n+1}}{A_{n+1}} + \frac{T_{n+1} b_{n+1}}{2 Z_{n+1}} \tag{8.75}$$

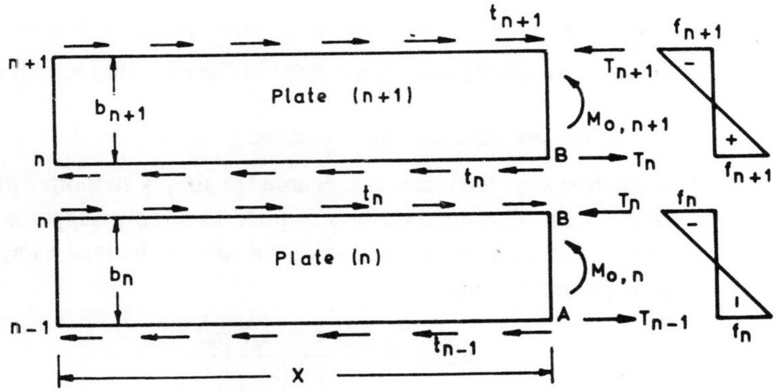

Fig. 8.10 Free edge stresses and edge shears for *n*th and (*n* + 1)th plates

where Z_{n+1} , A_{n+1} and b_{n+1} stand for the modulus of section, area and width of (*n* + 1) plate respectively. In a similar way, the fibre stress at *B* of plate (*n*) may be written as

$$-\frac{M_{o,n}}{Z_n}-\frac{T_{n-1}\,b_n}{2\,Z_n}+\frac{T_{n-1}}{A_n}-\frac{T_n}{A_n}-\frac{T_n\,b_n}{2\,Z_n} \tag{8.76}$$

where Z_n, A_n and b_n again stand for modulus of section, area and width of plate *n* respectively.

[$Z_{n+1} = \dfrac{d_{n+1}\,b_{n+1}^2}{6}$ and $Z_n = \dfrac{d_n b_n^2}{6}$ where d_n and d_{n+1}

are the thicknesses of n and (n+1) plates respectively] .

Since the fibre stress at *B* for plates *AB* and *BC* has to be the same, the two expressions may be equated to obtain

$$\frac{T_{n-1}}{A_n}+2\left(\frac{T_n}{A_n}+\frac{T_n}{A_{n+1}}\right)+\frac{T_{n+1}}{A_{n+1}}=-\frac{1}{2}\left(\frac{M_{0,n}}{Z_n}+\frac{M_{0,n+1}}{Z_{n+1}}\right) \tag{8.77}$$

This relation is called the three-shear equation. It is interesting to note that this equation is similar to the three-moment equation for continuous beams. Applying the above edge-shear equation at each joint, a system of equations are set up, solving which the edge shears can be determined in terms of the unknown transverse moments, m_2, m_3, etc.

(h) For determining the unknown transverse moments, the condition that net angular change at the joints should be zero, is used. The angular change caused due to various deformations, is given below.

(1) Change in angle caused by the slope of the plate due to slab action.

The slopes are calculated in two steps.

(i) In the first step, the plates are regarded as simply supported at the joints (Fig. 8.11). Considering the nth plate as simply supported at joints $(n-1)$ at n, its slope $\omega_{n,\,n-1}$ at joint n can be obtained using area-moment theorem. Thus

$$\omega_{n,\,n-1} = \frac{(p_n \cos \phi_n)\, b_n^3}{24\, EJ_n} \tag{8.78}$$

where $J_n = d_n^3/12$, is the moment of inertia of the plate due to slab action. Noting that $b_n \cos \phi_n = h_n$, the slope equation may be rewritten as

$$\omega_{n,\,n-1} = \frac{p_n\, h_n\, b_n^2}{2\, Ed_n^3} \tag{8.79}$$

It should be noted that p_n is the first Fourier component of the actual load $\bar{p}_n$ or $p_n = (4/\pi)\, \bar{p}_n$.

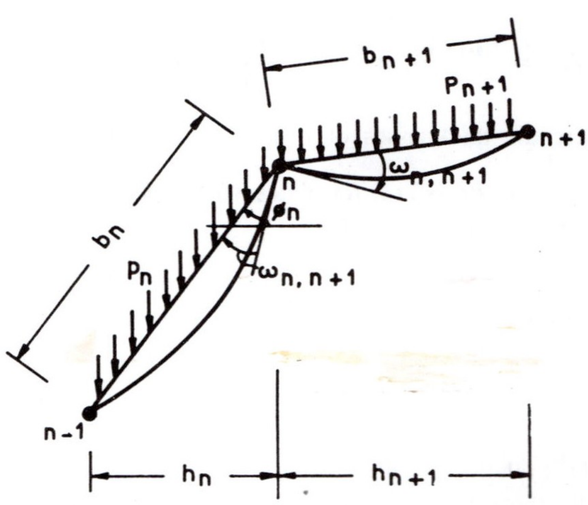

Fig. 8.11 Angle change caused by loads

Similarly,

$$\omega_{n,\,n+1} = \frac{p_{n+1}\; h_{n+1}\; b_{n+1}^2}{2\; Ed_{n+1}^3} \tag{8.80}$$

Thus the total angle change at joint n is $(\omega_{n,\,n-1} + \omega_{n,\,n+1})$.

(ii) Next, the change in angle caused by the unknown joint moment is calculated (Fig. 8.12). Applying area-moment theorem to plate n, the slope at joint n can be obtained as

$$\theta_{n,\,n-1} = \frac{b_n}{6\,EJ_n}\,(2m_n + m_{n-1}) \tag{8.81}$$

Similarly

$$\theta_{n,\,n+1} = \frac{b_{n+1}}{6\,EJ_{n+1}}\,(2m_n + m_{n+1}) \tag{8.82}$$

Hence the total change in the angle at joint n will be

$$(\theta_{n,\,n-1} + \theta_{n,\,n+1})$$

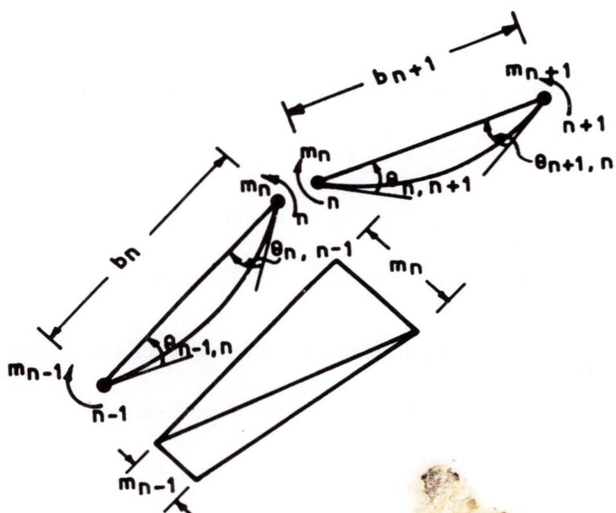

Fig. 8.12 Angle change caused by unknown transverse moments at the joints

(2) Angle change caused by in-plane plate deflections.

The in-plane plate deflections are computed in two steps and then the angular change caused by the plate deflections is computed.

(i) The in-plane deflection v_n, caused by the resultant plate load R_n, can be computed from

$$v_n = \frac{1}{EI_n} (L/\pi)^4 \; R_n \tag{8.83}$$

where $I_n = d_n b_n^3/12$

(ii) Next the in-plane deflection v'_n, caused due to edge shear, is computed. Referring to Fig. 8.13, the moment at the central section of the plate caused by a pair of edge shears T_n and T_{n-1} is

$$\frac{T_n b_n}{2} + \frac{T_{n-1}\, b_n}{2} \tag{8.84}$$

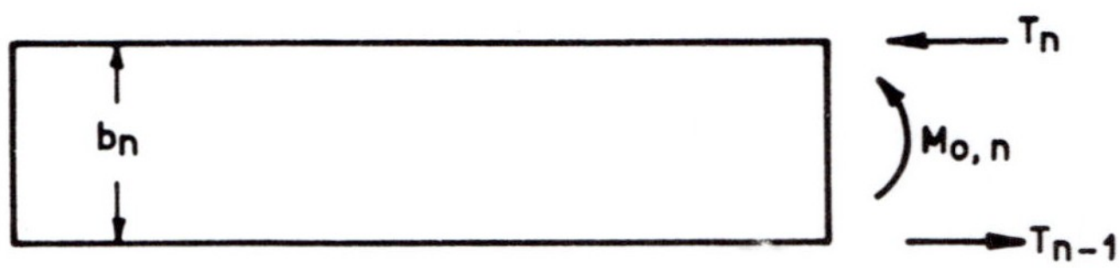

Fig. 8.13 Bending moment and edge shears acting on a typical *n*th plate

Remembering that T_n and T_{n-1} are the central amplitudes of a sine wave,

$$-EI_n \frac{d^2 v'_n}{dx^2} = \frac{T_n + T_{n-1}}{2}\; b_n \sin \frac{\pi x}{L} \tag{8.85}$$

Integrating Eq. (8.85) twice with respect to x,

$$v'_n = \frac{1}{EI_n} \frac{T_n + T_{n-1}}{2} (L/\pi)^2 \; b_n \sin \frac{\pi x}{L} \tag{8.86}$$

Hence, the magnitude of the deflection at the centre ($x = L/2$)

$$v'_n = \frac{1}{EI_n} \left(\frac{T_n + T_{n-1}}{2} \right) (L/\pi)^2 \; b_n \tag{8.87}$$

The total in-plane deflection is

$$v_n = \frac{1}{EI_n} (L/\pi)^4 \left[R_n + \frac{T_n + T_{n-1}}{2} (\pi/L)^2 \; b_n \right] \tag{8.88}$$

(iii) The plate rotation caused due to the in-plane deflection is computed next. In Fig. 8.14, v_n and v_{n+1} stand for the plate deflections taking place in the plane of the plates (n) and (n + 1); $w_{n,n-1}$, $w_{n,n+1}$, $w_{n-1,n}$ and $w_{n+1,n}$ are deflections of the plates at right angles to their planes occurring at the joints. Thus $w_{n,n+1}$ is the deflection at the joint n of the plate connecting joints n and (n + 1).

Referring to Fig. 8.14,

$$v_n = (PQ + QR) = w_{n,\,n-1}\tan\gamma_n + \frac{v_{n+1}}{\cos\gamma_n}$$

or

$$w_{n,\,n-1} = v_n\cot\gamma_n - \frac{v_{n+1}}{\sin\gamma_n} \tag{8.89}$$

Also,

$$\begin{aligned} w_{n,\,n+1} &= ST = (SQ + QT) \\ &= v_{n+1}\tan\gamma_n + \left(v_n - \frac{v_{n+1}}{\cos\gamma_n}\right)\frac{1}{\sin\gamma_n} \\ &= \frac{v_n}{\sin\gamma_n} - v_{n+1}\cot\gamma_n \end{aligned} \tag{8.90}$$

Similar expressions may be written for $w_{n-1,\,n}$ and $w_{n+1,\,n}$

Thus,

$$w_{n-1,\,n} = \frac{v_{n-1}}{\sin\gamma_{n-1}} - v_n\cot\gamma_{n-1} \tag{8.91}$$

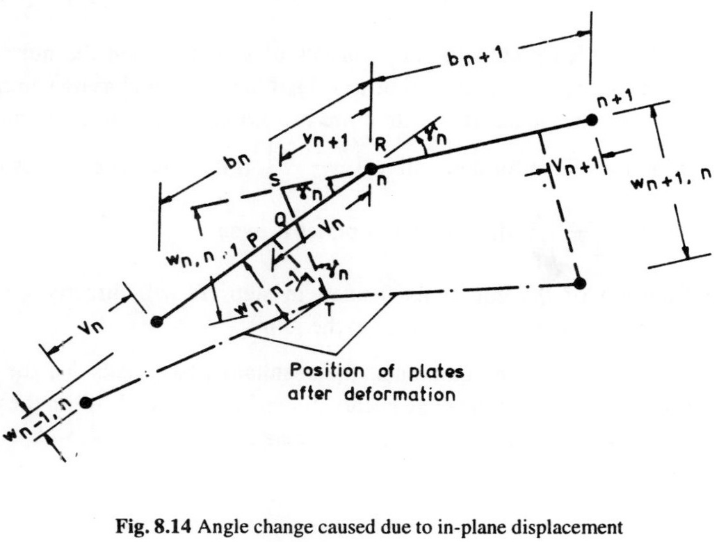

Fig. 8.14 Angle change caused due to in-plane displacement

and

$$w_{n+1,\,n} = v_{n+1} \cot \gamma_{n+1} - \frac{v_{n+2}}{\sin \gamma_{n+1}} \tag{8.92}$$

These expressions enable the rotation of plates n and $(n + 1)$ to be calculated. Denoting these by ψ_n and ψ_{n+1} .

$$\psi_n = \frac{1}{b_n} (w_{n,\,n-1} - w_{n-1,\,n})$$

$$= \frac{1}{b_n} \left[v_n (\cot \gamma_n + \cot \gamma_{n-1}) - \frac{v_{n+1}}{\sin \gamma_n} - \frac{v_{n-1}}{\sin \gamma_{n-1}} \right] \tag{8.93}$$

and

$$\psi_{n+1} = \frac{1}{b_{n+1}} \left[v_{n+1} (\cot \gamma_{n+1} + \cot \gamma_n) - \frac{v_{n+2}}{\sin \gamma_{n+1}} - \frac{v_n}{\sin \gamma_n} \right] \tag{8.94}$$

The angle change caused due to plate rotation is $(\psi_{n+1} - \psi_n)$.

(i) At the joints, no angie change can occur, as the adjoining plates are monolithically connected to form rigid joints. Hence the sum of the reductions in angle worked out in steps (1) and (2) must be set to zero, i.e.,

$$(\theta_{n,\,n-1} + \theta_{n,\,n+1}) + (\omega_{n,\,n-1} + \omega_{n,\,n+1}) + (\psi_{n+1} - \psi_n) = 0 \tag{8.95}$$

If the folded plate structure consists of n plates, then the number of equations to be formed will be $(n - 3)$, if the structure has no symmetry. On the other hand, if the structure has symmetry, then the number of equations to be formed will be $\left(\frac{n - 3}{2}\right)$, if the number of plates is odd and $\left(\frac{n - 2}{2}\right)$, if the number of plates is even.

(j) Solution of the equations formed in step (i) will directly give the unknown transverse moments at the joints.

(k) Knowing the joint moments, the resultant plate loads R_n, the plate moments $M_{o,n}$ and the edge shears T_n can be computed. With these, the fibre stresses in the plate can be computed at the central as well as other sections.

8.4.2.2 Simpson's method[8.10]

The method proposed by Simpson for the analysis of simply supported folded plate involves a series of moment and stress distributions, which could be done by hand computation. It may be recalled, in the Whitney method, the basic structure chosen is a folded plate hinged at the joints on which the effects of joint moments are subsequently superimposed in the form of additional ridge loads. In the Simpson method, the basic structure selected is a folded plate with rigid joints. To start with, the ridges are assumed nondeflecting and this portion of the analysis is identical to Winter and Pei method. The effects of ridge-displacements are subsequently accounted for in the Simpson method by allowing each plate to rotate by an arbitrary amount, which will be corrected later, by using a correction factor. The final results are obtained by superposing the rigid joint solution (no-rotation) over the rotation solution. The method is outlined below with reference to a particular cross-section of the folded plate (Fig. 8.15).

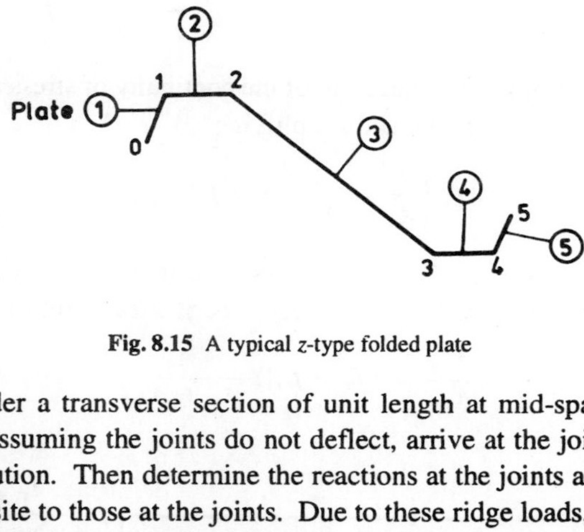

Fig. 8.15 A typical z-type folded plate

(a) Consider a transverse section of unit length at mid-span of the given folded plate Assuming the joints do not deflect, arrive at the joint moments by moment distribution. Then determine the reactions at the joints and apply forces equal and opposite to those at the joints. Due to these ridge loads, the plate loads are determined using Eqs. (8.65) and (8.66). Then determine the resultant plate loads R_n. Calculate the bending stress caused by the resulting plate loads, assuming that each plate acts independently. The bending stress at the top and the bottom fibre of the plate is computed from

$$M_{o,n} = \frac{R_n L^2}{8} \quad \text{and} \quad f_b \text{ or } f_t = \pm \frac{M_{o,n}}{Z_n} \tag{8.96}$$

where f_b and f_t are the bottom and top fibre stress and Z_n is the modulus of section of nth plate. The bending stresses computed as above will be designated as free edge stresses. It is obvious that the bending stress at a common joint of two plates, computed using the above equation will not be the same. In order to establish compatibility of stress at a joint, edge shears are to be introduced. The magnitude of these edge shears are determined using the three-shear Eq. (8.77). Instead of writing this edge shear equation at each joint and then solving a resulting set of simultaneous equations, a distribution procedure similar to moment distribution can be developed. This is possible after recognising the similarity between three-shear equation and three moment equation. Since the stresses are to be distributed to make it compatible at a joint, the distribution procedure is called as stress-distribution procedure. As is done in the case of moment-distribution procedure, it is necessary to first establish a procedure to determine the distribution and carry over factors.

(b) Stress distribution: Consider two plates (n) and (n + 1) having a common joint n and secured by the application of edge shears. When plates (n) and (n + 1) are regarded as bending independently, fibre stress f_{n+1} and f_n develop at point B of plates AB and BC (Fig. 8.16). The application of edge shears has an effect on the values of f_n and f_{n+1} so that they become equal. Referring to Fig. 8.16, first consider the effect of edge shear T_n only.

$$\frac{T_n}{A_{n+1}} + \frac{T_n\, b_{n+1}}{2\, Z_{n+1}} + f_{n+1} = -\frac{T_n}{A_n} - \frac{T_n b_n}{2\, Z_n} + f_n \tag{8.97}$$

This relation is nothing but a statement of the continuity of stress at B. Transposing terms in the above equation and simplifying

$$4T_n\left(\frac{1}{A_n} + \frac{1}{A_{n+1}}\right) = (f_n - f_{n+1}) \tag{8.98}$$

It may be seen from Eq. (8.97) that the stress f_{n+1} is to be corrected by the addition of a stress $4T_n/A_{n+1}$ to account for the effect of edge shear. But from Eq. (8.98),

$$\frac{4T_n}{A_{n+1}} = (f_n - f_{n+1})\,\frac{A_n}{A_n + A_{n+1}} \tag{8.99}$$

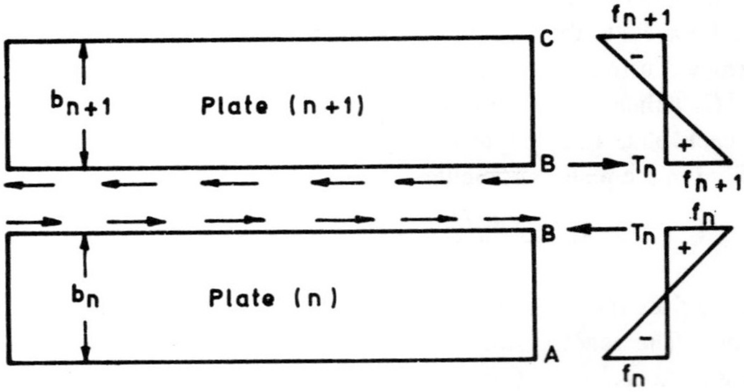

Fig. 8.16 Free edge stresses for a typical nth and (n + 1)th plate and edge shear at a typical nth joint

Similarly, the stress f_n is to be corrected by the addition of

$$-(f_n - f_{n+1}) \cdot \left(\frac{A_{n+1}}{A_n + A_{n+1}} \right) \tag{8.100}$$

From Eqs. (8.99) and (8.100), it is obvious that distribution factors for $(n + 1)$th and nth plate will be $A_n/(A_n + A_{n+1})$ and $A_{n+1}/(A_n + A_{n+1})$ respectively. The application of the edge shear T_n at B will also induce stresses at A and C, which are respectively

$$\frac{T_n}{A_{n+1}} - \frac{T_n\, b_{n+1}}{2\, Z_{n+1}} = -\frac{2T_n}{A_{n+1}} = -\frac{1}{2}\,(f_n - f_{n+1})\,\frac{A_n}{A_n + A_{n+1}} \tag{8.101}$$

and

$$-\frac{T_n}{A_n} + \frac{T_n\, b_n}{2\, Z_n} = \frac{2T_n}{A_n} = \frac{1}{2}\,(f_n - f_{n+1})\,\frac{A_{n+1}}{A_n + A_{n+1}} \tag{8.102}$$

Equations (8.101) and (8.102) may be visualised as carry-overs of the stresses distributed at B. It can be easily seen that the carry-over factor is –1/2. With the distribution factors and carry-over factor known, stress distribution can be carried out similar to moment distribution. It is to be noted that in applying the distribution process described here, proper signs are to be attached to f_n and f_{n+1}, which are regarded as positive, if tensile.

By using the stress distribution procedure, the stress compatibility at the common joint can be established. This solution will be referred to as no-rotation solution.

(c) The effects of joint displacements have now to be accounted for by considering the rotations of plates 2, 3 and 4. The first and the last plates are regarded as cantilevers (Fig. 8.15). Consider that the joint 2 will deflect by an arbitrary amount Δ_{20} below the level of joint 1 (Fig. 8.17). The fixing moment induced at 2 as a result is equal to

$$\frac{3EJ_2\, \Delta_{20}}{b_2^2} = \frac{3EJ_2\, \psi_{20}}{b_2} \quad \text{where } \psi_{20} = \frac{\Delta_{20}}{b_2} \tag{8.103}$$

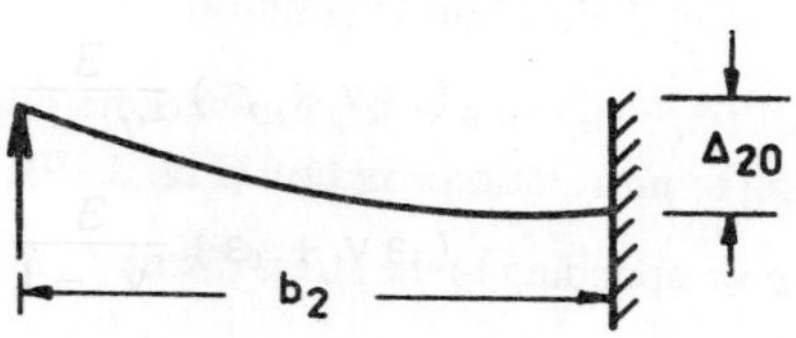

Fig. 8.17 Rotation of plate 2 due to arbitrary displacement Δ_{20}.

As Δ_{20} is arbitrary, ψ_{20} is an arbitrary rotation of plate 2. If ψ_{20} is such that the magnitude of moment induced is 3, then $\psi_{20} \doteqdot b_2/EJ_2$. The arbitrary rotation and actual rotation of the plate are clearly related by an unknown constant k_2 such that $\psi_2 = k_2 \psi_{20}$. The arbitrary moment of 3 at joint 2 is next distributed by the moment distribution procedure. The resulting joint moments and reactions are then found. Forces equal and opposite to the reactions are applied at the joints and resolved along the plates as plate loads. The free edge stresses caused by these loads are next determined. Stress compatibility at the common edge is realized by stress distribution. The resulting stresses will be referred to as Case II solution corresponding to an arbitrary rotation of plate 2.

(d) Next consider the effect of an arbitrary rotation of plate 3 (Fig. 8.18). As before, $\psi_3 = k_3 \psi_{30}$. The moment induced at joints 2 and 3 is $6EJ_3\Delta_{30}/b_3^2 = 6EJ_3 \psi_{30}/b_3$. Let the arbitrary rotation ψ_{30} be such that the magnitude of the moments induced is 6. Hence $\psi_{30} = b_3/EJ_3$. Distribute the moments of 6 units each at joints 2 and 3 by moment distribution. Arrive at the reactions at the joints and apply forces opposite to these at the joints. Resolve these forces into plate loads and compute the free edge stresses, correct these by stress distribution to achieve stress compatibility at the common edges. The resulting stresses will be referred to as the Case III solution corresponding to the arbitrary rotation ψ_{30} of plate 3. In a similar way, the case IV solution corresponding to an arbitrary rotation ψ_{40} of plate 4 is worked in the same manner as the case III solution. It should be noted that in this case

$$\psi_4 = k_4 \psi_{40} \text{ and } \psi_{40} = b_4/EJ_4 \tag{8.104}$$

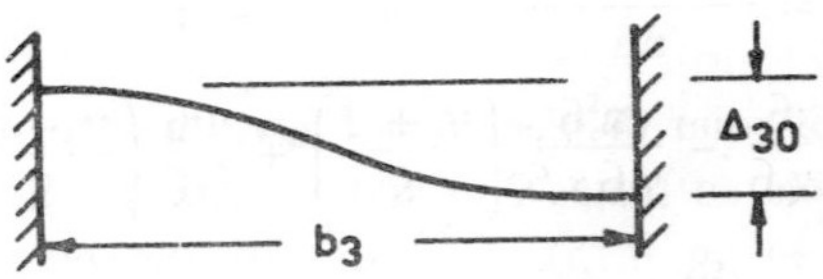

Fig. 8.18 Rotation of plate 3 due to arbitrary displacement Δ_{30}

(e) The in-plane deflections are now calculated both for the case of no-rotation as well as rotation solutions.

(i) Deflection corresponding to no-rotation solution

Let f_t and f_b be the final fibre stresses at the top and the bottom of the plate n at mid-span, corresponding to no-rotation solution (Fig. 8.19).

The plate moment corresponding to the stress distribution shown in Fig. 8.19 is

$$\frac{1}{2}(f_b - f_t)\, b_n d_n\, (b_n/6) \text{ or } \frac{1}{12}(f_b - f_t)\, b_n^2\, d_n \tag{8.105}$$

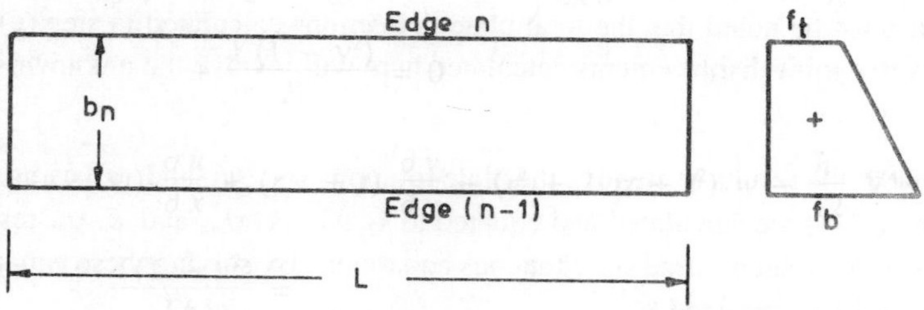

Fig. 8.19 Final longitudinal stress variation in a typical *n*th plate

If p' is the uniformly distributed load producing the moment given in Eq. (8.105), then

$$\frac{p' L^2}{8} = \frac{1}{12} (f_b - f_t)\, b_n^2\, d_n \tag{8.106}$$

The downward deflection for a plate, subjected to an uniform load of p' per unit length, at mid-span is $(5/384) \times (p' L^4/EI_n)$. Substituting for p' from Eq. (8.106) and noting that $I_n = d_n b_n^3/12$, the plate deflection v_n at mid-span can be computed as

$$v_n = \frac{5}{48} \frac{L^2}{b_n} (f_b - f_t) \tag{8.107}$$

(ii) Deflection corresponding to arbitrary rotations

Assuming that f_t and f_b are fibre stresses at mid-span due to arbitrary rotation of *n*th plate, the bending moment is identical to that given in Eq. (8.105) (Fig. 8.19). In this case (simply supported case), it is assumed that the rotation angle (and hence the corresponding plate loads) varies along the span as a half-wave of a sine curve. Two integrations of this loading will yield the bending moment, and at the centre of the span it will be proportional to $\psi_{no}\ (L^2/\pi^2)$. Similarly, the mid-span deflection is proportional to $\frac{\psi_{no}}{EI_n}\ (L^4/\pi^4)$. Hence, the deflection at mid-span may be obtained by multiplying the bending moment at that section by $\frac{1}{EI_n}\ (L^2/\pi^2)$. But, it is already shown that the bending moment in the *n*th plate is $\frac{1}{12}\ (f_b - f_t)\ d_n b_n^2$. Hence, the deflection at mid-span due to arbitrary rotation of the plate is

$$\frac{L^2}{\pi^2\, Eb_n} (f_b - f_t) \tag{8.108}$$

(f) From the plate deflections calculated in step (e), the transverse joint-displacements $w_{n-1,n}$, $w_{n+1,n}$, ..., etc., can be computed using Eqs. (8.91) and (8.92). It must be noted that the total plate deflections calculated in step (e) and the transverse joint-displacements calculated here will involve the unknown constants k_2, k_3 and k_4.

(g) From the results of step (f), the plate rotations ψ_2, ψ_3 and ψ_4 using Eqs. (8.93) and (8.94) are calculated and equated to $k_2\,\psi_{20}$, $k_3\,\psi_{30}$ and $k_4\,\psi_{40}$ respectively, to obtain a set of three simultaneous equations. By solving these equations k_2, k_3 and k_4 are determined.

(h) The final fibre stress (longitudinal) in the folded plate is obtained by combining the stresses of no-rotation solution with k_2 times the stresses of case II solution (step c), k_3 times the stresses of case III solution and k_4 times the stresses of case IV solution (step d). A similar procedure is adopted for determining the final transverse moments. For an unsymmetrical problem, the Simpson method leads to $(n-2)$ simultaneous equations, while for a symmetric problem, it leads to $(n-2)/2$ equations if the number of plates is even and $(n-3)/2$ equations if the number of plates is odd (n is the number of plates).

8.4.2.3 Ordinary folded plate theory (other support conditions)

As mentioned earlier, both Whitney's and Simpson's methods are applicable to a simply supported folded plate. However, it is common nowadays to use continuous folded plates for roofing large areas. The analysis of continuous folded plates has hence received much attention and methods based on ordinary folded plate theory have been presented by some investigators. Some of them are just extension of the procedure developed for simply supported folded plates and these will be described here briefly.

Ramaswamy[8.11] has suggested a simple method of analysis for continuous folded plates. Basically, the method is an extension of Simpson method. In this method, first it is necessary to determine the relations connecting fibre stresses and deflection due to plate action (continuous beam) at mid-span for the case of (i) no-joint displacement (no rotation) (ii) considering joint displacement (rotation case). For the case of no-rotation solution, the expressions for bending moment at the center of each span could be obtained directly, treating each plate as a continuous beam subjected to uniformly distributed load (corresponding to the plate load). For the case of rotation solution, the continuous beam is assumed to be loaded with a load proportional to the shape of the elastic line of the deflected continuous beam. For this pattern of loading, equations for bending moment and deflection at the center of each span can be obtained. Using these modified equations for stresses and deflection, the analysis is carried out in an identical way as in Simpson's method. This method perhaps, will be more suited for two or three equal span continuous folded plates.

A more general method applicable for prismatic as well as nonprismatic folded plates with different support conditions including continuous support has been developed by Beaufait[8.12]. The method is similar to Simpson method, except that the true deflected shape is used instead of an assumed deflected shape. In the plate action, instead of using the mid-section and the elastic curve of the beam, the beam is divided into a number of segments and at each segment, the longitudinal stress and deflection are computed. The analysis at each of these segments is carried in an identical way, as in Simpson method, for no-rotation and rotation solution.

Another method suggested by Mousa et al[8.13] for the analysis of continuous folded plates is more convenient for hand computation and will be described here. This method essentially follows the Simpson's method, except that the elastic curve of the individual plates in the beam-action analysis is formulated in terms of trigonometric series. In the Simpsons' method, for beam-action analysis (for no-rotation case), familiar strength of materials equations are used for computing the fibre stresses as well as the in-plane deflections.

In the method suggested by Mousa et al.[8.13], the beam-action analysis is done in the following way. The differential equation governing the displacement of a prismatic beam subjected to an arbitrary loading $q(x)$ is given by

$$\frac{d^4 v}{dx^4} = \frac{q(x)}{EI} \tag{8.109}$$

where E is the modulus of elasticity and I the moment of inertia of the beam. A beam simply supported on the two outer edges and continuous over t intermediate supports and subjected to applied load $q(x)$ is shown in Fig. 8.20. The beam can be analysed as a simply supported beam subjected to the applied load $q(x)$ and the redundant reactions R_1, R_2, R_3, ..., R_t (Ref. 8.14). The applied load and the redundant reactions can be represented by Fourier series as

$$q(x) = \sum_{m=1}^{\infty} A_m \sin \frac{m\pi x}{L} \tag{8.110}$$

$$R_k = \sum_{m=1}^{\infty} A_m^k \sin \frac{m\pi x}{L} \quad (k = 1, 2, ..., t) \tag{8.111}$$

in which

$$A_m = \frac{2}{L} \int_0^L q(x) \sin \frac{m\pi x}{L} \, dx$$

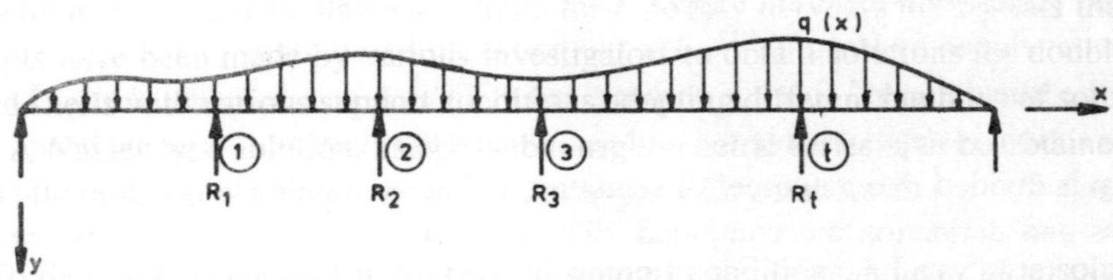

Fig. 8.20 A continuous beam with t intermediate supports

and $$A_m^k = \frac{2}{L} \lim_{\lambda \to 0} \int_{\beta L-\lambda}^{\beta L+\lambda} \frac{R_k}{2\lambda} \sin \frac{m\pi x}{L}\, dx = \frac{2R_k}{L} \sin m\pi\beta$$

in which L is the longitudinal span and β is the ratio of the distance between the end support and redundant reaction R to the total span length (Fig. 8.21). The boundary conditions for the beam are

$$v''(0) = v(0) = v(L) = v''(L) = 0 \tag{8.112}$$

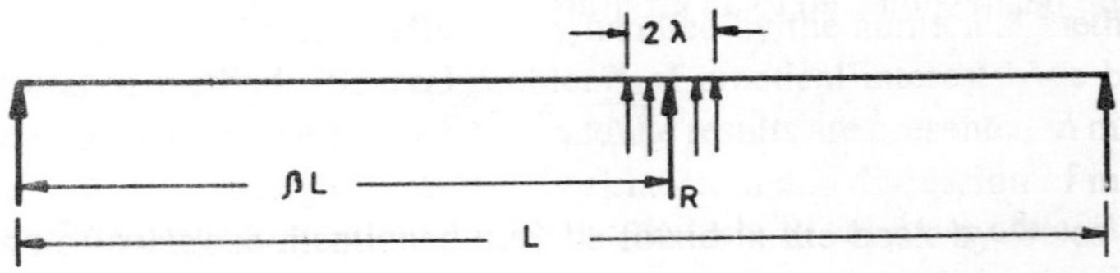

Fig. 8.21 A two span continuous beam

The expression for v satisfying the above boundary conditions can be taken as

$$v(x) = \sum_{m=1}^{\infty} B_m \sin \frac{m\pi x}{L} \tag{8.113}$$

Now the total load acting on the beam can be represented by $p(x)$ and consists of both external load $q(x)$ as well as the redundant reactions R_k.

Hence the resultant loading may be expressed as

$$p(x) = \sum_{m=1}^{\infty} \left[A_m - \sum_{k=1}^{t} A_m^k \right] \sin \frac{m\pi x}{L} \tag{8.114}$$

Substituting Eqs. (8.113) and (8.114) in Eq. (8.109), we get

$$B_m = \left(\frac{L}{m\pi}\right)^4 \left(\frac{1}{EI}\right) \left(A_m - \sum_{k=1}^{t} A_m^k\right) \tag{8.115}$$

Hence, the equation for the elastic curve can be written as

$$v(x) = \left(\frac{L}{\pi}\right)^4 \frac{1}{EI} \sum_{m=1}^{\infty} \frac{1}{m^4} \left(A_m - \sum_{k=1}^{t} R_k \sin m\pi\beta \right) \sin \frac{m\pi x}{L} \qquad (8.116)$$

For unyielding intermediate supports, the displacements at their supports vanish, i.e.,

$$v(x) = 0, \ (x = 1, 2, ..., t) \qquad (8.117)$$

in which, x is the distance about x-axis to the particular intermediate support.

Substituting Eq. (8.114) in Eq. (8.116) yields.

$$\sum_{k=1}^{t} R_k D_k = \frac{L}{2} D_\xi \ (k = 1, 2, ..., t) \qquad (8.118)$$

where

$$D_\xi = \sum_{m=1}^{\infty} \frac{A_m}{m^4} \sin m\pi L_l$$

$$D_k = \sum_{m=1}^{\infty} \frac{1}{m^4} \sin m\pi\beta \sin m\pi L_l$$

Equation (8.118) gives a set of simultaneous equations, which can be solved to determine the redundants R_1, R_2, ..., etc. Substituting the calculated reactions and the Fourier coefficient in Eq. (8.116), the expression for the elastic curve of the individual plate supported on intermediate rigid supports can be calculated.

The effect of the joint displacements (rotation of plates) can be done in an identical way as in the case of Simpson method applied to simply supported folded plate.

Following the procedure suggested by Mousa et al.[8.13] recently Chandrashekhara and Singh[8.15] have suggested a procedure for the analysis of cantilever folded plates. In this, the beam action analysis is done by selecting beam functions[8.16] satisfying the boundary conditions of a cantilever beam. They have also indicated that solutions for clamped-clamped and clamped-supported folded plate can be obtained in a similar way by selecting suitable beam functions.

8.5 Prestressed Folded Plates

For long spans, the longitudinal tensile stress becomes very large requiring large quantities of steel. Further, with large quantity of steel, placing of steel becomes difficult as there would be congestion of reinforcement and concreting also becomes very difficult. Hence, in such cases prestressing can be resorted to, to reduce the longitudinal tensile stress and thus steel. The longitudinal prestressing also reduces the transverse moments as well as the deflection of the structure.

The analysis of prestressed folded plate can be done by suitably modifying Whitney or Simpson method. In these methods, while calculating the longitudinal bending stress (due to plate loads) and deflection, the effect of prestressing force may be incorporated. Except for this small change, the rest of the procedure in the analysis remains the same.

8.6 Beam Method

The beam method as applied to folded plate structure involves the calculation of the longitudinal stresses using the well known beam flexure formula. It assumes that the variation of longitudinal stress across the entire cross-section of the structure is planar and as a result, the cross-section is supposed to move parallel to itself and will maintain its original shape even after deflection. The main and serious disadvantage of this method is that the transverse moments which exist because of monolithic joints cannot be determined.

It may be pointed out here that Evans and Rockey[8.17] have critically evaluated the methods of analysis available for simply supported folded plate structures. They have shown that an ordinary method allowing for relative joint displacements is satisfactory for the analysis of folded plate structures, in which the individual plate length to width ratio is greater than three. They have concluded that an ordinary method neglecting joint displacements, and beam method can lead to large inaccuracies and in certain cases this could be in excess of 100%. Hence, it must be said here that the ordinary method neglecting joint displacements and beam method should be used with caution.

Example 8.1

Analysis of northlight folded plate roof using Whitney's method:

The geometry of the folded plate with the dimensions is shown in Fig. 8.22. The span of the folded plate roof is taken as 18.25 m. The unit weight of concrete is assumed to be 2400 kg/m^3. It is assumed that a uniform live load of 73.25 kg/m^2 of surface area is acting on the folded plate. The following data can be taken from Fig. 8.22.

(i) Geometrical dimensions

Plate	Plate width b_n, m	Horizontal projection h_n, m	Inclination to horizontal ϕ_n	Angle between the previous plate and next plate γ_n	Thickness $d_n \times 10^{-2}$m
1	0.62	0.108	80°	80°	9
2	1.105	1.105	0	40.59°	10
3	3.75	2.85	319.41°	319.41°	9
4	1.105	1.105	0	280°	10
5	0.62	0.108	80°	—	9

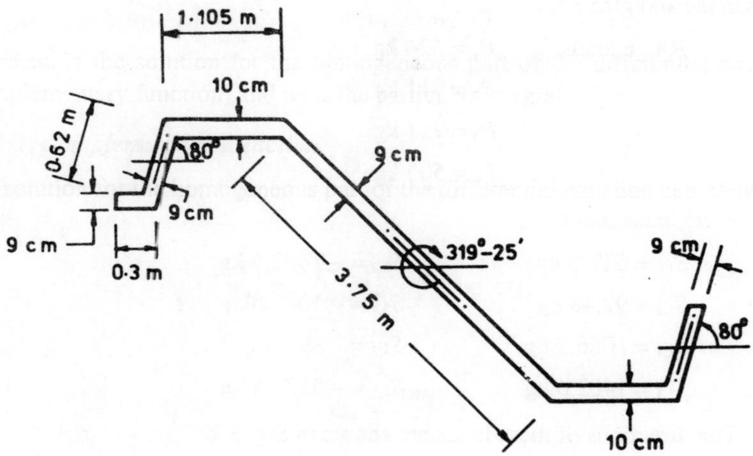

Fig. 8.22 Northlight folded plate

(ii) Geometrical Properties

Plate	A_n, m^2	Z_n, m^3	I_n, m^4	J_n, m^4
1	0.0558	0.5766×10^{-2}	0.1787×10^{-2}	0.6075×10^{-4}
2	0.1105	0.2035×10^{-1}	0.1124×10^{-1}	0.8333×10^{-4}
3	0.3375	0.2109	0.3955	0.6075×10^{-4}
4	0.1105	0.2035×10^{-1}	0.1124×10^{-1}	0.8333×10^{-4}
5	0.0558	0.5766×10^{-2}	0.1787×10^{-2}	0.6075×10^{-4}

(iii) Calculation of ridge loads, P_n

The loads per meter length of the plates are first calculated:

Plate 1 = 179.33 kg

Plate 2 = 346.14 kg

Plate 3 = 1084.69 kg

Plate 4 = 346.14 kg

Plate 5 = 179.33 kg

Knowing the load on each plate (per meter length), the ridge loads are calculated. Only the first term in the Fourier series is considered. Additional loads of 59.5 kg/m and 44.5 kg/m at joints 0 and 5 are considered which are due to sunshade and glazing.

Ridge loads: $P_1 = 524$ kg

$P_2 = 911$ kg

$P_3 = 911$ kg

$P_4 = 505$ kg

(iv) Plate loads due to P_n

$S_{1,0} = 532.5$ kg	$S_{3,2} = -1402.5$ kg
$S_{1,2} = 92.48$ kg	$S_{3,4} = -1066.5$kg
$S_{2,1} = 1066.5$ kg	$S_{4,3} = -89.1$ kg
$S_{2,3} = 1402.6$ kg	$S_{4,5} = -513.15$ kg

The directions of these loads are shown in Fig. 8.23.

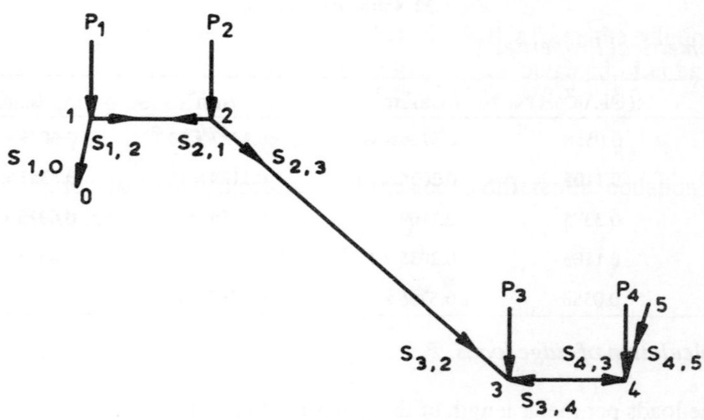

Fig. 8.23 Plate loads

(v) Additional ridge loads P_n due to transverse moments

The known moments m_1 and m_4 at joints 1 and 4 are (computed taking Plate 1 and 5 as cantilevers).

$$m_1 = -\frac{4}{\pi}(59.5 \times 0.26 + 179.33 \times 0.054) = -31.99 \text{ kg.m}$$

$$m_4 = -\frac{4}{\pi}(44.5 \times 0.1075 + 179.33 \times 0.054) = -18.41 \text{ kg.m}$$

(Sagging moments are taken as positive)

$$\Delta P_1 = \frac{m_2 - m_1}{1.105} = (0.905m_2 + 28.95)$$

$$\Delta P_2 = -\frac{m_2 - m_1}{1.105} + \frac{m_3 - m_2}{2.95} = (-28.95 - 1.26m_2 + 0.35m_3)$$

$$\Delta P_3 = \frac{m_2 - m_3}{2.85} + \frac{m_4 - m_3}{1.105} = (0.35m_2 - 1.26m_3 - 16.64)$$

$$\Delta P_4 = \frac{m_3 - m_4}{1.105} = (0.905m_3 + 16.64)$$

(vi) Additional plate loads due to P_n

$$\Delta S_{1,0} = 0.919m_2 + 29.4$$
$$\Delta S_{1,2} = 0.16m_2 + 5.1$$
$$\Delta S_{2,1} = -1.469m_2 + 0.411m_3 - 33.89$$
$$\Delta S_{2,3} = -1.934m_2 + 0.540m_3 - 44.57$$
$$\Delta S_{3,2} = -0.54m_2 + 1.934m_3 + 25.62$$
$$\Delta S_{3,4} = -0.41m_2 + 1.470m_3 + 19.48$$
$$\Delta S_{4,3} = -0.16m_3 - 2.93$$
$$\Delta S_{4,5} = -0.919m_3 - 16.89$$

(vii) Resultant plate loads R_n

$$R_n = (S_{n,n-1} - S_{n-1,n}) + (\Delta S_{n,n-1} - \Delta S_{n-1,n})$$
$$R_1 = 0.919m_2 + 561.94$$
$$R_2 = -1.629m_2 + 0.411m_3 + 935.05$$
$$R_3 = 1.394m_2 + 1.39m_3 - 2734.96$$
$$R_4 = 0.41m_2 - 1.626m_3 + 955.00$$
$$R_5 = 0.919m_3 + 530.04$$

(viii) Plate moments, M_0, n

$$M_{0,n} = R_n L^2 / \pi^2$$
$$M_{0,1} = 31.01m_2 + 18963.41$$
$$M_{0,2} = -55.00m_2 + 13.86m_3 + 31554.31$$
$$M_{0,3} = 47.02m_2 + 47.02m_3 - 92294.2$$
$$M_{0,4} = 13.85m_2 - 55m_3 + 32227.8$$
$$M_{0,5} = 31.01m_3 + 17886.9$$

(ix) Edge-shear equations

$$\frac{T_{n-1}}{A_n} + 2T_n\left(\frac{1}{A_n} + \frac{1}{A_{n+1}}\right) + \frac{T_{n+1}}{A_{n+1}} = -\frac{1}{2}\left(\frac{M_{0,n}}{Z_n} + \frac{M_{0,n+1}}{Z_{n+1}}\right)$$

Joint 1

$$4T_1\left(\frac{1}{A_1} + \frac{1}{A_2}\right) + \frac{2T_2}{A_2} = -\left(\frac{M_{0,1}}{Z_1} + \frac{M_{0,2}}{Z_2}\right)$$

Joint 2

$$\frac{2T_1}{A_2} + 4T_2\left(\frac{1}{A_2} + \frac{1}{A_3}\right) + \frac{2T_3}{A_3} = -\left(\frac{M_{0,2}}{Z_2} + \frac{M_{0,3}}{Z_3}\right)$$

Joint 3

$$\frac{2T_2}{A_3} + 4T_3\left(\frac{1}{A_3} + \frac{1}{A_4}\right) + \frac{2T_4}{A_4} = -\left(\frac{M_{0,3}}{Z_3} + \frac{M_{0,4}}{Z_4}\right)$$

Joint 4

$$\frac{2T_3}{A_4} + 4T_4\left(\frac{1}{A_4} + \frac{1}{A_5}\right) = -\left(\frac{M_{0,4}}{Z_4} + \frac{M_{0,5}}{Z_5}\right)$$

Substituting for $A_1, A_2, A_3, \ldots, A_5$, $Z_1, Z_2, \ldots, Z_5$ and $M_{0,1}, M_{0,2}, \ldots, M_{0,5}$, in the above equations and after solving the four equations, T_1, T_2, T_3, and T_4 are determined as

$$T_1 = -36.302m_2 - 1.854m_3 - 43895.1$$

$$T_2 = 68.55m_2 - 26.57m_3 - 5735.8$$

$$T_3 = -26.57m_2 + 68.56m_3 - 7241.6$$

$$T_4 = -1.854m_2 - 36.302m_3 - 42218.9$$

(x) Plate deflections

$$v_n = \frac{1}{EI_n}(L/\pi)^4\left[R_n + (T_{n-1} + T_n)(\pi/L)^2(b_n/2)\right]\sin\frac{\pi x}{L}$$

$$v_1 = \frac{10^4}{E}(37.30m_2 - 1.085m_3 + 1011)$$

$$v_2 = \frac{10^4}{E}(-11.16m_2 - 0.555m_3 + 1240.5)$$

$$v_3 = \frac{10^4}{E}(1.073m_2 + 1.073m_3 - 995.1)$$

$$v_4 = \frac{10^4}{E}(-0.554m_2 - 11.16m_3 + 1471)$$

$$v_5 = \frac{10^4}{E}(-1.085m_2 + 37.30m_3 + 9161.5)$$

(xi) Calculation of angle changes at the joints

(a) Angle change due to plate deflections

$$\psi_n = \frac{1}{b_n}\left[v_n(\cot\gamma_n + \cot\gamma_{n-1}) - \frac{v_{n+1}}{\sin\gamma_n} - \frac{v_{n-1}}{\sin\gamma_{n-1}}\right]$$

$$\psi_{n+1} = \frac{1}{b_{n+1}}\left[v_{n+1}(\cot\gamma_{n+1} + \cot\gamma_n) - \frac{v_{n+2}}{\sin\gamma_{n+1}} - \frac{v_n}{\sin\gamma_n}\right]$$

Joint 2

$$\psi_2 = \frac{10^4}{E}(-49.798m_2 - 1.173m_3 - 6471.6)$$

$$\psi_3 = \frac{10^4}{E}(4.380m_2 - 4.380m_3 + 91.15)$$

Joint 3

$$\psi_4 = \frac{10^4}{E}(1.185m_2 + 49.72m_3 + 5237.8)$$

(b) Angle change due to loads

$$\omega_n = \frac{4}{\pi}\left[\frac{p_n b_n^2 h_n}{2Ed_n^3} + \frac{p_{n+1} b_{n+1}^2 h_{n+1}}{2Ed_{n+1}^3}\right]$$

$$\omega_2 = \frac{10^4}{E}(1038.4),\quad \omega_3 = \frac{10^4}{E}(1038.4)$$

(c) Angle change due to transverse moments

Joint 2

$$\theta_{2,1} = \frac{b_2}{6EJ_2}(2m_2 + m_1) = \frac{10^4}{E}(0.44m_2 - 7.07)$$

$$\theta_{2,3} = \frac{10^4}{E}(2.058m_2 + 1.029m_3)$$

Joint 3

$$\theta_{3,2} = \frac{10^4}{E}(1.029m_2 + 2.058m_3)$$

$$\theta_{3,4} = \frac{10^4}{E}(0.442m_2 - 4.063)$$

Total angle change at each joint

$$(\omega_{n,n-1} + \omega_{n,n+1}) + (\theta_{n,n-1} + \theta_{n,n+1}) + (\psi_{n+1} - \psi_n)$$

Joint 2

$$5.669m_2 - 0.218m_3 + 759.41 = 0$$

Joint 3

$$-0.218m_2 + 5.669m_3 + 618.1 = 0$$

On solving the above equations

$$m_2 = -138.36 \text{ kg.m}$$
$$m_3 = -114.52 \text{ kg.m}$$

(xii) Calculation of T_n and $M_{0,n}$

Substituting the values of m_2 and m_3 in the expressions in steps (viii) and (ix) for $M_{0,n}$ and T_n, we get

$$M_{0,1} = 14737.2 \text{ kg.m}$$
$$M_{0,2} = 37\,687.9 \text{ kg.m}$$
$$M_{0,3} = -104547.6 \text{ kg.m}$$
$$M_{0,4} = 36\,644.5 \text{ kg.m}$$
$$M_{0,5} = 14\,398.4 \text{ kg.m}$$
$$T_1 = -38\,809.4 \text{ kg}$$
$$T_2 = -12\,206.3 \text{ kg}$$
$$T_3 = -11\,366.8 \text{ kg}$$
$$T_4 = -37\,930.3 \text{ kg}$$

Longitudinal stresses (Fig. 8.24)

Joint	Stress in kg/m^2	Stress in kg/cm^2
0	1164860	116.48
1	226156.4	22.62
2	–707660.4	–70.77
3	707684.8	70.77
4	–221898.2	–22.19
5	–1137608	–113.76

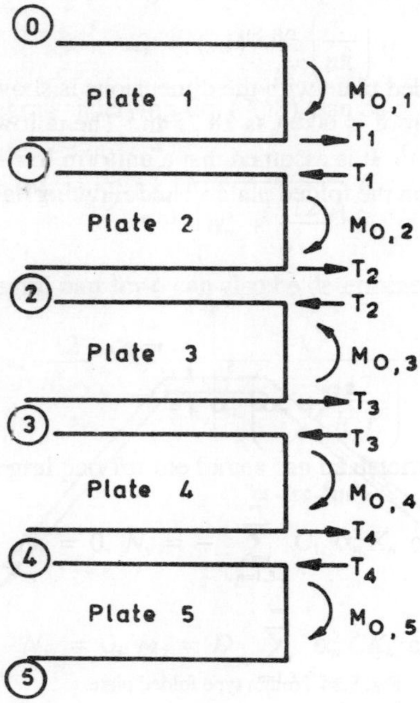

Fig. 8.24 Edge shear and bending moment on individual plates

The variations of longitudinal stress over the cross-section at mid-span is shown in Fig. 8.25.

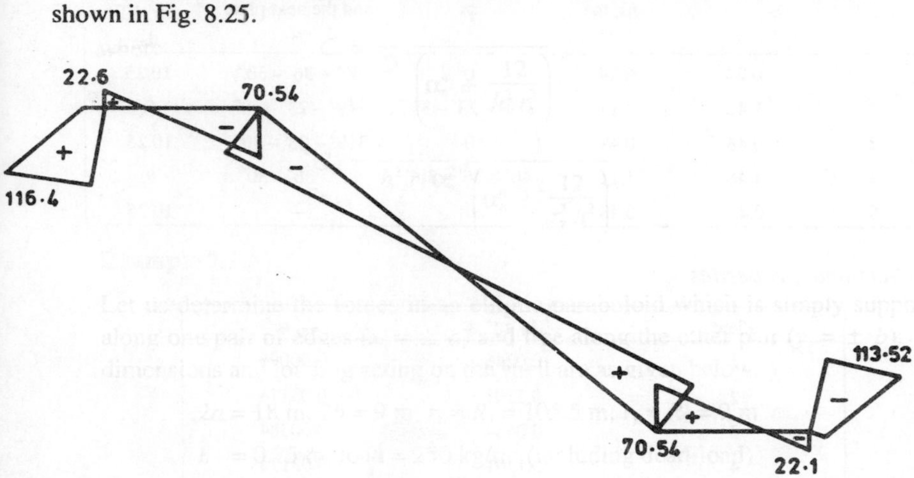

Fig. 8.25 Longitudinal stress variation at mid-span (stress in kg/cm^2)

Example 8.2

Analysis of a trough type folded plate roof using Simpson's method.

(i) Data

The geometry of the folded plate with the dimensions is shown in Fig. 8.26. The span of the folded plate roof is taken as 18.25 m. The unit weight of concrete is assumed to be 2400 kg/m^3. It is assumed that a uniform live load of 73.25 kg/ m^2 of surface area is acting on the folded plate. The following data can be taken from Fig. 8.26.

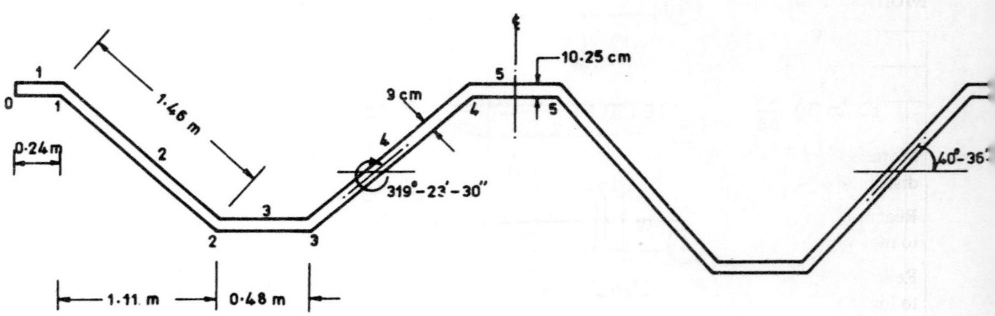

Fig. 8.26 Trough type folded plate

(a) Geometrical properties

Plate	Plate width b_n, m	Horizontal projection h_n, m	Inclination to horizontal ϕ_n	Angle between previous plate and the next plate γ_n	Thickness of plate in m × 10^{-2} d_n
1	0.24	0.24	0	40° – 36′ – 30″	10.25
2	1.46	1.11	319° – 23′ – 30″	319° – 23′ – 30″	9
3	0.48	0.48	0	319° – 23′ – 30″	10.25
4	1.46	1.11	40° – 36′ – 30″	40° – 36′ – 30″	9
5	0.48	0.48	0	—	10.25

(b) Sectional properties

Plate	A_n, m^2	Z_n, m^3
1	0.0246	0.00096
2	0.1301	0.03174
3	0.0484	0.00384
4	0.1301	0.03174
5	0.0484	0.00384

(c) Loads and fixed-end moments

Plate	Load, kg	Fixed-end moments, kg.m
1	76.62	9.19
2	419.74	38.86
3	153.12	6.0
4	419.74	38.86
5	153.24	6.0

(d) No-rotation solution

Moment distribution (no-rotation)

	1		2		3		4	
D.F.	0	1	0.14	0.86	0.82	0.18	0.18	0.82
	-9.19	38.86	−38.86	6.0	−6.0	38.86	−38.86	6.0
Moments after distribution	−9.19	9.19	−42.95	42.95	−31.87	−31.87	−33.42	33.42
Reactions due to moment		30.41↓	30.41↑	23.26↑	23.26↓	1.4↓	1.4↑	
Reactions due to loads	76.62↑	209.87↑	209.87↑	76.62↑	76.62↑	209.87↑	209.87↑	76.62↑
Total reactions		256.08↑		340.16↑		261.83↑		287.89↑
Ridge loads		256.08↓		340.16↓		261.83↓		287.89↓

Calculations of plate loads

$S_{1,0} = 256.08 \times 1.1664 = 298.68$ kg/m

$S_{1,2} = 256.08 \times 1.5364 = 393.44$ kg/m

$S_{2,1} = 340.16 \times -1.5364 = -522.62$ kg/m

$S_{2,3} = 340.16 \times -1.1664 = -396.76$ kg/m

$S_{3,2} = 261.83 \times -1.1664 = -305.38$ kg/m

$S_{3,4} = 261.83 \times -1.5364 = -402.24$ kg/m

$S_{4,3} = 287.89 \times 1.5364 = 442.31$ kg/m

$S_{4,5} = 287.89 \times 1.1664 = 335.79$ kg/m

From Fig. 8.27, the resultant plate loads can be obtained as

$R_1 = 298.68$ kg/m

$R_2 = -916.06$ kg/m

$R_3 = 91.38$ kg/m

$R_4 = 844.55$ kg/m

$R_5 = 0$

Plate	Longitudinal stresses due to plate loads				Free edge stresses t/m²	Stresses after distribution t/m²
	Load R t/m	$M = RL^2/8$ t.m	Z m³	f t/m²		
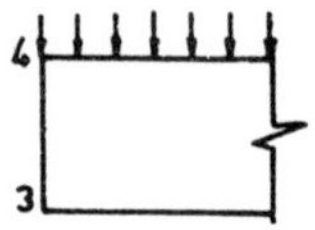	0.845	35.18	0.03173	1108.73	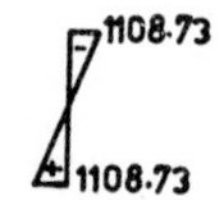	
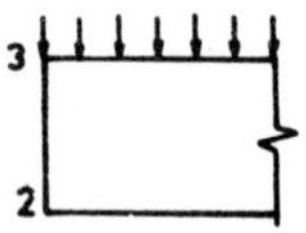	0.091	3.83	0.00384	996.03	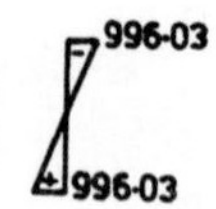	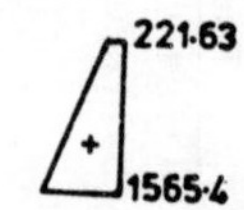
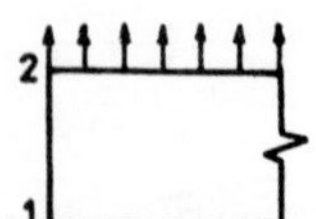	0.916	38.13	0.03174	1202.58	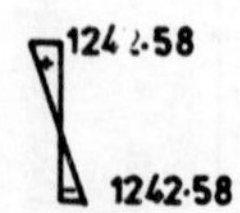	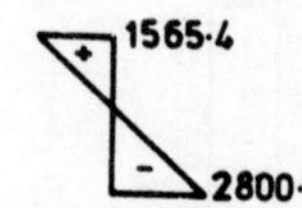
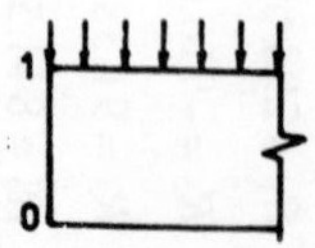	0.299	12.43	0.00096	12947.9	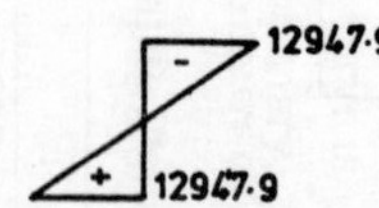	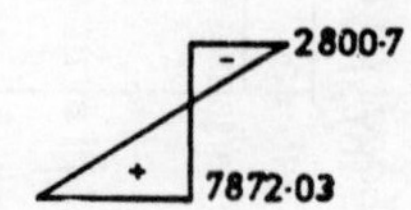

Stress distribution (No-rotation)

	0		1		2		3		4
D.F.		0.84	0.16	0.27	0.73	0.73	0.27	0.27	0.73
	12947.9	-12947.9	-1202.58	1202.58	996.03	-996.03	1108.73	-1108.73	
	-4933.05	9866.1	-1879.25	939.63					
			154.71	-309.47	836.71	-418.36			
					-920.95	1841.9	-681.2	340.6	
							-103.7	207.4	-560.7
Stresses after distribution (t/m^2)	7872.03	-2800.7	-2800.7	1565.4	1565.4	211.63	211.63	-424.3	-424.3

(e) Effect of joint displacements – Arbitrary rotation of plates

Arbitrary rotation of plate 2 : Case II solution

		1		2		3		4
D.F.	0	1	0.14	0.86	0.82	0.18	0.18	0.82
Initial Moments (t-m)		0	3					
Moments after distribution (t-m)	0	0	2.49	–2.49	–0.27	0.27	0.1	–0.1
Reactions due to moments		2.24↑	2.24↓	5.77↓	5.77↑	0.33↑	0.33↓	
Total reactions		2.24↑	8.01↓		6.10↑		0.33↓	
Ridge load		2.24↓	8.01↑		6.10↓		0.33↑	

Plate loads: $R_1 = 2.61$ t/m, $R_2 = 8.89$ t/m, $R_3 = -16.5$ t/m, $R_4 = 8.89$ t/m, $R_5 = 0$

Longitudinal stresses

Plate	Load t/m	$M = RL^2/\pi^2$ t-m	Z m^3	f t/m^2	Free edge stresses t/m^2	Stresses after distribution t/m^2
 4–3	8.89	300	0.03174	9454.7	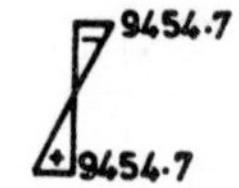 − 9454.7 / + 9454.7	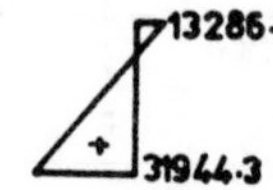 13286.7 / + 31944.3
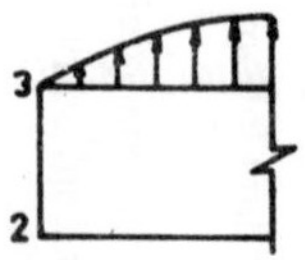 3–2	16.5	556.8	0.00384	1 45 000	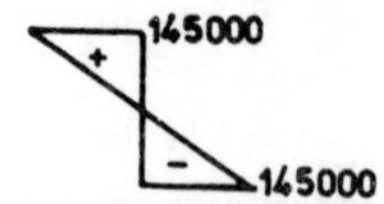 + 145000 / − 145000	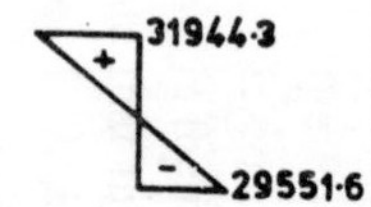 + 31944.3 / − 29551.6
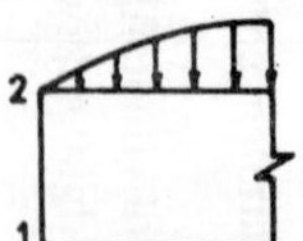 2–1	8.89	300	0.03174	9454.7	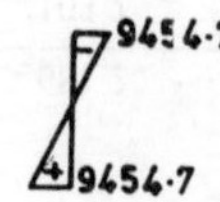 − 9454.7 / + 9454.7	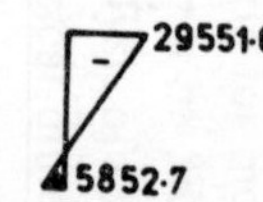 − 29551.6 / 5852.7
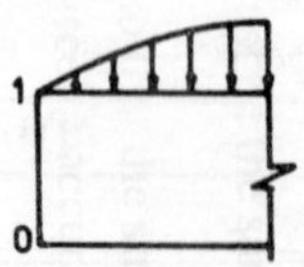 1–0	2.61	88.08	0.00096	91 750	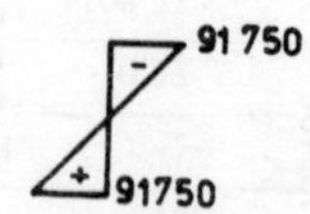 − 91 750 / + 91750	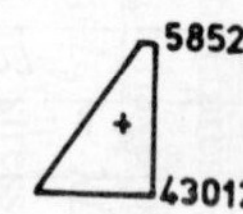 5852.7 / + 43012

Arbitrary rotation of plate 3: Case III solution

	1		2		3		4	
D.F.	0	1	0.14	0.86	0.82	0.18	0.18	0.82
Initial moment (t-m)				6	6			
Moment after distribution		0	–0.6	0.6	0.7	–0.7	–0.27	0.27
Reaction due to moment		0.54↓	↑0.54	2.71↑	↓2.71	0.87↓	↑0.87	
Total reactions		0.54↓	↑3.25		↓3.58		↑0.87	
Ridge loads (t/m)		0.54↑	↓3.25		↑3.58		↓0.87	

Plate loads: $R_1 = -0.63$ t/m, $R_2 = -4.2$ t/m, $R_3 = 8.04$ t/m, $R_4 = -4.2$ t/m, $R_5 = 0$

Longitudinal stresses

Plate	Load t/m	$M = RL^2/\pi^2$ t.m	Z m^3	f t/m^2	Free edge stresses t/m^2	Stresses after distribution t/m^2
	4.2	141.73	0.03174	4466.75	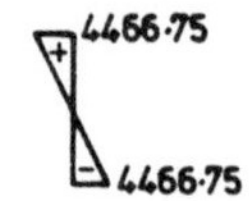	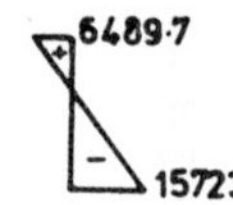
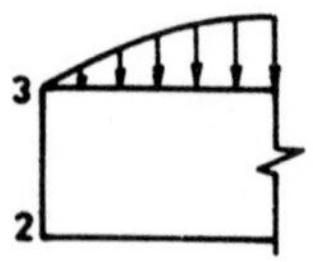	8.04	271.32	0.00384	70656.25	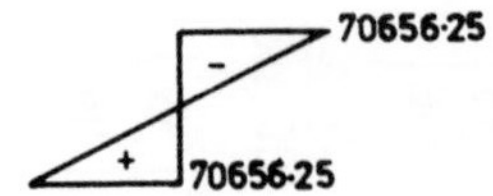	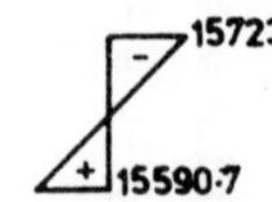
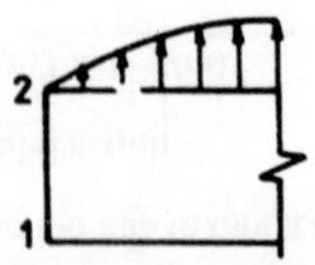	4.2	141.73	0.01174	4466.75	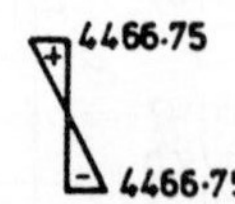	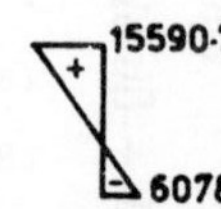
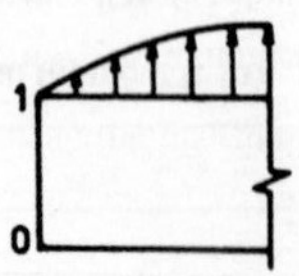	0.63	21.26	0.00096	22145.8	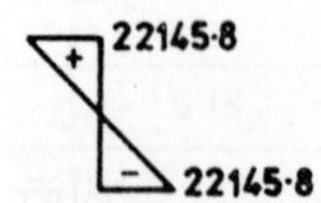	

Arbitrary rotation of plate 4: Case IV solution

		1		2		3		4
Moment after distribution (t-m)	0	0	0.36	–0.36	–4.07	4.07	3.79	–3.79
Reaction due to moment		0.32↑	0.32↓	9.23↑	9.23↑	7.08↑	7.08↓	
Ridge loads (t/m)		0.32↓	9.35↑			16.31↓	7.08↑	

Plate loads: $R_1 = 0.373$ t/m, $R_2 = 14.18$ t/m, $R_3 = -30.163$ t/m, $R_4 = 14.181$ t/m, $R_5 = 0$

Longitudinal stresses

Plate	Load t/m	$M = RL^2/\pi^2$ t.m	Z m^3	f t/m^2	Free edge stresses t/m^2	Stresses after distribution t/m^2
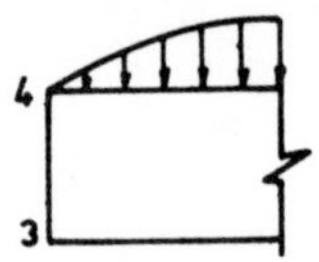	14.181	478.5	0.03174	15082.1	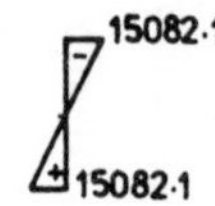	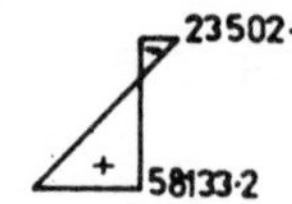
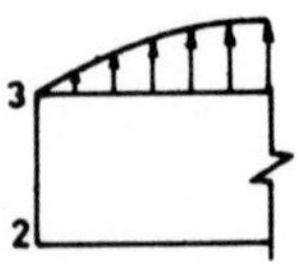	30.1	1017.9	0.00384	265075.3	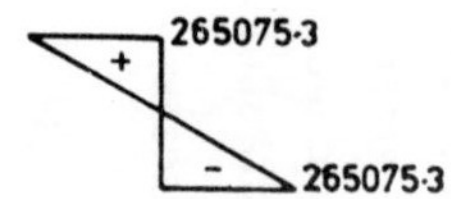	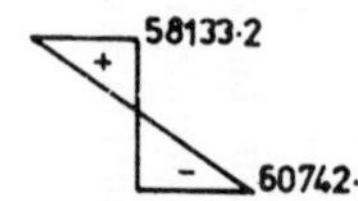
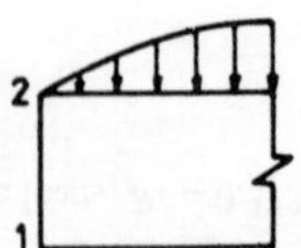	14.18	478.5	0.03174	15082.1	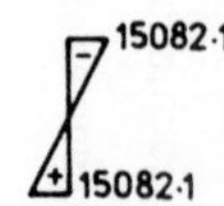	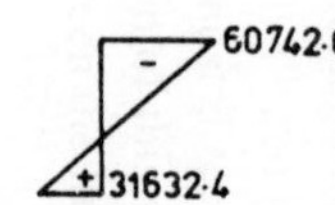
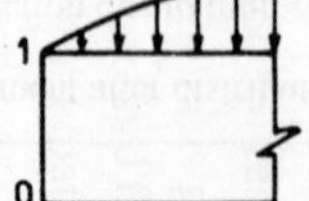	0.373	12.587	0.00384	3277.8	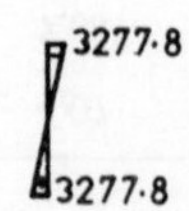	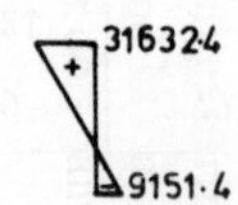

(f) Plate deflections $v_n(m)$

Case	Formula	v_1	v_2	v_3	v_4	v_5
	$v_n = \frac{5(f_b - f_t)L^2}{48Eb_n}$	$\frac{1542832.5}{E}$	$\frac{-103751.7}{E}$	$\frac{97126.6}{E}$	$\frac{15349.2}{E}$	0
II	$v_n = \frac{(f_b - f_t)L^2}{\pi^2 Eb_n}$	$\frac{5224951.6}{E}$	$\frac{818331.3}{E}$	$\frac{-4323454.7}{E}$	$\frac{1045464.5}{E}$	0
III	$v_n = \frac{(f_b - f_t)L^2}{\pi^2 Eb_n}$	$\frac{-285513.1}{E}$	$\frac{-500853.4}{E}$	$\frac{2201502.2}{E}$	$\frac{-513422}{E}$	0
IV	$v_n = \frac{(f_b - f_t)L^2}{\pi^2 Eb_n}$	$\frac{-5734586.6}{E}$	$\frac{2135146.2}{E}$	$\frac{-8357535.2}{E}$	$\frac{1886923.6}{E}$	0

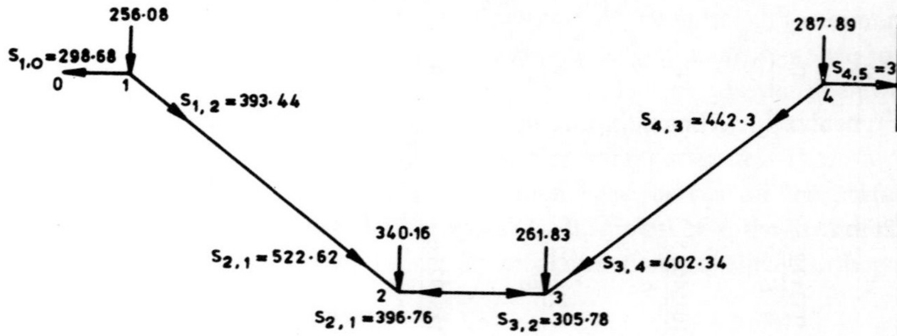

Fig. 8.27 Plate loads

(g) Plate rotations ψ_2, ψ_3 and ψ_4

$$\psi_2 = \frac{1}{h_2}\left[v_2(\cot\gamma_1 + \cot\gamma_2) - \frac{v_1}{\sin\gamma_1} - \frac{v_3}{\sin\gamma_2}\right] = \left(\frac{v_3 - v_1}{0.9503}\right)$$

$$\psi_3 = \frac{1}{-h_3}\left[v_3(\cot\gamma_2 + \cot\gamma_3) - \frac{v_2}{\sin\gamma_2} - \frac{v_4}{\sin\gamma_3}\right]$$

$$= -4.86v_3 + \frac{v_2 + v_4}{0.3124}$$

$$\psi_4 = \frac{1}{h_4}\left[v_4(\cot\gamma_3 + \cot\gamma_4) - \frac{v_3}{\sin\gamma_3} - \frac{v_5}{\sin\gamma_4}\right] = \frac{v_3}{0.9543}.$$

$$\frac{EJ_2}{b_2}\psi_{20} = 1, \quad \psi_{20} = \frac{b_2}{EJ_2} = \frac{1.46}{E\left[\frac{1}{12}\times 1\times(9\times 10^{-2})^3\right]}$$

$$\psi_{20} = \frac{0.2403\times 10^5}{E}, \quad \psi_{30} = \frac{b_3}{EJ_3} = \frac{5.349\times 10^3}{E}$$

$$\psi_{40} = \frac{b_4}{EJ_4} = \frac{0.2403\times 10^5}{E}$$

Now the actual rotations ψ_2, ψ_3 and ψ_4 can be written in terms of arbitrary rotations ψ_{20}, ψ_{30} and ψ_{40} and the unknown constants k_2, k_3 and k_4.

$$\psi_2 = \psi_{20}\times k_2 = \frac{0.2403\times 10^5}{E}\times k_2$$

$$\psi_3 = \psi_{30}\times k_3 = \frac{5.349\times 10^3}{E}\times k_3$$

$$\psi_4 = \psi_{40}\times k_4 = \frac{0.2403\times 10^5}{E}\times k_4$$

The values of the actual rotations ψ_2, ψ_3 and ψ_4 obtained in the previous step in terms of the arbitrary rotations will be equated to their values obtained in terms of plate deflections. This will result in three simultaneous equations in the unknown constants k_2, k_3 and k_4. Thus

$$\psi_2 = \left(\frac{0.2403 \times 10^5}{E}\right) \times k_2 = \frac{v_3 - v_1}{0.9503}$$

$$22835.7\, k_2 = -\,1445705.9 - 9548406.3\, k_2 + 2487115.3\, k_3 - 2622948.6\, k_4$$

or

$$-\,1445705.9 - 9571242\, k_2 + 2487115.3\, k_3 - 2622948.6\, k_4 = 0 \qquad (1)$$

$$\psi_3 = \left(\frac{5.349 \times 10^3}{E}\right) \times k_3 = -\,4.86\, v_3 + \frac{v_2 + v_4}{0.3124}$$

$$-\,755011.7 + 50553363\, k_2 - 13951343\, k_3 + 53492265\, k_4 = 0 \qquad (2)$$

$$\psi_4 = \left(\frac{0.2403 \times 10^5}{E}\right) k_4 = \frac{v_3}{0.9543}$$

$$97126.6 - 4323454.7\, k_2 + 2201502.2\, k_3 - 8380370.9\, k_4 = 0 \qquad (3)$$

Solving the above three simultaneous equations, we get

$$k_2 = -\,0.00255755,\ k_3 = 0.81229615,\ k_4 = 0.22838664$$

(h) Calculation of longitudinal stresses and transverse moments

Once the values of the constants k_2, k_3 and k_4 are determined, the longitudinal stresses at all edges are calculated as the stresses due to the no rotation solution plus k_2 times the stresses of the Case II solution, plus k_3 times the stresses of Case III solution, plus k_4 times the stresses of the Case IV solution. The transverse moments are also obtained in a similar way.

The longitudinal stresses and transverse moments at mid-span are given below.

Longitudinal stresses

Joint	No rotation solution	Case II	Case III	Case IV	Final t/m²	Stresses kg/cm²
0	7872.03	–110	–6587.3	–2090	–915.27	–91.5
1	–2800.7	–14.97	–4937.3	7224.4	–528.57	–52.8
2	1565.4	75.58	12664.3	–13872.8	432.58	43.2
3	221.63	–81.69	–12771.7	13276.8	645.04	64.5
4	–424.3	33.98	5271.6	–5367.7	–486.46	–48.6

Transverse moments kg-m

Joint	No rotation solution	Case II	Case III	Case IV	Final moments kg-m
0	0	0	0	0	0
1	–9.19	0	0	0	–9.19
2	–42.95	–6.37	–487.4	82.2	–454.5
3	–31.87	0.7	563.6	–929.5	–392.07
4	–33.52	–0.2	–219.3	865.6	612.7

The variation of longitudinal stress over the cross-section at mid-span is shown in Fig. 8.28.

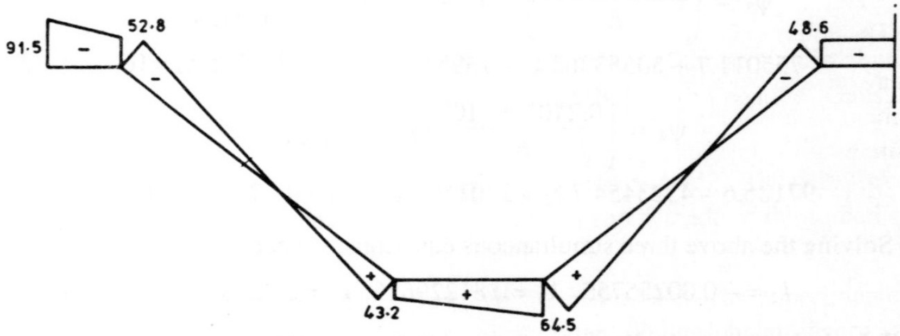

Fig. 8.28 Longitudinal stress variation at mid-span (Stress in kg/cm^2)

8.7 Design of Reinforcements

For a reinforced concrete folded plate, the reinforcements are to be designed to resist the following stresses or forces:

(a) Longitudinal stress (σ_x) wherever it is tensile.

(b) Diagonal tension caused by the combined action of longitudinal and shear stresses.

(c) Transverse moment.

The design of reinforcements to resist the longitudinal stress and transverse moments can be easily computed. However, for designing reinforcement to resist diagonal tension, one has to compute the principal tensile stress due to the combined effect of longitudinal and shear stresses and if this tensile stress exceeds the permissible limit, then reinforcement has to be provided. To calculate the principal stresses, the following procedure may be adopted.

For a simply supported folded plate, the edge shear variation can be written as

$$T = T_{\max} \frac{4x}{L}\left(1 - \frac{x}{L}\right)$$

where T_{max} is the value of edge shear at mid-span, L is the span of the folded plate.

The rate of variation of this edge shear per unit thickness gives the shear stress. Hence, shear stress can be computed from

$$\tau = \frac{1}{d}\frac{\partial T}{\partial x} = \frac{4T_{max}}{dL}\left(1 - \frac{2x}{L}\right)$$

The principal stresses can then be computed from

$$\sigma_{1,2} = \frac{\sigma_x}{2} \pm \sqrt{(\sigma_x/2)^2 + \tau^2}$$

where σ_x is the longitudinal stress at the point under consideration.

As an illustration, let us consider the example of trough type of folded plate discussed earlier.

(a) Design of reinforcements for transverse moment

It may be seen from table for transverse moments that at joint 2 we have a negative moment (causing tension at the top) of 454.5 kg-m/m while at joint 4, we have a positive moment (causing tension at the bottom) of 612.7 kg-m/m.

Area of steel required for resisting the negative moment can be computed as

$$A_{st} = \frac{454.5 \times 100}{1400 \times 0.87 \times 6.5} = 5.74 \text{ cm}^2$$

(where safe stress in steel = 1400 kg/cm^2 and effective depth = 6.5 cm). Provide 8 mm bars at 10 cm c/c at the top.

Area of steel required for resisting the positive moment can be computed as

$$A_{st} = \frac{612.7 \times 100}{1400 \times 0.87 \times 6.5} = 7.74 \text{ cm}^2$$

Provide 10 cm bars at 10 cm c/c at the bottom.

Hence, provide two layers of steel throughout the cross-section, with 8 mm bars at 10 cm c/c at the top and 10 mm bars at 10 cm c/c at the bottom.

The spacing of the rods could be decreased as we go towards the support, so as to economise the use of steel.

(b) Longitudinal reinforcement (Fig. 8.28)

Plate 1 is completely in compression and hence no reinforcement is required. However, provide nominal reinforcement of 8 mm bars, three in number in plate 1.

Plate 2 is partly in compression and partly in tension. The tensile zone of plate 2 is limited to a length of 0.67 m. Hence, reinforcement required to resist tension can be computed as

$$A_{st} = \frac{0.67}{2} \times \frac{43.2 \times 100 \times 8}{1400} = 9.27 \text{ cm}^2$$

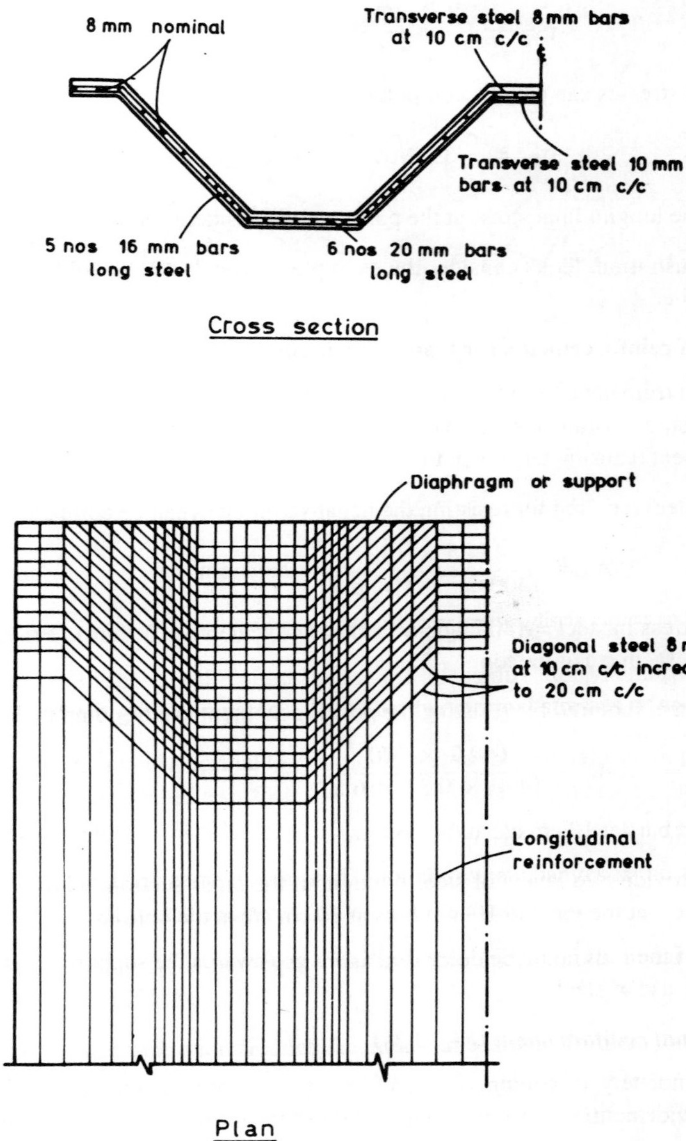

Fig. 8.29 Reinforcement details for a trough type folded plate

Hence, provide five bars of 16 mm in the tensile zone.

Plate 3 is completely in tension. The reinforcement required to resist this tension can be computed as

$$A_{st} = \left(\frac{43.2 + 64.5}{2}\right) \times \frac{0.48 \times 100 \times 10.25}{1400} = 18.92 \text{ cm}^2$$

Provide six bars of 20 mm dia in the bottom plate.

(c) Diagonal reinforcement

In this example, the principal tensile stress works out to less than the permissible value. Hence, provide nominal diagonal reinforcement of 8 mm bars at 10 cm c/c, which can be increased to 20 cm c/c after 1/8th span.

The arrangement of reinforcements is shown in Fig. 8.29.

REFERENCES

8.1 Ehlers, G., 'Ein neues Konstruktionprinzip', *Bauingenieur*, Vol. 9, 1930, p. 125.

8.2 Phase I Report on Folded Plate Construction, Task Committee on Folded Plate Construction of the Committee on Masonry and Reinforced Concrete, *Journal of the Structural Division, Proc. ASCE,* Vol. 89, No. ST 6, 1963, pp. 365–406.

8.3 Goldberg, J.E. and H.L. Leve, 'Theory of prismatic folded plate structures', *Publication of International Association for Bridge and Structural Engineering,* Vol. 17, 1957, pp. 59–86.

8.4 ————, D. Glauz and A.V. Setlur, 'Computer analysis of folded plate structures' *Proc. Seventh Congress, International Association for Bridge and Structural Engineering*, 1964, pp. 55–64.

8.5 Mast, P.E., 'New method for exact analysis of folded plates', *Jl. of the Structural Div., Proc. ASCE,* Vol. 93, No. ST 2, 1967, pp. 453–476.

8.6 Goldberg, J.E., M.J. Gutzwiller and R.H. Lee, 'Analytical and model studies of continuous folded plates', *Journal of Engineering Mechanics Division, Proc. ASCE,* Vol. 94, No. EM5, 1968, pp. 1127–1158.

8.7 Reiss, M. and Michael Yitzhak, 'Analysis of short folded plates', *Jl. of Structural Divn., Proc. ASCE,* Vol. 91, No. ST 5, 1965, pp. 233–254.

8.8 Winter, G. and M. Pei, 'Hipped plate construction', *Journal of the American Concrete Institute, Proc.,* Vol. 43, 1947, pp. 505–531.

8.9 Whitney, C.S., B.G. Anderson and H. Birnbaum, 'Reinforced concrete folded plate construction', *Journal of the Structural Division, Proc. ASCE,* Vol. 85, No. ST 8, 1959, pp. 15–43.

8.10 Simpson, H., 'Design of folded plate roofs', *Journal of the Structural Division, Proc. ASCE,* Vol. 84, No. ST 3, 1958, pp. 1508–1 — 1508–21.

8.11 Ramaswamy, G.S., *Design and Construction of Concrete Shell Roofs,* McGraw-Hill, 1968.

8.12 Beaufait, G.W., 'Analysis of continuous folded plate surface', *Journal of the Structural Division, Proc. ASCE,* Vol. 91, No. ST 6, 1965, pp. 117-140.

8.13 Mousa, A.M., R.A. Parmelee and S.L. Lee, 'Approximate analysis of continuous prismatic shells', *Publication, International Association for Bridge and Structural Engineering,* Vol. 28, No. 1, 1968, p. 103.

8.14 Lee, S.L., 'Analysis of continuous beams by Fourier series', *Journal of the Engineering Mechanics Division, Proc. ASCE,* Vol. 83, No. EM 4, 1957, pp. 1399–1 — 1399–13.

8.15 Chandrashekhara, K. and D.P. Singh, 'Theoretical and experimental analysis of cantilever folded plate', *Journal of the Institution of Engineers (India),* Vol. 57, Part CI4, 1977, pp. 172–176.

8.16 Sundara Raja Iyengar, K.T. and S. Anantharamu, 'A series solution for beam problems', *Journal of the Institution of Engineers (India),* Vol. 45, No. 5, CI3, 1964, pp. 371–393.

8.17 Evans, H.R. and K.C. Rockey, 'A critical review of the methods for folded plate structures', *Proc. Instn. Civ. Engrs.,* Vol. 49, 1971, pp. 171–192.

Chapter Nine

Experimental Analysis of Shell Structures

9.1 INTRODUCTION

Many times, the geometry and supporting conditions used for certain shell roofs are so complex that rigorous mathematical solutions cannot be obtained. However, it is possible to obtain approximate solutions for such problems through computer based numerical methods, like finite difference and finite element methods. Often, the accuracy of the results obtained from the numerical methods is not known. Hence, an experimental study will be of particular importance, in that it can notonly be used to provide direct solution for a complex problem but also be used to establish the accuracy of the results obtained from numerical methods. From this point of view, experimental stress analysis has a greater role to play now, than it did some two or three decades back. While a more realistic experimental stress analysis can be carried over on an actual structure, so that all the factors affecting the behaviour of the structure could be taken care of, such a study often becomes impracticable or uneconomical. Hence, normally, one carries out the experimental study on a model of actual structure, reduced to some scale, in which all the variables affecting the behaviour of the structure are faithfully represented. In summarising, it may be said that the model analysis is carried out for any one of the following purposes:

(a) To check the assumptions or approximations made in the theoretical analysis.

(b) As a tool for the design of a structure.

(c) To develop methods based on ultimate load concept.

In the first case, the model analysis may be carried out:

(i) To examine the implications of the assumptions made regarding the structural behaviour which many times are made to simplify the theoretical analysis.

(ii) To examine the implications of the assumptions made in the theoretical analysis, like for example material behaviour.

(iii) To verify the accuracy of the results obtained from the numerical and other approximate methods.

In the second case, the model analysis results are directly interpreted to predict the prototype behaviour within the elastic range and such a model analysis is often referred as linear elastic model analysis. By making use of the dimensional analysis and theory of models, it is possible to determine the stresses and displacements in the prototype from the results of the elastic model analysis. Hence, the linear elastic model analysis can be directly used for the design of a structure.

In the third case, the model is essentially used to get the failure pattern and ultimate load, from which, methods based on limit analysis can be developed. Model analysis carried out for any of the above three purposes is often referred as direct model analysis. In contrast, the indirect model analysis deals with obtaining the influence lines for the applied unit force or displacement. It should be noted that indirect model analysis has limited applications in structural analysis and design and hence, will not be discussed here further.

Generally, the direct model analysis, whether elastic or ultimate, involves the following steps:

(i) Establishing model-prototype relations through dimensional analysis.

(ii) Selection of a suitable model material.

(iii) Fabrication of model and loading system.

(iv) Selection of methods to measure displacements, strains or stresses in the model.

(v) Interpretation of the results.

9.2 DIMENSIONAL ANALYSIS AND THEORY OF MODELS

In the design of models, the relationship between the dimensions of the prototype and model must be established with certain imposed conditions. The two commonly imposed conditions are:

(i) The stresses in model and prototype are equal or occur in some predetermined ratio.

(ii) The deformations of the model and prototype may be in some predetermined ratio but a limitation is placed on the deformations of the structure.

Normally, in model analysis, a model which is geometrically similar to prototype is used. In such a case, any one of the above conditions is adequate. On the other hand, if the model is not geometrically similar to the prototype, then both the above conditions are to be imposed. A geometrically similar model would have all its dimensions scaled from the dimensions of the prototype by a constant factor.

The design of the model can be done based on dimensional analysis, such that the experimental data later can be interpreted to predict the behaviour of the prototype. Buckingham[9.1] in 1915, enunciated the Pi-theorem, which laid the foundation for the dimensional analysis. The Buckingham Pi-theorem is stated as follows:

If there are n physical quantities necessary to specify a physical law and if there are i dimensions involved in these quantities, then there are $(n - i)$ independent numerics. In this, each of the independent dimensionless terms are called as Pi-terms.

In problems of mechanics, we have three fundamental dimensions, viz. force, length and time. If we are interested only in the static analysis, then the fundamental dimensions reduce to two. Before we start determining the dimensionless or Pi-terms, it is first essential to identify the variables for a given physical problem. For example, if we consider the shell problem for a model analysis, the variables as we know would be: length (L), width (B) or radius of the shell (R), thickness of shell (h), modulus of elasticity (E), Poisson's ratio (ν), displacement (u, v or w), load (q per unit area) and stress (σ).

Hence, there are eight variables in a shell problem involving two dimensions and hence, we can formulate six dimensionless or Pi-terms.

There are no set procedures for determining the Pi-terms, but by and large, they may be selected by a fairly formalised method. In this connection, Buckingham suggests that as few physical quantities as possible should be included in Pi-terms. It is suggested that if there are i dimensions, a maximum of $(i + 1)$ quantities may be included in each term. Following these guidelines we may now write the Pi-terms for the shell problem. Since Poisson's ratio is dimensionless, it must appear as one Pi-term. Hence, the six Pi-terms by inspection can be written as

$$\pi_1 = \nu,\ \pi_2 = \frac{L}{B} \text{ or } \frac{L}{R},\ \pi_3 = \frac{L}{h},\ \pi_4 = \frac{q}{E},\ \pi_5 = \frac{\sigma}{E},\ \pi_6 = \frac{w}{L} \text{ or } \frac{w}{R}$$

Any other nondimensional quantities can be formulated from the above six Pi-terms. After having formed the non-dimensional terms, we say that these nondimensional parameters should be the same for model and prototype. This means

$$\nu_m = \nu_p,\ \frac{L_m}{B_m} = \frac{L_p}{B_p},\ \frac{L_m}{h_m} = \frac{L_p}{h_p},\ \frac{q_m}{E_m} = \frac{q_p}{E_p},\ \frac{\sigma_m}{E_m} = \frac{\sigma_p}{E_p},\ \frac{w_m}{L_m} = \frac{w_p}{L_p}$$

The first relation indicates that the Poisson's ratio for model and prototype should be the same. Many times, this condition cannot be fulfilled and we will discuss later the implications of this in the model analysis of shell structures. The second and third relations indicate that the geometrical dimensions have been scaled down from the prototype. If λ is the scale factor, then $L_p = \lambda L_m$, $B_p = \lambda B_m$ and $h_p = \lambda h_m$. Using the fourth and fifth relation, the stress in prototype $\sigma_p = \sigma_m (E_p/E_m)$ or the load to be applied on the model $q_m = q_p (E_m/E_p)$. It is obvious from the above relations, that we need to select any two from the following three scales, viz.

$$\frac{L_p}{L_m}, \frac{E_p}{E_m}, \frac{q_p}{q_m}$$

Normally, in most of the model analysis, the geometrical scale factor is first fixed and later a suitable model material is chosen. This fixes the factor (E_p/E_m) and then one can work out what load should be applied on the model in relation to prototype.

From the above description, it is clear that the dimensional analysis is a very general procedure and one need only know the variables of the given physical system. If, by mistake or oversight, one omits a variable, then it is likely that the model analysis results cannot be correctly interpreted to predict the prototype behaviour. In order to overcome this difficulty, if one specifies more variables, some of them not relevant, then the number of nondimensional parameters which should be formed will increase and unnecessarily complicate the problem. Hence, it is essential to identify the variables of a physical system correctly, before applying the dimensional analysis.

9.3 MODEL MATERIAL

Before considering the various model materials, it is necessary to examine first certain requirements which must be fulfilled by model materials in respect of similarity, manufacturing and testing of the model. The following are the necessary requirements for a model material:

(a) The stress-strain relationship of the model material and prototype must be similar.

(b) Poisson's ratio of the model and prototype material must be the same.

(c) The modulus of elasticity should be sufficiently low, so that the strains and displacements could be measured with a high degree of accuracy.

(d) The material should be such that a model of complex geometry could easily be fabricated without undue introduction of stresses.

The first requirement fixes somewhat, the type of model material. If linear elastic model analysis is to be carried out, then the first requirement specifies that the stress-strain relation should be linear. If on the other hand, the model analysis is to be carried out to determine the ultimate load, then the rheological behaviour of the model material should be the same as the prototype. The third requirement largely determines the scale of the model. For a given load and modulus of elasticity of the model material, the magnitude of displacements and strains depend upon the size of the model. Hence, depending on the sensitivity of the available measuring apparatus, the size of the model can easily be worked out.

For the elastic model analysis, a wide variety of materials, like steel, aluminium, plastics, etc., are available. Of these, plastics have been widely used in elastic model analysis of shell structure. Some of the plastics which have the requisite properties for model analysis are the acrylic and epoxy resins. Plastics, in general, have time dependent deformation, and hence to satisfy the requirement of linear stress-strain relation, the tests have to be carried out in a short duration of time (normally in about 20 to 30 min). The value of the Poisson's ratio for most of the plastics vary between 0.35 and 0.4, whereas for concrete (if the prototype shell is made of concrete), the Poisson's ratio is between 0.15 and 0.2. Though there is a difference in the Poisson's ratio between the prototype and model material in this case, some limited study made on cylindrical shells has indicated that the effect of Poisson's ratio is not predominant on stress resultants like N_x, N_y, N_{xy} and M_y, which are normally used in the design of concrete shells. The acrylic plastics are normally called as thermoplastics as they tend to become soft or rubbery when heated to a temperature ranging from 110° to 200°C. The most commonly used acrylic plastics are plexiglas or perspex. These are available in sheet form with thickness varying from 1 to 10 mm and generally are transparent. The modulus of elasticity of this material varies from 25000–35000 kg/cm^2 and Poisson's ratio would be 0.35. This being thermoplastic, the shell can be easily moulded to get different geometrical shapes either by vacuum forming or draping. A model of complex geometric shape can also be made by joining together elements, made of this material, by using solvents like trichloroethylene or polymerizable cements.

On the other hand, epoxy resins with varying mechanical properties are available under different trade names. The widely used epoxy resins in India are Araldite CY 230 and Araldite CT 200. These epoxy resins are marketed by M/s Ciba and Co., Bombay. The manufacturer supplies suitable hardeners for use along with these resins for making a casting. However, it is also possible to use other types of hardeners with these resins to obtain material having different mechanical and optical properties[9.2]. It must be noted that the plastics, in general, are susceptible to temperature variations and in order to eliminate the residual stresses in the model, the testing of the model should be done in temperature controlled conditions.

If it is required to determine the ultimate strength of a prototype shell through a model, then it is necessary to select a model material which represents the behaviour of concrete up to failure. Materials like gypsum plaster, cement mortar (micro-concrete) could be used in such a case as these materials have the same stress-strain characteristics as concrete[9.3]. Reinforced concrete shell also can be simulated by using threaded steel wires for reinforcement and any one of the above material for concrete.

9.4 FABRICATION OF MODEL AND LOADING SYSTEM

The model fabrication technique generally varies depending upon the nature of the model to be fabricated. So far as shell models are concerned, the technique of making models varies with the type of shell surface, namely developable and nondevelopable. Shell models having developable surface can be easily manufactured while those having nondevelopable surface cannot be easily manufactured since, while forming the model, the surface will be subjected to stretching and twisting, thus causing the variation in the shell thickness. Further, the techniques of manufacturing shell models also depend on the type of material used for the models like plastics, sheet metal or mortar. If plastics are used for shell models, then the shell surface could be obtained using a vacuum forming process. For shells with developable surface, the model can be prepared easily, using the open mould draping technique. If sheet metal is used for making the model, then a die is prepared first for the required shell surface and later the sheet metal is inserted in the die and pressed. Mortar models, reinforced or unreinforced, can be fabricated easily, by using prepared form work in wood. There are certain fabrication and technical difficulties inherent in the use of models. If the analysis is to be made on small scale models, accuracy of fabrication is essential. The tolerances placed on the dimensions of the prototype structure must be scaled down by the same factor that is used for fixing the dimensions of the model.

Generally, the loads that have to be considered in the analysis of shell roofs are (a) dead weight of the shell and (b) uniform live load. Sometimes, the shell roofs are to be analysed for wind loading, which is asymmetrical, and point loads. However, most of the model analysis of shell roofs are done by considering uniform load (both live and dead loads) and point loads. Uniform distributed loading is derived by using any one of the following techniques:

(i) by placing small weights on the shell surface.

(ii) by applying a series of point loads which are closely spaced, and

(iii) by pneumatic loading (pressure loading).

Each of the above methods have specific applications and when considered from a general point of view, have their own advantages and disadvantages.

Apart from mechanical loading, many times, the prototype structures are subjected to thermal loading and it is necessary to determine the thermal stresses in the prototype. A study on thermal stresses using models present two difficulties: (a) the application of a given temperature variation, (b) the influence of this temperature on the material and measuring apparatus. For this reason, very few studies have been made on this aspect.

9.5 OBSERVATIONS ON THE MODEL

Prediction of the behaviour of a structure by means of model analysis implies in a general way, the determination of displacements, strains and stresses. From the design point of view, it is important to determine the stresses developed under the action of working loads. For the determination of the safety factor, it is necessary to determine the magnitude of loading which causes failure.

9.5.1 Measurement of Displacements and Strains

The measurement of displacement in the models is carried out by means of dial gauges with a sensitivity varying from 0.01 to 0.1 mm and vary rarely to 0.001 mm. The measurement of strains is one of the most important aspects, as this permits the determination of stresses once the relation between stress and strain is known. The measurement of strain is normally done on the surface of the models, as the interior strain measurement involves considerable difficulty.

Among the strain gauges used in the measurement of strain on models, mention can be made of Huggenberger extensometer, acoustic strain gauge and electrical resistance strain gauge[9.4]. The gauge length of these strain gauges varies from 15 cm to 3 mm. The gauge length of the strain gauge to be used in a particular study is decided based on the size of the model and accuracy required. The strain gauges referred above permit as a general rule, measurement of strain of the order of 1 to 30×10^{-6}.

The direction of principal stresses (stress trajectories) on the surface of the models made of plastics or metal can easily be obtained by the use of brittle coating technique[9.5]. The knowledge of stress trajectories has the advantage of permitting a great reduction in the number of observations to be made with the strain gauges for obtaining the magnitudes of principal strains and stresses. If the stress-strain relationship is not linear and creep has to be considered, then it is not easy to determine the stresses from the measurement of strains.

Grid and Moire methods can be used to determine the displacements directly. The essential difference between Grid and Moire method is that, in the Grid method, the displacements are obtained at discrete points while in the Moire method, the complete displacement field can be obtained. Hence, the Grid method is often referred as point-by-point method while the Moire method is called as whole field method. In the Grid method[9.5], lines or dots are marked on the surface of the specimen and the change in the distance between points of lines or dots as a consequence of the deformation of the specimen is determined. This method is perhaps the easiest one to understand, and is the most direct of all experimental methods of stress analysis. An important limitation of this method is that, when displacements are small, the change in length between the lines or dots cannot be very accurately measured.

The Moire effect[9.6,9.7], as understood in strain analysis, is produced by two sets of gratings. The word gratings means here, arrays of alternately opaque and transparent lines or dots. For strain analysis purposes, Moire fringes can be produced by using any one of the following two techniques:

(a) By directly placing two transparent gratings one over the other.

(b) By using two projected images focussed on the same plane.

In the first technique, one grating is reproduced on the model and is called as the model or specimen grating and the other is used as a reference or master grating. When the model is subjected to deformation, the density (number of lines per unit length) of grating changes and because of the difference between the specimen and master gratings, an interference pattern is formed. The interference pattern is called as the Moire fringe pattern and gives the relative displacement in a direction normal to the grating. Hence, to determine the two in-plane displacement components, namely u and v, the gratings have to be first oriented in the y-direction to get the u-displacement field and later in x-direction to get the v-displacement field. By measuring the displacement in the radial or z-direction, all the displacement components namely u, v and w at a point can be determined. First, the strains can be determined using the measured displacements in the strain-displacement relations and later stresses using the stress-strain relationship. It should be noted that in this procedure, the total stress (i.e. both membrane and bending) at a point could be determined. Since, in this method, the in-plane displacements are determined from the Moire pattern, the Moire method is often referred as in-plane Moire technique.

The second technique mentioned above was developed by Ligtenberg[9.8] for the stress analysis of bent plates. This has been extended by Josselin de Jong[9.9] for the stress analysis of shells. The procedure developed by Josselin de Jong uses two identical transparent models separated by a constant distance, the space between them being filled with a material having different refractive index from that of the models. Equal and opposite loads are applied to the models, resulting in the formation of the refraction Moire pattern. It can be shown that this pattern gives the slope at a point, from which the curvatures can be determined and finally, the bending stress can be determined. Since, in this method, the Moire pattern is formed because of the out-of-plane displacement, the method is referred as out-of-plane Moire method.

The determination of stresses in two and three dimensional models can be done by using photoelasticity[9.10,9.11]. The photoelastic method has the advantage of being more rapid and in general, gives more accurate results compared to strain-gauge technique. Further, the photoelastic method is a whole-field method and hence, observations can be made over the entire area of the model. This method has been applied to a wide variety of stress problems in many branches of engineering and large number of practical problems have been effectively solved using this method. Apart from the requirement of the model material enumerated earlier, the material for photoelastic work should, in addition, satisfy the requirement of being transparent, birefringent and optically sensitive. Considerable amount of study has been made during the last two decades, to find out suitable materials for making photoelastic models. In recent years, epoxy resins, like Araldite CY 230 and Araldite CT 200 mentioned earlier, are widely used for photoelastic work, as it is possible to cast models of complex shape using these resins.

Photoelastic analysis, as it is ordinarily understood, concerns itself in determining the difference and direction of principal stresses in a stressed transparent model by means of a polariscope. This difference in principal stresses is directly proportional to the retardation (fringe order) and is equal to twice the maximum shear stress. Several techniques have been developed for simulating the loads, particularly dead load[9.12, 9.13], as well as for solving shell problems like frozen stress technique[9.14], embedded polarised technique, composite model technique[9.15, 9.16], etc.

9.6 MODEL TESTS ON SHELL STRUCTURES

We have, in the above paragraphs, described the procedure for designing models, choice of model materials and experimental methods that could be used to determine the strains and stresses in the model. Most of the model tests are done to examine the boundary conditions and basic assumptions made in the theoretical analysis on strength and stability. Depending upon the type of information needed, shell models have been prepared using materials like plastic or aluminium alloy as well as cement mortar and gypsum. Several publications[9.17-9.31] are there, describing the tests on shell models using various types of materials loading and measuring techniques. From this, it is very evident that large number of shell-model tests have been done simulating reinforced or prestressed concrete shell structures. The study in most of the cases is not only aimed at examining the behaviour of shell under working load and compare it with the theory, but also obtain ultimate load. The measuring techniques, very widely used in most of the model tests, have been generally direct strain measurement using mechanical or electrical resistance strain gauges and deflections using dial gauges.

Occasionally, full-scale shell roofs have been tested to failure and several examples of this type of experimental work have been reported[9.32] The object of the prototype tests, many times, is to verify the results obtained from small-scale model tests using different types of materials for the model preparation.

9.7 CONCLUDING REMARKS

With the increasing use of shell roof structures, there has been considerable activity on the development of suitable model material, measuring and testing techniques. This has now reached a stage where the model tests are able to provide accurate and reliable data, not only to verify the theoretical solutions but also for design. With the types of supports provided in practice for shell structures, proper visualisation of the boundary conditions for a theoretical analysis becomes somewhat difficult. In such cases, the model analysis appears to provide a satisfactory procedure to obtain the requisite knowledge of shell behaviour. With the wide range of model materials and measurement techniques now available, there is no difficulty in obtaining the required information accurately. Further, a model test gives a designer a physical feeling of the implications of the support or boundary conditions on the shell behaviour and provide sufficient information to improve his engineering judgement.

REFERENCES

9.1 Buckingham, E. 'Model experiments and the form of empirical equations', *Trans ASME,* Vol. 37, 1915, pp. 263–296.

9.2 Leven, M.M., 'Epoxy resins for photoelastic use', *photoelasticity,* Pergamon Press, New York, 1963, pp. 145–165.

9.3 Johnson, R. Paul, 'Strength tests on scaled-down concrete suitable for model with a note on mix design', *Magazine of concrete research,* Vol. 14, No. 40, 1962, pp. 47–53.

9.4 Dally, J.W. and W.F. Riley, *Experimental Stress Analysis*, McGraw-Hill Book Co., 1978.

9.5 Durelli. A.J., E. Phillips and C.H. Tsao, *Introduction to the Theoretical and Experimental Analysis of Stress and Strain,* McGraw-Hill Book Co., 1958.

9.6 Durelli, A.J. and V.J. Parks, *Moire Analysis of Strain,* Prentice-Hall Inc., 1970.

9.7 Theocaris, P.S., *Moire Fringe in Strain Analysis*, Pergamon Press, 1969.

9.8 Ligtenberg, F.K. 'The Moire method — a new experimental method for the determination of moments in small slab models', *Proc. SESA,* Vol. 12, No. 2, 1955, pp. 83–98.

9.9 Jong, G. de Josselin, 'Refraction Moire analysis of curved surfaces', *Proc. of the Symposium on Shell Research,* Delft, Edited by A.M. Hass and A.L. Bouma, North-Holland Publishing Co., Amsterdam, 1961, pp. 302–307.

9.10 Billington, D.P. and Mark, R., 'Small-scale model analysis of thin shells' *Jl. ACI,* Vol. 62, No. 6, 1965, pp. 673–688.

9.11 Morris, W.J., 'The photoelastic investigation of structural shells with particular reference to cylindrical shells', *Proc. of the Symposium on Shell Research,* Delft, Edited by A.M. Hass and A.L. Bouma, North-Holland Publishing Co., Amsterdam, 1961, pp. 353–355.

9.12 Brown, E.H. and S.L. Chow, 'The photoelastic analysis of gravity stresses in shells', *Proc. World Conference on Shell Structures,* California, National Academy of Sciences — National Research Council, Washington D.C. Publication No. 1187, 1962, pp. 305–310.

9.13 Chandrashekhara, K. and S.P. Srinivasan, 'Photoelastic analysis of free standing stairs', *Jl. of Structural Div., Proc. ASCE,* Vol. 98, No. ST 12, 1972, pp. 2836–2841.

9.14 Chandrashekhara, K. and K. Abraham Jacob, 'Photoelastic analysis of pyramidal hipped plate structure', *Bulletin IASS,* No. 55, 1974, pp. 37–44.

9.15 Franz, G. and W. Teepe, 'Untersuchungen an Schalen-modellen aus kunstoff', *Proc. of the Symposium on Shell Research,* Delft, Edited by A.M. Hass and A.L. Bouma, North-Holland Publishing Co., Amsterdam, 1961, pp 182–199.

9.16 Kuske, A. and G. Robertson, *Photoelastic Stress Analysis,* John Wiley, 1974.

9.17 Rowe, R.E., 'Experimental methods in the study of the behaviour of shell roofs', *Proc. of the the World Conference on Shell Structures,* California, National Academy of Sciences — National Research Council, Washington D.C., Publication No. 1187, 1962, pp. 223–234.

9.18 Enami, Akora, 'The investigation of ultimate load analysis of reinforced concrete prismatic folded plate structure', *Ibid.,* pp. 245–254.

9.19 Yu, C.W. and L.B. Kriz, 'Tests of a hyperbolic paraboloid reinforced concrete shell', *Ibid.,* pp. 261–274.

9.20 Rowe, R.S. and J.F. Mirza, 'An experimental investigation of small-scale hyperbolic paraboloids', *Ibid.,* pp. 275–278.

9.21 Dayaratnam, P. and K.H. Gerstle, 'Buckling of hyperbolic paraboloids', *Ibid.,* pp. 289–296.

9.22 Loo, T.C. and R.M. Evan-Iwanowski, 'Deformations and collapse of spherical domes subjected to uniform pressure and normal concentrated loads at apex', *Ibid.*, pp. 297–304.

9.23 Munro, J., 'Some tests on thin shells of reinforced mortar', *Ibid.*, pp. 311–318.

9.24 Rowe, R.E., 'Tests on four types of hyperbolic shells', *Proc. of the Symposium on Shell Research*, Delft, Edited by A.M. Hass and A.L. Bouma, North-Holland Publishing Co., Amsterdam, 1961, pp. 16–35.

9.25 Brennan, P.J., 'Experimental studies of hyperbolic paraboloid structures under static and dynamic loads', *Ibid.*, pp. 36–46.

9.26 Lauletta, E., 'Statics of hyperbolic paraboloidal shells studied by means of shell models', *Ibid.*, pp. 47–57.

9.27 Munro, J. and B.M. Ahuja, 'An investigation of the strain distribution in reinforced concrete shallow thin shells of negative Gaussian curvature', *Ibid.*, pp. 58–78.

9.28 Bouma,A.L., A.C. Van Riel, H. Van Kotan and W.J. Beranek, 'Investigations on models of eleven cylindrical shells made of reinforced and prestressed concrete' *Ibid.*, pp. 79–101.

9.29 Rühle, H., 'Die Verwendung von Gipsmodellen für experimentelle Untersuchungen von doppeltgekrümmten Wellenschalenträgern und Kegelstumpfschalen und ihre ergebnisse', *Ibid.*, pp. 116–136.

9.30 Schmidt, H., 'Ergebnisse von Beulversuchen mit doppelt gekrümmten Schalenmodellen aus Aluminium', *Ibid.*, pp. 159–181.

9.31 Arcan, M. and E.Nicolau, 'Experimental stress analysis on shells by models of plastic', *Ibid.*, pp. 277–281.

9.32 Zalewski, W., 'Experimental methods as a help in the design of shell structures in Poland', *Ibid.*, pp. 269–276.

Appendix I

Determination of Roots of the Characteristic Equation

I. Solution with Trigonometric Expression in the Longitudinal Direction:

It has been shown in Chapter 4 that the solution for w can be taken as

$$w = e^{\rho\theta} \cos \alpha_m x \tag{1}$$

where, $\alpha_m = \dfrac{m\pi}{L}$, L is the length of the shell and m is an odd integer

Introducing the above expression for w in the homogeneous part of the differential equation (Eq. 4.12), results in the following eighth degree polynomial equation in ρ,

$$\left(\frac{\rho^2}{\alpha_m^2 R^2} - 1\right)^4 + \frac{4}{\varepsilon^4} = 0 \tag{2}$$

where $\dfrac{1}{\varepsilon^4} = \dfrac{3\,(1 - \nu^2)}{\alpha_m^4 R^2 h^2}$

Eq. (2) being an eighth degree polynomial in ρ will have eight roots namely $\rho_1, \rho_2, \rho_3, \ldots, \rho_8$. We will now proceed to determine these roots.

$$\text{Let } \left(\frac{\rho^2}{\alpha_m^2 R^2} - 1\right) = n \tag{3}$$

Then Eq. (2) can be written as

$$n^4 + \frac{4}{\varepsilon^4} = 0 \tag{4}$$

The above equation can be split as

$$\left(n^2 + \frac{2i}{\varepsilon^2}\right)\left(n^2 - \frac{2i}{\varepsilon^2}\right) = 0 \tag{5}$$

where $i = \sqrt{-1}$

The above equation can be rewritten as

$$\left\{n^2 + \frac{1}{\varepsilon^2}(1 + i)^2\right\}\left\{n^2 - \frac{1}{\varepsilon^2}(1 + i)^2\right\} = 0 \tag{6}$$

Equating each of the expressions on the left hand side to zero, we get

$$\left\{n^2 + \frac{1}{\varepsilon^2}(1 + i)^2\right\} = 0 \tag{7a}$$

$$\left\{n^2 - \frac{1}{\varepsilon^2}(1 + i)^2\right\} = 0 \tag{7b}$$

From Eq. (7a), we can determine two roots as

$$n_{1,2} = \pm i\,\frac{(1 + i)}{\varepsilon} \tag{8a}$$

and from Eq. (7b), the other two roots can be determined as

$$n_{3,4} = \pm\frac{1}{\varepsilon}(1 + i) \tag{8b}$$

Since $n = \left(\dfrac{\rho^2}{\alpha_m^2 R^2} - 1\right)$, we can determine ρ as

$$\rho_{1,2} = \pm\,\alpha_m R\sqrt{(1 + n)}$$

Hence,

$$\rho_{1,2,3,4} = \alpha_m R\sqrt{(1 + n_{1,2,3,4})} \tag{9a}$$

$$\rho_{5,6,7,8} = -\alpha_m R\sqrt{(1 + n_{1,2,3,4})} \tag{9b}$$

For example, the first root ρ_1 can be written as

$$\rho_1 = \alpha_m R\sqrt{(1 + n_1)}$$

Substituting for n_1 from Eq. (8a), we get

$$\rho_1 = \alpha_m R\sqrt{(1 + i(1 + i)/\varepsilon)}$$

or

$$\rho_1 = \alpha_m R\sqrt{\{(1/\varepsilon)(\varepsilon + i - 1)\}}$$

In the above equation, the term under the square root can be expanded as

$$\sqrt{(\varepsilon - 1) + i} = \frac{1}{\sqrt{2}}\left\{\sqrt{\sqrt{(\varepsilon - 1)^2 + 1} + (\varepsilon - 1)} + i\sqrt{\sqrt{(\varepsilon - 1)^2 + 1} - (\varepsilon - 1)}\right\}$$

Hence, ρ_1 can be determined as

$$\rho_1 = \frac{\alpha_m R}{\sqrt{\varepsilon}}\left[\sqrt{\left\{\sqrt{(\varepsilon-1)^2+1}+(\varepsilon-1)\right\}/2}\right.$$

$$\left.+\ i\sqrt{\left\{\sqrt{(\varepsilon-1)^2+1}-(\varepsilon-1)\right\}/2}\ \right]$$

It is obvious that root ρ_1 is complex and in general can be written as

$$\rho_1 = \lambda(j_1 + ik_1) \tag{10}$$

where $\lambda = \dfrac{\alpha_m R}{\sqrt{\varepsilon}} = \sqrt[8]{3\ (1-\nu^2)}\ \sqrt{\alpha_m R}\ \sqrt[4]{(R/h)}$

$$j_1 = \sqrt{\left\{\sqrt{1+(1-\varepsilon)^2} - (1-\varepsilon)\right\}/2}$$

$$k_1 = \sqrt{\left\{\sqrt{1+(1-\varepsilon)^2} + (1-\varepsilon)\right\}/2}$$

Following the above procedure, the other seven roots viz. ρ_2, ρ_3 ,..., ρ_8 can be determined.

II. Solution with Trigonometric Expression in the Circumferential Direction:

It has been shown in Chapter 6, that the solution for w in the case of a cylindrical shell of revolution can be taken as

$$w = e^{\rho\bar{x}} \cos m\theta \tag{11}$$

where $\bar{x} = x/L$ and m is an integer.

Substituting the above expression for w in Eq. (6.8), we get the following eighth degree polynominal equation in ρ

$$(\rho^2 - m^2)^4 + 4\lambda^4\ \rho^4 = 0 \tag{12}$$

where $\lambda^4 = 3\ (1-\nu^2)\ (R/h)^2$

Eq. (12) will have eight roots viz. ρ_1, ρ_2, ρ_3 ,..., ρ_8 and we will now describe the procedure for determining these roots.

Taking the square root of Eq. (12), we get

$$(\rho^2 - m^2)^2 = \pm\ 2i\ \lambda^2\ \rho^2 \tag{13}$$

where $i = \sqrt{-1}$

Eq. (13) can be rewritten as

$$(\rho^2 - m^2)^2 = \pm\ (1 + i)^2\ \lambda^2\ \rho^2 \tag{14}$$

By taking the square root of Eq. (14), we get

$$(\rho^2 - m^2) = \pm\ (1 + i)\ \lambda\rho \tag{15a}$$

and

$$(\rho^2 - m^2) = \pm\ (1 - i)\ \lambda\rho \tag{15b}$$

from which the eight roots can be determined.

Let us, for example, consider the first root ρ_1 of Eq. (13) and represent it in the complex form as

$$\rho_1 = (c + id)$$

where c and d are real quantities. Substituting the above form of the root in Eq. (15a) and after separating the real and imaginary parts, we get

$$\alpha\beta - m^2 - \lambda\beta = 0 \tag{16a}$$

$$\alpha^2 - \beta^2 - 2\,\lambda\alpha = 0 \tag{16b}$$

where, $\alpha = (c + d)$ and $\beta = (c - d)$

Eliminating α from Eq. (16b) using Eq. (16a) we get

$$\beta^4 + \lambda^2\,\beta^2 - m^4 = 0 \tag{17}$$

whose roots are

$$\beta^2 = -\frac{\lambda^2}{2} + \sqrt{(\lambda^2/2)^2 + m^4}$$

or

$$\beta = \pm\left\{-\frac{\lambda^2}{2} + \sqrt{(\lambda^2/2)^2 + m^4}\right\}^{1/2} = \Omega$$

From Eq. (16a), we can find α as

$$\alpha = \frac{m^2 + \lambda\beta}{\beta} = \lambda + \frac{m^2}{\beta} = \lambda + \frac{m^2}{\Omega}$$

Further, we have

$$c = \frac{1}{2}\,(\alpha + \beta) = \frac{1}{2}\left[\lambda + \frac{m^2}{\Omega} + \Omega\right]$$

$$d = \frac{1}{2}\,(\alpha - \beta) = \frac{1}{2}\left[\lambda + \frac{m^2}{\Omega} - \Omega\right]$$

The root corresponding to this choice is

$$\rho_2 = (c - id)$$

By following the above procedure, the other roots can be determined.

Appendix II

Tables of 'G' Functions

A short table of 'G' functions namely G_1, G_2, G_3 and G_4 and their first derivative which appear in the solution of the differential equation (Eq. 5.37) for a conical shell subjected to axisymmetric edge loading is given here covering a range of $0 \leq \alpha \leq 10$ in steps of 0.1. The values of 'G' functions given in the table has been taken from Hampe and have been cross checked with the tables of ber, bei, ker, kei functions given by Lowell. For $\alpha > 10$, the asymptotic formulas can be used and are given below:

$$G_1 \approx \frac{\exp \frac{\alpha}{\sqrt{2}}}{\sqrt{2\pi\alpha}} \cos\left(\frac{\alpha}{\sqrt{2}} - \frac{\pi}{8}\right)$$

$$G_2 \approx -\frac{\exp \frac{\alpha}{\sqrt{2}}}{\sqrt{2\pi\alpha}} \sin\left(\frac{\alpha}{\sqrt{2}} - \frac{\pi}{8}\right)$$

$$G_3 \approx \sqrt{2/\pi\alpha}\ \exp \frac{-\alpha}{\sqrt{2}} \sin\left(\frac{\alpha}{\sqrt{2}} + \frac{\pi}{8}\right)$$

$$G_4 \approx -\sqrt{2/\pi\alpha}\ \exp \frac{-\alpha}{\sqrt{2}} \cos\left(\frac{\alpha}{\sqrt{2}} + \frac{\pi}{8}\right)$$

$$G'_1 \approx \frac{\exp \frac{\alpha}{\sqrt{2}}}{\sqrt{2\pi\alpha}} \cos\left(\frac{\alpha}{\sqrt{2}} + \frac{\pi}{8}\right)$$

$$G'_2 \approx -\frac{\exp \frac{\alpha}{\sqrt{2}}}{\sqrt{2\pi\alpha}} \sin\left(\frac{\alpha}{\sqrt{2}} + \frac{\pi}{8}\right)$$

$$G'_3 \approx -\sqrt{2/\pi\alpha}\ \exp \frac{-\alpha}{\sqrt{2}} \sin\left(\frac{\alpha}{\sqrt{2}} - \frac{\pi}{8}\right)$$

$$G'_4 \approx \sqrt{2/\pi\alpha}\ \exp \frac{-\alpha}{\sqrt{2}} \cos\left(\frac{\alpha}{\sqrt{2}} - \frac{\pi}{8}\right)$$

Table of 'G' Functions

α	G_1	G_2	G_3	G_4	G'_1	G'_2	G'_3	G'_4
0.0	1.00000	0.00000	0.50000	–	0	0	0	–
0.1	1.00000	−0.00250	0.49456	−1.54092	−0.00006	−0.05000	−0.09293	6.34134
0.2	0.99998	−0.01000	0.48264	−1.10335	−0.00050	−0.10000	−0.14192	3.13405
0.3	0.99987	−0.02250	0.46671	−0.85130	−0.00169	−0.14999	−0.17462	2.04983
0.4	0.99960	−0.04000	0.44805	−0.67649	−0.00400	−0.19997	−0.19704	1.49737
0.5	0.99902	−0.06249	0.42754	−0.54489	−0.00781	−0.24992	−0.21212	1.15852
0.6	0.99798	−0.08998	0.40581	−0.44126	−0.01350	−0.29980	−0.22165	0.92726
0.7	0.99625	−0.12245	0.38336	−0.35739	−0.02143	−0.34956	−0.22683	0.75818
0.8	0.99360	−0.15989	0.36056	−0.28831	−0.03199	−0.39915	−0.22857	0.62856
0.9	0.98975	−0.20227	0.33773	−0.23078	−0.04554	−0.44846	−0.22756	0.52576
1.0	0.98438	−0.24957	0.31512	−0.18252	−0.06245	−0.49740	−0.22433	0.44220
1.1	0.97714	−0.30173	0.29293	−0.14187	−0.08308	−0.54581	−0.21933	0.37300
1.2	0.96763	−0.35870	0.27130	−0.10755	−0.10781	−0.59352	−0.21293	0.31490
1.3	0.95543	−0.42041	0.25038	−0.78594 10^{-1}	−0.13697	−0.64034	−0.20510	0.26562
1.4	0.94008	−0.48673	0.23024	−0.54193	−0.17093	−0.68601	−0.19712	0.22349
1.5	0.92107	−0.55756	0.21097	−0.33699	−0.21001	−0.73025	−0.18819	0.18728
1.6	0.89789	−0.63273	0.19262	−0.16571	−0.25454	−0.77274	−0.17883	0.15605

α	G_1	G_2	G_3	G_4	G'_1	G'_2	G'_3	G'_4
1.7	0.86997	−0.71204	0.17522	−0.02350 10^{-1}	−0.30484	−0.81310	−0.16920	0.12903
1.8	0.83672	−0.79526	0.15878	0.09356	−0.36118	−0.85093	−0.15943	0.10564
1.9	0.79752	−0.88212	0.14333	0.18883	−0.42384	−0.88574	−0.14965	0.85389 10^{-1}
2.0	0.75173	−0.97229	0.12885	0.26525	−0.49307	−0.91701	−0.13993	0.67864
2.1	0.69869	−0.10654 10	0.11534	0.32535	−0.56906	−0.94418	−0.13037	0.52727
2.2	0.63769	−0.11610	0.10277	0.37140	−0.65200	−0.96661	−0.12103	0.39685
2.3	0.56805	−0.12585	0.91123 10^{-1}	0.40534	−0.74202	−0.98361	−0.11196	0.28487
2.4	0.48905	−0.13575	0.80368	0.42891	−0.83920	−0.99443	−0.10320	0.18915
2.5	0.39997	−0.14572	0.70471	0.44365	−0.94358	−0.99827	−0.94790 10^{-1}	0.10778
2.6	0.30009	−0.15569	0.61398	0.45089	−0.10551 10	−0.99426	−0.86752	0.03906
2.7	0.18871	−0.16557	0.53108	0.45183	−0.11738	−0.98149	−0.79104	−0.01849
2.8	0.06511	−0.17529	0.45563	0.44752	−0.12993	−0.95897	−0.71858	−0.06620
2.9	−0.07137	−0.18472	0.38723	0.43888	−0.14314	−0.92566	−0.65022	−0.10526
3.0	−0.22138	−0.19376	0.32545	0.42672	−0.15698	−0.88048	−0.58596	−0.13672
3.1	−0.38553	−0.20228	0.26990	0.41176	−0.17141	−0.82230	−0.52580	−0.16154
3.2	−0.56438	−0.21016	0.22016	0.39461	−0.18636	−0.74992	−0.46967	−0.18055
3.3	−0.75841	−0.21723	0.17583	0.37582	−0.20177	−0.66214	−0.41749	−0.19452
3.4	−0.96804	−0.22334	0.13653	0.35585	−0.21755	−0.55769	−0.36916	−0.20414
3.5	−0.11936 10	−0.22832	0.10188	0.33511	−0.23361	−0.43530	−0.32456	−0.21001

α	G_1	G_2	G_3	G_4	G'_1	G'_2	G'_3	G'_4
3.6	−0.14353 10	−0.23199 10	0.71499 10^{-2}	0.31395 10^{-1}	−0.24983 10	−0.29366	−0.28354 10^{-1}	−0.21269 10^{-1}
3.7	−0.16933	−0.23413	0.45054	0.29267	−0.26608	−0.13149	−0.24596	−0.21265
3.8	−0.19674	−0.23454	0.22199	0.27150	−0.28222	0.05253	−0.21166	−0.21034
3.9	−0.22576	−0.23300	0.02617	0.25066	−0.29807	0.25965	−0.18047	−0.20614
4.0	−0.25634	−0.22927	−0.13993	0.23032	−0.31347	0.49114	−0.15222	−0.20040
4.1	−0.28843	−0.22309	−0.27922	0.21062	−0.32818	0.74817	−0.12674	−0.19342
4.2	−0.32195	−0.21422	−0.39432	0.19167	−0.34200	0.10319 10	−0.10386	−0.18546
4.3	−0.35679	−0.20236	−0.48771	0.17356	−0.35465	0.13433	−0.83404 10^{-2}	−0.17677
4.4	−0.39283	−0.18726	−0.56188	0.15633	−0.36588	0.16833	−0.65209	−0.16755
4.5	−0.42991	−0.16860	−0.61885	0.14006	−0.37537	0.20526	−0.49115	−0.15797
4.6	−0.46784	−0.14610	−0.66075	0.12475	−0.38280	0.24520	−0.34963	−0.14820
4.7	−0.50639	−0.11946	−0.68939	0.11042	−0.38782	0.28818	−0.22600	−0.13836
4.8	−0.54531	−0.08837	−0.70646	0.09707	−0.39006	0.33422	−0.11872	−0.12856
4.9	−0.58429	−0.05252	−0.71365	0.08470	−0.38911	0.38331	−0.02643	−0.11890
5.0	−0.62301	−0.01160	−0.71225	0.07329	−0.38453	0.43541	0.05220	−0.10946
5.1	−0.66107	−0.03467	−0.70359	0.06280	−0.37589	0.49046	0.11846	−0.10030
5.2	−0.69803	0.08658	−0.68890	0.05322	−0.36270	0.54835	0.17355	−0.91447 10^{-2}

α	G_1	G_2	G_3	G_4	G'_1	G'_2	G'_3	G'_4
5.3	−0.73344 10	0.14443 10	−0.66922 10^{-2}	0.04449 10^{-1}	−0.34445 10	0.60892 10	0.21858 10^{-2}	−0.83011 10^{-2}
5.4	−0.76674	0.20845	−0.64549	0.03660	−0.32064	0.67199	0.25463	−0.74959
5.5	−0.79736	0.27890	−0.61856	0.02949	−0.29070	0.73729	0.28267	−0.67331
5.6	−0.82466	0.35597	−0.58919	0.02312	−0.25410	0.80454	0.30362	−0.60143
5.7	−0.84794	0.43986	−0.55804	0.17446 10^{-2}	−0.21024	0.87336	0.31834	−0.53401
5.8	−0.86644	0.53068	−0.52270	0.12424	−0.15855	0.94333	0.32759	−0.47108
5.9	−0.87937	0.62854	−0.49268	0.08009	−0.09844	0.10139 10^{2}	0.33212	−0.41261
6.0	−0.88583	0.73347	−0.45942	0.04157	−0.02931	0.10846	0.33257	−0.35853
6.1	−0.88491	0.84545	−0.42629	0.08246 10^{-3}	0.04943	0.11547	0.32954	−0.30873
6.2	−0.87561	0.96437	−0.39361	−0.20312	0.13835	0.12235	0.32358	−0.26310
6.3	−0.85688	0.10901 10^{2}	−0.36149	−0.44507	0.23802	0.12901	0.31519	−0.22417
6.4	−0.82762	0.12223	−0.33063	−0.64734	0.34899	0.13536	0.30481	−0.18368
6.5	−0.78669	0.13607	−0.30074	−0.81365	0.47174	0.14129	0.29285	−0.14954
6.6	−0.73287	0.15047	−0.27211	−0.94757	0.60675	0.14670	0.27964	−0.11887
6.7	−0.66492	0.16538	−0.24484	−1.05247	0.75442	0.15146	0.26552	−0.91452 10^{-3}
6.8	−0.58155	0.18074	−0.21902	−1.13150	0.91510	0.15543	0.25076	−0.67099
6.9	−0.48146	0.19644	−0.19470	−1.18762	0.10891 10^{2}	0.15847	0.23559	−0.45606
7.0	−0.36329	0.21239	−0.17191	−1.22360	0.12765	0.16041	0.22024	−0.26771

α	G_1	G_2	G_3	G_4	G'_1	G'_2	G'_3	G'_4
7.1	−0.22571 10	0.22848 10^2	−0.15066 10^{-2}	−1.24198 10^{-3}	0.14774 10^2	0.16109 10^2	0.20486 10^{-2}	−0.10394 10^{-3}
7.2	−0.06737	0.24456	−0.13093	−1.24514	0.16918	0.16033	0.18968	0.03717
7.3	0.11308	0.26049	−0.11271	−1.23524	0.19194	0.15792	0.17475	0.15750
7.4	0.31695	0.27609	−0.95966 10^{-3}	−1.21427	0.21600	0.15367	0.16022	0.25887
7.5	0.54550	0.29116	−0.80651	−1.18404	0.24130	0.14736	0.14616	0.34300
7.6	0.79994	0.30458	−0.66715	−1.14619	0.26777	0.13875	0.13266	0.41156
7.7	0.10814 10^2	0.31882	−0.54099	−1.10220	0.29532	0.12763	0.11976	0.46611
7.8	0.13909	0.33092	−0.42741	−1.05339	0.32382	0.11373	0.10752	0.50813
7.9	0.17293	0.34147	−0.32754	−1.00094	0.35314	0.09681	0.95946 10^{-3}	0.53901
8.0	0.20974	0.35017	−0.23530	−0.94591	0.38311	0.07660	0.85072	0.56005
8.1	0.24957	0.35667	−0.15536	−0.88922	0.41353	0.05286	0.74903	0.57246
8.2	0.29245	0.36061	−0.08525	−0.83167	0.44415	0.02530	0.65437	0.57735
8.3	0.33840	0.36159	−0.02425	−0.77397	0.47472	−0.00634	0.56670	0.57575
8.4	0.38738	0.35920	0.02832	−0.71671	0.50492	−0.04232	0.48587	0.56862
8.5	0.43936	0.35298	0.07315	−0.66040	0.53442	−0.08390	0.41172	0.55682
8.6	0.49423	0.34246	0.11088	−0.60547	0.56281	−0.12832	0.34403	0.54114
8.7	0.55187	0.32714	0.14216	−0.55227	0.58967	−0.17883	0.28254	0.52229

α	G_1		G_2		G_3		G_4		G'_1		G'_2		G'_3		G'_4	
8.8	0.61210	10^{2}	0.30651	10^{2}	0.16789	10^{-3}	–0.50110	10^{-3}	0.61451	10^{2}	–0.23465	10^{2}	0.22698	10^{-3}	0.50091	10^{-3}
8.9	0.67469		0.28003		0.18775		–0.45216		0.63682		–0.29598		0.17706		0.47757	
9.0	0.73936		0.24713		0.20318		–0.40563		0.65601		–0.36299		0.13247		0.45278	
9.1	0.80756		0.20724		0.21441		–0.36164		0.6714[illegible]		–0.43583		0.09289		0.42701	
9.2	0.87350		0.15976		0.22191		–0.32025		0.68246		–0.51460		0.05799		0.40064	
9.3	0.94208		0.10412		0.22615		–0.28125		0.68831		–0.59936		0.02759		0.37403	
9.4	0.10110	10^{3}	0.03969		0.22754		–0.24544		0.68821		–0.69012		0.00085		0.34746	
9.5	0.10795		–0.03411		0.22647		–0.21201		0.68132		–0.78684		–0.02194		0.32126	
9.6	0.11470		–0.11787		0.22331		–0.18119		0.66674		–0.88940		–0.04105		0.29547	
9.7	0.12126		–0.21218		0.21837		–0.15290		0.64353		–0.99763		–0.05722		0.27044	
9.8	0.12754		–0.31758		0.21196		–0.12707		0.61070		–0.11112	10^{3}	–0.06944		0.24626	
9.9	0.13343		–0.43459		0.20434		–0.10361		0.56720		–0.12299		–0.08129		0.22306	
10.0	0.13884		–0.56370		0.19577		–0.82417	10^{-4}	0.51195		–0.13531		–0.08971		0.20091	

Name Index

Subject Index